Teacher Guide

Volume 2

Developed by Education Development Center, Inc.
through National Science Foundation
Grant No. ESI-0099093

EDC

Published and distributed by:

Math

www.Math.SchoolSpecialty.com

Think Math! Teacher Guide   1358059

Printing 4 – 6/2010   978-0-15-359416-8

Webcrafters, Madison, WI

This program was funded in part through the National Science Foundation under Grant No. ESI-0099093. Any opinions, findings, and conclusions or recommendations expressed in this program are those of the authors and do not necessarily reflect the views of the National Science Foundation.

Principal Investigator

E. Paul Goldenberg

Curriculum Design and Pedagogy Oversight

E. Paul Goldenberg Lynn Goldsmith Nina Shteingold

Research

Director: Lynn Goldsmith Sabita Chopra Suenita Lawrence
Nina Arshavsky Sophia Cohen Katherine Schwinden
Cynthia Char Andrea Humez Eugenia Steingold

Editorial

Director: Frances Fanning Nicholas Bozard Eric Karnowski

Writing

Director: Eric Karnowski

Jean Benson Stacy Grossman Paisley Rossetti
Abigail Branch Andrea Humez Nina Shteingold
Sara Cremer Suenita Lawrence Kate Snow
E. Paul Goldenberg Debora Rosenfeld Julie Zeringue

Graphics and Design

Directors: Laura Koval Jessica Cummings E. Charles Snow
and Korynn Kirchwey Jennifer Putnam Jenny Wong

Project Management

Directors: Eric Karnowski Amy Borowko Alexander Kirchwey Kimberly Newson
and Glenn Natali Nannette Feurzeig Helen Lebowitz David O'Neil
Kim Foster June Mark Cynthia Plouff

Mathematics Reviewers

Richard Askey, Professor of Mathematics, Emeritus
University of Wisconsin, Madison, Wisconsin

Harvey Keynes, Professor of Mathematics
University of Minnesota, Minneapolis, Minnesota

Roger Howe, Professor of Mathematics
Yale University, New Haven, Connecticut

David Singer, Professor of Mathematics
Case Western Reserve University, Cleveland, Ohio

Sherman Stein, Professor of Mathematics, Emeritus
University of California at Davis, Davis, California

Additional Mathematics Resource

Al Cuoco, Center Director, Center for Mathematics Education, Education Development Center, Newton, Massachusetts

Advisors

Peter Braunfeld June Mark
David Carraher Ricardo Nemirovsky
Carole Greenes James Newton
Claire Groden Judith Roitman
Deborah Schifter

Evaluators

Douglas H. Clements Mark Jenness
Cynthia Halderson Julie Sarama

Acknowledgement

We especially want to acknowledge the inspiration we derived from two special works and their visionary authors: *Vision in Elementary Mathematics*, by W. W. Sawyer, and *Math Workshop* by Robert Wirtz and his colleagues.

Sawyer and Wirtz understood the power of puzzlement, curiosity, and surprise—for teachers as well as for children. They crafted problems that provide not only essential practice, but the added bonus of ideas and surprises for the observant child. These discovery opportunities foreshadow later learning, so that when children must master hard ideas in later grades, the ideas are already well underway.

Part of Sawyer's "vision" was literally about vision—the power of graphic images and formats that capture mathematical ideas and processes and that reduce the sole reliance on words. Clear, precise mathematical language is essential, of course, but jumpstarting ideas without words helps not only the English Language Learner, but all children, and builds secure concepts to which they can attach their growing mathematical vocabulary. Both *Vision* and *Math Workshop* introduced a technique of teaching—for occasional use—in which the teacher, playfully, is absolutely silent! This change of pace rivets children's attention as they watch eagerly for clues—after all, there's nothing to listen for—and creates an almost electric charge in the classroom.

Sawyer also recognized children as great language learners, who acquire even the formal language of algebra if it is not just "another thing to learn," but is seen as a convenient "shorthand" for expressing ideas and patterns that the children are eager to describe.

Finally, both works recognized teachers as intelligent, college-educated adults. *Math Workshop* showed the utmost respect for teachers, giving flexibility as well as guidance, and recognizing that only through the teacher's complete engagement, judgment, and thoughtful teaching can a lesson really work.

We gratefully acknowledge what we learned, over many years, from these mentors, and hope that our work lives up to the brilliance and uncanny insight and foresight they brought to mathematics.

E. Paul Goldenberg, Principal Investigator

Think Math! Contents

Contents

Think Math! Contents

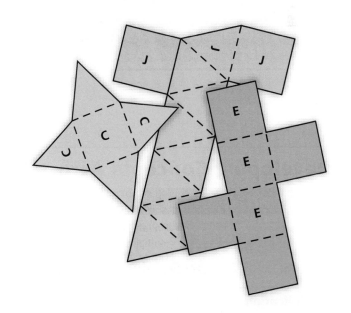

Big Idea Use multiplication and division concepts to arrive at a process for dividing large numbers

Developing a Division Algorithm

About the Chapter

In this chapter, students work with multiplication and division concepts to arrive at a process for dividing large numbers. Seeing multiplication and division as related operations allows students to reason through division in a meaningful way. The connection is also helpful when students consider division with remainders.

The Division Process While the chapter leads students to use a process very much like the long division algorithm, students should approach the algorithm as a process of "carving away" at the dividend, rather than a rote series of steps that focus on digits rather than the meanings of the numbers. The process requires underestimating a quotient, using multiplication and subtraction to see how close the estimate is to the actual quotient, then modifying the estimate. This is similar to the guess and check problem

solving strategy; however, students do not check a new estimate each time. They only work with the amount by which their estimate was incorrect, and add the corrections to the original estimate at the end of the process.

Interpreting Remainders When division doesn't work out "nicely"—if the quotient is not a whole number—students have a new issue to contend with: What should I do with the remainder? The connection between multiplication and division suggests going beyond thinking of the remainder as "leftovers," and the chapter introduces giving a quotient as a number with a fractional part, written either as a fraction or as a decimal. In a real-world problem context, however, a different question must be considered: Should the remainder be ignored (round down), used as a fraction (report exact answer), or be accommodated by including another whole object (round up)?

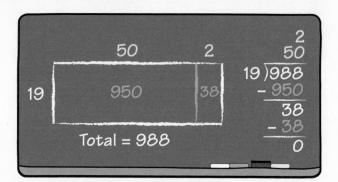

Developing Concepts Across the Grades

Topic	Prior Learning	Learning in Chapter 8	Later Learning
Division	• Find the missing factor in multiplication sentences Grade 4, Chapter 13	• Divide with large numbers using an area model • Interpret remainders Lessons 8.1–8.9	• Find quotients with terminating and repeating decimals Grade 6
Multiplication	• Multiply multi-digit numbers • Multiply 2-digit numbers by multiples of 10 Grade 4, Chapter 6	• See the connection between multiplication and division • Use multiplication to check division Lessons 8.1, 8.2	• Multiply by powers of 10 • Scientific notation Grade 6
Estimation	• Use rounding and compatible numbers to estimate quotients Grade 4, Chapter 13	• Use rounding and compatible numbers to estimate solutions to multiplication and division problems Lesson 8.5	• Estimate products and quotients of fractions Grade 6

Chapter Planner

Lesson	Objectives	NCTM Standards	Vocabulary	Materials/Resources

CHAPTER 8 World Almanac For Kids • Vocabulary • Games • Challenge
Teacher Guide pp. 637A–637F, Student Handbook pp. 130–131, 142–146

Lesson	Objectives	NCTM Standards	Vocabulary	Materials/Resources
1 Exploring Missing Factors PACING 1 DAY **Teacher Guide** pp. 638–645 **Lesson Activity Book** pp. 151–152 **Student Handbook** Student Letter p. 129 Explore p. 132	• To solve problems using multiplication and division	1, 2, 6, 7, 8, 9, 10	division	**For the students:** ■ School-Home Connection TR: SHC29–SHC30 ■ P62, E62, SR62
2 Connecting Multiplication and Division PACING 1 DAY **Teacher Guide** pp. 646–653 **Lesson Activity Book** pp. 153–154	• To use division to solve problems • To use multiplication to solve problems • To see connections between multiplication and division	1, 2, 6, 7, 8, 9, 10	dividend divisor factor product quotient remainder	**For the students:** ■ TR: AM65 ■ P63, E63, SR63
3 Dividing Using Multiplication and the Area Model PACING 1 DAY **Teacher Guide** pp. 654–663 **Lesson Activity Book** pp. 155–156 **Student Handbook** Explore p. 133 Game p. 144 Review Model p. 134	• To divide with large numbers using an area model • To use multiplication to solve problems involving whole numbers	1, 2, 6, 7, 8, 9, 10	break partition separate split	**For the students:** ■ sets of cards numbered 1–12 ■ P64, E64, SR64
4 Recording the Steps in Division PACING 1 DAY **Teacher Guide** pp. 664–673 **Lesson Activity Book** pp. 157–158 **Student Handbook** Review Model p. 135	• To use division to solve problems involving whole numbers • To use an area model to determine the partial quotients that make up the total quotient	1, 2, 6, 7, 8, 9, 10	compatible numbers	**For the students:** ■ P65, E65, SR65 **Science Connection:** **Gravity** **Teacher Guide** p. 636

NCTM Standards 2000
1. Number and Operations
2. Algebra
3. Geometry
4. Measurement
5. Data Analysis and Probability
6. Problem Solving
7. Reasoning and Proof
8. Communication
9. Connections
10. Representation

Key
AG: Assessment Guide
E: Extension Book
LAB: Lesson Activity Book
P: Practice Book
SH: Student Handbook
SR: Spiral Review Book
TG: Teacher Guide
TR: Teacher Resource Book

MATH GLOSSARY in **Student Handbook** p. 266

Planner (continued)

Chapter Planner (continued)

Lesson	Objectives	NCTM Standards	Vocabulary	Materials/ Resources
5 **Dividing and Recording Division Efficiently** PACING 1 DAY **Teacher Guide** pp. 674–683 **Lesson Activity Book** pp. 159–160 **Student Handbook** Game p. 145	• To use division to solve problems involving whole numbers • To use rounding and compatible numbers to estimate solutions to multiplication and division problems	1, 2, 6, 7, 8, 9, 10	approximation estimation	**For the students:** ■ sets of cards numbered 1–9 ■ P66, E66, SR66 **Social Studies Connection:** **Presidential Election Years** Teacher Guide p. 636
6 **Using Multiplication to Check Division** PACING 1 DAY **Teacher Guide** pp. 684–691 **Lesson Activity Book** pp. 161–162	• To use multiplication to check division • To use division to solve problems involving whole numbers	1, 2, 6, 7, 8, 9, 10	inverse	**For the students:** ■ TR: AM66, AM67 ■ pencils ■ paper cips ■ P67, E67, SR67
7 **Investigating Remainders** PACING 1 DAY **Teacher Guide** pp. 692–701 **Lesson Activity Book** pp. 163–164 **Student Handbook** Explore p. 136 Review Model p. 137	• To use multiplication and division to solve problems involving whole numbers • To explore remainders	1, 2, 6, 7, 8, 9, 10	remainder	**For the students:** ■ square tiles ■ P68, E68, SR68
8 **Interpreting Remainders in Word Problems** PACING 1 DAY **Teacher Guide** pp. 702–709 **Lesson Activity Book** pp. 165–166 **Student Handbook** Explore p. 138	• To use division to solve problems involving whole numbers • Given a context, to decide whether to ignore remainders or to add them as fractions or decimals to the quotient	1, 2, 6, 7, 8, 9, 10	reasonable	**For the students:** ■ P69, E69, SR69
9 **Another Option for Interpreting Remainders** PACING 1 DAY **Teacher Guide** pp. 710–717 **Lesson Activity Book** pp. 167–168 **Student Handbook** Review Model p. 139	• To use division to solve problems • Given a context, to decide whether to ignore remainders, to add them as fractions or decimals to the quotient, or to round up the quotient	1, 2, 6, 7, 8, 9	rounding up the quotient	**For the students:** ■ calculators ■ P70, E70, SR70 **Literature Connection:** **Using Math to Fly a Jumbo Jet** Teacher Guide p. 636

Chapter Planner *(continued)*

Lesson	Objectives	NCTM Standards	Vocabulary	Materials/Resources
10 **Problem Solving Strategy and Test Prep** **PACING 1 DAY** **Teacher Guide** pp. 718–723 **Lesson Activity Book** pp. 169–170 **Student Handbook** Review Model pp. 140–141	• To practice the problem solving strategy *draw a picture* • To articulate the steps and strategies used to solve problems • To prepare for standardized tests	1, 2, 6, 7, 8, 9, 10		

CHAPTER 8 Assessment TG pp. 726–727, **LAB** pp. 171–172, **AG** pp. AG77–AG80	**For the students:** ■ Chapter 8 Test pp. AG77–AG78

Planning Ahead

In **Lesson 8.2,** students will use Cuisenaire® Rods in the Extension Activity.

In **Lesson 8.3,** students will play *200 Zoom* in small groups. Each group will need four sets of cards numbered from 1 to 12.

In **Lesson 8.5,** students will play *Don't Overestimate* in pairs. Each pair will need four sets of cards numbered 1–9.

In **Lesson 8.7,** they will use grid paper on the Review Model page.

In **Lesson 8.8,** they will use adding machine tape in the Intervention Activity.

Games

Use the following games for skills practice and reinforcement of concepts.

Lesson 8.3 ▶
200 Zoom provides an opportunity for students to practice multiplication and addition in the context of playing a game.

200 Zoom

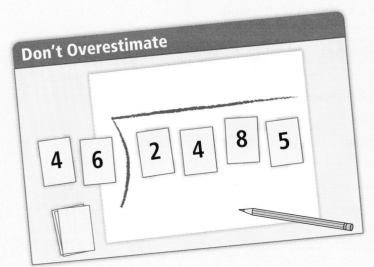

Don't Overestimate

◀ **Lesson 8.5** *Don't Overestimate* provides an opportunity for students to practice estimating partial quotients.

Developing Problem Solvers

Open-Ended Problem Solving

The Headline Story in the Daily Activities section provides an open-ended situation where students can pose and solve problems. For each story, there are many possible responses.

Headline Stories can be found on TG pages 639, 647, 655, 665, 675, 685, 693, 703, 711.

Leveled Problem Solving

Leveled Problem Solving provides an opportunity for students to apply learning from the lesson to a real-life situation. Problems are leveled by ability to allow students of all ability levels to become successful problem solvers. Each Leveled Problem Solving begins with a real-life scenario upon which three problems are built.

The levels of problems are:

❶ Basic Level	❷ On Level	❸ Above Level
students who need extra support	students working at grade level	students who are ready for more challenging problems

Leveled Problem Solving can be found on TG pages 645, 652, 662, 672, 682, 691, 700, 709, and 717.

The World Almanac for Kids Feature is designed to stimulate student interest in the math concepts they are about to learn. Students use data to solve problems and explain solutions. The Chapter 8 Project can be found on SH pages 130–131.

Write Math **Reflect and Summarize the Lesson** poses a problem or question for students to think and write about. This feature can be found on TG pages 644, 651, 661, 671, 681, 690, 699, 708, 716, and 720.

Other opportunities to write about math can be found on LAB pages 154, 156, 158, 160, and 170.

Problem Solving Strategies

The focus of **Lesson 8.10** is the strategy *draw a picture*. However, students will use a variety of problem solving strategies as they work through the chapter. The chart below shows strategies that may be useful in completing each lesson.

Strategy	Lesson(s)	Description
✓ Draw a Picture	8.3, 8.4, 8.7, 8.10	Draw pictures of area models; and use a grid to illustrate how remainders can be written as fractions
Guess and Check	8.3–8.6	Guess and check to find appropriate partial quotients
Look for a Pattern	8.2–8.8	Relate multiplication and division
Make a Model	0, 0, 0	Use an area model to show division
Make a Table	8.4	Make a table of useful multiples to use in solving division problems
Solve a Simpler Problem	8.3–8.5	Break an array into smaller ones to solve a division problem
Use Logical Reasoning	8.2, 8.4, 8.6, 8.7	Connect multiplication and division; use compatible numbers to estimate; and interpret remainders in word problems
Write an Equation	8.2	Write sentences in a multiplication/division fact family

Meeting the Needs of All Learners

Differentiated Instruction

Extra Support	On Level	Enrichment
Intervention Activities TG pp. 645, 652, 662, 672, 682, 691, 700, 709, 717	**Practice Book** pp. P62–P70	**Extension Activities** TG pp. 645, 652, 662, 672, 682, 691, 700, 709, 717
	Spiral Review Book pp. SR62–SR70	**Extension Book** pp. E62–E70
	LAB Challenge LAB pp. 152, 154, 156, 158, 160, 162, 164, 166, 168	**LAB Challenge** LAB pp. 152, 154, 156, 158, 160, 162, 164, 166, 168
Lesson Notes **Basic Level** TG pp. 650, 686, 698	**Lesson Notes** **On Level** TG pp. 670, 698	**Lesson Notes** **Above Level** TG pp. 650, 660, 687
Leveled Problem Solving **Basic Level** TG pp. 645, 652, 662, 672, 682, 691, 700, 709, 717	**Leveled Problem Solving** **On Level** TG pp. 645, 652, 662, 672, 682, 691, 700, 709, 717	**Leveled Problem Solving** **Above Level** TG pp. 645, 652, 662, 672, 682, 691, 700, 709, 717

English Language Learners

Suggestions for addressing the needs of children learning English as a second language are included in the Developing Mathematical Language section at the beginning of most lessons.

ELL activities for this chapter can be found on TG pages 639, 647, 655, 665, 675, 685, 693, 703, and 711.

The Multi-Age Classroom

Grade 4	• Students on this level should be able to complete the lessons in Chapter 8 but might need some additional practice with key concepts and skills. • Give students more practice with division.	See Grade 5, Intervention Activities, Lessons 8.1–8.9. See Grade 4, Lessons 2.6–2.8, 13.1–13.6.
Grade 5	• Students on this level should be able to complete the lessons in Chapter 8 with minimal adjustments.	See Grade 5, Practice pages P62–P70.
Grade 6	• Students on this level should be able to complete the lessons in Chapter 8 and to extend division concepts and skills. • Give students extended work with repeating and terminating quotients.	See Grade 5, Extension pages E62–E70.

Cross Curricular Connections

Science Connection

Math Concept: multiplication and division

Gravity

- Ask students what they know about gravity. Discuss how different planets exert different forces of gravity.

- Show how much a person who weighs 120 pounds on Earth would weigh on Mercury.

Weight on Planet of 1 Pound on Earth			
Planet	Weight	Planet	Weight
Mercury	0.38	Saturn	0.92
Venus	0.90	Uranus	0.89
Mars	0.38	Neptune	1.12
Jupiter	2.36		

- Using the data in the table, weights of items on other planets can be found. The Mercury weight for a 120-pound person on Earth would be: 0.38×120 lb $= 45.6$ lb

- Tell students an object will weight 944 pounds on Jupiter. Have them estimate, then use a calculator to find, the weight on Earth. Discuss how they found their answers. 400 lb

- Assign a planet to pairs of students, and have them find the weight of the 120-pound person on that planet. Venus: 108 lb; Mars: 45.6 lb; Jupiter: 283.2 lb; Saturn: 110.4 lb; Uranus: 106.8 lb; Neptune: 134.4 lb

Lesson 8.4

Social Studies Connection

Math Concept: division

Presidential Election Years

- Discuss with students when the last presidential election was held. Ask them how often such an election is held and when the election before the last one was held. Write the years on the board, and ask students whether they notice any pattern in the numbers. Possible answers: all even years, all divisible by 2

- Ask students to work backward from the most recent year you have written on the board and write the years of the previous five elections.

- Lead students to see that for over 200 years, every presidential election year has been divisible by 4.

- Challenge students to name the years of the twentieth-century U.S. presidential elections. Have them check their answers by multiplication. 1900, 1904, 1908, 1912, 1916, 1920, 1924, 1928, 1932, 1936, 1940, 1944, 1948, 1952, 1956, 1960, 1964, 1968, 1972, 1976, 1980, 1984, 1988, 1992, 1996

Lesson 8.5

Literature Connection

Math Concept: division

Using Math to Fly a Jumbo Jet
By Wendy and David Clemson and Chris Perry

Students will be able to apply their knowledge about division while interpreting data about jumbo jets. Teachers and students alike will enjoy the challenging problems and information presented in this book.

Lesson 8.9

School-Home Connection

A reproducible copy of the School-Home Connection letter in English and Spanish can be found in the *Teacher Resource Book,* pages SHC29–SHC32. Encourage students to play *Divide and Divide Again,* found on the School-Home Connection page, with a family member. Students will work with the concept of remainders in division in **Lessons 8.7–8.9.**

Assessment Options

There are many opportunities in *Think Math!* to assess students' understanding of concepts, skills, and problem solving. Learning Goals for Chapter 8 are provided below. The assessment options provide opportunities to evaluate whether or not students have retained learning from prior experiences. Choose the forms of assessment that best meet the needs of your students.

Chapter 8 Learning Goals

	Learning Goals	Lesson Number
8-A	Use multiplication and division of whole numbers to solve problems and multiplication to check division	8.1, 8.2, 8.6
8-B	Divide numbers with up to a 3-digit dividend and a 2-digit divisor using an area model or division record	8.3, 8.4, 8.5
8-C	Write remainders using whole numbers and fractions and interpret remainders in a given context	8.7, 8.8, 8.9
8-D	Apply problem solving strategies such as *draw a picture* to solve problems	8.10

✔ Informal Assessment

Ongoing Assessment
Provides insight into students' thinking to guide instruction (TG pp. 648, 651, 656, 666, 667, 676, 686, 694, 704, and 714)

Reflect and Summarize the Lesson
Checks understanding of lesson concepts (TG pp. 644, 651, 661, 671, 681, 690, 699, 708, 716, 720)

Snapshot Assessment
Mental Math and Quick Write
Offers a quick observation of students' progress on chapter concepts and skills (TG pp. 724–725)

Performance Assessment
Provides quarterly assessment of Chapters 8–11 concepts using real-life situations
Assessment Guide
pp. AG219–AG227

✔ Formal Assessment

Standardized Test Prep
Problem Solving Test Prep
Prepares students for standardized tests
Lesson Activity Book p. 170 (TG p. 721)

Chapter 8 Review/Assessment
Reviews and assesses students' understanding of the chapter
Lesson Activity Book pp. 171–172 (TG p. 726)

Chapter 8 Test
Assesses the chapter concepts and skills
Assessment Guide
Form A pp. AG77–AG78
Form B pp. AG79–AG80

Benchmark 3 Assessment
Provides quarterly assessment of Chapters 8–11 concepts and skills
Assessment Guide
Benchmark 3A pp. AG93–AG100
Benchmark 3B pp. AG101–AG108

World Almanac for Kids

Use the World Almanac for Kids feature, *Marching Bands,* found on pp. 130–131 of the **Student Handbook,** to provide students with an opportunity to practice their problem solving skills by solving real world problems.

FACT • ACTIVITY 1

❶ The missing factor tells how many rows of 10 marchers are in the band of 350.

❷ 35; Possible answers: 350 ÷ 10 = 35 rows of marchers

❸ 70 rows of marchers; Possible explanation: When the band is divided into rows with half the number of marchers, the number of rows doubles.

❹ There will be 14 marchers in each of the 25 rows.

25

14
Total = 350 members

Student Handbook p. 130

FACT·ACTIVITY 2

If you study a band instrument, it is likely to be one of three types: woodwind, brass, or percussion.

Use area models for 1–3.

❶ Suppose the OMTAAMB band has 320 brass players, 128 woodwind players, and 112 percussion players. Group each section of the band so that there are 16 members in each row. How many rows will each section of the marching band have?

Brass: 320 ÷ 16 = ■

Woodwind: 128 ÷ 16 = ■

Percussion: 112 ÷ 16 = ■

❷ If two of the drummers cannot march, what happens to the arrangement of percussion marchers?

❸ Write a division sentence which shows the number of complete rows and the number of marchers left over if there are only 110 percussion marchers. Then check your answer using multiplication.

CHAPTER PROJECT

Pretend you are the band director for a marching band. Decide on the number of people in your band and how many are in each section (brass, percussion, and woodwind). Some bands also have flag twirlers, called color guards. Decide if they will be a part of your band.

Then, develop 3 different marching arrangements (formations) for the different sections of your band. Your first formation should be an attempt to have the band march into the stadium in equal rows. Use area models on grid paper, multiplication, and related division sentences for help if you wish. (Hint: The sections can be "rectangles" of different sizes.) Decide what you will do if there are "remainders."

Present your formations to the class. Use equations to explain the number of rows and the number of people in each row for each section.

ALMANAC
Fact

The One More Time Around Again Marching Band (OMTAAMB) is the world's largest marching band. There are about 560 members in the band from far away places including Japan and New Zealand. The band played at the 2000 Olympic Games in Sydney, Australia.

Student Handbook p. 131

FACT·ACTIVITY 2

❶ Brass: 320 ÷ 16 = 20 rows;
Woodwind: 128 ÷ 16 = 8 rows;
Percussion: 112 ÷ 16 = 7 rows

❷ There will not be an equal number of marchers in each row.

❸ 110 ÷ 16 = 6 r14. The remainder of 14 shows that one row will have 14 instead of 16 marchers. Check: (6 × 16) + 14 = 110.

CHAPTER PROJECT

Possible response: This is one arrangement for 92 band members:

```
X X X X X X X X X X X X X
X X X X X X X X X X X X X  brass
```

```
        X X X X X X X
        X X X X X X X  percussion
        X X X X X X X
```

```
X X X X      X X      X X X X
X X X X      X X      X X X X
X X X X      X X      X X X X
X X X X              X X X X
woodwinds            woodwinds
```

```
        X X X X
        color guard
```

Brass: 26 people, 26 ÷ 2 = 13, 2 rows of 13

Percussion: 24 people, 24 ÷ 3 = 8, 3 rows of 8

Woodwind: 32 people, 32 ÷ 2 = 16; 16 ÷ 4 = 4, 2 sets of 4 rows of 4

Color guard: 10 people, 1 row of 4 and 3 rows of 2

Vocabulary

To reinforce vocabulary concepts, invite students to complete the vocabulary activities on pp. 142–143 of the **Student Handbook.** Encourage students to record their answers in their math journals.

Many responses are possible.

⑬ Possible response: If the *divisor* is 19 and the *dividend* is 684, use compatible numbers 600 ÷ 20 to estimate the first partial product of the *quotient.* The first partial *quotient* is 30 because 20 × 30 = 600. Then multiply 19 × 30 to get 570, and subtract 684 − 570 to get 114. Use compatible numbers again to estimate 114 ÷ 19. These compatible numbers are 120 ÷ 20, which is 6. So, 684 ÷ 19 = 30 + 6 = 36.

⑭ Possible response: Divide the *dividend* by the *divisor*, and write the *quotient.* If there is something left over after you subtract the last partial product, that amount is the remainder.

⑮ Possible response: Multiplication undoes division. The two factors in the multiplication problem are the *divisor* and the *quotient* in the division problem. The *product* in the multiplication problem is the *dividend* in the division problem. So, multiply the *quotient* and the *divisor* to see whether they equal the *dividend.* For example, if 615 ÷ 41 = 15, then 15 × 41 = 615.

Chapter **8** Vocabulary

Choose the best vocabulary term from Word List A for each sentence.

❶ To __?__ a number is to break it into smaller parts that total the given number. **partition**

❷ When deciding how to report a remainder, you need to make the most sensible or __?__ choice. **reasonable**

❸ In division, the __?__ is the number that is left over when one number does not divide into another evenly. **remainder**

❹ In a division problem, the number you divide into is called the __?__. **dividend**

❺ The result of multiplying two or more numbers together is a(n) __?__. **product**

❻ Multiplication and division are __?__ operations because each undoes the other. **inverse**

❼ In a division problem, the number you divide by is called the __?__. **divisor**

❽ An approximation and a(n) __?__ are both guesses that are near an exact answer. **estimation**

❾ In division, adding 1 to the quotient and dropping the remainder is called __?__. **rounding up the quotient**

❿ __?__ are numbers used to estimate the quotient of a division problem. **compatible numbers**

Word List A
- approximation
- compatible numbers
- dividend
- division
- divisor
- estimation
- factor
- inverse
- output
- partition
- product
- quotient
- reasonable
- remainder
- rounding up the quotient

Complete each analogy using the best term from Word List B.

⑪ Addend is to sum as __?__ is to product. **factor**

⑫ Subtraction is to difference as division is to __?__. **quotient**

Word List B
- dividend
- divisor
- factor
- quotient

🗨 Talk Math

Discuss with a partner what you have just learned about division. Use the vocabulary terms *dividend*, *divisor*, and *quotient*.

⑬ How can you use compatible numbers to find a partial quotient?

⑭ How do you know whether a division problem has a remainder?

⑮ How can you use multiplication to check a division problem?

142 Chapter 8

Student Handbook p. 142

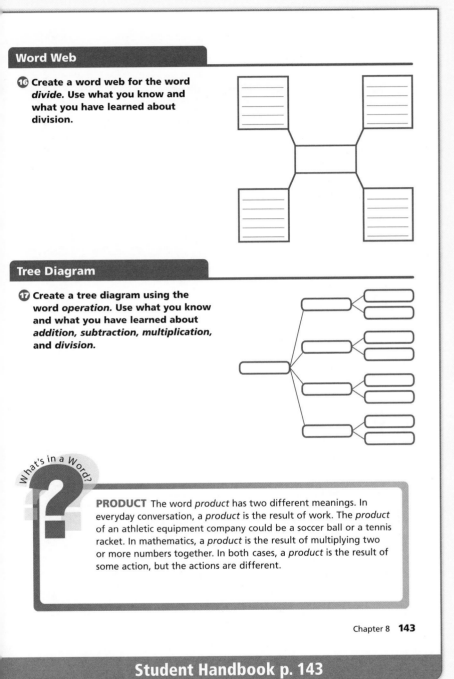

Word Web

16 Create a word web for the word *divide*. Use what you know and what you have learned about division.

Tree Diagram

17 Create a tree diagram using the word *operation*. Use what you know and what you have learned about *addition, subtraction, multiplication,* and *division*.

What's in a Word?

PRODUCT The word *product* has two different meanings. In everyday conversation, a *product* is the result of work. The *product* of an athletic equipment company could be a soccer ball or a tennis racket. In mathematics, a *product* is the result of multiplying two or more numbers together. In both cases, a *product* is the result of some action, but the actions are different.

Chapter 8   **143**

Student Handbook p. 143

16 Many answers are possible. One example is provided.

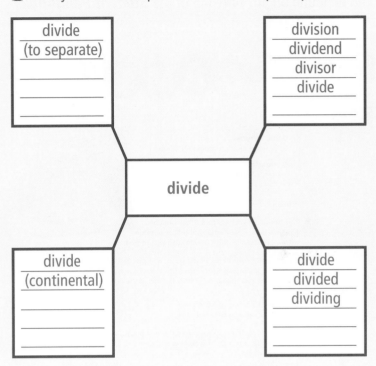

17 Many answers are possible. One example is provided.

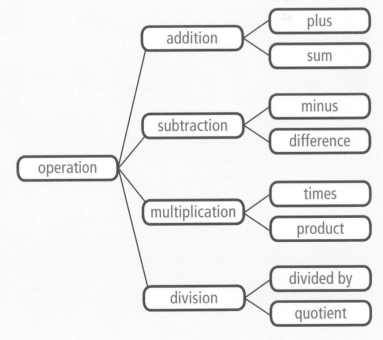

Chapter 8 — Developing a Division Algorithm

Games

200 Zoom in **Lesson 8.3** provides an opportunity for students to practice multiplication and addition in the context of playing a game. ***Don't Overestimate*** in **Lesson 8.5** provides an opportunity for students to practice estimating partial quotients. These games can be found on pp. 144–145 of the ***Student Handbook.***

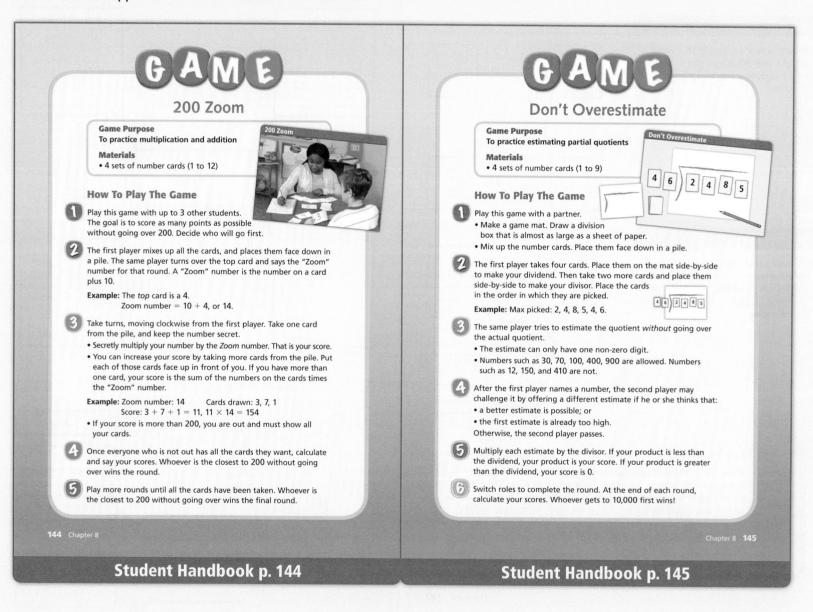

200 Zoom

Game Purpose
To practice multiplication and addition

Materials
• 4 sets of number cards (1 to 12)

How To Play The Game

1. Play this game with up to 3 other students. The goal is to score as many points as possible without going over 200. Decide who will go first.

2. The first player mixes up all the cards, and places them face down in a pile. The same player turns over the top card and says the "Zoom" number for that round. A "Zoom" number is the number on a card plus 10.

   Example: The *top* card is a 4.
   Zoom number = 10 + 4, or 14.

3. Take turns, moving clockwise from the first player. Take one card from the pile, and keep the number secret.
   • Secretly multiply your number by the *Zoom* number. That is your score.
   • You can increase your score by taking more cards from the pile. Put each of those cards face up in front of you. If you have more than one card, your score is the sum of the numbers on the cards times the "Zoom" number.

   Example: Zoom number: 14   Cards drawn: 3, 7, 1
   Score: 3 + 7 + 1 = 11, 11 × 14 = 154
   • If your score is more than 200, you are out and must show all your cards.

4. Once everyone who is not out has all the cards they want, calculate and say your scores. Whoever is the closest to 200 without going over wins the round.

5. Play more rounds until all the cards have been taken. Whoever is the closest to 200 without going over wins the final round.

144 Chapter 8

Student Handbook p. 144

Don't Overestimate

Game Purpose
To practice estimating partial quotients

Materials
• 4 sets of number cards (1 to 9)

How To Play The Game

1. Play this game with a partner.
   • Make a game mat. Draw a division box that is almost as large as a sheet of paper.
   • Mix up the number cards. Place them face down in a pile.

2. The first player takes four cards. Place them on the mat side-by-side to make your dividend. Then take two more cards and place them side-by-side to make your divisor. Place the cards in the order in which they are picked.

   Example: Max picked: 2, 4, 8, 5, 4, 6.

3. The same player tries to estimate the quotient *without* going over the actual quotient.
   • The estimate can only have one non-zero digit.
   • Numbers such as 30, 70, 100, 400, 900 are allowed. Numbers such as 12, 150, and 410 are not.

4. After the first player names a number, the second player may challenge it by offering a different estimate if he or she thinks that:
   • a better estimate is possible; or
   • the first estimate is already too high.
   Otherwise, the second player passes.

5. Multiply each estimate by the divisor. If your product is less than the dividend, your product is your score. If your product is greater than the dividend, your score is 0.

6. Switch roles to complete the round. At the end of each round, calculate your scores. Whoever gets to 10,000 first wins!

Chapter 8 145

Student Handbook p. 145

Challenge

The Challenge activity *Quotient Families* challenges students to determine how the four division problems in a "quotient family" are alike. This activity can be found on p. 146 of the *Student Handbook.*

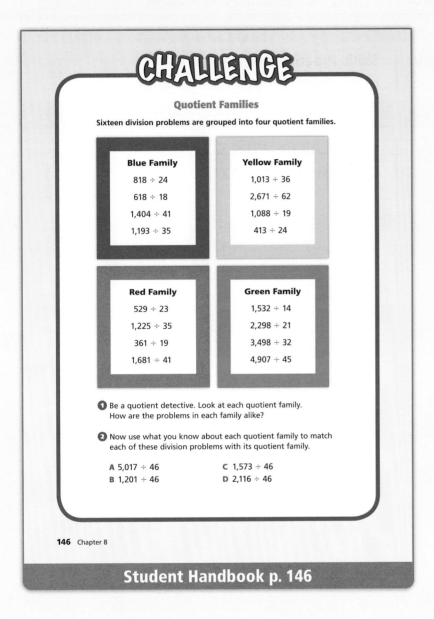

CHALLENGE

Quotient Families

Sixteen division problems are grouped into four quotient families.

Blue Family

818 ÷ 24

618 ÷ 18

1,404 ÷ 41

1,193 ÷ 35

Yellow Family

1,013 ÷ 36

2,671 ÷ 62

1,088 ÷ 19

413 ÷ 24

Red Family

529 ÷ 23

1,225 ÷ 35

361 ÷ 19

1,681 ÷ 41

Green Family

1,532 ÷ 14

2,298 ÷ 21

3,498 ÷ 32

4,907 ÷ 45

❶ Be a quotient detective. Look at each quotient family. How are the problems in each family alike?

❷ Now use what you know about each quotient family to match each of these division problems with its quotient family.

A 5,017 ÷ 46   C 1,573 ÷ 46

B 1,201 ÷ 46   D 2,116 ÷ 46

146 Chapter 8

Student Handbook p. 146

❶ The Blue Family has the same 2-digit quotient, 34. Remainders are different.

The Yellow Family has different quotients, but each has the same remainder: 5.

In the Red Family, the quotient is equal to the divisor.

The Green Family has the same 3-digit quotient, 109. Remainders are different.

❷ **A** Green Family

B Yellow Family

C Blue Family

D Red Family

Lesson 1 Exploring Missing Factors

NCTM Standards 1, 2, 6, 7, 8, 9, 10

Lesson Planner

STUDENT OBJECTIVE ·
- To solve problems using multiplication and division

1 | Daily Activities (TG p. 639)

Open-Ended Problem Solving/Headline Story	Skills Practice and Review— Finding the Greatest Multiple of 10

2 | Teach and Practice (TG pp. 640–645)

MATERIALS

A **Reading the Student Letter** (TG pp. 640–641)

B **Exploring Division** (TG pp. 641–642)

C **Using Puzzles to Solve Postage Problems** (TG p. 643)

D **Finding Missing Factors** (TG p. 644)

- 📖 LAB pp. 151–152
- 📖 SH pp. 129, 132

3 | Differentiated Instruction (TG p. 645)

Leveled Problem Solving (TG p. 645)	Practice Book P62
Intervention Activity (TG p. 645)	Extension Book E62
Extension Activity (TG p. 645)	Spiral Review Book SR62

Lesson Notes

About the Lesson

Long division is a process whose essential steps are finding multiples of the divisor that are less than the dividend (or the amount remaining after subtracting from the dividend). The activities in this lesson require this same type of thinking. The work helps students see the connection between multiplication and division of large numbers and prepares them for the division work in this chapter.

Use with Lesson Activity Book pp. 151–152.

Developing Mathematical Language

Vocabulary: division

Division and multiplication are inverse operations; *division* undoes multiplication. Because of this relationship, finding the missing factor in a multiplication sentence is a precursor to *division*. Finding the missing factor provides students with a direct link to the *division* concepts of finding the number in each equal group or the number of equal groups.

Review the meaning of *division*.

Beginning Display 15 counters. Explain that finding how many go into equal groups is one type of division. Have students show how they would divide the counters into 3 equal groups. Write $15 \div 3 = 5$ on the board.

Intermediate Write $3 \times \blacksquare = 15$ and $15 \div 3 = \blacksquare$. Ask students to explain how the number sentences are related. Suggest the use of pictures as needed. Then encourage students to explain how they think of *division*.

Advanced Ask students to define *division*. Then write $3 \times \blacksquare = 15$ and $15 \div 3 = \blacksquare$. Discuss how thinking of a missing factor can help solve a *division* problem.

Open-Ended Problem Solving

After writing this story on the board, ask your students to share their ideas. Encourage students to consider the situation where there is the same number of students per grade.

 ### Headline Story

The Moss School has 600 students in kindergarten through fifth grade. There are as close to 18 students per class as possible. What can you say about the number of classes?

Possible responses: I divided 600 by 18 and got 33 with a remainder of 6. That would be 33 classes, but 6 classes would have 19 students. Since there are 6 grades, there would be about 100 students in each grade. There could be 5 classes of 20 students for each grade.

 ## Skills Practice and Review

Finding the Greatest Multiple of 10

Have students estimate the value of expressions like $250 \div 6$ by finding the largest multiple of 10 that is still less than $250 \div 6$. For example, 50 is too large because 50×6 is 300, which is more than 250. Forty will work, because 40×6 is 240, and 240 is less than 250. You might want to ask students to name the multiples in order and ask if each is the largest until the class reaches one that is too big. In our example, the student would count $6 \times 10 = 60$, $6 \times 20 = 120$, $6 \times 30 = 180$, $6 \times 40 = 240$ (close), $6 \times 50 = 300$ (too big). Here are some other problems you might try.

$304 \div 4$ 70	$266 \div 7$ 30	$531 \div 9$ 50
$395 \div 5$ 70	$384 \div 12$ 30	

whole class · 10 MIN

A Reading the Student Letter

NCTM Standards 1, 2, 6, 7, 8, 9, 10

Purpose To introduce the chapter content

Introduce The Student Letter reminds students of some of the things they have learned in the past about multiplication, and about connections between multiplication and division. Have students read the letter independently. You may want to take an extra minute or two to let students try the first two problems posed in the letter—using 35×74 to find 70×74, and completing the related sentences. This will give you and them a sense of how much they already know. The rest of the letter gives students a hint of what might remain for them to learn about connections between multiplication and division.

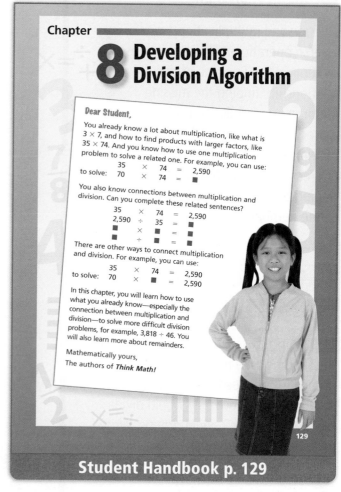

Student Handbook p. 129

Task The questions in the letter ask students to think about ways they can use simple multiplication facts to find more difficult facts and to find quotients. Ask students to discuss the questions with a partner.

Share Ask students to share their answers to the questions in the letter with the class.

• To use $35 \times 74 = 2{,}590$ to find 70×74, notice that 70 is twice 35. So, the desired product must be twice 2,590, or 5,180.

• Completing the related sentences for $35 \times 74 = 2{,}590$:

$$35 \times 74 = 2{,}590$$
$$2{,}590 \div 35 = 74$$
$$74 \times 35 = 2{,}590$$
$$2{,}590 \div 74 = 35$$

- To use $35 \times 74 = 2{,}590$ to find the missing number in $70 \times ? = 2{,}590$, notice that 70 is 35 multiplied by 2. Since the second product is the same as the first, the factor 74 must be *divided* by 2: $74 \div 2 = 37$.

Talk Math

❷ How can you use $12 \times 19 = 228$ to find 24×19? Explain your method.
Possible explanation: 24 is twice 12, so the product I am looking for must be twice 228, or 456.

❷ How can you use $26 \times 34 = 884$ to find the missing number in $? \times 68 = 884$? Explain your method. Possible explanation: 68 is 34 times 2. The products are the same, so the missing number must be 26 divided by 2, or 13.

B Exploring Division

small groups or whole class 15 MIN

NCTM Standards 1, 2, 6, 7, 8, 9, 10

Purpose To divide a quantity by considering amounts of different magnitudes (tens and ones) for the divisor

Introduce Have students work together in pairs or small groups to try to solve the problem on Explore: Shipping Stamps. As they work, observe what strategies they're using. Some may multiply four (the number of packages) by various multiples of 10 to find the one closest to 152. Others may notice that 152 has a 2 in the ones place and begin reciting or listing multiples of 4 to find those that have a 2 in the ones place.

Task After students have had a few minutes to work on the problem, gather them together to report on their progress and share their strategies.

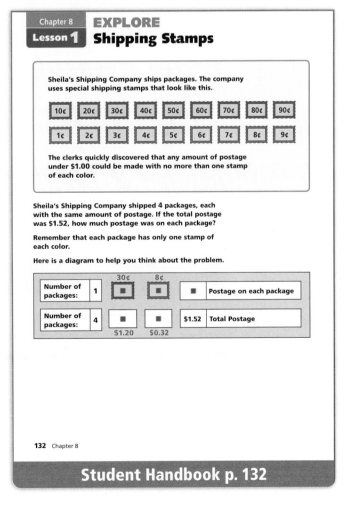

Student Handbook p. 132

Teacher Story

"One of my students mentioned that using one stamp of each color to make an amount under $1.00 is the same as using a 2-digit number to record an amount under 100. I think others may have thought about it, but he was the only one to verbalize it!"

Talk Math

❷ **How did you begin the process of figuring out how many of each type of stamp was needed?** Possible answers: I figured out the number of blue stamps first because I could quickly find out what multiple was too large—40¢. I thought about the ones, or green stamps first and knew the total needed to end in 2.

❷ **What two possibilities for green stamps produce a total cost that ends in 2?** A 3¢ stamp because 4 × 3 = 12, or an 8¢ stamp because 4 × 8 = 32.

This experience may have prompted some students to decide that they can't be sure about the ones stamps (green) until they decide on the tens stamps (blue).

At this point you may want to copy the diagram from the bottom of the Explore page onto the board. Ask students to tell you the largest tens stamp that can be used 30¢ and write it into the square representing the tens stamp. Ask students to then figure out how much of the $1.52 postage for the 4 packages is paid by the tens stamps. $1.20

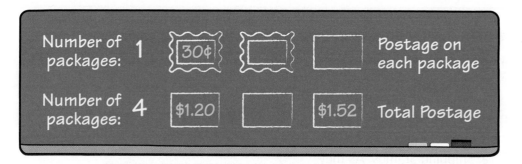

Students are now likely to see that the difference between $1.20 and $1.52 is 32¢, or four 8¢ stamps. Complete the diagram.

Practice
Try a few more examples by erasing all the numbers and entering a new number of packages and the total postage. Some students may prefer to reason about the ones stamps first, and you might write the possibilities that they come up with off to the side.

Number of Packages	Total Postage	Stamps Used
6	$3.72	60¢, 2¢
8	$3.92	40¢, 9¢
12	$9.12	70¢, 6¢

Use with Lesson Activity Book pp. 151–152.

Using Puzzles to Solve Postage Problems

Purpose To divide using a puzzle format

Introduce Introduce multiplication puzzles as a way to solve problems like the postage problems in Activity B. Draw the first puzzle below on the board.

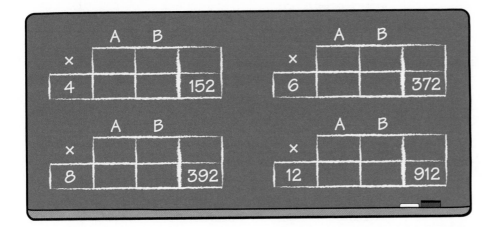

Task Tell students that **A marks the place for the value of the tens stamp, and B marks the place for the value of ones stamp.** Fill in the table one number at a time to match the numbers produced in the previous activity. Although some students may want to think about the value of the ones stamps first and record these numbers somewhere or keep them in mind, start with box A for this demonstration.

As in the Explore page in Activity B, begin with the total number of blue (tens) stamps for 4 packages (30 × 4). Write 30 in box A and write 120 into the box directly below box A. Next, write the difference between 120 and 152 (32) into the box between them. Write 8 into box B. Sum 30 and 8 to fill in the last box.

Remind students of the context of the problem as you point to the individual numbers, saying something like, "4 packages with 38¢ of postage on each is a total of $1.52."

Follow the same procedure to complete the other three puzzles with the class's help.

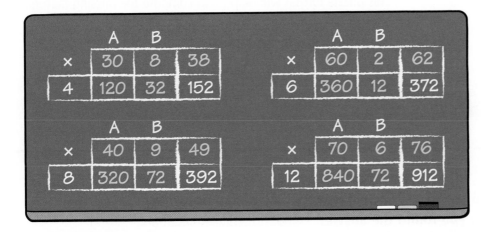

individuals

20 MIN

Purpose To divide by finding missing factors

NCTM Standards 1, 2, 6, 9, 10

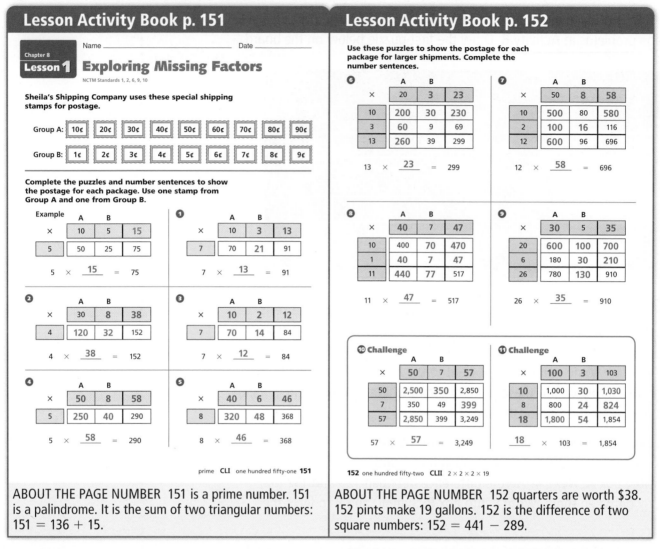

Lesson Activity Book p. 151

Name _____ Date _____

Chapter 8
Lesson 1 **Exploring Missing Factors**
NCTM Standards 1, 2, 6, 9, 10

Sheila's Shipping Company uses these special shipping stamps for postage.

Group A: 10¢ 20¢ 30¢ 40¢ 50¢ 60¢ 70¢ 80¢ 90¢

Group B: 1¢ 2¢ 3¢ 4¢ 5¢ 6¢ 7¢ 8¢ 9¢

Complete the puzzles and number sentences to show the postage for each package. Use one stamp from Group A and one from Group B.

Example

×	A 10	B 5	15
5	50	25	75

5 × **15** = 75

①

×	A 10	B 3	13
7	70	21	91

7 × **13** = 91

②

×	A 30	B 8	38
4	120	32	152

4 × **38** = 152

③

×	A 10	B 2	12
7	70	14	84

7 × **12** = 84

④

×	A 50	B 8	58
5	250	40	290

5 × **58** = 290

⑤

×	A 40	B 6	46
8	320	48	368

8 × **46** = 368

prime **CLI** one hundred fifty-one **151**

Lesson Activity Book p. 152

Use these puzzles to show the postage for each package for larger shipments. Complete the number sentences.

⑥

×	A 20	B 3	23
10	200	30	230
3	60	9	69
13	260	39	299

13 × **23** = 299

⑦

×	A 50	B 8	58
10	500	80	580
2	100	16	116
12	600	96	696

12 × **58** = 696

⑧

×	A 40	B 7	47
10	400	70	470
1	40	7	47
11	440	77	517

11 × **47** = 517

⑨

×	A 30	B 5	35
20	600	100	700
6	180	30	210
26	780	130	910

26 × **35** = 910

⑩ Challenge

×	A 50	B 7	57
50	2,500	350	2,850
7	350	49	399
57	2,850	399	3,249

57 × **57** = 3,249

⑪ Challenge

×	A 100	B 3	103
10	1,000	30	1,030
8	800	24	824
18	1,800	54	1,854

18 × 103 = 1,854

152 one hundred fifty-two **CLII** 2 × 2 × 2 × 19

ABOUT THE PAGE NUMBER 151 is a prime number. 151 is a palindrome. It is the sum of two triangular numbers: 151 = 136 + 15.

ABOUT THE PAGE NUMBER 152 quarters are worth $38. 152 pints make 19 gallons. 152 is the difference of two square numbers: 152 = 441 − 289.

Teaching Notes for LAB page 151

Have students work on the page independently or in pairs. Students complete missing-factor puzzles and related number sentences. By now, students should be familiar with these puzzles and their connection to number sentences.

Teaching Notes for LAB page 152

The puzzles on the page ask students to figure out the postage for larger numbers of packages. Students may end up using all four operations—addition, subtraction, multiplication, and division—to complete the puzzles. Again, their familiarity with this puzzle format will help them compute the missing factors.

Challenge Problem This problem asks students to find the missing factor in a different location.

Reflect and Summarize the Lesson

 Write Math

Suppose you spent $1.68 to buy 6 erasers. If each eraser cost the same, how much did each eraser cost? Explain how you found the answer. $0.28; Possible explanation: I know that 6 × 20 = 120 is less than 168 and 6 × 30 = 180 is greater, So, the tens digit is 2. The difference is 168 − 120 = 48. But I know that 6 × 8 = 48. So, the cost is 20 + 8 = 28 cents.

Use with Lesson Activity Book pp. 151–152.

Leveled Problem Solving

There are 45 tacks in a small box. There 58 small boxes of tacks.

❶ Basic Level

How many tacks are there in all? How many tacks are in half the boxes? Explain. 2,610 tacks in all: 45 × 58 = 2,610. Half the packages have half the total number, or 1,305 tacks.

❷ On Level

A large box has twice as many tacks as a small box. How many large boxes hold the same number of tacks as 58 small boxes? Explain. 29 large boxes; 45 × 58 = 2,610. When you double one factor, halve the other: 90 × 29 = 2,610.

❸ Above Level

The economy pack has one third as many tacks as a small box. How many economy packs hold the same number of tacks as 58 small boxes? Explain. 174 economy packs: 15 × 174 = 2,610

Intervention

Activity Factor Patterns

Display this table.

56	×	18	=	1,008
28	×	36	=	1,008
14	×	72	=	1,008

Have students solve for the missing factors. Discuss with the class the pattern formed by the factor pairs. Then have students use the pattern to create their own tables and have their classmates complete them.

Practice

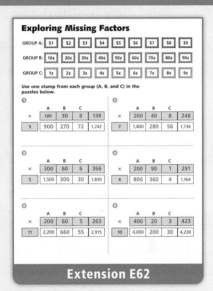

Practice P62

Extension

Extension E62

Spiral Review

Spiral Review Book page SR62 provides review of the following previously learned skills and concepts:

• locating positive mixed numbers on a number line

• applying the problem solving strategy *solve a simpler problem*

You may wish to have students work with partners to complete the page.

Spiral Review SR62

Extension Activity
Factor Sandwich

Show students these number sentences. Have students work in pairs to find the two multiples of 10 between which the missing factors lie.

70 × ■ = 5,000 70 and 80

38 × ■ = 780 20 and 30

■ × 53 = 1,600 30 and 40

■ × 42 = 3,450 80 and 90

Lesson 2 Connecting Multiplication and Division

NCTM Standards 1, 2, 6, 7, 8, 9, 10

Lesson Planner

STUDENT OBJECTIVES
- To use division to solve problems
- To use multiplication to solve problems
- To see connections between multiplication and division

1 Daily Activities (TG p. 647)

Open-Ended Problem Solving/Headline Story	Skills Practice and Review—Finding the Greatest Multiple of 10

2 Teach and Practice (TG pp. 648–651)

	MATERIALS
(A) **Multiplying, Un-Multiplying, Dividing, and Un-Dividing** (TG pp. 648–649)	• TR: Activity Master, AM65
(B) **Connecting Multiplication and Division** (TG p. 650)	• LAB pp. 153–154
(C) **Connecting "Un-Multiplication" to Division** (TG p. 651)	

3 Differentiated Instruction (TG p. 652)

Leveled Problem Solving (TG p. 652)	Practice Book P63
Intervention Activity (TG p. 652)	Extension Book E63
Extension Activity (TG p. 652)	Spiral Review Book SR63

Lesson Notes

About the Lesson

In this lesson, students use fact families and related multiplication facts to divide. They already know the fact-family connections between multiplication and division. They also know how products like 7×3, 7×6, 7×12, and 7×24 are related: the second factor doubles in each succeeding product, so the products must double, too. Students use this knowledge and the fact that multiplication and division are inverse operations to find quotients that are related to previously determined products.

About the Mathematics

To understand division, students need to learn what division is, when it is the correct operation to use, and how to divide. Division is the undoing of multiplication. If $a \times b = c$, then $a = c \div b$, as long as neither a nor b is 0.

Division is used when we need to find *how many* of one quantity are represented by another quantity. For example, how many hours are represented by 7,200 seconds? It is also used when we need to know *how big* a quantity results if another quantity is separated into equal parts. For example, how big will classes be if 1,000 students are split among 45 classrooms? As for *how* to divide, that is the subject of much of this chapter.

Developing Mathematical Language

Vocabulary: dividend, divisor, factor, product, quotient, remainder

When there is no *remainder,* the *quotient* and *divisor* can be thought of as *factors* and the *dividend* can be thought of as their *product.* Show these relationships on the board:

> When there is no remainder:
>
> $$\frac{\text{quotient}}{\text{divisor}\,)\overline{\text{dividend}}}$$
>
> dividend ÷ divisor = quotient
>
> $$\frac{\text{factor}}{\text{factor}\,)\overline{\text{product}}}$$
>
> product ÷ factor = factor

Familiarize students with the terms *dividend, divisor, factor, product,* and *quotient.*

Beginning Display this division: $6)\overline{24}$ with quotient 4. Point to each number, identify it as the *dividend, divisor,* or *quotient,* and have students repeat its name. Then identify each number as a *factor* or *product.*

Intermediate Display this division: $5)\overline{30}$ with quotient 6. Have students identify the *dividend, divisor,* and *quotient.* Then have them rewrite the division, substituting the terms *factor* and *product* for *dividend, divisor,* and *quotient.*

Advanced Have pairs of students write a division sentence, substitute the terms *dividend, divisor,* and *quotient* for the numbers, and then substitute the terms *factor* and *product.*

Open-Ended Problem Solving

Read the Headline Story to the students. Encourage them to think of creative scenarios that incorporate information from the story.

 Headline Story

> **Sam Houston Elementary School has nearly 1,000 children from kindergarten through 5th grade, with about the same number of students in each grade. Most classes have close to 25 students. No class has more than 25 students. What can you figure out from this information?**

Possible responses: 4 classes would have about 100 children, so 1,000 children would require about 40 classes. If there were 42 classes and the same number of classrooms for each of the 6 grades, there would be 7 classrooms for each grade.

Skills Practice and Review

Finding the Greatest Multiple of 10

If 6 friends collected 258 shells on the beach, about how many shells would each friend get? Show students how to estimate 258 ÷ 6 by systematically guessing and checking to find the largest multiple of 10 that is still less than 258 ÷ 6. Begin with a guess of 30: 30 × 6 = 180, which is less than 258. Therefore, 30 is a good guess, but is it the largest multiple of 10 that is less than 258 ÷ 6. Try 50: it is too high, because 50 × 6 is 300, which is greater than 258. Try 40: 40 × 6 is 240, which is smaller than 258. So, 40 is the largest multiple of 10 that is still less than 258 ÷ 6.

Now have students estimate on their own, using 280 shells and 5 friends 50 shells, 312 shells and 4 friends 70 shells, and 574 shells and 7 friends 80 shells.

| **Teach and Practice**

individuals or small groups

20 MIN

Materials
- For each student: AM65

NCTM Standards 1, 2, 6, 7, 8, 9, 10

✓ Ongoing Assessment
- Do students know the basic multiplication facts through 12 × 12?
- Can students write fact families for any given multiplication or division fact?

Ⓐ Multiplying, Un-Multiplying, Dividing, and Un-Dividing

Purpose To understand division as un-multiplication and multiplication as un-division

Introduce Tell students that un-multiplying and un-dividing are made-up words that draw attention to the way multiplication and division "un-do" each other.

- multiply: 5 × 6 = 30
  un-multiply by dividing: 30 ÷ 6 = 5
- divide: 28 ÷ 4 = 7
  un-divide by multiplying: 7 × 4 = 28

Task Have students complete Activity Master 65: Multiplying, Un-Multiplying, Dividing and Un-Dividing on their own or in small groups. Most students already have at least a general understanding of related products and the relationship between multiplication and division. This activity helps them consolidate those ideas so they can use them.

Problem 1 reminds students that they can solve multiplication problems by using related facts. Students can find 12 × 28 by doubling 12 × 14. If they don't know 12 × 14, they can find it by doubling 12 × 7 or by adding 12 × 4 and 12 × 10. And if they don't know 12 × 7, they can double 6 × 7. This is the "double or add" strategy they learned earlier this year.

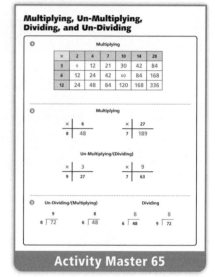

Activity Master 65

The diagrams in Problem 2 represent small sections of a multiplication table. In the first part, two factors are shown and students must find the product. The second part shows un-multiplying: the product and one factor are known, and students must un-multiply to find the other factor.

Use with Lesson Activity Book pp. 153–154.

- If you think students would find additional practice and review helpful, you might have them work through another horizontal or vertical "missing factor" problem, like one of these:

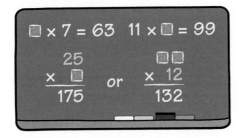

- The goal, at this point, is for students to understand division as simply un-multiplication. You might write this on the board to summarize.

> **Multiplication**
> The question is: $7 \times 9 = ?$
> What's the answer? 63
>
> **Division**
> The question is: $7 \times ? = 63$.
> What's the answer? 9

Problem 3 is like Problem 2 and has the same purpose, but the diagrams are pared down even further, and the labels are different. The un-dividing problems are again portions of a multiplication table. You can also think of them as arrays with the numbers of rows and columns shown, or as rectangles with their lengths and heights shown. The diagrams are drawn so that the "dividing" problems show the familiar "division box" with the dimensions of the array or rectangle shown and one number missing.

Talk Math

❓ Jodie found that the product of her age and 15 is 180. What is the product of her age and 30? Explain your method. 360; Possible explanation: 30 is twice 15, so the product I'm looking for must be twice 180; $180 \times 2 = 360$.

❓ What are the division sentences in the fact family that includes $3 \times 8 = 24$? $24 \div 3 = 8$ and $24 \div 8 = 3$

Possible Discussion

To take the discussion of the multiplication table on Activity Master 65 a bit further, you might challenge the class to multiply 26 by 5 mentally using the related problem 26×10. The method is to halve the product of 26×10, because 5 times a number is half 10 times that number: $26 \times 10 = 260$, so $26 \times 5 = 130$.

Teacher Story

❝I have some students who still have not memorized their multiplication facts. For each of these students, I keep an individualized list of the facts they have not memorized. Every day I give some of these students a sticky note showing three facts to work on. I keep track of the facts I assign to each student and, if possible, quiz them on the facts the next day. Sometimes I assign division facts rather than multiplication facts. Once a student knows the facts, I cross them off the relevant list and give the student three new facts. My students seem to be better able to manage working on a few facts at a time than they would if I were to assign the entire list at once.❞

Purpose To practice "un-multiplication" (division)

NCTM Standards 1, 2, 6, 7, 8, 9, 10

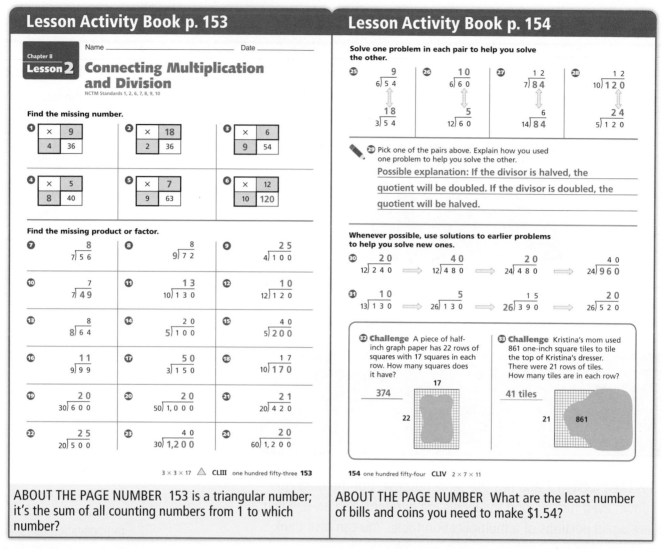

Lesson Activity Book p. 153

ABOUT THE PAGE NUMBER 153 is a triangular number; it's the sum of all counting numbers from 1 to which number?

Lesson Activity Book p. 154

ABOUT THE PAGE NUMBER What are the least number of bills and coins you need to make $1.54?

Teaching Notes for LAB page 153

Have students complete the page individually or with partners. The page gives students practice with the idea of un-multiplying.

Students can think of Problems 1–6 as multiplication problems that are missing various parts.

Differentiated Instruction Basic Level/Above Level
Problems 7–24 have equal content, but Problems 16–24 use larger numbers. You may decide to assign only Problems 7–15 to basic-level problem solvers and only Problems 16–24 to above-level problem solvers. Or, you may decide that the practice and challenge of both sets of problems are worthwhile for all students.

Teaching Notes for LAB page 154

In each pair in Problems 25–28, students will probably find that one problem is easier to solve than the other. That may be because the numbers are smaller or more familiar, or because a memorized fact is involved. In each case, students can use the solution to the easier problem to solve the more difficult one.

Challenge Problems Both of these problems present realistic dimensions of real-world objects. Because students are just learning division, the problems can be solved in one-step so as not to distract students from the new skill they are learning.

Connecting "Un-Multiplication" to Division

Purpose To provide a visual model of "un-multiplication" as division

Introduce Remind students of some of the connections between multiplication and division that they know. Then say that not only are the operations related, but so are the multiplication and division diagrams that have been used in this lesson.

Task Ask students to determine how a picture of an array simplifies to a multiplication table and a division box. Draw figures like those below to guide students' thinking.

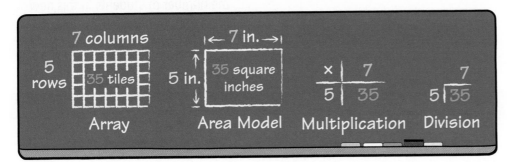

Share Ask students to share their conclusions.

- These are all different ways of showing the same thing.
- This shows the connection between arrays area models, the multiplication statement, and the division statement.

Ongoing Assessment

- Do students understand how to find the number of tiles in a rectangular array for which they know the number of rows and the number of columns?
- Do students know how to find the area of a rectangle whose length and width are given?

Reflect and Summarize the Lesson

 Write Math

How can you use the fact that 16 × 14 = 224 to find 16 × 28? How can you use it to find 8 × 14? Possible explanation: 28 is twice 14, so 16 × 28 must be twice 16 × 14, which is 2 × 224, or 448. Since 8 is half of 16, 8 × 14 must be half of 16 × 14, which is half of 224, or 112.

Leveled Problem Solving

The Smith School band marches in two groups: 14 rows of 7 students and 8 rows of 13 students.

❶ Basic Level

How many students are in the band? Explain. 202 students: $14 \times 7 = 98$, $8 \times 13 = 104$, $98 + 104 = 202$

❷ On Level

How many more students are in the larger than the smaller group? Explain. 6 more students: $104 - 98 = 6$

❸ Above Level

More students join the band. Now the first group has 14 rows of 14 students. The second group has 8 rows of 26 students. Compare the number of students in this new band with the original. There are twice as many in the new band.

| **Intervention** | **Practice** | **Extension** |

Activity Multiplication/ Division Fact Families

Write a multiplication fact on the chalkboard. Ask a volunteer to name the other three facts in the multiplication/division fact family.

$6 \times 8 = 48 \qquad 48 \div 8 = 6$
$8 \times 6 = 48 \qquad 48 \div 6 = 8$

Continue by giving the other multiplication or division facts and having students name the other facts.

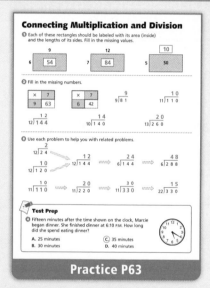

Practice P63

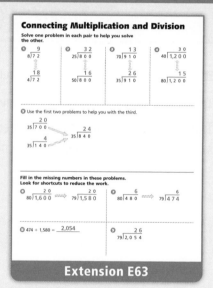

Extension E63

Spiral Review

Spiral Review Book page SR63 provides review of the following previously learned skills and concepts:

• using results of a survey to complete a graph and analyze the data

• completing input-output tables

You may wish to have students work with partners to complete the page.

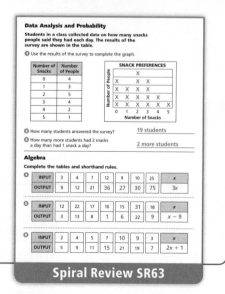

Spiral Review SR63

Extension Activity Division Meaning

Use Cuisenaire® Rods to model. The white rod = 1.

• How many groups of 2 are in 8? There are 4 reds in 1 brown, so $8 \div 2 = 4$.

• Can I divide 8 into 2 equal groups? There are 2 purples in 1 brown, so $8 \div 2 = 4$.

Have students make up stories that show the two meanings, then make models using rods to explain their thinking.

Teacher's Notes 🍎

Daily Notes . . .

Quick Notes

More Ideas

Lesson 3 Dividing Using Multiplication and the Area Model

NCTM Standards 1, 2, 6, 7, 8, 9, 10

Lesson Planner

STUDENT OBJECTIVES
- To divide with large numbers using an area model
- To use multiplication to solve problems involving whole numbers

1 | Daily Activities (TG p. 655)

Open-Ended Problem Solving/Headline Story	Skills Practice and Review— Ten Times, Five Times

2 | Teach and Practice (TG pp. 656–661)

MATERIALS

(A) **Exploring Division of Large Numbers** (TG pp. 656–658)

(B) **Dividing Using Multiplication and the Area Model** (TG p. 659)

(C) **Playing a Game: 200 Zoom** (TG p. 660)

- sets of cards numbered 1–12
- 📖 LAB pp. 155–156
- 📖 SH pp. 133–134, 144

3 | Differentiated Instruction (TG p. 662)

Leveled Problem Solving (TG p. 662)	Practice Book P64
Intervention Activity (TG p. 662)	Extension Book E64
Extension Activity (TG p. 662)	Spiral Review Book SR64

Lesson Notes

About the Lesson

Any process for dividing large numbers relies on the connection between multiplication and division, and on the ability to partition the dividend into smaller numbers. Using area as a model, students can see the divisor as one dimension of a rectangle, and division as the process of finding the other dimension when the area is known. Breaking the dividend into smaller, more convenient numbers allows students to find the missing factor bit by bit. For example, if students know that 25×10 is 250 and 25×2 is 50, they can solve $925 \div 25$ by breaking 925 into $250 + 250 + 250 + 50 + 50 + 50 + 25$. The area model would show $925 = 25 \times (10 + 10 + 10 + 2 + 2 + 2 + 1)$, or simply $925 = 25 \times 37$. This means that $925 \div 25 = 37$. In **Lesson 8.4,** students will begin to write vertical records of this process.

Use with Lesson Activity Book pp. 155–156.

Developing Mathematical Language

Vocabulary: break, partition, separate, split

To *partition* a number is to *break* it into smaller, not necessarily equal numbers whose sum is the given number. You may choose to teach the word *partition* to your students, or they may use more common words such as *break, separate,* and *split.* The term that students use in this lesson to talk about how they *break* apart an area model is unimportant. You may decide to discourage use of the word "divide" in this context, to avoid confusion with the main topic of this chapter, namely, the operation of *partitioning* a number into equal smaller numbers.

Familiarize students with the synonyms *break, split,* and *separate.*

Beginning Show students two groups of 12 counters: one group in which all 12 are together and one group that has been *separated* into 2 equal groups. Ask students to use the synonyms to describe the *separated* group.

Intermediate Have students use 24 counters. Ask them to put the counters into 3 equal groups. Ask them to use the synonyms to complete the sentence "I can ____ the 24 counters into 3 groups."

Advanced Have students separate 20 counters into two groups. Tell them that they can *divide* the counters into two equal groups or *split* them into groups that do not have to be equal. Ask them to identify how their counters have been *separated.*

Open-Ended Problem Solving

Read the Headline Story to the students. Encourage them to think of creative ways to solve the problem.

 Headline Story

> **The students in Mr. Stein's class will call every family in school to ask for volunteers. There are 3 classes in each grade from kindergarten through fifth grade. There are about 23 students in each class. They assume each family has 2 children in the school. About how many families will each student call?**

Possible responses: There are about 23 × 3 = 69 children in each grade, and about 6 × 69 = 414 children in the school. There are 414 ÷ 2 = 207 families in the school. 207 ÷ 23 = 9 So, each student in Mr. Stein's class will call about 9 families.

Skills Practice and Review

Ten Times, Five Times

Ask students to multiply 24 × 5 in their heads. If any find the correct answer (120), ask how they did it. If students don't mention it, say they could find the answer by multiplying 24 × 10 and dividing the result by 2.

Present pairs of multiplication problems, an even number times 10 followed by the same number times 5 (for example, 14 × 10 followed by 14 × 5). Ask students to explain how they can find the product mentally. Once students see the pattern, skip the "help" step (multiplying by 10) and have them multiply even numbers by 5.

individuals or whole class ⏱ **20 MIN**

NCTM Standards 1, 2, 6, 7, 8, 9, 10

Ⓐ Exploring Division of Large Numbers

Purpose To explore division of large numbers

Introduce You may choose to have students work independently on Explore: Multiplying and Un-Multiplying for about five minutes before beginning a group discussion. Or you may have the class work together as a group from the beginning.

✔**Ongoing Assessment**

• Can students accurately subtract numbers of up to 4 digits?

• Can students accurately multiply numbers of up to 4 digits by 1-digit numbers, by 10, by multiples of 10, and by 100?

Problem **A tile layer set 925 square tiles in 25 equal rows. How many tiles were in each row?**

Before discussing strategies for breaking 925 into 25 rows, say:

Estimate the row length and explain how you found your estimate. Possible estimate: 30; possible explanation: I rounded 925 to 900 and 25 to 30. 900 ÷ 30 = 30.

Have students compare the estimate to the answer they got to the Explore problem.

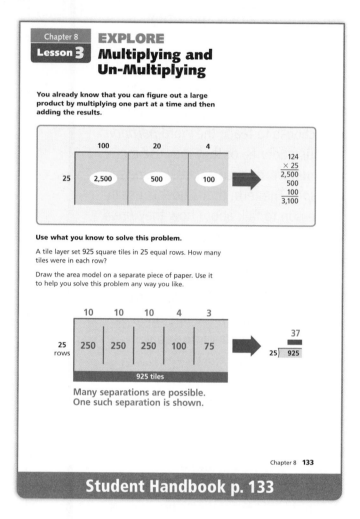

Student Handbook p. 133

Ask students to explain how they used the area model at the bottom of the Explore page to solve the problem 925 ÷ 25. Students may suggest various partitions. Following the model at the top of the page, some students may suggest 250, 250, 250, 100, 75 as their partitions, and write 10, 10, 10, 4, and 3 above the array.

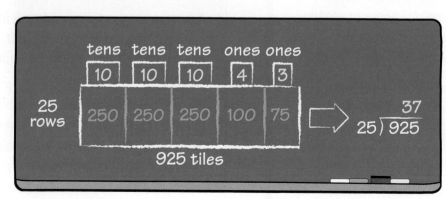

The blue number in each of the 5 sections tells the number of tiles in that section. The yellow number at the top tells the width of the section (the number of columns). For example, the first section has 25 rows (as they all do) and is 10 tiles wide, so it contains 250 tiles.

- The student who made the sketch kept mental notes about how much of the area model was left after each chunk was removed. After removing the first 750 tiles ($250 + 250 + 250 = 750$), $925 - 750 = 175$ tiles remained. After removing 100 more tiles, $175 - 100 = 75$ tiles remained.

Many other reasonable cuts are possible as students guess and check various partitionings.

Share Ask students to name the key steps they must carry out to divide a large number by partitioning.

- They must show the number of tiles in each part of the area model.
- They must show how wide each part is (how many tiles across).
- They must figure out how much of the area model is left.
- They must summarize by finding the width of an entire row of the area model.

Problem To give students an opportunity to practice what they have learned, have the class work together to find 2,783 ÷ 23.

The divisor 23 is a bit tougher to work with than 25. It will be used on LAB page 156.

Talk Math

❷ Could there be 100 tiles in each row? Explain. Yes! $100 \times 23 = 2,300$, and we have over 2,700 to begin with so we can cut the area model with a line, write 100 at the top, and write 2,300 inside.

❷ How much of the area model is left? Explain how you know. 483; to find out, I subtracted: $2,783 - 2,300 = 483$.

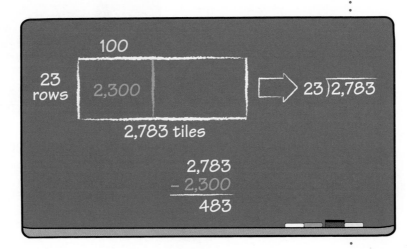

Students might now attack 483 bit by bit, cutting off 230 and seeing what's left. Or, they may recognize that they could cut off a section 20 tiles across. Either way, help them record what they've done, and remind them to subtract to find how much is left.

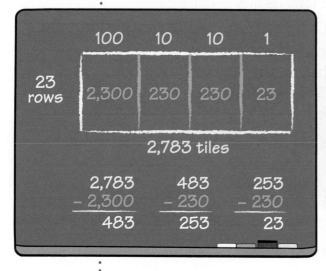

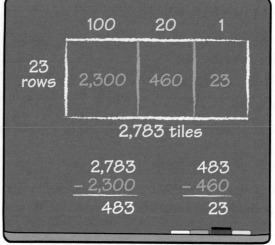

Finally, make sure students summarize their results. No matter how they partitioned the area model, they will find that it has 121 tiles (the sum of the yellow numbers) in each row.

$$121$$
$$23 \overline{)2{,}783}$$

 Talk Math

❷ Brianna wanted to divide 678 ÷ 20. The array shows her first step.

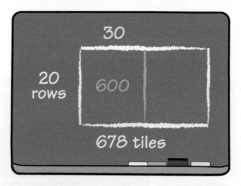

How much of the area model is left? Explain how you know. 78 tiles; Possible explanation: 678 is the number of tiles in the area model. If I carve out 600 tiles, there will be 78 left.

Use with Lesson Activity Book pp. 155–156.

Dividing Using Multiplication and the Area Model LAB pp. 155–156

Purpose To practice dividing large numbers using an area model

NCTM Standard 1

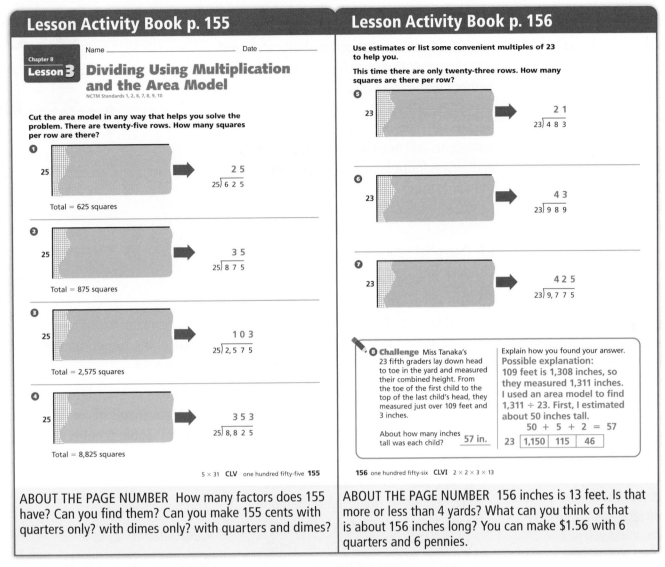

Lesson Activity Book p. 155

Name _____ Date _____

Chapter 8 Lesson 3 **Dividing Using Multiplication and the Area Model**
NCTM Standards 1, 2, 6, 7, 8, 9, 10

Cut the area model in any way that helps you solve the problem. There are twenty-five rows. How many squares per row are there?

1 25 → $25\overline{)625}$ = 25
Total = 625 squares

2 25 → $25\overline{)875}$ = 35
Total = 875 squares

3 25 → $25\overline{)2,575}$ = 103
Total = 2,575 squares

4 25 → $25\overline{)8,825}$ = 353
Total = 8,825 squares

5 × 31 **CLV** one hundred fifty-five **155**

ABOUT THE PAGE NUMBER How many factors does 155 have? Can you find them? Can you make 155 cents with quarters only? with dimes only? with quarters and dimes?

Lesson Activity Book p. 156

Use estimates or list some convenient multiples of 23 to help you.

This time there are only twenty-three rows. How many squares are there per row?

5 23 → $23\overline{)483}$ = 21

6 23 → $23\overline{)989}$ = 43

7 23 → $23\overline{)9,775}$ = 425

8 Challenge Miss Tanaka's 23 fifth graders lay down head to toe in the yard and measured their combined height. From the toe of the first child to the top of the last child's head, they measured just over 109 feet and 3 inches.

About how many inches tall was each child? **57 in.**

Explain how you found your answer. Possible explanation: 109 feet is 1,308 inches, so they measured 1,311 inches. I used an area model to find 1,311 ÷ 23. First, I estimated about 50 inches tall.
50 + 5 + 2 = 57

| 23 | 1,150 | 115 | 46 |

156 one hundred fifty-six **CLVI** 2 × 2 × 3 × 13

ABOUT THE PAGE NUMBER 156 inches is 13 feet. Is that more or less than 4 yards? What can you think of that is about 156 inches long? You can make $1.56 with 6 quarters and 6 pennies.

Teaching Notes for LAB page 155

Have students complete the page individually or with partners.

Students practice the method discussed in Activity A, breaking each area model into conveniently smaller partitions to determine the number of squares in each row. This is an opportunity for you to observe and see who understands the method and who still needs help with the logic of the process. The divisors on this page are all 25, and multiples of 25 are generally easy for students to find and subtract.

Teaching Notes for LAB page 156

The divisors on this page are all 23. Students may find it helpful to prepare a list of multiples of 23 (some by doubling or by multiplying by 10) before they begin.

For Problem 7, you may want to suggest to students that they begin by finding a multiple of 23 that is less than 97.

Challenge Problem This problem uses the idea of "average height" without giving a rule for finding it. Students may find "about how many inches tall" each child is by dividing.

ⒸPlayingaGame: *200 Zoom*

Materials

• For each small group:
4 sets of cards
numbered 1–12

NCTM Standards 1, 2, 6, 7, 8, 9, 10

Possible Discussion

Success in *200 Zoom* requires that you know when to stop drawing cards. If the Zoom is 16 and you have a 2, you should probably take another card, because your score is only 32. If your second card is a 12, however, you've gone over, because your total, 14, times the Zoom is too great. If your second card is a 10, that's perfect. It adds 160 points to your score, for a total of 192. You are now so close you should stop. What if your second card is an 8? Your card total, 10, times the Zoom is only 160. Someone else could beat you. But there's a risk if you pick again: you will go over unless you pick a 1 or a 2, not a very likely possibility. Keep in mind that the other players also must be careful not to go over. All in all, 160 is not a bad score.

Differentiated Instruction

Above Level Encourage strong students to work out and discuss strategies for winning *200 Zoom*. Ask these questions:

• When does it make sense to draw another card?

• When does it make sense NOT to draw another card?

Purpose To practice multiplication and addition in the context of playing a game

Goal The object of this game, *200 Zoom,* is to accumulate points through multiplication and addition, and thereby achieve the greatest score without exceeding 200 points.

Prepare Materials Each group of 2 to 4 students will need a deck of numbered cards containing four of each number from 1 to 12 (48 cards total).

How to Play

❶ One player shuffles the cards and places the deck face down.

❷ The player who shuffled the cards turns the top card face up. The player announces the "Zoom" number for that round, which is 10 plus the value of the turned-up card. For example, if a 4 is turned up, the Zoom number is 14.

❸ Moving clockwise from the shuffler, each player takes one card from the deck, keeping its value secret. The player secretly calculates his or her score, which is the value of his or her card times the Zoom number.

❹ Players may draw additional cards, if they wish, to increase their score. When a player holds more than one card, the player's score is the sum of the numbers on his or her cards times the Zoom number. Any cards drawn after the first card must be placed faced up in front of the player.

> **Example**
>
> Zoom number: 17
>
> Cards drawn: 2, 6, 3
>
> Score: $2 + 6 + 3 = 11$
>
> $\qquad 11 \times 17 = 187$

❺ If a player's score exceeds 200, that player is out and must turn all of his or her cards face up for others to see.

❻ Once all players still in the game have drawn as many cards as they want, the players calculate and announce their scores. The player with the greatest score that is not over 200 wins the round.

❼ Play continues until all cards have been drawn from the deck. The winner of the final round is the player with the greatest score not over 200 when the last card has been taken.

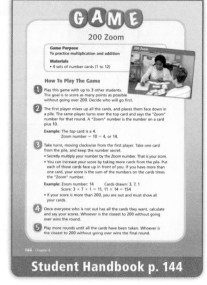

Student Handbook p. 144

Reflect and Summarize the Lesson

Write Math

Explain how to use an area model to find 675 ÷ 15. 45; Possible explanation: First I draw a rectangle and label the left side 15 (for the number of rows) and the bottom 675 (for the total number of tiles). Then I find multiples of 15 that I carve out of the model. Each time I carve out a part, I write how wide that part is, above the model. When I have carved out as many multiples of 15 as I can, I add the numbers above the model to find the total width.

Review Model ....

Refer students to Review Model: Dividing Using an Area Model in the *Student Handbook* to see how they can use an area model to help them divide with whole numbers.

✔**Check for Understanding**

❶ 15

❷ 25

❸ 38

❹ 32

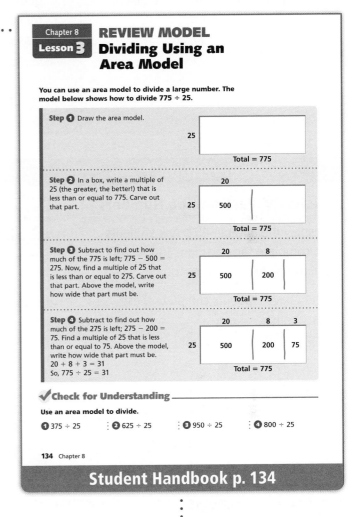

Student Handbook p. 134

3 | Differentiated Instruction

Leveled Problem Solving

A rectangular floor has 37 rows of square tiles.
There are 1,591 tiles in the floor.

❶ Basic Level

Are there more than or fewer than 100 tiles in a row? Explain.
There are fewer than because 37×100 is 3,700, and 3,700 is greater than 1,591.

❷ On Level

Use partitioning to make a first guess at the number of tiles in a row on the floor. Explain your reasoning. Possible answer: less than 100 because 37×100 is greater than 1,591. A good guess would be a multiple of 10 whose product with 37 is close to 1,591.

❸ Above Level

How many tiles in a row are on the floor? Show your work.
43 tiles in a row; possible answer:

	10	10	10	10	3
37	370	370	370	370	111

$10 + 10 + 10 + 10 + 3 = 43$

Intervention	Practice	Extension

Activity Partitioning Numbers

Display the number 492. Ask students to complete the partition: $100 + 100 + 100 + \blacksquare + 90 + \blacksquare$ 100, 2

Then have students complete these partitions:

$208 = 100 + \blacksquare + \blacksquare$ 100, 8
$166 = \blacksquare + \blacksquare + \blacksquare$ 100, 60, 6

Help students connect this to writing whole numbers in expanded form.

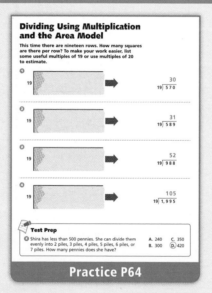

Practice P64

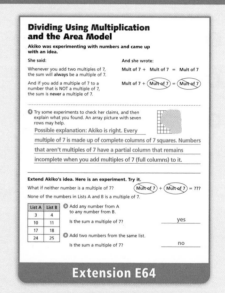

Extension E64

Spiral Review

Spiral Review Book page SR64 provides review of the following previously learned skills and concepts:

- writing coordinates for the vertices of a reflected figure
- applying the problem solving strategy *look for a pattern*

You may wish to have students work with partners to complete the page.

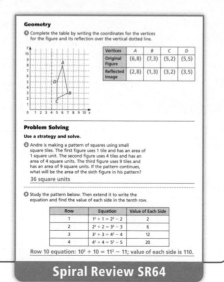

Spiral Review SR64

Extension Activity
Guess or Guess Again

Have students estimate the quotient $43\overline{)3,196}$. Ask:

- Would 100 be a reasonable first guess? Why? No; 43×100 is greater than the dividend, 3,196.

- Would 80 be a reasonable first guess? Why? Yes; using compatible numbers I would think $3,200 \div 40 = 80$.

Now compare a first guess for $39\overline{)5,123}$ to the above. A first guess of 125 makes sense if you use compatible numbers: $5,000 \div 40 = 125$.

Use with Lesson Activity Book pp. 155–156.

Teacher's Notes 🍎

Daily Notes . . .

Quick Notes

More Ideas

Lesson 4 Recording the Steps in Division

NCTM Standards 1, 2, 6, 7, 8, 9, 10

Lesson Planner

STUDENT OBJECTIVES
- To use division to solve problems involving whole numbers
- To use an area model to determine the partial quotients that make up the total quotient

1 Daily Activities (TG p. 665)

Open-Ended Problem Solving/Headline Story	Skills Practice and Review—Five, Fifty, and Five Hundred Times

2 Teach and Practice (TG pp. 666–671)

MATERIALS

(A) **Using Compatible Numbers to Estimate** (TG p. 666)

(B) **Making Tables for Multiples of Divisors** (TG pp. 667–668)

(C) **Making a Record** (TG p. 669)

(D) **Recording the Steps in Division** (TG p. 670)

- 📖 LAB pp. 157–158
- 📖 SH p. 135

3 Differentiated Instruction (TG p. 672)

Leveled Problem Solving (TG p. 672)	Practice Book P65
Intervention Activity (TG p. 672)	Extension Book E65
Extension Activity (TG p. 672)	Spiral Review Book SR65
Science Connection (TG p. 636)	

Lesson Notes

About the Lesson

This lesson introduces an organized process for performing and recording division. It is based on the area model used for multiplication, which by now is very familiar to students, and on the connection between multiplication and division. All practice problems in the lesson use the same divisor. Students build a table of useful multiples of that divisor before they begin to divide. That way, they can focus their attention on the process of division, and avoid the distraction of having to stop to perform other calculations.

About the Mathematics

Below are two ways students might divide $2,641 \div 19$.

```
 19│2,641              19│2,641
   −1,900   100          −1,900   100
      741                   741
   −  380    20          −  570    30
      361                   171
   −  190    10          −  171     9
      171
   −   95     5
       76
   −   76     4
```

(continued on page R3)

Developing Mathematical Language

Vocabulary: compatible numbers

Compatible numbers are easy to use and are chosen to simplify the calculation of an estimate. Students should understand that sensibly chosen *compatible numbers* are not right or wrong, though some may yield better estimates than others. For example, the quotient 407 ÷ 55 may usefully be estimated using the *compatible numbers* 400 ÷ 50, 420 ÷ 60, 350 ÷ 70, 400 ÷ 40, or any of several other pairs. The first two, however, yield estimates closer to the actual quotient than the others do.

Remind students about the term *compatible numbers*.

Beginning Show students these pairs of numbers: 190 and 17, 240 and 30, 170 and 40. Remind students that *compatible* means "easy to use." Ask them to point to a pair that is compatible and explain why.

Intermediate Show students the division 418 ÷ 57. Ask them to tell whether each of the following uses *compatible numbers* to estimate the quotient:

> 420 ÷ 60 yes
> 420 ÷ 50 no
> 400 ÷ 50 yes
> 400 ÷ 60 no

Advanced Show students the following division: 349 ÷ 43. Ask them to write as many pairs of *compatible numbers* as they can to estimate the quotient.
Possible answers: 320 ÷ 40, 350 ÷ 50, 360 ÷ 40

1 | Daily Activities

Open-Ended Problem Solving

Read the Headline Story to the students. Encourage them to think of creative ways to approach the problem. Note that although students do not yet have a formal procedure for finding a solution, they can make estimates and approach the problem in non-standard ways.

 Headline Story

> Mr. Wong has between 300 and 1,000 small prizes to divide evenly among his 19 students. He will give away as many prizes as possible. What is the greatest number of prizes that could be left over? Is it possible for each student to get 60 prizes?

Possible responses: 18 prizes because if 19 or more were left over, each student would get another prize. Since 19 is less than but close to 20, and 20 × 60 = 1,200, each student could not receive 60 prizes.

Skills Practice and Review

Five, Fifty, and Five Hundred Times

Repeat the Skills Practice and Review activity from **Lesson 8.3,** increasing the challenge enough to keep students alert and involved. You might start with problems like the ones in the first two columns below. When students are comfortable with even numbers, graduate to odd numbers (third column), multiplying first by 10, then by 5.

14 × 5 70	42 × 50 2,100	25 × 10 250	25 × 5 125
24 × 50 1,200	68 × 50 3,400	21 × 10 210	21 × 5 105
620 × 5 3,100	16 × 5 80	41 × 10 410	41 × 5 205
36 × 5 180	16 × 50 800	31 × 10 310	31 × 5 155
52 × 500 26,000	16 × 500 8,000	63 × 10 630	63 × 5 315

whole class · 10 MIN

A Using Compatible Numbers to Estimate

NCTM Standards 1, 2, 6, 7, 8, 9, 10

Purpose To estimate using compatible numbers

Introduce If you have not already done so, write the Headline Story on TG p. 665 on the board. Ask students to reread the story about Mr. Wong and his prizes.

✔ **Ongoing Assessment**

• Do students know basic division facts?

• Can students find the quotients of numbers one or both of which are 10 times the numbers in basic division facts; e.g., 560 ÷ 8 (70) and 720 ÷ 90 (8)?

Problem Ask students how they could estimate the number of small prizes each of Mr. Wong's 19 students would receive if he had exactly 893 prizes to give away. If no one mentions compatible numbers, remind the class that they can estimate the answer to a problem by replacing the numbers in the problem with numbers that are easier to calculate with. Such easier numbers are called *compatible numbers*. You might show these two examples of compatible numbers:

• To estimate 373 ÷ 31, students might recognize that 31 is close to 30 and 373 is close to 360, which is a multiple of 30. So, 360 and 30 would be good compatible numbers to choose. Since 36 ÷ 3 is 12, 360 ÷ 30 is also 12. So, 373 ÷ 31 is about 12.

• To estimate 438 ÷ 6, students might recognize that 42 is a multiple of 6 and choose compatible numbers 420 and 6. So, 438 ÷ 6 is about 420 ÷ 6, or 70.

Share To answer the question about Mr. Wong, write 19)‾893 on the board. Ask students to suggest some compatible numbers they could use to estimate the quotient. They might choose 800 ÷ 20 40, 880 ÷ 20 44, or 900 ÷ 20 45. In each case, ask students if they think the resulting estimate is too high or too low. Learning to make this judgment will prove enormously useful for students as they begin to find exact quotients.

💬 **Talk Math**

❓ At Hatfield Elementary School, there are 504 students in 7 classes. Each class has the same number of students. What is a good estimate of the number of students in each class? Explain your reasoning. Possible answer: 70 students; possible explanation: I used the compatible numbers 490 and 7: 490 ÷ 7 = 70.

❓ Marcel worked 32 hours and earned $232. What is a good estimate of the amount that he earned each hour? Explain your reasoning. Possible answer: $7; possible explanation: I used the compatible numbers 210 and 30: 210 ÷ 30 = 21 ÷ 3 = 7.

Use with Lesson Activity Book pp. 157–158.

Making Tables for Multiples of Divisors

Purpose To make a table of useful multiples of 19

NCTM Standards 1, 2, 6, 7, 8, 9, 10

Introduce Mention that in Activity A, students estimated the quotient 893 ÷ 19. Now they will find the quotient exactly.

Task **Remind students that the quotient 893 ÷ 19 also completes the multiplication sentence 19 × ■ = 893. The first step in finding the quotient will be to make a table of multiples of 19.** To find multiples in this lesson, students will use only the strategies of doubling and of multiplying by 5. (**Lesson 8.5** will use all of the single-digit multiples, plus 10 times those multiples.)

Set up a table of multiples (shown below), writing only the factors (the row and column labels shown in white). Ask students to help you input the products. Start with the most "obvious" products, × 1 and × 10, shown in blue. You may need to remind students about doubling strategies to obtain the pink products. The yellow products can be found by halving the × 10 product or by adding the entries under × 1 and × 4. Leave this table visible for the rest of the lesson.

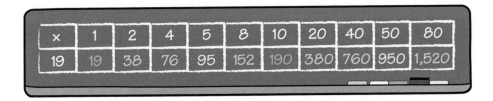

×	1	2	4	5	8	10	20	40	50	80
19	19	38	76	95	152	190	380	760	950	1,520

Now use the table to divide 893 ÷ 19.

• Draw an area model to represent the problem.

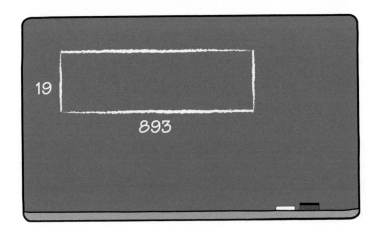

- Ask students to use the table to help them make a good first estimate of how many prizes Mr. Wong can give to each of his 19 students. The table shows that he can give 40 prizes to each because doing so will use up 760 of his 893 prizes. (This also agrees with the estimates students made in Activity A.) Draw a section of the diagram to represent 760 prizes. Fill in the numbers 40 and 760 where they belong (shown in yellow and blue, below).

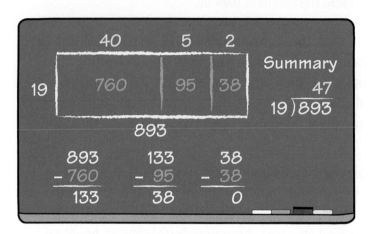

- Ask students to find how many prizes Mr. Wong had left to give away. Since 760 have been given away, there are $893 - 760 = 133$ prizes left. (This subtraction can be recorded anywhere, but it may be best to do so under the block that represents 760.)

- Ask students to use the table to make additional estimates until all the prizes are gone. The table shows that he can give 5 more prizes to each student, using up 95 of the remaining 133 prizes. Record these numbers. Then, he can give 2 more prizes to each student, using up the remaining 38 prizes. (You or your students may want to show the final subtraction to complete the step.)

- Finally, ask students to summarize and answer the question asked: How many prizes can Mr. Wong give to each student? First, 40 were given away, then 5, then 2. So, the total is $40 + 5 + 2 = 47$.

Talk Math

? Suppose that in the first step above, you had estimated 20 prizes rather than 40. Could you still have found the answer? Explain. Yes; Possible explanation: 20 prizes for each student represents 380 total prizes. Removing 380 from the original 893 would have left $893 - 380 = 513$. Now I could take 20 more for each student, leaving $513 - 380 = 133$, the number that remained after the first subtraction when the original estimate of 40 was made. After that, I could continue as in the original solution.

? Suppose that in the first step above, you had estimated 50 prizes rather than 40. Could you still have found the answer? Explain. No; Possible explanation: 50 prizes for each student represents 950 prizes, which was more than the number of prizes Mr. Wong began with.

Use with Lesson Activity Book pp. 157–158.

Making a Record

Purpose To show the division process in a standard record

Introduce Point out that there are many ways to record the steps used in division. In this activity, students will learn one method.

Problem **How many prizes would each of Mr. Wong's 19 students receive if he had 988 prizes to give away?** Solve the problem as a class, organizing the solution process into a vertical division record:

- Write the division problem 19)988 on the board, and draw the corresponding area model.
- When students suggest the first estimate (50), using the table of multiples of 19, write 50 and the corresponding multiple (950) in both the diagram of the area model and the record. (Shown in yellow and blue in both.)
- Show how the subtraction can be shown easily in the record.
- Have students suggest how to proceed. They will probably see that $38 = 2 \times 19$, so with 38 prizes left, each student will receive 2 prizes.
- Don't forget to have students write the summary!
- You might tell students that this record style is the one most people are used to seeing.

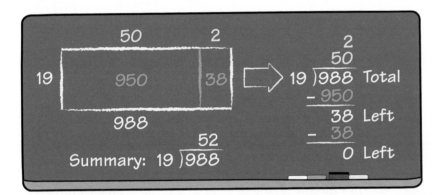

Talk Math Write the problem below on the board and then ask this question.

? Francine made the record to find the number of prizes each of Mr. Wong's students would receive if he had 342 prizes to give away. How many prizes would each student receive? Explain how Francine found the answer.

18 prizes; Possible explanation: she added the two numbers, 10 and 8, at the top of the record.

$$
\begin{array}{r}
8 \\
10 \\
19\overline{)342} \\
-190 \\
\hline
152 \\
-152 \\
\hline
0
\end{array}
$$

Purpose To practice recording the steps in division

NCTM Standards 1, 2, 6, 7, 8, 9, 10

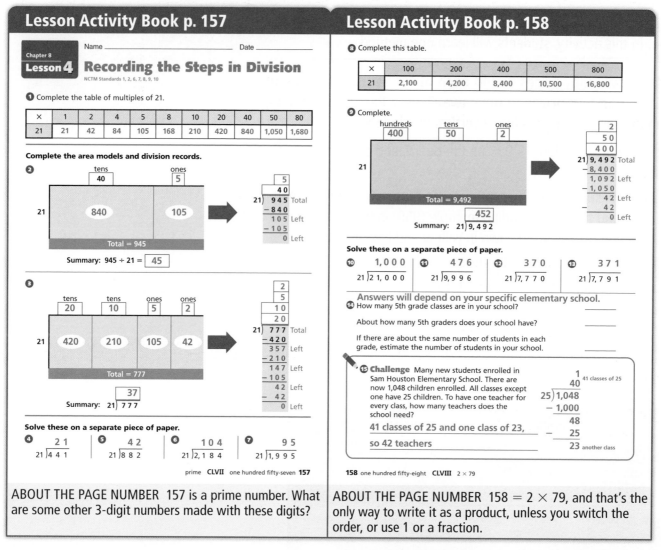

Lesson Activity Book p. 157

Name _____ Date _____

Chapter 8 Lesson 4 Recording the Steps in Division
NCTM Standards 1, 2, 6, 7, 8, 9, 10

❶ Complete the table of multiples of 21.

×	1	2	4	5	8	10	20	40	50	80
21	21	42	84	105	168	210	420	840	1,050	1,680

Complete the area models and division records.

❷ Summary: 945 ÷ 21 = 45

❸ Summary: 21)777 = 37

Solve these on a separate piece of paper.

❹ 21)441 = 21 ❺ 21)882 = 42 ❻ 21)2,184 = 104 ❼ 21)1,995 = 95

prime **CLVII** one hundred fifty-seven **157**

Lesson Activity Book p. 158

❽ Complete this table.

×	100	200	400	500	800
21	2,100	4,200	8,400	10,500	16,800

❾ Complete.

Summary: 21)9,492 = 452

Solve these on a separate piece of paper.

❿ 1,000 / 21)21,000 ⓫ 476 / 21)9,996 ⓬ 370 / 21)7,770 ⓭ 371 / 21)7,791

Answers will depend on your specific elementary school.
⓮ How many 5th grade classes are in your school? _____

About how many 5th graders does your school have? _____

If there are about the same number of students in each grade, estimate the number of students in your school. _____

⓯ **Challenge** Many new students enrolled in Sam Houston Elementary School. There are now 1,048 children enrolled. All classes except one have 25 children. To have one teacher for every class, how many teachers does the school need?

41 classes of 25 and one class of 23, so 42 teachers

1 40 41 classes of 25
25)1,048
−1,000
48
−25
23 another class

158 one hundred fifty-eight **CLVIII** 2 × 79

ABOUT THE PAGE NUMBER 157 is a prime number. What are some other 3-digit numbers made with these digits?

ABOUT THE PAGE NUMBER 158 = 2 × 79, and that's the only way to write it as a product, unless you switch the order, or use 1 or a fraction.

Teaching Notes for LAB page 157

Have students complete the page individually or with partners.

Differentiated Instruction **On Level** Students may use either area models or vertical records. Some students will not need to record numbers in the models and will rely solely on the vertical records. If students try this but make a lot of mistakes, suggest they use the area models first to check their work. Encourage them to make connections between the models and the records.

Teaching Notes for LAB page 158

For Problem 10, the division 21)21,000 is an easy problem with big numbers. For Problem 12, the division 21)7,770 is related to 21)777 on LAB page 157.

Challenge Problem The challenge problem refers back to the Headline Story from **Lesson 8.2.** It is another multi-step real-world problem that requires thinking and attention to what is being asked.

Reflect and Summarize the Lesson

Write Math

How many prizes would each of Mr. Wong's 19 students receive if he had 475 prizes to give away? **Show your work.** 25 prizes; A possible division record is shown below.

$$
\begin{array}{r}
5 \\
2\,0 \\
19\overline{)475} \\
-380 \\
\hline
95 \\
-95 \\
\hline
0
\end{array}
\qquad
\text{Summary: } 19\overline{)475}\!\!\!\!^{25}
$$

Review Model

Refer students to Review Model: Finding Multiples in the **Student Handbook** to see how they can use mental math strategies to complete a table of multiples.

✔ Check for Understanding

×	1	2	3	4	5	6	7	8	9	10
16	16	32	48	64	80	96	112	128	144	160

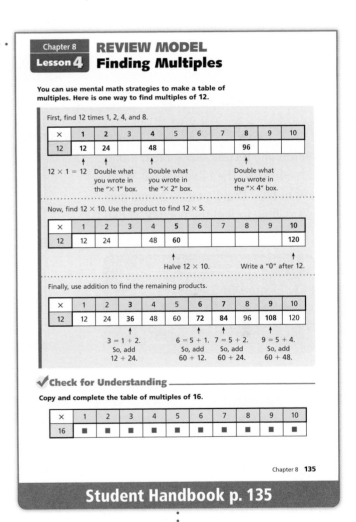

Chapter 8 Lesson 4 — **REVIEW MODEL** **Finding Multiples**

You can use mental math strategies to make a table of multiples. Here is one way to find multiples of 12.

First, find 12 times 1, 2, 4, and 8.

×	1	2	3	4	5	6	7	8	9	10
12	12	24		48				96		

12 × 1 = 12   Double what you wrote in the "× 1" box.   Double what you wrote in the "× 2" box.   Double what you wrote in the "× 4" box.

Now, find 12 × 10. Use the product to find 12 × 5.

×	1	2	3	4	5	6	7	8	9	10
12	12	24		48	60					120

Halve 12 × 10.   Write a "0" after 12.

Finally, use addition to find the remaining products.

×	1	2	3	4	5	6	7	8	9	10
12	12	24	36	48	60	72	84	96	108	120

3 = 1 + 2. So, add 12 + 24.   6 = 5 + 1. So, add 60 + 12.   7 = 5 + 2. So, add 60 + 24.   9 = 5 + 4. So, add 60 + 48.

✔ Check for Understanding

Copy and complete the table of multiples of 16.

×	1	2	3	4	5	6	7	8	9	10
16	■	■	■	■	■	■	■	■	■	■

Chapter 8 **135**

Student Handbook p. 135

Leveled Problem Solving

**The library volunteers have 962 books to pack.
They want to pack 26 books in each carton.**

❶ Basic Level

Draw an area model that can be used to find the number of cartons they need. Possible model:

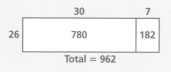

	30	7
26	780	182

Total = 962

❷ On Level

They have 30 cartons. Do they have enough for all the books? Explain your reasoning. no; possible answer: $30 \times 26 = 780$ and $780 < 962$

❸ Above Level

How many cartons will they need? Explain your work. 37 cartons; $962 \div 26 = 37$

Intervention

Activity Area Models

Give students the following problem.

The top of a rectangular table is made with 640 tiles. The table top has 16 rows of tiles. Draw an area model and discuss how to find the number of tiles in each row.

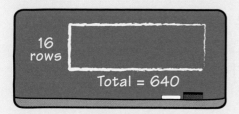

16 rows

Total = 640

Practice

Recording the Steps in Division

❶ Complete the table of multiples of 27.

×	1	2	4	5	8	10	20	40	50	80
27	27	54	108	135	216	270	540	1,080	1,350	2,160

❷ Complete the area model and division record.

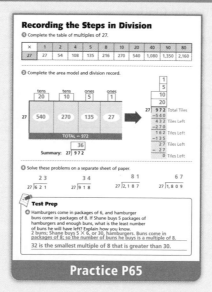

tens 20	tens 10	ones 5	ones 1
540	270	135	27

27 | 540 | 270 | 135 | 27

TOTAL = 972

Summary: 27√972 36

	1
	5
	10
	20

27 | 972 Total Tiles
−540
432 Tiles Left
−270
162 Tiles Left
−135
27 Tiles Left
− 27
0 Tiles Left

❸ Solve these problems on a separate sheet of paper.

27√6 2 1   27√9 1 8   27√2,1 8 7   27√1,8 0 9
  2 3   3 4   8 1   6 7

Test Prep

❹ Hamburgers come in packages of 6, and hamburger buns come in packages of 8. If Shane buys 5 packages of hamburgers and enough buns, what is the least number of buns he will have left? Explain how you know.
2 buns; Shane buys 5 × 6, or 30, hamburgers. Buns come in packages of 8; so the number of buns he buys is a multiple of 8.
32 is the smallest multiple of 8 that is greater than 30.

Practice P65

Extension

Recording the Steps in Division

Jonathan experimented with multiples of 3.

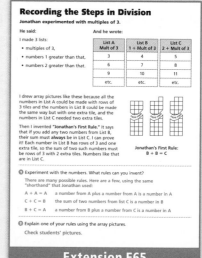

He said:

I made 3 lists:
• multiples of 3,
• numbers 1 greater than that,
• numbers 2 greater than that.

List A Mult of 3	List B 1 + Mult of 3	List C 2 + Mult of 3
3	4	5
6	7	8
9	10	11
etc.	etc.	etc.

I drew array pictures like these because all the numbers in List A could be made with rows of 3 tiles and the numbers in List B could be made the same way but with one extra tile, and the numbers in List C needed two extra tiles.

Then I invented "Jonathan's First Rule." It says that if you add any two numbers from List B, their sum must always be in List C. I can prove it! Each number in List B has rows of 3 and one extra tile, so the sum of two such numbers must be rows of 3 with 2 extra tiles. Numbers like that are in List C.

Jonathan's First Rule: B + B = C

❶ Experiment with the numbers. What rules can you invent?
There are many possible rules. Here are a few, using the same "shorthand" that Jonathan used:

A + A = A   a number from A plus a number from A is a number in A
C + C = B   the sum of two numbers from list C is a number in B
B + C = A   a number from B plus a number from C is a number in A

❷ Explain one of your rules using the array pictures.
Check students' pictures.

Extension E65

Spiral Review

Spiral Review Book page SR65 provides review of the following previously learned skills and concepts:

• finding the product of 2-digit factors
• converting between customary measurement units

You may wish to have students work with partners to complete the page.

Number and Operations

Complete each partial product. Then write the final product.

❶ 26 × 19
26 × 10 = 260
26 × 9 = 234
494

❷ 84 × 37
84 × 30 = 2,520
84 × 7 = 588
3,108

❸ 71 × 26
71 × 20 = 1,420
71 × 6 = 426
1,846

❹ 55 × 44
55 × 40 = 2,200
55 × 4 = 220
2,420

❺ 18 × 92
18 × 90 = 1,620
18 × 2 = 36
1,656

❻ 23 × 62
23 × 60 = 1,380
23 × 2 = 46
1,426

❼ 184 × 15
184 × 10 = 1,840
184 × 5 = 920
2,760

❽ 207 × 26
207 × 20 = 4,140
207 × 6 = 1,242
5,382

❾ 318 × 29
318 × 20 = 6,360
318 × 9 = 2,862
9,222

Measurement

Complete the table.

❿ Ounces	32	96	16	8	64	128	72
Pounds	2	6	1	$\frac{1}{2}$	4	8	$4\frac{1}{2}$

⓫ Pounds	2,000	4,000	10,000	3,000	1,000	1,500	2,500
Tons	1	2	5	$1\frac{1}{2}$	$\frac{1}{2}$	$\frac{3}{4}$	$1\frac{1}{4}$

⓬ Pounds	$2\frac{1}{2}$	5	$1\frac{1}{2}$	$3\frac{1}{4}$	7	$4\frac{1}{2}$	9
Ounces	40	80	24	52	112	68	144

Spiral Review SR65

Extension Activity
Work Backward

Challenge students to work backward to create an area model of this division problem.

17√731
−170
561
−340
221
−170
51
−51
0

3
10
20
10

	10	20	10	3
17	170	320	170	31

Total = 731

Summary: 17√731   43

Teacher's Notes 🍎

Daily Notes . . .

Quick Notes

More Ideas

_____

_____

_____

_____

_____

_____

_____

_____

_____

_____

_____

_____

_____

_____

_____

_____

_____

_____

_____

_____

_____

_____

Lesson 5 Dividing and Recording Division Efficiently

NCTM Standards 1, 2, 6, 7, 8, 9, 10

Lesson Planner

STUDENT OBJECTIVES
- To use division to solve problems involving whole numbers
- To use rounding and compatible numbers to estimate solutions to multiplication and division problems

1 | Daily Activities (TG p. 675)

| Open-Ended Problem Solving/Headline Story | Skills Practice and Review— Is the Quotient in the Thousands? |

2 | Teach and Practice (TG pp. 676–681)

MATERIALS

Ⓐ **Creating a Table of Multiples for Division** (TG p. 676)

Ⓑ **Dividing Efficiently With the Table** (TG pp. 677–678)

Ⓒ **Playing a Game: _Don't Overestimate!_** (TG pp. 679–680)

Ⓓ **Dividing and Recording Division Efficiently** (TG p. 681)

- sets cards numbered 1–9
- 📖 LAB pp. 159–160
- 📖 SH p. 145

3 | Differentiated Instruction (TG p. 682)

Leveled Problem Solving (TG p. 682)

Intervention Activity (TG p. 682)

Extension Activity (TG p. 682)

Social Studies Connection (TG p. 636)

Practice Book P66

Extension Book E66

Spiral Review Book SR66

Lesson Notes

About the Lesson

This lesson and the previous lesson focus on division, the mathematical process by which a quotient is computed. The process involves approximating the quotient, checking to see how close it is to the exact quotient, then taking another step that improves the approximation. This lesson highlights efficiency— getting the best possible first approximation, then getting the best possible improvement at each step. The Headline Story focuses on using division as a problem-solving tool.

Use with Lesson Activity Book pp. 159–160.

Developing Mathematical Language

Vocabulary: approximation, estimation

The words *estimation* and *approximation* both refer to a guess at an answer, preferably an educated guess. To find a quotient using the standard algorithm, a solver must first *estimate/approximate* several partial quotients. This lesson emphasizes efficiency in finding partial quotients—making the best possible *estimation/approximation* at each step, rather than wild guesses. This reduces the number of calculations and the amount of time needed to find a quotient, and thereby lessens the possibility of error.

Familiarize students with the terms *estimate (estimation)* and *approximate (approximation)*.

Beginning Write on the board: $29\overline{)609}$ with 21 above. Show students the following numbers:

20, 30, 40

Ask students to point to the best estimate of the quotient. Repeat with other exercises.

Intermediate Write on the board: $39\overline{)792}$ Ask: "What would be your first *estimate* of the quotient?" Following a response, tell students, "Your *estimate* is an *approximation* of the answer." Use other examples to help students see that making an *estimate* leads to an *approximation*.

Advanced Write on the board: $43\overline{)280}$ Ask: "What is an *estimate* of the quotient?" Following a response, invite a volunteer to "estimate the quotient."

Open-Ended Problem Solving

Read the Headline Story to the students. Encourage them to think of creative ways to solve the problem.

 Headline Story

> **Five million minutes! Is that greater than a day? a week? a month? a year? your age?**

Possible responses: Students may divide 5,000,000 minutes by 60 by hand or on a calculator to find the number of hours (over 83,000), and may divide again by 24 to find the number of days (almost 3,500), which is less than 10 years ($10 \times 365 = 3{,}650$).

Skills Practice and Review

Is the Quotient in the Thousands?

Write a problem like $28\overline{)11{,}256}$ on the board. Ask students if the quotient is in the thousands, hundreds, tens, or ones. To find the answer, students could use multiplication or compatible numbers. Have students use both of these methods.

Multiplication	Compatible Numbers
Try multiples of 10 in descending order.	**Approximate the solution.**
$28 \times 1{,}000 = 28{,}000$ and $28{,}000 > 11{,}256$, so the quotient is not in the thousands.	$11{,}256 \div 28$ is about the same as $12{,}000 \div 30$ and $12{,}000 \div 30 = 400$.
$28 \times 100 = 2{,}800$ and $2{,}800 < 11{,}256$, so the quotient is in the hundreds.	The compatible numbers were close to the actual numbers and gave a result in the hundreds, so the quotient is in the hundreds.

Continue with other problems. Students should not find exact quotients, only rough estimates of whether quotients are in the thousands, hundreds, tens, or ones.

whole class 10 MIN

NCTM Standards 1, 2, 6, 7, 8, 9, 10

A Creating a Table of Multiples for Division

Purpose To create a table of multiples to help solve a division problem

Introduce In today's Headline Story, students converted numbers of minutes and seconds into more understandable numbers of larger units. Put Activity A in a similar context by asking this question:

- A baby is 384 hours old. How can you figure out how many days old that is? Divide 384 by 24.

- What can you do to simplify the task of dividing 384 by 24? Possible response: Make a table of multiples of 24.

✔ Ongoing Assessment

- Do students know how to multiply by 10 mentally?

- Do students know that 5 times a number is half of 10 times the number?

- Do students know that 4 times a number is twice 2 times the number, and that 8 times a number is twice 4 times the number?

Task Start a table of multiples of 24 on the board. Use only single-digit factors for the column heads, as shown below. Ask students to help you fill in the multiples.

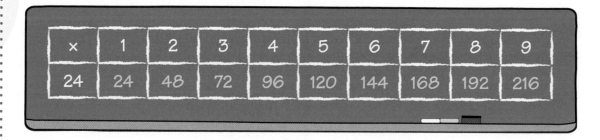

×	1	2	3	4	5	6	7	8	9
24	24	48	72	96	120	144	168	192	216

Encourage students to use familiar strategies such as doubling and adding to find the multiples, but allow them to use any strategies they are comfortable with.

Share Ask students to share their methods for finding multiples. One possible line of attack would be to start with $1 \times 24 = 24$, double successively to get 2×24, 4×24, and 8×24, then modify multiplication by 10 to get 5×24 (half of 10×24) and 9×24 ($10 \times 24 - 24$). The remaining multiples can be found using sums and differences of multiples already found.

Finally, ask students to use the table to find $384 \div 24$ and to share their methods. Students might reason that $24 \times 10 = 240$ and $384 - 240 = 144$; $144 = 24 \times 6$. So, $384 \div 24 = 10 + 6 = 16$.

💬 Talk Math

❓ If $1 \times 18 = 18$, what is 4×18? Explain how you found the answer. 72; Possible explanation: 2×18 is twice 1×18, or 36, and 4×18 is twice 2×18, which is twice 36, or 72.

❓ If $1 \times 28 = 28$, what is 5×28? Explain. 140; Possible explanation: $10 \times 28 = 280$, so 5×280 is half of 280, or 140.

Teacher Story

"Whenever my students are multiplying by 9, I always encourage them to multiply by 10, then subtract. For example:
$23 \times 9 =$
$23 \times 10 - 23 =$
$230 - 23 = 207$"

Use with Lesson Activity Book pp. 159–160.

B **Dividing Efficiently With the Table**

Purpose To find partial quotients efficiently

Introduce Give the class this problem: A baby is 6,552 hours old. How many days old is that?

Task Direct students to use the table from Activity A to find partial quotients for the division 24)6,552. Students will need to decide whether to use numbers from the table, or multiples of those numbers and 10 or 100.

- Ask: Do you expect the quotient 24)6,552 to be in the thousands or hundreds? Why? Possible response: hundreds; possible explanation: 24,000 is too large, but 2,400 is less than 6,552.

To help them solve the division problem, students may want to create a table of multiples of 24 multiplied by 10, 20, 30, and so on. Help students see that they can create this table from the first one.

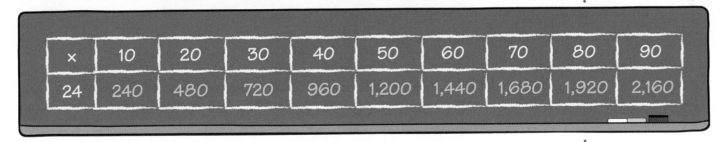

×	10	20	30	40	50	60	70	80	90
24	240	480	720	960	1,200	1,440	1,680	1,920	2,160

If students need more help, they may wish to create a table of multiples of 24 multiplied by 100, 200, 300, and so on.

- Have students find the partial quotients and partial dividends as in **Lesson 8.4,** but this time have them choose the greatest possible partial quotient. You might sketch both the area model and the division record on the board, or help students do so.

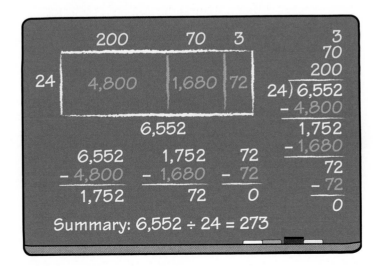

Division shows that a baby who is 6,552 hours old is 273 days old.

• Ask: How many weeks old is the baby?

Students should see that they can find the answer by dividing 273 ÷ 7. Have students make a table of multiples of 7 if they need it (many will not). Write 7)273 and ask if the quotient is in the hundreds (no, because a hundred 7s is still greater than 273,) or tens (yes, because 10 × 7 is only 70.) Have students complete the division, using an appropriate record.

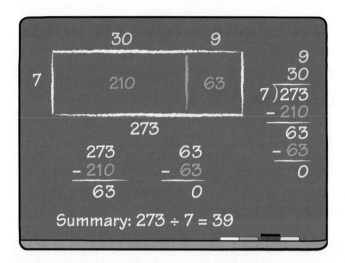

Talk Math

❷ Do you expect the quotient 24)1,800 to be in the hundreds or tens? Why? tens; Possible explanation: 100 × 24 = 2,400, which is greater than 1,800, while 70 × 24 = 1,680, which is less than 1,800.

❷ Do you expect the quotient 24)2,800 to be in the hundreds or tens? Why? hundreds; Possible explanation: 100 × 24 = 2,400, which is less than 2,880. So the quotient must be in the hundreds.

Use with Lesson Activity Book pp. 159–160.

Playing a Game: *Don't Overestimate*

Purpose To practice estimating partial quotients

Goal The object of this game, *Don't Overestimate,* is to collect the most points by giving the best underestimates. For example, if the problem is $24\overline{)2,746}$, and a player estimates the quotient to be 80, the player wins 1,920 points, because $80 \times 24 = 1,920$, and 1,920 doesn't "go over" (it is less than) 2,746. But it's possible to do better. A player who estimates the quotient to be 100 gets 2,400 points because $100 \times 24 = 2,400$, and that's still not over 2,746. Caution players not to get greedy! If their estimate goes over, they'll get no points at all!

Prepare Materials On an $8\frac{1}{2} \times 11$ standard sheet of paper, sketch a division box large enough to fill the page. This is the "mat."

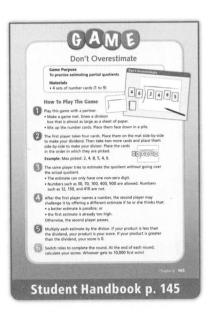

Student Handbook p. 145

Materials
- For each pair: 4 sets of cards numbered 1–9

NCTM Standards 1, 2, 6, 7, 8, 9, 10

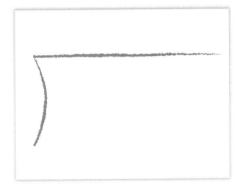

For playing cards, use a deck of 36 cards with four each of the numbers, 1 to 9. Shuffle and place the deck face down.

How to Play

❶ The first player draws four cards. Using the mat, the player places the cards face up, side by side, in the order drawn, to form the dividend. The player then draws two more cards and places them face up to form a 2-digit divisor.

Example:

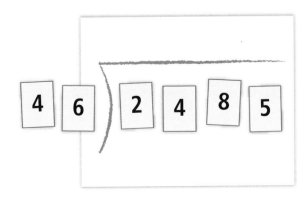

Possible Discussion

Students are likely to benefit from a brief discussion of strategy before they play *Don't Overestimate!* If you overestimate when it is your turn to go first, you score 0. The second player can score a lot of points with very little thinking—all that player needs to do is not go over. If your estimate is too low, you get a score, but the second player (with some good thinking) can get a score greater than yours. If your estimate is the greatest possible that does not exceed the actual quotient, the second player can still score but cannot get a greater score than yours.

The second player may want to challenge every estimate by offering a higher one, because if the challenge fails, there will be no penalty.

② The same player attempts to estimate the quotient *without going over* the actual quotient by naming a number that has a single non-zero digit. (Numbers like 30, 70, 100, 400, and 900, for example, are allowed, but 12, 150, and 410 are not.)

③ The second player may challenge the first player's estimate by offering a different estimate, if the player thinks:

   A that under the same rules for choosing numbers, a better estimate is possible; or

   B that the first estimate is already too high.

Otherwise, the second player passes.

④ Players check each estimate by multiplying it by the divisor. Any product that does not exceed the original dividend is added to the score of the player who made the estimate. If a product exceeds the original dividend, the player scores 0.

⑤ To complete the round, the second player draws the cards and makes the first estimate.

⑥ At the end of each round, players should calculate their scores to that point. When at least one player reaches 10,000 points, the game is over. The player with the highest score wins.

Dividing and Recording Division Efficiently LAB pp. 159–160

individuals **20 MIN**

Purpose To divide efficiently

NCTM Standards 1, 2, 6, 7, 8, 9, 10

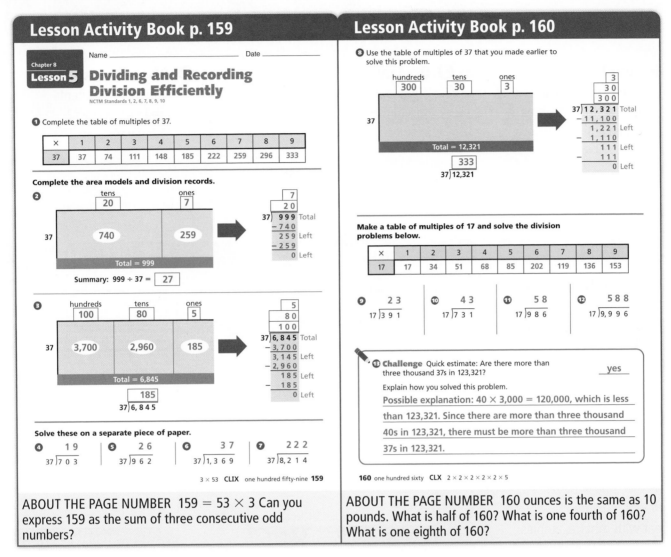

Lesson Activity Book p. 159

ABOUT THE PAGE NUMBER 159 = 53 × 3 Can you express 159 as the sum of three consecutive odd numbers?

Lesson Activity Book p. 160

ABOUT THE PAGE NUMBER 160 ounces is the same as 10 pounds. What is half of 160? What is one fourth of 160? What is one eighth of 160?

Teaching Notes for LAB page 159
Have students complete the page individually or with partners.

Problems 2 and 3 assist students by structuring the division process and the record. The four problems at the bottom of the page leave students to complete these steps on their own. The repeated use of the divisor 37 allows students to focus their attention as much as possible on the process of division without being distracted by multiplication.

Teaching Notes for LAB page 160
The division at the top of the page illustrates that even with a much larger dividend than students saw on LAB page 159, the division process—and, in this case, even the number of steps—is unchanged.

Challenge Problem Students may use the compatible numbers 120,000 and 40 to estimate: 120,000 ÷ 40 = 3,000. Because 37 is less than 40, there must be even more 37s in 120,000 than there are 40s. So, there must be more than three thousand 37s in 120,000, and even more in 123,321.

Reflect and Summarize the Lesson

 Write Math

Kevin wants to divide 21)‾966. What is the most efficient first partial quotient he can write? Explain your reasoning. 40; Possible explanation: Since 9 × 21 = 189 and 189 is less than 966, I knew the first partial quotient had to be greater than 9. I multiplied 21 by 10, 20, 30, and so on, until I found the greatest multiple of 21 that ended in 0 and was less than 966. That multiple was 840, which is 40 × 21.

3 | Differentiated Instruction

**Taft School has 754 students in 29 classes.
Each class has the same number of students.**

❶ Basic Level

What is a reasonable estimate of the number of students in each class? Explain. 24; Possible explanation: I used compatible numbers. 750 ÷ 30 = 25

❷ On Level

What is the most efficient first partial product? Explain. Possible answer: 20 because 20 × 29 = 580, which is less than 754, but 30 × 29 = 870, which is greater than 754.

❸ Above Level

How many students are in each class? Show your work.

26 students in each class

```
        1
        5
       20
  29)754
     −580
      174
     −145
       29
     − 29
        0
```

Intervention

Activity Estimating Quotients

Show students the division 3,694 ÷ 76. Have them complete the following multiplication sentences:

10 × 76 = ■760   100 × 76 = ■7,600

Ask: "How do these multiplications help you know whether the quotient will be a number of tens or hundreds?" Since 100 × 76 = 7,600, there must be fewer than 100 groups of 76 in 3,694. So the quotient must be a number of tens. Repeat with other examples.

Practice

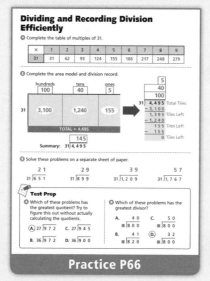

Practice P66

Extension

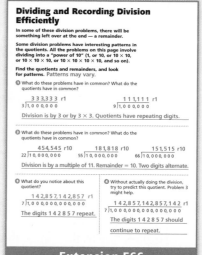

Extension E66

Spiral Review

Spiral Review Book page SR66 provides review of the following previously learned skills and concepts:

- writing equivalent fractions and decimals
- applying the problem solving strategy *draw a picture*

You may wish to have students work with partners to complete the page.

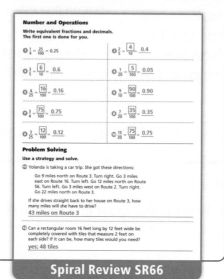

Spiral Review SR66

Extension Activity
Efficient Estimates

Have pairs of students write problems in which a 4-digit number is divided by a 2-digit number. Challenge them to:

- Name the greatest place in the quotient, and
- Find the most efficient first partial quotient.

For example, for 72)5,362 the most efficient first partial quotient is 70 because 70 × 72 = 5,040, the greatest product of a multiple of 10 and 72 that is less than 5,362.

Teacher's Notes 🍎

Daily Notes . . .

Quick Notes

More Ideas

Lesson 6 Using Multiplication to Check Division

NCTM Standards 1, 2, 6, 7, 8, 9, 10

Lesson Planner

STUDENT OBJECTIVES
- To use multiplication to check division
- To use division to solve problems involving whole numbers

1 | Daily Activities (TG p. 685)

| Open-Ended Problem Solving/Headline Story | Skills Practice and Review—Estimating Using Compatible Numbers |

2 | Teach and Practice (TG pp. 686–690)

Ⓐ **Exploring Multiplication as a Check for Division** (TG pp. 686–687)

Ⓑ **Related Divisions** (TG pp. 688–689)

Ⓒ **Using Multiplication to Check Division** (TG p. 690)

MATERIALS
- TR: Activity Masters AM66–AM67
- pencils, paper clips
- 📖 LAB pp. 161–162

3 | Differentiated Instruction (TG p. 691)

Leveled Problem Solving (TG p. 691)	Practice Book P67
Intervention Activity (TG p. 691)	Extension Book E67
Extension Activity (TG p. 691)	Spiral Review Book SR67

Lesson Notes

About the Lesson

Students who learn to divide by following a memorized set of rules—divide, multiply, subtract, bring down, repeat—may never notice that the multiplication step is actually a check for the previous step in the division process. Each time students divide, they follow with a multiplication that undoes that division step, so that they can see how much further they must go to complete the division. So familiar are the steps that students may see nothing new or surprising about using multiplication as a check for division.

Judge how comfortable your students are with division at this point, and use your judgment to help you decide where to place the emphasis in the lesson.

About the Mathematics

When dividing, students perform all of the multiplication steps they take when they check their work. As a result, if they do their arithmetic correctly, a check is unnecessary. Since they may make errors, however, checking is a good idea. Because they have seen that dividing is un-multiplying, students should see why the checking method works, and why it makes sense to use it to check complex divisions they perform on a calculator.

Use with Lesson Activity Book pp. 161–162.

Developing Mathematical Language

Vocabulary: inverse

Multiplication and division are *inverse* operations. Each operation un-does the other. That explains why multiplication can be used to check division. For the same reason, addition can be used to check the *inverse* operation of subtraction: $15 - 8 = 7$; Check: $7 + 8 = 15$? yes

Familiarize students with the term *inverse*.

Beginning Show students the following multiplication sentence: $8 \times 4 = 32$

Show the following sentences and ask students to point to the sentences that show the *inverse* operation of the sentence above:

$36 \div 4 = 9$ $32 \div 4 = 8$ $32 \div 8 = 4$
$32 \div 4 = 8, \; 32 \div 8 = 4$

Intermediate Show students the following multiplication: $9 \times 8 = 72$

Ask them to use the same numbers to write two sentences that show the *inverse* operation. Then show the following division: $48 \div 8 = 6$

Ask students to write two sentences that show the *inverse* operation. $72 \div 8 = 9$, $72 \div 9 = 8$; $6 \times 8 = 48$, $8 \times 6 = 48$

Advanced Have students use two factors and their product, such as 4, 6, and 24, to write a multiplication sentence. Then have them write a sentence to show the *inverse* operation. Provide another example (3, 9, 27). Have students write a division sentence and again, write a sentence for the *inverse* operation. Possible answers: $4 \times 6 = 24$, $24 \div 6 = 4$; $27 \div 3 = 9$, $9 \times 3 = 27$

---

1 | Daily Activities

Open-Ended Problem Solving

Read the Headline Story to the students. Encourage your students to create challenging problems.

Headline Story

There are about 235 million egg-laying hens in the United States. A laying hen produces roughly 250 to 300 eggs per year. In 2005, the population of the United States was estimated at about 295 million people. Ask some mathematical questions that you can answer using this information.

Possible responses: About how many eggs are produced in the U.S. per year? How many dozens is that? (235,000,000 hens $\times$ 300 eggs per hen per year = 70,500,000,000 eggs per year; 70,500,000,000 eggs $\div$ 12 = 5,875,000,000 dozen eggs)

Skills Practice and Review

Estimating Using Compatible Numbers

Have students estimate quotients by choosing compatible numbers close to the dividend and divisor. Possible problems are given below.

Problem	Possible compatible numbers	Actual quotient	Problem	Possible compatible numbers	Actual quotient
$252 \div 6$	$240 \div 6$	42	$576 \div 12$	$600 \div 12$	48
$504 \div 12$	$480 \div 12$	42	$576 \div 24$	$600 \div 25$	24
$504 \div 7$	$490 \div 7$	72	$497 \div 7$	$490 \div 7$	71
$574 \div 7$	$560 \div 7$	82	$642 \div 3$	$630 \div 3$	214

individuals or whole class   **15 MIN**

Materials
- For each student: AM66

NCTM Standards 1, 2, 6, 7, 8, 9, 10

✓ Ongoing Assessment

- Notice the methods students use to complete both the division and the multiplication on Activity Master 66: Checking Division. While the goal is for students eventually to be able to divide without using area models, some may still find them helpful. You will need to decide when to push students to wean themselves from this model and when to encourage them to stay with the model.

Differentiated Instruction

Basic Level While working on Activity Master 66: Checking Division, some students may find it useful to draw and label a 32 × 29 area model to compute the partial products.

	20	9
30	600	270
2	40	18

$32 \times 29 = 600 + 270 + 40 + 18 = 928$

Ⓐ Exploring Multiplication as a Check for Division

Purpose To explore multiplication as a check for division

Introduce Have students work independently on Activity Master 66: Checking Division.

Task Direct students to the following challenges, which appear on Activity Master 66: Checking Division.

Finish the division record to find 928 ÷ 32. Many methods are possible. One such method is shown.

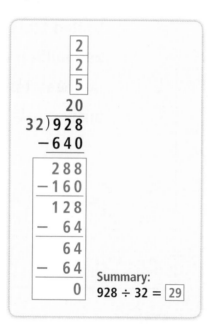

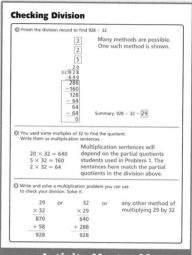

Activity Master 66

You used some multiples of 32 to find the quotient. Write them as multiplication sentences.

Multiplication sentences will depend on the partial quotients students used in Problem 1. The sentences here match the partial quotients in the division above.

$20 \times 32 = 640$

$5 \times 32 = 160$

$2 \times 32 = 64$

Write and solve a multiplication problem you can use to check your division.

29 × 32; several multiplication methods are possible. One such method is shown.

$$\begin{array}{r} 29 \\ \times\ 32 \\ \hline 870 \\ +\ 58 \\ \hline 928 \end{array}$$

Share When students have completed both the division and the multiplication check, have them discuss places where the division and multiplication records match up.

- When there is no remainder, the factors in each multiplication are the divisor and quotient in the division.
- The product in the multiplication is the dividend in the division.
- Other numbers may match, as well, depending on the methods students used.

Noting connections like the above may help students better to see why multiplication and division each undo (or check) the other.

Talk Math

❷ Tawny divided 910 ÷ 26 and got the quotient 35. How can she check her work? Was she right? Possible answer: She can multiply 26 × 35 to see if the product is 910. It is, so she was right.

❷ Arlen divided 726 ÷ 22 and got the quotient 32. How can he check his work? Was he right? Possible answer: He can multiply 22 × 32 to see if the product is 726. It is not, so he was not right.

Differentiated Instruction

Above Level If your students are very independent, you might ask them to solve 32)928 without using Activity Master 66: Checking Division. Students should get 29 as the quotient, but they may find the partial quotients in a variety of ways. When they are finished, ask for suggestions on how they could check their answer. If no one suggests multiplication, remind them of the inverse connection between division and multiplication, and that they used multiplication to check each partial quotient when they were dividing.

Materials

• For each student:
AM67, pencil, paper clip

NCTM Standards 1, 2, 6, 7, 8, 9, 10

B Related Divisions

Purpose To solve related division problems

Introduce Have students make spinners out of a paper clip, a pencil, and the circles on Activity Master 67: Related Division Problems:

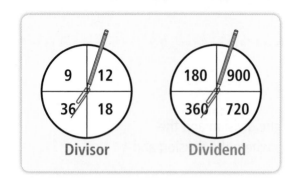

Divisor   Dividend

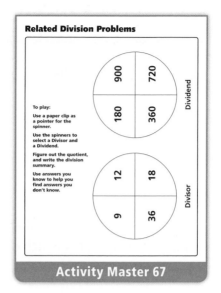

Activity Master 67

Task Direct students to spin the paper clips, choose a divisor and a dividend, record the problem, and find the quotient. Then have them repeat the activity several more times, spinning and finding additional quotients. Ask students to find later quotients, if they can, with the aid of previously solved problems.

Before students begin this activity, challenge them to find the number of division problems the spinners can select. There are 4 possible divisors and, for each of them, 4 possible dividends, so there are 4 × 4, or 16 possible division problems.

Next, ask students to name two or three of the "easiest" problems the spinners can select. Possible answers: 180 ÷ 18, 360 ÷ 36, and 900 ÷ 9 Point out that the "harder" problems can all be solved by using the easiest problems as shortcuts. For example, since 900 ÷ 9 = 100, 900 ÷ 18 = 50, and 900 ÷ 36 = 25.

Though the spinners give this activity a game-like feel, and students may enjoy working in pairs, there is no competitive element to the activity. Because all the problems the spinners can select are related, looking for those relationships will make the work easy and fun for students. Problems will repeat, as they are selected randomly. Tell students that they don't need to write or solve a given problem more than once. 9)$\overline{900}$ should be easy for students, and that can help them solve 18)$\overline{900}$. That, in turn, can help them solve 36)$\overline{900}$. Similarly, 36)$\overline{360}$ should be easy and should help students to find both 36)$\overline{180}$ and 18)$\overline{360}$. Dividing by 12 will require more thinking for most students, but 36)$\overline{360}$ can help them find 12)$\overline{360}$, and 12)$\overline{360}$ can help them find 12)$\overline{180}$.

Talk Math

? How can knowing that $800 \div 8 = 100$ help you find $800 \div 16$? Possible answer: Since 16 is twice 8, the quotient $800 \div 16$ should be half the quotient $800 \div 8$. So, $800 \div 16$ is half of 100, or 50.

? How can knowing that $300 \div 25 = 12$ help you find $150 \div 25$? Possible answer: Since 150 is half of 300, the quotient $150 \div 25$ should be half the quotient $300 \div 25$. So, $150 \div 25$ is half of 12, or 6.

individuals 15 MIN

Purpose To use multiplication to check division

NCTM Standards 1, 2, 6, 7, 8, 9, 10

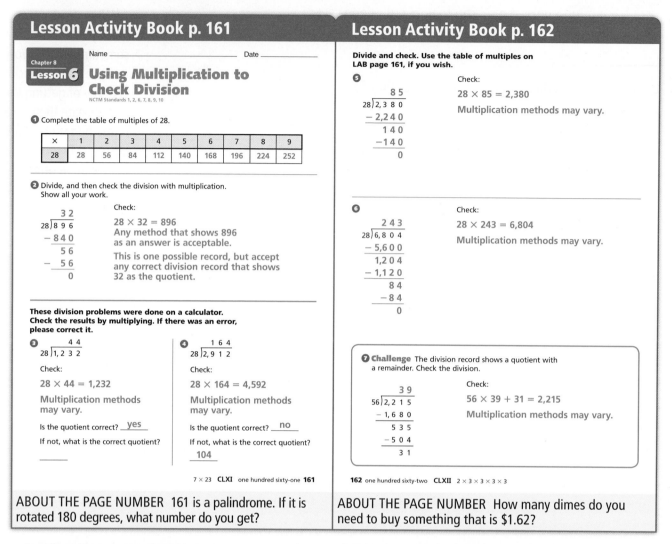

Lesson Activity Book p. 161

Chapter 8
Lesson 6 **Using Multiplication to Check Division**
NCTM Standards 1, 2, 6, 7, 8, 9, 10

Name _____ Date _____

❶ Complete the table of multiples of 28.

×	1	2	3	4	5	6	7	8	9
28	28	56	84	112	140	168	196	224	252

❷ Divide, and then check the division with multiplication. Show all your work.

```
      3 2
28 ) 8 9 6
   − 8 4 0
      5 6
    −  5 6
         0
```
Check:
$28 \times 32 = 896$
Any method that shows 896 as an answer is acceptable.
This is one possible record, but accept any correct division record that shows 32 as the quotient.

These division problems were done on a calculator. Check the results by multiplying. If there was an error, please correct it.

❸
```
        4 4
28 ) 1, 2 3 2
```
Check:
$28 \times 44 = 1,232$
Multiplication methods may vary.
Is the quotient correct? __yes__
If not, what is the correct quotient?
_____

❹
```
      1 6 4
28 ) 2, 9 1 2
```
Check:
$28 \times 164 = 4,592$
Multiplication methods may vary.
Is the quotient correct? __no__
If not, what is the correct quotient?
__104__

7 × 23 **CLXI** one hundred sixty-one **161**

Lesson Activity Book p. 162

Divide and check. Use the table of multiples on LAB page 161, if you wish.

❺
```
        8 5
28 ) 2, 3 8 0
   − 2, 2 4 0
        1 4 0
      − 1 4 0
            0
```
Check:
$28 \times 85 = 2,380$
Multiplication methods may vary.

❻
```
        2 4 3
28 ) 6, 8 0 4
   − 5, 6 0 0
      1, 2 0 4
    − 1, 1 2 0
           8 4
         − 8 4
            0
```
Check:
$28 \times 243 = 6,804$
Multiplication methods may vary.

❼ **Challenge** The division record shows a quotient with a remainder. Check the division.
```
          3 9
56 ) 2, 2 1 5
   − 1, 6 8 0
        5 3 5
      − 5 0 4
          3 1
```
Check:
$56 \times 39 + 31 = 2,215$
Multiplication methods may vary.

162 one hundred sixty-two **CLXII** 2 × 3 × 3 × 3 × 3

ABOUT THE PAGE NUMBER 161 is a palindrome. If it is rotated 180 degrees, what number do you get?

ABOUT THE PAGE NUMBER How many dimes do you need to buy something that is $1.62?

Teaching Notes for LAB page 161
Have students complete the page individually or with partners. To solve Problem 2, students may choose to stack partial quotients.

Students should be permitted to use any method of multiplication they choose to check their divisions.

Teaching Notes for LAB page 162
To solve Problems 5 and 6, students may choose to stack partial quotients.

Challenge Problem Checking a problem that has a remainder requires students to think about which numbers from the division record they will use, how they will use them, and where multiplication fits in. Multiplying 56 × 39 gives a product very close to the dividend. The remainder indicates exactly how close to the dividend it is.

Reflect and Summarize the Lesson

 Write Math

Chrissy divided 27)3,348 and found the quotient 124. How can she check to see if her answer is correct? She can multiply 27 × 124. If the product is 3,348, she is correct. If the product is not 3,348, she is not correct.

3 | Differentiated Instruction

Leveled Problem Solving

There are 830 raffle tickets for sale. Each student volunteer has 30 tickets to sell.

❶ Basic Level
Were all 830 tickets used up by giving each volunteer 30? Explain. No; 830 cannot be evenly divided by 30, so some tickets were left over.

❷ On Level
How many student volunteers could have gotten 30 tickets each? Show your work.
27 volunteers; $27 \times 30 = 810$

❸ Above Level
After all 27 of the student volunteers took 30 tickets to sell, the remaining tickets were divided among 4 students. How many did they each get? Explain.
5 tickets each; $27 \times 30 = 810$, $830 - 810 = 20$, $20 \div 4 = 5$

| Intervention | Practice | Extension |

Activity Inverse Operations

Present a division problem, such as:

Ask students to write a multiplication sentence that corresponds to the division.

$\blacksquare \times 19 = 323$

Have students solve the division sentence and then use the corresponding multiplication to check their work. You may wish to suggest that they use a grid to find partial products.

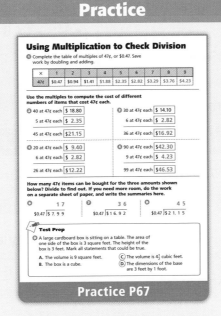

Practice P67

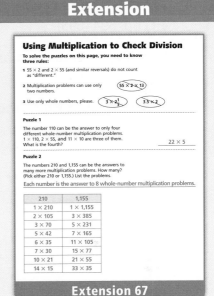

Extension 67

Spiral Review

Spiral Review Book page SR67 provides review of the following previously learned skills and concepts:

- completing a table to show the pattern of square number differences
- finding mode, range, and median for data shown in a graph

You may wish to have students work with partners to complete the page.

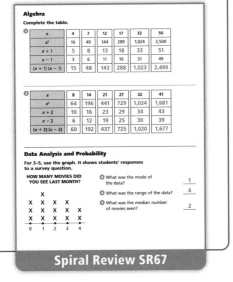

Spiral Review SR67

Extension Activity
Mystery Number

Challenge students to find missing terms by using the appropriate inverse operation.

Present the following division:

Have students use what they have learned about the inverse nature of multiplication and division to find the missing term, in this case the remainder.

$762 - (17 \times 43) = \blacksquare$

Present other divisions with missing terms.

Lesson 7 Investigating Remainders

NCTM Standards 1, 2, 6, 7, 8, 9, 10

Lesson Planner

STUDENT OBJECTIVES
- To use multiplication and division to solve problems involving whole numbers
- To explore remainders

1 Daily Activities (TG p. 693)

Open-Ended Problem Solving/Headline Story	Skills Practice and Review— Is the Quotient Reasonable?

2 Teach and Practice (TG pp. 694–699)

	MATERIALS
Ⓐ **What is the Largest Possible Remainder?** (TG pp. 694–695)	• square tiles
Ⓑ **Writing Remainders as Fractions** (TG pp. 696–697)	• 📖 LAB pp. 163–164 • 📖 SH pp. 136–137
Ⓒ **Investigating Remainders** (TG p. 698)	

3 Differentiated Instruction (TG p. 700)

Leveled Problem Solving (TG p. 700)	Practice Book P68
Intervention Activity (TG p. 700)	Extension Book E68
Extension Activity (TG p. 700)	Spiral Review Book SR68

Lesson Notes

About the Lesson

Your students are gaining skill in dividing when the dividend is a multiple of the divisor. They know that the quotient will be a whole number, and that there will be no remainder.

They may not know, however, what to do when the quotient is not a whole number and there is a remainder. At first, it may seem to them that the method they learned for checking division doesn't work. When there is a remainder, multiplying quotient by divisor to see if the dividend results isn't enough.

There's an extra step that involves adding in the remainder. In this lesson, students will see that the checking method remains the same even when there is a remainder. They will begin to incorporate the remainder as a fractional part of the quotient. And although they haven't yet learned to multiply fractions, they will still see that, if they express the remainder as a fractional part of the quotient, the rule that "multiplication undoes division" still holds: if $b \div a = c$, then $b \times c = a$.

Use with Lesson Activity Book pp. 163–164.

Developing Mathematical Language

Vocabulary: remainder

In division, the *remainder* is the number that is left over when a divisor fails to divide a dividend evenly. Students may wonder why it is called a *remainder* rather than a "remainer." Tell them that between the 9th and 16th centuries, the French inserted the letter *d* in the root word, and there it has remained ever since.

Familiarize students with the term *remainder.*

Beginning Display the following division model:

Tell students that the model shows 10 ÷ 3. Ask students to tell how many are left after the division and point to the *remainder.* 1 Repeat with other division sentences.

Intermediate Show students the following division problem: 5)12

Ask: "Will this division come out even?" no Model the division.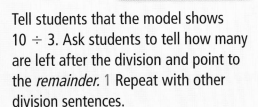

Ask a student to point to the *remainder.* 2

Advanced Show students this problem:

$$\begin{array}{r} 2 \\ 4\overline{)11} \\ -8 \\ \hline 3 \end{array}$$

Ask them to point to the whole-number quotient and the *remainder.* Repeat with other division problems.

Open-Ended Problem Solving

Read the Headline Story to the students. Encourage them to think of creative ways to solve the problem.

 Headline Story

Suppose that every day someone in your class helps the kindergartners at the crosswalk. A different student helps each day. How many times will each of you get to help?

Possible responses: There are 180 days in our school year. I divided 180 by 26, the number of students in our class, and got 6 and a remainder of 24. So, 6 turns per student × 26 students uses up 156 days, with 24 days left. On those 24 days, most of us could get a 7th turn.

Skills Practice and Review

Is the Quotient Reasonable?

Remind students that they might make errors when dividing, even if they use a calculator. One way to judge the reasonableness of the quotient is to round and then estimate. First, round the divisor and the calculated quotient so that each has only one non-zero digit. Next, multiply. Finally, compare the product to the actual dividend.

Example:
$$55\overline{)13{,}640}^{\,248} \rightarrow 60\overline{)\phantom{13{,}640}}^{\,200}$$

60 × 200 = 12,000   12,000 is close to 13,640.
So, the quotient is reasonable.
Ask if these quotients are reasonable.

8,034 ÷ 39 = 267 no	22,608 ÷ 72 = 314 yes
22,494 ÷ 46 = 489 yes	55,412 ÷ 61 = 89 no
9,888 ÷ 206 = 48 yes	34,124 ÷ 449 = 706 no

individuals
10 MIN

NCTM Standards 1, 2, 6, 7, 8, 9, 10

A What is the Largest Possible Remainder?

Purpose To explore the relationship between the divisor and the remainder in a division

Introduce Before students work independently on Explore: What Remainders Are Possible?, point out that in most of the divisions they have performed so far, the dividend has been a whole-number multiple of the divisor. As a result, the division has come out "evenly." The quotient is a whole number.

$19 \times 27 = 513$, so $513 \div 27 = 19$ exactly

Mention that, in this exploration, students will investigate divisions that do not come out evenly.

You may wish to read and discuss the two divisions at the top of the page as a class. The difference between the two is that, on the left, 0 remains after the last subtraction. The quotient is exactly 28. On the right, 1 remains after the last subtraction. The quotient is close to 32, but not exactly 32.

✔ Ongoing Assessment

• Can students accurately complete a division record showing division by 1- and 2-digit whole numbers?

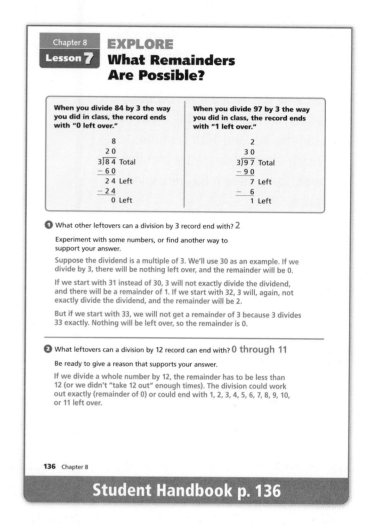

Student Handbook p. 136

Task Direct students to the following challenges, which appear on Explore: What Remainders Are Possible?

What other leftovers can a division by 3 record end with? 2

Students should conclude after completing Problem 1 that, when dividing by 3, only three different leftovers are possible after the final subtraction— 0, 1, and 2. If they are unsure of why this should be so, ask the following questions:

Use with Lesson Activity Book pp. 163–164.

- Suppose 3 were left over after what you thought was the final subtraction.

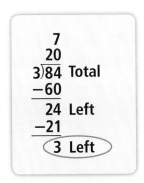

How would you know that it was **not** the final subtraction? Possible response: You could divide the 3 that remained by the divisor 3, and place another partial quotient of 1 above the current quotient of $20 + 7 = 27$.

- Suppose 4 were left over after what you thought was the final subtraction. How would you know that it was **not** the final subtraction? Possible response: You could divide the 4 that remained by the divisor 3, and place another partial quotient of 1 above the current quotient.

Students should see that you could ask the same question about possible leftovers of 5, 6, 7, and so on. In every case, students could continue dividing by 3 and writing one or more additional partial quotients in the record.

What leftovers can a division by 12 record end with?
0, 1, 2, 3, 4, 5, 6, 7, 8, 9, 10, or 11

For reasons similar to those in Problem 1, the only possible leftovers are whole numbers less than 12. If students were to find a leftover of 12 or more, they could continue dividing by 12 and writing one or more additional partial quotients in the record.

Share Ask students to share their discoveries about remainders. Students should understand that only remainders that are less than the divisor are possible.

Talk Math

❷ Why must a remainder always be less than the divisor? Possible answer: If the record shows a remainder greater than the divisor, it will be possible to continue with the division process, finding additional partial quotients and making the quotient greater.

❷ Jon wants to separate his baseball cards into 6 stacks. If he divides by 6 to find the number of cards there will be in each pile, what are the possible remainders his division record might end with? 0, 1, 2, 3, 4, or 5

Materials
- For each student: square tiles

NCTM Standards 1, 2, 6, 7, 8, 9, 10

B Writing Remainders as Fractions

Purpose To write remainders as fractions

Introduce Ask for a student volunteer. Invite the student to solve the following problem using square tiles on an overhead projector or on a table where all can see them, or arrays drawn on the board.

Problem **Ask: How can you arrange 31 tiles to fill as many 5-tile columns as possible?** Here is one possible correct response:

- After a student makes an appropriate picture, write the associated number sentence $(5 \times 6) + 1 = 31$. Invite another student to explain how the sentence fits the picture. Possible explanation: 5×6 refers to 6 columns each containing 5 tiles; 1 refers to the extra tile; the entire sentence represents 31 tiles.

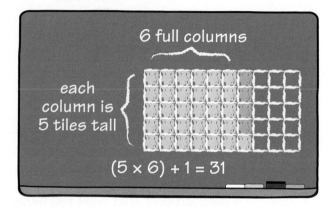

6 full columns

each column is 5 tiles tall

$(5 \times 6) + 1 = 31$

- Point out that $31 \div 5$ really asks, "What can I multiply by 5 to give 31?" State that the number cannot be 6. It must be greater than 6 because $6 \times 5 = 30$. But it can't be as great as 7 because $7 \times 5 = 35$. Challenge students with this question: Can you find the number?

Some students may be able to work out the quotient from their understanding of fractions and decimals. Since they are looking for a number between 6 and 7, they may try fractions or decimals in that interval. Help them use tiles to see whether their answers work. For example, if they guess "six and a half," use tiles to build a 6-by-5 array (to represent all 5 of the sixes in 31). Then add a "half-tile" for each of the 5 rows. Alternatively, add six and a half tiles 5 times, but put only 6 tiles in each column; have students imagine the half tiles, or draw and label one in the proper place. Since you need more than 31 tiles to do this, six and a half is too great.

If any students find the answer $(6\frac{1}{5})$ on their own, offer generous congratulations! However the class arrives at the answer, show how it fits the first arrangement of 31 tiles:

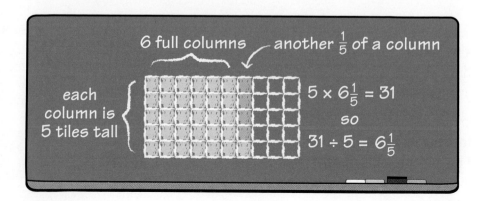

6 full columns — another $\frac{1}{5}$ of a column

each column is 5 tiles tall

$5 \times 6\frac{1}{5} = 31$

so

$31 \div 5 = 6\frac{1}{5}$

Use with Lesson Activity Book pp. 163–164.

Give the class a new problem: How can you show $5\overline{)32}$ using tiles? Then restate the problem: What number can I multiply by 5 to give 32?

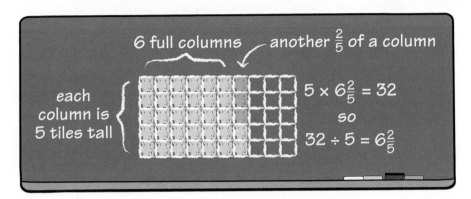

Many students will be unsure of what to make of $5 \times 6\frac{2}{5}$ or even $5 \times \frac{2}{5}$. You may want to introduce multiplication of fractions now, although this is not necessary, as the topic will be explored in a later chapter.

Share Remind students that in Activity A, they saw that only certain remainders are possible in a division. Ask students to explain how that conclusion relates to this activity. They should see that no matter how many tiles they start with, if they fill as many 5-tile columns as possible, no more than 4 tiles can be left over. In other words, a partially filled column can be only $\frac{1}{5}$, $\frac{2}{5}$, $\frac{3}{5}$, or $\frac{4}{5}$ full.

Talk Math

❷ Each column in an array is 8 tiles tall. The array contains 3 full columns, plus a partially filled column containing 5 tiles. What number sentence can you write to describe the number of tiles in the array?
$(8 \times 3) + 5 = 29$

❷ What division problem can you write to describe the number of 8-tile tall columns in the array above? Possible answer: $29 \div 8$; Some students may be able to go further and write $29 \div 8 = 3\frac{5}{8}$.

Teacher Story

"When my class checks division with fractional quotients, I like to briefly introduce the idea of multiplication of fractions. Some of my students like seeing that $5 \times \frac{1}{5}$ is 1 and that $5 \times \frac{2}{5}$ should be twice as great. Others prefer it when I say that 5×2 apples is 10 apples, so 5×2 fifths is 10 fifths. They already know that $\frac{10}{5}$ is 2, so are usually quick to volunteer that last step!"

individuals **20 MIN**

Purpose To practice division with fractional remainders

NCTM Standards 1, 2, 6, 7, 8, 9, 10

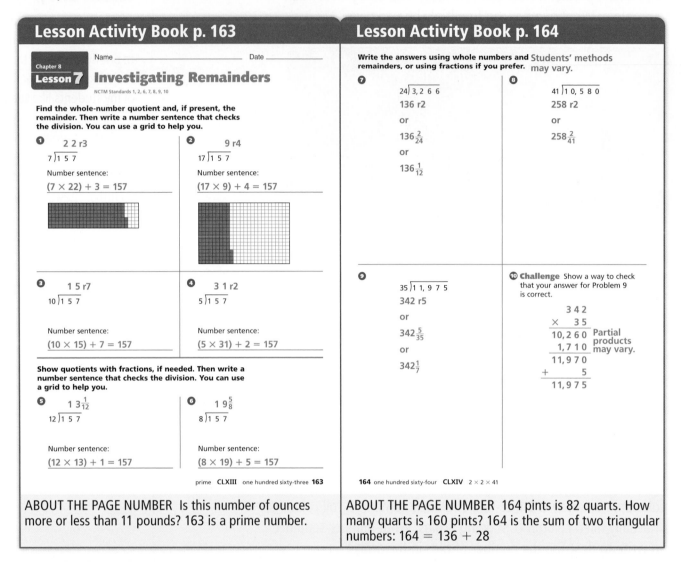

Lesson Activity Book p. 163

Name _____ Date _____

Chapter 8
Lesson 7 **Investigating Remainders**
NCTM Standards 1, 2, 6, 7, 8, 9, 10

Find the whole-number quotient and, if present, the remainder. Then write a number sentence that checks the division. You can use a grid to help you.

1   2 2 r3
7) 1 5 7

Number sentence:
(7 × 22) + 3 = 157

2   9 r4
17) 1 5 7

Number sentence:
(17 × 9) + 4 = 157

3   1 5 r7
10) 1 5 7

Number sentence:
(10 × 15) + 7 = 157

4   3 1 r2
5) 1 5 7

Number sentence:
(5 × 31) + 2 = 157

Show quotients with fractions, if needed. Then write a number sentence that checks the division. You can use a grid to help you.

5 $1\,3\frac{1}{12}$
12) 1 5 7

Number sentence:
(12 × 13) + 1 = 157

6 $1\,9\frac{5}{8}$
8) 1 5 7

Number sentence:
(8 × 19) + 5 = 157

prime **CLXIII** one hundred sixty-three **163**

Lesson Activity Book p. 164

Write the answers using whole numbers and remainders, or using fractions if you prefer. Students' methods may vary.

7   24) 3, 2 6 6
136 r2
or
$136\frac{2}{24}$
or
$136\frac{1}{12}$

8   41) 1 0, 5 8 0
258 r2
or
$258\frac{2}{41}$

9   35) 1 1, 9 7 5
342 r5
or
$342\frac{5}{35}$
or
$342\frac{1}{7}$

10 Challenge Show a way to check that your answer for Problem 9 is correct.

      3 4 2
  ×   3 5
  10,2 6 0   Partial
   1,7 1 0   products
  11,9 7 0   may vary.
  +   5
  11,9 7 5

164 one hundred sixty-four **CLXIV** 2 × 2 × 41

ABOUT THE PAGE NUMBER Is this number of ounces more or less than 11 pounds? 163 is a prime number.

ABOUT THE PAGE NUMBER 164 pints is 82 quarts. How many quarts is 160 pints? 164 is the sum of two triangular numbers: 164 = 136 + 28

Teaching Notes for LAB page 163

Have students complete the page individually or with partners.

Make sure students know what the words *quotient* and *remainder* refer to and how to check a quotient (multiply the divisor by the whole-number quotient and add the remainder).

Differentiated Instruction Basic Level/On Level Small grids are provided for optional student use for Problems 1 and 2. Some students may wish to use graph paper or square tiles to complete Problems 3–6.

Teaching Notes for LAB page 164

For the problems on this page, students may choose whether to show division with remainders or with complete quotients including fractions.

Challenge Problem To check, students should multiply the whole-number quotient (342) times the divisor (35), and to the product (11,970) add the remainder (5). The sum (11,975) is the dividend.

Reflect and Summarize the Lesson

Write Math

Find $19 \div 5$. Write the remainder as a fraction. $3\frac{4}{5}$

Review Model ....

Refer students to Review Model: Dividing Using a Grid in the *Student Handbook* to see how to use a grid to find both the quotient and the remainder in a division problem.

✔ Check for Understanding

1 5 r3 or $5\frac{3}{5}$

2 6 r4 or $6\frac{4}{9}$

3 7 r6 or $7\frac{6}{7}$

4 13

5 23 r1 or $23\frac{1}{4}$

6 9 r7 or $9\frac{7}{8}$

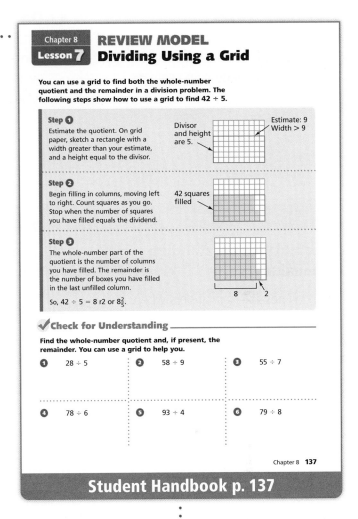

Student Handbook p. 137

3 | Differentiated Instruction

Leveled Problem Solving

The school librarian wants to divide 329 books as evenly as possible among 9 shelves. Any leftover books will be displayed in the front of the library.

❶ Basic Level

Estimate the number of books that will be on each shelf. Explain how you made your estimate. . About 40 books; possible answer: use compatible numbers, 320 ÷ 8 = 40.

❷ On Level

What is the greatest number of books that can possibly be left over in the division you would use to solve this problem? Explain. 8 books; if the divisor is 9, the greatest possible remainder is 8.

❸ Above Level

How many books will be on each shelf? How many will be displayed in the front of the library? Show your work. 36 books on each shelf; 5 displayed in the front of the library.

Intervention

Activity Understanding Remainders

List all possible remainders when the divisor is 5, 6, 7, 8, and 9. Ask students to describe the pattern they see. The remainders are all of the whole numbers less than the divisor. Lead students to see that if a divisor is described by a variable n, the possible remainders are $n - 1$, $n - 2$, $n - 3$, all the way to $n - n$.

Practice

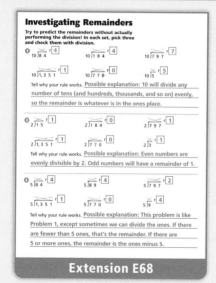

Practice P68

Extension

Investigating Remainders

Extension E68

Extension Activity Division Models

Have pairs of students write the division problem that corresponds to the model.

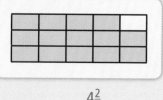

$$3\overline{)14} \quad 4\tfrac{2}{3}$$

Challenge students to draw other division models and write the corresponding division problems and solutions.

Spiral Review

Spiral Review Book page SR68 provides review of the following previously learned skills and concepts:

• writing a pair of fractions with a common denominator to compare them

• converting between customary measurement units

You may wish to have students work with partners to complete the page.

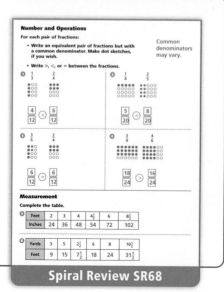

Spiral Review SR68

---

700 Chapter 8 • Lesson 7

Use with Lesson Activity Book pp. 163–164.

Teacher's Notes 🍎

Daily Notes . . .

Quick Notes

More Ideas

Lesson 8 Interpreting Remainders in Word Problems

NCTM Standards 1, 2, 6, 7, 8, 9, 10

Lesson Planner

- To use division to solve problems involving whole numbers
- Given a context, to decide whether to ignore remainders or to add them as fractions or decimals to the quotient

1 Daily Activities (TG p. 703)

Open-Ended Problem Solving/Headline Story	Skills Practice and Review—Is the Quotient Reasonable?

2 Teach and Practice (TG pp. 704–708)

MATERIALS

Ⓐ **What Do You Do About the Remainder?** (TG pp. 704–705)

Ⓑ **Interpreting Remainders in Word Problems** (TG p. 706)

Ⓒ **Creating Word Problems** (TG pp. 707–708)

- 📖 LAB pp. 165–166
- 📖 SH p. 138

3 Differentiated Instruction (TG p. 709)

Leveled Problem Solving (TG p. 709)	Practice Book P69
Intervention Activity (TG p. 709)	Extension Book E69
Extension Activity (TG p. 709)	Spiral Review Book SR69

Lesson Notes

About the Lesson

When a quotient is not a whole number, the solver must decide what to do about the remainder. If the problem has no real-world context, there are three ways to report the remainder: as a whole number of "leftovers," as a fraction, or as a decimal. If the quotient is the answer to a real-world problem, however, there are choices to make. Is the remainder relevant to the answer, or can I just ignore it? If it is relevant, will the quotient make sense with a fractional or decimal remainder, or shall I round up to the next whole number? This lesson and **Lesson 8.9** will provide students with the background to choose sensibly.

Developing Mathematical Language

Vocabulary: reasonable

Is a given estimate *reasonable?* Which is the most *reasonable* way to express a remainder? As students advance in their study of mathematics, they will encounter more and more problems with multiple possible answers, the correct one of which they can find by choosing *reasonably.*

Familiarize students with the term *reasonable.*

Beginning Display this problem.

$$\begin{array}{r} 36\ r\blacksquare \\ 22\overline{)801} \end{array}$$

Show students 9, 29, and 39 as possible remainders, and ask them to point to the only *reasonable* one. Repeat with other division expressions.

Intermediate Display this problem.

$$\begin{array}{r} 40\ r10 \\ 24\overline{)970} \end{array}$$

Tell the class that the division represents the number of cartons of 24 water bottles that can be made from 970 bottles. Ask students what they think is the most *reasonable* thing to do with the remainder. Ignore it.

Advanced Present the following problem: "Sixteen students paid a total of $184 for the class field trip to the science museum. How much did each student pay?" Have students do the division, and decide on the most *reasonable* way to handle the remainder. 184 ÷ 16 = $11.50; write the remainder as a decimal.

Open-Ended Problem Solving

Read the Headline Story to the students. Encourage them to think of creative ways to solve the problem.

Headline Story

To figure the volume of a rectangular box, multiply length × width × height. If a rectangular box has a volume of 60 cubic units and a height of 4 units, what are some possibilities for its other two dimensions?

Possible responses: Because the height is 4, length × width × 4 = 60. Length × width must be 15, because 15 × 4 = 60. So, length and width could be 3 and 5 or 1 and 15 or 2 and $7\frac{1}{2}$.

Skills Practice and Review

Is the Quotient Reasonable?

Write the following division expressions on the board. Direct students first to round the divisor and possible quotients, then to multiply and choose the correct quotient. Ask them to provide a number sentence that justifies each choice. Possible number sentences are given.

2,640 ÷ 24 =	110 or 11?	110; 100 × 20 = 2,000
8,446 ÷ 41 =	26 or 206?	206; 200 × 40 = 8,000
11,620 ÷ 35 =	332 or 32?	332; 300 × 40 = 12,000
14,472 ÷ 54 =	168 or 268?	268 ; 300 × 50 = 15,000
22,940 ÷ 62 =	307 or 370?	370; 400 × 60 = 24,000
11,956 ÷ 98 =	122 or 211?	122; 100 × 100 = 10,000
5,396 ÷ 76 =	710 or 71?	71; 70 × 80 = 5,600
14,194 ÷ 47 =	32 or 302?	302; 300 × 50 = 15,000
8,184 ÷ 88 =	993 or 93?	93; 90 × 90 = 8,100
21,320 ÷ 41 =	52 or 520?	520; 500 × 40 = 20,000

individuals or
whole class

🕙 **10 MIN**

NCTM Standards 1, 2, 6, 7, 8, 9, 10

A What Do You Do About the Remainder?

Purpose To explore two interpretations of the remainder in a division problem, and to learn that the correct interpretation depends on the context

Introduce Have students work independently on Explore: What Do I Do About the Remainder? Explain that the goal of the activity is to explore how the statement of a problem can affect the way the remainder is expressed.

Problems Direct students to the following problems, which appear on Explore: What Do I Do About the Remainder? Both problems involve sharing money. In Problem 1, the remaining pennies cannot be shared evenly, so the remainder is ignored. In Problem 2, the remaining dollars can be split into halves and shared evenly, so the remainder is not ignored.

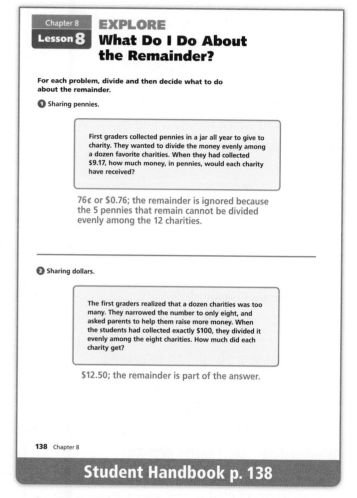

Chapter 8

Lesson 8

EXPLORE

What Do I Do About the Remainder?

For each problem, divide and then decide what to do about the remainder.

❶ Sharing pennies.

First graders collected pennies in a jar all year to give to charity. They wanted to divide the money evenly among a dozen favorite charities. When they had collected $9.17, how much money, in pennies, would each charity have received?

76¢ or $0.76; the remainder is ignored because the 5 pennies that remain cannot be divided evenly among the 12 charities.

❷ Sharing dollars.

The first graders realized that a dozen charities was too many. They narrowed the number to only eight, and asked parents to help them raise more money. When the students had collected exactly $100, they divided it evenly among the eight charities. How much did each charity get?

$12.50; the remainder is part of the answer.

138 Chapter 8

Student Handbook p. 138

• First graders collected pennies in a jar all year to give to charity. They wanted to divide the money evenly among a dozen favorite charities. When they had collected $9.17, how much money, in pennies, would each charity have received? 76¢ or $0.76

To find the amount each charity would receive, divide 917 pennies by 12.

After the last subtraction, 5 pennies remain. Since they cannot be divided evenly among 12 charities, they should be ignored. Each charity would receive 70¢ + 6¢ = 76¢, or $0.76.

$$\begin{array}{r} 6 \\ 70 \\ 12\overline{)917} \\ -840 \\ \hline 77 \\ -72 \\ \hline 5 \end{array}$$

- The first graders realized that a dozen charities was too many. They narrowed the number to only eight, and asked parents to help them raise more money. When the students had collected exactly $100, they divided it evenly among the eight charities. How much did each charity get? $12.50

  To find the amount each charity would receive, divide $100 by 8.

  After the last subtraction, 4 dollars remain. Since 4 dollars can be divided evenly among 8 charities, with each charity receiving $0.50, 4 dollars should not be ignored. Each charity received $10 + $2 + $0.50, or $12.50.

```
       2
      10
  8)100
   - 80
      20
    - 16
       4
```

Share When students are finished, ask them to share ideas. If your students work well together, a discussion of what to do with the remainder can generate some good give and take. The important idea to bring out is that a remainder affects an answer in different ways, depending on the problem.

- In the pennies problem, the whole-number quotient is the answer in its totality. The "extra" represented by the remainder is ignored.

- In the dollars problem, the whole-number quotient is only part of the answer. The remainder must be converted to a fraction of a dollar and then incorporated into the answer.

Summarize by reiterating the two ways of handling remainders illustrated by this activity: ignore the remainder or convert it to a fraction or a decimal. The choice of which to use will depend on the context of the problem.

Talk Math

❷ Can 391 pennies be divided evenly among 23 students? Explain your reasoning. Yes; possible explanation: each student will receive exactly 17 pennies. There is no remainder.

❷ Can 148 pennies be divided evenly among 5 students? Explain your reasoning. No; possible explanation: each student will receive 29 pennies, but there is a remainder of 3 pennies, which cannot be divided evenly among 5 students.

❷ Can 148 dollars be divided evenly among 5 students? Explain your reasoning. Yes; possible explanation: each student will receive $29 plus the $3 remainder divided equally among 5 students. Since $3.00 ÷ 5 = $0.60, each student will receive $29.60.

B **Interpreting Remainders in Word Problems** LAB pp. 165–166

 individuals 👤 ⏰ **20 MIN**

Purpose To interpret remainders in division problems

NCTM Standards 1, 2, 6, 7, 8, 9, 10

Lesson Activity Book p. 165

Name _____ Date _____

Chapter 8
Lesson 8 **Interpreting Remainders in Word Problems**
NCTM Standards 1, 2, 6, 7, 8, 9, 10

Decide what to do when there is a remainder—ignore it or include it as a fraction or a decimal.

1 How many 24-foot jump ropes can be made from a rope that is 100 feet long?

Solution: __4 jump ropes__

What should you do about the remainder?

__ignore it__

$$\begin{array}{r} 4 \\ 24\overline{)100} \\ -96 \\ \hline 4 \end{array}$$

2 Nathan used lots of tennis balls when practicing his serve. At the end of practice, he gathered up 59 tennis balls and put them back into cans. If each can holds 3 tennis balls, how many cans will he fill?

Solution: __19 cans__

What should you do about the remainder?

__ignore it__

$$\begin{array}{r} 9 \\ 10 \\ 3\overline{)59} \\ -30 \\ \hline 29 \\ -27 \\ \hline 2 \end{array}$$

3 Altogether, the 32 students in Ms. Rosenfeld's class raised $456 at the bake sale. The money will be divided up to pay for each student's admission and snack for a field trip. How much money is available for each student?

Solution: __$14.25__

What should you do about the remainder?

__show it as a decimal__

$$\begin{array}{r} 4 \\ 10 \\ 32\overline{)456} \\ -320 \\ \hline 136 \\ -128 \\ \hline 8 \end{array}$$

$4\frac{8}{32} = 14\frac{1}{4} = \$14.25$

3 × 5 × 11 **CLXV** one hundred sixty-five **165**

Lesson Activity Book p. 166

4 My large plastic bottle holds 196 ounces of water. How many cups of water is that? (1 cup = 8 oz)

Solution: __$24\frac{1}{2}$ cups__

What should you do about the remainder?

__show it as a fraction__

$$\begin{array}{r} 24 \\ 8\overline{)196} \\ -160 \\ \hline 36 \\ -32 \\ \hline 4 \end{array}$$
4 oz = $\frac{1}{2}$ cup

5 The bagel bakery advertised a "Baker's Dozen Sale": buy a dozen bagels and get an extra bagel free. The first batch they made was 20 dozen bagels. How many bags of 13 bagels will that make?

Solution: __18 bags__

What should you do about the remainder?

__ignore it__

$$\begin{array}{r} 8 \\ 10 \\ 13\overline{)240} \\ -130 \\ \hline 110 \\ -104 \\ \hline 6 \end{array}$$
12 bagels per doz × 20 doz = 240 bagels

6 Challenge A rope is 408 ft long. If it is cut into 32 shorter pieces, what is the length of each piece? Write your answer in feet and inches.

Solution: __12 ft 9 in.__

What should you do about the remainder?

__show it as a fraction then__

__use it to get the number__

__of inches__

$$\begin{array}{r} 2 \\ 10 \\ 32\overline{)408} \\ -320 \\ \hline 88 \\ -64 \\ \hline 24 \end{array}$$
$12\frac{24}{32} = 12\frac{3}{4}$
$\frac{3}{4}$ of 12 = 9 in.

166 one hundred sixty-six **CLXVI** 2 × 83

ABOUT THE PAGE NUMBER Can you make 165 cents without pennies? without pennies and nickels? with only dimes?

ABOUT THE PAGE NUMBER Is 166 inches more or less than 20 feet?

Teaching Notes for LAB page 165

Have students complete the page individually or with partners.

To solve the problems correctly, students must understand their contexts and interpret their remainders correctly. In Problem 1, a partial jump rope doesn't make sense, and in Problem 2, the question asks about full cans of balls, so in both contexts, the remainder should be ignored. In Problem 3, the remainder is a fraction of a dollar and should be written as a decimal.

Teaching Notes for LAB page 166

As on LAB page 165, students must interpret remainders correctly to solve the problems correctly. In Problem 4, partial cups make sense, so the remainder should be included. In Problem 5, a partial bag makes no sense, so the remainder should be ignored.

Challenge Problem This problem is similar to Problems 1 and 3 on LAB page 165. This problem asks students to interpret the remainder as a fraction and then use it to convert feet to inches.

Creating Word Problems

Purpose To consider situations that suggest different ways of dealing with a remainder when dividing

Introduce Tell students that they will review the story problems on LAB pages 165 and 166 to discuss how the contexts of the stories helped them to know how to handle the remainders.

Task Ask students to begin by discussing the contexts of problems where the remainder was ignored.

Materials
• For each student: completed LAB pp. 165–166

NCTM Standards 1, 2, 6, 7, 8, 9

Talk Math

❓ What should you do about the remainder 4 in Problem 1 and why? Possible answer: You ignore the remainder because the question asks for the number of 24-foot jump ropes. Part of a jump rope is not a jump rope.

❓ What do you do about the remainder in Problem 2 and why? Possible answer: You ignore the remainder because the question asks for the number of full cans and not remaining loose balls.

❓ Now look at Problem 5. What should you do about the remainder and why? Possible answer: You ignore the remainder because the question asks for the number of bags of 13 bagels.

Briefly discuss with students how these three situations are alike. If necessary, prompt students by asking questions such as these:

❓ In Problems 1 and 2, what things do the questions as about? Jump ropes and cans of tennis balls

❓ Do fractions of these things make sense? Possible answers: you either have a whole jump rope or you don't have one at all; you could have a fraction of a can, but the problem asks about full cans.

Now direct students to the other story problems on the LAB pages.

❓ Problem 3 asks how much money will be available for each student's admission and snack? What did you get for the remainder and what did you do about it? Possible answer: The remainder was 8, but it's part of a dollar, so I knew that it was $\frac{8}{32}$ or $\frac{1}{4}$ of a dollar. That's 25¢, so I added it to the dollar amount.

❓ What did you do about the remainder in Problem 4 and why? Possible answer: The remainder was 4, which is $\frac{4}{8}$ or $\frac{1}{2}$ a cup. I added it to the whole number of cups.

Briefly discuss with students how these situations are alike. If necessary, prompt students by asking questions similar to these.

❓ Does each question ask for a number of whole things? yes

❓ Do any of the questions ask about things that may be described with partial amounts? yes

Concept Alert

In order to help students make clear distinctions between contexts that suggest different ways of dealing with remainders, two types of situations are emphasized in this lesson (ignoring the remainder or recording it as a fraction or decimal). In the next lesson, students will investigate contexts that warrant rounding the quotient up, and will also practice distinguishing among all three types of situations.

❷ In each of these stories, why does the remainder matter to the answer? Possible answer: For the money, the leftover dollars could be divided evenly by using cents instead of dollars. With the water bottle, it makes sense to talk about a half cup, so there's no need to ignore the remainder.

❷ In each of these stories, does the remainder, or extra amount, change how you would answer the question concerning the number of whole things? Possible answer: Yes, you add it on to the whole number amount. You write it as a fraction or a decimal.

Help your students see that in Problems 3 and 4, parts of the units (things the problems ask about) make sense (unlike in Problems 1, 2 and 5).

Practice Ask students to think of other division situations where the context calls for either ignoring the remainder or including it. Have them begin with a question, such as "How many full boxes?" or "How many horses?" or "How many boxes?" Then ask them to try to use numbers to create division situations.

If any students make up problems where the context calls for the whole number to be rounded up (such as the number of buses needed transport all people), compliment them on thinking of a situation where the remainder is not included as a fraction or decimal, and tell them that you will save the problem to look at more closely during the next lesson.

After students have made up a few problems where the remainder should be ignored, ask them to think about situations where the remainder should be included as part of the answer. Again, you might ask students to begin by thinking of questions. If they need help getting started, you might give the following examples: "How many hours?" "How many miles?" Then, as time allows, ask volunteers to create examples of this type of division situation.

Reflect and Summarize the Lesson

Write Math

Think of a division word problem about a situation in your school where you would ignore the remainder in the solution. Then think of a problem where you would write the remainder in the solution as a fractiion or a decimal. Possible problems: There are 190 books to put on shelves. If each shelf holds 15 books, how many shelves will be filled with books? (12; ignore the remainder) The school cafeteria collected $117 for box lunches for the school picnic. If 52 students each bought a box lunch, how much did each lunch cost? ($2.25; write the remainder as a decimal).

3 Differentiated Instruction

Leveled Problem Solving

Students fill up one row of the auditorium before beginning the next row. There are 588 seats with 28 in each row.

❶ Basic Level

How many rows of seats are in the auditorium? Explain. 21 rows; 588 ÷ 28 = 21

❷ On Level

If there are 396 students in the auditorium, how many rows are filled? Explain. 14 rows; 396 ÷ 28 = 14 r4, so 14 rows are filled, and there are 4 students in the 15th row.

❸ Above Level

If there are 468 students in the auditorium, how many rows are used? How many students are in the last row used? Explain. 17 rows; 20 students; 468 ÷ 28 = 16 r20, so there will be 20 students in the 17th row.

Intervention

Activity Understanding Remainders

Give students a 20-inch piece of adding machine tape, scissors, and a ruler. Tell them to make as many 6-inch sections as possible. When students have finished, relate the activity to this division sentence:

$$6\overline{)20} = 3\ r2$$

Discuss why the remainder in this situation is dropped and the solution is 3. A 6-inch piece cannot be made from the remainder.

Practice

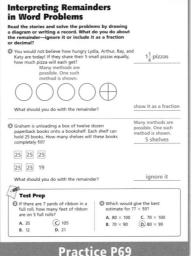

Practice P69

Extension

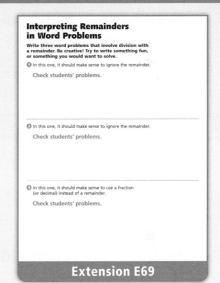

Extension E69

Spiral Review

Spiral Review Book page SR69 provides review of the following previously learned skills and concepts:

- describing the faces in a net and naming the figure formed by the net
- applying the problem solving strategy *act it out-make a model*

You may wish to have students work with partners to complete the page.

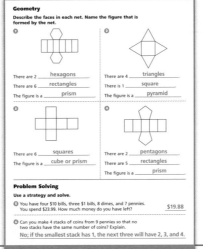

Spiral Review SR69

Extension Activity
Interpreting Remainders

Present this information:
- There are 20 players on a team.
- A car holds 6 people.
- Pizza for the team costs $50.

Challenge pairs of students to write and solve three division problems for this information: one in which it is reasonable for the remainder to be dropped, one in which the remainder should be expressed as a fraction or decimal, and one in which the remainder forces the quotient to be rounded up to the next whole number.

Lesson 9 Another Option for Interpreting Remainders

NCTM Standards 1, 2, 6, 7, 8, 9

Lesson Planner

STUDENT OBJECTIVES
- To use division to solve problems
- Given a context, to decide whether to ignore remainders, to add them as fractions or decimals to the quotient, or to round up the quotient

1 Daily Activities (TG p. 711)

Open-Ended Problem Solving/Headline Story	Skills Practice and Review—Is the Quotient Reasonable?

2 Teach and Practice (TG pp. 712–716)

	MATERIALS
Ⓐ **Introducing a Third Option** (TG p. 712)	• calculators
Ⓑ **Interpreting Remainders in Word Problems** (TG p. 713)	• 📖 LAB pp. 167–168
Ⓒ **Comparing Calculator Answers to Hand-Calculated Answers** (TG p. 714–715)	• 📖 SH p. 139

3 Differentiated Instruction (TG p. 717)

Leveled Problem Solving (TG p. 717)	Practice Book P70
Intervention Activity (TG p. 717)	Extension Book E70
Extension Activity (TG p. 717)	Spiral Review Book SR70
Literature Connection (TG p. 636)	

Lesson Notes

About the Lesson

In the previous lesson, students explored division situations where it made sense to ignore the remainder or to report it as a fraction or a decimal. In this lesson, students encounter situations where the remainder calls for rounding the quotient up to the next whole number.

About the Mathematics

You may wish to show students how to convert a calculator quotient into a quotient consisting of a whole number and a remainder. The whole-number parts will be the same. To find the remainder, multiply the decimal part of the quotient by the original divisor.

Calculator: $107 \div 44 = 2.431818181818$
Subtract 2: $2.431818181818 - 2 = 0.431818181818$
Multiply by the divisor: 0.431818181818×44.

If you get something like 18.999999999 simply round to the remainder, 19. So, $107 \div 44 = 2$ r19.

Check: $(2 \times 44) + 19 = 88 + 19 = 107$.

Use with Lesson Activity Book pp. 167–168.

Developing Mathematical Language

Vocabulary: rounding up the quotient

Students might be familiar with rounding to a given place, such as to the nearest ten or hundred. Or they might use rounding to determine whether an answer is reasonable. *Rounding up the quotient* is sometimes used when there is a remainder when dividing—the quotient is rounded up to the next whole number. You may wish to distinguish this method of rounding from rounding to the nearest one when rounding decimals. Emphasize that the main purpose of *rounding up the quotient* is to interpret the remainder.

Review the term *rounding up the quotient* with students.

Beginning Write the division sentence 20 ÷ 3 = 6 r2. Explain that *rounding up the quotient* can be used when there is a remainder. Have students cross out the *r2* and then circle the *6* as a reminder to add 1 to round up. This quotient rounds up to 7.

Intermediate Display the division sentences 20 ÷ 3 = 6 r2, 17 ÷ 2 = 8 r1, and 13 ÷ 3 = 4 r1. Talk about what *rounding up the quotient* means. Ask students to explain how they would round up each quotient. 7, 9, 5

Advanced Have students discuss what they think *rounding up the quotient* means.

Open-Ended Problem Solving

Write the following story on the board. In order to create a situation that calls for including the remainder as a fraction or a decimal, you might give a hint that students think about something that can be measured or something that can be divided up into less than 1.

 Headline Story

> **Make up two different division story problems that use 28 ÷ 8. Use one situation that calls for ignoring the remainder and the other that calls for including it as fraction or decimal.**

Possible responses: Eight books fit in a box. If there are 28 books, how many boxes will be filled? Ignore the remainder, because the question asks about full boxes. If you just change the question to, "How many boxes will be used?" you can include the remainder as a fraction, so the answer will be, $3\frac{1}{2}$.

Skills Practice and Review

Is the Quotient Reasonable?

Write the following division expressions on the board and ask students to use both rounding and compatible numbers to determine the reasonable quotient. Ask them to provide a number sentence that justifies each choice. Possible number sentences are given.

1,920 ÷ 24 =	800 or 80?	80; 80 × 20 = 1,600 80 × 25 = 2,000
22,608 ÷ 72 =	314 or 3,140?	314; 314 × 70 = 21,980 314 × 75 = 23,550
10,640 ÷ 56 =	190 or 19?	190; 190 × 60 = 11,400 190 × 50 = 9,500

 whole class 5 MIN

NCTM Standards 1, 2, 6, 7, 8, 9, 10

A Introducing a Third Option

Purpose To explore a third interpretation of the remainder in a division problem, that of rounding the quotient to the next greater whole number

Introduce Review the results of Activity A in **Lesson 8.8,** where students saw that, depending on the context of a problem, a remainder might be either ignored or converted to a fraction or decimal. Tell students, that you are going to ask them a very tricky question.

Problem **Present the following problem to students.**

Jonah noticed that the cookies he wanted to buy were packaged by the dozen. He wanted enough cookies for 25 people. How many packages should he buy?

Students should be able to compute that $25 \div 12 = 2$ r1 mentally. The remainder cannot be ignored in this problem, because if Jonah buys just 2 packages, there won't be enough cookies for everyone. Assuming he can't buy part of a package, he will have to buy 3 whole packages. So, in this problem, it makes sense to round up the quotient, 2 r1, to the next larger whole number, 3. Draw students' attention to the fact that this problem does not fit any of last lesson's cases.

Talk Math Then read this problem to the students and discuss the solution.

❓ Tennis balls are sold in canisters each containing 3 balls. Mr. Parks wants each of his 14 tennis students to have a ball. How many canisters must he buy? Explain your reasoning. 5 canisters; Possible explanation: $14 \div 3 = $ r2. If he buys just 4 canisters, containing $4 \times 3 = 12$ balls, not everyone will get a ball. So he must round to next greater whole number and buy 5 canisters, containing $5 \times 3 = 15$ balls. Since he has 14 students, he will have $15 - 14 = 1$ extra ball.

Use with Lesson Activity Book pp. 167–168.

Interpreting Remainders in Word Problems
LAB pp. 167–168

individuals 👤 ⏰ **20 MIN**

Purpose To interpret remainders in division problems

NCTM Standards 1, 2, 6, 7, 9

Lesson Activity Book p. 167

Name _____ Date _____

Chapter 8 Lesson 9

Another Option for Interpreting Remainders

NCTM Standards 1, 2, 6, 7, 9

Decide what to do when there is a remainder—ignore it (round down), include it as a fraction or a decimal, or round up.

1 Four classes of fifth graders—a total of 107 students and adults—will travel by bus to Colonial Jamestown for a field trip. Forty-four people may ride on one bus. How many buses will be needed?

Solution: __3 buses__

$$44)\overline{107} \quad \begin{array}{r} 2 \\ -88 \\ \hline 19 \end{array}$$

What should you do about the remainder?
__round up__

2 180 people bought tickets to see a play. 22 people can fit in each row of seats. If the people fill in as many rows as possible, how many rows will have people seated in them?

Solution: __9 rows__

$$22)\overline{180} \quad \begin{array}{r} 8 \\ -176 \\ \hline 4 \end{array} \quad 8\frac{4}{22}$$

What should you do about the remainder?
__round up__

3 The Cape Cod ferry can take 30 cars at a time. How many trips must the ferry make to take 366 cars?

Solution: __13 trips__

$$30)\overline{366} \quad \begin{array}{r} 12 \\ -300 \\ \hline 66 \\ -60 \\ \hline 6 \end{array}$$

What should you do about the remainder?
__round up__

prime **CLXVII** one hundred sixty-seven **167**

Lesson Activity Book p. 168

4 Ms. Lawrence wants to give some special pencils to her 26 students. If she orders 11 dozen pencils and wants to give each student the same number of pencils, how many pencils will each student get?

$12 \times 11 = 132$

Solution: __5 pencils__

$$26)\overline{132} \quad \begin{array}{r} 5 \\ -130 \\ \hline 2 \end{array}$$

What should you do about the remainder?
__ignore it__

5 Marya was surprised when she saw on her pedometer that she had walked 135 miles in the last 30 days. If she walked about the same distance every day, about how many miles did she walk each day?

Solution: __$4\frac{1}{2}$ miles__
__4.5 miles__

$$4\frac{15}{30} = 4\frac{1}{2}$$
$$30)\overline{135} \quad \begin{array}{r} -120 \\ \hline 15 \end{array}$$

What should you do about the remainder?
__include it as a fraction or decimal__

6 Challenge We laid pencils side by side until the total width was a whole number of inches. We found that 24 pencils, side by side, measured 7 inches. We found some boxes that were $3\frac{1}{2}$ inches wide and held only one layer of pencils. How many of the smaller boxes would we need to hold 100 pencils? Explain.

Solution: __9 boxes__

If 24 pencils, side by side, measure _____
7 inches, then $23\frac{1}{2}$-inch wide box _____
will hold 12 pencils. _____

$$12)\overline{100} \quad \begin{array}{r} 8 \\ -96 \\ \hline 4 \end{array}$$

What should you do about the remainder?
__round up__

168 one hundred sixty-eight **CLXVIII** $2 \times 2 \times 2 \times 3 \times 7$

| **ABOUT THE PAGE NUMBER** How many quarters would you need to buy something for $1.67? 167 is a prime. | **ABOUT THE PAGE NUMBER** 168 inches is 14 feet. How many inches are in 15 feet? |

Teaching Notes for LAB page 167

Have students work independently or with partners. In order to solve the problems, students must interpret the remainders correctly. They decide whether to ignore the remainder, add it on as a fraction or decimal, or round the quotient up to the next whole number.

Teaching Notes for LAB page 168

As on LAB page 167, students must interpret remainders correctly to solve the problems. In Problem 4, the extra pencils are ignored because each student must get the same number of pencils. In Problem 5, remaining miles may be included as either a fraction or a decimal.

Challenge Problem In this problem, students must realize that, because only 12 pencils will fit in a box, they must perform an extra step.

Materials
- For each students: calculator, LAB pp. 167–168

NCTM Standards 1, 2, 6, 7, 8, 9 ,10

✓ **Ongoing Assessment**
- Can students use a calculator to perform simple arithmetic operations?
- Can students round decimals up or down to the nearest whole number?

Comparing Calculator Answers to Hand-Calculated Answers

Purpose To compare calculator answers to hand-calculated answers

Introduce Write the following on the board:

Have students use their calculators to divide 5 by 3. Then ask:

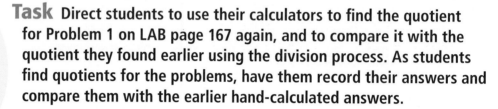
5 ÷ 3 = 1 r2

- Did you get the same quotient that I wrote on the board? no
- Why was your answer different? Possible answer: Calculators do not express quotients with remainders. When a quotient has a remainder, a calculator will give an exact quotient if the decimal portion of the quotient comes to an end. In this example, 1.66666666, the decimal does not come to an end, so the quotient is not exact.

Task Direct students to use their calculators to find the quotient for Problem 1 on LAB page 167 again, and to compare it with the quotient they found earlier using the division process. As students find quotients for the problems, have them record their answers and compare them with the earlier hand-calculated answers.

The quotient given by the calculator will look something like 2.431818. . . . (The final digits will depend on how many digits the calculator displays.) Students are likely to remember, from previous study, how to round a decimal up or down to the nearest whole number. Review this skill, if necessary. The quotient that they found by hand (not including the remainder) is the same as the calculator answer rounded down. The correct answer is the same as the calculator answer rounded up. Ask:

- Why is the correct answer not 2? Two buses would not be enough to carry 107 students.
- Why is the correct answer not 2.4318 . . .? It isn't possible to drive or ride in 0.4318 of a bus.

Continue with Problem 3, which is similar to Problem 1. The quotient 12.2 for the division problem 366 ÷ 30 doesn't make sense. To transport all the cars, we must round up the quotient to 13.

Next, direct students to use their calculators to find the quotient for Problem 4 on LAB page 168 again, and to compare it with the quotient they found earlier. The calculator shows (correctly) that 132 ÷ 26 = 5.0769 . . . . However, it is silly to think of giving 0.0769. . . pencils. Only a whole number of pencils can be given. Here we don't round up, because we won't be able to give each student another pencil. So, to get a sensible answer, we ignore the remainder, or, in the case of the calculator answer, round 5.0769 down to 5.

In Problem 5 on LAB page 168, no rounding is required, because fractions of a mile make sense. According to the calculator, the number of miles she walked each day is 135 ÷ 30 = 4.5, the exact and correct answer.

Practice

For additional practice, pose the following problems.

- How many 8-ounce cups are needed if I pour the water in my 196-ounce plastic bottle of water into cups? 25 cups

- On a hot day, Jen sold 8-ounce cups of water for 10¢ each. She used a full 196-ounce bottle of water to fill the cups. If she sold as many cups as she could fill, how much money did she earn? $2.40

Share Ask students to summarize what they have learned in the activity. They may say that they must always perform division calculations correctly, whether they are working by hand or with a calculator. But even then, their work is not finished. If there is a remainder, they must think about what it means and then decide whether to ignore it, write it as a decimal or fraction, or round up to the next greater whole number.

Talk Math Have students solve these problems and discuss their answers.

❷ Every taxi holds 4 passengers. How many taxis are needed to transport 13 passengers? Explain your reasoning. 4 taxis; Possible explanation: 12 passengers will need $12 \div 4 = 3$ taxis. The 13th passenger will need a fourth taxi.

❷ Jeff used a calculator to solve a problem like one above. The display indicated that 11.75 taxis were needed to take some passengers to the airport. How many taxis were needed? Explain your reasoning. 12 taxis; Possible explanation: Since it isn't possible to have 11.75 taxis, Jeff should round up to next greater whole number, 12, which indicates 12 taxis.

Reflect and Summarize the Lesson

Write Math

What three options do you have if a real-world division problem has a remainder? Give an example to illustrate each option. Ignore the remainder, convert the remainder to a fraction or decimal, or round up the quotient to the next greater whole number; Possible examples:

- ignore – If 28 pennies are divided evenly among 5 students, how many pennies will each student receive? 5 pennies

- convert – If $28 is divided equally among 5 students, how much money will each student receive? $5.60

- round up – If 28 teachers go to lunch and each table seats 5 people, how many tables are needed? 6 tables

Review Model

Refer students to Review Model: Interpreting Remainders in the *Student Handbook* to see how to interpret remainders in division problems.

✔ Check for Understanding

❶ 5 buses; round to the next whole number because 4 buses will not be enough.

❷ 21 boxes; ignore the remainder because the muffins that are left over will not fill a box.

❸ $14.50; write the remainder as a decimal because a part of a dollar makes sense.

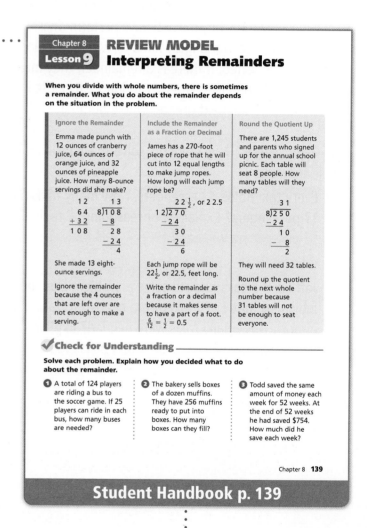

Student Handbook p. 139

3 | Differentiated Instruction

Leveled Problem Solving

There are 85 students registered for a dance camp.
The maximum number of students in each class is 15.

❶ Basic Level

Will 6 classes be enough? Explain. Yes, 85 ÷ 15 = 5 r10, so round the quotient up to the next whole number, 6.

❷ On Level

How many classes are needed for all the students who registered? Explain. 6 classes; 85 ÷ 15 = 5 r10, so 5 classes would not be enough for all of the students.

❸ Above Level

How many students will be in each class if the classes are divided as equally as possible? 5 classes with 14 students and 1 class with 15 students

---

Intervention

Activity Remainder Roses

Present the following problem.

There are 14 roses. Each small vase holds 4 roses. How many vases are needed to hold all of the roses? 4 vases

Ask students to draw a picture to illustrate the problem. Discuss the different solutions. Although 4 vases are needed, there might be 3 vases with 4 roses and 1 vase with 2 roses or 2 vases with 4 roses and 2 vases with 3 roses.

Practice

Another Option for Interpreting Remainders

Solve. Decide what to do when there is a remainder— ignore it (round down), include it as a fraction or a decimal, or round up. Show your work.

❶ Some mini-vans can carry 7 people. How many 7-person mini-vans will be needed to take 18 people to a museum?

$$7\overline{)18} \quad \begin{array}{r} 2 \\ -14 \\ \hline 4 \end{array}$$

Solution: __3__ mini-vans

What should you do about the remainder? __round up__

❷ There are 350 seats in the auditorium where the fifth-grade graduation will be held. If each of the 58 fifth graders gets an equal number of tickets, how many will each fifth grader get?

$$58\overline{)350} \quad \begin{array}{r} 6 \\ -348 \\ \hline 2 \end{array}$$

Solution: __6__ tickets

What should you do about the remainder? __ignore it__

❸ A class of fifth graders sold homemade cheese pizzas as a fundraiser. They sold 20 pizzas and made $165. If the price of each pizza was the same, how much did each pizza cost?

$$20\overline{)165} \quad 8\tfrac{5}{20}=8\tfrac{1}{4} \quad \begin{array}{r} -160 \\ \hline 5 \end{array}$$

Solution: __$8.25__

What should you do about the remainder? __include it as a decimal__

Test Prep

❹ Alvin had fewer than 100 pennies. He found he could divide them evenly into 2 piles, 3 piles, 4 piles, 5 piles, or 6 piles. How many pennies did he have? Explain how you know.

60 pennies; Possible explanation: 60 is the only number less than 100 that is divisible by 2, 3, 4, 5, and 6.

Practice P70

Extension

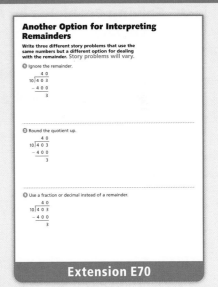

Another Option for Interpreting Remainders

Write three different story problems that use the same numbers but a different option for dealing with the remainder. Story problems will vary.

❶ Ignore the remainder.

❷ Round the quotient up.

❸ Use a fraction or decimal instead of a remainder.

Extension E70

Spiral Review

Spiral Review Book page SR70 provides review of the following previously learned skills and concepts:

- identifying factors and common factors for two numbers
- practicing addition and subtraction by completing Cross Number Puzzles

You may wish to have students work with partners to complete the page.

Number and Operations

List the factors for the two numbers. Then list any common factors for the two numbers.

❶ 18 1, 2, 3, 6, 9, 18
28 1, 2, 4, 7, 14, 28
Common factors 1, 2

❷ 24 1, 2, 3, 4, 6, 8, 12, 24
40 1, 2, 4, 5, 8, 10, 20, 40
Common factors 1, 2, 4, 8

❸ 16 1, 2, 4, 8, 16
20 1, 2, 4, 5, 10, 20
Common factors 1, 2, 4

❹ 48 1, 2, 3, 4, 6, 8, 12, 16, 24, 48
64 1, 2, 4, 8, 16, 32, 64
Common factors 1, 2, 4, 8, 16

❺ 21 1, 3, 7, 21
32 1, 2, 4, 8, 16, 32
Common factors 1

❻ 25 1, 5, 25
10 1, 2, 5, 10
Common factors 1, 5

❼ 81 1, 3, 9, 27, 81
45 1, 3, 5, 9, 15, 45
Common factors 1, 3, 9

❽ 36 1, 2, 3, 4, 6, 9, 12, 18, 36
19 1, 19
Common factors 1

Reasoning and Proof

Complete the Cross Number Puzzle.

34	92	126
59	23	82
93	115	208

75	81	156
49	84	133
124	165	289

19	24	43
66	58	124
85	82	167

Spiral Review SR70

Extension Activity
Rafts and Rules

Present this problem:

There are 27 students and 6 adults who want to take a scenic raft ride. Each raft holds 5 people plus 1 guide. Can everyone go if there must be at least one adult in addition to the guide on each raft? Explain. No; 7 rafts are needed to hold everyone but there are only 6 adults.

Have students work in pairs to solve the problem. Discuss why it is not enough to round up the quotient to solve the problem.

Lesson 10 Problem Solving Strategy and Test Prep

NCTM Standards 1, 2, 6, 7, 8, 9, 10

Lesson Planner

STUDENT OBJECTIVES ....
- To practice the problem solving strategy *draw a picture*
- To articulate the steps and strategies used to solve problems
- To prepare for standardized tests

Problem Solving Strategy:
Draw a Picture (TG pp. 719–720, 722–723)

MATERIALS

Ⓐ **Discussing the Problem Solving Strategy: Draw a Picture** (TG p. 719)

Ⓑ **Solving Problems by Applying the Strategy** (TG p. 720)

- 📖 LAB p. 169
- 📖 SH pp. 140–141

Problem Solving Test Prep (TG p. 79)

Ⓒ **Getting Ready for Standardized Tests** (TG p. 721)

- 📖 LAB p. 170

Lesson Notes

About Problem Solving

Problem Solving Strategy: Draw a Picture

The problem solving strategy *draw a picture* is an excellent strategy to use with division problems. It allows students to visualize the process of division as they whittle away at the dividend by removing multiples of the divisor. LAB pages 169–170 assess students' understanding of the process of long division and its connection to multiplication.

Skills Practice and Review

Wanted: Quotient or Remainder?

Read the following problems to students. Ask whether the question asks for a quotient or a remainder. If students say "quotient," have them specify whether it is the exact quotient, the quotient rounded up, or the quotient rounded down.

- Cupcakes are sold in packages of 8. How many packages are needed so that 20 people can each have a cupcake? quotient, rounded up

- Cupcakes are sold in packages of 10. If enough packages are bought so that 26 people each have a cupcake, how many extra cupcakes will there be? remainder

- A community garden is 50 feet long and 9 feet wide. Four people will share it equally. How large a plot will each get? quotient, exact

- A community garden is 60 feet long and 4 feet wide. How many gardeners can get an 8-foot-long plot? quotient, rounded down

Use with Lesson Activity Book pp. 169–170.

Problem Solving Strategy

A | Discussing the Problem Solving Strategy: Draw a Picture

whole class 15 MIN

NCTM Standards 1, 2, 6, 7, 8, 9, 10

Purpose To share strategies for solving problems and focus on the problem solving strategy, *draw a picture*

Introduce Remind students that throughout this chapter they have been drawing pictures to divide whole numbers. You might draw an area model on the board to show a division "picture."

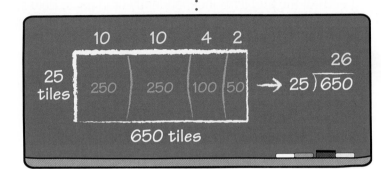

Point out that drawing a picture allows a problem solver to "see" the problem in a different way. Sometimes that alone will be enough to provide a solution. Even if it does not, a picture often suggests an approach to solving a problem that was not evident earlier.

Introduce the following problem.

Problem **There are 12 square tables in the math lab. The tables are all the same size. Each table can seat 1 person on a side. If the tables are pushed together to form a rectangle, what is the greatest number of people that can be seated?**

Share Have students share their strategies for solving the problem. Drawing a quick sketch will allow students to try many possible answers quickly. Some may begin by trying a 3 × 4 rectangle, the closest rectangle to a square that is possible. A picture shows that 14 people can be seated.

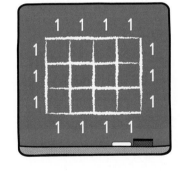

Some students may notice a disadvantage to arranging the tables as above. Two tables are wasted in the middle, where no people can be seated. This may suggest that a long narrow arrangement makes more sense. One or two more sketches should lead them to the correct solution.

This arrangement allows the greatest number of people to be seated, 26.

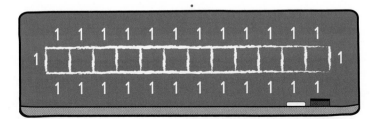

💬 Talk Math

❓ How many people can be seated if the tables are arranged in a 2 × 6 rectangle? 16 people

❓ What is the largest number of people that can be seated if the tables do not have to touch each other? 48 people

Solving Problems by Applying the Strategy LAB p. 169

NCTM Standards 1, 2, 6, 7, 8, 9, 10

Purpose To practice the problem solving strategy, *draw a picture*

Teaching Notes for LAB page 169

Students practice the problem solving strategy *draw a picture* by solving each of the problems independently or in pairs. Help students get started with Problem 1 by asking questions such as the following:

 Read to Understand

What do you know from reading the problem? There are 6 dozen, or 72, cookies. Eleven children will share them equally.

What do you need to find out? the number of cookies that will be left for Juan's father

 Plan

How can you solve this problem? Possible answer: You could draw a picture to show the number of cookies given to the children. Then you could use the picture to find the number of cookies that are left.

 Solve

What picture can you draw that would help you solve the problem? Possible answer: You could draw 11 plates, 1 for each child's cookies, and use tally marks (or dots) to represent the cookies as you count and distribute them. The cookies that are left when there aren't enough left to give each child another one are left for Juan's father. Then you could see how many cookies remain after all of the children receive their cookies. Possible drawing:

      ⇐ **left over**

 Check

Look back at the original problem. Did you answer the question that was asked? Does your answer make sense? How do you know?

Students can use this method to solve the other problems on LAB page 169. Supplement the questions above with ones that are tailored to Problems 2 and 3.

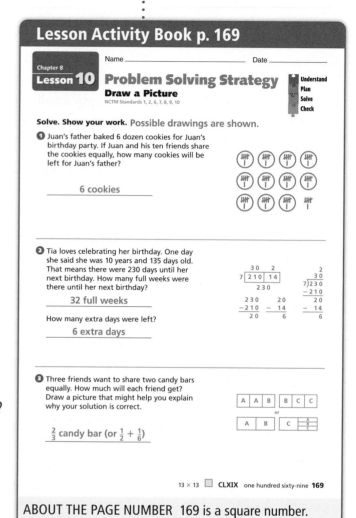

Lesson Activity Book p. 169

Name _____ Date _____

Chapter 8
Lesson 10 **Problem Solving Strategy**
Draw a Picture
NCTM Standards 1, 2, 6, 7, 8, 9, 10

Understand
Plan
Solve
Check

Solve. Show your work. Possible drawings are shown.

1. Juan's father baked 6 dozen cookies for Juan's birthday party. If Juan and his ten friends share the cookies equally, how many cookies will be left for Juan's father?

   6 cookies

2. Tia loves celebrating her birthday. One day she said she was 10 years and 135 days old. That means there were 230 days until her next birthday. How many full weeks were there until her next birthday?

   32 full weeks

   How many extra days were left?

   6 extra days

3. Three friends want to share two candy bars equally. How much will each friend get? Draw a picture that might help you explain why your solution is correct.

   $\frac{2}{3}$ candy bar (or $\frac{1}{2} + \frac{1}{6}$)

13 × 13 ☐ CLXIX one hundred sixty-nine **169**

ABOUT THE PAGE NUMBER 169 is a square number. It is also the sum of two square numbers. Do you know which ones?

Reflect and Summarize the Lesson

 Write Math How does drawing a picture help you solve a problem? Possible answer: A picture gives you a visual image of the information in the problem. Seeing the information that way may suggest an approach to solving the problem that you hadn't thought of before.

C Getting Ready for Standardized Tests LAB p. 170

individuals
20 MIN

Purpose To prepare students for standardized tests

NCTM Standards 1, 2, 6, 7, 8, 9, 10

Lesson Activity Book p. 170

Problem Solving Test Prep

Choose the correct answer.

1 Ryan divides his model car collection into groups of 8 cars. There are 3 cars left over. How many cars would be left over if he divided his collection into groups of 4?

A. 8
B. 6
C. 3
D. 2

2 Jada stacks boxes to make a pyramid display in a store window. Each row has one fewer box than the row below it. If the bottom row has 9 boxes, how many boxes are in the display?

A. 35
B. 45
C. 55
D. 72

Show What You Know

Solve each problem. Explain your answer.

3 The streets in Morgan's town run north-south and east-west. She leaves her house on her bike, rides 5 blocks north, 4 blocks east, 6 blocks south, and 1 block west. What is the least number of blocks she must ride to get home?

4 blocks; Possible answer: Draw the streets as a grid and then trace the path. When Morgan stops, she is 3 blocks east and 1 block south of her house, a total of 4 blocks.

4 Albert, Carlo, Jamie, and Steve do odd jobs on the weekends. One Saturday, Albert earned more than Carlo but less than Jamie. Steve earned more than Jamie. Using this information, is it possible to put the boys in order from greatest to least earnings? If so, put them in order, and explain your answer. If not, explain what other information you would need.

Yes; Steve, Jamie, Albert, Carlo; Possible answer: Using the second sentence, you can order Albert, Carlo, and Jamie from greatest to least: Jamie, Albert, Carlo. Using the third sentence, you can place Steve as earning the most.

170 one hundred seventy **CLXX** 2 × 5 × 17

ABOUT THE PAGE NUMBER How many dimes do you need to make $1.70? how many nickels?

Teaching Notes for LAB page 170

The test items on this page were written in the same style and are arranged in the same format as those on many state assessments. The test is cumulative and is designed for students to apply a variety of problem solving strategies, including *draw a picture, look for a pattern,* and *use logical reasoning.* Students might share the strategies they use.

The item analysis chat below highlights one of the possible strategies that may be used for each item.

Show What You Know

Written Response

Direct students' attention to Problems 3 and 4. Explain that they must decide how to solve the problems. Then have students write an explanation of how they know their answer is correct. To provide more space for students to communicate their thinking about these problems, you may wish to have them write their responses and explanations on a separate sheet of paper. Use the Scoring Rubric below to evaluate their understanding.

Item Analysis Chart

Item	Strategy
1	Use Logical Reasoning
2	Look for a Pattern
3	Draw a Picture
4	Use Logical Reasoning

Scoring Rubric

2	• Demonstrates complete understanding of the problem and chooses an appropriate strategy to determine the solution
1	• Demonstrates a partial understanding of the problem and chooses a strategy that does not lead to a complete and accurate solution
0	• Demonstrates little understanding of the problem and shows little evidence of using any strategy to determine a solution

Review Model..

Refer students to the Problem Solving Strategy Review Model: Draw a Picture in the *Student Handbook* to review a model of the four steps they can use with problem solving strategy, *draw a picture.*

Additional problem solving practice is also provided.

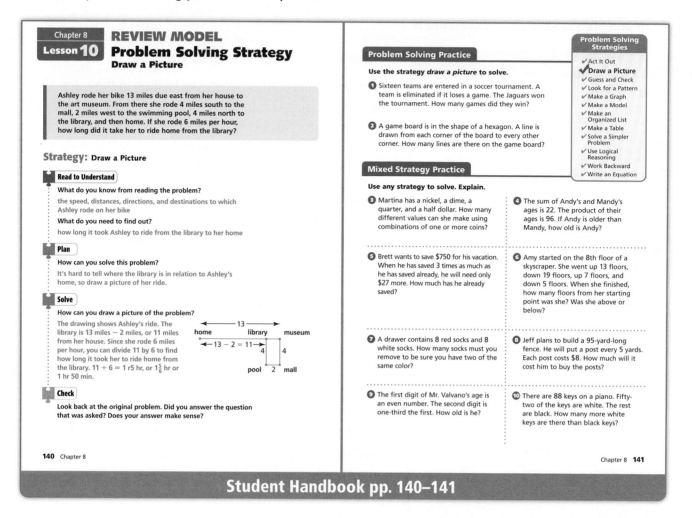

Student Handbook pp. 140–141

Task **Have students read the problem at the top of the Review Model page. Then discuss.**

💬 Talk Math

❓ Look at the drawing on this page. Which way do you move to show east? left west? right north? up south? down

❓ If Ashley rides 8 miles per hour, will it take more time or less time to ride home from the library? Explain. Less time; if she rides faster it will take less time.

❓ What other strategy could you use to solve this problem? Answers will vary. Possible answer: You could *make a model* and *act it out* by using one-inch tiles to make a path to represent the distances and directions Ashley rode her bike. Each tile could represent one mile of the path.

Use with Lesson Activity Book pp. 169–170.

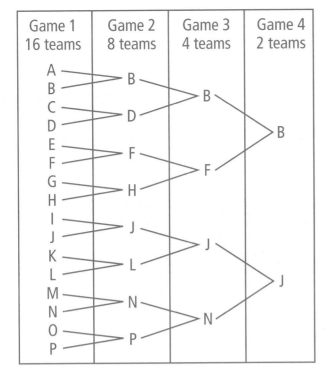

Game 1 16 teams	Game 2 8 teams	Game 3 4 teams	Game 4 2 teams

So, if the Jaguars win 4 games, they will win the tournament.

❷ 15 lines; you can *draw a picture* of the game board and then draw a line from each of the six corners to every other corner. From the first vertex you will draw 5 lines, from the second 4 lines, from the third 3 lines, from the fourth 2 lines, and from the fifth 1 line.

Mixed Strategy Practice

❸ 15 values; you can *make an organized list* of all the possible combinations and then find out how many different values the coins have.

Coins	Value	Coins	Value
n	5¢	d, q	35¢
d	10¢	d, h	60¢
q	25¢	q, h	75¢
h	50¢	n, d, q	40¢
n, d	15¢	n, d, h	65¢
n, q	30¢	n, q, h	80¢
n, h	55¢	d, q, h	85¢
		n, d, g, h	90¢

2 Numbers - Sum of 22	Product
11, 11	121 - too big
9, 13	117 - too big
7, 15	105 - too big
6, 15	96 - just right!

❺ $241; you can *work backward* to solve the problem. First subtract $27 from the amount he wants to save: $750 − $27 = $723. Then divide $723 by 3 to find the amount he has saved: $723 ÷ 3 = $241.

❻ 4 floors below; you can *draw a picture* to solve the problem. Draw a vertical number line with numbers 0 to 25 to represent the floors of the skyscraper. Begin at 8 and move up and down to show where Amy landed each time she went up and down on the elevator. She ended on the 4th floor which is 4 floors below the 8th floor, where she started.

❼ 3 socks; you can *use logical reasoning* to solve the problem. If you take 1 sock you will have 1 color. If you take 2 socks, you might pick 1 red and 1 white—2 different colors. If you take 3 socks, at least 2 will have to be the same color.

❽ $160; you can *solve a simpler problem* to help you find the number of posts he will read and then write an equation to find the total cost. If he had a 25-yard fence, he would need a post at the beginning of the fence and then at 5 yd, 10 yd, 15 yd, 20 yd, and 25 yd—6 posts in all. For a 95-yard fence he needs 20 posts. 20 × $8 = $160.

❾ 62; you can *guess and check* and *use logical reasoning* to solve the problem. The first digit must be 2, 4, 6, or 8. One-third of 6 is 2. One-third of the other even numbers is not a whole number, so he must be 62.

❿ 16 more white keys; you can *write equations* to solve the problem. Subtract the number of white keys from the total number of keys to find the number of black keys: 88 − 52 = 36. Then subtract the number of black keys from the number of white keys to find how many more white keys than black keys there are: 52 − 36 = 16.

Purpose To provide students with an opportunity to demonstrate understanding of Chapter 8 concepts and skills

MATERIALS
- LAB pp. 171–172
- Chapter 8 Test (Assessment Guide) pp. AG77–AG78

Chapter 8 Learning Goals and Assessment Options

These learning goals are assessed in many ways throughout the chapter. The chart below correlates each learning goal to specific formal and informal assessment options.

	Learning Goals	Lesson Number	Snapshot Assessment	Chapter Review Item Number	Chapter Test Item Number
				LAB pp. 171–172	Assessment Guide pp. AG77–AG78
8-A	Use multiplication and division of whole numbers to solve problems and multiplication to check division	8.1, 8.2, 8.3	1, 2, 3, 4, 7	1–6, 8	1–5, 8
8-B	Divide numbers with up to a 3-digit dividend and a 2-digit divisor using an area model or division record	8.3, 8.4, 8.5	5, 8	7–11	6–13
8-C	Write remainders using whole numbers and fractions and interpret remainders in a given context	8.7, 8.8, 8.9	9, 10, 11	9–11	9–16
8-D	Apply problem solving strategies such as *draw a picture* to solve problems	8.10	6, 12	12	17–19

Snapshot Assessment

The following Mental Math and Quick Write questions and tasks provide a quick, informal assessment of students' understanding of Chapter 8 concepts, skills, and problem solving strategies.

whole class 10 MIN

Mental Math This oral assessment uses mental math strategies and can be used with the whole class.

❶ How can you use the fact $12 \times 16 = 192$ to find 12×32? Answers may vary. Possible explanation: 32 is twice 16, so 12×32 must be twice 12×16 which is 192×2 or 384.
(Learning Goal 8-A)

❷ How can you use the fact $11 \times 18 = 198$ to find 11×36? Answers may vary. Possible explanation: 36 is twice 18, so 11×36 must be twice 11×18 which is 198×2 or 396.
(Learning Goal 8-A)

❸ If $32 \times 7 = 224$, what is $224 \div 7$? 32
(Learning Goal 8-A)

❹ What could you do to check your quotient in a division problem? Answers may vary. Possible answer: you can multiply the quotient by the divisor to see if you get the dividend.
(Learning Goal 8-A)

5 Explain how to use an area model to find 420 ÷ 12? Draw a rectangle, label the left side 12 for the number of rows, and the bottom 420 for the total number of tiles. Then find multiples of 12 taken out of the model. Each time a part is taken, write how wide that part is above the model. When all parts have been taken from the model, add the numbers above the model to find the width.
(Learning Goal 8-B)

6 How could 8 friends share 3 dozen cookies equally? Possible answer: Each friend could have 4 whole cookies, and there would be 4 cookies left over. Each one of the remaining cookies could be split in half, then each friend would have $4\frac{1}{2}$ cookies altogether.
(Learning Goal 8-D)

Quick Write This informal written assessment can be administered to small groups or the whole class. Read each question and have the students record responses on their write-on boards. Encourage students to listen and think about the questions before responding.

7 Write a division sentence from the same related sentences:
- 123 × 4 = 492 492 ÷ 4 = 123 or 492 ÷ 123 = 4
- 305 × 12 = 3,660 3,660 ÷ 12 = 305 or 3,660 ÷ 305 = 12
- Divide 255 by 15 and get 17 for an answer. How could you check your answer to see if it is correct? Multiply 15 × 17 and get 255.
(Learning Goal 8-A)

8 Solve the problem 345 ÷ 5 using a division record.
- What is the quotient? 69
(Learning Goal 8-B)

$$\begin{array}{r} 9 \\ 60 \\ 5\overline{)345} \\ -300 \\ \hline 45 \\ 45 \\ \hline 0 \end{array}$$

9 How can you arrange 23 tiles to fill as many 4-tile columns as possible? Student could make a picture of 5 full 4-tile columns, with 3 remaining tiles. Some students will be able to find the answer of 5 full columns without the picture.
- What is a division sentence which matches this problem? 23 ÷ 4 = 5 r3 or $5\frac{3}{4}$
- What fraction of the 6th column would be filled with the 3 remaining tiles? $\frac{3}{4}$
(Learning Goal 8-C)

10 Mrs. Tyo had 248 paperback books in a classroom library. She wanted to divide them equally among her 18 students.
- Estimate the number of books each student will receive. Possible estimate: 12
- How many books will each student have? 13 books
- How many paperback books remain? 14 books remain
(Learning Goal 8-C)

11 Draw an array in which each column is 4 tiles tall with 7 full columns, plus a partially filled column containing 3 tiles.
- Write a number sentence to describe the array. (4 × 7) + 3 = 31
- What division sentence could you write to describe the array? 31 ÷ 4 = 7 r3
(Learning Goal 8-C)

12 There are 137 students and 7 classroom teachers in Grade 5. If each classroom is supposed to have about the same number of students, how many students will be in each classroom? Accept any reasonable work shown that shows 3 of the classrooms will have 19 students each, and 4 classrooms will have 20 students each.
(Learning Goal 8-D)

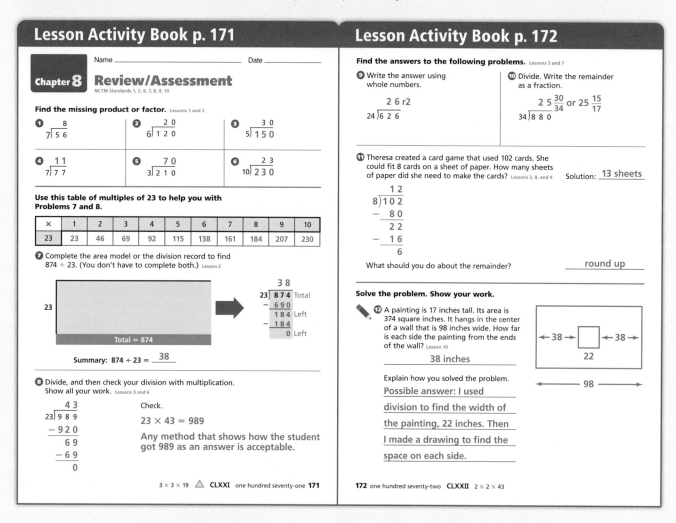

Chapter **8** ASSESSMENT

Formal Assessment

Chapter Review/Assessment The Chapter 8 Review/Assessment on *Lesson Activity Book* pages 171–172 assesses students' understanding of the division algorithm and problem solving. Students should be able to complete these pages independently.

Lesson Activity Book p. 171

Name _____ Date _____

Chapter 8 **Review/Assessment**
NCTM Standards 1, 2, 6, 7, 8, 9, 10

Find the missing product or factor. Lessons 1 and 2

1 8 / 7)56
2 20 / 6)120
3 30 / 5)150

4 11 / 7)77
5 70 / 3)210
6 23 / 10)230

Use this table of multiples of 23 to help you with Problems 7 and 8.

×	1	2	3	4	5	6	7	8	9	10
23	23	46	69	92	115	138	161	184	207	230

7 Complete the area model or the division record to find 874 ÷ 23. (You don't have to complete both.) Lesson 2

23 | Total = 874

38
23)874 Total
− 690
184 Left
− 184
0 Left

Summary: 874 ÷ 23 = __38__

8 Divide, and then check your division with multiplication. Show all your work. Lessons 3 and 6

43
23)989
− 920
69
− 69
0

Check.
23 × 43 = 989
Any method that shows how the student got 989 as an answer is acceptable.

3 × 3 × 19 △ CLXXI   one hundred seventy-one **171**

Lesson Activity Book p. 172

Find the answers to the following problems. Lessons 3 and 7

9 Write the answer using whole numbers.

26 r2
24)626

10 Divide. Write the remainder as a fraction.

$25\frac{30}{34}$ or $25\frac{15}{17}$
34)880

11 Theresa created a card game that used 102 cards. She could fit 8 cards on a sheet of paper. How many sheets of paper did she need to make the cards? Lessons 3, 8, and 9

Solution: __13 sheets__

12
8)102
− 80
22
− 16
6

What should you do about the remainder?   __round up__

Solve the problem. Show your work.

12 A painting is 17 inches tall. Its area is 374 square inches. It hangs in the center of a wall that is 98 inches wide. How far is each side the painting from the ends of the wall? Lesson 10

__38 inches__

←38→ [ ] ←38→
22
←——— 98 ———→

Explain how you solved the problem.
Possible answer: I used division to find the width of the painting, 22 inches. Then I made a drawing to find the space on each side.

172 one hundred seventy-two   CLXXII   2 × 2 × 43

Extra Support Students who have difficulty with items on the Chapter 8 Review/Assessment may need review of the lesson where development of the concept was provided. You can use the Intervention Activity to increase students' understanding before the Chapter Test is given.

Chapter Test Use the Chapter 8 Test in the *Assessment Guide* to assess concepts, skills, and problem solving from the chapter and to prepare students for standardized tests. The Chapter Test and other test items are also available online.

Chapter Notes

Quick Notes

More Ideas

Attributes of Two-Dimensional Figures

About the Chapter

In this chapter, students take a deeper look at attributes of two-dimensional figures, particularly triangles and quadrilaterals, than they had in previous years. As students find new ways to classify triangles and quadrilaterals, they focus on the angles and sides that form these polygons.

Classifications Triangles are generally classified in two ways: by the lengths of their sides (*scalene, isosceles,* and *equilateral*) and by the sizes of their angles (*acute, right,* and *obtuse*). In this chapter, students consider how the two classifications are related (for example, an equilateral triangle must be acute). Quadrilaterals are also classified in different ways, frequently in terms of their sides (both lengths of different sides and whether there are pairs of parallel sides). As with triangles, quadrilaterals can often be classified in more than one way. For example, every square, without exception, is also a rectangle, and every rectangle, without exception is also a parallelogram.

Importance of Angles In previous years, students learned to Identify parallel and perpendicular lines and to distinguish obtuse and acute angles by comparing them to right angles. In this chapter, they begin to develop a deeper understanding of how all of the attributes of figures are related to one another.

For example, they see that the three angles of a triangle fit together to create a straight angle, and

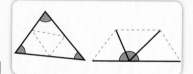

that angles that are opposite each other when two lines cross, or angles in a Z-shape formed by a line intersecting parallel lines, are congruent.

Using such ideas, students become detectives, using logical reasoning to make deductions about other angles in a figure.

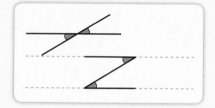

They see not only *that* the three angles of a triangle make a straight angle; they create an informal proof that shows *why* that must be true.

Developing Concepts Across the Grades

Topic	Prior Learning	Learning in Chapter 9	Later Learning
Angles	• Compare and order angles by sides • Classify angles as acute, right, or obtuse Grade 4, Chapter 4	• Use a protractor to measure angles to the nearest 5° • Determine angle measures using relationships among angles formed when a line intersects a pair of parallel lines Lessons 9.1, 9.2, 9.5, 9.6	• Identify corresponding angles in similar figures Grade 6
Triangles	• Classify triangles by the number of sides of equal length • Symmetry in triangles Grade 4, Chapter 4	• Classify triangles using congruent parts and perpendicular sides • Construct congruent triangles Lessons 9.2, 9.3, 9.4	• Measure volume of triangular prisms Grade 6
Quadrilaterals	• Find and describe rules for classifying parallelograms Grade 4, Chapter 4	• Classify quadrilaterals by their attributes Lessons 9.7, 9.8	• Write a proportion to find an unknown length Grade 6

Chapter Planner

Lesson	Objectives	NCTM Standards	Vocabulary	Materials/Resources

CHAPTER 9 World Almanac • Vocabulary • Games • Challenge
Teacher Guide pp. 735A–735F, Student Handbook pp. 148–149, 162–166

1 Investigating Angles

PACING 1 DAY

Teacher Guide
pp. 736–743
Lesson Activity Book
pp. 173–174
Student Handbook
Student Letter p. 147
Explore p. 150

- To review the concept of an angle and its size
- To explore the relationship of angle sizes in a triangle

3, 4, 7, 8, 9

∠
angle
acute angle
obtuse angle
right angle
straight angle
vertex

For the students:
- School-Home Connection TR: SHC33–SHC34
- straightedges, blank paper, scissors, crayons or markers (optional)
- P71, E71, SR71

Literature Connection:
Sir Cumference and the Great Knight of Angleland
Teacher Guide p. 734

2 Classifying Angles and Triangles

PACING 1 DAY

Teacher Guide
pp. 744–751
Lesson Activity Book
pp. 175–176
Student Handbook
Explore p. 151
Game p. 164
Review Model p. 152

- To classify triangles using congruent parts and perpendicular sides
- To use a protractor to measure angles to the nearest 5°

3, 4, 6, 7, 8

equilateral triangle
isosceles triangle
scalene triangle
congruent
perpendicular

For the teacher:
- demonstration protractor
- transparency of AM68 (optional)

For the students:
- rulers
- protractors
- color counters
- paper clips
- pencils
- TR: AM68, AM69
- P72, E72, SR72

Social Studies Connection:
National Flags
Teacher Guide p. 734

3 Constructing Triangles

PACING 1 DAY

Teacher Guide
pp. 752–759
Lesson Activity Book
pp. 177–178
Student Handbook
Review Model p. 153

- To construct congruent triangles
- To practice measuring and drawing segments and angles

3, 4, 6, 8, 10

congruent figures

For the teacher:
- demonstration protractor
- straightedges

For the students:
- protractors
- straightedges
- scissors
- tape
- P73, E73, SR73

4 Constructing Similar Triangles

PACING 1 DAY

Teacher Guide
pp. 760–767
Lesson Activity Book
pp. 179–180
Student Handbook
Explore p. 154

- To draw and measure angles using a protractor
- To identify congruent angles and shapes and identify similar shapes
- To recognize that the sum of the angle measures in a triangle is 180°

3, 4, 6, 8

similar

For the students:
- protractors
- centimeter rulers
- scissors
- unlined 8.5 × 11 in. paper
- TR: AM70–AM73
- P74, E74, SR74

NCTM Standards 2000
1. Number and Operations
2. Algebra
3. Geometry
4. Measurement
5. Data Analysis and Probability
6. Problem Solving
7. Reasoning and Proof
8. Communication
9. Connections
10. Representation

Key
AG: Assessment Guide
E: Extension Book
LAB: Lesson Activity Book
P: Practice Book
SH: Student Handbook
SR: Spiral Review Book
TG: Teacher Guide
TR: Teacher Resource Book

MATH GLOSSARY in **Student Handbook** p. 266

Planner (continued) ➡

Chapter Planner *(continued)*

Lesson	Objectives	NCTM Standards	Vocabulary	Materials/Resources
5 Angles Formed by Intersecting Lines PACING 1 DAY **Teacher Guide** pp. 768–773 **Lesson Activity Book** pp. 181–182 **Student Handbook** Explore p. 155, Game p. 165	• To find the measures of angles formed by two intersecting lines, given the measure of one of the angles • To practice measuring and drawing angles using protractors	1, 3, 4, 6, 7, 8, 9	opposite angles	**For the students:** ■ protractors ■ compasses ■ small counters ■ TR: AM74–AM76 ■ P75, E75, SR75
6 Angles Formed by a Line Intersecting Parallel Lines PACING 1 DAY **Teacher Guide** pp. 774–783 **Lesson Activity Book** pp. 183–184 **Student Handbook** Review Model p. 156	• To determine angle measures using relationships among angles formed when a line intersects a pair of parallel lines	1, 3, 4, 6, 7, 8, 9	‖	**For the teacher:** ■ transparency of AM78 (optional) ■ protractors **For the students:** ■ TR: AM77–AM78 ■ P76, E76, SR76
7 Comparing and Classifying Quadrilaterals PACING 1 DAY **Teacher Guide** pp. 784–791 **Lesson Activity Book** pp. 185–186 **Student Handbook** Explore p. 157, Review Model p. 158	• To classify quadrilaterals according to attributes • To review definitions and properties of a parallelogram, a rectangle, and other special quadrilaterals	3, 6, 7, 8, 9	quadrilateral kite parallelogram rectangle rhombus square trapezoid	**For the teacher:** ■ transparency of AM79 (optional) **For the students:** ■ P77, E77, SR77 **Science Connection:** **Snow Crystals** **Teacher Guide p. 734**
8 Investigating Quadrilaterals PACING 1 DAY **Teacher Guide** pp. 792–799 **Lesson Activity Book** pp. 187–188 **Student Handbook** Explore p. 159, Review Model p. 158	• To identify quadrilaterals by their attributes • To see that the sum of the angle measures in a quadrilateral is 360°	3, 4, 6, 7, 8, 9	concave convex	**For the students:** ■ TR: AM80–AM86 ■ protractors ■ P78, E78, SR78
9 Problem Solving Strategy and Test Prep PACING 1 DAY **Teacher Guide** pp. 800–805 **Lesson Activity Book** pp. 189–190 **Student Handbook** Review Model pp. 160–161	• To practice the problem solving strategy *look for a pattern* • To articulate the steps and strategies used to solve problems • To prepare for standardized tests	1, 2, 3, 4, 6, 7, 8, 10		**For the students:** ■ TR: AM85–AM86 ■ protractors

CHAPTER 9 Assessment
TG pp. 806–809, LAB pp. 191–192, AG pp. AG81–AG84

For the students:
■ Chapter 9 Test pp. AG81–AG82

Games

Use the following games for skills practice and reinforcement of concepts.

Lesson 9.2 ▶

Triangle Maze provides an opportunity for students to practice identifying different kinds of triangles by their attributes.

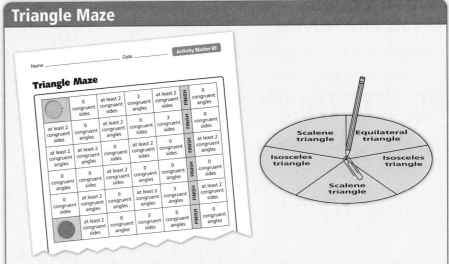

Triangle Maze

First to 360°

◀ **Lesson 9.5** *First to 360°* provides an opportunity for students to draw angles of specific measures.

Lesson 9.8 ▶

Quadrilateral Name Game provides an opportunity for students to match quadrilaterals with their attributes.

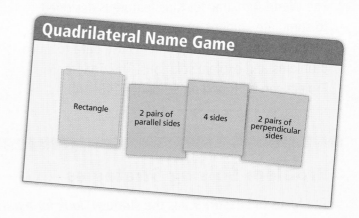

Quadrilateral Name Game

Planning Ahead

Throughout this chapter, students will be using protractors and both inch and centimeter rules.

In **Lesson 9.2,** students will be playing *Triangle Maze.* Each pair of students will need a copy of AM69: *Triangle Maze,* two different color counters or other small objects, and a pencil and a paper clip to make a spinner.

In **Lesson 9.4,** students will need tangram cutouts for both the Intervention and Extension activities.

In **Lesson 9.5,** each pair of students will need one game board, AM74–AM76: *First to 360°* Game Board 1, 2, or 3. Each player needs to prepare a piece of paper by using a compass to draw a circle with one radius drawn in. Alternatively, you might draw this circle and duplicate it for students. They will share a collection of small counters and will each need a protractor.

In **Lesson 9.8,** each group of 3 to 5 students will need a set of Name Cards (cut from AM85) and a set of Attribute Cards (cut from AM86). For best results, photocopy each page onto card stock, possibly with all Name Cards in one color and all Attribute Cards on another color.

Developing Problem Solvers

Open-Ended Problem Solving

The Headline Story in the Daily Activities section of every lesson provides an open-ended problem for students to complete. For each story, there are many possible responses.

Headline Stories can be found on TG pages 737, 745, 753, 761, 769, 775, 785, and 793.

Leveled Problem Solving

Leveled Problem Solving provides an opportunity for students to apply learning from the lesson to a real-life situation. Problems are leveled by ability to allow students of all ability levels to become successful problem solvers. Each Leveled Problem Solving begins with a real-life scenario upon which three problems are built.

The levels of problems are:

❶ Basic Level	❷ On Level	❸ Above Level
students needing extra support	students working at grade level	students who are ready for more challenging problems

Leveled Problem Solving can be found on TG pages 742, 751, 759, 766, 773, 783, 791, and 798.

The World Almanac for Kids feature is designed to stimulate student interest in the math concepts they are about to learn. Students use data to solve problems and explain solutions. The Chapter 9 Project can be found on SH pages 148–149.

Write Math **Reflect and Summarize the Lesson** poses a problem or question for students to think and write about. This feature can be found on TG pages 741, 750, 758, 765, 772, 782, 790, 797, and 802.

Other opportunities to write about math can be found on LAB pages 174, 177, 178, 184, 188, 189, and 190.

Problem Solving Strategies

The focus of **Lesson 9.9** is the strategy, *look for a pattern.* However, students will use a variety of problem solving strategies as they work through the chapter. The chart below shows strategies that may be useful in completing each lesson.

Strategy	Lesson(s)	Description
Act It Out	9.2	Measure angles with a protractor.
Draw a Picture	9.1, 9.2, 9.3	Draw angles to show angle classification; use a protractor to draw angles of a given measure; draw triangles when given the measures of two angles and the length of the side between them or the lengths of two sides and the measure of the angle between them; and draw an angle similar to a given angle.
✔ Look for a Pattern	9.3, 9.9	Recognize congruence of angles and similarity of triangles; and determine geometric patterns.
Make a Model	9.1	Show that the three angles in any triangle form a straight angle (180°); and show that the sum of the measures of the four angles in any quadrilateral is 360°.
Use Logical Reasoning	9.2, 9.5, 9.6, 9.7, 9.8, 9.9	Determine attributes of triangles and quadrilaterals to classify them; determine that opposite angles formed by intersecting lines are congruent; use straight angles, opposite angles, and angles formed by a line intersecting parallel lines to find unknown angle measures; and find geometric patterns.

Meeting the Needs of All Learners

Differentiated Instruction

Extra Support	On Level	Enrichment
Intervention Activities TG pp. 742, 751, 759, 766, 773, 783, 791, 798	**Practice Book** pp. P71–P78	**Extension Activities** TG pp. 742, 751, 759, 766, 773, 783, 791, 798
	Spiral Review Book pp. SR71–SR78	**Extension Book** pp. E71–E78
	LAB Challenge LAB pp. 174, 176, 180, 182, 184, 186, 188 SH p. 166	**LAB Challenge** LAB pp. 174, 176, 180, 182, 184, 186, 188 SH p. 166
Lesson Notes **Basic Level** TG pp. 746, 748, 762, 772	**Lesson Notes** **On Level** TG pp. 763, 772	**Lesson Notes** **Above Level** TG pp. 763, 772
Leveled Problem Solving **Basic Level** TG pp. 742, 751, 759, 766, 773, 783, 791, 798	**Leveled Problem Solving** **On Level** TG pp. 742, 751, 759, 766, 773, 783, 791, 798	**Leveled Problem Solving** **Above Level** TG pp. 742, 751, 759, 766, 773, 783, 791, 798

English Language Learners

Suggestions for addressing the needs of students learning English as a second language are included in the Developing Mathematical Language section at the beginning of most lessons.

ELL activities for this chapter can be found on TG pages 737, 745, 753, 761, 769, 775, 785, and 793.

The Multi-Age Classroom

Grade 4	• Students on this level should be able to complete the lessons in Chapter 9 but might need some additional practice with key concepts and skills. • Give students more practice with angles and triangles.	See Grade 5, Intervention Activities, Lessons 9.1–9.8. See Grade 4, Lessons 4.1–4.4.
Grade 5	• Students on this level should be able to complete the lessons in Chapter 9 with minimal adjustments.	See Grade 5, Practice pages P71–P78.
Grade 6	• Students on this level should be able to complete the lessons in Chapter 9 and to extend concepts and skills related to two-dimensional geometric shapes. • Give students extended work with similar figures.	See Grade 5, Extension pages E71–E78.

Cross Curricular Connections

Science Connection

Math Concept: classifying triangles and quadrilaterals

Snow Crystals

- Tell students that snowflakes and snow crystals are made of ice. A snowflake can be just one snow crystal or several that are stuck together. The basic shape of a snow crystal is a hexagonal prism. Two faces of the prism are hexagons.

- Have students identify any shapes they recognize in a hexagonal prism. hexagons, rectangles
- Have students draw a regular hexagon. Have them draw one or two segments each from one vertex to another and identify any shapes they find. Have students justify their answers. Possible answers: rectangle, trapezoid, isosceles triangle, scalene triangle

Lesson 9.7

Social Studies Connection

Math Concept: classifying angles and triangles

National Flags

- Tell students that countries, states, and even cities and clubs use flags as emblems.
- Show students pictures of the flags of Iceland and Jamaica.

Iceland   Jamaica

- Have students classify the angles in each flag. Iceland: all right angles; Jamaica: each black triangle has all acute angles, each green triangle has 2 acute and 1 obtuse angle.
- Have students classify the triangles in the Jamaican flag. Black triangles are equilateral triangles; green triangles are obtuse triangles.

Lesson 9.2

Literature Connection

Math Concept: finding angles

Sir Cumference and the Great Knight of Angleland
By Cindy Neuschwander
Illustrated by Wayne Geehan

This is an exciting tale of the squire Radius and his quest to find the lost King Lell. Students will learn about acute, obtuse, right, and straight angles and how to use a protractor to measure them.

Lesson 9.1

School-Home Connection

A reproducible copy of the School-Home Connection letter in English and in Spanish can be found in the *Teacher Resource Book,* pages SHC33–SHC36.

Encourage students to play *Stake a Quadrilateral Claim,* found on the School-Home Connection page, with a family member. Students will work with the concept of quadrilaterals in **Lessons 9.7** and **9.8.**

Assessment Options

There are many opportunities in *Think Math!* to assess students' understanding of concepts, skills, and problem solving. Learning Goals for Chapter 9 are provided below. The assessment options provide opportunities to evaluate whether or not students have retained learning from prior experiences. Choose the forms of assessment that best meet the needs of your students.

Chapter 9 Learning Goals

	Learning Goals	Lesson Number
9-A	Draw, classify, and determine the measures of angles by measuring with a protractor and by using known measures of other angles	9.1–9.6
9-B	Classify triangles, construct triangles, and recognize similar triangles	9.2–9.4
9-C	Classify quadrilaterals, determine the sum of the measures of the angles of a quadrilateral, and sketch lines of symmetry in a quadrilateral	9.7, 9.8
9-D	Apply problem solving strategies such as *look for a pattern* to solve problems	9.9

✓ Informal Assessment

Ongoing Assessment
Provides insight into students' thinking to guide instruction (TG pp. 741, 748, and 755)

Reflect and Summarize the Lesson
Checks understanding of lesson concepts
(TG pp. 741, 750, 758, 765, 772, 782, 790, 797, 802)

Snapshot Assessment
Mental Math and Quick Write
Offers a quick observation of students' progress on chapter concepts and skills
(TG pp. 806–807)

Performance Assessment
Provides quarterly assessment of Chapters 8–11 concepts using real-life situations
Assessment Guide pp. AG219–AG224

✓ Formal Assessment

Standardized Test Prep
Problem Solving Test Prep
Prepares students for standardized tests
Lesson Activity Book p. 190 (TG p. 803)

Chapter 9 Review/Assessment
Reviews and assesses students' understanding of the chapter
Lesson Activity Book pp. 191–192 (TG p. 808)

Chapter 9 Test
Assesses the chapter concepts and skills
Assessment Guide
Form A pp. AG81–AG82
Form B pp. AG83–AG84

Benchmark 3 Assessment
Provides quarterly assessment of Chapters 8–11 concepts and skills
Assessment Guide
Benchmark 3A pp. AG93–AG100
Benchmark 3B pp. AG101–AG108

Attributes of Two-Dimensional Figures

World Almanac for Kids

Use the World Almanac for Kids feature, *Patterns in Play,* found on pp. 148–149 of the **Student Handbook,** to provide students with an opportunity to practice using their problem solving skills by solving real world problems.

FACT•ACTIVITY 1

❶ $x = 130°$; $y = 50°$

❷ obtuse; 100°, 40°, 40°

❸ about 4 cm

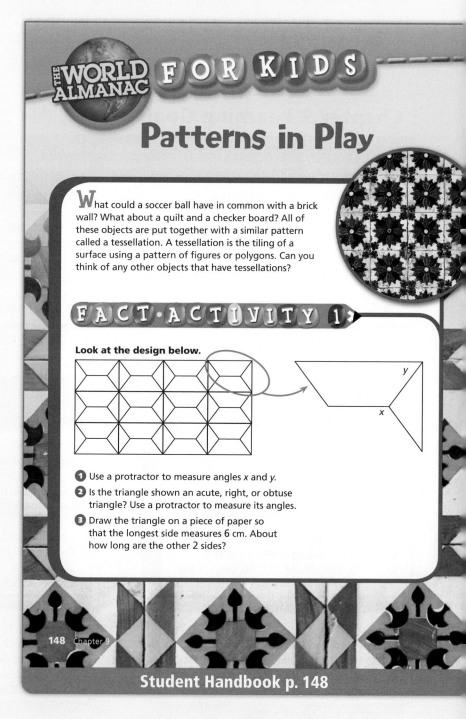

THE WORLD ALMANAC FOR KIDS

Patterns in Play

What could a soccer ball have in common with a brick wall? What about a quilt and a checker board? All of these objects are put together with a similar pattern called a tessellation. A tessellation is the tiling of a surface using a pattern of figures or polygons. Can you think of any other objects that have tessellations?

FACT•ACTIVITY 1

Look at the design below.

❶ Use a protractor to measure angles *x* and *y.*

❷ Is the triangle shown an acute, right, or obtuse triangle? Use a protractor to measure its angles.

❸ Draw the triangle on a piece of paper so that the longest side measures 6 cm. About how long are the other 2 sides?

148 Chapter 9

Student Handbook p. 148

FACT·ACTIVITY 2

M.C. Escher is the father of modern tessellation art. The design below is an example of tessellation art. The white and green triangles are congruent.

Trace the enlargement of the single set of figures. Shade the sections blue, yellow, and green as shown. Use your drawing to answer the questions below.

1 Look at the blue quadrilateral. Which angle is congruent to *x*? Label the congruent angle *x*.

2 Find other angles that are congruent to *x*. Label them *x*, also.

3 Look at the yellow quadrilateral. Which angle is congruent to *y*? Label it *y*. Which angle is congruent to *z*? Label it *z*.

CHAPTER PROJECT

Make your own tessellating pattern. Draw a triangle or quadrilateral on an index card. Within the figure, draw 2 segments to divide your figure into 3 smaller figures (triangles or quadrilaterals).

Cut out the 3 figures and trace multiple copies of each one on a different color of construction paper. Cut out at least 10 pieces of each figure. Arrange and glue the pieces to a larger sheet of cardboard or poster board to form a tessellating pattern. Remember, there should be no gaps or open spaces between figures. Display your tessellation in your classroom.

ALMANAC Fact

M.C. Escher created over 2,000 drawings and sketches and about 450 lithographs, woodcuts, and engravings.

Student Handbook p. 149

FACT·ACTIVITY 2

1 – 3 See diagram below.

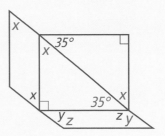

CHAPTER PROJECT

Sample answer:

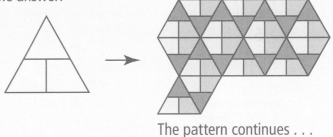

The pattern continues . . .

To reinforce vocabulary concepts, invite students to complete the vocabulary activities on pp. 162–163 of the *Student Handbook.* Encourage students to record their answers in their math journals.

Many responses are possible.

⓭ Possible response: A triangle is scalene if no two of its sides are *congruent.* It can have a *right angle* with two *acute angles* or an *obtuse angle* with two *acute angles,* or every angle can be an *acute angle.*

⓮ Possible response: When two lines intersect, they form four angles. If the lines are perpendicular, then each of the four angles is a *right angle* and they all would be *congruent.* If the lines are not perpendicular, then each angle is either an *acute angle* or an *obtuse angle.* Pairs of opposite angles are *congruent.*

⓯ Possible response: A parallelogram is a quadrilateral with two pairs of sides that are parallel to each other. If every angle is a *right angle,* then the parallelogram is a rectangle. If all four sides are congruent, then the parallelogram is a rhombus. If the parallelogram does not have *right angles,* then it has 2 *acute angles* and 2 *obtuse angles.* Opposite sides of a parallelogram are *congruent.* Opposite angles of a parallelogram are *congruent.*

Chapter 9 Vocabulary

Choose the best vocabulary term from Word List A for each sentence.

1 An angle that forms a square corner is called a(n) __?__. right angle

2 A polygon with four sides is called a(n) __?__. quadrilateral

3 Two figures are __?__ if they have the same shape and the same or a different size. similar

4 A quadrilateral with two pairs of parallel sides, two pairs of congruent sides, and four right angles is a(n) __?__. rectangle

5 Figures with the same size and shape are __?__. congruent figures

6 An angle with a measure less than a right angle is a(n) __?__. acute angle

7 A triangle that has three congruent sides is a(n) __?__. equilateral triangle

8 A quadrilateral with four congruent sides and two pairs of parallel sides is a(n) __?__. rhombus

9 A quadrilateral with two pairs of parallel sides and two pairs of congruent sides is a(n) __?__. parallelogram

10 Two lines that intersect at right angles are __?__. perpendicular

Word List A

acute angle
concave
congruent figures
convex
equilateral triangle
isosceles triangle
kite
obtuse angle
opposite angles
parallel (∥)
parallelogram
perpendicular
quadrilateral
rectangle
rhombus
right angle
scalene triangle
similar
straight angle
trapezoid
vertex

Complete each analogy using the best term from Word List B.

11 Rectangle is to __?__ as equilateral triangle is to triangle. quadrilateral

12 Acute angle is to equilateral triangle as __?__ is to rectangle. right angle

Word List B

right angle
congruent figures
quadrilateral
square

Talk Math

Discuss with a partner what you have just learned about attributes of two-dimensional figures. Use the vocabulary terms *acute angle, obtuse angle, right angle,* and *congruent.*

13 How can you tell whether a triangle is a scalene triangle?

14 How can you describe the angles formed by two intersecting lines?

15 How can you describe a parallelogram?

162 Chapter 9

Student Handbook p. 162

Degrees of Meaning Grid

16 Create a degrees of meaning grid. Start at least two rows with the word *triangle* and at least two rows with the word *quadrilateral*. Use what you know and what you have learned about quadrilaterals and triangles.

General	Less General	Specific

Analysis Chart

17 Create an analysis chart. List various polygons. Show the greatest number of right angles, acute angles, obtuse angles, and pairs of parallel sides the polygons can have.

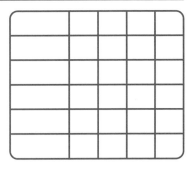

What's in a Word?

KITE There is a small hawk called a *kite* because the word *kite* sounds a bit like the bird's cry. Toy *kites* are made of paper, lightweight wood, and string. Because toy *kites* hover and glide like the bird, they were named after it. The quadrilateral *kite* gets its name from the toy because its shape is like the shape of some toy *kites*.

Chapter 9 **163**

Student Handbook p. 163

---

16 Many answers are possible. One example is provided.

General	Less General	Specific
triangle	isosceles triangle	pennant
triangle	equilateral triangle	traffic yield sign
quadrilateral	rectangle	square
quadrilateral	parallelogram	rectangle
quadrilateral	rhombus	square

17 Many answers are possible. One example is provided.

	right angles	acute angles	obtuse angles	pairs of parallel sides
rectangle	4	0	0	2
equilateral triangle	0	3	0	0
square	4	0	0	2
right triangle	1	2	0	0

Games

Triangle Maze in **Lesson 9.2** provides an opportunity for students to practice identifying the attributes of different kinds of triangles. *First to 360°* in **Lesson 9.5** provides an opportunity for students to draw angles of specific measures. These games can be found on pp. 164-165 of the *Student Handbook*.

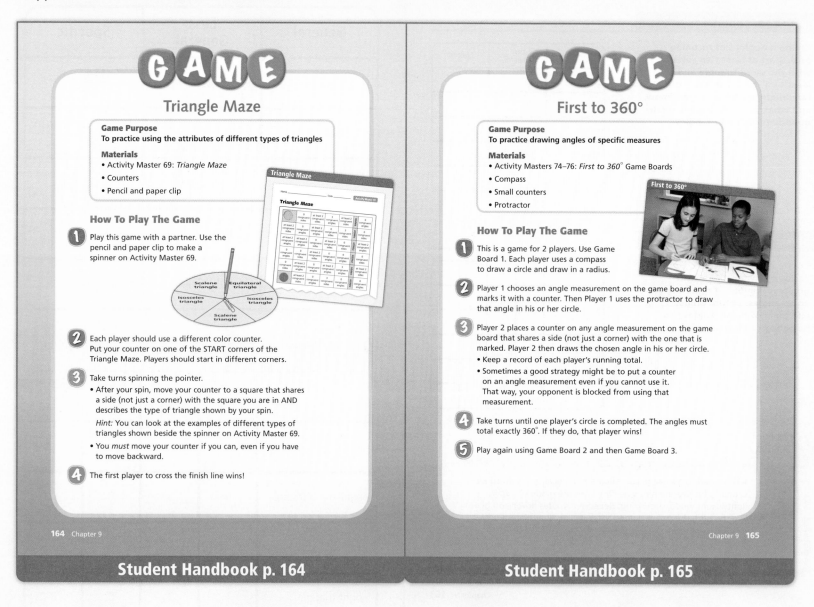

GAME

Triangle Maze

Game Purpose
To practice using the attributes of different types of triangles

Materials
• Activity Master 69: *Triangle Maze*
• Counters
• Pencil and paper clip

How To Play The Game

1. Play this game with a partner. Use the pencil and paper clip to make a spinner on Activity Master 69.

2. Each player should use a different color counter. Put your counter on one of the START corners of the Triangle Maze. Players should start in different corners.

3. Take turns spinning the pointer.
   • After your spin, move your counter to a square that shares a side (not just a corner) with the square you are in AND describes the type of triangle shown by your spin.
   Hint: You can look at the examples of different types of triangles shown beside the spinner on Activity Master 69.
   • You *must* move your counter if you can, even if you have to move backward.

4. The first player to cross the finish line wins!

164 Chapter 9

Student Handbook p. 164

GAME

First to 360°

Game Purpose
To practice drawing angles of specific measures

Materials
• Activity Masters 74–76: *First to 360°* Game Boards
• Compass
• Small counters
• Protractor

How To Play The Game

1. This is a game for 2 players. Use Game Board 1. Each player uses a compass to draw a circle and draw in a radius.

2. Player 1 chooses an angle measurement on the game board and marks it with a counter. Then Player 1 uses the protractor to draw that angle in his or her circle.

3. Player 2 places a counter on any angle measurement on the game board that shares a side (not just a corner) with the one that is marked. Player 2 then draws the chosen angle in his or her circle.
   • Keep a record of each player's running total.
   • Sometimes a good strategy might be to put a counter on an angle measurement even if you cannot use it. That way, your opponent is blocked from using that measurement.

4. Take turns until one player's circle is completed. The angles must total exactly 360°. If they do, that player wins!

5. Play again using Game Board 2 and then Game Board 3.

Chapter 9 165

Student Handbook p. 165

Challenge

The Challenge activity *Exterior Angles* challenges students to measure the exterior angles of polygons and then find a pattern in the sum of these measures. This activity can be found on p. 166 of the *Student Handbook.*

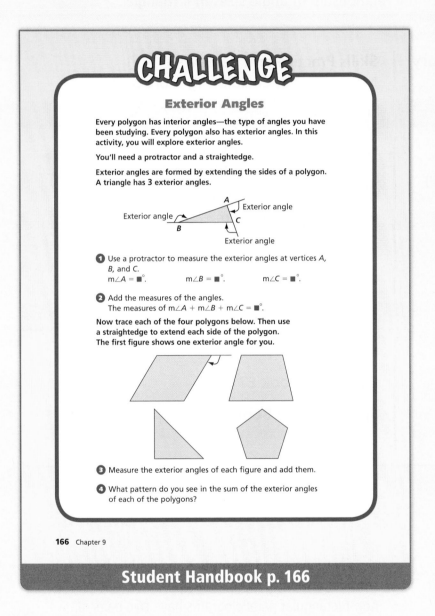

Student Handbook p. 166

❶ m∠A = 90°   m∠B = 160°   m∠C = 110°

❷ 360°

❸ Parallelogram: 120° + 60° + 120° + 60° = 360°
Triangle: 135° + 135° + 90° = 360°
Trapezoid: 77° + 77° + 103° + 103° = 360°
Pentagon: 72° + 72° + 72° + 72° + 72° = 360°

❹ The sum of the exterior angles for any polygon is 360°.

Lesson 1 Investigating Angles

NCTM Standards 3, 4, 7, 8, 9

Lesson Planner

STUDENT OBJECTIVES
- To review the concept of an angle and its size
- To explore the relationship of angle sizes in a triangle

1 Daily Activities (TG p. 737)

Open-Ended Problem Solving/Headline Story	Skills Practice and Review— Mental Sums: Calculating Store Sales

2 Teach and Practice (TG pp. 738–741)

	MATERIALS
Ⓐ **Reading the Student Letter** (TG p. 738)	• straightedges, blank paper, scissors, crayons or markers (optional)
Ⓑ **Experimenting with Triangles** (TG p. 739)	• 📖 LAB pp. 173–174
Ⓒ **Creating Angles and Classifying by Size** (TG p. 740)	• 📖 SH pp. 147, 150
Ⓓ **Classifying and Comparing Angles** (TG p. 741)	

3 Differentiated Instruction (TG p. 742)

Leveled Problem Solving (TG p. 742)	Practice Book P71
Intervention Activity (TG p. 742)	Extension Book E71
Extension Activity (TG p. 742)	Spiral Review Book SR71
Literature Connection (TG p. 734)	

Lesson Notes

About the Lesson

This lesson introduces the idea of angle size. Using numbers to describe the size of angles will be studied in **Lesson 9.2**. In this lesson, students use the torn-off corners of a triangle to investigate sums of angle measures. Even though each student in the class begins with a unique triangle, they all get similar results—a fact that students may find surprising and intriguing.

This lesson also reviews *acute, right,* and *obtuse* angles. Students will need these terms as they

classify triangles in **Lesson 9.2** and as they begin to consider attributes of quadrilaterals. (For example, non-rectangular parallelograms have two pairs of congruent angles, a pair of acute angles and a pair of obtuse angles.) As they learn to use a protractor, students must decide whether the angle is acute (smaller than a right angle) or obtuse (larger than a right angle) in order to choose the appropriate scale on the protractor.

Use with Lesson Activity Book pp. 173–174.

Developing Mathematical Language

Vocabulary: ∠, **angle, acute angle, obtuse angle, right angle, straight angle, vertex**

This lesson introduces the angle notation (∠) and one method of naming an *angle:* using only the *vertex* (for example, ∠A). As you write the notation on the board, you can read it out loud: "angle A." Students will likely not need any other explanation of this notation. Take care to draw the angle sign (∠) with a horizontal bottom to distinguish it from the "less than" sign (<).

Review the terms *angle, acute angle, obtuse angle, right angle,* and *straight angle* with students.

Beginning Discuss the words *acute,* and *obtuse.* Tell students that acute means "sharp or pointed" and *obtuse* can mean "blunt or not sharp." Have students bend one of their arms at the elbow to show each type of angle.

Intermediate Draw each of the four types of angles on the board. Randomly point to the various angles, and have students name them orally.

Advanced Have students choose any two types of angles and compare them using one or two complete sentences.

Open-Ended Problem Solving

Read this story aloud or write it on the board. Encourage students to find as many possibilities as they can.

 Headline Story

> **I'm thinking of a number written with five digits. It's a decimal between 26 and 27, and it has only even digits. All its digits are different.**

Possible responses: The first two digits of the number are 2 and 6. Many numbers are possible. The smallest number is 26.048. Other numbers are 26.084, 26.408, 26.480, 26.804, and 26.840. These six numbers differ only by the order of the digits after the decimal point.

Skills Practice and Review

Mental Sums: Calculating Store Sales

Tell students about a small retail store. The store keeps track of how many items were sold each week. Give students some numbers of items sold, in hundreds, and have them find sums and differences. Record the weekly and total sales in a table.

For example: In the first week of the year, the store sold 300 CDs. (Write 300.) The next week it sold 400. (Write 400.) How many more were sold the second week? How many were sold in the two weeks together? (Write 700.)

Sales	
Weekly	**Total**
300	
400	700
500	1,200

Sometimes, give sales figures as a two-step problem, like this: Then the store had a sale and sold *100 more CDs than it did the previous week.* Now how many CDs has it sold this week? (Write 500.) How many more CDs did the store sell that week than the first week? Now how many CDs has it sold this year? (Write 1,200.)

whole class **10 MIN**

A Reading the Student Letter

NCTM Standards 3, 4, 8

Purpose To introduce the content of the chapter

Introduce Have students read the letter independently before discussion.

Task Begin discussion of the letter by asking students about the first two angles.

💬 **Talk Math**

❓ **What are some ways to describe these two angles?**
Possible answers: The first one is closed up more than the second one. The first one is smaller than a right angle and the second one is bigger than a right angle.

❓ **The first angle's sides are longer than the second angle's but we say that the second angle is bigger than the first. How could you explain this thinking?**
Possible answer: The length of the sides doesn't matter. You could extend the sides of the second angle to the same length as those for the first angle and compare them. The second angle opens up more than the first one so it's bigger.

Student Handbook p. 147

Concept Alert

As students' understanding of angle develops, their attention will focus on the measure of the opening between rays or line segments, and they will more readily ignore irrelevant features, such as the *lengths* of the sides. When the angles are not part of a polygon, students are particularly likely to confuse short angle sides with a small angle size. Help students focus on how much the angle *opens;* you might even extend, or shorten, the lines used to form the angle and ask if the angle opens more or less than it did before.

Purpose To show that the three angles in any triangle form a straight angle

Introduce To complete this Explore page, each student will need a piece of paper, a straightedge, a pair of scissors, and optionally, crayons or markers.

Task Have students work through Explore:
An Experiment with a Triangle in small groups.
Encourage students to read each instruction carefully before drawing anything. Emphasize that students should use a straightedge to draw all line segments and that each student will draw a unique triangle.

These pictures show the sequence of steps in the experiment.

Materials
• For each student: piece of blank paper, straightedge, scissors, crayons or markers (optional)

NCTM Standards 3, 4, 8, 9

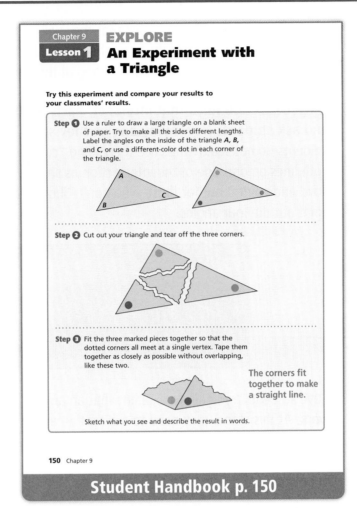

Student Handbook p. 150

💬 **Talk Math**

❓ What did you notice when you placed the three dotted corners together so that they all met at a single vertex? Possible answer: They can be arranged to form a straight line.

❓ Look around at the various ways others may have taped the corners together. What did you notice? No matter how the corners were taped together, they can still be arranged to form a line.

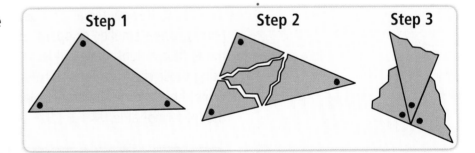

Step 1   Step 2   Step 3

Share Ask volunteers to show what they did with their triangle pieces, preferably on the overhead so everyone can see. Discuss their observations, including the fact that despite the variety of starting triangles, all the results were the same. Point out that as students added each new piece, they formed a new angle. Because the sides of the angle formed by all three pieces lie along a straight line, the angle is called a *straight angle.*

Use with Lesson Activity Book pp. 173–174.

(C) Creating Angles and Classifying by Size

NCTM Standards 3, 4, 8

Purpose To compare angles in order to classify them as acute, obtuse, right, or straight

Introduce Explain to students that they will be continuing the discussion of the term *angle* in this activity. In mathematics, thinking about definitions can help students develop a deeper understanding of the work they do.

Teacher Story

"One of my students drew a straight angle after I drew an obtuse angle. When it came to classifying in the table, some students wanted to call it obtuse, but others wanted it to have its own category. I left the question open and made a small research project out of it, asking students to find definitions of *obtuse*. We learned some mathematics and had a good discussion about multiple meanings— including non-mathematical meanings—of a word!"

Task Draw two lines that intersect, each continuing past the intersection, and ask students how many angles they see. (There are four, but sometimes students do not see them, since there is no "corner.") Use a piece of paper to cover both lines on one side of the intersection as shown below. Ask if they see an angle now, and point it out for those who don't. Show the intersecting lines again, and point out the four angles.

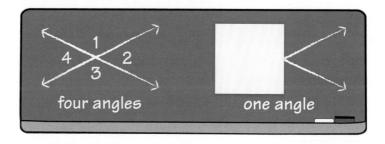

Have students try again to explain what an angle is, since "corner" may not always work. At this stage, they need to see that an angle is formed by two lines (or parts of lines) coming together at a point. Be sure students also know that this point is called the *vertex* of the angle. Most will be familiar with *vertex* and *vertices* as parts of polygons.

Ask some students to come up, one by one, and draw an angle that looks different from all the others. If necessary, draw an obtuse or right angle yourself after the first two or three have been drawn to remind students that angles don't have to be acute.

Practice Review the angle classifications *right* (for example, a corner of a piece of paper), *acute* (smaller, or opens less, than a right angle), and *obtuse* (larger, or opens more, than a right angle but less than a straight angle). Start a table on the board using those classifications as column heads, and label the angles that students drew. Write the angles in the proper place as students correctly identify them, as shown in the following table.

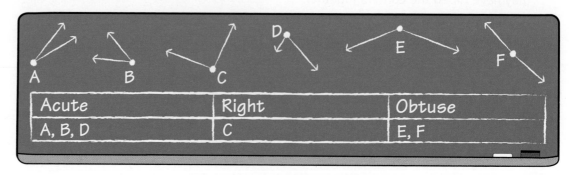

Acute	Right	Obtuse
A, B, D	C	E, F

Use with Lesson Activity Book pp. 173–174.

Purpose To classify angles as acute, right, or obtuse and to compare angle measures

NCTM Standards 3, 4, 7, 8

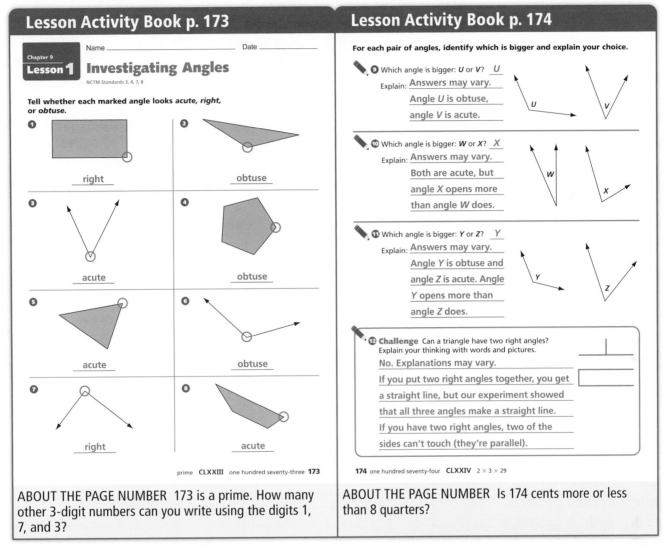

ABOUT THE PAGE NUMBER 173 is a prime. How many other 3-digit numbers can you write using the digits 1, 7, and 3?

ABOUT THE PAGE NUMBER Is 174 cents more or less than 8 quarters?

Teaching Notes for LAB page 173

Have students work on the page independently.

Students classify angles as acute, right, or obtuse.

✓ **Ongoing Assessment** Make note of any students who do not readily recognize the various types of angles; they will need to learn additional strategies. Encourage them to use a corner of the page for comparison.

Teaching Notes for LAB page 174

Students compare the sizes of two angles and explain their reasoning. Some students may be distracted by the line lengths, even though they are irrelevant. In Problems 9 and 11, one angle is obtuse and the other is acute; Problem 10 may be the most difficult, since both angles are acute, though one clearly opens more than the other.

Challenge Problem This problem asks students to consider whether a triangle can have two right angles. Students may need to try creating such a triangle to see why it's not possible.

Reflect and Summarize the Lesson

Write Math **Draw and label four different angles: an acute angle, a right angle, an obtuse angle, and a straight angle. Exlain how you know the angles you drew are correct.** Possible answer: An acute angle is smaller than a right angle; a right angle has a square corner; an obtuse angle is bigger than a right angle and smaller than a straight angle; a straight angle forms a straight line.

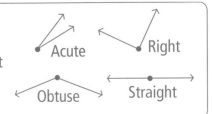

Leveled Problem Solving

Chris drew an angle and then placed the corner of a sheet of paper at the vertex of the angle.

❶ Basic Level

The corner of the paper exactly fit in the angle. What type of angle did Chris draw? Explain. A right angle; a right angle is a square corner.

❷ On Level

When he tried to fit the corner of the paper in the angle, some of the corner was outside the angle. What type of angle did he draw? Explain. An acute angle; an acute angle cannot contain a square corner.

❸ Above Level

When he put the square corner in the angle, part of the angle was left over. What type of angle did he draw? An obtuse or straight angle; it can contain a square angle and have space left over.

Intervention	Practice	Extension

Activity Comparing Angles

Without giving any instructions as to lengths of sides or size of angle, have students draw any angle on a sheet of paper. Ask two students at a time to stand next to each other, hold up their angles for everyone to see, and name the larger angle. After several pairs of students have shown their angles, invite five students to arrange themselves in order from smallest to largest angle.

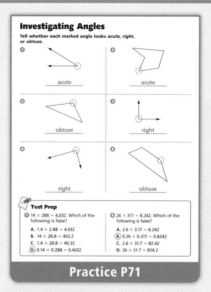

Practice P71

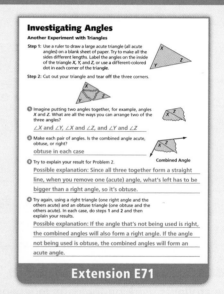

Extension E71

Spiral Review

Spiral Review Book page SR71 provides review of the following previously learned skills and concepts:

• determining the median, mode, and range of data displayed in a graph

• applying the problem solving strategy *make a table*

You may wish to have students work with partners to complete the page.

Spiral Review SR71

Extension Activity
Active Angles

Hold 2 pencils horizontally side by side. Begin to rotate one of the pencils slowly until it has made a $\frac{1}{4}$ turn. Ask: *What type of angle* can be *described as a $\frac{1}{4}$ turn?* right angle *What type of angle is less than a $\frac{1}{4}$ turn?* acute angle Continue rotating one pencil until the two pencils are eraser-to-eraser forming a straight line. Ask: *What type of angle can be described as a $\frac{1}{2}$ turn?* straight angle *What type of angle is greater than a $\frac{1}{4}$ turn, but less than a $\frac{1}{2}$ turn?* obtuse angle

---

Teacher's Notes 🍎

Daily Notes . . .

Quick Notes

More Ideas

Lesson 2 Classifying Angles and Triangles

NCTM Standards 3, 4, 6, 7, 8

Lesson Planner

STUDENT OBJECTIVES
- To classify triangles using congruent parts and perpendicular sides
- To use a protractor to measure angles to the nearest 5°

1 Daily Activities (TG p. 745)

Open-Ended Problem Solving/Headline Story	Skills Practice and Review— Totaling Store Sales

2 Teach and Practice (TG pp. 746–749)

MATERIALS

Ⓐ **Measuring Angles** (TG p. 746)

Ⓑ **Classifying Triangles** (TG p. 747)

Ⓒ **Measuring and Classifying Angles and Triangles** (TG p. 748)

Ⓓ **Playing a Game: Triangle Maze** (TG p. 749)

- TR: Activity Masters, AM68, AM69
- transparency of AM68 (optional)
- demonstration protractor (for the chalkboard or for the overhead projector)
- protractors, rulers
- color counters, pencil, paper clip
- 📖 LAB pp. 175–176
- 📖 SH pp. 151–152

3 Differentiated Instruction (TG p. 751)

Leveled Problem Solving (TG p. 751)	Practice Book P72
Intervention Activity (TG p. 751)	Extension Book E72
Extension Activity (TG p. 751)	Spiral Review Book SR72
Social Studies Connection (TG p. 734)	

Lesson Notes

About the Lesson

As part of refining their ability to analyze attributes of two-dimensional figures, students begin to consider relationships among angles. Later in this chapter, students will need to recognize the connection between parallel sides in certain quadrilaterals and the congruence of particular angles formed by those sides.

In this lesson, students measure angles using a protractor and use numbers to describe the size of an angle.

In previous grades, students classified triangles by their largest angle (acute, right, or obtuse) and by their number of congruent sides (scalene, isosceles, or equilateral). In this lesson, they see how these classifications connect to each other by answering questions such as, "If a triangle is right, can it also be scalene?" or, "If a triangle is equilateral, can it also be obtuse?" They see that the number of congruent angles also allows them to classify triangles as scalene, isosceles, and equilateral.

Use with Lesson Activity Book pp. 175–176.

Developing Mathematical Language

Vocabulary: equilateral triangle, isosceles triangle, scalene triangle, congruent, perpendicular

Each line segment or side of a *scalene triangle* is a different length. At least two sides of an *isosceles triangle* are *congruent,* or equal in length. All three sides of an *equilateral triangle* are *congruent.* Lines and parts of lines are *perpendicular* to each other if they meet at a right angle. If two line segments or angles have the same measure, they match exactly, and so they are *congruent.*

Review the terms *scalene triangle, isosceles triangle, equilateral triangle,* and *perpendicular* with students.

Beginning Tell students that when line segments are *perpendicular* they look like an addition sign and make 4 square corners. Have students use their forearms to show *perpendicular* line segments.

Intermediate Draw a *scalene triangle,* an *isosceles triangle,* and an *equilateral triangle* on the board. Have students identify them orally as you randomly point to each one.

Advanced Have partners discuss the properties of each of the three different types of triangles.

1 | Daily Activities

Open-Ended Problem Solving

After students have investigated the problem, make a table of the class's experiments and have students look for a pattern.

 Headline Story

> Draw 6 or fewer points on a piece of paper. Connect each point to all the other points. How many line segments did you draw?

Possible responses: For 1 point, you can draw 0 segments. For 2 points, you can draw 1 segment. For 3 points, you can draw 3 segments. (It's a triangle.) For 4 points you can draw 6 segments. For 5 points, you can draw 10 segments and for 6 points you can draw 15 segments. (Some students who have used *Think Math!* in earlier grades may recognize the numbers of segments as the triangular numbers.)

Skills Practice and Review

Totaling Store Sales

Remind students of the small store described in the previous lesson. As before, give students numbers of items sold, but this time include numbers with a non-zero tens digit (such as 310 or 570 items), and have them find the total sales for the given weeks. (Students will have more to keep in mind than they did in the previous lesson, so let them focus on finding sums. Differences will be included in the next lesson.) Record the weekly sales and the totals each time. Keep the pace fast and lively.

2 | Teach and Practice

Ⓐ Measuring Angles

Materials
- For the teacher: demonstration protractor
- For each student: ruler, protractor, AM68

NCTM Standards 4, 8

Differentiated Instruction

Basic Level Students might use a corner of a piece of paper to determine if an angle is acute, right, or obtuse.

Concept Alert

These are some common errors students may make while measuring angles.

- Students may not place the "center" of the protractor at the angle's vertex.
- Students may position the protractor upside down along one side of the angle.
- Students may read the angle measurement from wrong scale on the protractor.

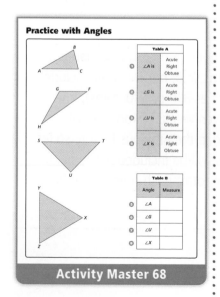

Activity Master 68

Purpose To practice measuring angles using protractors

Introduce Students will be figuring out how large the angles are on AM68: Practice with Angles. In Table A, they need to determine if the designated angles are acute, right, or obtuse. Have them complete this part as a class. To complete Table B, students will need to know how to use a protractor. Refer them to Explore: How to Use a Protractor. Read the Explore page as a class while you demonstrate some of the steps using your demonstration protractor.

Task Have students read and independently follow the directions on Explore: How to Use a Protractor. Provide support when needed. (Students often find protractors difficult to use at first).

Chapter 9 EXPLORE
Lesson 2 How to Use a Protractor

Follow these steps to use a protractor to measure angles.

❶ Match the circle in the center of the straight side of the protractor to the vertex of the angle you want to measure.

❷ Match the zero mark on the protractor to one of the lines, or parts of lines, that form the angle.

❸ The other line, or part of a line, must cross the curved side of the protractor. Read the measurement from the curved side. For **acute** angles, use the smaller number. For **obtuse** angles, use the larger number.

Chapter 9 **151**

Student Handbook p. 151

Once students understand how to use a protractor, have them work in pairs or small groups to measure the angles and complete Table B of AM68: Practice with Angles. Observe students as they work, as it is likely that some will need help placing their protractors correctly or deciding which number to choose for the angle measure. Students will use AM68 again in the next activity.

Ask students to think about how measuring the angles in Table B might help them check that they have completed Table A correctly.

💬 Talk Math

❓ Does the measurement you got with a protractor for ∠A match the classification you chose in Table A? How do you know if you're correct? Possible answer: The angle measures 30° and an acute angle is less than 90°.

❓ What if you measured ∠U and got 89°? Were you wrong if you predicted that it was a right angle? Possible answers: It is very difficult to measure exactly with a protractor and all measurements are really estimates. Chances are it is close enough to 90° to be considered a right angle.

Use with Lesson Activity Book pp. 175–176.

Classifying Triangles

Purpose To classify triangles as scalene, isosceles, or equilateral

Introduce Go over the Review Model: Classifying Triangles with your class. As you refer to *right* triangles, check to see whether students know what *perpendicular* means. (Two lines are perpendicular if they form a right angle.) Point out that students have two names for the same angle: *right angle* and *90° angle.* They can also say that the sides of the angle are *perpendicular.*

The definitions for isosceles and equilateral triangles include the term *congruent.* Use the term in context and indicate that it means "equal measure." Two segments or two angles are congruent if they have the same measure.

Task **To give your students practice in classifying triangles by their sides, have them use rulers to measure and classify the triangles on AM68: Practice with Angles.** Have students record the length of each side and then determine which type triangle is shown most often on the page. (The lengths are probably easiest to measure in centimeters.) You may want to show a transparency of the page and do the activity together. Students should find that the isosceles triangles are shown most often since △ ABC and △ STU are isosceles, △ FGH is scalene, and △ XYZ is equilateral.

When all the triangles are classified, have students measure all the angles in the isosceles and equilateral triangles, compare the angles within each triangle, and record their observations using words, pictures, and numbers.

Talk Math

❓ What parts of △ XYZ are congruent? all the sides and all the angles

❓ What parts of △ ABC and △ STU are congruent? two of the sides and two of the angles

Extend Have students discuss their observations. While the angles seem to be congruent, we can't be certain our measurements are accurate. In fact, there is always some amount of error when measuring. Students don't yet have the knowledge to prove these angles must be congruent, but some may recall that isosceles triangles have a line of symmetry.

Have a volunteer cut out and fold △ ABC or △ STU along a line of symmetry and see that the angles in question match each other.

Although △ STU is isosceles, it can be classified another way.

❓ What kind of angles—acute, obtuse, or right—does the triangle have?
It has one right angle and two acute angles.

❓ What can you say about sides SU and TU? They're congruent and perpendicular.

❓ What are two ways you can classify △ STU? isosceles and right

Materials
- For the teacher: transparency of AM68 (optional)
- For each student: AM68, protractor and ruler

NCTM Standards 4, 8

Possible Discussion

As students compare angle measures in this activity, some may notice that, in triangles, the largest angle is opposite the longest side, and the smallest angle is opposite the shortest side. Here's a demonstration that may help students see why it makes sense: Get two pencils, pens, or other long objects to represent two sides of a triangle. Hold the pencils together to share a vertex, and put the other ends against a flat surface to represent the third side of the triangle (or have students imagine the third side). As you make the angle formed by the pencils larger, what happens to the length of the side opposite that angle? (It also gets larger.) What happens to the length as the angle gets smaller? (It also gets smaller.) So longer sides are opposite larger angles, and shorter sides are opposite smaller angles.

Measuring and Classifying Angles and Triangles LAB pp. 175–176

Purpose To measure angles with protractors and to use angle and side measures to classify triangles

NCTM Standards 3, 4, 7, 9

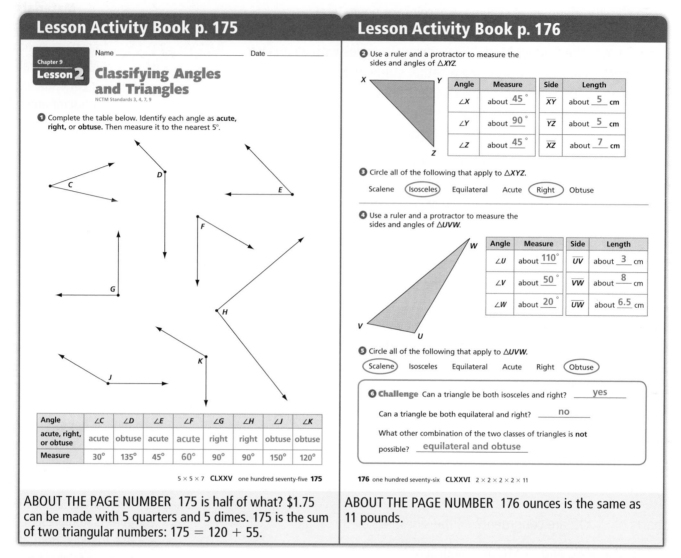

Lesson Activity Book p. 175

Name _____ Date _____

Chapter 9
Lesson 2 **Classifying Angles and Triangles**
NCTM Standards 3, 4, 7, 9

❶ Complete the table below. Identify each angle as **acute, right,** or **obtuse**. Then measure it to the nearest 5°.

Angle	∠C	∠D	∠E	∠F	∠G	∠H	∠J	∠K
acute, right, or obtuse	acute	obtuse	acute	acute	right	right	obtuse	obtuse
Measure	30°	135°	45°	60°	90°	90°	150°	120°

5 × 5 × 7 **CLXXV** one hundred seventy-five **175**

ABOUT THE PAGE NUMBER 175 is half of what? $1.75 can be made with 5 quarters and 5 dimes. 175 is the sum of two triangular numbers: 175 = 120 + 55.

Lesson Activity Book p. 176

❷ Use a ruler and a protractor to measure the sides and angles of △*XYZ*.

Angle	Measure	Side	Length
∠X	about 45°	$\overline{XY}$	about 5 cm
∠Y	about 90°	$\overline{YZ}$	about 5 cm
∠Z	about 45°	$\overline{XZ}$	about 7 cm

❸ Circle all of the following that apply to △*XYZ*.

Scalene (Isosceles) Equilateral Acute (Right) Obtuse

❹ Use a ruler and a protractor to measure the sides and angles of △*UVW*.

Angle	Measure	Side	Length
∠U	about 110°	$\overline{UV}$	about 3 cm
∠V	about 50°	$\overline{VW}$	about 8 cm
∠W	about 20°	$\overline{UW}$	about 6.5 cm

❺ Circle all of the following that apply to △*UVW*.

(Scalene) Isosceles Equilateral Acute Right (Obtuse)

❻ **Challenge** Can a triangle be both isosceles and right? _____ yes _____

Can a triangle be both equilateral and right? _____ no _____

What other combination of the two classes of triangles is **not** possible? equilateral and obtuse

176 one hundred seventy-six **CLXXVI** 2 × 2 × 2 × 2 × 11

ABOUT THE PAGE NUMBER 176 ounces is the same as 11 pounds.

Teaching Notes for LAB page 175

Students classify angles as acute, right, or obtuse and measure them with a protractor. Students should be able to complete the page independently, although you may want to have them check their answers (and placement and reading of the protractor) with a partner.

✔**Ongoing Assessment** As protractors are new tools, expect students to need some time to get used to them. As they measure the angles using protractors and the triangles on the next page using protractors and rulers, watch for students who are having trouble; they may need extra help to complete these pages.

Teaching Notes for LAB page 176

Students are asked to measure the sides and angles of two triangles. They use this information to classify the triangles by their largest angle and the number of congruent sides (or angles) using the terms *acute, right, obtuse, scalene, isosceles,* and *equilateral.*

Differentiated Instruction Basic Level If students with weak measurement skills choose to measure the sides of the triangles in inches, suggest they try centimeters as well. The triangles are rather small, so centimeters may be a better unit choice (and, in fact, the lengths are close to whole numbers of centimeters).

Challenge Problem This problem asks students to consider what combinations of the two classes (acute, right, or obtuse, and scalene, isosceles, or equilateral) are impossible.

D Playing a Game: *Triangle Maze*

Purpose To give students additional practice with the features of different classes of triangles in the context of a game

Goal The object of the game, *Triangle Maze,* is to be the first player to move through a maze connecting triangle types and their features.

Prepare Materials Each pair of students will need AM69: *Triangle Maze,* two different color counters or other small objects, and a pencil and a paper clip to make a spinner like this.

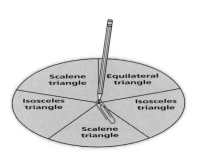

Materials
- For each pair: AM69, two different color counters, pencil, paper clip

NCTM Standards 3, 7, 8

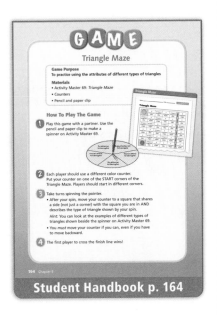

Student Handbook p. 164

How to Play

❶ Each player puts a counter or token on a corner marked START. Players should start in different corners.

❷ Players take turns spinning the pointer to generate a type of triangle.

❸ After spinning, the player moves his or her token to any square that

    A shares a side (not just a corner) with the square the token is currently on, and

    B describes the type of triangle indicated by the spinner.

For example, if the spinner landed on "Equilateral triangle," the player can move up, down, left, or right to any square marked *3 congruent angles, 3 congruent sides, at least 2 congruent angles,* or *at least 2 congruent sides.* Players can refer to the examples of each type of triangle shown beside the spinner.

❹ Players *must* move the token if at all possible, even if it means moving backward (away from the finish line).

❺ The first player to cross the finish line, entering the last column of squares, wins.

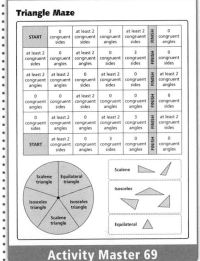

Activity Master 69

Reflect and Summarize the Lesson

Write Math

Draw a triangle. Is your triangle acute, right, or obtuse? Tell how you know. Is your triangle scalene, isosceles, or equilateral? Tell how you know. Check students' drawing and responses. They should describe the measure of the angles of the triangle to explain whether it is acute, right, or obtuse. They should describe the lengths of the sides of the triangle to explain whether it is scalene, isosceles, or equilateral.

Review Model . . . .

Refer students to Review Model: Classifying Triangles in the *Student Handbook* to see how to classify triangles by the measure of their angles and by the lengths of their sides.

✔ **Check for Understanding**

❶ acute

❷ obtuse

❸ acute

❹ right

❺ equilateral

❻ scalene

❼ isosceles

❽ equilateral

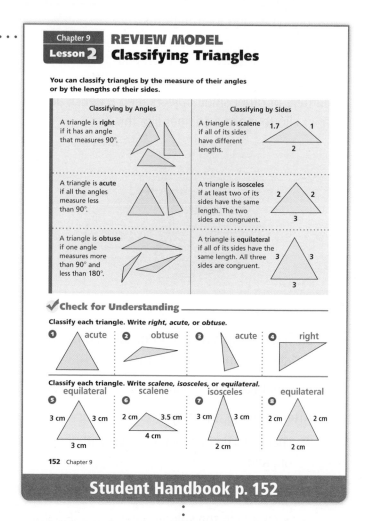

Use with Lesson Activity Book pp. 175–176.

Leveled Problem Solving

Jenice draws a triangle and then writes a description of it.

❶ Basic Level

All sides of the triangle are congruent. What else could she say about the triangle? Explain. All angles are congruent; in an equilateral triangle, all angles as well as sides are congruent.

❷ On Level

No two sides of the triangle are congruent. What else could she say about the triangle? Explain. It is scalene, and no angles are congruent: it could be an acute, right, or obtuse triangle.

❸ Above Level

The triangle has a right angle and no congruent sides. What else could she say about the triangle? Explain. It is scalene, and no angles are congruent; the two other angles are acute angles.

Intervention

Activity Choosing a Scale

Ask students to name any two angle measures that are at the same point on the protractor. Then ask them to explain how they will decide which measure to use if an angle crosses the protractor at that point. Encourage them to include reference to a right angle in their answers. If the angle is less than a right angle (or square corner), you use the lesser number. If the angle is greater than a right angle (or square corner) you use the greater number.

Practice

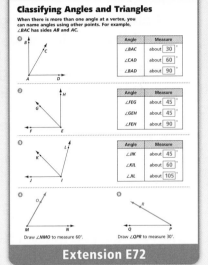

Practice P72

Extension

Extension E72

Spiral Review

Spiral Review Book page SR72 provides review of the following previously learned skills and concepts:

- using rounding and compatible numbers to estimate solutions to multiplication and division problems
- practicing using coordinates to identify points on a coordinate grid

You may wish to have students work with partners to complete the page.

Spiral Review SR72

Extension Activity
Protractor Pattern

Have students look at the pairs of angle measures named at each point on a protractor. Ask them to describe any pattern they see. Elicit that the sum of the two measures is always 180°. Challenge students to explain why this pattern is found on a protractor. Except for a right angle, the two measures named at any one point on a protractor refer to an acute and an obtuse angle formed by a ray extending from the straight line at the bottom of the protractor.

Lesson Planner

STUDENT OBJECTIVES
- To construct congruent triangles
- To practice measuring and drawing line segments and angles

1 Daily Activities (TG p. 753)

Open-Ended Problem Solving/Headline Story	Skills Practice and Review— Calculating Store Sales

2 Teach and Practice (TG pp. 754–758)

MATERIALS

(A) **Drawing an Angle** (TG p. 754)

(B) **Constructing a Triangle Given Two Sides and the Angle between Them** (TG p. 755)

(C) **Constructing a Triangle Given Two Angles and the Side between Them** (TG p. 756)

(D) **Constructing Triangles** (TG p. 757)

- demonstration protractor
- protractors
- straightedges
- scissors
- tape
- LAB pp. 177–178
- SH p. 153

3 Differentiated Instruction (TG p. 759)

Leveled Problem Solving (TG p. 759)	Practice Book P73
Intervention Activity (TG p. 759)	Extension Book E73
Extension Activity (TG p. 759)	Spiral Review Book SR73

Lesson Notes

About the Lesson

If you were told that a certain figure had *three* sides, each 2 cm long, there is only one figure it could be. In this lesson, students learn that they can draw a unique triangle knowing only two of its sides and the angle between them, or only two of its angles and the side between them.

By doing these constructions, students see that all the triangles constructed with the same side-angle-side measures are congruent to each other—that is, there is only one such shape, though it could be in lots of different positions—and, likewise, that all triangles constructed with the same angle-side-angle measures are congruent to each other. In their later study of geometry, students will encounter these ideas as formal ways to show triangle congruence, but today they're developing these ideas informally as they build skills with measurement and drawing.

About the Mathematics

It is easy to perform experiments to see why knowing all the side lengths of a triangle tells you the exact shape of the triangle, while knowing all the sides of a four-sided figure does not. Cut straws that are, say, 4 inches, 6 inches, and 8 inches in length, and arrange

(continued on page R3)

Developing Mathematical Language

Vocabulary: congruent figures

In the previous lesson, students encountered the term *congruent* applied to line segments and angles. In previous years, students of *Think Math!* have referred to two figures with the same size and shape, or two figures that match when one is placed over the other as *congruent*. A more formal meaning for congruence is discussed during this lesson: for two polygons to be congruent, each pair of corresponding parts (for example, sides or angles) must be congruent.

Review the term *congruent figures* with students.

Beginning Review with students that *congruent figures* have the same size and shape. Show students several pattern blocks, and have them find the ones that are *congruent*.

Intermediate Have each student cut out a figure. As a group, compare the figures and determine whether any of the figures are *congruent figures*. If none of the figures is congruent, discuss how you could create two *congruent figures*.

Advanced Have students use their own words to describe *congruent figures*.

---

1 | Daily Activities

Open-Ended Problem Solving

This problem may be read to students and they can share their ideas orally.

 Headline Story

> One side of an isosceles triangle measures 5 cm. What can you say about the triangle?

Possible responses: One of the other sides can measure 5 cm, and the third side could then have some other length. Or, both second and third sides could be the same length, but different from 5 cm. If all three sides are 5 cm long, then the triangle would be both isosceles and equilateral! The angles that are opposite each of the congruent sides will have the same measures. The triangle could be acute, obtuse, or right.

Skills Practice and Review

Calculating Store Sales

As in **Lessons 9.1** and **9.2,** describe the small retail store. This time, as you give students numbers of items it sells each week (perhaps in tens rather than hundreds, but adjust this according to your class), have them compare sales from week to week indicating the differences as "up" or "down" so much from the week before. Also, have them find total sales for the given weeks. Record the weekly sales and the totals each time. Use numbers that are large enough to represent a bit of a challenge to your class but still allow you to keep the pace fast and lively.

whole class | 10 MIN

A Drawing an Angle

Materials
- For the teacher: demonstration protractor, straightedge
- For each student: protractor, straightedge

NCTM Standards 3, 4, 6, 8

Purpose To draw an angle of specified measure with a protractor

Introduce Tell the class you're thinking of a particular triangle, and ask if someone can draw it for you. (With no information, this may seem silly, but someone may offer a triangle anyway.) Begin giving clues and ask if they think they have enough information: The length of one side is 6 inches. The length of a second side is 8 inches. Those two sides are perpendicular. (At this point there is enough information, and the triangle is reasonably easy to draw using grid paper to make sure that the angle between the two sides is a right angle.)

Task Ask students to think about how they would construct a triangle if they were given the lengths of two sides and if the angle given between them was different from 90°, say 45° or 60°. Demonstrate drawing an angle of a specified measure, with students following along at their desks.

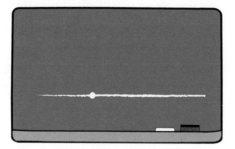 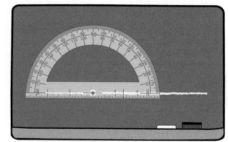

- Draw a segment (of a specified length) and choose an endpoint to be the vertex.
- Place the "center" of the protractor at the vertex you've chosen, and align the bottom edge of the protractor with the line, just as if you were going to measure an angle. (The zero mark on the protractor will be on the segment if the segment is long enough. You can extend the segment if you like.)

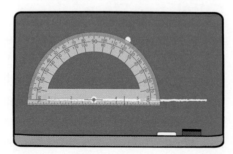 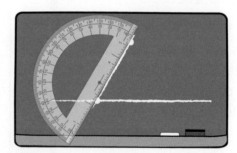

- Find the proper degree mark (60°, or whatever angle you've chosen) on the protractor, and put a small dot at that mark.
- Use a ruler or the side of the protractor to connect the vertex and the small dot.

Practice Decide if your students need to draw another angle on their own or if they can proceed directly to the next activity. They will get more opportunities to draw angles of specific sizes later.

Use with Lesson Activity Book pp. 177–178.

Constructing a Triangle Given Two Sides and the Angle between Them

Purpose To construct a triangle when the lengths of two sides and the measure of the angle between them is given

Introduce Ask the class whether two side lengths and the measure of the angle between them is enough information to let them draw the triangle you're thinking of, or if they might end up with a different triangle.

Task Have the whole class work together through the Side-Angle-Side example on Review Model: Constructing Triangles. Read out one instruction at a time, and walk around to check students' work briefly before moving on to the next step.

After students have constructed △ABC, ask them to cut it out carefully and compare it to the triangles other students constructed. As long as students were fairly accurate

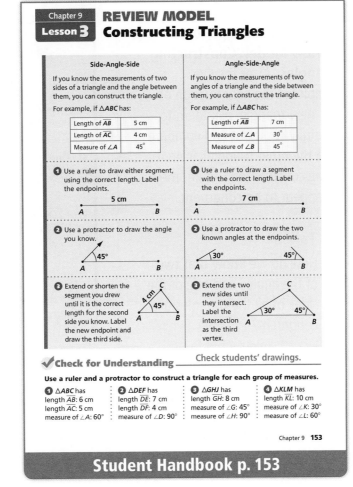

Student Handbook p. 153

with the construction, the triangles should all appear to be *congruent*. You can informally show congruence by placing one triangle on top of another and seeing that the triangles (within reasonable error) coincide.

Use students' new understanding of congruent sides and angles to make this idea more formal: all corresponding angles and corresponding sides of the triangles are congruent. (Corresponding sides or angles are the ones that are in the same place when the figures are matched up against each other.)

Share Ask students to share their ideas about why all the triangles look the same. A possible response might be something like, "We know that two of the sides are the same length, and the angle shows how much the two sides will open up. That tells you what the third side has to be. It couldn't be different for different people." You can illustrate this idea with two pencils: if the angle has to open a certain amount, is there another way to make that third side? How many different lengths are possible for the third side?

Ongoing Assessment

Observe your students as they use the centimeter ruler and the protractor.

• Are they matching one endpoint of the segment they want to measure with the zero mark on the ruler?

• Or, are they matching one endpoint to any whole centimeter marking and determining the measurement by finding the difference?

Some students may still be overly casual about matching one end of the segment to a known point on the ruler before reading out the length, and this will be evident in their construction. Many students are still likely to be relatively unskilled with protractors. Check to see if students are lining their protractors up correctly, and when necessary refer them to Explore: How to Use a Protractor on SH p. 151 from **Lesson 9.2.**

C Constructing a Triangle Given Two Angles and the Side between Them

Materials
- For each student: protractor, straightedge, scissors

NCTM Standards 3, 4, 8, 10

Possible Discussion

This activity provides an opportunity to bring up the sum of the angles in a triangle. Remind students that they know the angles of a triangle form a straight angle, then ask them what the measure of a straight angle is. If they need a hint, put two straws or pencils together to form an angle. Have the student use the protractor to measure the angle; move one straw to make the angle wider and have them measure again. Do this several times, and, finally, move the straw to form a straight angle with the other one, and once again ask for the angle measure. Students should see that the measure of a straight angle (and so the sum of the measures of the angles inside a triangle too) is 180°. Students will discuss this again in **Lesson 9.4**.

Purpose To construct triangles given two angle measures and the side length between them

Introduce Similar to the previous activity, pose this question: What if the given information is two angles and the length of the side between them?

Task Have the whole class work through the Angle-Side-Angle example on Review Model: Constructing Triangles. After they've completed the construction of this new triangle, ask them to carefully cut it out and compare it to the other triangles from the same construction. Again, they all appear to be congruent.

💬 **Talk Math**

❓ How do we know that two of the angles and one of the sides of all the triangles are congruent? Possible answer: We all constructed them using the same information.

❓ Is there a way we can know that the third angle of all the triangles is congruent? Possible answer: All the angles of a triangle need to add up to a straight angle, so if we know the measurements of two angles, we can figure out the third.

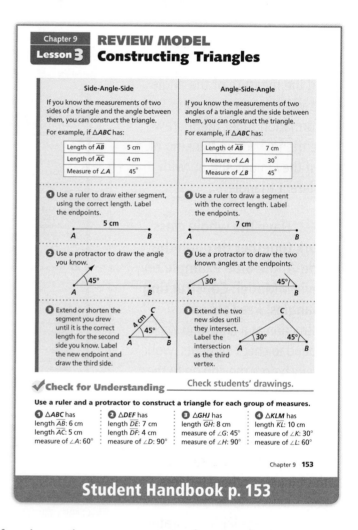

Student Handbook p. 153

Extend Challenge students to consider whether they will always construct congruent triangles given the measures of the three angles. Students are likely to think that they will. After all, the congruent triangles that they just constructed had the same size corresponding angles.

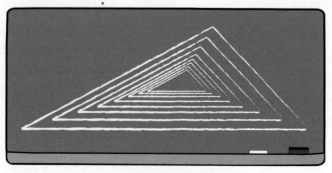

To help students see that fixing the three angles of a triangle still allows for making triangles that are not congruent, sketch a drawing on the board similar to the one at the left.

Help students to conclude that triangles can have the same three angle measures, but different side lengths.

Constructing Triangles LAB pp. 177–178

NCTM Standards 3, 4, 8, 10

Purpose To construct triangles given two angle measures and the length of the side between them or given the lengths of two sides and the angle measure between those sides

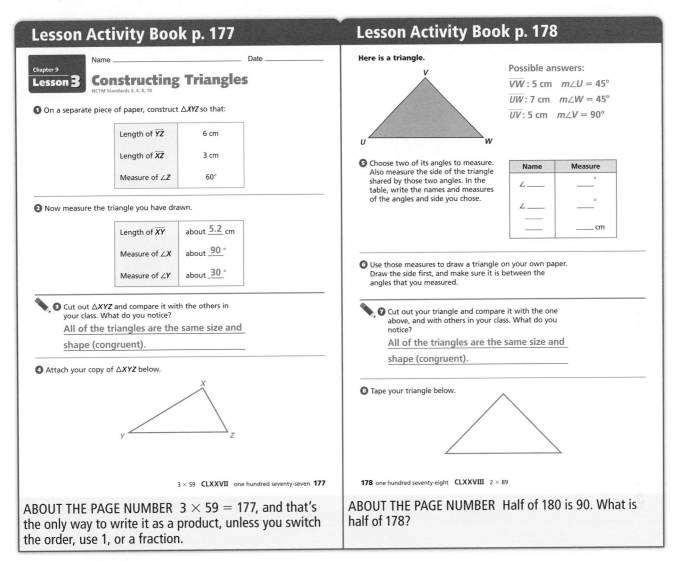

Lesson Activity Book p. 177

Chapter 9 Lesson 3 **Constructing Triangles**
NCTM Standards 3, 4, 8, 10

Name _____ Date _____

1 On a separate piece of paper, construct △*XYZ* so that:

Length of $\overline{YZ}$	6 cm
Length of $\overline{XZ}$	3 cm
Measure of ∠*Z*	60°

2 Now measure the triangle you have drawn.

Length of $\overline{XY}$	about 5.2 cm
Measure of ∠*X*	about 90 °
Measure of ∠*Y*	about 30 °

3 Cut out △*XYZ* and compare it with the others in your class. What do you notice?

All of the triangles are the same size and shape (congruent).

4 Attach your copy of △*XYZ* below.

3 × 59 **CLXXVII** one hundred seventy-seven **177**

ABOUT THE PAGE NUMBER 3 × 59 = 177, and that's the only way to write it as a product, unless you switch the order, use 1, or a fraction.

Lesson Activity Book p. 178

Here is a triangle.

Possible answers:
$\overline{VW}$: 5 cm   m∠*U* = 45°
$\overline{UW}$: 7 cm   m∠*W* = 45°
$\overline{UV}$: 5 cm   m∠*V* = 90°

5 Choose two of its angles to measure. Also measure the side of the triangle shared by those two angles. In the table, write the names and measures of the angles and side you chose.

Name	Measure
∠ ___	___ °
∠ ___	___ °
___	
___	___ cm

6 Use those measures to draw a triangle on your own paper. Draw the side first, and make sure it is between the angles that you measured.

7 Cut out your triangle and compare it with the one above, and with others in your class. What do you notice?

All of the triangles are the same size and shape (congruent).

8 Tape your triangle below.

178 one hundred seventy-eight **CLXXVIII** 2 × 89

ABOUT THE PAGE NUMBER Half of 180 is 90. What is half of 178?

Teaching Notes for LAB page 177

Students are asked to construct a triangle given two side lengths and the measure of the angle between them. Ask students to label the vertices of their triangles to match the information they're using. This will help them complete Problem 2. When they cut out the triangle and compare it with another student's, they know what to expect, but this step might help any student who misunderstood the instructions to spot an error. Since students tape the triangle to the bottom of the page, you'll also be able to compare it to the intended triangle shown in the answers.

Teaching Notes for LAB page 178

Students choose two angles of △*UVW* and a side between them to measure. Then they use those measurements to make a copy of the triangle. Again, it's helpful if students label the vertices as they draw each piece of the triangle.

Reflect and Summarize the Lesson

Write Math

Describe the steps you would use to draw a triangle if you knew the lengths of two sides and the measure of the angle between them. Draw a line segment the length of one side. Use a protractor to draw the angle with the vertex of the angle at one of the endpoints of the segment. Extend or shorten the second segment you drew until it is the correct length for the second side. Label the new endpoint and draw the third side.

Describe the steps you would use to draw a triangle if you knew the measure of two angles and the length of the side between them. Draw a segment the length of the side and label the endpoints. Use a protractor to draw the two known angles at the endpoints. Extend the two new sides until they intersect. Label the intersection as the third vertex.

Review Model

Refer students to Review Model: Constructing Triangles in the **Student Handbook** to see how to construct a triangle when you know the lengths of two sides and the measure of the angle between them, or the measure of two angles and the length of the side between them.

✔ Check for Understanding

Check students' drawings.

❶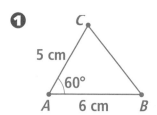

❷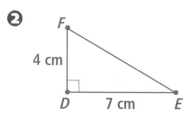

❸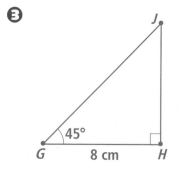

❹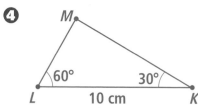

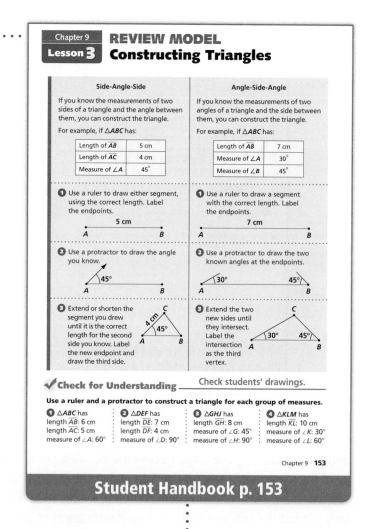

Student Handbook p. 153

Use with Lesson Activity Book pp. 177–178.

3 | Differentiated Instruction

Leveled Problem Solving

Zhu and Rob each draw a triangle.

❶ Basic Level

Both triangles have all of their sides congruent to sides in the other triangle. Are the triangles congruent? Explain. Yes; if you know the lengths of all 3 sides, a triangle can have only one shape, so they have to be congruent.

❷ On Level

Each triangle has a 3-inch side, a 2-inch side, and a 49° angle between them. Are they congruent? Explain. Yes, only one triangle can have 2 given sides and a given angle between them. They have to be congruent.

❸ Above Level

Each triangle has the same angles. Are they congruent? Explain. Maybe; triangles can have 3 congruent angles and not be congruent. These could be the same shape but different sizes.

Intervention

Activity Drawing Triangles

Give students verbal directions for drawing a triangle using side-angle-side. Tell them to draw a horizontal 5-inch segment. Then have them construct a 60° angle at one end and make the other arm of the triangle 4 inches. Have them complete the triangle. Ask: *Will everyone's triangle be congruent? How could we tell?* Yes; you could place the triangles on top of one another to check.

Practice

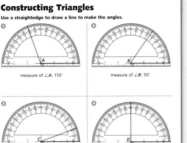

Practice P73

Extension

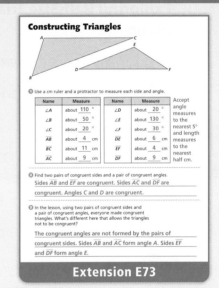

Extension E73

Spiral Review

Spiral Review Book page SR73 provides review of the following previously learned skills and concepts:

- using algebraic notation to continue patterns in input-output tables
- applying the problem solving strategy *act it out*

You may wish to have students work with partners to complete the page.

Spiral Review SR73

Extension Activity
Side, Side, Angle?

Challenge students to decide whether you will always know the shape of a triangle if you know 2 sides and the angle at the end of one of the sides. Ask them to demonstrate or explain why their answers are correct.

The triangles do not have to be congruent. $\overline{AB}$ and $\overline{DE}$, $\overline{AC}$ and $\overline{DF}$, ∠C and ∠F are

congruent, but the triangles are not.

Lesson 4 Constructing Similar Triangles

NCTM Standards 3, 4, 6, 8

Lesson Planner

STUDENT OBJECTIVES
- To draw and measure angles using a protractor
- To identify congruent angles and shapes and identify similar shapes
- To recognize that the sum of the angle measures in a triangle is 180°

1 Daily Activities (TG p. 761)

Open-Ended Problem Solving/Headline Story	Skills Practice and Review— Totaling Store Sales

2 Teach and Practice (TG pp. 762–765)

MATERIALS

Ⓐ **Exploring Half-Size Triangles**
(TG pp. 762–763)

Ⓑ **Making the Large Triangle** (TG p. 764)

Ⓒ **Recognizing Congruence and Similarity**
(TG p. 765)

- TR: Activity Masters, AM70–AM73
- protractors, centimeter rulers
- unlined $8\frac{1}{2} \times 11$ in. paper
- scissors
- 📖 LAB pp. 179–180
- 📖 SH p. 154

3 Differentiated Instruction (TG p. 766)

Leveled Problem Solving (TG p. 766)	Practice Book P74
Intervention Activity (TG p. 766)	Extension Book E74
Extension Activity (TG p. 766)	Spiral Review Book SR74

Lesson Notes

About the Lesson

In this lesson, students further investigate the relationships among angle measures in triangles, this time looking at congruent and similar triangles. The corresponding sides of similar figures have different lengths, but the corresponding angles must have the same measure. Students create a half-size copy of a triangle (by halving the side lengths), and observe that the angles are unchanged, seeing again that the lengths of the segments along the sides of the angle don't affect the measure of the angle itself. The fact that the measures of a triangle's interior angles must always sum to 180° also helps students see that the corresponding angles in similar triangles can't change in the same way that the side lengths change.

Use with Lesson Activity Book pp. 179–180.

Developing Mathematical Language

Vocabulary: similar

Figures of the same shape but not necessarily of the same size are called *similar*. A picture and an enlargement of that picture are *similar*. Students will discover that if two triangles have corresponding angles, the triangles must be *similar*. If two figures are congruent, they are also *similar*.

Review the term *similar* with students.

Beginning Remind students that *similar* means "having the same shape but not necessarily the same size." Have students draw a rectangle or a triangle. Then have them draw a *similar* shape.

Intermediate Draw several *similar* squares, rectangles, and triangles on the board. Have students say the word *similar* when you point to any shape *similar* to one of the squares. Repeat for the rectangles and triangles.

Advanced Discuss with students that when the word *similar* is used in everyday conversation, it has the more general meaning of "being alike in some way." Have students give examples of both uses of *similar*. For example, "Kyle's jacket is *similar* to Enrique's jacket because the jackets are the same color," and "A square and a smaller square are *similar*."

Open-Ended Problem Solving

Write this problem on the board and encourage students to use an organized strategy to solve.

 Headline Story

> In the U.S., we can write May 2, 2007 as 5/2/2007. In Europe and South America, the same date is written 2/5/2007. How many other dates in the year are unclear if you don't know where the writer is from?

Possible responses: There are 12 months, so you only have to worry about the first 12 days of each month. Except, if the number of the month and the date are the same, then it's written the same way. So, in each month there are eleven dates that can be misread. This gives 12 × 11, or 132 dates per year.

Skills Practice and Review

Totaling Store Sales

Describe the small store again, give sales figures (such as 317 or 574 items), and have students find total sales for the given weeks. Continue to encourage mental math, modeling, if necessary, by "checking" students' answers this way: "317 + 574, that's 800 . . . 880 . . . and 11 . . . 891." Some students may still feel the need to work out the answers on paper, so expect them to need a little more time to answer than they did in the previous lessons. For some students, confidence is the biggest issue, and it can be a great boost to them to point out that every mark they make on paper represents a computation that they've already done in their heads! Have students calculate sums only. Record the weekly sales and the totals each time.

small groups

20 MIN

Materials
- For each student: AM70–AM73, ruler, protractor

NCTM Standards 3, 4, 6, 8

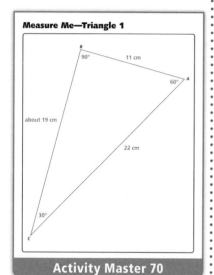

Measure Me—Triangle 1

Activity Master 70

Differentiated Instruction

Basic Level Students who still have difficulty with the protractor should be reassured that measurements are estimates (time, length, weight, and so on). Because the protractor is an especially unfamiliar measurement tool and requires careful placement, alignment, and reading, errors in angle measurement can still be expected. Proficiency does not happen all at once, but develops over a few years with experience. With that experience, students will also gradually learn to visualize and sketch the approximate size of common angles such as 30°, 45°, 60°, 90°, and 120°.

(A) Exploring Half-Size Triangles

Purpose To construct a triangle similar to a given triangle

Introduce Have students work in groups of three or four. Each student will need a copy of Explore: Shrinking a Triangle and one of the Measure Me Activity Masters. All students in a group should have the same version of the page (the same triangle). Before students start working, clarify that measurements are estimates and are not exact.

Task Have students complete Explore: Shrinking a Triangle in their groups. After students finish drawing their smaller triangles, have students compare the small and large triangles, discussing what changed and what remained the same. Clearly, the side lengths have changed. (Some students may recall the term *similar,* used to describe figures that have the same shape but not the same size. If not, remind them of this term.)

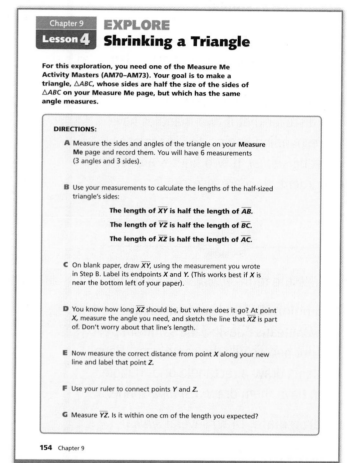

Chapter 9
Lesson 4 **EXPLORE**
Shrinking a Triangle

For this exploration, you need one of the Measure Me Activity Masters (AM70–AM73). Your goal is to make a triangle, △*ABC*, whose sides are half the size of the sides of △*ABC* on your Measure Me page, but which has the same angle measures.

DIRECTIONS:

A Measure the sides and angles of the triangle on your **Measure Me** page and record them. You will have 6 measurements (3 angles and 3 sides).

B Use your measurements to calculate the lengths of the half-sized triangle's sides:

The length of $\overline{XY}$ is half the length of $\overline{AB}$.
The length of $\overline{YZ}$ is half the length of $\overline{BC}$.
The length of $\overline{XZ}$ is half the length of $\overline{AC}$.

C On blank paper, draw $\overline{XY}$, using the measurement you wrote in Step B. Label its endpoints *X* and *Y*. (This works best if *X* is near the bottom left of your paper).

D You know how long $\overline{XZ}$ should be, but where does it go? At point *X*, measure the angle you need, and sketch the line that $\overline{XZ}$ is part of. Don't worry about that line's length.

E Now measure the correct distance from point *X* along your new line and label that point *Z*.

F Use your ruler to connect points *Y* and *Z*.

G Measure $\overline{YZ}$. Is it within one cm of the length you expected?

154 Chapter 9

Student Handbook p. 154

If students do not also report that the angle measures remain the same, draw their attention to the angles, and ask what they observe.

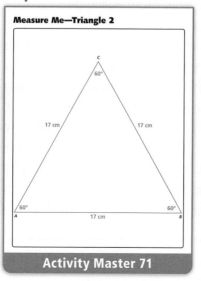

Measure Me—Triangle 2

Activity Master 71

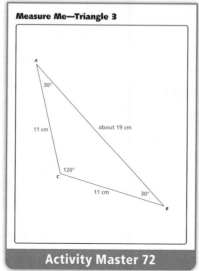

Measure Me—Triangle 3

Activity Master 72

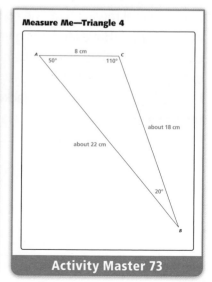

Measure Me—Triangle 4

Activity Master 73

Students often expect that when they cut the sides in half, the angles will become half-size as well. Challenge them to imagine what a "triangle" would look like if its angles were half the measure of their original triangle's angles. Suggest they consider their triangle as a concrete example, if necessary. Remind students that they know that the angles of the original (large) triangle, when put together, form a straight angle; then ask what the put-together angles would look like if all three were cut in half. It would be a right angle, not a straight angle, so the half-size angles couldn't make a triangle. Use this opportunity to help students conclude that the sum of the angle measures in a triangle must be 180°. Have them use their individual triangles to check this result.

Talk Math

❷ Within each group, are the small triangles congruent? yes

❷ Within each group, are the small triangles congruent to the original triangle? no

❷ How are the corresponding angles in the similar triangles (the original and one made with half length sides) related? The angles are the same.

Help students conclude the important characteristic of similar figures: while corresponding sides are not congruent, corresponding angles must be.

Differentiated Instruction

On Level/Above Level
Students who enjoy challenges and/or seem adept at using a protractor to draw angles may enjoy drawing their own large triangles from which to make half-size triangles. Challenge them to use the measurements of two angles and the side between them to construct the half-size triangle.

Materials

- For each student:
  AM70–AM73 from
  Activity A, scissors

NCTM Standards 3, 4, 6, 8

B Making the Large Triangle

Purpose To discover that a "half-size" triangle has one-fourth the area of the original triangle

Introduce Have each student cut out two copies of the small triangle constructed during Activity A. (To get the second copy, they can either cut two layers simultaneously or trace one cutout to make a new copy.)

Task Have students work together to find out how many copies of the small triangle fit within $\triangle ABC$ so that it is completely covered with no spaces or overlaps. Let students experiment until they are able to agree that four copies fit inside $\triangle ABC$.

Concept Alert

Students may be surprised to find that halving the dimensions of a triangle did not halve the area. In fact, halving the dimensions produced a triangle with one-fourth the area of the original triangle. One way to think about this relationship is to think about the opposite—doubling. What happens when you double the dimensions of a rectangle? Do you get double the area? No. You get four times the area.

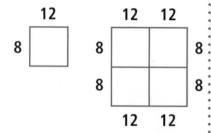

This happens because (2 × length) × (2 × width) = 4 (length × width).

💬 Talk Math

❷ What can you say about the side lengths of the original $\triangle ABC$ and the small triangle? Possible answer: The corresponding sides of the small triangle are half the length of the sides of $\triangle ABC$ (or the corresponding sides of $\triangle ABC$ are twice the length of the sides of the small triangle).

❷ What can you say about the area of the original $\triangle ABC$ compared to the area of the small triangle? Possible answer: The small triangle's area is $\frac{1}{4}$ the area of $\triangle ABC$ (or the area of $\triangle ABC$ is 4 times that of the small triangle).

Purpose To recognize similar figures and congruent angles

NCTM Standards 3, 4

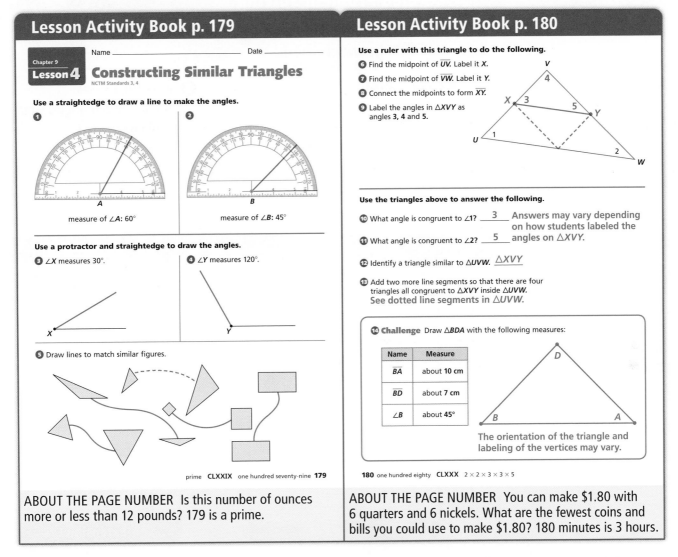

Lesson Activity Book p. 179

Name _____ Date _____

Chapter 9
Lesson 4 **Constructing Similar Triangles**
NCTM Standards 3, 4

Use a straightedge to draw a line to make the angles.

❶ (protractor) **A** — measure of ∠A: 60°

❷ (protractor) **B** — measure of ∠B: 45°

Use a protractor and straightedge to draw the angles.

❸ ∠X measures 30°.

❹ ∠Y measures 120°.

❺ Draw lines to match similar figures.

prime CLXXIX one hundred seventy-nine **179**

Lesson Activity Book p. 180

Use a ruler with this triangle to do the following.

❻ Find the midpoint of $\overline{UV}$. Label it **X**.

❼ Find the midpoint of $\overline{VW}$. Label it **Y**.

❽ Connect the midpoints to form $\overline{XY}$.

❾ Label the angles in △XVY as angles 3, 4 and 5.

Use the triangles above to answer the following.

❿ What angle is congruent to ∠1? __3__ Answers may vary depending on how students labeled the angles on △XVY.

⓫ What angle is congruent to ∠2? __5__

⓬ Identify a triangle similar to △UVW. __△XVY__

⓭ Add two more line segments so that there are four triangles all congruent to △XVY inside △UVW. See dotted line segments in △UVW.

⓮ **Challenge** Draw △BDA with the following measures:

Name	Measure
$\overline{BA}$	about **10 cm**
$\overline{BD}$	about **7 cm**
∠B	about **45°**

The orientation of the triangle and labeling of the vertices may vary.

180 one hundred eighty CLXXX $2 \times 2 \times 3 \times 3 \times 5$

ABOUT THE PAGE NUMBER Is this number of ounces more or less than 12 pounds? 179 is a prime.

ABOUT THE PAGE NUMBER You can make $1.80 with 6 quarters and 6 nickels. What are the fewest coins and bills you could use to make $1.80? 180 minutes is 3 hours.

Teaching Notes for LAB page 179

Have students work on the page independently.

Students draw angles in Problems 1–4. In Problem 5, they connect similar figures.

Teaching Notes for LAB page 180

Students connect the midpoints of the sides of a triangle to make smaller congruent triangles that are similar to triangle *UVW*. (If students say that they have forgotten what a *midpoint* is, ask them what they think it should mean. Most will either recall the meaning or figure it out from the parts of the word.) They also identify congruent angles in similar triangles.

Challenge Problem This problem asks students to create a triangle using three measurements like they did in **Lesson 9.3**, but without step-by-step instructions. You may want to remind them of their work in that lesson or refer them to the Review Model on SH p. 153.

Reflect and Summarize the Lesson

 Write Math **Suppose you draw two similar triangles. The one has sides with these lengths: 6 inches, 8 inches, and 10 inches. The other has sides with these lengths: 3 inches, 4 inches, and 5 inches. Explain how the measures of the angles and the areas of these two triangles are related.** The measures of the angles in the two triangles are approximately equal. The area of the larger triangle is 4 times the area of the smaller triangle.

Leveled Problem Solving

Estéban has cut out a triangle. He finds the midpoints of two sides and draws a line between them.

❶ Basic Level

How many times longer is a side of the original triangle than a side of the smaller triangle? Explain. 2 times; a midpoint cuts a line segment into 2 equal parts.

❷ On Level

Are the two triangles congruent? Explain. No; they have the same shape but not the same size.

❸ Above Level

Are the two triangles similar? Explain. Yes; corresponding angles are congruent.

Intervention

Activity Tangram Triangles

Display cutouts of the five triangles in a tangram set. Ask students whether they can name any pairs of congruent triangles and any pairs of similar triangles. For each pair named, have students justify the choice by reference to relative side lengths and relative angle measures. All 3 different triangles are similar isosceles right triangles. There are 2 pairs of congruent triangles (the largest and the smallest).

Practice

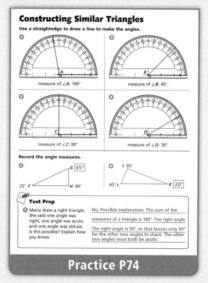

Practice P74

Extension

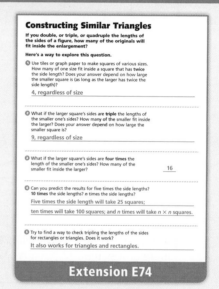

Extension E74

Spiral Review

Spiral Review Book page SR74 provides review of the following previously learned skills and concepts:

• generating equivalent fractions
• constructing a frequency graph

You may wish to have students work with partners to complete the page.

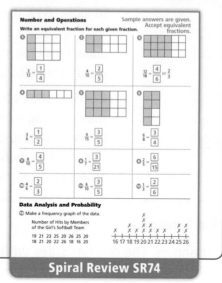

Spiral Review SR74

Extension Activity
Area and Tangram Triangles

Have pairs of students use or make two sets of tangram cutouts. Challenge them to use pieces to demonstrate (without using a ruler) that when you halve the side lengths of a triangle, the area of the triangle is divided by 4. Students can compare side lengths of the largest and smallest triangles using copies of the smallest triangle to see that the side lengths are in the ratio 2:1. They can cover the largest triangle with 4 copies of the smallest triangle, demonstrating that the areas are in the ratio 4:1.

Teacher's Notes 🍎

Daily Notes . . .

Quick Notes

More Ideas

Lesson 5 · Angles Formed by Intersecting Lines

NCTM Standards 1, 3, 4, 6, 7, 8, 9

STUDENT OBJECTIVES

STUDENT OBJECTIVES
- To find the measures of angles formed by two intersecting lines, given the measure of one of the angles
- To practice measuring and drawing angles using protractors

Lesson Planner

1 Daily Activities (TG p. 769)

| Open-Ended Problem Solving/Headline Story | Skills Practice and Review— Calculating Store Sales |

2 Teach and Practice (TG pp. 770–772)

	MATERIALS
Ⓐ Measuring Angles Formed by Intersecting Lines (TG p. 770)	• TR: Activity Masters, AM74–AM76
Ⓑ Determining Angle Measures (TG p. 771)	• protractors • compasses
Ⓒ Playing a Game: *First to 360°* (TG p. 772)	• small counters • 📖 LAB pp. 181–182 • 📖 SH p. 155, 165

3 Differentiated Instruction (TG p. 773)

Leveled Problem Solving (TG p. 773)	Practice Book P75
Intervention Activity (TG p. 773)	Extension Book E75
Extension Activity (TG p. 773)	Spiral Review Book SR75

Lesson Notes

About the Lesson

When two lines intersect, the four angles formed are related in predictable ways. Knowing these relationships allows us to puzzle out sizes of many angles when sizes of only a few angles are known.

Students will learn and use two facts about these angle relationships. When two lines intersect, the measures of any two angles that share a side sum to 180° and the measures of any two opposite angles

(see angles marked in green in the figures below) are equal.

Use with Lesson Activity Book pp. 181–182.

Developing Mathematical Language

Vocabulary: opposite angles

Angles described in this lesson as *opposite* angles are sometimes formally called *vertical* angles. If that terminology is important in your state or district, make sure students learn the term without confusing the idea with what it means for a line to be vertical. Used with angles, "vertical" does not in any way imply "straight up and down"; instead, the word *vertical* refers to the fact that the opposite angles touch only at their *vertex* (and share the same lines as sides). Because the word has such strong associations with a completely different meaning, we do not use it, and we recommend not using it.

Review the term *opposite angles* with students.

Beginning Discuss the meaning of the word *opposite* as being "at the other end or side." Use examples such as "the opposite side of the classroom" or "she sits at the opposite end of the table." Point out that *opposite angles* are on the opposite sides of an intersection point. Draw two intersecting lines on the board. Have students point to pairs of *opposite angles*.

Intermediate Have students draw two intersecting lines on paper. Then have them label a pair of *opposite angles*.

Advanced Have students explain how to locate pairs of *opposite angles*.

Open-Ended Problem Solving

Prompt students by asking questions such as, "Can the product be 36?" and "Does the product have to be a whole number?"

 Headline Story

> **A number between 4 and 5 is multiplied by a number between 7 and 8. What can you say about the product?**

Possible responses: The product is between 28 and 40. If the factors are both closer to the smaller numbers, the product is closer to 28; if the factors are both closer to the larger numbers, the product is closer to 40. If the factors are 4.8 and 7.5, the product is 36. If the factors are 4.5 and 7.5 (in the middle of the two ranges), the product is 33.75 (less than the middle of the product range, which is 34).

Skills Practice and Review

Calculating Store Sales

Describe the small store, and use three-digit numbers like 459 or 603 as the weekly sales figures, similar to the skills practice in the previous lesson. Have students compare sales from week to week, recording the size of the ups and downs, and the total sales for the year to date. Encourage and, if necessary, model mental math, but recognize that some students will need to use pencil and paper even if they can calculate mentally, and they may need extra time to answer. As always, keep the pace fast and lively.

individuals or pairs **15 MIN**

Materials
• For each student: protractor

NCTM Standards 1, 3, 4, 6, 8

Ⓐ **Measuring Angles Formed by Intersecting Lines**

Purpose To discover that opposite angles formed by intersecting lines are congruent

Introduce Students will each need a copy of Explore: Angles Formed by Intersecting Lines. Students need to remember that a straight angle measures 180° in order to complete Problem 1, which you may want to do as a class.

Task When students have worked through to at least Problem 4, discuss how they found their answers and the observations they made.

Talk Math

❓ How are you able to answer Problem 1 without using a protractor? Each pair of angles forms a straight angle and straight angles measure 180°.

❓ How does knowing that m∠F is approximately 60° help you to figure out the measure of ∠E? (Problem 3) ∠F and ∠E form a straight angle. So, the measure of ∠E is 180° − 60° = 120°.

❓ What does knowing that ∠F and ∠E and ∠F and ∠H form straight angles tell you about ∠E and ∠H (Problem 4)? Since ∠F is part of both straight angles, ∠E and ∠H must be congruent.

❓ Explain your answer to Problem 6. Possible answers: Both ∠E + ∠G and ∠E + ∠F form straight angles and the sum of their measures is 180°. Since ∠E is part of both pairs, ∠G must be congruent to ∠F.

Help students conclude that opposite angles formed by intersecting lines are congruent.

Practice Have students use their protractors to measure the angles and verify that opposite angles have the same measure.

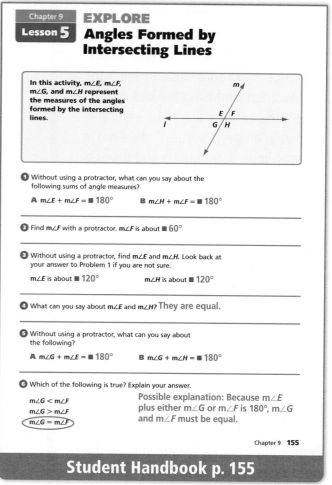

Student Handbook p. 155

Use with Lesson Activity Book pp. 181–182.

Purpose To use straight angles and opposite angles to find unknown angle measures

NCTM Standards 1, 3, 4, 7, 9

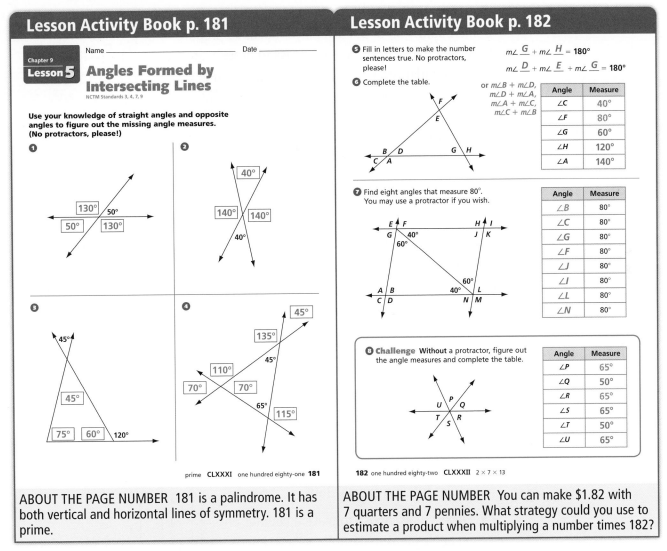

Lesson Activity Book p. 181

Chapter 9
Lesson 5 **Angles Formed by Intersecting Lines**
NCTM Standards 3, 4, 7, 9

Use your knowledge of straight angles and opposite angles to figure out the missing angle measures. (No protractors, please!)

① 130° 50° / 50° 130°

② 40° / 140° 140° / 40°

③ 45° / 45° / 75° 60° 120°

④ 45° / 135° / 45° / 110° / 70° 70° / 65° 115°

prime CLXXXI one hundred eighty-one **181**

ABOUT THE PAGE NUMBER 181 is a palindrome. It has both vertical and horizontal lines of symmetry. 181 is a prime.

Lesson Activity Book p. 182

⑤ Fill in letters to make the number sentences true. No protractors, please!

$m\angle \underline{G} + m\angle \underline{H} = 180°$
$m\angle \underline{D} + m\angle \underline{E} + m\angle \underline{G} = 180°$

⑥ Complete the table.

or $m\angle B + m\angle D$,
$m\angle D + m\angle A$,
$m\angle A + m\angle C$,
$m\angle C + m\angle B$

Angle	Measure
∠C	40°
∠F	80°
∠G	60°
∠H	120°
∠A	140°

⑦ Find eight angles that measure 80°. You may use a protractor if you wish.

Angle	Measure
∠B	80°
∠C	80°
∠G	80°
∠F	80°
∠J	80°
∠I	80°
∠L	80°
∠N	80°

⑧ **Challenge** Without a protractor, figure out the angle measures and complete the table.

Angle	Measure
∠P	65°
∠Q	50°
∠R	65°
∠S	65°
∠T	50°
∠U	65°

182 one hundred eighty-two CLXXXII 2 × 7 × 13

ABOUT THE PAGE NUMBER You can make $1.82 with 7 quarters and 7 pennies. What strategy could you use to estimate a product when multiplying a number times 182?

Teaching Notes for LAB page 181
This page provides students with opportunities to continue practicing the strategies they've learned for determining angle measures. They recognize that opposite angles are congruent and have equal measures.

Teaching Notes for LAB page 182
Students use angles given in diagrams and tables to determine unknown angle measures.

Challenge Problem This problem requires that students use computation as well as knowledge about opposite and straight angles to determine angle measures.

pairs | 15 MIN

C Playing a Game: *First to 360°*

Materials
- For each pair: AM74–AM76, small counters, compasses, protractors

NCTM Standards 1, 3, 6

Purpose To practice drawing angles of specific measures

Goal The object of the game, *First to 360°* is to be the first to fill in a circle with angles totaling 360°.

Prepare Materials Each pair of students will share one game board, AM74–AM76: *First to 360°* Game Board 1, 2, or 3. Each player needs to prepare a piece of paper by using a compass to draw a circle with one radius drawn in. Alternatively, you might draw this circle and duplicate it for students. They will share a collection of small counters and will each need a protractor. Depending on your class, you might demonstrate the game first for the class.

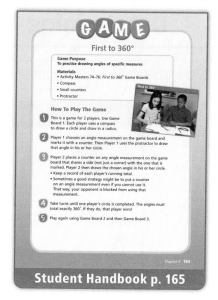

Student Handbook p. 165

Differentiated Instruction

Basic Level Use AM75: *First to 360°* Game Board 2.

On Level Use AM74: *First to 360°* Game Board 1.

Above Level Use AM76: *First to 360°* Game Board 3.

How to Play

❶ One player chooses an angle measurement on the game board and marks it with a counter. Then, the player uses a protractor to draw that angle into that player's circle.

❷ The other player must then place a counter on any angle measurement in a space on the game board that shares a side (not just a vertex) with one that is already marked. That player draws the chosen angle into that player's circle.

❸ Players may want to keep both their own and their partner's running totals of angle measures on their papers.

❹ Players continue alternating turns until one player's circle is completed with angles totaling exactly 360°.

❺ Players may choose to place a counter on an angle measurement that they cannot use (it is greater than the difference that remains in the circle) to block the other player from being able to use it.

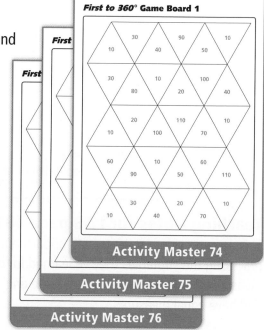

Extend Two alternate game boards are provided for various levels of challenge.

Activity Master 74

Activity Master 75

Activity Master 76

Reflect and Summarize the Lesson

 Write Math

Draw a pair of intersecting lines. Label the four angles formed at the intersection *A, B, C,* and *D.* Without using a protractor, name four pairs of angles that each form a straight angle. Then name an angle that has the same measure as angle *A.* For the intersecting lines shown here, ∠*A* and ∠*B,* ∠*B* and ∠*C,* ∠*C* and ∠*D,* and ∠*D* and ∠*A* each form a straight angle, and ∠*C* has the same measure as ∠*A.*

D/A
C/B

Use with Lesson Activity Book pp. 181–182.

Leveled Problem Solving

**George draws a triangle whose angles are 60°, 72°, and 48°.
Then he extends each side of the triangle.**

❶ Basic Level

Can he find an angle of 120° in his drawing? Explain. Yes; the angle outside the triangle on the same side of the 60° angle is 120° because the two angles add to a straight angle, 180°.

❷ On Level

Can he find an angle of 108° in his drawing? Explain. Yes; the angle outside the triangle on the same side of the 72° angle is 108° because the two angles add to a straight angle, 180°.

❸ Above Level

How many angles of different measures are in his drawing? Explain. 6; the angles of the triangle and another angle at each vertex: 120° (at 60°), 108° (72°), and 132° (48°).

Intervention

Activity Rotating Angles

Display two pencils, straws, or other thin straight sticks so that they intersect to form right angles. Ask students to describe what they see. Then rotate one of the sticks around the point of intersection, and ask students to describe pairs of angles that appear to be congruent and pairs that appear to add to 180°. Continue to rotate one stick, asking students to look for patterns. Opposite angles will always be congruent; angles on the same side of the stick will add to 180°.

Practice

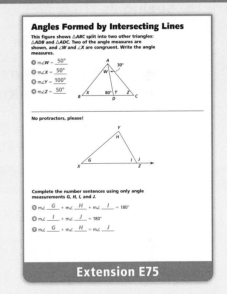

Practice P75

Extension

Angles Formed by Intersecting Lines

This figure shows △ABC split into two other triangles: △ADB and △ADC. Two of the angle measures are shown, and ∠W and ∠X are congruent. Write the angle measures.

❶ m∠W = 50°
❷ m∠X = 50°
❸ m∠Y = 100°
❹ m∠Z = 50°

No protractors, please!

Complete the number sentences using only angle measurements G, H, I, and J.

❺ m∠ _G_ + m∠ _H_ + m∠ _I_ = 180°
❻ m∠ _I_ + m∠ _J_ = 180°
❼ m∠ _G_ + m∠ _H_ = m∠ _J_

Extension E75

Spiral Review

Spiral Review Book page SR75 provides review of the following previously learned skills and concepts:

- converting measurement units
- given a context, deciding whether to ignore remainders or add them as fractions or decimals to the quotient, or round up

You may wish to have students work with partners to complete the page.

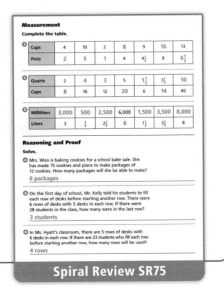

Spiral Review SR75

Extension Activity
Extended Triangles

Have students draw a triangle using 3 intersecting segments. Have them measure (or estimate) each angle inside the triangle. There are 9 angles outside the triangle whose sides are the intersecting lines. Challenge students to use the measures or estimates of the angles of the triangle to find the measures of each of the 9 angles. Then have them explain how they used the concepts of opposite angles and straight angles to solve the problem.

Lesson 6 Angles Formed by a Line Intersecting Parallel Lines

NCTM Standards 1, 3, 4, 6, 7, 8, 9

Lesson Planner

STUDENT OBJECTIVE
- To determine angle measures using relationships among angles formed when a line intersects a pair of parallel lines

1 Daily Activities (TG p. 775)

| Open-Ended Problem Solving/Headline Story | Skills Practice and Review— Adding and Subtracting Town Distances |

2 Teach and Practice (TG pp. 776–782)

Ⓐ **Seeing Zs** (TG p. 776)

Ⓑ **Angle Measures in Zs** (TG pp. 777–778)

Ⓒ **Finding Angle Measures When Measures of Other Angles Are Known** (TG p. 779)

Ⓓ **Reviewing Strategies for Finding Angle Measures** (TG pp. 780–781)

MATERIALS

- transparency of AM78 (optional)
- TR: Activity Masters, AM77–AM78
- protractors
- 📖 LAB pp. 183–184
- 📖 SH p. 156

3 Differentiated Instruction (TG p. 783)

Leveled Problem Solving (TG p. 783)	Practice Book P76
Intervention Activity (TG p. 783)	Extension Book E76
Extension Activity (TG p. 783)	Spiral Review Book SR76

Lesson Notes

About the Lesson

In this lesson, students will learn that the angles inside the "Z" shape (formed when a line intersects two parallel lines) are congruent. They will see *why* these angles are congruent, and they will use this result to figure out other angles.

About the Mathematics

In this lesson, we use the fact that two parallel lines will intersect a third line at the same angle. The lesson appeals to the intuitive notion of parallel—drawn in exactly the same direction. Just imagining a line "sliding," remaining parallel to itself, suggests that the lines will cross another line at the same angle. There is another way to show that these lines *must* intersect the third line at the same angle. It uses no more information than your students already know, but takes sophisticated reasoning that will make sense to you, but is generally hard for children: showing that all other situations are impossible, so what you are asserting is the only possibility.

(continued on page R4)

Use with Lesson Activity Book pp. 183–184.

Developing Mathematical Language

Vocabulary: ‖

Conveniently, the symbol for *parallel* looks like two vertical, parallel lines. Students need to recognize that *a*‖*b* means that line *a* is parallel to line *b*.

Review the term *parallel* (‖) with students.

Beginning Have students stretch one of their arms straight out. Then ask them to do the same with the other arm so that the arms are *parallel*. Have students repeat the activity placing the initial arm straight out in a different direction.

Intermediate Write the word *parallel* on the board. Ask students to find the *parallel* line segments in the word. Students should notice the three letter *l*s look like *parallel* line segments.

Advanced Have students identify *parallel* lines in familiar objects, such as books, windows, or desks.

Open-Ended Problem Solving

While students work on this headline story, encourage them to explain how they came up with their facts about the sketch.

 Headline Story

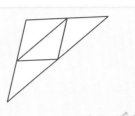

What can you say about the figures in this picture?

Possible responses: There are 5 triangles in the picture; four seem congruent and the fifth is similar, to each of them; its area is four times greater than the area of each of the smaller ones; each of its sides is twice as long as the corresponding side of a smaller triangle. There are three parallelograms in the picture and 3 trapezoids. It looks like there are 3 pairs of parallel segments.

 MENTAL MATH

Skills Practice and Review

Adding and Subtracting Town Distances

Tell students about some towns along the same highway, and give distances between successive towns. For example, Alphaville is 4.6 miles from Betaboro; Betaboro is 9.2 miles from Gammatown; and Gammatown is 3.9 miles from Delta City. A picture would be helpful.

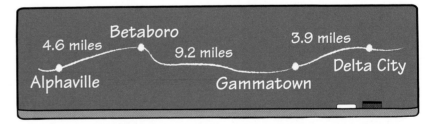

Ask students about the distances between various towns, or how much farther one town is from another. For example, Alphaville to Gammatown is 4.6 + 9.2, or 13.8 miles. Betaboro to Delta City is 9.2 + 3.9, or 13.1 miles. Which is farther: Alphaville to Gammatown, or Betaboro to Delta City? How much farther? Alphaville to Gammatown, 0.7 miles further.

Add distances as needed to give all students a chance to answer.

individuals
10 MIN

Ⓐ Seeing Zs

Materials
• For each student: AM77

NCTM Standards 3, 6, 8

Purpose To find hidden figures—first, trapezoids in a design; then, Zs in lines intersecting parallel lines

Introduce Ask students if they are familiar with "hidden picture" activities in which they search for "camouflaged" letters, numbers, or figures. Remind them that sometimes the lines or figures that are hidden are also turned, or rotated so that they are not always easy to see immediately. If your students are unfamiliar with the symbol for parallel, show it to them as they will see it on the Activity Master.

Task Hand out copies of AM77: Hidden Trapezoids and Zs and give students a few minutes to trace over as many trapezoids and Zs as they are able to find.

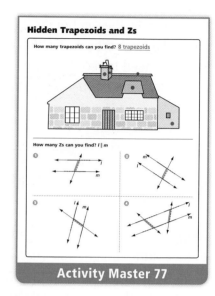

Activity Master 77

💬 Talk Math

❓ There are eight trapezoids in the picture at the top of the page. What did you notice about them? Possible answer: Even though they are all trapezoids, they don't all look the same because their angles and side lengths may be different.

❓ How can you describe a trapezoid? Possible answer: It is a quadrilateral that has one pair of parallel sides.

❓ How many Zs did you find in each figure at the bottom of the page and what do you notice about them? Possible answers: There are two Zs for each intersecting line that crosses a pair of parallel lines. Sometimes, they really don't look that much like the letter Z, because they're turned around or "stretched."

Angle Measures in Zs

Purpose To discover that when a line intersects a pair of parallel lines, the angles within the "elbows" of a Z are congruent

Introduce Project AM78: Drawing Another Intersecting Line or draw only lines *l* and *m* on the board (making sure that the angle marked *F* is a 60° angle). Label the angles *E, F, G,* and *H,* and write the corresponding angle measures as shown. This diagram is the same as on the page students completed in Explore: Angles Formed by Intersecting Lines in **Lesson 9.5.** Tell them that you will now construct another line that intersects line *l* and that they will find the angle measures.

Draw line *n* so that the angle marked *S* below measures 60°. (If you're drawing on the board, use a protractor or sketch *n* and tell students to imagine that line *n* is drawn at the same angle to line *l* as line *m*.) Label the four angles as shown below (*R, S, T,* and *U*) but don't indicate the measure of angle *S* yet.

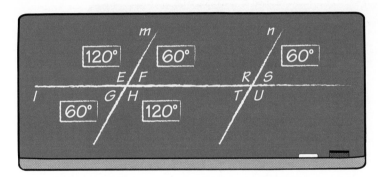

Help students see that lines *m* and *n* are parallel, and so they are at the same angle to line *l*. (You might gesture with your hands to show the parallel relationship between lines *m* and *n*. Also, see About the Math for another way to understand why these lines must cross line *l* at the same angle.) Show students how to record this kind of relationship by saying "*m* is parallel to *n*" as you write "*m* ∥ *n*" on the board. Ask students what the measure of angle *S* is, and mark it on your sketch as shown above.

Task Ask students to figure out the measures of the other angles **without using a protractor and to explain how they know the measures.** Their reasoning may depend on which angles they find first, but they must use their knowledge of straight angles and opposite angles. For example:

- m∠*T* is 60° because ∠*T* is opposite ∠*S*, which measures 60°.
- m∠*R* is 120° because ∠*S* measures 60°, and since the two angles form a straight angle, the sum of their angle measures must be 180°.
- m∠*U* is 120° because m∠*R* = 120° and opposite angles have the same measure (or because m∠*S* (or m∠*T*) is 60° and the two angles form a straight angle).

Now, draw a "Z" shape over parts of all three lines, as shown in yellow on p. 778. (If you are using the overhead projector, do this on a blank transparency placed on top of the original. If you are drawing on the board, you may want to

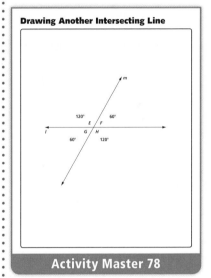

Drawing Another Intersecting Line

Activity Master 78

sketch a heavy chalk line near the lines, but not directly on them, since you will erase it later.) Ask students what they notice about the angles in the elbows of the Z (the ones labeled ∠F and ∠T). (Both angles have the same measure.)

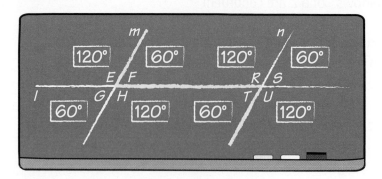

Remove this Z and draw the other one, as shown below in blue. Students should notice that the angles in the elbows of this Z also have the same measure.

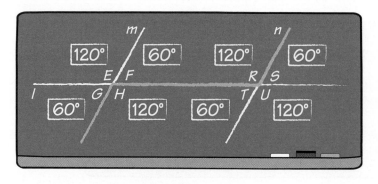

To test that this observation works for any line that crosses parallel lines—regardless of the angle—draw another pair of parallel lines (as accurately as you can), then draw a line crossing it at an unknown angle. Have a student suggest a measure for one of the angles. Label two congruent angles on the same side of the intersecting line (such as the ones labeled *F* and *S* below) with that value.

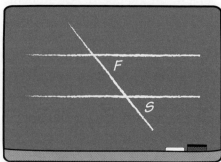

Now, have students use the straight angles and opposite angles to figure out the remaining measures. Have them find the Zs and see that the angles in the elbows are either both the suggested measure or both 180° minus that measure. Confirm that their observation will be true whenever two parallel lines have another line crossing them: the angles in the elbows of the Zs will have the same measure.

Use with Lesson Activity Book pp. 183–184.

Finding Angle Measures When Measures of Other Angles Are Known LAB pp. 183–184

individuals
15 MIN

NCTM Standards 1, 3, 4, 7, 8, 9

Purpose To use knowledge of straight angles, opposite angles, and corresponding angles formed by the intersection of a line with two parallel lines to find missing angle measures

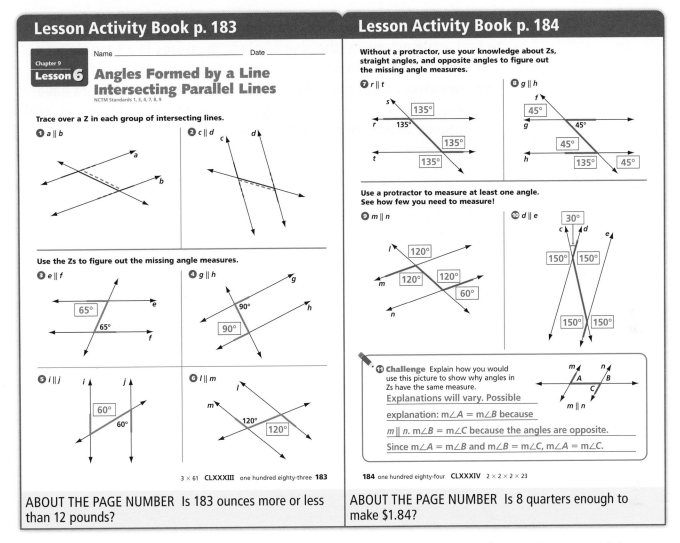

Teaching Notes for LAB page 183

Students should work independently on the page.

Although the directions ask students to find only one Z at the top of the page, they may find two in each figure. At the bottom of the page, students indicate that angles within Zs are congruent.

Teaching Notes for LAB page 184

Students use their knowledge of angles in Zs, of angles that form a straight angle, and of opposite angles to determine angle measures when a line intersects a pair of parallel lines. In Problems 9 and 10, students may use protractors, but are challenged to find angle measures by measuring as few angles as they can.

Challenge Problem This problem asks students to use their accumulated knowledge of angles to explain why two angles are congruent.

Use with Lesson Activity Book pp. 183–184.

Reviewing Strategies for Finding Angle Measures

Purpose To review strategies for finding angle measures when measures of other angles are known

Task To review the four facts learned thus far that students can use to find angle measures (the sum of angle measures in a triangle is 180°; the sum of the measures of angles that form a straight angle is 180°, opposite angles have the same measure; angles within Zs have the same measure), draw a picture, specify some angle measures, and ask students to determine the unknown angle measures. Ask for the explanations.

Talk Math

❓ If you know two of a triangle's angle measures, how can you find the third angle? Possible answer: The sum of the measures of all three angles is 180°, so you can subtract the sum of the two known angles from 180° to get the measure of the third angle.

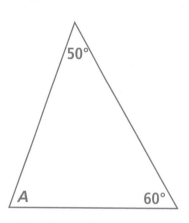

$$50° + 60° + m\angle A = 180°$$
$$m\angle A = 180° - 50° - 60°$$
$$m\angle A = 70°$$

❓ If you know the measure of one of two angles that make up a straight angle, how can you find the measure of the other one? Possible answer: The sum of the measures of all angles that make up a straight angle is 180°, so you can subtract the angle measure you know from 180°.

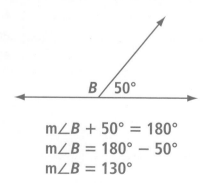

$$m\angle B + 50° = 180°$$
$$m\angle B = 180° - 50°$$
$$m\angle B = 130°$$

❷ If two lines intersect, what do you know about the angles that are opposite each other? Possible answer: Opposite angles are congruent and have equal measures.

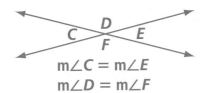

$$m\angle C = m\angle E$$
$$m\angle D = m\angle F$$

❷ When a line intersects a pair of parallel lines, what do you know about the angles within a Z? Possible answer: The angles inside a Z are congruent and have equal measures.

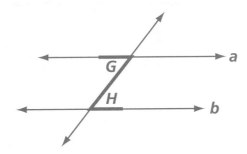

Extend Ask student who complete the challenge problem on LAB p. 184 to share an explanation. Draw the figure on the board so that all students may follow the explanation.

Write Math

Look at these three lines. Lines *a* and *b* are parallel and angle ∠D measures 60°. What are the measures of the other angles? Explain how you know. ∠F, ∠R, and ∠T measure 60°. ∠E, ∠G, ∠S, and ∠U measure 120°. Explanations will vary, but should indicate students' understanding of the angles formed by Zs, and the fact that straight angles are 180°.

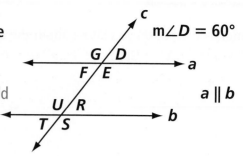

m∠D = 60°

a ∥ b

Review Model

Refer students to the Review Model: Angle Measures in the **Student Handbook** to see how to use their knowledge of straight angles, opposite angles and Zs to find the measures of angles.

✔ **Check for Understanding**

❶ m∠A = 70°

m∠B = 80°

m∠C = 30°

❷ m∠D = 120°

m∠E = 60°

m∠F = 120°

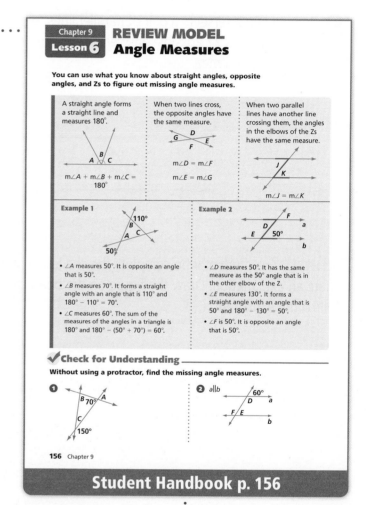

Student Handbook p. 156

Use with Lesson Activity Book pp. 183–184.

3 | Differentiated Instruction

Leveled Problem Solving

Lourdes draws a triangle. Then she draws a line parallel to the base through the top vertex. There are 6 angles in all.

❶ Basic Level
The triangle is equilateral. What are the measures of all the angles in her drawing? Explain. 5 angles measure 60°, 1 measures 180°; 3 angles of the triangle and, Z angles measure 60°, and the angle on top measures 180°.

❷ On Level
The triangle is isosceles. The base angles are 75°. What are the measures of the other angles? Explain. 30°, 75°, 180°; top angle of triangle measures 30°, Z angles measure 75°, straight angle at top measures 180°.

❸ Above Level
The triangle is isosceles right. What are the measures of all the angles? Explain. 90°, 45°, 180°; right angle measures 90°, Z angles measure 45°, straight angle measures 180°.

Intervention

Activity Cutting Parallel Lines

Show 2 parallel pencils, straws, or other thin straight sticks. Place a third stick so that it cuts through the other two. Ask students to estimate any one of the angles formed and then to name the measures of all other angles based on that estimate. Rotate the third stick and ask students to again estimate any angle and name the other based on the estimate. Have students justify their responses by referring to opposite angles, Z angles, or straight angles.

Practice

Practice P76

Extension

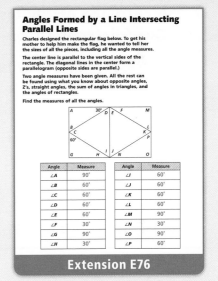

Extension E76

Extension Activity
More Than Two Lines

Have pairs of students draw 3 parallel line segments. Then have them draw a segment that crosses all 3 (but not at a right angle). Challenge them to measure any one angle with a protractor and to use that measure to find the measures of all other angles in the figure. For each angle whose measure they write, have them write an explanation of how they found the measure. Remind them to refer to opposite angles, angles within a Z, and straight angles.

Spiral Review

Spiral Review Book page SR76 provides review of the following previously learned skills and concepts:

- using the pattern of multiplying by 10
- applying the problem solving strategy *draw a picture*

You may wish to have students work with partners to complete the page.

Spiral Review SR76

Lesson 7 | Comparing and Classifying Quadrilaterals

NCTM Standards 3, 6, 7, 8, 9

Lesson Planner

STUDENT OBJECTIVES
- To classify quadrilaterals according to attributes
- To review definitions and properties of a parallelogram, a rectangle, and other special quadrilaterals

1 Daily Activities (TG p. 785)

Open-Ended Problem Solving/Headline Story	Skills Practice and Review—Adding and Subtracting Kite String Lengths

2 Teach and Practice (TG pp. 786–789)

A Exploring Parallelograms (TG pp. 786–787)

B Identifying Attributes of Other Quadrilaterals (TG pp. 787–788)

C Attributes of Quadrilaterals (TG p. 789)

MATERIALS
- transparency of AM79 (optional)
- LAB pp. 185–186
- SH p. 157–158

3 Differentiated Instruction (TG p. 791)

Leveled Problem Solving (TG p. 791)

Intervention Activity (TG p. 791)

Extension Activity (TG p. 791)

Science Connection (TG p. 734)

Practice Book P77

Extension Book E77

Spiral Review Book SR77

Lesson Notes

About the Lesson

Students have learned to identify polygons by their most specific names. As students mature mathematically, they progress from merely naming shapes to analyzing and comparing their properties, and recognizing family relationships. This lesson focuses on the classification of quadrilaterals according to four properties: the number of congruent angles, the number of congruent sides, the number of pairs of parallel sides, and the number of right angles. By looking at properties, students see that a square has all the properties needed to qualify as a rhombus, a rectangle, and as a parallelogram. Students also investigate the lines of symmetry in various quadrilaterals.

About the Mathematics

Parallelograms are defined as having two pairs of *parallel* sides—the idea of parallel sides is built directly into the name of these figures—but students will already have noticed that the parallel sides are also *congruent*. However, the mere presence of a pair of parallel sides is not enough to explain why these sides are congruent: a trapezoid has one pair of parallel sides, but they are *not* congruent.

Developing Mathematical Language

Vocabulary: quadrilateral, kite, parallelogram, rectangle, rhombus, square, trapezoid

Students who had *Think Math!* in previous years already have some experience with most of these terms—but they may not have previously sorted them. Also, *kite* and *rhombus* may be new terms. Students are being asked to identify all of the categories that a particular quadrilateral belongs to, so they need to understand relationships such as the following. All *rectangles* are *parallelograms*. A *parallelogram* is a *rectangle* only if all of its angles are congruent. All *rhombuses* are *parallelograms*. If a *rhombus* is also a *rectangle*, it's a *square*.

Review the terms *quadrilateral, kite, trapezoid, parallelogram, rhombus, rectangle,* and *square* with students.

Beginning Relate the specific names of the different types of *quadrilaterals* to the names of different family members. The term *quadrilateral* is similar to a last name. Both Jaime Gomez and Carlos Gomez are members of the Gomez family, but they are different people.

Intermediate Remind students that a *quadrilateral* means "a polygon with four sides." Point out that the *quad-* part of the word means "four."

Advanced Have students verbally compare any two types of *quadrilaterals,* such as *trapezoid* and *rhombus.*

Open-Ended Problem Solving

After writing the story on the board, prompt students by asking questions such as, "Does the sum have to be a whole number?" and "Do the addends have to be whole numbers?"

 Headline Story

> **A number between 4 and 5 is added to a number between 7 and 8. What can you say about the sum?**

Possible responses: The sum is between 11 and 13. If the two numbers are both closer to the smaller numbers (4 and 7), the sum is 11 and a little more. ($4.1 + 7.05 = 11.15$; $4.45 + 7.4 = 11.85$) If the two numbers are both closer to the larger numbers (5 and 8), the sum is 12 and a little more. ($4.51 + 7.55 = 12.06$; $4.9 + 7.96 = 12.86$) If one number is closer to the smaller number, and the other is closer to the larger, then the sum is closer to 12 than to 11 or 13. ($4.1 + 7.55 = 11.65$; $4.51 + 7.4 = 11.94$) The sum could be exactly 12. ($7.55 + 4.45 = 12$)

Skills Practice and Review

Adding and Subtracting Kite String Lengths

Tell students a story about a child flying a kite. Have the child in the story let out string, or wind some in, and have your students tell how far the kite is from the child. Record the answers so students can keep track of the current distance. For example:

To get the kite in the air, the child used 5 meters of string. She let out 3.6 meters of string to make the kite go higher. How far is the kite from the child? 8.6 meters She let out another 7.8 meters of string to let it go really high. How far away is the kite now? 16.4 meters It was a bit too windy when the kite was so high, so she wound 2.7 meters of string back onto the spool. How far away is the kite now? 13.7 meters

pairs or whole class

20 MIN

NCTM Standards 3, 6, 8

A Exploring Parallelograms

Purpose To identify the attributes of polygons, specifically parallelograms

Introduce Students will each need a copy of Explore: Sorting Figures. Let them work in pairs to identify the rules that govern whether or not the figures in Problem 1 belong to Set P. The point of the exploration is not for students to assign a name to the figures in Set P. Rather, they need to consider the *attributes* that all the figures in Set P share, but that the other figures do not have. Students may identify the figures in Set P as parallelograms; instead of responding yes or no to this, encourage them to write the necessary rules without using the names of any polygons (although they may use the word *polygon* in one of the rules.)

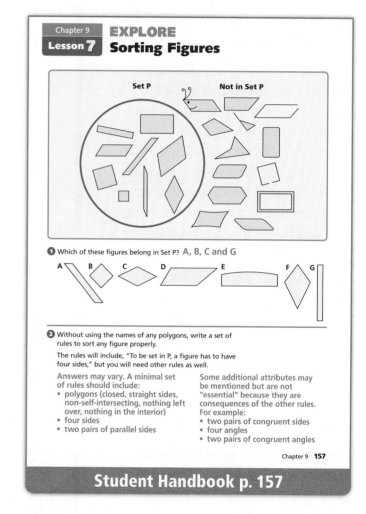

Student Handbook p. 157

Task Discuss with students their answers to Problem 2 on the Explore to verify that **they have noticed the important attributes.** Record their rules on the board for everyone to see, and then identify these three *essential attributes*—a minimal set of rules without which figures that aren't in Set P might be included.

- polygons
- four sides
- two pairs of parallel sides

If students don't mention all of these essential attributes, have students generate them by pointing out figures that are not part of the set but match the other two rules. Have students check that these three attributes are enough to correctly identify all the figures as belonging to Set P or not. Ask students if they know a name that applies to all the figures in the set, but to none of the figures that aren't in the set. If students don't suggest *parallelogram,* remind them of this word.

Often, students also list other properties that they notice, but that aren't true for all the figures in Set P. For example, students may say things like "It can have right angles." About any such rules that students list, ask if the rule fits *all* the figures in Set P or only some. Does it fit *any* figures outside of Set P? Use the attributes named by students that fit only *some* of the figures in Set P (whether or not these attributes also describe other figures) to name special parallelograms. For example, "Its sides can be perpendicular to each other, and if they are, then it is a special parallelogram called a rectangle."

Ask students to show parallelograms in Set P that have additional properties, for example, a right angle, or all congruent sides. Ask them for a specific name for these parallelograms.

 Talk Math

❷ What name describes all parallelograms that have a right angle? rectangle

❷ What name describes all parallelograms that have four congruent angles? rectangle

❷ What name describes all parallelograms that have four congruent sides? rhombus

❷ What name describes all parallelograms have four congruent sides and four congruent angles? square

 B ## Identifying Attributes of Other Quadrilaterals

whole class 15 MIN

Materials
• For the teacher: transparency of AM79 (optional)

NCTM Standards 3, 8

Purpose To identify attributes of special cases of parallelograms and of other quadrilaterals—trapezoids and kites, and to be exposed to the notation used to indicate congruent sides and angles

Introduce Show students a transparency of AM79: Classifying Quadrilaterals or draw the quadrilaterals on the board, and point out the notation for congruent sides and angles. Tell students that congruent parts, whether sides or angles, have the same marks.

Task Have students look at **Figure 1 and identify all the congruent parts**—two pairs of congruent sides (noted by one tic mark or two), and two pairs of congruent angles (noted by one arc or two) of the parallelogram. Point out the notation that shows the pairs of parallel sides, and then ask students to supply as many names for the figure as they can. (If they forget to mention *polygon* and *quadrilateral,* you can remind them that these terms apply as well.) By identifying congruent parts students will list many of the properties of a parallelogram. (Parallelograms have two pairs of congruent sides and two pairs of congruent angles.)

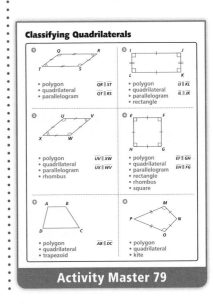
Activity Master 79

Concept Alert

A kite, just like a parallelogram, has two pairs of congruent sides. Unlike in a parallelogram, in a kite congruent sides share a vertex.

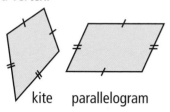

kite   parallelogram

Some people consider a rhombus a special case of a kite because is has two pairs of congruent sides that share vertices. However, some people don't consider a rhombus a special case of a kite because it has two pairs of parallel sides.

A trapezoid may have one pair of non-parallel, congruent sides.

Possible Discussion

This figure fits the rules for a kite discussed in the activity, but it's not a kite! So we need to add one more rule: kites can't "cave in" on themselves. (The formal term is *concave;* kites must be *convex.*) Tell students that this year, they'll only be working with quadrilaterals that don't "cave in" like this. They can remember that kites actually look like toy kites.

Go through Figures 2–4 in a similar manner. Explain symbols for the right angles. Ask students what else they can say about a right angle and the sides that form it. The angle is 90°; the sides are perpendicular. Ask students for the special name for each of the figures, and for a property each has that is not shared by all the parallelograms. Figure 2 has four congruent angles, but not four congruent sides, and is a rectangle; Figure 3 has four congruent sides, but not four congruent angles, and is a rhombus; and Figure 4 has both properties so it is a rhombus and a rectangle, and thus is a square.

Figures 5 and 6 are not parallelograms, but they do have special names: *trapezoid* and *kite.* The markings and notes about parallel lines give the essential attributes of these figures. Ask students to list the attributes they can see.

Trapezoid	Kite
Quadrilateral (four-sided polygon)	Quadrilateral (four-sided polygon)
One pair of parallel sides	No parallel sides
	Two pairs of congruent sides

Finally, review what a line of symmetry is. In past years, students may have used mirrors to find lines of symmetry. When a mirror is placed on a line of symmetry, the part of the figure on the paper and its reflection in the mirror together form an image of the original figure. Have students show lines of symmetry (if any) for each of the Figures 1–6.

Show a line of symmetry on one of the figures (the trapezoid and the parallelogram that is neither a rhombus nor rectangle have no lines of symmetry) and point out that the corresponding parts on either side are congruent.

Use with Lesson Activity Book pp. 185–186.

Attributes of Quadrilaterals LAB pp. 185–186

  15 MIN

Purpose To recognize attributes of congruity, parallelism, and perpendicularity of sides and angles in quadrilaterals

NCTM Standards 3, 7, 9

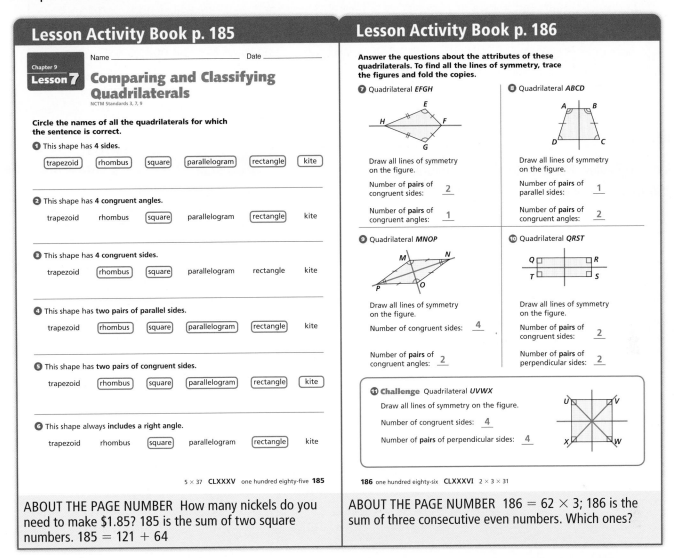

Lesson Activity Book p. 185

Name _____ Date _____

Chapter 9
Lesson 7 **Comparing and Classifying Quadrilaterals**
NCTM Standards 3, 7, 9

Circle the names of all the quadrilaterals for which the sentence is correct.

❶ This shape has **4 sides.**

(trapezoid) (rhombus) (square) (parallelogram) (rectangle) (kite)

❷ This shape has **4 congruent angles.**

trapezoid   rhombus   (square)   parallelogram   (rectangle)   kite

❸ This shape has **4 congruent sides.**

trapezoid   (rhombus)   (square)   parallelogram   rectangle   kite

❹ This shape has **two pairs of parallel sides.**

trapezoid   (rhombus)   (square)   (parallelogram)   (rectangle)   kite

❺ This shape has **two pairs of congruent sides.**

trapezoid   (rhombus)   (square)   (parallelogram)   (rectangle)   (kite)

❻ This shape always **includes a right angle.**

trapezoid   rhombus   (square)   parallelogram   (rectangle)   kite

5 × 37   **CLXXXV**   one hundred eighty-five **185**

Lesson Activity Book p. 186

Answer the questions about the attributes of these quadrilaterals. To find all the lines of symmetry, trace the figures and fold the copies.

❼ Quadrilateral **EFGH**

Draw all lines of symmetry on the figure.

Number of **pairs** of congruent sides: _2_

Number of **pairs** of congruent angles: _1_

❽ Quadrilateral **ABCD**

Draw all lines of symmetry on the figure.

Number of **pairs** of parallel sides: _1_

Number of **pairs** of congruent angles: _2_

❾ Quadrilateral **MNOP**

Draw all lines of symmetry on the figure.

Number of congruent sides: _4_

Number of **pairs** of congruent angles: _2_

❿ Quadrilateral **QRST**

Draw all lines of symmetry on the figure.

Number of **pairs** of congruent sides: _2_

Number of **pairs** of perpendicular sides: _2_

⓫ **Challenge** Quadrilateral **UVWX**

Draw all lines of symmetry on the figure.

Number of congruent sides: _4_

Number of **pairs** of perpendicular sides: _4_

186 one hundred eighty-six   **CLXXXVI**   2 × 3 × 31

ABOUT THE PAGE NUMBER How many nickels do you need to make $1.85? 185 is the sum of two square numbers. 185 = 121 + 64

ABOUT THE PAGE NUMBER 186 = 62 × 3; 186 is the sum of three consecutive even numbers. Which ones?

Teaching Notes for LAB page 185
You might suggest that students use a copy of Review Model: Classifying Quadrilaterals in the **Student Handbook,** to assist them with the LAB page. They may work on the page independently or with partners.

Teaching Notes for LAB page 186
Students should trace the quadrilaterals and fold the tracings to confirm that they have found lines of symmetry.

Challenge Problem This problem asks students about the square, which has the most lines of symmetry among the quadrilaterals.

Use with Lesson Activity Book pp. 185–186.

Chapter 9 • Lesson 7 **789**

Reflect and Summarize the Lesson

Write Math

Look at the figures in Problems 8 and 9 on LAB page 186. How are Quadrilateral *ABCD* and Quadrilateral *MNOP* alike? How are they different? What special quadrilateral names apply to these two quadrilaterals? Possible answers: Both quadrilaterals are polygons and have 2 pairs of congruent angles; Quadrilateral *ABCD* has 1 pair of parallel sides and 1 line of symmetry; Quadrilateral *MNOP* has 4 congruent sides and 2 lines of symmetry. Quadrilateral *ABCD* is a polygon, a quadrilateral, and a trapezoid. Quadrilateral *MNOP* is a polygon, a quadrilateral, a parallelogram, and a rhombus.

Review Model ⋯⋯⋯⋯⋯⋯⋯⋯⋯⋯⋯⋯⋯⋯⋯⋯

Refer students to Review Model: Classifying Quadrilaterals in the *Student Handbook* to see how to classify quadrilaterals.

✔ Check for Understanding

❶ polygon, quadrilateral, parallelogram, rhombus

❷ polygon, quadrilateral, trapezoid

❸ polygon, quadrilateral, parallelogram, rectangle

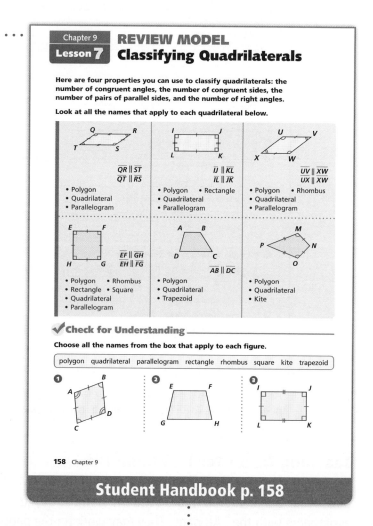

Student Handbook p. 158

3 | Differentiated Instruction

Leveled Problem Solving

Alyssa is drawing a quadrilateral.

❶ Basic Level
All the angles are right angles. What type of quadrilateral could it be? Explain. Any rectangle, including a square; all rectangles have 4 right angles.

❷ On Level
The figure has two pairs of parallel sides. What type of quadrilateral could it be? Explain. Any parallelogram; all parallelograms have 2 pairs of parallel sides.

❸ Above Level
The figure has at least one right angle. What type of quadrilateral could it be? Explain. You cannot tell; it could be any quadrilateral with a right angle.

Intervention	Practice	Extension

Activity A Family Tree

Draw a Quadrilateral Family Tree.

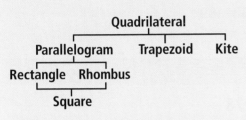

Discuss with students how, as you move down the tree, figures possess attributes of those above them plus new ones.

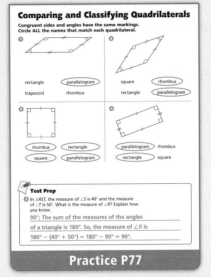

Practice P77

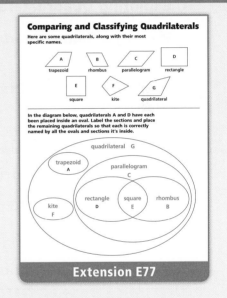

Extension E77

Spiral Review

Spiral Review Book page SR77 provides review of the following previously learned skills and concepts:

- classifying triangles
- identifying a number based on characteristics of its digits

You may wish to have students work with partners to complete the page.

Spiral Review SR77

Extension Activity
Family Members?

Display the Quadrilateral Family Tree from the Intervention Activity.

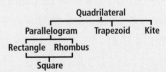

Ask students to write an explanation of why trapezoids and kites each have their own branch. Parallelograms have 2 pairs of parallel sides. But trapezoids have only one pair of parallel sides, and kites might have no pairs of parallel sides.

Lesson 8 Investigating Quadrilaterals

NCTM Standards 3, 4, 6, 7, 8, 9

Lesson Planner

STUDENT OBJECTIVES
- To identify quadrilaterals by their attributes
- To see that the sum of the angle measures in a quadrilateral is 360°

1 Daily Activities (TG p. 793)

Open-Ended Problem Solving/Headline Story	Skills Practice and Review—Making a Triangle

2 Teach and Practice (TG pp. 794–797)

	MATERIALS
Ⓐ **Exploring Quadrilaterals** (TG pp. 794–795)	• TR: Activity Masters, AM80–AM86
Ⓑ **Playing a Game: *Quadrilateral Name Game*** (TG p. 796)	• protractors
Ⓒ **Angle Measures in Quadrilaterals** (TG p. 797)	• 📖 LAB pp. 187–188 • 📖 SH pp. 158–159

3 Differentiated Instruction (TG p. 798)

Leveled Problem Solving (TG p. 798)	**Practice Book P78**
Intervention Activity (TG p. 798)	**Extension Book E78**
Extension Activity (TG p. 798)	**Spiral Review Book SR78**
Cross Curricular Connection (TG p. 734)	

Lesson Notes

About the Lesson

In **Lesson 9.1** of the chapter, students put together the cut-off corners of triangles to see that the angles always combined to make a straight angle. They later found that this meant the angle measures in a triangle must have a sum of 180°. This lesson echoes that work as students cut off the corners of quadrilaterals and put them together, completely filling the space around a single vertex and finding that the measures of the angles must sum to 360°.

About the Mathematics

In this lesson, students informally investigate the sum of the measures of the internal angles of a

quadrilateral. The discovery that the sum of the measures of the angles of any (convex) quadrilateral is 360° follows from the fact that a quadrilateral can be split along one diagonal into two triangles and that the sum of the measures of the angles in a triangle is 180°.

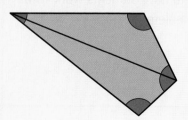

Use with Lesson Activity Book pp. 187–188.

Developing Mathematical Language

Vocabulary: concave, convex

Students can experience the differences between *concave* and *convex* polygons by examining sets of each type. As they look at a group of triangles and parallelograms, for example, you may want to point out that all polygons of these types must be *convex* because it is impossible to draw a line segment from one vertex to another that goes outside the figure when all angles inside must be less than 180°.

Concave polygons, on the other hand, always have at least one angle that is greater than 180°. A line segment that is outside the figure can always be drawn between two vertices. *Concave* figures are also identifiable from their "cave-like" hollowed-out section that actually gives them their name.

Review the terms *concave* and *convex* with students.

Beginning Discuss the word *cave* with students. If possible, show a picture of a cave. Help students see the relationship between the shape of a cave and a *concave* figure.

Intermediate Have students draw and label different *convex* and *concave* figures on the board.

Advanced Ask students to explain how a *concave* figure is like a cave.

Open-Ended Problem Solving

Write the following story on the board and ask students to be prepared to justify all their responses.

 Headline Story

A > B and C > D. Compare the following:

A + C ● B + D

A + D ● B + C

A − D ● B − C

What else could you say?

Possible responses: A + C must be greater than B + D, because the sum of two larger numbers is greater than the sum of two smaller numbers. A + D can be equal to, greater than, or less than B + C, because it depends on what numbers you use for A, B, C, and D. A − D is greater than B − C, because A − D is subtracting a smaller number from a larger number, and B − C is subtracting a larger number from a smaller one. Both A − D and B − C could be less than 0. You can't tell whether A − C or B − D is larger.

Skills Practice and Review

Making a Triangle

Have a student provide an angle measure. Say another angle measure and ask students whether the two angles given could be angles in a triangle. If so (because their sum is less than 180°), ask what the measure of the third angle would be. If these angles couldn't be two angles of a triangle, ask why not. Try to keep the activity fast-paced and lively.

whole class — 20 MIN

Materials
- For each student:
  AM80–AM84,
  protractors

NCTM Standards 3, 6, 8

A Exploring Quadrilaterals

Purpose To discover that the sum of the angles in a quadrilateral is 360°

Introduce This activity is very similar to the triangle exploration in the first lesson of the chapter, except that now students begin with a quadrilateral. Each student will need Explore: An Experiment with a Quadrilateral and one of the Quadrilateral Experiment Activity Masters (AM80–AM84). Take a minute to point out that none of the quadrilaterals "cave in" like ◁ does. (The results they will observe in this lesson only hold true for convex quadrilaterals.) Draw or show some other examples like the ones on the next page and ask students whether they cave in. (The red areas show where the concave polygons cave in.)

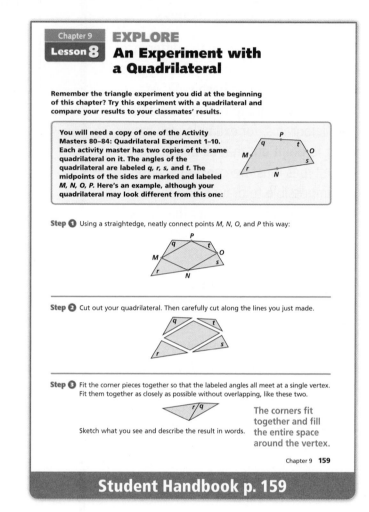

Chapter 9 **EXPLORE**
Lesson 8 **An Experiment with a Quadrilateral**

Remember the triangle experiment you did at the beginning of this chapter? Try this experiment with a quadrilateral and compare your results to your classmates' results.

You will need a copy of one of the Activity Masters 80–84: Quadrilateral Experiment 1–10. Each activity master has two copies of the same quadrilateral on it. The angles of the quadrilateral are labeled q, r, s, and t. The midpoints of the sides are marked and labeled M, N, O, P. Here's an example, although your quadrilateral may look different from this one:

Step ❶ Using a straightedge, neatly connect points M, N, O, and P this way:

Step ❷ Cut out your quadrilateral. Then carefully cut along the lines you just made.

Step ❸ Fit the corner pieces together so that the labeled angles all meet at a single vertex. Fit them together as closely as possible without overlapping, like these two.

Sketch what you see and describe the result in words.

The corners fit together and fill the entire space around the vertex.

Chapter 9 **159**

Student Handbook p. 159

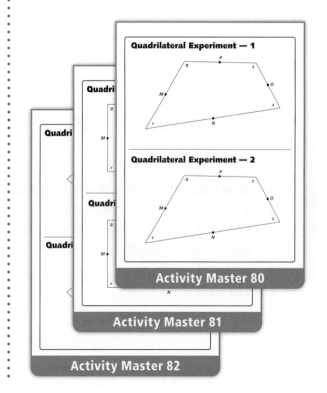

Quadrilateral Experiment — 1

Quadrilateral Experiment — 2

Activity Master 80

Activity Master 81

Activity Master 82

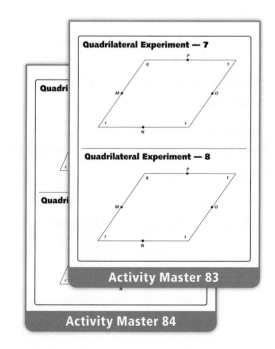

Quadrilateral Experiment — 7

Quadrilateral Experiment — 8

Activity Master 83

Activity Master 84

Use with Lesson Activity Book pp. 187–188.

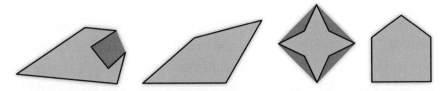

Task Have students cut out one of the quadrilaterals on their activity master and use it to perform the experiment suggested on the **Explore page.** In the final step of the experiment, students fit the cut-off corners together in any of these (and other) ways, showing that the four angles of the quadrilateral, together, completely surround a point (fill 360°).

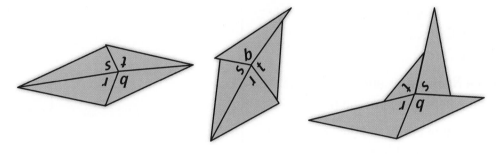

Have students display their arrangements alongside the other (still intact) quadrilateral, and let them see the various arrangements their classmates made. (To allow other observations to be made, be sure the unused center pieces from the cut quadrilaterals are visible.)

💬 Talk Math

❷ What do you notice happens when you put all four angles of a quadrilateral together? Possible response: They completely fill in all the space around one point (or vertex).

❷ If your quadrilateral is a rectangle, how can that help you know the sum of the angle measures? Possible response: Each right angle measures 90°, so four of them would equal 360°.

❷ What do you now know about the sum of the angle measures in all these quadrilaterals? Possible response: The sum of the measures of all angles in a quadrilateral is 360°.

Practice Give students additional experience with this new fact by having the class measure three of the angles in a quadrilateral and calculate the fourth. If your students are measuring angles with ease, you can also have them measure all the angles in their quadrilaterals and verify that the sum of the measures is (close to) 360°. Measurement error may cause the sum to be off by a few degrees.

Possible Discussion

As students complete the experiment in Activity A and see what their classmates have done, they may notice and be surprised that the unused center polygon appears to be a parallelogram—in fact, some students may have rearranged the four triangles to form a congruent parallelogram. They can't prove that the polygon is a parallelogram yet—that will take more geometry in later grades—but the observation is correct. Encourage any observations the students make, and enjoy the surprises. The only observation essential for this lesson, however, is that placing the four triangles so that the labeled corners meet at a single point fills up all the space around that point—that is, the sum of the angle measures is 360°.

B **Playing a Game:** *Quadrilateral Name Game*

Purpose To match quadrilaterals with their attributes

Goal To be the first player in the group to run out of Attribute Cards

Prepare the Materials Each group of 3 to 5 students will need a set of Name Cards (cut from AM85) and a set of Attribute Cards (cut from AM86). For best results, photocopy each page onto card stock, possibly with all Name Cards in one color and all Attribute Cards on another color. Save these cards for use in the Skills Practice and Review activity in **Lesson 9.9.** Let students use the **Lesson 9.7** Review Model: Classifying Quadrilaterals, SH p. 158, as needed to identify or confirm correct plays.

How to Play

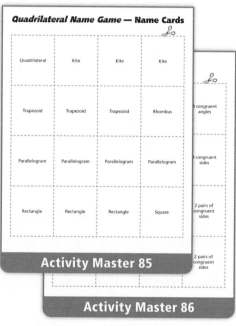

1 For 3 or 5 players, remove the Attribute Card that says "4 sides" and play with only 15 Attribute Cards. For 4 players, use all 16 Attribute Cards.

2 Mix up the Name Cards and stack them face down where everyone can reach.

3 Mix the Attribute Cards and deal them, face down, so each player has the same number of cards. Players may look at their cards.

4 Turn the top Name Card face up so everyone can see.

5 Players take turns discarding Attribute Cards that match the displayed Name Card until no one has a card with attributes that match the specified polygon. Players may not repeat Attribute Cards for a specific polygon.

6 The other players should challenge a play that they think is incorrect, using the **Lesson 9.7** Review Model: Classifying Quadrilaterals, SH p. 158, to resolve conflicts as needed. *Remember: Only one card with a particular attribute can be played for the same Name Card.*

For example, if the current Name Card is "Square," a player may play "4 congruent angles," "2 pairs of parallel sides," "4 congruent sides," "4 sides," "2 pairs of perpendicular sides," or "2 pairs of congruent sides." A player may not play "0 pairs of parallel sides" or "1 pair of parallel sides."

7 If a player can't play a new attribute, the player says, "Pass."

8 Play continues until no one can play a new attribute.

9 The last player to play a card removes all the played cards to a discard pile and then turns over a new Name Card. Play begins again with the player to his or her left.

10 The first player to run out of cards wins.

C # Angle Measures in Quadrilaterals LAB pp. 187–188

Purpose To use knowledge about angles to figure out various angle measures in quadrilaterals

NCTM Standards 3, 4, 6, 7, 9

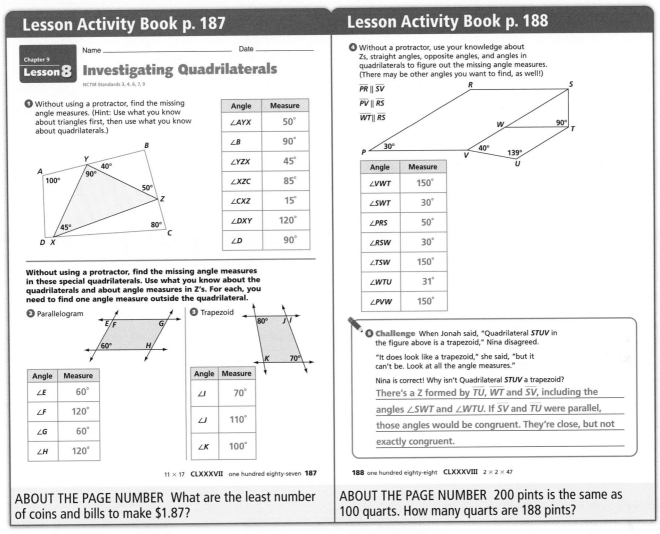

Lesson Activity Book p. 187

Name _____ Date _____

Chapter 9
Lesson **8** **Investigating Quadrilaterals**
NCTM Standards 3, 4, 6, 7, 9

❶ Without using a protractor, find the missing angle measures. (Hint: Use what you know about triangles first, then use what you know about quadrilaterals.)

Angle	Measure
∠AYX	50°
∠B	90°
∠YZX	45°
∠XZC	85°
∠CXZ	15°
∠DXY	120°
∠D	90°

Without using a protractor, find the missing angle measures in these special quadrilaterals. Use what you know about the quadrilaterals and about angle measures in Z's. For each, you need to find one angle measure outside the quadrilateral.

❷ Parallelogram

Angle	Measure
∠E	60°
∠F	120°
∠G	60°
∠H	120°

❸ Trapezoid

Angle	Measure
∠I	70°
∠J	110°
∠K	100°

11 × 17   **CLXXXVII**   one hundred eighty-seven **187**

Lesson Activity Book p. 188

❹ Without a protractor, use your knowledge about Zs, straight angles, opposite angles, and angles in quadrilaterals to figure out the missing angle measures. (There may be other angles you want to find, as well!)

$\overline{PR} \parallel \overline{SV}$
$\overline{PV} \parallel \overline{RS}$
$\overline{WT} \parallel \overline{RS}$

Angle	Measure
∠VWT	150°
∠SWT	30°
∠PRS	50°
∠RSW	30°
∠TSW	150°
∠WTU	31°
∠PVW	150°

✎ ❺ **Challenge** When Jonah said, "Quadrilateral *STUV* in the figure above is a trapezoid," Nina disagreed.

"It does look like a trapezoid," she said, "but it can't be. Look at all the angle measures."

Nina is correct! Why isn't Quadrilateral *STUV* a trapezoid?

There's a Z formed by $\overline{TU}$, $\overline{WT}$ and $\overline{SV}$, including the angles ∠SWT and ∠WTU. If $\overline{SV}$ and $\overline{TU}$ were parallel, those angles would be congruent. They're close, but not exactly congruent.

188 one hundred eighty-eight   **CLXXXVIII**   2 × 2 × 47

ABOUT THE PAGE NUMBER What are the least number of coins and bills to make $1.87?

ABOUT THE PAGE NUMBER 200 pints is the same as 100 quarts. How many quarts are 188 pints?

Teaching Notes for LAB page 187

Have students complete the page independently.

The page asks students to use what they know about sums of angle measures in triangles and quadrilaterals, and about the measures of angles in a Z formation to figure out the measures of missing angles.

If students aren't familiar with the labeling of angles used on the LAB page, explain that the middle letter indicates the vertex of the angle and the first and third letter indicate the endpoints of the segments that form the angle at that vertex.

Teaching Notes for LAB page 188

This page has a more complex figure. Students use their knowledge of angles to find missing angle measures.

Challenge Problem This problem requires students to recognize that two angles can appear congruent, but in fact, not be. Students must use their knowledge about angles to show that the two lines are not parallel.

Reflect and Summarize the Lesson

 Write Math

Look at Problem 1 on LAB page 187. Explain how you found the measure of ∠AYX, the measure of ∠B, and the measure of ∠D. Possible answers: ∠AYB is a straight angle so the sum of the measures of the three angles at the vertex *Y* must equal 180°: 180° − 40° = 140°; 140° − 90° = 50°. The sum of the measures of the angles of a triangle is 180º, so to find the measure of ∠B, subtract the sum of the other two angles from 180°; 180° − (40° + 50°) = 90°. The measure of the sum of the angles of a quadrilateral is 360°, so to find the measure of ∠D, subtract the sum of the other three angles from 360°. 360° − (100° + 90° + 80°) = 90°.

Use with Lesson Activity Book pp. 187–188.

Chapter 9 • Lesson 8 **797**

3 | Differentiated Instruction

Jaleel is drawing a quadrilateral.

❶ Basic Level

All the angle measures are the same. What type of quadrilateral could it be? Explain. Any rectangle, including a square; all rectangles have 4 right angles.

❷ On Level

The figure has 3 angles that measure 67°, 110°, and 117°. What is the measure of the remaining angle? Explain. 66°; $360 - (67 + 110 + 117) = 66$

❸ Above Level

Three of the angles measure 50°, 130°, and 130°. What type of quadrilateral could it be? Explain. any non-rectangular parallelogram or an isosceles trapezoid

---

Intervention	Practice	Extension

Activity Quadrilateral Angle Measures

Display a variety of quadrilaterals on the board. Ask a volunteer to draw a diagonal on any figure. Discuss what is shown: A diagonal creates 2 triangles; the sum of the measures of any triangle's angles is 180°; the sum of the measures of the quadrilateral's angles must be twice that, or 360°. Repeat with the other quadrilaterals. Ask students to summarize what they have seen.

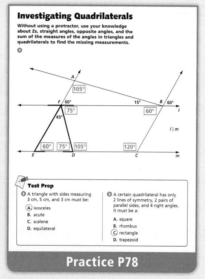

Practice P78

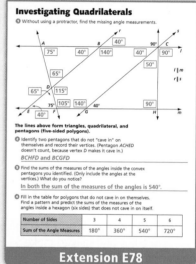

Extension E78

Spiral Review

Spiral Review Book page SR78 provides review of the following previously learned skills and concepts:

- practicing adding and subtracting decimals
- estimating and finding weight in customary units

You may wish to have students work with partners to complete the page.

Spiral Review SR78

Extension Activity
Consecutive Angle Sums

Ask pairs of students to draw several parallelograms, including rectangles, rhombuses, and squares. In each figure, have students consecutively name the angles *A, B, C,* and *D.* Then have them measure each angle and find the sum of the measures of pairs of consecutive angles. Ask students to describe what they notice about the sums. Elicit that in any parallelogram, the sum of the measures any pair of consecutive angles is 180°.

Teacher's Notes 🍎

Daily Notes . . .

Quick Notes

More Ideas

Problem Solving Strategy and Test Prep

NCTM Standards 1, 2, 3, 4, 6, 7, 8, 10

Lesson Planner

STUDENT OBJECTIVES
- To practice the problem solving strategy *look for a pattern*
- To articulate the steps and strategies used to solve problems
- To prepare for standardized tests

Problem Solving Strategy:
Solve a Simpler Problem (TG pp. 801–802, 804–805)

MATERIALS

(A) **Discussing the Problem Solving Strategy: Look for a Pattern** (TG p. 801)

(B) **Solving Problems by Applying the Strategy** (TG p. 802)

- TR: Activity Masters, AM85–AM86
- protractors
- 📖 LAB p. 189
- 📖 SH pp. 160–161

Problem Solving Test Prep (TG p. 803)

(C) **Getting Ready for Standardized Tests** (TG p. 803)

- 📖 LAB p. 190

Lesson Notes

About Problem Solving

Problem Solving Strategy: Look for a Pattern

The problem solving strategy *look for a pattern* has been used by students in this chapter to look for relationships among triangles and among quadrilaterals and to find unknown angle measures using knowledge of opposite angles, straight angles, and Zs that occur when two parallel lines are crossed by a third line.

This lesson also assesses students' understanding of attributes of triangles and quadrilaterals and of the angles and sides that form these polygons.

Skills Practice and Review

Attributes of Quadrilaterals

Make two separate piles of the Name Cards and Attribute Cards from the *Quadrilateral Name Game.* Shuffle the Name Cards and place them in a pile face down. Remove any duplicate cards from the Attribute Cards and place them in another pile face down. Turn over the top Name Card, read the name of the shape and ask students to name as many attributes as they can. Remind students that they should name the number or pairs of parallel and/or perpendicular sides, and congruent sides or angles. At your choice, you may use the Attribute Cards by turning them over one at a time and asking students to respond *yes* or *no* if the shape has the attribute described on the card.

Use with Lesson Activity Book pp. 189–190.

Problem Solving Strategy

A Discussing the Problem Solving Strategy: Look for a Pattern

whole class · 15 MIN

NCTM Standards 1, 2, 6, 7, 8, 10

Purpose To share strategies for solving problems and focus on the problem solving strategy, *look for a pattern*

Introduce Remind students that throughout this chapter they have been looking for patterns to find relationships among triangles and among quadrilaterals and to find unknown angle measures using knowledge of opposite angles, straight angles, and Zs that occur when two parallel lines are crossed by a third line. Then record the following problem and pattern of counters on the board.

Problem Sophia used counters to make the first four figures in this pattern. How many counters will she need in all to continue this pattern until she has six figures in all?

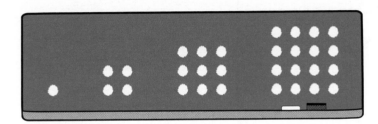

Share Have students share their strategies for solving the problem. Students will likely look for a pattern in the four figures shown and use the pattern to determine the fifth and sixth figures. Be sure they understand that the problem asks for the total number of counters they will need, not just the counters they need to make the sixth figure.

💬 Talk Math

❷ What pattern do you see in the first four figures of this pattern?
Possible answer: Each figure is an array with 1 more row and 1 more column that the figure before it.

❷ How many counters will Sophia need to make the fifth figure? 5×5, or 25 counters

❷ How many counters will she need to make the sixth figure? 6×6, or 36 counters

❷ How can you find the number of counters Sophia needs to make the first six figures in the pattern? I need to find the sum of the counters in each figure in the pattern: $1 + 4 + 9 + 16 + 25 + 36 = 91$. So, she needs 91 counters.

Solving Problems by Applying the Strategy LAB p. 189

individuals or whole class — 15 MIN

NCTM standards 2, 3, 4, 6, 8, 10

Purpose To practice the problem solving strategy, *look for a pattern*

Teaching Notes for LAB page 189

Have students look at the first problem on LAB page 189 and, if available, put up a transparency of the page. Give students a few minutes to work on the first problem. Then have students share their strategies for solving the problem. If students don't suggest it, show how to use the problem solving strategy *look for a pattern* to solve the problem. You may want to ask questions like these to guide the discussion.

Read to Understand

What do you know from reading the problem? Kurt used green and white triangles to make a figure with 24 rows.

What do you need to find out? how many small triangles there are

Plan

How can you solve this problem? You can look for a pattern in the total number of triangles in one row, in two rows, in three rows, and so on.

Solve

How many total triangles are in the first few rows? In one row there is 1 triangle; in two rows there are 1 + 3, or 4, triangles; in three rows there are 1 + 3 + 5, or 9, triangles.

Do you see a pattern in these numbers? 1, 4, and 9 are all square numbers.

How many total triangles are in 24 rows? in *n* rows? There are 24 × 24, or 576, triangles in 24 rows. There are *n* × *n* triangles in *n* rows.

Check

Look back at the original problem. Does your answer make sense? How do you know?

Allow students to work independently or with a partner to solve the other problem on the page. When most students have completed the page, you might ask a couple of students to describe the specific strategies they used to solve the problem.

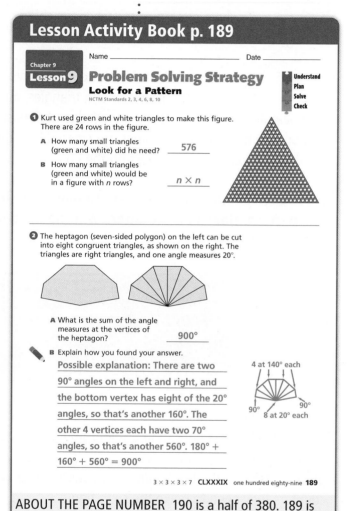

Lesson Activity Book p. 189

Name _____ Date _____

Chapter 9 — Lesson 9

Problem Solving Strategy
Look for a Pattern
NCTM Standards 2, 3, 4, 6, 8, 10

Understand / Plan / Solve / Check

1 Kurt used green and white triangles to make this figure. There are 24 rows in the figure.

A How many small triangles (green and white) did he need? 576

B How many small triangles (green and white) would be in a figure with *n* rows? *n* × *n*

2 The heptagon (seven-sided polygon) on the left can be cut into eight congruent triangles, as shown on the right. The triangles are right triangles, and one angle measures 20°.

A What is the sum of the angle measures at the vertices of the heptagon? 900°

B Explain how you found your answer.
Possible explanation: There are two 90° angles on the left and right, and the bottom vertex has eight of the 20° angles, so that's another 160°. The other 4 vertices each have two 70° angles, so that's another 560°. 180° + 160° + 560° = 900°

4 at 140° each
90° 90°
8 at 20° each

3 × 3 × 3 × 7 **CLXXXIX** one hundred eighty-nine **189**

ABOUT THE PAGE NUMBER 190 is a half of 380. 189 is a half of what?

Reflect and Summarize the Lesson

Write Math

How does looking for a pattern help you solve a problem like the one above?
Possible answer: If you can find a pattern, it simplifies your work. You don't need to count the triangles in each row and then find the sum for all those numbers.

802   **Chapter 9 • Lesson 9**

Use with Lesson Activity Book pp. 189–190.

C **Getting Ready for Standardized Tests** LAB p. 190

 individuals 20 MIN

NCTM Standards 1, 2, 3, 5, 6, 8, 10

Purpose To prepare students for standardized tests

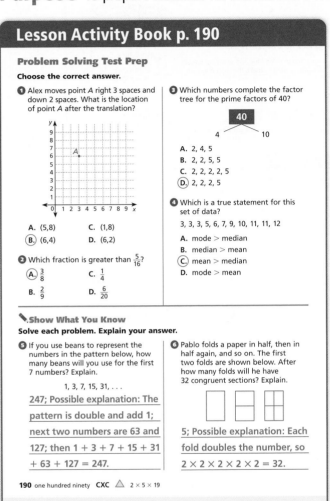

Teaching Notes for LAB page 190

The test items on this page are written in the same style and arranged in the same format as those on many state assessments. The page is cumulative and is designed for students to apply a variety of problem solving strategies including *draw a picture, write an equation,* and *look for a pattern.* Have students share the strategies they use.

The Item Analysis Chart below highlights one of the possible strategies that may be used for each item.

Show What You Know

Written Response

Direct students' attention to Problems 5 and 6. Explain that they must decide how to solve the problems. Then have students write an explanation of how they know their answer is correct. To provide more space for students to communicate their thinking about these problems, you may wish to have them write their responses and explanations on a separate sheet of paper. Use the Scoring Rubric below to evaluate their understanding.

Item Analysis Chart

Item	Strategy
1	Act it out, draw a picture
2	Write an equation
3	Draw a picture or diagram, guess and check
4	Write an equation
5	Look for a pattern
6	Look for a pattern

Scoring Rubric

2	• Demonstrates complete understanding of the problem and chooses an appropriate strategy to determine the solution
1	• Demonstrates a partial understanding of the problem and chooses a strategy that does not lead to a complete and accurate solution
0	• Demonstrates little understanding of the problem and shows little evidence of using any strategy to determine a solution

Review Model...

Refer students to the Problem Solving Strategy Review Model: Look for a Pattern in the *Student Handbook* pp. 160–161 to review a model of the four steps they can use with the problem solving strategy, *look for a pattern*.

Additional problem solving practice is also provided.

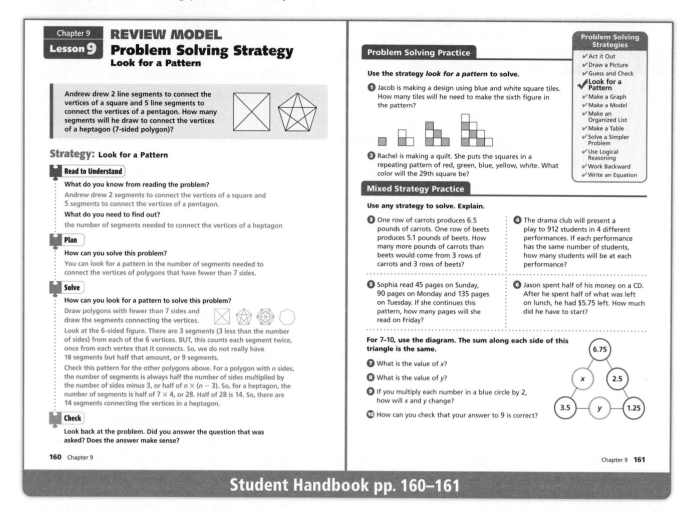

Student Handbook pp. 160–161

Task Have students read the problem at the top of the Review Model page. Then discuss.

💬 Talk Math

❓ **How does drawing the polygons help you solve this problem?** Possible answer: When you draw the figures you can see the number of lines you need to connect the vertices.

❓ **Look at the diagram of the pentagon with segments drawn. Describe a pattern that allows you to figure out how many segments to draw between vertices?** Possible answer: I multiplied the number of vertices (5) by the number of vertices minus 3 (5 − 3 = 2) and then took half the product. 5 × 2 = 10 and half of 10 is 5.

1 21 tiles: you can *look for a pattern* in the number of tiles used to make the four figures in the pattern: 1, 3, 6, 10. A pattern is add 2 to the first number to get the second ($1 + 2 = 3$), add 3 to the second number to get the third ($3 + 3 = 6$), add 4 to the third number to get the fourth ($6 + 4 = 10$). So, for the fifth number, add 5 to the fourth number ($10 + 5 = 15$) and for the sixth number, add 6 to the fifth number ($15 + 6 = 21$). So, there will be 21 tiles in the sixth figure.

2 yellow: you can *look for a pattern.* These colors repeat: red, green, blue, yellow, white. Red squares will be 1st, 6th, 11th, 16th, 21st, 26th. So, the 27th will be green, the 28th will be blue, and the 29th will be yellow.

3 4.2 more pounds of carrots; you can *write multiplication equations* to find how many pounds of carrots and beets were produced: $3 \times 6.6 = 19.5$; $3 \times 5.1 = 15.3$. Then, subtract to find how many more pounds of carrots than beets were produced: $19.5 - 15.3 = 4.2$

4 228 students; you can *write a division equation* to solve: $912 \div 4 = 228$

5 270 pages; you can *look for a pattern* in the number of pages she read each day: 45, 90, 135. Each day she read 45 more pages than the day before. So, on Wednesday she read $135 + 45$, or 180, pages; on Thursday she read $180 + 45$, or 225, pages; on Friday she read $225 + 45$, or 270, pages.

6 $23.00; you can *work backward* to find how much Jason had to start. Multiply $5.75 by 2 to find how much he had before he bought lunch: $\$5.75 \times 2 = \$11.50$. Then multiply by 2 again to find how much he had before he spent half on a CD: $\$11.50 \times 2 = \$23.00$.

7 0.25; you can *write equations* to find both *x* and *y.* First add the numbers on the side of the triangle with all blue circles to find what the total should be: $6.75 + 2.5 + 1.25 = 10.5$. Then to find *x*, subtract 6.75 and 3.5 from 10.5: $10.5 - 6.75 = 3.75$; $3.75 - 3.5 = 0.25$.

8 5.75; to find *y* subtract 3.5 and 1.25 from 10.5: $10.5 - 3.5 = 7.00$; $7.00 - 1.25 = 5.75$.

9 *x* and *y* will also be multiplied by 2. *x* will be 0.5; *y* will be 11.5; You can *use logical reasoning.* If you multiply each number along the side with the three blue circles by 2, then the sum will also be multiplied by 2. The same will be true for the other two sides, so both *x* and *y* will also have to be multiplied by 2.

10 Possible answer: I can multiply all the numbers by 2 and see if the three sums along the sides of the triangle are the same: $13.5 + 5.0 + 2.5 = 21.0$; $13.5 + 0.5 + 7.0 = 21.0$; $7.0 + 11.5 + 2.5 = 21.0$. The sums are the same. I can *use logical reasoning* to help me decide how to check the answer to #9.

Attributes of Two-Dimensional Figures

NCTM Standards 1, 2, 3, 4, 6, 7, 9, 10

Purpose To provide students with an opportunity to demonstrate understanding of Chapter 9 concepts and skills

MATERIALS
- LAB pp. 191–192
- Chapter 9 Test (Assessment Guide pp. AG81–AG82)

Chapter 9 Learning Goals and Assessment Options

These learning goals are assessed in many ways throughout the chapter. The chart below correlates each learning goal to specific formal and informal assessment options.

	Learning Goals	Lesson Number	Snapshot Assessment	Chapter Review Item Numbers	Chapter Test Item Numbers
				LAB pp. 191–192	Assessment Guide pp. AG81–AG82
9-A	Draw, classify, and determine the measures of angles by measuring with a protractor and by using known measures of other angles	9.1–9.6	1, 2	1–5, 7, 8	1–4, 6
9-B	Classify triangles, construct triangles, and recognize similar triangles	9.2–9.4	3, 5	6, 9	5, 7
9-C	Classify quadrilaterals, determine the sum of the measures of the angles of a quadrilateral, and sketch lines of symmetry in a quadrilateral	9.7, 9.8	4, 6, 9	10–13	8–11
9-D	Apply problem solving strategies such as *look for a pattern* to solve problems	9.9	10	14	12

Snapshot Assessment

whole class 10 MIN

The following Mental Math and Quick Write questions and tasks provide a quick, informal assessment of students' understanding of Chapter 9 concepts, skills, and problem solving strategies.

Mental Math This oral assessment uses mental math strategies and can be used for the whole class.

① The sum of the interior angles of every triangle, no matter the shape or size, is always _____°. 180°
When two lines intersect, the opposite angles are _____. congruent, or the same measure
(Learning Goal 9-A)

② Find the missing angle of the triangle, then tell if the missing angle is acute, right, or obtuse:
- 40°, 60° 80° acute
- 45°, 45° 90° right
- 50°, 30° 100° obtuse
- 62°, 38° 80° acute
(Learning Goal 9-A)

③ Similar triangles have the same _____, but may have different _____. shape; sizes
(Learning Goal 9-B)

④ The sum of the interior angles of every quadrilateral, no matter the size or shape, is always _____°. 360°
(Learning Goal 9-C)

5 Is the statement always true, sometimes true, or false? If false, why?

- Every equilateral triangle has 3 congruent sides. always true
- An equilateral triangle could have a right angle. False; there must be 3 congruent angles, 60° each.
- A scalene triangle has angle measures of 30°, 60°, and 90°. sometimes true
- A right triangle has two 90° angles. False; there can only be one right angle in a triangle.

(Learning Goal 9-B)

6 What is the most exact name for:

- a parallelogram with 90° angles? rectangle
- a parallelogram with 4 congruent sides? rhombus
- a parallelogram with 4 congruent sides and 4 congruent angles? square
- Name the polygon which has exactly 2 pair of parallel sides. Parallelogram; caution against rectangle, rhombus, and square since they require more than just 2 pair of parallel sides.

(Learning Goal 9-C)

Quick Write This informal written assessment can be administered to small groups or the whole class. Read each question and have the students record responses on their write-on boards. Encourage students to listen and think about the questions before responding.

For 7 and 8, students will need a protractor.

7 Using a protractor, create intersecting line segments by following the directions:

- Draw a horizontal line segment, label it *m*
- Now draw another line segment which intersects line segment *m* at a 60° angle; label it *n*
- Label the 2 largest angles *A* and *C*. Label the 2 smaller angles *B* and *D* Check student drawings.
- If angle *B* has a measure of 60°, what is the measure of opposite angle *D*? 60°
- What do you know about opposite angles *A* and *C*? same measure, 120°
- What is the sum of the measures angles *A* and *B*? 180°

(Learning Goal 9-A)

8 Using a protractor, draw the following triangle:

- It has a base of 2 inches.
- An adjacent leg is 2 inches.
- The long side (hypotenuse) is about 3 inches.
- The angle opposite the longest side is 90°.
- One of the other angles is 45°. Check student drawings for reasonable accuracy.
- What is the measure of the third angle? 45°
- Is it acute, right, or obtuse? acute
- Classify the triangle you made. right, isosceles

(Learning Goal 9-B)

9 Draw the figure, then draw all lines of symmetry. How many lines of symmetry are in a:

- rectangle? 2 • rhombus? 2 • parallelogram? 0, 2, or 4

Check lines of symmetry in student drawings.

- A parallelogram has 3 interior angles labeled with 110°, 110°, and 70° degrees. What is the measure of the 4th angle? Explain how you know. 70°; Possible explanation: Opposite angles in a parallelogram are congruent.

(Learning Goal 9-C)

10 Determine the missing values in this record of a basketball tournament:

Round	1	2	3	4	5	6
Number of teams	128	64	32	16	8	4

How many rounds are necessary to determine a final winner? 7

(Learning Goal 9-D)

Chapter 9 ASSESSMENT

Formal Assessment

Chapter Review/Assessment The Chapter 9 Review/Assessment on *Lesson Activity Book* pages 191–192 assesses students' understanding of two-dimensional figures and problem solving. Students should be able to complete these pages independently.

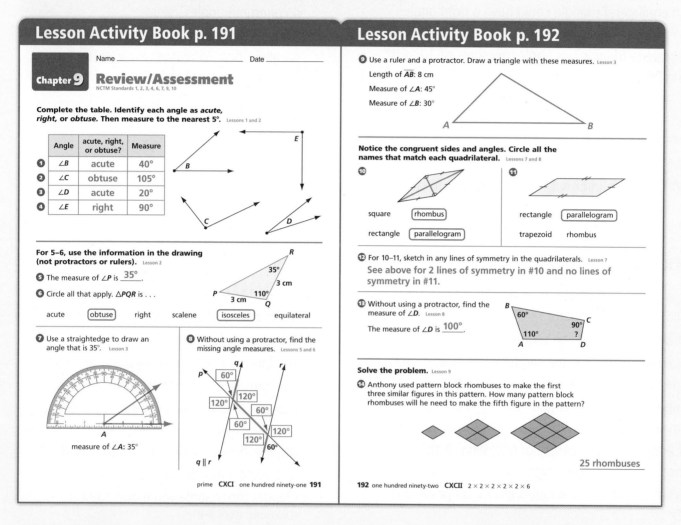

Extra Support Students who have difficulty with items on the Chapter 9 Review/Assessment may need review of the lesson where development of the concept was provided. You can use the Intervention Activity to increase students' understanding before the Chapter Test is given.

Chapter Test Use the Chapter 9 Test in the *Assessment Guide* to assess concepts, skills, and problem solving from the chapter and to prepare students for standardized tests. The Chapter Test and other test items are also available online.

Chapter Notes

Quick Notes

More Ideas

Big Idea Find perimeter and area of two-dimensional figures including parallelograms and trapezoids

Area and Perimeter

About the Chapter

This chapter begins by reviewing units of measurement, and then focuses on students' understanding of perimeter and area of two-dimensional figures. Building on what they already know, students reason geometrically to develop shape-specific formulas.

Finding Perimeter Instead of simply measuring and then summing the lengths of the sides of polygons, students first use words to describe this process and then develop simpler shorthand formulas specific to parallelograms.

Finding Area The idea that the area of a figure equals the sum of the areas of its parts is central to understanding *why* formulas for area work. Students use this fact and their knowledge of how to find the area of a rectangle to discover the formula for the area of a parallelogram. They cut a parallelogram along a line perpendicular to a base, and then put the parts back together to create a rectangle with the same base and height.

Students discover the formula for the area of a triangle by putting two congruent triangles together to see that each is half the area of a parallelogram and they use similar reasoning to determine the formula for the area of a trapezoid.

Students begin to recognize that they can also find the areas of polygons that are neither parallelograms nor trapezoids by splitting the polygon up into shapes for which they have area formulas.

Considering Perimeter and Area Together Students explore the idea that polygons that have the same area may have very different shapes and perimeters.

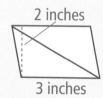

2 inches

3 inches

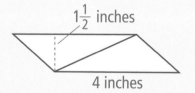

$1\frac{1}{2}$ inches

4 inches

Developing Concepts Across the Grades

Topic	Prior Learning	Learning in Chapter 10	Later Learning
Area and Perimeter	• Find perimeters and areas of shapes made with squares • Estimate area in standard units Grade 4, Chapter 5	• Connect models for perimeter and area with appropriate formulas • Use simpler figures such as triangles to find perimeter and area of more complex figures Lessons 10.1–10.6	• Find surface areas for pyramids and cylinders Grade 6
Measurement	• Draw, measure, and compare shapes in square inches and square centimeters • Compare models of standard square units Grade 4, Chapter 5	• Select and use appropriate units to measure length, perimeter, and area • Find and measure heights of parallelograms Lessons 10.1–10.4	• Convert measurements units between systems Grade 6
Understand and Use Variables	• Find a missing dimension in an array of tiles Grade 4, Chapter 2	• Connect models for perimeter and area with appropriate formulas • Use formulas for the areas of triangles, parallelograms, and trapezoids Lessons 10.3–10.5	• Use volume formulas for pyramids and cylinders Grade 6

Chapter Planner

Lesson	Objectives	NCTM Standards	Vocabulary	Materials/Resources

Chapter 10 World Almanac for Kids • Vocabulary • Games • Challenge
Teacher Guide pp. 817A–817D, Student Handbook pp. 168–169, 178–182

1 **Length and Perimeter**

PACING 1 DAY

Teacher Guide pp. 818–825
Lesson Activity Book pp. 193–194
Student Handbook Student Letter p. 167

- To select and use appropriate units to measure length and perimeter

1, 3, 4, 6, 7, 8, 9

area
perimeter
scale

For the students:
- School-Home Connection TR: SHC37–SHC38
- TR: AM87
- centimeter and inch rulers
- P79, E79, SR79

Literature Connection:
The Silk Road: Using a Map to Measure Distances
Teacher Guide p. 816

2 **Perimeter Formulas**

PACING 1 DAY

Teacher Guide pp. 826–833
Lesson Activity Book pp. 195–196
Student Handbook Explore p. 170
Game p. 180
Review Model p. 171

- To measure length and perimeter
- To connect models for perimeter with appropriate formulas

1, 2, 3, 4, 7, 8, 9

parallelogram
rectangle
rhombus
square
trapezoid
congruent
parallel
perpendicular
right angle

For the students:
- TR: AM88–AM89
- paper clips
- P80, E80, SR80

3 **Area of Parallelograms**

PACING 1 DAY

Teacher Guide pp. 834–841
Lesson Activity Book pp. 197–198

- To connect models for perimeter and area with appropriate formulas
- To select and use appropriate units and formulas for perimeter and area of parallelograms

1, 3, 4, 6, 7, 8, 9

base
height

For the teacher:
- index cards
- scissors

For the students:
- TR: AM90
- centimeter and inch rulers
- scissors
- P81, E81, SR81

Physical Education Connection:
Tennis Court
Teacher Guide p. 816

NCTM Standards 2000
1. Number and Operations
2. Algebra
3. Geometry
4. Measurement
5. Data Analysis and Probability
6. Problem Solving
7. Reasoning and Proof
8. Communication
9. Connections
10. Representation

Key
AG: Assessment Guide
E: Extension Book
LAB: Lesson Activity Book
P: Practice Book
SH: Student Handbook
SR: Spiral Review Book
TG: Teacher Guide
TR: Teacher Resource Book

MATH GLOSSARY in **Student Handbook** p. 266

Planner (continued)

Chapter Planner (continued)

Lesson	Objectives	NCTM Standards	Vocabulary	Materials/ Resources
4 **Measuring to Find Areas of Parallelograms** PACING **1** DAY **Teacher Guide** pp. 842–849 **Lesson Activity Book** pp. 199–200 **Student Handbook** Game p. 181 Review Model p. 172	• To select and use appropriate units and formulas for perimeter and area of parallelograms • To find and measure heights of parallelograms	1, 3, 4, 6, 7, 8, 9, 10	measuring height of a parallelogram	**For the Students:** ■ TR: AM88–AM89, AM91 ■ centimeter rulers ■ index cards or half sheets of paper ■ tape ■ paper clips ■ P82, E82, SR82
5 **Area of Triangles and Trapezoids** PACING **1** DAY **Teacher Guide** pp. 850–859 **Lesson Activity Book** pp. 201–202 **Student Handbook** Explore p. 173 Review Model p. 174	• To use the formula for the area of a parallelogram to find the formulas for the areas of a triangle and a trapezoid	1, 2, 3, 4, 6, 7, 8, 9, 10	trapezoid	**For the students:** ■ TR: AM92 ■ centimeter and inch rulers ■ tape ■ scissors ■ P83, E83, SR83
6 **Area and Perimeter of Other Polygons** PACING **1** DAY **Teacher Guide** pp. 860–867 **Lesson Activity Book** pp. 203–204 **Student Handbook** Explore p. 175	• To use simpler figures, such as triangles, to find the perimeter and area of more complex figures	1, 3, 4, 6, 7, 8, 9	polygon	**For the students:** ■ TR: AM93–AM94 ■ centimeter rulers ■ scissors ■ tape ■ P84, E84, SR84 **Social Studies Connection:** **State Areas** **Teacher Guide** p. 816
7 **Problem Solving Strategy and Test Prep** PACING **1** DAY **Teacher Guide** pp. 868–873 **Lesson Activity Book** pp. 205–206 **Student Handbook** Review Model pp. 176–177	• To practice the problem solving strategy *solve a simpler problem* • To articulate the steps and strategies used to solve problems • To prepare for standardized tests	1, 3, 4, 6, 7, 8, 9		**For the students:** ■ centimeter rulers

CHAPTER 10 Assessment
TG pp. 874–877, **LAB** pp. 207–208, **AG** pp. AG85–AG88

For the students:
■ Chapter 10 Test pp. AG85–AG86

Games

Use the following games for skills practice and reinforcement of concepts.

Perimeter Race

Lesson 10.2 ▶

Perimeter Race provides an opportunity for students to practice finding perimeters of rectangular figures

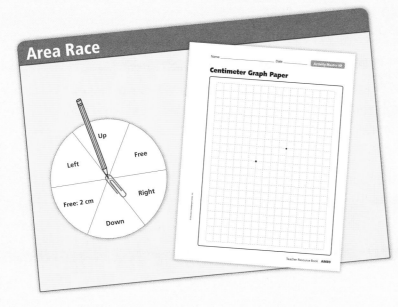

Area Race

◀ Lesson 10.4 *Area Race* provides an opportunity for students to practice finding areas of rectangular figures.

Planning Ahead

In **Lessons 10.1, 10.3, 10.4, 10.5, 10.6,** and **10.7,** students will use inch and centimeter rulers. They will also need scissors and tape in some of these lessons.

In **Lesson 10.2,** students will be playing *Perimeter Race.* Each pair of students will need a copy of AM88: Directions Spinner, AM89: Centimeter Graph Paper, and a pencil and a paper clip to make a spinner.

In **Lesson 10.3,** the teacher uses index cards and in **Lesson 10.4** students use index cards.

In **Lesson 10.4,** students will be playing *Area Race.* Each pair of students will need a copy of AM88: Directions Spinner, AM89: Centimeter Graph Paper, and a pencil and a paper clip to make a spinner.

In the Extension activity in **Lesson 10.1** and in the Skills Practice and Review in **Lesson 10.5,** students use square tiles.

In the Extension activity in **Lesson 10.2,** students use string and in **Lesson 10.4** they use centimeter grid paper. In both the Intervention and Extension activities in **Lesson 10.6,** they use geoboards.

Developing Problem Solvers

Open-Ended Problem Solving

The Headline Story in the Daily Activities section of every lesson provides an open-ended problem for students to complete. For each story there are many possible responses.

Headline Stories can be found on TG pages 819, 827, 835, 843, 851, and 861.

Headline Story

Leveled Problem Solving

Leveled Problem Solving provides an opportunity for students to apply learning from the lesson to a real-life situation. Problems are leveled by ability to allow students of all ability levels to become successful problem solvers. Each Leveled Problem Solving begins with a real-life scenario upon which three problems are built.

The levels of problems are:

❶ Basic Level	❷ On Level	❸ Above Level
students needing extra support	students working at grade level	students who are ready for more challenging problems

Leveled Problem Solving can be found on TG pages 825, 832, 840, 849, 858, and 866.

THE WORLD ALMANAC FOR KIDS

The World Almanac for Kids feature is designed to stimulate student interest for the math concepts they are about to learn. Students use data to solve problems and explain solutions. The Chapter 10 Project can be found on SH pages 168–169.

Write Math

Reflect and Summarize the Lesson poses a problem or question for students to think and write about. This feature can be found on TG pages 824, 831, 839, 848, 857, 865, and 870.

Other opportunities to write about math can be found on LAB pages 196, 197, 204, and 206.

Problem Solving Strategies

The focus of **Lesson 10.7** is the strategy *solve a simpler problem*. However, students will use a variety of problem solving strategies as they work through the chapter. The chart below shows strategies that may be useful in completing each lesson.

Strategy	Lesson(s)	Description
Act It Out	10.1, 10.3, 10.4, 10.5, 10.7	Use centimeter and inch rulers to measure length.
Draw a Picture	10.4	Make a sketch to help solve an area problem.
Make a Model	10.3, 10.5, 10.6	Cut an index card in two and rearrange the pieces to show that the area of the two figures is the same; cut a parallelogram to show it has the same area as a rectangle with the same base and height; put two congruent triangles (or two congruent trapezoids) together to form a parallelogram to show how areas are related; and use a constant number of square tiles to make various figures of different shapes with the same area.
Solve a Simpler Problem	10.6, 10.7	Split an odd-shaped figure into triangles (or other figures with known areas) and then sum the areas of the triangles to find the area of the odd-shaped figure.
Use Logical Reasoning	10.1, 10.7	Use a diagram with a given scale to determine actual length or distance; and use known area formulas to find area formula for other figures.
Write an Equation	10.2, 10.5	Write a formula for the perimeter of a parallelogram, a triangle, and a trapezoid.

Meeting the Needs of All Learners

Differentiated Instruction		
Extra Support	**On Level**	**Enrichment**
Intervention Activities TG pp. 825, 832, 840, 849, 858, 866	**Practice Book** pp. P79–P84	**Extension Activities** TG pp. 825, 832, 840, 849, 858, 866
	Spiral Review Book pp. SR79–SR84	**Extension Book** pp. E79–E84
	LAB Challenge LAB pp. 194, 196, 198, 200, 202, 204 SH p. 182	**LAB Challenge** LAB pp. 194, 196, 198, 200, 202, 204 SH p. 182
Lesson Notes **Basic Level** TG pp. 836, 846	**Lesson Notes** **On Level** TG pp. 839, 846	**Lesson Notes** **Above Level** TG p. 839
Leveled Problem Solving **Basic Level** TG pp. 825, 832, 840, 849, 858, 866	**Leveled Problem Solving** **On Level** TG pp. 825, 832, 840, 849, 858, 866	**Leveled Problem Solving** **Above Level** TG pp. 825, 832, 840, 849, 858, 866

English Language Learners

Suggestions for addressing the needs of students learning English as a second language are included in the Developing Mathematical Language section at the beginning of most lessons.

ELL activities for this chapter can be found on TG pages 819, 827, 835, 843, 851, and 861.

The Multi-Age Classroom

Grade 4	• Students on this level should be able to complete the lessons in Chapter 10 but might need some additional practice with key concepts and skills. • Give students more practice with area and perimeter.	See Grade 5, Intervention Activities, Lessons 10.1–10.6. See Grade 4, Lessons 5.1–5.6.
Grade 5	• Students on this level should be able to complete the lessons in Chapter 10 with minimal adjustments.	See Grade 5, Practice pages P79–P84.
Grade 6	• Students on this level should be able to complete the lessons in Chapter 10 and to extend concepts and skills related to area and perimeter. • Give students extended work with area formulas.	See Grade 5, Extension pages E79–E84.

Cross Curricular Connections

Social Studies Connection

Math Concept: finding area of complex figures

State Areas

- Tell students that rivers, lakes, mountains, or lines of longitude or latitude create the boundaries of countries and states.

- Have each student trace an outline of one of the state of the continental United States from social studies textbook or from a reference book.

- Have students use their rulers to divide the state into polygons, if necessary, and to measure to estimate the area in square inches or square centimeters of the traced figure.

- Help students use the map scale and calculate the estimated area for their chosen state.

Lesson 10.6

Physical Education Connection

Math Concept: area of a rectangle

Tennis Court

- Tell students that tennis is a popular sport played on a rectangular court. Players use a racket to hit a tennis ball over a net that divides the court in half. The game can be played either by two players or four players. When only two players play, it is called singles. When four players play, it is called doubles.

- Show students the following bird's-eye view of one half of a tennis court. Tell students that, in a singles game, the ball is allowed to land in the back court and in the forecourt but not in either alley.

- Have students write a word problem about area that requires the information from the diagram to solve. Then have pairs of students trade papers and solve the problems.

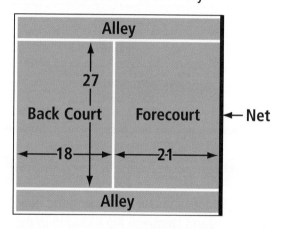

Lesson 10.3

Literature Connection

Math Concept: measurement

The Silk Road: Using a Map to Measure Distances
By Janey Levy

Travel to the Far East with your students as they discover and explore the silk road. Using the silk road as a background, your students will learn how to measure distances on a map and how to use a scale to convert from map measurements to real world distances.

Lesson 10.1

School-Home Connection

A reproducible copy of the School-Home Connection letter in English and in Spanish can be found in the *Teacher Resource Book,* pages SHC39–SHC40.

Encourage students to try *Area Challenges,* found on the School-Home Connection page, with a family member. Students will work with the concept of area in **Lessons 10.3, 10.4,** and **10.5.**

Assessment Options

There are many opportunities in *Think Math!* to assess students' understanding of concepts, skills, and problem solving. Learning Goals for Chapter 10 are provided below. The assessment options provide opportunities to evaluate whether or not students have retained learning from prior experiences. Choose the forms of assessment that best meet the needs of your students.

Chapter 10 Learning Goals

	Learning Goals	Lesson Number
10-A	Use appropriate units and formulas for perimeter and area of two-dimensional figures	10.1–10.6
10-B	Use given measurements or ruler measurements to find the perimeters of two-dimensional figures	10.1, 10.2
10-C	Use given measurements or ruler measurements to find the areas of two-dimensional figures	10.3–10.6
10-D	Apply problem solving strategies such as *solve a simpler problem* to solve problems	10.7

✓ Informal Assessment

Ongoing Assessment
Provides insight into students' thinking to guide instruction (TG pp. 823, 829, 839, 845, 846, 856, 865)

Reflect and Summarize the Lesson
Checks understanding of lesson concepts (TG pp. 824, 831, 839, 848, 857, 865, 870)

Snapshot Assessment
Mental Math and **Quick Write**
Offers a quick observation of students' progress on chapter concepts and skills (TG pp. 874–875)

Performance Assessment
Provides quarterly assessment of Chapters 8–11 concepts using real-life situations
Assessment Guide pp. AG219–AG224

✓ Formal Assessment

Standardized Test Prep
Problem Solving Test Prep
Prepares students for standardized tests
Lesson Activity Book p. 206 (TG p. 871)

Chapter 10 Review/Assessment
Reviews and assesses students' understanding of the chapter
Lesson Activity Book pp. 207–208 (TG p. 876)

Chapter 10 Test
Assesses the chapter concepts and skills
Assessment Guide
Form A pp. AG85–AG86
Form B pp. AG87–AG88

Benchmark 3 Assessment
Provides quarterly assessment of Chapters 8–11 concepts and skills *Assessment Guide*
Benchmark 3A pp. AG93–AG100
Benchmark 3B pp. AG101–AG108

World Almanac for Kids

Use the World Almanac for Kids feature, *Up, Up, and Away!*, found on pp. 168–169 of the ***Student Handbook***, to provide students with an opportunity to practice using their problem solving skills by solving real world problems.

FACT • ACTIVITY 1

1 $P = 1\frac{1}{2} + 1\frac{1}{2} + 1 + 1 = 5$ in.

2 5 ft

3 280 centimeters; Possible answer: Use a formula: $4 \times 70 = 280$ cm or add the length of each side: $70 + 70 + 70 + 70 = 280$ cm.

4 Possible answer: $P = 14$ in; 14 ft

Student Handbook p. 168

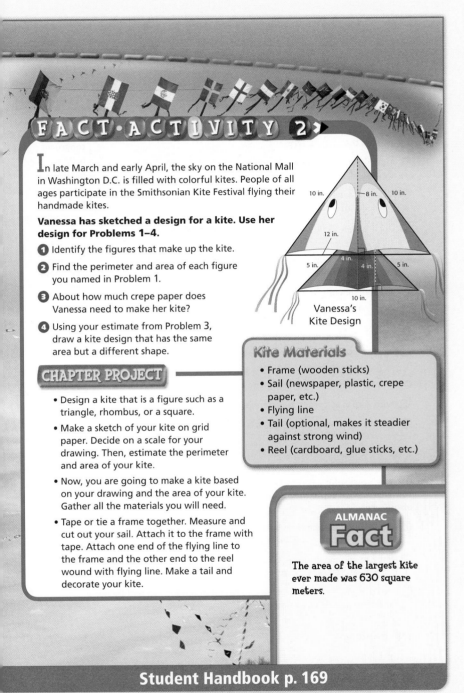

FACT·ACTIVITY 2

In late March and early April, the sky on the National Mall in Washington D.C. is filled with colorful kites. People of all ages participate in the Smithsonian Kite Festival flying their handmade kites.

Vanessa has sketched a design for a kite. Use her design for Problems 1–4.

1 Identify the figures that make up the kite.

2 Find the perimeter and area of each figure you named in Problem 1.

3 About how much crepe paper does Vanessa need to make her kite?

4 Using your estimate from Problem 3, draw a kite design that has the same area but a different shape.

CHAPTER PROJECT

- Design a kite that is a figure such as a triangle, rhombus, or a square.

- Make a sketch of your kite on grid paper. Decide on a scale for your drawing. Then, estimate the perimeter and area of your kite.

- Now, you are going to make a kite based on your drawing and the area of your kite. Gather all the materials you will need.

- Tape or tie a frame together. Measure and cut out your sail. Attach it to the frame with tape. Attach one end of the flying line to the frame and the other end to the reel wound with flying line. Make a tail and decorate your kite.

Vanessa's Kite Design

10 in. — 8 in. — 10 in.
12 in.
5 in. — 4 in. — 4 in. — 5 in.
10 in.

Kite Materials

- Frame (wooden sticks)
- Sail (newspaper, plastic, crepe paper, etc.)
- Flying line
- Tail (optional, makes it steadier against strong wind)
- Reel (cardboard, glue sticks, etc.)

ALMANAC Fact

The area of the largest kite ever made was 630 square meters.

Student Handbook p. 169

FACT·ACTIVITY 2

1 triangle, trapezoid

2 triangle: $P = 32$ in., $A = 48$ in.^{2}; trapezoid: $P = 24$ in., $A = 28$ in.^{2}

3 $48 + 28 = 76$; about 80 in.^{2}

4 Possible answer: a 10 in. $\times$ 8 in. rectangle

CHAPTER PROJECT

Sample answer:

My drawing is a 3-inch square. The scale for my drawing is 1 inch = 1 foot. The perimeter of my kite is 12 feet and the area of my kite is 9 square feet.

Vocabulary

To reinforce vocabulary concepts, invite students to complete the vocabulary activities on pp. 178–179 of the **Student Handbook.** Encourage students to record their answers in their math journals.

Many responses are possible.

12 Possible response: First, choose one side to be the *base,* and measure it. Next, extend the base, if necessary, to draw a line *perpendicular* to the *base* from a vertex that is not on the base to the base. Then measure the distance from the vertex to the *base.* That is the *height.* Finally, multiply the length of the *base* and the length of the *height* to find the area of the parallelogram.

13 Possible response: First, choose one side of the triangle to be the *base,* and measure it. Next, extend the *base,* if necessary, to draw a line *perpendicular* to the base from the vertex not on the *base.* Then measure the distance from the vertex to the *base.* That is the *height.* Finally, multiply the length of the *base* and the length of the *height* and divide the product by 2 to find the area of the triangle.

14 Possible response: A trapezoid has two bases, and they are parallel to each other. Measure each *base,* and add them. Next, draw a line *perpendicular* to the bases, and measure the distance between the two bases. That is the *height.* Finally, multiply the sum of the lengths of the two bases by the length of the *height* and divide the product by 2. The result is the area of the trapezoid.

Chapter 10 Vocabulary

Choose the best vocabulary term from Word List A for each sentence.

1 The measurement of space inside a plane figure is called the __?__. area

2 A quadrilateral with exactly one pair of parallel sides is a(n) __?__. trapezoid

3 A closed plane figure formed by three or more line segments is called a(n) __?__. polygon

4 The distance from the base to the farthest point of a plane figure is the __?__ of the figure. height

5 A(n) __?__ has opposite sides that are both parallel and congruent. parallelogram

6 A rectangle with four sides of equal length is a(n) __?__. square

7 Two __?__ lines intersect to form four right angles. perpendicular

8 A quadrilateral with four equal sides is a(n) __?__. rhombus

9 Sides of a polygon that have the same length are __?__. congruent

Word List A

area
base
congruent
height
parallel
parallelogram
perimeter
perpendicular
polygon
rectangle
rhombus
right angle
scale
square
trapezoid

Complete each analogy using the best term from Word List B.

10 Index card is to corner as rectangle is to __?__. right angle

11 Fence is to backyard as __?__ is to polygon. perimeter

Word List B

area
parallel
perimeter
right angle

Talk Math

Use the vocabulary terms *base, height,* and *perpendicular* to discuss with a partner what you have just learned about area.

12 How can you measure the base and height of a parallelogram and then use those measurements to find its area?

13 How can you measure the base and height of a triangle and then use those measurements to find its area?

14 How can you measure the base and height of a trapezoid and then use those measurements to find its area?

178 Chapter 10

Student Handbook p. 178

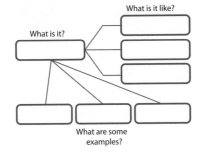
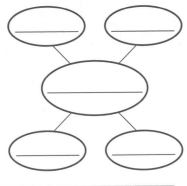
15 Many answers are possible. One example is provided.

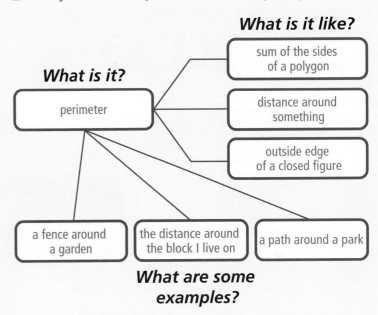

16 Many answers are possible. One example is provided.

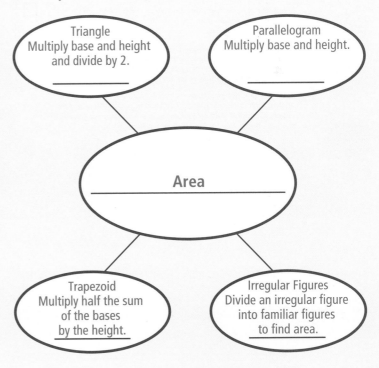

Games

Perimeter Race, in **Lesson 10.2** provides an opportunity for students to practice finding perimeters of rectangular figures. *Area Race,* in **Lesson 10.4** provides an opportunity for students to practice finding areas of rectangular figures. These games can be found on pp. 180–181 of the *Student Handbook.*

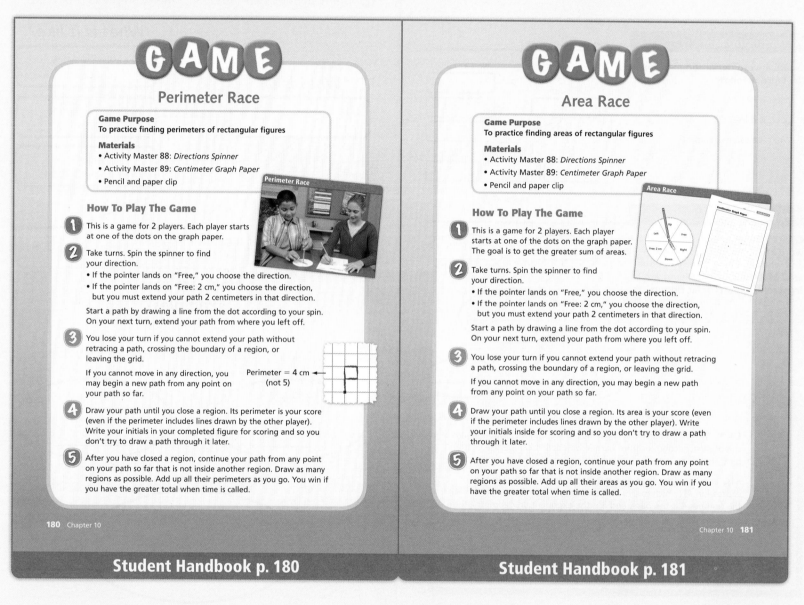

Student Handbook p. 180

Student Handbook p. 181

Challenge

The Challenge activity *Area, Area, Area,* challenges students to use what they have learned about area, division, and fractions to find the areas of parts of figures. This activity can be found on p. 182 of the *Student Handbook.*

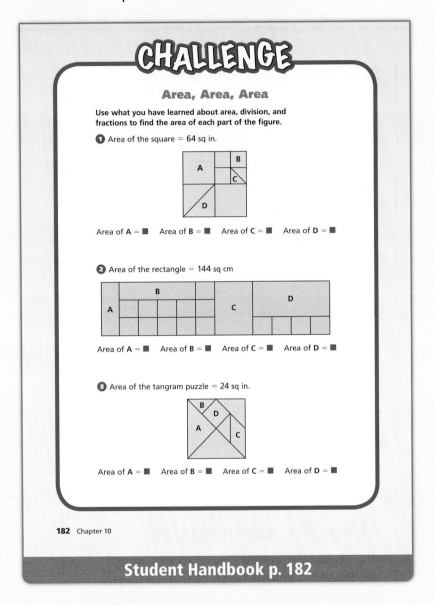

❶ Area of A = 16 sq in.; Area of B = 4 sq in.; Area of C = 2 sq in.; Area of D = 8 sq in.

❷ Area of A = 12 sq cm; Area of B = 16 sq cm; Area of C = 24 sq cm; Area of D = 32 sq cm

❸ Area of A = 6 sq in.; Area of B = 1.5 sq in.; Area of C = 3 sq in.; Area of D = 3 sq in.

Lesson 1 Length and Perimeter

NCTM Standards 1, 3, 4, 6, 7, 8, 9

Lesson Planner

STUDENT OBJECTIVE
- To select and use appropriate units to measure length and perimeter

1 | Daily Activities (TG p. 819)

Open-Ended Problem Solving/Headline Story | Skills Practice and Review—
Using Estimation To Place the Decimal Point

2 | Teach and Practice (TG pp. 820–824)

Ⓐ **Reading the Student Letter** (TG p. 820)

Ⓑ **Choosing Units of Measure** (TG pp. 821–822)

Ⓒ **Finding Perimeters** (TG p. 823)

Ⓓ **Selecting and Using Perimeter Formulas** (TG p. 824)

MATERIALS

- TR: Activity Master, AM87
- centimeter and inch rulers
- 📖 LAB pp. 193–194
- 📖 SH p. 167

3 | Differentiated Instruction (TG p. 825)

Leveled Problem Solving (TG p. 825)

Intervention Activity (TG p. 825)

Extension Activity (TG p. 825)

Literature Connection (TG p. 816)

Practice Book P79

Extension Book E79

Spiral Review Book SR79

Lesson Notes

About the Lesson

As an introduction to this chapter, students first distinguish among units of length, weight, and capacity. They then compute perimeters by measuring the sides of figures in inches or centimeters, and then finding the total of the side lengths. They also record formulas for finding perimeter, and apply these formulas on the LAB pages.

About the Mathematics

To compute perimeters and areas throughout this chapter, students begin by using a ruler to measure side lengths or the height of a figure. All measurements are, by their nature, approximate and therefore only give a certain level of precision and accuracy. Though the imprecision of measurements is not the focus of this chapter, the "=" sign is avoided whenever measurements are recorded to maintain mathematical correctness.

Use with Lesson Activity Book pp. 193–194.

Developing Mathematical Language

Vocabulary: area, perimeter, scale

The *perimeter* of a polygon is the sum of the lengths of its sides. Sometimes one or more side lengths are missing in a diagram. You may need to remind students that they must determine the missing lengths before they can compute the *perimeter* of a polygon.

The *area* of a polygon is the measure of the space inside it. Students might also relate to *area* as a general region, such as a playground *area*.

Scale is the ratio between two sets of measurements, for example 1 cm : 5 mi. Students might be familiar with the *scale* on a map, and those who have worked with model airplanes, cars, or dollhouses might also have a sense of *scale* relating to the actual size of an object.

Familiarize students with the terms *perimeter* and *area.*

Beginning Have students draw a square on paper. Ask them color the *perimeter* red. Then have them color the *area* inside it yellow.

Intermediate Give students a long piece of string and several square sheets of paper. Ask students to use them to demonstrate *perimeter* and *area* of a desk top.

Advanced Have students explain the difference between *area* and *perimeter.*

Open-Ended Problem Solving

For this Headline Story, suggest that students draw pictures.

 Headline Story

There are no more than 6 points on a piece of paper. How many segments have endpoints at any two of these points?

Possible responses: For 1 point, you can draw 0 segments. For 2 points, you can draw 1 segment. For 3 points, you can draw 3 segments. (It's a triangle.) For 4 points you can draw 6 segments (a quadrilateral with both of its diagonals). For 5 points, you can draw 10 segments. For 6 points, you can draw 15 segments.

Skills Practice and Review

Using Estimation To Place the Decimal Point

One by one, write these (incorrect) number sentences on the board. After you write each sentence, have students verify that it is incorrect. Then say that it can be corrected by putting in a decimal point, and ask students where the decimal point should go. Use questions like the ones below to guide students, as needed.

$$12 + 4.8 = 168$$

Would 1.68 be reasonable? no
Why or why not? The sum should be about 17 because you can round 4.8 to 5 and see that $12 + 5 = 17$.

$$4.2 + 10.6 = 148 \quad 14.8 \qquad 14.5 + 13.5 = 280 \quad 28.0$$
$$17.8 - 12.5 = 530 \quad 5.30$$

Remind students they can use the estimation strategies—rounding and compatible numbers—to help them place the decimal point.

whole class 5 MIN

NCTM Standards 3, 4, 8

A Reading the Student Letter

Purpose To introduce the measures of perimeter and area

Introduce The Student Letter is designed to spur interest and curiosity. Have students read and discuss the letter. Don't worry if students' knowledge of perimeter and area is not solid at this point, as they will learn much more about these measurements throughout the chapter.

Problem **What do you already know about two-dimensional figures, and their perimeter and area?**

Students may remember parallelograms and trapezoids from grade 4, and they may remember that the perimeter is the length of the border of a figure and that the area is the amount of space inside a figure.

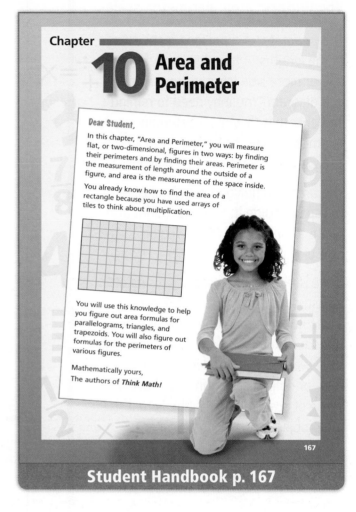

Chapter

10 **Area and Perimeter**

Dear Student,

In this chapter, "Area and Perimeter," you will measure flat, or two-dimensional, figures in two ways: by finding their perimeters and by finding their areas. Perimeter is the measurement of length around the outside of a figure, and area is the measurement of the space inside.

You already know how to find the area of a rectangle because you have used arrays of tiles to think about multiplication.

You will use this knowledge to help you figure out area formulas for parallelograms, triangles, and trapezoids. You will also figure out formulas for the perimeters of various figures.

Mathematically yours,
The authors of *Think Math!*

167

Student Handbook p. 167

Concept Alert

Some students may think that a parallelogram is a special case of the trapezoid since it meets the conditions of having 4 sides and one pair of parallel sides. In fact, a trapezoid has *exactly* one pair of parallel sides, so any quadrilateral that has parallel sides is either a parallelogram or a trapezoid, but not both.

 Talk Math

❷ How are parallelograms and trapezoids the same? They both have 4 sides. They both have at least one pair of parallel sides.

❷ How are parallelograms and trapezoids different? Parallelograms have two pairs of parallel sides while trapezoids have exactly one pair of parallel sides.

B Choosing Units of Measure

Purpose To review units of measure for length, weight, and volume

Introduce Ask your students what they know about the U.S. customary and metric measurement systems. They may know that the customary system is "customary" only in the United States, and that the metric system is standard in most of the world. They may also know that the metric system is based on powers of 10, but the customary system is based on other numbers: 12 (inches and feet), 3 (feet and yards), 4 (quarts and gallons), 16 (ounces and pounds; fluid ounces and pints), and so on. They might even know that people tend to use fractions with U.S. customary units (e.g., $\frac{1}{3}$ cup) while people generally use decimals with metric units because they are neatly organized around powers of 10 (e.g., 3.6 meters).

Talk Math

? What do the prefixes *milli-, centi-,* and *kilo-* mean? *Milli-* means one-thousandth, *centi-* means one-hundredth, and *kilo-* means one thousand.

? Why might students need to learn about the metric system? The metric system is widely used in science. It is often used when very large or very small measurements are needed. We may purchase products made in other countries with metric specification or parts. For example, you may need a set of metric wrenches to work on certain machines.

Task **State a unit of measure, and have students say if it is a unit of** *length, weight,* **or** *capacity.* **Then ask students to say whether the unit is a** *customary* **or** *metric* **unit.** You might also ask students to give an example of something measured with each unit. If any students are unclear about the meaning of *capacity,* you might describe it as the measurement of how much a container can hold. Record the information in a table like this.

Teacher Story

"I like to make a table of units of measure to help my students distinguish among the different types of measurement (length, weight, and capacity), and match each unit to the appropriate system (metric or customary). We add words to the chart as we see them or think of them throughout the year."

Unit	What It Measures	Customary or Metric?	What One Might Measure with It
gram	weight	metric	paperclip, grape, things that weigh very little
mile	length	customary	large distances, e.g., between schools
milliliter	capacity	metric	cough medicine, liquids in science labs
millimeter	length	metric	very short distances, e.g., the width of a dime
inch	length	customary	short lengths/distances, ribbon, child's height
kilogram	weight	metric	medium weight, large package
kilometer	length	metric	foot race (used in few contexts in U.S.)
quart	capacity	customary	medium liquid quantity, milk, water
fluid ounce	capacity	customary	small liquid quantity, water
ounce	weight	customary	piece of mail, a few grapes

Use with Lesson Activity Book pp. 193–194.

It may be worth clarifying the use of *ounce* for two different kinds of measures. Although the capacity ounce measure is technically a *fluid ounce,* it is often shortened to just *ounce.* For now, it is enough for your students to know that *ounce* names two different units of measurement, one of capacity and one of weight.

Because this chapter focuses on length, perimeter, and area, you might make a separate table of customary and metric units for length. For example, the table might include: inch (in.), foot (ft), yard (yd), mile (mi), centimeter (cm), meter (m), and kilometer (km).

To review, ask students to solve the following problems by selecting an appropriate unit of length.

- What is the perimeter of your math book? Possible answers: 40 inches, 100 centimeters

- What is the perimeter of this room? Possible answers: 80 feet, 28 yards, 25 meters

- What is the distance between your home and the library? Possible answers: 2 miles, 2 kilometers

Extend Have students measure the length of 5 classroom objects. Ask students to choose the unit of measure they would use to measure the length of each object. Then use that unit of measure to measure the length of each object to the nearest inch, foot, or yard.

C Finding Perimeters

Purpose To measure lengths and find perimeters

Introduce Give students Activity Master 87: Measuring Lengths and a ruler that has both inches and centimeter markings. Explain that students will measure in both inches and centimeters on this page, and review the symbol for line segments if necessary.

Task Have students complete AM87: Measuring Lengths independently. **Students must select and use appropriate units to measure the perimeter in Problems 7 and 8.**

Your students may have worked with perimeter before, but they may not have performed measurements themselves. Ask students to discuss what measurements they made and how they found the perimeters in Problems 7 and 8 of AM87. Write the different methods students used on the board so that students can begin to connect the written formulas with the figures. (Students will further explore these formulas in the next lesson, so you don't need to spend much time on them now.)

Materials
• For each student: AM87, centimeter and inch ruler

NCTM Standards 1, 3, 4, 7, 8, 9

Measuring Lengths

Measure each line segment to the nearest centimeter (cm).

$\overline{AB}$ 13 cm
$\overline{CD}$ 9 cm
$\overline{EF}$ 3 cm

Measure each line segment to the nearest $\frac{1}{2}$ inch (in).

$\overline{GH}$ 1$\frac{1}{2}$ in.
$\overline{IJ}$ 3$\frac{1}{2}$ in.
$\overline{KL}$ 3 in.

Measure the sides of each parallelogram to the nearest centimeter. Find the perimeter and record in cm.

6 cm
4 cm
Perimeter 20 cm
6 cm

3 cm
5 cm
4 cm
Perimeter 16 cm
5 cm
3 cm

Activity Master 87

💬 Talk Math

❓ Did you need to measure all 4 sides of the parallelograms in Problems 7 to 8 find the perimeters? No; since the figures are parallelograms, each side has a parallel partner with the same length.

❓ How could you find the perimeters in Problems 7 and 8 by measuring only two sides of each parallelogram? To find the perimeter of each figure, you could double the sum of the two unequal sides (2 × (short side length + long side length)), or double each individual side length (short side length × 2 + long side length × 2). You could also add all 4 sides individually: short side + long side + short side + long side.

Tell students you want to decorate the perimeter of a book case in your room. Have students select and use formulas to find the perimeter of the book case.

✓ Ongoing Assessment

• Watch for students who need support using a ruler to measure line segments. For example, some students may not match up the zero mark on the ruler to the endpoint of the line segment.

• Watch for students who struggle to record the length to the nearest centimeter or half-inch, and show them how to round their measurements.

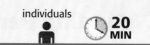

Purpose To practice finding the perimeters of various figures

NCTM Standards 1, 4, 6

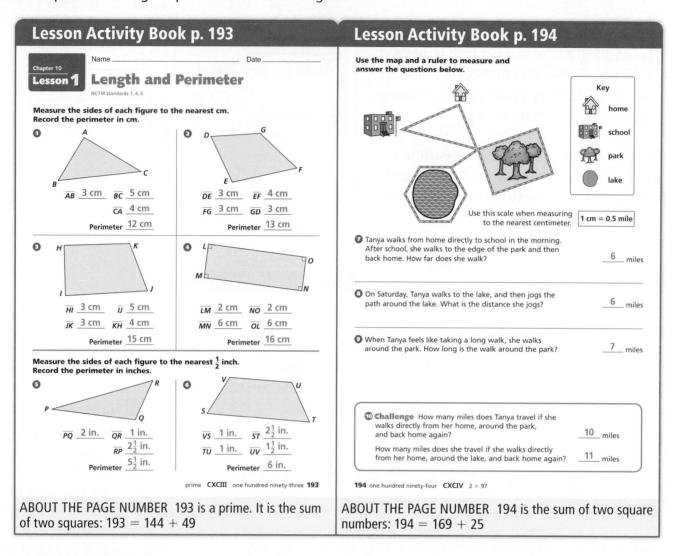

Lesson Activity Book p. 193

Chapter 10
Lesson 1 **Length and Perimeter**
NCTM Standards 1, 4, 6

Measure the sides of each figure to the nearest cm.
Record the perimeter in cm.

❶
$\overline{AB}$ 3 cm $\overline{BC}$ 5 cm
$\overline{CA}$ 4 cm
Perimeter 12 cm

❷
$\overline{DE}$ 3 cm $\overline{EF}$ 4 cm
$\overline{FG}$ 3 cm $\overline{GD}$ 3 cm
Perimeter 13 cm

❸
$\overline{HI}$ 3 cm $\overline{IJ}$ 5 cm
$\overline{JK}$ 3 cm $\overline{KH}$ 4 cm
Perimeter 15 cm

❹
$\overline{LM}$ 2 cm $\overline{NO}$ 2 cm
$\overline{MN}$ 6 cm $\overline{OL}$ 6 cm
Perimeter 16 cm

Measure the sides of each figure to the nearest $\frac{1}{2}$ inch.
Record the perimeter in inches.

❺
$\overline{PQ}$ 2 in. $\overline{QR}$ 1 in.
$\overline{RP}$ $2\frac{1}{2}$ in.
Perimeter $5\frac{1}{2}$ in.

❻
$\overline{VS}$ 1 in. $\overline{ST}$ $2\frac{1}{2}$ in.
$\overline{TU}$ 1 in. $\overline{UV}$ $1\frac{1}{2}$ in.
Perimeter 6 in.

prime **CXCIII** one hundred ninety-three **193**

ABOUT THE PAGE NUMBER 193 is a prime. It is the sum of two squares: 193 = 144 + 49

Lesson Activity Book p. 194

Use the map and a ruler to measure and answer the questions below.

Key
home
school
park
lake

Use this scale when measuring to the nearest centimeter. 1 cm = 0.5 mile

❼ Tanya walks from home directly to school in the morning. After school, she walks to the edge of the park and then back home. How far does she walk?   6 miles

❽ On Saturday, Tanya walks to the lake, and then jogs the path around the lake. What is the distance she jogs?   6 miles

❾ When Tanya feels like taking a long walk, she walks around the park. How long is the walk around the park?   7 miles

❿ **Challenge** How many miles does Tanya travel if she walks directly from her home, around the park, and back home again?   10 miles

How many miles does she travel if she walks directly from her home, around the lake, and back home again?   11 miles

194 one hundred ninety-four **CXCIV** 2 × 97

ABOUT THE PAGE NUMBER 194 is the sum of two square numbers: 194 = 169 + 25

Teaching Notes for LAB page 193

Students measure and record side lengths and find perimeters. The right angles indicated in the figure in Problem 4 show that this figure is a rectangle, and some students may realize that they therefore do not need to measure all four sides.

For Problems 1–4, they measure to the nearest centimeter, and for Problems 5 and 6, they measure to the nearest half-inch.

Teaching Notes for LAB page 194

Students solve word problems that involve a map, scale, and ruler. Students may find it helpful to write the length of each section of road on the map. You may need to remind some students to convert their centimeter measurements to miles.

Challenge Problem Students calculate the mileage of longer routes that include perimeters.

Reflect and Summarize the Lesson

Write Math

Explain how you could find the perimeter of the cover of your Student Handbook.

Possible answer: Since the cover of the Student Handbook is a rectangle, I could measure the long side once and the short side once, and then find 2 × the length of the long side + 2 × the length of the short side to find the perimeter.

3 | Differentiated Instruction

Leveled Problem Solving

A standard sheet of paper is a rectangle $8\frac{1}{2}$ inches wide and 11 inches long.

❶ Basic Level
What is the perimeter of a standard sheet of paper? Explain. 39 in.; $8\frac{1}{2} + 8\frac{1}{2} + 11 + 11 = 39$

❷ On Level
If you find its perimeter by adding the width and length and then multiplying by 2, what will be the 2 factors in the multiplication? Explain. $19\frac{1}{2}$ and 2; add $8\frac{1}{2}$ and 11 to get $19\frac{1}{2}$, and then multiply by 2.

❸ Above Level
If you tape 2 sheets of paper along the short side, what is the perimeter of this larger paper? Explain. 61 in.; long side is 22 in., short side is $8\frac{1}{2}$ in.; $2 \times 22 + 2 \times 8\frac{1}{2} = 44 + 17 = 61$.

Intervention

Activity Understanding Perimeter

Display various quadrilaterals and triangles. For each figure, ask students how many *different* lengths they will need to measure in order to find its perimeter. Draw a chart on the board to list the figures that require one measurement (rhombuses), two measurements (parallelograms – non-rhombuses), three measurements (scalene triangles, isosceles trapezoids), and four measurements (other trapezoids)

Practice

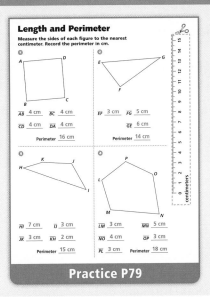

Practice P79

Extension

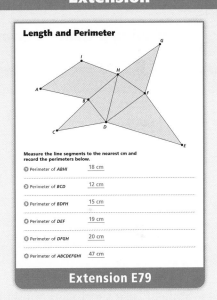

Extension E79

Extension Activity
Work Backward

Provide pairs of students with several square tiles. Tell them that each side of each tile is 1 unit. Ask them to make figures with a given perimeter. Have groups compare figures. For example, ask students to use 4 tiles to make a figure whose perimeter is exactly 10 units. Some figures might not look the same; for example:

Both figures use 4 tiles and have perimeters of 10 units.

Spiral Review

Spiral Review Book page SR79 provides review of the following previously learned skills and concepts:

- identifying congruent angles and figures and identifying similar figures
- measuring lengths to the nearest $\frac{1}{8}$ inch and nearest centimeter

You may wish to have students work with partners to complete the page.

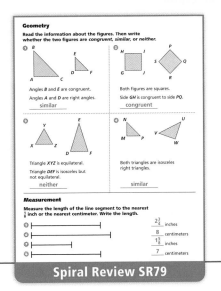

Spiral Review SR79

Lesson 2 Perimeter Formulas

NCTM Standards 1, 2, 3, 4, 7, 8, 9

Lesson Planner

STUDENT OBJECTIVES
- To measure length and perimeter
- To connect models for perimeter with appropriate formulas

1 | Daily Activities (TG p. 827)

Open-Ended Problem Solving/Headline Story	Skills Practice and Review—Selecting Units of Measure

2 | Teach and Practice (TG pp. 828–831)

	MATERIALS
(A) **Exploring Perimeter** (TG p. 828)	• TR: Activity Masters, AM88–AM89
(B) **Using Perimeter Formulas** (TG p. 829)	• paper clips
(C) **Playing a Game: *Perimeter Race*** (TG p. 830)	• 📖 LAB pp. 195–196
	• 📖 SH pp. 170–171, 180

3 | Differentiated Instruction (TG p. 832)

Leveled Problem Solving (TG p. 832)	Practice Book P80
Intervention Activity (TG p. 832)	Extension Book E80
Extension Activity (TG p. 832))	Spiral Review Book SR80

Lesson Notes

About the Lesson

Students use shorthand notation to generate formulas for finding the perimeter of a parallelogram (including the special case of a rhombus). They use the same symbol for each side of a figure that has an equal length. For example, if they use s to stand for the shorter side of the parallelogram and l to stand for the longer side of the parallelogram, they might generate the following formulas for perimeter:

$$P = s + s + l + l \quad P = 2s + 2l \quad P = 2 \times (s + l)$$

Similarly, for rhombuses (and squares) that have 4 equal sides, students might generate $P = 4s$ or $P = 4l$.

Use with Lesson Activity Book pp. 195–196.

Developing Mathematical Language

Vocabulary: parallelogram, rectangle, rhombus, square, trapezoid, congruent, parallel, perpendicular, right angle

Specific vocabulary improves the clarity and precision of communication. Mathematics depends heavily on clear and precise communication, so learning to use precise mathematical vocabulary is an important skill. Throughout the chapter, whenever students are explaining their ideas or referring to particular figures or parts of figures, encourage them to use specific figure names, such as *parallelogram, rectangle, square, rhombus,* and *trapezoid.* When they refer to attributes of lines and angles, they should use terms such as *congruent, parallel, right angle,* and *perpendicular.*

Familiarize students with the terms *parallelogram, rectangle, square, trapezoid, congruent, parallel,* and *right angle.*

Beginning Write the words *parallel* and *parallelogram* on the board. Have a volunteer circle the part of *parallelogram* that is the same as *parallel.* Draw *parallelograms* on the board and have volunteers point to sides that are *parallel.*

Intermediate Write the terms *congruent, parallel,* and *right angle* on the board. Encourage students to use those terms in discussing attributes of a *parallelogram, a rectangle,* and *a square.*

Advanced Have pairs of students compare a *parallelogram* to a *trapezoid.*

Open-Ended Problem Solving

This Headline Story contains no numbers, and barely any constraints. The goal is for students to think of the pieces of information that are needed to respond to such a situation. As students consider the variables in the situation, they may want to pick plausible values that offer a possible solution.

 Headline Story

> Dave plans to fence in a rectangular region of his yard for his dog. How might he decide the shape and size of the area to fence in?

Possible responses: First he might decide where he wants the region to be, and how much of the yard he wants to use. He could measure the sides of the dog's space to figure out the amount of fencing he will need. He might try different side lengths for the dog's region to see how the perimeter changes. He might therefore make the rectangular region more square-like than oblong in order to use less fencing for the same area.

Skills Practice and Review

Selecting Units of Measure

Have students choose the appropriate unit of measure (length, weight, or capacity) for each of the following situations. You or your students might also make up additional questions.

- Is the distance between towns measured in kilograms or miles? miles
- Is the distance around a lake measured in kilometers or centimeters? kilometers
- Is the weight of a bunch of paper clips measured in grams or cups? grams
- Is the amount of juice in a glass measured in gallons or fluid ounces? fluid ounces

individuals
or pairs

15
MIN

NCTM Standards 1, 2, 3, 4, 7, 8, 9

Ⓐ Exploring Perimeter

Purpose To describe how to find the perimeter of any parallelogram

Introduce Have students look at Explore: Perimeter of Parallelograms. Some students may be uncertain about the use of letters instead of numbers as labels for the side lengths. You may need to remind them that the letters simply stand for "some number," but that the same letter stands for the same number.

To prepare students for completing the page, ask them to describe some of the attributes of parallelograms. Students should mention that parallelograms have two pairs of parallel sides and that opposite sides are congruent. Students might also mention that rectangles, squares, and rhombuses are special types of parallelograms.

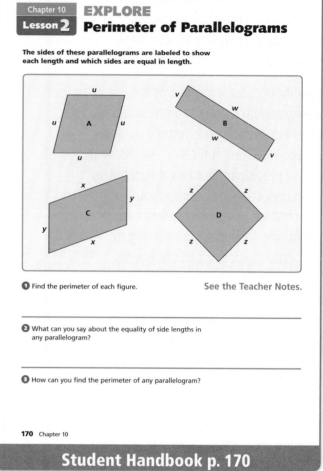

Chapter 10
Lesson 2

EXPLORE

Perimeter of Parallelograms

The sides of these parallelograms are labeled to show each length and which sides are equal in length.

❶ Find the perimeter of each figure.   See the Teacher Notes.

❷ What can you say about the equality of side lengths in any parallelogram?

❸ How can you find the perimeter of any parallelogram?

170   Chapter 10

Student Handbook p. 170

Task Have students complete **Explore: Perimeter of Parallelograms.**

Students may work independently or with a partner. Once students have completed the page, have them share their answers and record their methods for finding perimeter by writing an equation on the board.

💬 **Talk Math**

❓ How did you find the perimeter of figure A? I added the four sides together.

❓ How could you record your method with a formula? $P = u + u + u + u$, or $P = 4u$

❓ How could you record your method of finding the perimeter of figure C with a formula? $P = x + y + x + y$, or $P = 2x + 2y$, or $P = 2 \times (x + y)$

❓ How can you find the perimeter of any parallelogram? Possible answer: I can add together the lengths of all of its sides. (While this is true, it is not specific to parallelograms. Therefore, encourage a more specific answer.) Since parallelograms have two pairs of equal-length sides, I could add the lengths of two not parallel sides to each other and then double that amount. If the parallelogram is a rhombus, I could quadruple the length of any side.

Using Perimeter Formulas LAB pp. 195–196

individuals 25 MIN

Purpose To practice finding perimeters of parallelograms by using a formula

NCTM Standards 1, 3, 4, 7, 9

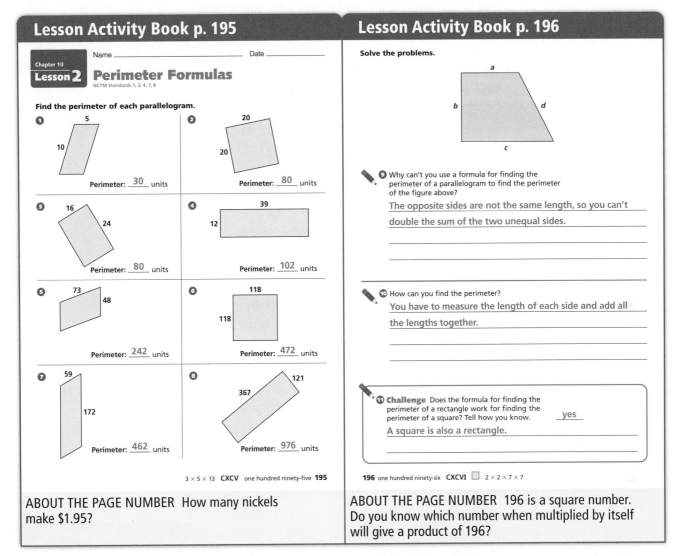

Teaching Notes for LAB page 195

Students use two given side lengths to find the perimeter of each parallelogram. Students should use the formulas they discussed in the previous activity. For the squares in Problems 2 and 6, students can multiply the length of one side by 4 since all 4 sides are the same length.

✓**Ongoing Assessment** Ask students for the formulas they are using to find the perimeter of the parallelograms on this page. This will help you to see whether students are being efficient in their work, or whether they need more practice recognizing that opposite sides of parallelograms have the same lengths.

Teaching Notes for LAB page 196

Students analyze the formula for finding the perimeter of a parallelogram and situations where it can be used.

Challenge Problem Students consider whether the formula for finding the perimeter of a rectangle also applies to finding the perimeter of a square.

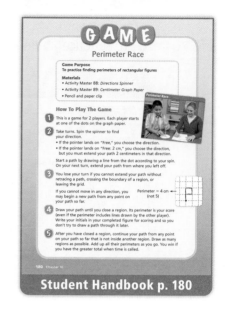
C Playing a Game: *Perimeter Race*

Materials
- For each pair of students: AM88–AM89, pencil, paper clip

NCTM Standards 4

Purpose To practice finding perimeters of rectangular figures

Goal The object of the game, *Perimeter Race,* is to accumulate the largest total of perimeters. At the end of the time period, the player with the greater perimeter total wins.

Prepare Materials Students play in pairs. Each pair needs AM88: Directions Spinner, AM89: Centimeter Graph Paper, a pencil, and a paper clip. To use the spinner, a player spins the paper clip around the pencil point as the pencil is held vertically at the center of the spinner.

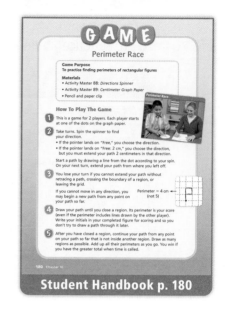

Student Handbook p. 180

How to Play

① Each player begins on one of the dots on the graph paper.

② Players alternate spinning the spinner to get a direction. They then extend the path (from where they left off in the previous turn) 1 cm in that direction along empty grid lines. If the spinner lands on "free," the player may choose the direction to move. If the spinner lands on "free: 2 cm," the player may still choose the direction to move, but must extend the path 2 cm in that direction.

If the path cannot be extended in the required direction because it would involve retracing a path, crossing the boundary of a region, or leaving the grid, it's the next player's turn. If a player has no possible moves in any direction, they may begin a new path from any point on their path thus far.

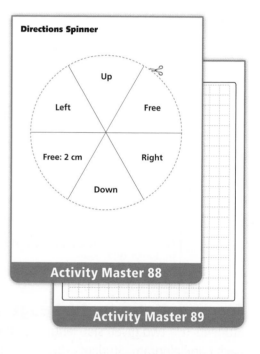

Activity Master 88

Activity Master 89

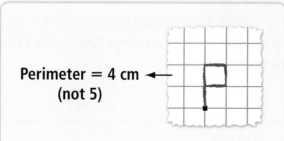

Perimeter = 4 cm ← (not 5)

③ Players continue drawing their paths (without crossing through squares) until they close a region. Their score is the perimeter of the enclosed region, even if the perimeter includes lines drawn by the other player. Players may find it helpful to shade or put an X in their completed figures so they don't try to draw paths through them later.

④ After closing a region, players may continue their path from any point on their path thus far. If a player's last extension of their path is enclosed in a region by the other player, they may also continue their path from any point on their path thus far that is not within an enclosed region.

⑤ Players keep a running total of their perimeters. The player with the higher perimeter total at the end of the game time is the winner.

Use with Lesson Activity Book pp. 195–196.

Reflect and Summarize the Lesson

Write Math What formula could you use to find the perimeter of this parallelogram? How would you use the formula to find the perimeter of a rectangle that is 6 inches long and 3 inches wide? Possible answers: $P = (2 \times l) + (2 \times s)$ or $P = 2 \times (l + s)$. To use the formula to find the number of inches in the perimeter I would replace the l in the formula with 6 and the s in the formula with 3: $P = (2 \times 6) + (2 \times 3) = 12 + 6 = 18$, or $P = 2 \times (6 + 3) = 2 \times 8 = 18$. So, the perimeter is 18 inches.

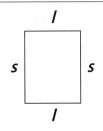

Review Model ....

Refer students to Review Model: Finding Perimeter in the *Student Handbook* to see how to find the perimeter of a parallelogram or other polygons.

✔ **Check for Understanding**

❶ $P = 9.6$ cm

❷ $P = 8$ cm

❸ $P = 8$ cm

❹ $P = 7.7$ cm

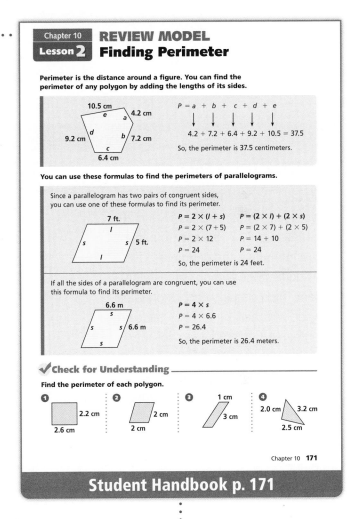

Student Handbook p. 171

Leveled Problem Solving

Lyle draws a trapezoid. One base is
12 centimeters longer than the other.

❶ Basic Level

If the longer base is
30 centimeters, what is the length
of the shorter base? Explain.
18 cm; subtract 12 from 30 to
find the shorter base.

❷ On Level

If the longer base is *x*, what is an
expression for the length of the
shorter base? Explain. *x* − 12;
the length of the shorter base is
found by subtracting 12 from
whatever number represents the
longer base.

❸ Above Level

If the length of the legs are 9 and
15 centimeters, and the shorter
base is 18 centimeters, what is
the perimeter of the trapezoid?
Explain. 72 cm; 18 + (18 + 12) +
9 + 15 = 18 + 30 + 24 = 72

Intervention

Activity Using Formulas

Display a parallelogram, and give
two side lengths, such as 12 and 20
centimeters. Ask students to name
ways of finding the perimeter. List
all suggestions without simplifying
them. Then simplify each expression
to see whether the result is the correct
perimeter (64 centimeters for the
given example). Review the order
of operations as they apply to each
expression, and discuss the errors in
the one(s) that did not work.

Practice

Perimeter Formulas
Find the perimeter of each parallelogram.

❶ 29 29   ❷ 33 99
Perimeter __116__ units   Perimeter __264__ units

❸ 339 112   ❹ 99 99
Perimeter __902__ units   Perimeter __396__ units

Test Prep
❺ Taylor used 64 feet of fencing to enclose a square
pen for his dog. How long is each side of the pen?
Explain how you know.
16 ft; Possible explanation: The four sides of a square all
have the same length. So, each side is 64 ÷ 4, or 16 feet.

Practice P80

Extension

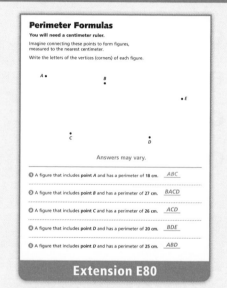

Perimeter Formulas
You will need a centimeter ruler.
Imagine connecting these points to form figures,
measured to the nearest centimeter.
Write the letters of the vertices (corners) of each figure.

A   *B*
   E
C   *D*

Answers may vary.

❶ A figure that includes **point A** and has a perimeter of **18 cm**. __ABC__
❷ A figure that includes **point B** and has a perimeter of **27 cm**. __BACD__
❸ A figure that includes **point C** and has a perimeter of **26 cm**. __ACD__
❹ A figure that includes **point D** and has a perimeter of **20 cm**. __BDE__
❺ A figure that includes **point D** and has a perimeter of **25 cm**. __ABD__

Extension E80

Spiral Review

Spiral Review Book page SR80 provides
review of the following previously learned
skills and concepts:

- using multiplication and division
  to solve problems involving whole
  numbers
- applying the problem solving strategy
  act it out-make a model

You may wish to have students work with
partners to complete the page.

Number and Operations
Solve.
❶ The baseball team uses the school vans to get to a game.
There are 25 players. Each van can hold 7 players. Each van
is filled before the next one is used. What is the greatest
number of students that will be in the van that is not full? __4 students__
❷ Mr. James fills in each row of his classroom with students
before starting another row. There are 27 students and
4 rows of seats. How many students will be in the last row? __3 students__
For 3–5, use this information.
A tour bus can carry 52 passengers. The minimum number
of passengers is 40 per bus. A group of 320 people is
going on a trip and wants to rent some buses.
❸ How many buses will the group need to rent? __7 buses__
❹ How many people will be on full buses? __312 people__
❺ Assuming the buses are full, how many people will not
be able to go on the trip if the company keeps to its plan? __8 people__

Problem Solving
Use a strategy and solve.
❻ Germaine has a CD cabinet that holds 50 CDs on 3 shelves.
He wants to arrange his 50 CDs so that the top shelf has
twice as many as the middle shelf and the bottom shelf
has no more than 10 CDs. How can he arrange the CDs
on the 3 shelves? Make a list of all the ways.
top 32, middle 16, bottom 2; top 30, middle 15, bottom 5;
top 28, middle 14, bottom 8
❼ Ms. Gomez marks out a grid on her classroom floor.
Roberto stands at one intersection on the grid. He walks
6 steps forward, turns right, walks 3 steps, turns left, and
walks 5 steps? He walks only on the grid lines, what is the
least number of steps he must take to get back to where
he began? __14 steps__

Spiral Review SR80

Extension Activity
Same Rectangle?

Provide pairs of students with a
24-cm piece of string whose ends are
taped together without overlapping,
cm rulers, and a sheet of cm graph
paper. Challenge students to find the
dimensions of as many rectangles as
they can, using the string, that have
a perimeter of 24 cm and sides with
whole numbers. Have them draw an
outline of each rectangle on the graph
paper. 1 cm × 11 cm, 2 cm × 10 cm,
3 cm by 9 cm, 4 cm × 8 cm, 5 cm ×
7 cm, 6 cm × 6 cm

Teacher's Notes 🍎

Daily Notes . . .

Quick Notes

More Ideas

Lesson 3 Area of Parallelograms

NCTM Standards 1, 3, 4, 6, 7, 8, 9

Lesson Planner

STUDENT OBJECTIVES
- To connect models for perimeter and area with appropriate formulas
- To select and use appropriate units and formulas for perimeter and area of parallelograms

1 Daily Activities (TG p. 835)

Open-Ended Problem Solving/Headline Story	Skills Practice and Review—Naming Units of Measure

2 Teach and Practice (TG pp. 836–839)

MATERIALS

(A) **Demonstrating Unchanged Area** (TG p. 836)

(B) **Finding a Rule for the Area of a Parallelogram** (TG pp. 837–838)

(C) **Using Area Formulas for Parallelograms** (TG p. 839)

- TR: Activity Master, AM90
- index cards
- scissors
- centimeter and inch rulers
- 📖 LAB pp. 197–198

3 Differentiated Instruction (TG p. 840)

Leveled Problem Solving (TG p. 840)	Practice Book P81
Intervention Activity (TG p. 840)	Extension Book E81
Extension Activity (TG p. 840)	Spiral Review Book SR81
Physical Education Connection (TG p. 816)	

Lesson Notes

About the Lesson

When a figure is cut into parts and the parts are then rearranged, the shape may change but the area will remain the same. In this lesson, students use this fact and their knowledge about finding the area of a rectangle to discover the formula for the area of a parallelogram. They cut a parallelogram perpendicular to a *base* and make a rectangle with the same base and height. Because the area, base, and height of the newly made rectangle are the same as those of the original parallelogram, the process of finding the area is the same for both: multiply the base times the height.

This lesson helps students to see why the area formula for parallelograms works. Students discover the formula themselves as a result of concrete manipulation of the figure. Because students are not simply memorizing a formula, they will be able to reconstruct the formula whenever they need to use it in the future. In **Lesson 10.5,** students will engage in similar activities to discover the area formulas for the area of triangles and trapezoids.

Use with Lesson Activity Book pp. 197–198.

Developing Mathematical Language

Vocabulary: base, height

The terms *base* and *height,* as used in geometry, have almost the same meaning they have in casual English. But, there is a subtle difference that can be confusing. In casual use, the *base* is at the bottom. However, just as a lamp may be turned upside down so that its *base* is no longer the lowest point, the mathematical *base* of a figure does not need to be horizontal or at the bottom of a figure. The *base* of a triangle or parallelogram can be any side we choose. Once we decide what side we are calling the *base,* the corresponding *height* is the distance from that side to the opposite side in the case of a parallelogram, or to the opposite vertex in the case of a triangle. Another name for the *height,* which students may be familiar with, is altitude.

Familiarize students with the terms *base* and *height.*

Beginning Discuss the word *height.* Then draw a parallelogram on the board, and discuss the *height* of the parallelogram as the distance straight up from the *base,* or bottom, of the figure to the top of the figure.

Intermediate Draw a parallelogram on the board. Show the *base* and *height* in two different colors. Name the color, and have students tell whether it is the *base* or *height* of the parallelogram.

Advanced Have students explain what the *base* and the *height* of a figure are.

Open-Ended Problem Solving

In responding to this Headline Story, students should consider how Dave might figure out and compare the costs of different size squares and rectangles that he might fence in.

 Headline Story

> While planning to fence in a rectangular part of his yard for his dog, Dave thought that part of his decision about the size and shape of the region should depend on the cost. He knows the cost of a foot of fencing.

Possible responses: Dave could measure the perimeters of different squares and rectangles that would fit in the yard. He could measure to the nearest foot and then multiply by the cost per foot to find the total cost for each of the figures. He might find that some of the possible configurations have the same perimeter and choose between these two by considering how much area is inside each fence.

Skills Practice and Review

Select Appropriate Units of Measure

Write the units of measure used below on the board. Then have students complete each of these sentences with as many reasonable measurement units as they can.

- The distance between home and school might be measured in . . . Possible answers: feet, yards, miles, meters, kilometers
- The perimeter of a playground might be measured in . . . Possible answers: feet, yards, meters
- The area of the ceiling . . . Possible answers: square feet, square meters
- The perimeter of a desk . . . Possible answers: inches, feet, centimeters

2 | Teach and Practice

Materials
- For the teacher: index cards, scissors

NCTM Standards 3, 6, 8, 9

Differentiated Instruction

Basic Level For students who remain unconvinced that the very different looking figure has the same area as the original rectangle, you might put the pieces back together as a rectangle to help them see that the new figure is made only from the parts of the original rectangle.

Ⓐ Demonstrating Unchanged Area

Purpose To review the concept of area and the process of finding the area of a rectangle

Introduce To give students additional experience selecting appropriate units of measure for area, ask the questions below.

- What unit of measure would you use to measure the area of the floor of a bedroom—square inches, square feet, square centimeters, or square miles? square feet

- What unit of measure would you use to measure the area of a city—square meters, square millimeters, square miles, or square feet? square miles

- What unit of measure would you use to measure the area of a football field—square centimeters, square inches, square kilometers, or square yards? square yards

Show students a rectangular index card, and remind them that rectangles can be thought of as rows and columns of unit squares. Students will likely remember that area is the amount of space inside a two-dimensional figure, and that we measure it as a number of square units in that amount of space. To check for this understanding, ask students how they could find the area of the rectangular index card. To find the area of a rectangular array, you multiply the number of rows by the number of columns. So for a 3-inch by 5-inch index card that effectively has 3 rows and 5 columns of 1-inch squares, that area is 15 square inches.

Task Cut the index card into two pieces, and rearrange the pieces so that the shape has changed. Ask students if the area has changed. no Rearrange the pieces again and ask for the area of the new figure. Students should realize that the area is still 15 square inches.

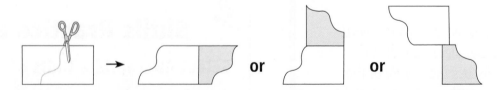

Practice Cut other index cards in different ways and repeat the process. Be careful not to combine pieces from two different cards, as this *will* change the area.

Use with Lesson Activity Book pp. 197–198.

Finding a Rule for the Area of a Parallelogram

Purpose To use the formula for the area of a rectangle to discover the formula for the area of a parallelogram

Introduce Give students AM90: Parallelogram and scissors, and have them cut out their parallelograms. Explain that they will be making a cut along one of the grid lines, and then rearranging the resulting two pieces into a rectangle. Once the parallelogram is cut into pieces that are rearranged into a rectangle, students should be able to find the area.

Task **Have students cut their parallelogram into two pieces (using exactly one cut), and rearrange the pieces to form a rectangle.** The grid lines are to help students cut a straight line. You might make extra parallelograms available so that students can try cutting in different places.

After students have experimented for a few minutes, discuss their findings as a class. Some students may have cut off a triangle and placed it on the other side of the remaining trapezoid to form a rectangle (as in the first diagram below). Others may have cut the parallelogram into two trapezoids and rearranged them into a rectangle (as in the second diagram). All students should have cut along the grid lines perpendicular to a base in order to be able to form a rectangle from the two pieces.

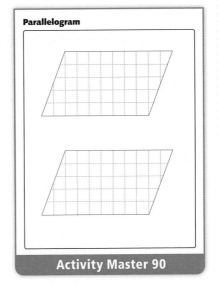

Parallelogram

Activity Master 90

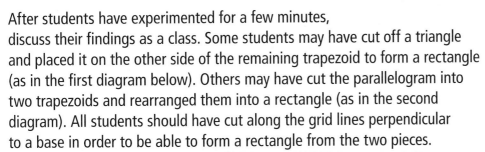

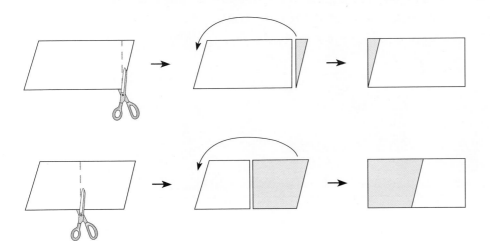

Materials
- For each student: AM90, scissors

NCTM Standards 1, 3, 7, 8, 9

Concept Alert

Sometimes materials refer to the *length* and *width* of a rectangle and describe area as *length* × *width*. But these terms can be ambiguous since the same side might appear to be the length in one orientation and the width in another orientation. Therefore, we use the terms *base* and *height* instead.

Height is the top-to-bottom measure when the *base* is horizontal. But since the base is not required to be horizontal, the *height* is not always vertical. Geometric figures, like all real-world objects, can be turned sideways or upside down. When students learn how to find the area of a rectangle, the words *base* and *height* mean the measurements of two perpendicular sides. Other parallelograms provide an opportunity for students to realize that the height is not always the measure of a side, but is the distance from the base to the opposite side.

Talk Math

❷ How does the area of the parallelogram compare to the area of the rectangle? The areas are the same.

❷ How could we compute the area of the rectangle? Multiply the base times the height.

❷ How can we find the length of the rectangle's base if we know the measurements of the original parallelogram? The base of the rectangle is the same as the base of the parallelogram.

❷ Look at the height of the rectangle. Where could we find that measurement on the original (uncut) parallelogram? The height of the rectangle is the same as the distance from the base of the parallelogram to the opposite side.

❷ What is a rule for finding the area of any parallelogram? The area of a parallelogram can be found in the same way that the area of a rectangle can be found, by multiplying the base times the height.

Have students find at least three parallelograms in the classroom. Then ask students to determine which one has the greatest area by having them use appropriate units to measure the areas.

Practice
Sketch several parallelograms on the board, and show the lengths of the base and the height to that base on the sketches. Ask students for the area of each parallelogram, based on those measurements. Students should use appropriate units to measure the area. To challenge students, you might label all side lengths of the parallelogram in addition to the height so that they must choose the numbers that are relevant to finding area.

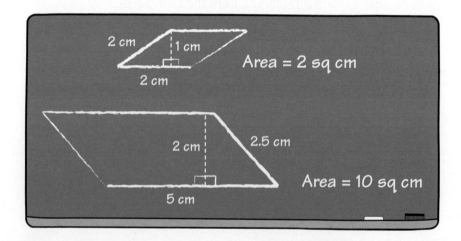

Use with Lesson Activity Book pp. 197–198.

Purpose To find the areas of parallelograms

NCTM Standards 1, 3, 4, 7, 9

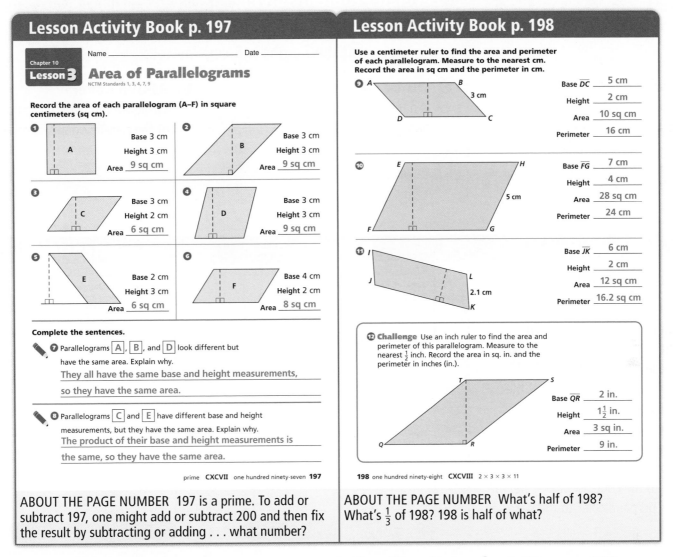

Teaching Notes for LAB page 197

Students find the area of parallelograms by multiplying the base and height of each. Students may need a reminder to record the areas in square centimeters. The height of each parallelogram is drawn to help students remember that the height measures the distance from a base to its opposite side, and is not the length of the side that is not parallel to the base.

Differentiated Instruction On Level/Above Level You might ask students whether congruent figures always have the same area, or whether all figures with the same area are congruent. The questions at the bottom of the page should help students see that not all figures with the same area are congruent. However, all congruent figures do have the same area.

Teaching Notes for LAB page 198

Students use a centimeter ruler to measure the base and height of each parallelogram and compute the area. Watch for students who use the length of a side as the height. Students also find the perimeter of each parallelogram.

✓ Ongoing Assessment Watch for students who use congruence of opposite sides to simplify their computations. There is no need to correct students who continue to measure all sides of the parallelogram since this method is merely inefficient, not incorrect.

Challenge Problem Students measure to the nearest half-inch and compute with fractions to find the area and perimeter of a parallelogram.

Reflect and Summarize the Lesson

 Write Math

Explain how the area of a rectangle with a base that is 3 cm and a height that is 4 cm compares to the area of a parallelogram with a base that is 3 cm and a height that is 4 cm. The areas are the same. Both have areas of 12 sq cm.

Leveled Problem Solving

Ali draws a parallelogram. The base is 16 centimeters. The sides are 10 centimeters and the height is 8 centimeters.

❶ Basic Level

Is the parallelogram a rectangle? Explain. No; since the height is different from one side length, it cannot be a rectangle.

❷ On Level

What is the perimeter of the parallelogram? Explain. 52 cm; $2 \times (16 + 10) = 2 \times 26 = 52$ cm

❸ Above Level

What are the perimeter and area of the parallelogram? Explain. 52 cm, 128 sq cm; $P = 2 \times (16 + 10) = 2 \times 26 = 52$; $A = 16 \times 8 = 128$

Intervention

Activity Base and Height

Display a nonrectangle parallelogram with a perpendicular line drawn from one vertex to the opposite side. Write these dimensions: length of base, length of a side, length of the perpendicular line. Ask students to name the values they would use to find the figure's area. Repeat with several parallelograms, leading students to the conclusion that *height* is always perpendicular to the base.

Practice

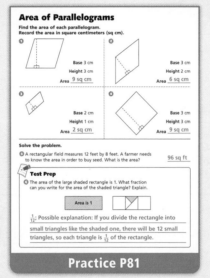

Practice P81

Extension

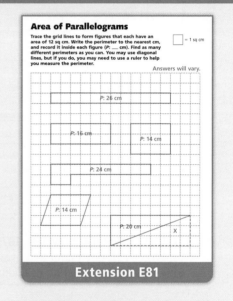

Extension E81

Spiral Review

Spiral Review Book page SR81 provides review of the following previously learned skills and concepts:

- observing patterns and making generalizations
- converting between cups, pints, quarts, and gallons

You may wish to have students work with partners to complete the page.

Spiral Review SR81

Extension Activity
Drawing Perpendiculars

Challenge students to draw a parallelogram so that it is not possible to draw a perpendicular from one base to the other inside the figure. Ask them to devise a way to find the height of this figure. An example is

Ask students to draw their results and explain why they think their drawings represent the height. Any line perpendicular to one base will cross the other base if that base is extended.

Teacher's Notes 🍎

Daily Notes . . .

Quick Notes

More Ideas

Lesson 4 Measuring to Find Areas of Parallelograms

NCTM Standards 1, 3, 4, 6, 7, 8, 9, 10

Lesson Planner

STUDENT OBJECTIVES
- To select and use appropriate units and formulas for perimeter and area of parallelograms
- To find and measure heights of parallelograms

1 Daily Activities (TG p. 843)

Open-Ended Problem Solving/Headline Story	Skills Practice and Review— Choosing Formulas for Area and Perimeter

2 Teach and Practice (TG pp. 844–848)

Ⓐ Measuring with a Wide Ruler (TG pp. 844–845)

Ⓑ Finding Areas and Perimeters (TG p. 846)

Ⓒ Playing a Game: *Area Race* (TG p. 847)

MATERIALS
- TR: Activity Masters, AM91, AM88–AM89
- centimeter rulers
- index cards or half sheets of paper
- tape
- paper clips
- 📖 LAB pp. 199–200
- 📖 SH pp. 172, 181

3 Differentiated Instruction (TG p. 849)

Leveled Problem Solving (TG p. 849)	Practice Book P82
Intervention Activity (TG p. 849)	Extension Book E82
Extension Activity (TG p. 849)	Spiral Review Book SR82

Lesson Notes

About the Lesson

Students practice identifying heights of parallelograms, and then measure these heights using a widened ruler to ensure they measure perpendicular to a base.

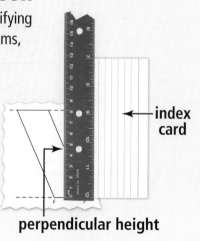

← index card

perpendicular height

They measure bases and practice using a formula to compute the area of parallelograms. After measuring the remaining side lengths, students also compute perimeters.

Use with Lesson Activity Book pp. 199–200.

Developing Mathematical Language

Vocabulary: measuring the height of a parallelogram

When *measuring the height of a parallelogram,* students need to be sure that the height is perpendicular to the base. The corner of an index card is a right angle, so students will use it to widen the ruler. This will help students align the (sometimes extended) base of a parallelogram with the zero mark on the ruler to *measure the height of a parallelogram.* Students will measure and use the height and base measurements in a formula to find the area of a parallelogram.

Familiarize students with the term *measuring the height of a parallelogram.*

Beginning Demonstrate measuring the height of a desk. Draw a parallelogram on the board. Measure different parts of the parallelogram and ask students to raise their hands when they notice you are *measuring the height of a parallelogram.*

Intermediate Draw one or more parallelograms on the board. Ask students to describe what you are doing as you are extending a base line, measuring the base, and *measuring the height of a parallelogram.*

Advanced Have students show that *measuring the height of a parallelogram* requires more steps than just measuring the length of the base.

Open-Ended Problem Solving

While students might make other mathematical observations, direct them to consider the possible areas of the garden in this Headline Story. They might draw pictures of the gardens.

 Headline Story

> A fence that is 24 yards long completely surrounds a garden.

Possible responses: If the garden is a square, it would be 6 yards on each side, and have an area of 36 square yards. If the garden is a non-square rectangle, there are many possibilities for its dimensions. One possibility is that the garden is 1 yard by 11 yards, with an area of 11 square yards. Another possibility is that the garden is 1.5 yards by 10.5 yards. The closer to a square the garden is, the greater its area.

Skills Practice and Review

Choosing Formulas for Area and Perimeter

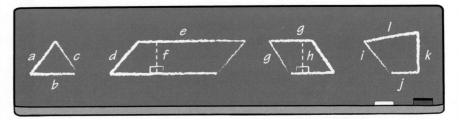

Ask students how they could find the perimeter for any of these figures, and have them record their formulas on the board. For example, to find the perimeter of the parallelogram they could write $2d + 2e$ or $2 \times (d + e)$. Then ask how they could find the area for either of the parallelograms, and again have them record their formulas on the board. Students might record $g \times h$ for the area of the rhombus.

To apply these formulas, replace the letters with actual numbers. Label some of the non-base sides with decimals so that students can practice adding decimal numbers when they find the perimeter.

individuals
15 MIN

A Measuring with a Wide Ruler

Materials
- For each student: AM91, centimeter ruler, tape, and index card or half sheet of paper

NCTM Standards 1, 3, 4, 8

Purpose To identify and measure the height of a parallelogram

Introduce Explain to students that they will be creating a wide centimeter ruler that will help them hold the measuring edge perpendicular to a base to help measure the heights of parallelograms. Students will be measuring with these rulers throughout the chapter so they should take care to assemble them as accurately as possible.

Measuring Heights

Use a wide ruler to help you make measurements perpendicular to a base.

① Measure the height in centimeters to Base $\overline{AB}$.

Base $\overline{AB}$ ___10 cm___
Height ___4 cm___
Area ___40 sq cm___

② Measure the height in centimeters to Base $\overline{CD}$.

Base $\overline{CD}$ ___7 cm___
Height ___6 cm___
Area ___42 sq cm___

③ Measure the height in centimeters to Base $\overline{EF}$.

Base $\overline{EF}$ ___3 cm___
Height ___8 cm___
Area ___24 sq cm___

Activity Master 91

To make their wide rulers, students should place a ruler on top of an index card or half sheet of paper, slide the centimeter edge of the ruler to the edge of the card (as if measuring the edge), and tape the ruler to the card. The excess paper should be along the inch side of the ruler. The "bottom" edge of the card should be in line with the centimeter ruler's zero mark. Students who have transparent rulers or rulers with a zero mark at the exact edge of the ruler may have an easier time with this than students with opaque rulers.

Give students AM91: Measuring Heights and demonstrate how to place the wide ruler along a base to measure the height.

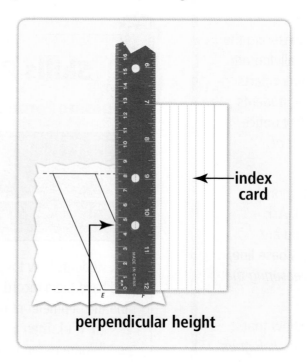

← index card

perpendicular height

Task **Have students complete AM91: Measuring Heights.** You may want your students to work on the page as a class to reach a consensus on the measurements. Students should notice the faint line extensions along the bases (and the sides parallel to the bases). These dotted lines are meant to help students line up the zero mark of their wide rulers and measure the height (the distance between the two parallel sides). In Problem 3, students will find that the height must be measured partly outside the parallelogram (due to its angles and narrowness), and that the line extensions will help them measure more accurately.

Talk Math

❷ How did you decide where to measure in order to find the height?
I measured the distance between the two dashed lines. Using my wide ruler I lined up the zero end with one of the dashed lines so that I knew I was measuring the perpendicular distance between the two dashed lines.

❷ How did you find the area of each parallelogram? I used the formula for area of a parallelogram: area = base × height.

✔ Ongoing Assessment

- As they measure on AM91: Measuring Heights, watch for students who continue to need support positioning the ruler correctly. Students' measurement experience has primarily been *along* a line, but to measure the height of a parallelogram, students must measure perpendicularly from one line to another.

- You might also observe students' ability to measure sides and round the measurements to the nearest centimeter.

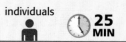
individuals
25 MIN

Purpose To practice measuring and using formulas to find the areas and perimeters of parallelograms

NCTM Standards 1, 3, 4, 6, 7, 9, 10

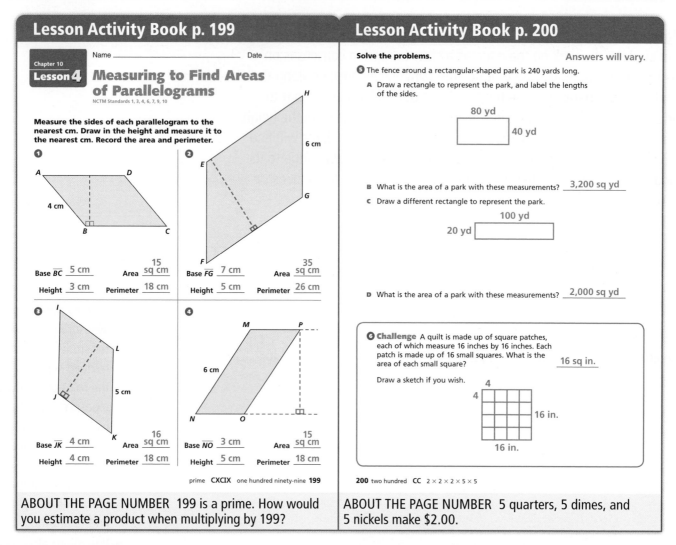

Teaching Notes for LAB page 199

Students identify and measure heights of parallelograms on this page. Make sure students realize they should draw in the heights. This will help you to identify the source of student errors (e.g., did they identify it incorrectly or measure it incorrectly). Students also measure the base so that they can multiply the base and height to find the area. The length of a non-base side of each parallelogram is given so that students can use the given measurement and their base measurement to find the perimeter of each figure.

Differentiated Instruction Below Level/On Level You might have students work in pairs to complete this page since they may not yet be comfortable finding heights in parallelograms.

Teaching Notes for LAB page 200

Students connect area and perimeter as they construct and label two different rectangles with the same perimeter. They then compute the areas of each rectangle to see that area can change when the perimeter remains unchanged. (The directions state to draw a rectangle. You may want to remind your students that it is also correct to draw a square since a square is a special case of a rectangle.)

✔Ongoing Assessment Continue watching for students who use the length of the non-base side as the height, as well as for students who forget to record area in square units.

Challenge Problem Students compute the area of a square made from a number of smaller squares of a given size.

Purpose To practice finding areas of rectangular figures

Goal The object of the game, *Area Race*, is to accumulate the larger total area. At the end of the time period, the player with the greatest area total wins.

Prepare Materials Students play this game in pairs. Each pair of students needs AM88: Directions Spinner, AM89: Centimeter Graph Paper, a pencil, and a paper clip. To use the spinner, a player spins the paper clip around the pencil point as the pencil is held vertically at the center of the spinner.

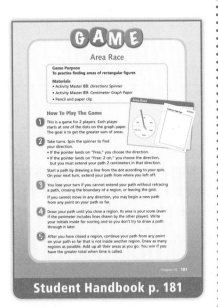

Student Handbook p. 181

Materials
• For each pair of students: AM88–AM89, pencil, paper clip

NCTM Standards 4, 6

How to Play

❶ Each player begins on one of the dots on the graph paper.

❷ Players alternate spinning the spinner to get a direction. They then extend the path 1 cm in that direction along empty grid lines. If the spinner lands on "free," the player may choose the direction to move. If the spinner lands on "free: 2 cm," the player may still choose the direction to move, but must extend the path 2 cm in that direction.

If the path cannot be extended in the required direction because it would involve retracing a path, crossing the boundary of a region, or leaving the grid, it's the next player's turn. If a player has no possible moves in any direction, they may begin a new path from any point on their path thus far.

❸ Players continue drawing their paths (without crossing through squares) until they close a region. Their score is the area of the enclosed region, even if the perimeter includes lines drawn by the other player. Players may find it helpful to shade or put an X in their completed shapes so they don't try to draw paths through them later.

❹ After closing a region, students may continue their path from any point on their path thus far. If a player's last extension of their path is enclosed in a region by the other player, they may also continue their path from any point on their path thus far that is not within an enclosed region.

❺ Players keep a running total of their areas. The player with the greater total area at the end of the game time is the winner.

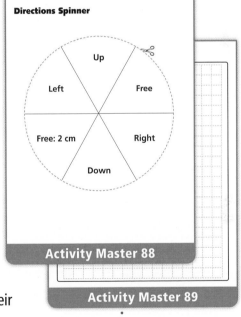

Directions Spinner

Up

Left

Free

Free: 2 cm

Right

Down

Activity Master 88

Activity Master 89

Extend Students might compute both the perimeter and the area for each region they enclose, keeping a separate running total for each measurement. There would then be two winners, one for the greatest area total and one for the greatest perimeter total. By paying attention to both area and perimeter, students can see that a larger area is not necessarily a larger perimeter, and vice versa.

Reflect and Summarize the Lesson

Write Math

Suppose you are given a drawing of a parallelogram. Explain what you would measure and how you would measure to help you find the area. First I would measure the length of the base. Then I would measure the height which is the distance from the base to the parallel side. To find the area I would multiply the length of the base by the length of the height. The answer would be in square units.

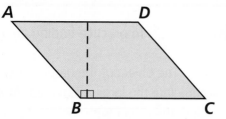

Review Model

Refer students to Review Model: Finding Area of a Parallelogram in the *Student Handbook* to see how the area of a parallelogram is related to the area of a rectangle and how to find the area of a parallelogram.

✔ **Check for Understanding**

❶ 50 sq ft

❷ 144 sq in.

❸ 4 sq cm

❹ 2.25 sq cm

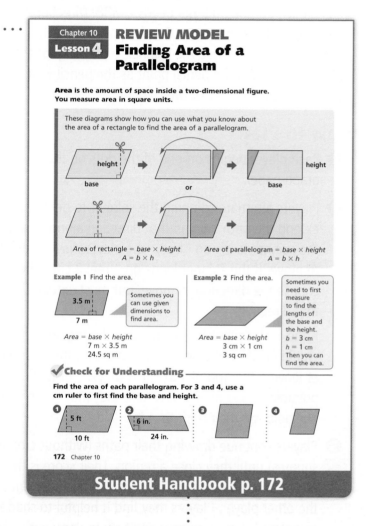

Student Handbook p. 172

Use with Lesson Activity Book pp. 199–200.

3 | Differentiated Instruction

Leveled Problem Solving

A rectangular room measures 12 feet by 20 feet. The floor will be covered with square tiles that are 2 feet on a side.

❶ Basic Level
What are the area and perimeter of each tile? Explain. Area: 4 square feet; multiply the length and width of one tile. Perimeter: 8 feet: add the side lengths of one tile.

❷ On Level
What are the area and perimeter of the room? Explain. Area: 240 sq ft; multiply the length and width of the room. Perimeter: 64 ft; add the length and width, and multiply the sum by 2.

❸ Above Level
How many tiles will be needed to cover the floor? 60 tiles; Possible explanation: find the room's area: 240 sq ft. Divide the area by the area of 1 tile, 4 sq ft. 240 ÷ 4 = 60

Intervention	Practice	Extension

Intervention

Activity Find a Pattern

Display several parallelograms. Write dimensions for the sides and the heights. For each figure, ask students to look for a pattern in the relationship between the side lengths and the height. Elicit that in nonrectangular parallelograms, the height will always be less than the side length that is not the base because the side is the hypotenuse of a right triangle for which the height is one of the legs.

Practice

Measuring to Find Areas of Parallelograms

Cut out the ruler on the right, if needed. Measure the sides and height of each parallelogram to the nearest cm. Record the area and perimeter for each figure.

① Base $\overline{BC}$ ___5 cm___
Height ___4 cm___
Area ___20 sq cm___
Perimeter ___20 cm___

② Base $\overline{EF}$ ___6 cm___
Height ___4 cm___
Area ___24 sq cm___
Perimeter ___22 sq cm___

Test Prep

③ Mario noticed that if he put 4 stickers on each page of his sticker album, he would have 2 left over. If he put 3 on each page, there would also be 2 left over. Mario had more than 10 stickers, but fewer than 30 stickers. How many stickers did he have?

A. 12 or 26 stickers
B. 14 or 26 stickers
C. 14 or 21 stickers
D. 13 or 25 stickers

Practice P82

Extension

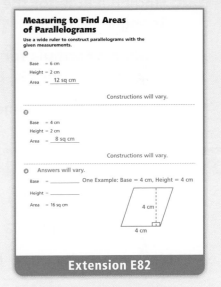

Measuring to Find Areas of Parallelograms

Use a wide ruler to construct parallelograms with the given measurements.

①
Base = 6 cm
Height = 2 cm
Area = ___12 sq cm___

Constructions will vary.

②
Base = 4 cm
Height = 2 cm
Area = ___8 sq cm___

Constructions will vary.

③ Answers will vary.
Base _____ One Example: Base = 4 cm, Height = 4 cm
Height = _____
Area = 16 sq cm

Extension E82

Spiral Review

Spiral Review Book page SR82 provides review of the following previously learned skills and concepts:

- identifying quadrilaterals by their attributes
- using lists of multiples to make generalizations about divisibility

You may wish to have students work with partners to complete the page.

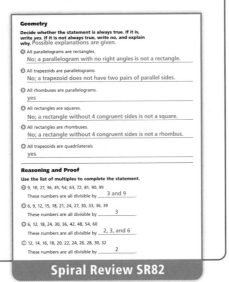

Geometry

Decide whether the statement is always true. If it is, write *yes*. If it is not always true, write *no*, and explain why. Possible explanations are given.

① All parallelograms are rectangles.
No; a parallelogram with no right angles is not a rectangle.

② All trapezoids are parallelograms.
No; a trapezoid does not have two pairs of parallel sides.

③ All rhombuses are parallelograms.
yes

④ All rectangles are squares.
No; a rectangle without 4 congruent sides is not a square.

⑤ All rectangles are rhombuses.
No; a rectangle without 4 congruent sides is not a rhombus.

⑥ All trapezoids are quadrilaterals.
yes

Reasoning and Proof

Use the list of multiples to complete the statement.

⑦ 9, 18, 27, 36, 45, 54, 63, 72, 81, 90, 99
These numbers are all divisible by ___3 and 9___

⑧ 6, 9, 12, 15, 18, 21, 24, 27, 30, 33, 36, 39
These numbers are all divisible by ___3___

⑨ 6, 12, 18, 24, 30, 36, 42, 48, 54, 60
These numbers are all divisible by ___2, 3, and 6___

⑩ 12, 14, 16, 18, 20, 22, 24, 26, 28, 30, 32
These numbers are all divisible by ___2___

Spiral Review SR82

Extension Activity
Perimeter-Area Relationship

Give pairs of students a sheet of centimeter graph paper. Ask them to draw as many rectangles as they can with a perimeter of 36 cm. For each, have pairs find and record the area. Areas will range from 17 sq cm (1 cm × 17 cm) to 81 sq cm (9 cm × 9 cm). Ask students to look for a pattern in how the shape of the rectangle is related to the area. Students should discover that as the shape approaches a square, the area increases.

Lesson 5 Area of Triangles and Trapezoids

NCTM Standards 1, 2, 3, 4, 6, 7, 8, 9, 10

Lesson Planner

STUDENT OBJECTIVE
- To use the formula for the area of a parallelogram to find the formulas for the areas of a triangle and a trapezoid

1 Daily Activities (TG p. 851)

Open-Ended Problem Solving/Headline Story	Skills Practice and Review— Choosing Formulas for Area and Perimeter

2 Teach and Practice (TG pp. 852–857)

MATERIALS

- (A) **Finding a Rule for the Area of a Triangle** (TG pp. 852–853)
- (B) **Finding a Formula for the Area of a Trapezoid** (TG pp. 854–855)
- (C) **Using Area and Perimeter Formulas** (TG p. 856)

- TR: Activity Master, AM92
- centimeter and inch rulers
- tape
- scissors
- LAB pp. 201–202
- SH pp. 173–174

3 Differentiated Instruction (TG p. 858)

Leveled Problem Solving (TG p. 858)	Practice Book P83
Intervention Activity (TG p. 858)	Extension Book E83
Extension Activity (TG p. 858)	Spiral Review Book SR83

Lesson Notes

About the Lesson

Students draw on their experience with finding a formula for the area of a parallelogram in **Lessons 10.3** and **10.4** to develop formulas for computing the areas of triangles and trapezoids. By putting two congruent triangles together, students see that the area of each triangle is half the area of the parallelogram they form.

Therefore, they can derive this formula:

Area of a triangle $= \frac{1}{2}$ area of a parallelogram $= \frac{1}{2} \times$ base $\times$ height

They use a similar method to derive the formula for the area of a trapezoid.

Area of a trapezoid $= \frac{1}{2}$ area of a parallelogram $= \frac{1}{2} \times$ (base 1 + base 2) $\times$ height

Use with Lesson Activity Book pp. 201–202.

Developing Mathematical Language

Vocabulary: trapezoid

In Geometry, the *trapezoid* is a quadrilateral in a class all its own. Exactly one pair of sides of a *trapezoid* is parallel. If no sides are parallel, then it is another quadrilateral. If two pairs of sides are parallel, then it is a parallelogram.

A *trapezoid* can have 0 or 2 right angles. It can have 0, 2, or 3 congruent sides. When two nonparallel sides of a trapezoid are congruent, it is called an isosceles *trapezoid.* The nonparallel sides are sometimes called the legs. The parallel sides are both considered bases and the lengths of both bases are used in the area formula.

Familiarize students with the term *trapezoid.*

Beginning Draw several shapes on the board, including at least one *trapezoid* Ask students which one is the *trapezoid.*

Intermediate Draw several quadrilaterals on the board, including at least one *trapezoid.* Have students name each shape.

Advanced Have students explain how to decide whether a quadrilateral is a *trapezoid,* a parallelogram, or neither.

Open-Ended Problem Solving

Students should consider how John might measure the area and perimeter of various objects in order to respond to this Headline Story. You might ask students to first consider ways of making more precise measurements, and then to consider ways of estimating.

 Headline Story

> **John wants to measure the area and perimeter of ____. He needs help.**

Possible responses: John could measure the top of a rectangular table (the area) and the edge around it (the perimeter) using a ruler. He might measure the sides in inches or feet and then calculate the area in square inches or square feet. John could use rope to measure the perimeter of a small, round pool, and then measure the rope by matching it up to a yardstick. Figuring out the pool's area would be harder, but John might make a rectangle around it, find the area of the rectangle, and then subtract some to make an estimate.

Skills Practice and Review

Choosing Formulas for Area and Perimeter

As in the previous lesson, sketch various triangles, parallelograms, and trapezoids on the board and label the lengths of their sides and heights with letters. Ask students how they could find the perimeter for any of these figures, and have them record their formulas on the board. For example, they could add all of the sides, or for a parallelogram they could double the sum of two not parallel sides. Then ask how they could find the area for any of the parallelograms, and again have them record their formulas on the board. Students might record *area = base × height* for the area.

To apply these formulas, replace the letters with actual numbers. Label some of the non-base sides with decimals so that students practice adding decimal numbers when they find the perimeter.

pairs

15 MIN

A Finding a Rule for the Area of a Triangle

Materials
- For each student: AM92, inch ruler, tape, scissors

NCTM Standards 1, 2, 3, 4, 7, 8, 9, 10

Purpose To discover the formula for finding the area of a triangle

Introduce Ask students how to find the area of a parallelogram. If necessary, remind them of how they cut a parallelogram into two pieces and rearranged the pieces to make a rectangle. Students should then recall that the area of a parallelogram is the product of its base and height.

Students will need AM92: Triangle and Trapezoid, Explore: Area of Triangles, scissors, tape, and an inch ruler. Explain to students that they will again be rearranging pieces to help them discover an area formula, this time for a triangle.

Task Have students work in pairs to complete Explore: Area of Triangles. On this page students put two congruent triangles together to form a parallelogram. Since students already know how to find the area of a parallelogram, they use this formula to discover the formula for the area of a triangle.

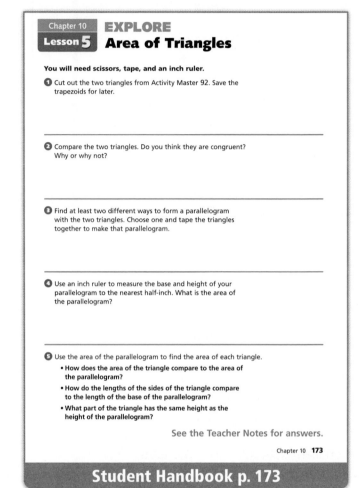

Chapter 10
Lesson 5

EXPLORE
Area of Triangles

You will need scissors, tape, and an inch ruler.

❶ Cut out the two triangles from Activity Master 92. Save the trapezoids for later.

❷ Compare the two triangles. Do you think they are congruent? Why or why not?

❸ Find at least two different ways to form a parallelogram with the two triangles. Choose one and tape the triangles together to make that parallelogram.

❹ Use an inch ruler to measure the base and height of your parallelogram to the nearest half-inch. What is the area of the parallelogram?

❺ Use the area of the parallelogram to find the area of each triangle.
- How does the area of the triangle compare to the area of the parallelogram?
- How do the lengths of the sides of the triangle compare to the length of the base of the parallelogram?
- What part of the triangle has the same height as the height of the parallelogram?

See the Teacher Notes for answers.

Chapter 10 **173**

Student Handbook p. 173

💬 **Talk Math**

❓ How do you know if the two triangles are congruent? Since they match up exactly when placed on top of each other, they are congruent.

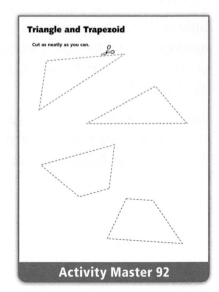

Triangle and Trapezoid

Cut as neatly as you can.

Activity Master 92

Use with Lesson Activity Book pp. 201–202.

❷ What are the possible parallelograms formed by the two triangles?

  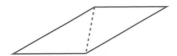

❷ How did you find the area of the parallelograms? I measured the base and height and then multiplied these two measures together to find the area in square inches.

 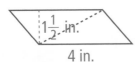 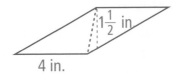

❷ How does the area of one of the triangles compare to the area of the parallelogram? The triangle's area is half the area of the parallelogram.

❷ What part of the triangle has the same measure as the base of the parallelogram? One side of the triangle is the base of the parallelogram, so its measure is the same.

❷ What part of the triangle has the same measure as the height of the parallelogram? The height of the parallelogram is the same as the height of the triangle.

Share Support your class in discovering a rule for finding the area of any triangle. Students should conclude that the area is half the area of the parallelogram, so its area is $\frac{1}{2} \times$ base $\times$ height. Write the formula in shorthand on the board so that students are familiar with it: Area of a triangle $= \frac{1}{2} \times b \times h$.

Practice Sketch several triangles on the board with the length of their sides and height labeled. Ask students to use the formula to find the area of these triangles.

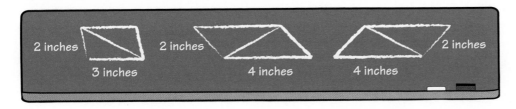

Use with Lesson Activity Book pp. 201–202.

Materials
- For each student: AM92, inch ruler, tape, scissors

NCTM Standards 1, 3, 4, 7, 8, 9, 10

B Finding a Formula for the Area of a Trapezoid

Purpose To discover the formula for finding the area of a trapezoid

Introduce Tell your students that they will again be rearranging two pieces into a parallelogram to help them discover another area formula, this time for a trapezoid. If necessary, review with students the fact that trapezoids have exactly one pair of parallel sides.

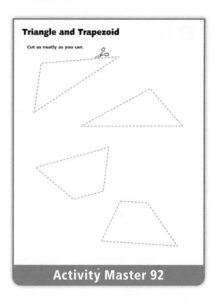

Triangle and Trapezoid
Cut as neatly as you can.

Activity Master 92

Task Have students cut out the two trapezoids on AM92: Triangle and Trapezoid and check that they are congruent. Then, tape them together to form a parallelogram.

There are only two ways students can position the trapezoids to make a parallelogram. Although they are oriented differently, these are the same parallelogram—one is a reflection of the other.

 **Talk Math**

❓ What is the area of the parallelogram? The base is 4 inches and the height is 1.5 inches, so the area is 4 in × 1.5 in, or 6 square inches.

❓ How does the area of the trapezoid compare to the area of the parallelogram? It's half the area.

❓ What parts of the trapezoid form the base of the parallelogram? The base of the parallelogram is the sum of the two parallel sides, or bases, of the trapezoid.

❓ What measure on the trapezoid matches the height of the parallelogram exactly? The height of the parallelogram is the same as the height, or perpendicular distance from one base to the other, of the trapezoid.

Use with Lesson Activity Book pp. 201–202.

Share Help your class find a rule for finding the area of any trapezoid. Students should conclude that because the area of the parallelogram is found by multiplying the base (which is the sum of the two bases of the trapezoid) by the height (which is also the height of the trapezoid), and since the trapezoid is half of the parallelogram, the area formula is $\frac{1}{2} \times$ (base 1 + base 2) $\times$ height. Written in shorthand, the formula is Area of a trapezoid $= \frac{1}{2} \times (b_1 + b_2) \times h$.

Practice Sketch several trapezoids on the board with the length of their sides and height labeled. Ask students to use the formula to find the area of these trapezoids.

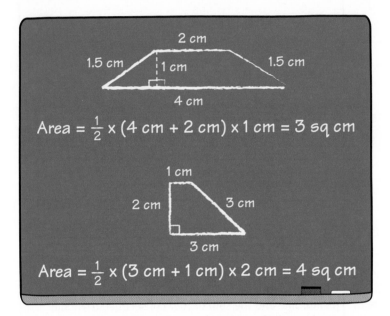

Using Area and Perimeter Formulas LAB pp. 201–202

Purpose To practice finding the area of triangles and trapezoids

NCTM Standards 1, 3, 4, 6, 7, 9

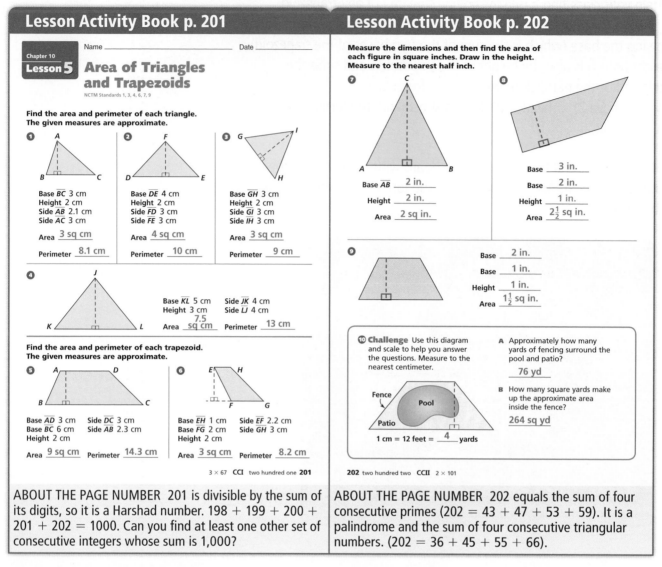

ABOUT THE PAGE NUMBER 201 is divisible by the sum of its digits, so it is a Harshad number. 198 + 199 + 200 + 201 + 202 = 1000. Can you find at least one other set of consecutive integers whose sum is 1,000?

ABOUT THE PAGE NUMBER 202 equals the sum of four consecutive primes (202 = 43 + 47 + 53 + 59). It is a palindrome and the sum of four consecutive triangular numbers. (202 = 36 + 45 + 55 + 66).

Teaching Notes for LAB page 201

Students do not need to measure on this page in order to compute the area and perimeter of the triangles and trapezoids. Measurements are given and are rounded to the nearest centimeter.

Concept Alert The areas in this and the previous lessons were given or recorded in square inches and square centimeters. Instead of asking students to record the units in this way, you might have them apply their understanding of exponents to the shorthand notation in.² or cm². While we say "4 square inches," we write "4 inches squared." Students often attempt to write the symbols in spoken order and end up with "4² in." However, this means "sixteen inches," not "four square inches."

Teaching Notes for LAB page 202

Students measure the bases and heights and compute the areas of the triangles and trapezoids. The space for recording the lengths of the two bases of the trapezoids in Problems 8 and 9 are intentionally not specified as "base 1" or "base 2" in order to emphasize that the two measurements are interchangeable in the formula.

✔ Ongoing Assessment Watch for students who use the formula for the area of a parallelogram instead of the formula for a triangle or trapezoid. Some students may need reminders to use the formulas they found in the two previous activities for the areas of triangles and trapezoids.

Challenge Problem Students use a centimeter ruler to measure a scaled diagram and convert feet to yards to find area and perimeter. You may want to review the meaning of scale with students before they begin working on this problem.

Reflect and Summarize the Lesson

Write Math

Explain how the area of a triangle with a base that is 3 cm and a height that is 4 cm compares to the area of a parallelogram with a base that is 3 cm and a height that is 4 cm. The area of the triangle is $\frac{1}{2}$ the area of the rectangle. The area of the rectangle is 12 sq cm and the area of the triangle is 6 sq cm.

Then, explain how you would find the area of a trapezoid with bases of 3 in. and 5 in. and a height of 4 inches. You can use the formula $A = \frac{1}{2} \times (b_1 + b_2) \times h$ to find the area of a trapezoid. So, the area is $\frac{1}{2} \times (3 + 5) \times 4 = \frac{1}{2} \times (8) \times 4 = 4 \times 4 = 16$, or 16 sq in.

Review Model

Refer students to Review Model: Finding Areas of Triangles and Trapezoids in the **Student Handbook** to see how the area of a triangle and the area of a trapezoid are related to the area of a parallelogram and how to find the area of a triangle and the area of a trapezoid.

✔ Check for Understanding

❶ 125 sq cm

❷ 36 sq in.

❸ 45 sq ft

❹ 62.5 sq m

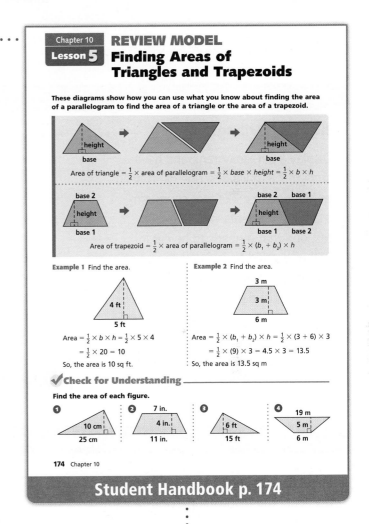

Leveled Problem Solving

Elijah draws a trapezoid and measures its bases and height.

❶ Basic Level

The lengths of the bases are 8 centimeters and 18 centimeters. The height is 12 centimeters. What is the area of the trapezoid? Explain. 156 sq cm;
$\frac{1}{2} \times 12 \times (8 + 18) = 156$

❷ On Level

The length of the bases are 14 centimeters and 8 centimeters. The area is 88 square centimeters. What is the height of the trapezoid? Explain. 8 cm; $88 = \frac{1}{2}$ $\times h \times (14 + 8) \rightarrow 88 = \frac{1}{2} \times h$ $(22) \rightarrow 88 = 4 \times 22$, so $h = 8$.

❸ Above Level

The length of one base is 10 centimeters. The height is 8 centimeters. The area is 64 square centimeters. What is the length of the other base? Explain. 6 cm; $\frac{1}{2} \times 8 \times (10 + 6) = 64$

Intervention	Practice	Extension

Activity Triangle Area

Display a parallelogram, and have students verbally describe what needs to be done to make two congruent triangles. Students will probably respond that it needs to be cut in half or divided by 2. Make the point that if students are more comfortable with the last description, they can think of the area of a triangle as $(b \times h) \div 2$ as well as $\frac{1}{2} \times b \times h$. Use several examples to show that the two expressions are equivalent.

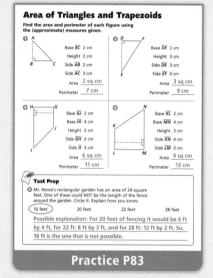

Practice P83

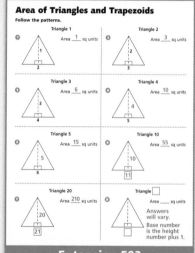

Extension E83

Spiral Review

Spiral Review Book page SR83 provides review of the following previously learned skills and concepts:

- multiplying decimals
- collecting data and constructing a frequency graph

You may wish to have students work with partners to complete the page.

Spiral Review SR83

Extension Activity
A Different Formula

Have students draw a rectangle, parallelogram, rhombus, square, trapezoid, and triangle. Have them measure the base and height of each figure. Ask them to draw a line through each figure, parallel to a base, halfway between the bases (for the triangle, halfway between the base and the upper vertex). Tell them to call this the *midline* (*m*). Have them measure it and look for a formula for the area of each figure that uses the midline.
$A = m \times h$

Teacher's Notes 🍎

Daily Notes . . .

Quick Notes

Lesson 6 Area and Perimeter of Other Polygons

NCTM Standards 1, 3, 4, 6, 7, 8, 9

Lesson Planner

STUDENT OBJECTIVE ·
- To use simpler figures, such as triangles, to find the perimeter and area of more complex figures

1 Daily Activities (TG p. 861)

| Open-Ended Problem Solving/Headline Story | Skills Practice and Review— Area and Perimeter with Square Tiles |

2 Teach and Practice (TG pp. 862–865)

Ⓐ **Exploring Polygons** (TG pp. 862–863)

Ⓑ **Finding Perimeters** (TG p. 864)

Ⓒ **Finding the Perimeter and Area of Polygons** (TG p. 865)

MATERIALS

- TR: Activity Masters, AM93–AM94
- centimeter rulers
- scissors
- tape
- 📖 LAB pp. 203–204
- 📖 SH p. 175

3 Differentiated Instruction (TG p. 866)

Leveled Problem Solving (TG p. 866)	Practice Book P84
Intervention Activity (TG p. 866)	Extension Book E84
Extension Activity (TG p. 866)	Spiral Review Book SR84
Social Studies Connection (TG p. 816)	

Lesson Notes

About the Lesson

Students use their knowledge of the formula for calculating the area of a triangle to calculate the area of polygons that are neither parallelograms nor trapezoids. They begin by splitting polygons into triangles so that they can then combine the areas of the triangles to find the total area of the polygon. Students also explore the idea that polygons that have the same area may have very different shapes and perimeters.

About the Mathematics

Students should be very familiar with the distributive property, which allows one to simplify a problem by breaking it into smaller, more manageable pieces, as this is how they learned to complete multi-digit multiplication, and division problems. In the same way that 46 can be broken into 40 + 6 to simplify arithmetic calculations, a polygon can be broken into triangles, parallelograms, or other simpler figures to simplify finding the area.

Use with Lesson Activity Book pp. 203–204.

Developing Mathematical Language

Vocabulary: polygon

The term *polygon* is used throughout the lesson. Although it is used synonymously with *figure,* you might remind your students that *polygons* are only one type of geometric figure. The word comes from the Greek root *poly,* which means "many," and *polygons* are figures with many angles. *Polygons* are a subset of two-dimensional figures, because, for example, a circle is a two-dimensional figure but not a *polygon.* In other words, all *polygons* are figures; not every figure is a *polygon.* You might even connect this to the relationship between squares and rectangles—squares are special rectangles; not every rectangle is a square.

Familiarize students with the term *polygon.*

Beginning Draw two sides of a figure on the board. Have a student complete it to form a *polygon.* Repeat with other students.

Intermediate Have students go to the board and draw a figure—either a *polygon* or a non-*polygon*—one at a time. As each student completes the figure, have the group say in unison whether it is a *polygon* or not a *polygon.*

Advanced Discuss with students the meanings of *poly-* as "many" and *-gon* as "angles." Have them explain how the meanings can help them remember what a *polygon* is like.

Open-Ended Problem Solving

Encourage students to use the formulas for the areas of a triangle and rectangle as they respond to this Headline Story. You might also ask students to draw the two triangles that could form the rectangle they describe in their responses.

 Headline Story

The area of a certain triangle is ____ square meters. The base measures 12 meters. The height is ____ . What is the area of a parallelogram with the same base and height measurements as the triangle?

Possible responses: If the triangle's area is 48 sq m, the height is 8 m, and so the parallelogram's area is 96 sq m. The parallelogram's area is always twice the triangle's area. If the triangle's area is 18 sq m, the height is 3 m, and the parallelogram's area is 36 sq m. The parallelogram's area is always a multiple of 12 since the base is 12 m.

Skills Practice and Review

Area and Perimeter with Square Tiles

Give students from 4 to 48 square tiles, and have them use a constant number of tiles (and therefore a constant area) to make various figures with various perimeters. At least one figure should be a rectangle, and students should create figures with at least 3 different perimeters. Students must match up the tiles' sides exactly for this activity. As students share their results, review the area and perimeter formulas for rectangles (and squares) by asking what shortcuts they could use to find the area and perimeter of their rectangular configurations.

example

non-example

individuals or whole class

15 MIN

Materials
• For each student: AM93

NCTM Standards 1, 3, 4, 6, 7, 8, 9

A Exploring Polygons

Purpose To find the area of a complex two-dimensional figure by splitting it into triangles

Introduce Ask students what area formulas they have learned so far. Students should mention the area formulas for a parallelogram, triangle, and trapezoid. If necessary, review these formulas with your students. You might remind students that they derived the formulas for a triangle and for a trapezoid by using two triangles or two trapezoids to form a parallelogram. This should help them to recreate the formulas. Each student will use Explore: Area and Perimeter of an Odd-Shaped Figure and AM93: Oddtown Playground.

Task Have students work individually or in pairs on the activity master to complete the activity on the Explore page. To find the odd-shaped figure's area, students should suggest splitting the figure into triangles. To find the perimeter, students should suggest adding the lengths of the sides. Since there are no obvious sides of equal lengths, students will need to find the length of each individual side.

To spur ideas for completing the activity, first pose the following problem to your students:

> "Suppose I said that the area of the map of the playground was just a bit over 30 square inches. How could you, with almost no work at all, prove me wrong?"

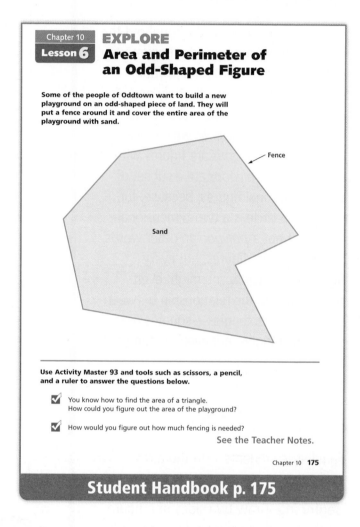

Chapter 10
Lesson 6

EXPLORE

Area and Perimeter of an Odd-Shaped Figure

Some of the people of Oddtown want to build a new playground on an odd-shaped piece of land. They will put a fence around it and cover the entire area of the playground with sand.

Fence

Sand

Use Activity Master 93 and tools such as scissors, a pencil, and a ruler to answer the questions below.

☑ You know how to find the area of a triangle. How could you figure out the area of the playground?

☑ How would you figure out how much fencing is needed?

See the Teacher Notes.

Chapter 10 **175**

Student Handbook p. 175

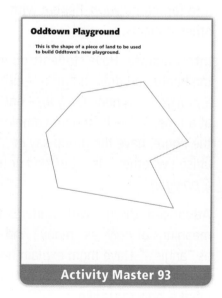

Oddtown Playground

This is the shape of a piece of land to be used to build Oddtown's new playground.

Activity Master 93

Students will likely begin by thinking about what area is and how they can bracket it easily. They might measure a 3-inch-by-5-inch rectangle and show that it is bigger than the figure. Others might break the map into seven triangular parts and show that each has less than 2 square inches in area to show that the most area the whole figure could cover is 14 square inches.

Once students have completed the page, discuss their strategies.

Talk Math

❓ **How many triangles did you find?** There are many different ways to split the odd-shaped figure into triangles, not always resulting in 5 triangles. Here is one way that does result in 5 triangles.

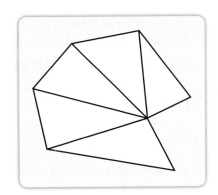

❓ **Could you split the figure into other shapes to find the area?** While it looks like you could form a trapezoid, triangle, and parallelogram by splitting the odd-shaped figure, you can't know for sure that the lines are parallel without further information. (However, if you only needed an estimate of the area, approximating the regions as a parallelogram and a trapezoid is a great strategy.)

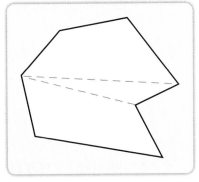

Practice Invite students to use a ruler to compute the area and perimeter of the odd-shaped figure on the activity master. Students should measure the base and height of each triangle (rounded to the nearest centimeter or half-inch), use the formula $A = \frac{1}{2} \times b \times h$ to find the approximate area of each triangle, and then add the areas together to get the approximate area of the whole polygon. The approximate area in centimeters is 117 sq cm, and in inches is 17.5 sq in. To find the perimeter, students should measure the length of each side and add the lengths together. If measuring in centimeters, the approximate perimeter is 46 cm. If measuring in inches, the approximate perimeter is 17.5 in.

Possible Discussion

Approximations are a part of people's everyday use of mathematics. If one didn't need an exact measurement of area, then one might simply recognize that a figure is close to a rectangle and calculate its area as if it were a rectangle. When exact measures are desired, however, acting on appearances of figures alone can lead to incorrect results. In this lesson students are discouraged from presuming a figure is of a certain type simply because it looks that way. Measurements, by their nature, are approximations, so they too are insufficient to determine exact results.

Materials
- For each student:
  TR: AM94, scissors, tape, centimeter ruler

NCTM Standards 1, 3, 4, 6, 7, 8, 9

Ⓑ Finding Perimeters

Purpose To construct a polygon from triangles, and then find its perimeter

Introduce Each student will need AM94: Polygon of Triangles, scissors, tape, and a ruler. Explain to your class that this activity asks them to do the opposite of what they did in the previous activity—begin with triangles and construct a polygon. There are many ways this can be done. Encourage students to try to construct polygons that they think might be different from what others are doing. Also tell students that their polygons may have points that "stick out," but that they should not overlap any of the triangles or pieces of triangles when they tape them together.

Task **Have students make a polygon from the triangles on AM94: Polygon of Triangles and then find the perimeter of the polygon.** Then ask small groups of students to line up their polygons from least to greatest perimeters.

💬 **Talk Math**

❓ **What do you notice about the polygons with smaller perimeters?** They are more "bunched up." The triangle pieces share more sides *inside* of the figure.

❓ **What do you notice about the polygons with larger perimeters?** They are more "stretched out." The perimeter becomes longer as more of the triangles' longer sides become sides (or outer edges) of the new polygon.

To help students see why points that are "sticking out" increase the perimeter, you might sketch a picture like the following on the board:

❓ **Do all of the polygons have the same area? How do you know?** Yes; since the same 5 triangles were used without any overlap to make all of the polygons, no area was gained or lost.

You may want to ask students to suggest a second cut for a triangle which will give an even greater perimeter. (see pink chalk dotted lines.)

Teacher Story

❝My students enjoyed making the variety of polygons out of the five triangles on AM94 so much that we decided to make a bulletin board display with them. They wrote the perimeter on the front of each one and we put them up in order from the least to greatest perimeter.❞

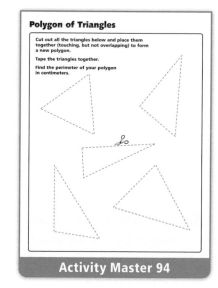

Polygon of Triangles

Cut out all the triangles below and place them together (touching, but not overlapping) to form a new polygon.

Tape the triangles together.

Find the perimeter of your polygon in centimeters.

Activity Master 94

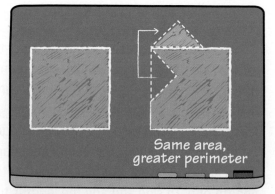

Same area, greater perimeter

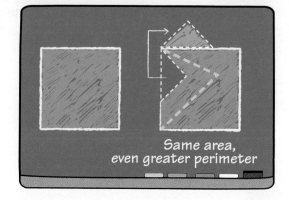

Same area, even greater perimeter

Use with Lesson Activity Book pp. 203–204.

Finding the Perimeter and Area of Polygons LAB pp. 203–204

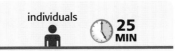
Purpose To use simpler figures to find the perimeter and area of more complex figures

NCTM Standards 1, 3, 7, 9

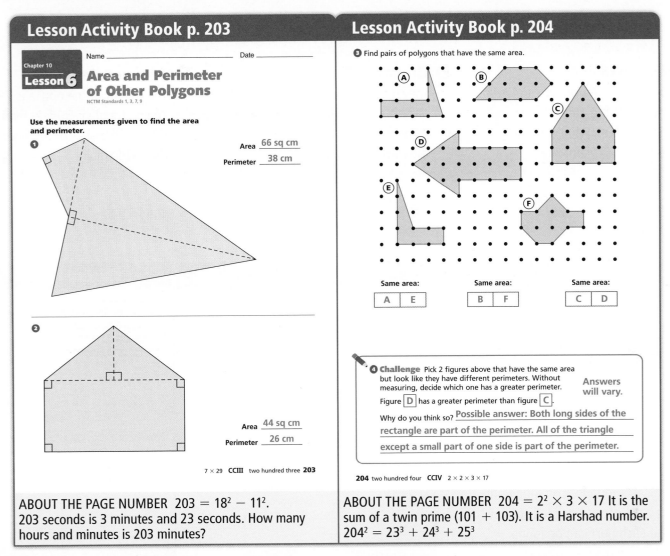

Lesson Activity Book p. 203

Chapter 10
Lesson 6 **Area and Perimeter of Other Polygons**
NCTM Standards 1, 3, 7, 9

Name _____ Date _____

Use the measurements given to find the area and perimeter.

❶

Area **66 sq cm**

Perimeter **38 cm**

❷

Area **44 sq cm**

Perimeter **26 cm**

7 × 29 CCIII two hundred three **203**

ABOUT THE PAGE NUMBER $203 = 18^2 - 11^2$.
203 seconds is 3 minutes and 23 seconds. How many hours and minutes is 203 minutes?

Lesson Activity Book p. 204

❸ Find pairs of polygons that have the same area.

Same area: A E

Same area: B F

Same area: C D

❹ **Challenge** Pick 2 figures above that have the same area but look like they have different perimeters. Without measuring, decide which one has a greater perimeter.

Answers will vary.

Figure **D** has a greater perimeter than figure **C**.

Why do you think so? Possible answer: Both long sides of the rectangle are part of the perimeter. All of the triangle except a small part of one side is part of the perimeter.

204 two hundred four CCIV 2 × 2 × 3 × 17

ABOUT THE PAGE NUMBER $204 = 2^2 \times 3 \times 17$ It is the sum of a twin prime (101 + 103). It is a Harshad number. $204^2 = 23^3 + 24^3 + 25^3$

Teaching Notes for LAB page 203

Students measure to find the area and perimeter of polygons made out of triangles and parallelograms.

✔**Ongoing Assessment** Watch for students who may still confuse the formula for the area of a parallelogram with the formula for the area of a triangle. You could quickly remind those students of how they put two congruent triangles together to make a parallelogram to help them reason through the relationship between the two formulas.

Teaching Notes for LAB page 204

Students find polygons that have the same area. The polygons with the same area are comprised of congruent figures, and it might help your students to think about cutting up each polygon and rearranging the pieces.

Challenge Problem In the previous activity, students discussed how figures with the same area can have different perimeters; the challenge here is to articulate, in writing, what attributes of polygons might lead to greater perimeters.

Reflect and Summarize the Lesson

Write Math

Explain how you can use what you know about finding the area of parallelograms, triangles, and trapezoids to find the area of an odd-shaped figure. Possible answer: I can break the odd-shaped figure up into simpler figures that are parallelograms, triangles, or trapezoids and then use the formulas I know for finding the areas of those figures to find the area of the odd-shaped figure.

3 | Differentiated Instruction

Leveled Problem Solving

Shondra draws a cross-section of a house. It shows a rectangle with an isosceles triangle on top of it.

❶ Basic Level

The rectangle's length is 3 times the height. If the area is 300 square feet, what are the dimensions? Explain. 30 ft × 10 ft; use *guess and check* to find that 30 × 10 = 300.

❷ On Level

The triangle represents the roof. It has an area of 300 square feet. If its height is 20 feet, how wide is the roof? Explain. 30 ft; use the triangle area formula: $300 = \frac{1}{2} \times b \times 20$. Guess and check to find that $b = 30$.

❸ Above Level

The height of the house is 28 feet. The rectangle is 30 feet by 8 feet. What is the area of the figure she draws? Explain. 540 sq ft; 30 × 8 = 240; 28 − 8 = 20; $\frac{1}{2} \times$ 20 × 30 = 300; and 240 + 300 = 540.

Intervention

Activity Breaking Up

Display a geoboard or use dot paper on the overhead. Draw the outline of a figure composed of polygons for which students have studied area formulas. Ask them to suggest ways to break the figure up into parallelograms, triangles, and trapezoids. In their descriptions, encourage them to use mathematical language. Continue until the figure has been subdivided so that the area of each part can be found using formulas students know.

Practice

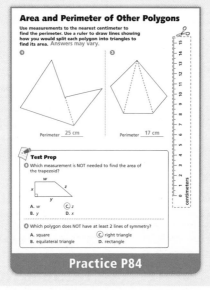

Practice P84

Extension

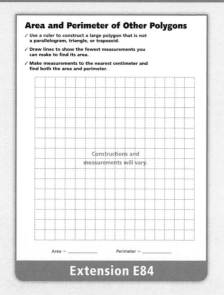

Extension E84

Spiral Review

Spiral Review Book page SR84 provides review of the following previously learned skills and concepts:

- representing mathematical relationships with input-output tables
- applying the problem solving strategy *look for a pattern*

You may wish to have students work with partners to complete the page.

Spiral Review SR84

Extension Activity
Area Challenge

Have students construct a triangle on a geoboard or dot paper so that no side is parallel to an edge. Challenge them to find a way of determining the area of the figure. You may want to help students recognize that a triangle can be surrounded by a rectangle that touches all 3 vertices so that the 3 outside triangles are all right triangles. Students can find the area of the rectangle and subtract the areas of the right triangles to find the area of the original one.

Use with Lesson Activity Book pp. 203–204.

Teacher's Notes 🍎

Daily Notes . . .

Quick Notes

More Ideas

Lesson 7

Problem Solving Strategy and Test Prep

NCTM Standards 1, 3, 4, 6, 7, 8, 9

Lesson Planner

STUDENT OBJECTIVES
- To practice the problem solving strategy *solve a simpler problem*
- To articulate the steps and strategies used to solve problems
- To prepare for standardized tests

Problem Solving Strategy:
Solve a Simpler Problem (TG pp. 869–870, 872–873)

MATERIALS

Ⓐ **Discussing the Problem Solving Strategy: Solve a Simpler Problem** (TG p. 869)

Ⓑ **Solving Problems by Applying the Strategy** (TG p. 870)

- centimeter rulers
- transparency of LAB p. 205 (optional)
- 📖 LAB p. 205
- 📖 SH pp. 176–177

Problem Solving Test Prep (TG p. 871)

Ⓒ **Getting Ready for Standardized Tests** (TG p. 871)

- 📖 LAB p. 206

Lesson Notes

About Problem Solving

Problem Solving Strategy: Solve a Simpler Problem

Students employ the problem solving strategy *solve a simpler problem* to find the area of complex figures by finding and summing the areas of simpler figures. Polygons can always be split into triangles, but with additional information (such as the location of parallel sides and right angles), they can also be split into parallelograms and trapezoids.

Students demonstrate their ability to find the perimeter and area of triangles, trapezoids, and parallelograms on the LAB pages.

Skills Practice and Review

Using Area Formulas

This practice works well as a silent activity. Make a table like the following, filling in one value and label in each column. Students fill in the spaces with measures that keep the areas consistent with the base and height lengths. Note that while it is not incorrect to use, for example, both feet and inches within a column, it makes the calculations more difficult. Encourage students to input numbers that make mental computation reasonable.

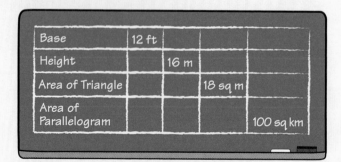

Base	12 ft			
Height		16 m		
Area of Triangle			18 sq m	
Area of Parallelogram				100 sq km

As a check, you may want to have students model the figures with square tiles, connecting these models to the area formulas they used to fill in the table.

Problem Solving Strategy

**(A) Discussing the Problem Solving Strategy:
Solve a Simpler Problem**

whole class

NCTM Standards 1, 3, 6, 7, 8, 9

Purpose To share strategies for solving problems and focus on the problem solving strategy, *solve a simpler problem*

Introduce Remind students that throughout this chapter they have been using the strategy *solve a simpler problem* to help them solve problems. They have, for example, used what they know about finding the area of a rectangle, to find the area of a parallelogram and then what they know about finding the area of a parallelogram to find the area of a triangle and the area of a trapezoid. Finally, they used what they know about finding the areas of these three polygons to find the areas of odd-shaped figures.

Record the following problem on the board or on a blank transparency. Ask a volunteer to read the problem. Then have the students begin working on the problem.

Problem Max made this sketch of the garden he is planting in his backyard. What is the area of his garden?

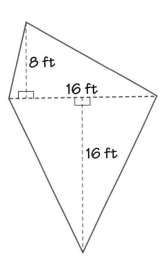

Share Have students share their strategies for solving the problem. Students will likely suggest finding and summing the areas of the two triangles shown on the sketch to find the area of the odd-shaped quadrilateral Max sketched for the garden.

 Talk Math

❷ What are the measures of the base and height of the smaller triangle? What is the area of the smaller triangle? The base is 16 feet and the height is 8 feet. You can use this formula to find the area of a triangle: $A = \frac{1}{2} \times b \times h$. So, the area of the smaller triangle is $\frac{1}{2} \times 16 \times 8$, or 64 sq ft.

❷ What are the measures of the base and height of the larger triangle? What is the area of the larger triangle? The base is 16 feet and the height is 16 feet. You can use the formula to find the area of the larger triangle, or, since the height of the larger triangle is twice the height of the smaller triangle, you can just double the area of the smaller triangle to find the area of the larger triangle: $2 \times 64 = 128$. So, the area of the larger triangle is 128 sq ft.

❷ What is the area of the odd-shaped quadrilateral garden? Explain how you know. 192 sq ft; The area of the quadrilateral is the sum of the areas of the two triangles that make up the quadrilateral: 64 sq ft + 128 sq ft = 192 sq ft.

Solving Problems by Applying the Strategy LAB p. 205

Purpose To practice the problem solving strategy, *solve a simpler problem*

Teaching Notes for LAB page 205

Have students look at the first problem on LAB page 205 and, if available, put up a transparency of the page. Give students a few minutes to work on the first problem. Then have students share their strategies for solving the problem. If students don't suggest it, show how to use the problem solving strategy *solve a simpler problem* to solve the problem. You may want to ask questions like these to guide the discussion.

 ### Read to Understand

What do you know from reading the problem? The swimming pool cover is a hexagon that has parallel segments labeled on the sketch.

What do you need to find out? the area and perimeter of a polygon that is not a parallelogram, triangle, or trapezoid

 ### Plan

How can you solve this problem? You can think about the strategies you might use. You might split the polygon into simpler figures whose area you know how to find.

 ### Solve

How might you use a simpler problem to solve the problem? The figure is already split into trapezoids, for which you know the area formula, and once you figure out the area of each trapezoid, you can add the areas together.

Is there more than one way to make a simpler problem? How do you know? Yes; you can split the polygon in various ways, for example into 6 triangles or 4 triangles and a rectangle.

 ### Check

Look back at the original problem. Does your answer make sense? How do you know?

Allow students to work independently or with a partner to solve the other problem on the page. When most students have completed the page, you might ask a couple of students to describe the specific strategies they used to solve the problem.

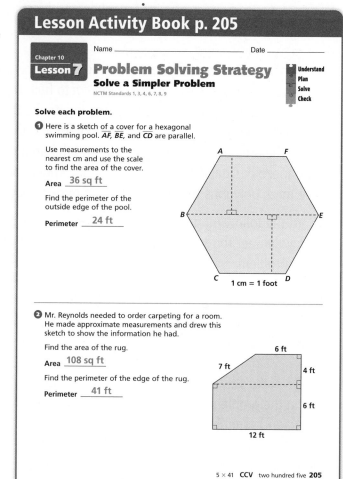

Lesson Activity Book p. 205

Chapter 10
Lesson 7 **Problem Solving Strategy**
Solve a Simpler Problem
NCTM Standards 1, 3, 4, 6, 7, 8, 9

Name _____ Date _____

Understand
Plan
Solve
Check

Solve each problem.

❶ Here is a sketch of a cover for a hexagonal swimming pool. *AF*, *BE*, and *CD* are parallel.

Use measurements to the nearest cm and use the scale to find the area of the cover.

Area __36 sq ft__

Find the perimeter of the outside edge of the pool.

Perimeter __24 ft__

1 cm = 1 foot

❷ Mr. Reynolds needed to order carpeting for a room. He made approximate measurements and drew this sketch to show the information he had.

Find the area of the rug.

Area __108 sq ft__

Find the perimeter of the edge of the rug.

Perimeter __41 ft__

6 ft
7 ft
4 ft
6 ft
12 ft

5 × 41 **CCV** two hundred five **205**

ABOUT THE PAGE NUMBER 205 is an odd, composite, natural number.

Reflect and Summarize the Lesson

 Write Math

How can using the strategy *solve a simpler problem* help you solve a problem about the area of an odd-shaped figure? Possible answer: You can split the odd-shaped figure into polygons, such as triangles, parallelograms, and trapezoids, and then find and sum the areas.

Problem Solving Test Prep

 C **Getting Ready for Standardized Tests** LAB p. 206

 individuals
 20 MIN

Purpose To prepare students for standardized tests

NCTM Standards 1, 2, 3, 6, 8

Lesson Activity Book p. 206

Problem Solving Test Prep

Choose the correct answer.

❶ What is the rule for the table?

Input	Output
4	14
2	8
6	20
9	29
7	23

A. $x + 10$ C. $2x + 6$
B. $4x - 2$ **D.** $3x + 2$

❷ Which is the only number of juice boxes that can be packed in cartons of 2, 3, 5, 6, or 9 with no boxes left over?

A. 800 C. 1,100
B. 900 D. 1,400

❸ Which number is NOT between the two given ones when the numbers are written in order?

999,809 and 1,001,034

A. 1,001,019 C. 999,900
B. 1,001,101 D. 999,810

❹ Which is NOT a correct name for all the figures?

A. polygons
B. quadrilaterals
C. parallelograms
D. simple closed figures

✎**Show What You Know**

Solve each problem. Explain your answer.

❺ What is the area of the figure?

10 ft
11 ft
20 ft

320 sq ft; area of large rectangle = 20 × 11 = 220, area of triangle = 20 × 10 ÷ 2 = 100, 220 + 100 = 320

❻ What is the area of the shaded frame around the picture?

9 in.
13 in.   7 in.
18 in.

171 sq in.; (13 × 18) − (9 × 7) = 234 − 63 = 171

206 two hundred six **CCVI** 2 × 103

ABOUT THE PAGE NUMBER 206 is the smallest number that can be written as the sum of 3 positive distinct squares in 5 ways.

Teaching Notes for LAB page 206

The test items on this page are written in the same style and arranged in the same format as those on many state assessments. The page is cumulative and is designed for students to apply a variety of problem solving strategies including *solve a simpler problem, look for a pattern, and use logical reasoning*. Students might share the strategies they use.

The Item Analysis Chart below highlights one of the possible strategies that may be used for each item.

Show What You Know

Written Response

Direct students' attention to Problems 5 and 6. Explain that they must decide how to solve the problems. Then have students write an explanation of how they know their answer is correct. To provide more space for students to communicate their thinking about these problems, you may wish to have them write their responses and explanations on a separate sheet of paper. Use the Scoring Rubric below to evaluate their understanding.

Item Analysis Chart

Item	Strategy
1	Look for a pattern
2	Use logical reasoning
3	Guess and check
4	Use logical reasoning
5	Solve a simpler problem
6	Solve a simpler problem

Scoring Rubric

2	• Demonstrates complete understanding of the problem and chooses an appropriate strategy to determine the solution
1	• Demonstrates a partial understanding of the problem and chooses a strategy that does not lead to a complete and accurate solution
0	• Demonstrates little understanding of the problem and shows little evidence of using any strategy to determine a solution

---

Review Model

Refer students to Problem Solving Review Model: Solve a Simpler Problem in the *Student Handbook* pp. 176–177 to review a model of the four steps they can use with the problem solving strategy, *solve a simpler problem.*

Additional problem solving practice is also provided.

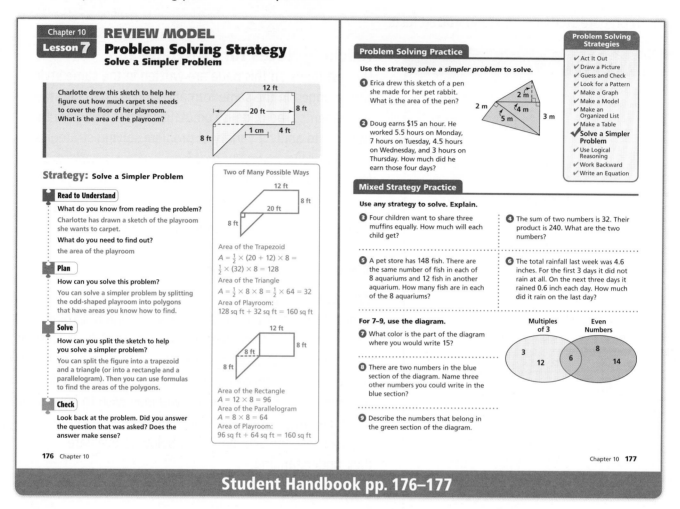

Student Handbook pp. 176–177

Task Have students read the problem at the top of the Review Model page. Then discuss.

Talk Math

❓ **What is the scale for the diagram Charlotte drew? What does scale mean?** The scale is 1 cm = 4 ft. The scale means that 1 centimeter on the diagram represents 4 feet in actual length.

❓ **What formulas are used to find the areas of a trapezoid and the area of a triangle?** For a trapezoid, a formula is $A = \frac{1}{2} \times (b_1 + b_2) \times h$ and for a triangle a formula is $A = \frac{1}{2} \times b \times h$.

❓ **For the first way shown to split the diagram, what does "20" in the equation represent?** 20 represents the actual length of one of the bases of the trapezoid. The base measures 5 cm and since the scale shows that 1 cm = 4 ft, then 5 cm = 20 feet.

Use with Lesson Activity Book pp. 205–206.

① 15 sq m; You can use the strategy *solve a simpler problem* by splitting the odd-shaped figure into triangles, finding the area of each triangle, and then finding the sum of the areas.

② $300; You can use the strategy *solve a simpler problem* by first finding the sum of the number of hours he worked in all during those four days: 5.5 + 7 + 4.5 + 3 = 20. Then, you can use what you know about multiplying by multiples 10: 20 × 15 = 300.

Mixed Strategy Practice

③ $\frac{3}{4}$ of a muffin; You can use the strategy *draw a picture* to show the 3 muffins with each muffin divided into fourths. Each child would get one fourth of each muffin, or $\frac{3}{4}$ muffin in all.

④ 12 and 20; You can *guess and check* to find the two numbers. You may want to *make a table* to organize your guesses. Choose two numbers with a sum of 32; then check to see if their product is 240.

Number 1	Number 2	Sum	Product	
16	16	32	256	too big
18	14	32	252	too big
24	8	32	192	too small
20	12	32	240	correct!

⑤ 17 fish; You can *work backward* and then *write an equation* to find the number of fish in each aquarium. First, subtract the 12 fish that are in another aquarium: 148 − 12 = 136. Then, divided the difference by 8 to find the number of fish in each of the other aquariums: 136 ÷ 8 = 17.

⑥ 2.8 in.; You can *write equations* to find how much it rained on the last day. First, multiply 0.6 in × 3 to find how much it rained on Days 4–6: 0.6 in. × 3 = 1.8 in. Then, subtract the product from 4.6 in. to find how much it rained on Day 7: 4.6 in. − 1.8 in. = 2.8 in.

⑦ Yellow; You can *use logical reasoning* to figure out where to write 15. 15 is a multiple of 3, but it is NOT an even number, so it goes in the yellow section of the diagram.

⑧ Numbers should be even numbers that are NOT multiples of 3. Possible answers: 2, 4, 10. You can *use logical reasoning* to name these three numbers.

⑨ These are even numbers that are multiples of 3. You can *use logical reasoning* to study the diagram. The numbers in the green section are in the oval for "Multiples of 3" and also in the oval for "Even Numbers", so these numbers must be both.

Area and Perimeter

NCTM Standards 1, 3, 4, 6, 7, 9, 10

Purpose To provide students with an opportunity to demonstrate understanding of Chapter 10 concepts and skills

MATERIALS
- LAB pp. 207–208
- Chapter 10 Test (Assessment Guide pp. AG85–AG86)

Chapter 10 Learning Goals and Assessment Options

These learning goals are assessed in many ways throughout the chapter. The chart below correlates each learning goal to specific formal and informal assessment options.

	Learning Goals	Lesson Number	Snapshot Assessment	Chapter Review Item Numbers	Chapter Test Item Numbers
				LAB pp. 207–208	Assessment Guide pp. AG85–AG86
10-A	Use appropriate units and formulas for perimeter and area of two-dimensional figures	10.1–10.6	1, 5, 6, 7, 8	1, 2, 5–9	1–4
10-B	Use given measurements or ruler measurements to find the perimeters of two-dimensional figures	10.1, 10.2	2, 9	1–8	7–9
10-C	Use given measurements or ruler measurements to find the areas of two-dimensional figures	10.3–10.6	3, 4, 10, 11	3–8	5, 6
10-D	Apply problem solving strategies such as *solve a simpler problem* to solve problems	10.7	12	9	10, 11

📷 Snapshot Assessment

The following Mental Math and Quick Write questions and tasks provide a quick, informal assessment of students' understanding of Chapter 10 concepts, skills, and problem solving strategies.

whole class · 10 MIN

Mental Math This oral assessment uses mental math strategies and can be used with the whole class.

1 How do you find the perimeter of any polygon?
Add the lengths of its sides.

- What is another way to find the perimeter of a rectangle or parallelogram? Add 2 lengths plus 2 widths; accept $2l + 2w$ or $2(l + w)$.
- Name an appropriate unit of measure for perimeter. Accept any linear unit, such as inches, meters, etc.
(**Learning Goal 10-A**)

2 Find the perimeter of:
- A rectangle, base is 10 cm, height is 5 cm 30 cm
- A rhombus, side is 3.5 m 14 m
- A parallelogram, base is 2 ft, side is 1.5 ft 7 ft

Describe the process you would use to find the perimeter of the classroom. Answers will vary; accept reasonable answers. Possible answer: I would measure the sides of the classroom in feet, then add the measurements together to get the perimeter.
(**Learning Goal 10-B**)

3 Find the area of:
- A rectangle, length is 5 miles, width is 4 miles 20 sq mi
- A triangle, base is 10 cm, height is 7 cm 35 sq cm
(Learning Goal 10-C)

4 James has a rectangular pool which measures 12 meters by 9 meters. What is the area of the pool cover? Explain how you found your answer. 108 square meters; multiply length times width, or 12 × 9 = 108
(Learning Goal 10-C)

Quick Write This informal written assessment can be administered to small groups or the whole class. Read each question and have the students record responses on their write-on boards. Encourage students to listen and think about the questions before responding.

5 If we put two congruent triangles together, we can form a parallelogram. This explains why the area of only one triangle is exactly _____ of the area of the parallelogram. half
(Learning Goal 10-A)

6 What is the area of a parallelogram that has a base of 4 meters and height of 3 meters? 12 square meters
(Learning Goal 10-A)

7 Write the formula for finding the area of a triangle. $A = \frac{1}{2} b \times h$
(Learning Goal 10-A)

8 What is the area of a right triangle that has a height of 6 inches a base of 8 inches and the longest side measure 10 inches? 24 square inches
(Learning Goal 10-A)

9 Find the perimeter of:
- An equilateral triangle; base is 4.3 in. 12.9 in.
- A square; side is 8 yd 32 yd
- A quadrilateral whose sides are 2 cm, 4 cm, 6 cm, and 3.5 cm 15.5 cm
(Learning Goal 10-B)

10 An "L" shape is made of a 4m-by-3m rectangle and a 2m-by-3m rectangle. What is the total area of the "L" shape? 18 square meters; find the area of the side, "L" 4 × 3 = 12, find the area of the base, "L" 2 × 3 = 6. Add the two areas together to find the total area, 12 + 6 = 18 square meters.
(Learning Goal 10-C)

11 Joyce is making a quilt, which is 3 yards long and 2.5 yards wide. What is the area of the quilt? Explain how you found your answer. 7.5 square yards; multiply length times width, or 3 × 2.5 = 7.5.
- The class wants to make a large pennant to hang on the wall in the cafeteria. They want the pennant to be 6 feet long. The side of the pennant is 4 feet. What is the total wall area covered by the pennant? 12 square feet
(Learning Goal 10-C)

12 Have the students sketch the table as you read the problem. The class had a table, which was originally rectangular in shape. Unfortunately, a corner of the table had broken off. The break was a straight line, leaving a perfectly triangular piece missing from the corner. The length on the complete side is 8 feet; the opposite side is 6 feet. The width on the complete end is 4 feet; the opposite width is 3 feet. Sketch the table top, show the broken corner, and label the side measurements. Find the total area of the table as it is now. 31 square feet
(Learning Goal 10-D)

Formal Assessment

Chapter Review/Assessment The Chapter 10 Review/Assessment on *Lesson Activity Book* pages 207–208 assesses students' understanding of perimeter and area of two-dimensional figures. Students should be able to complete these pages independently.

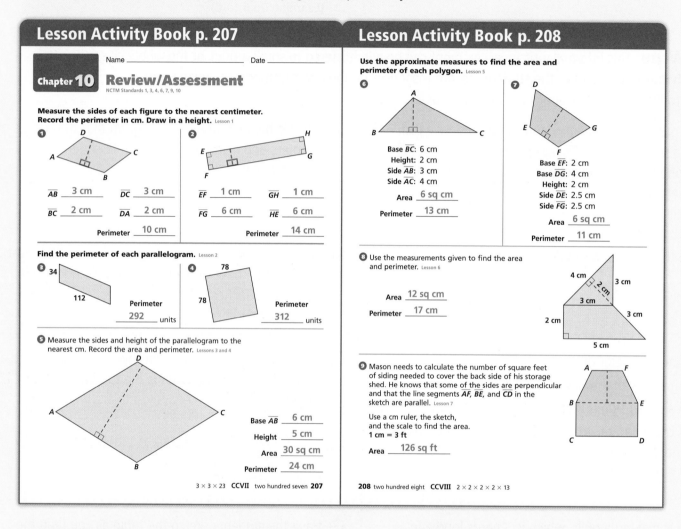

Extra Support Students who have difficulty with items on the Chapter 10 Review/Assessment may need review of the lesson where development of the concept was provided. You can use the Intervention Activity to increase students' understanding before the Chapter Test is given.

Chapter Test Use the Chapter 10 Test in the *Assessment Guide* to assess concepts, skills, and problem solving from the chapter and to prepare students for standardized tests. The Chapter Test and other test items are also available online.

Chapter Notes

Quick Notes

More Ideas

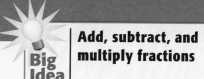

Big Idea | Add, subtract, and multiply fractions

Fraction Computation

About the Chapter

In this chapter, students add, subtract, and multiply fractions. In each case, the chapter shows how arithmetic with fractions is like arithmetic with whole numbers.

Adding and Subtracting Students have worked with the idea that we can only add or subtract like things since first grade: operating on numbers with the same place value and converting units of measure to a common unit are two examples. We *can* add yards and inches, but not simply by combining the numbers of each. The only way we can just "go by the numbers" is if the numbers are counting the same kinds of objects or quantities. Then we can just add or subtract the numbers. In the case of fractions, the same kinds of quantities refer to the size of the fractional pieces (which are expressed by the denominators of the fractions).

An Expanding View of Multiplication Multiplying with fractions, like multiplying with whole numbers, can be represented by area or combination" (intersecting line) models.

Contexts for Fraction Computation

Most of us encounter only simple fractions—halves, thirds, quarters, maybe eighths, and we need the basic understanding that allows us to deal with them. Beyond that, most of us don't use other fractions in any "everyday" way. The real importance of developing comfort with these other fractions is in preparing for algebra where situations involving fractions occur often.

$$\frac{3}{4} \times \frac{1}{4} \quad \frac{3}{16} \qquad \frac{3}{4} \times \frac{1}{9} \quad \frac{3}{36} = \frac{1}{12} \qquad \frac{3}{4} \times \frac{4}{5} \quad \frac{12}{20} = \frac{3}{5}$$

$$\frac{3}{4} \times \frac{7}{8} \quad \frac{21}{32} \qquad \frac{3}{4} \times \frac{6}{7} \quad \frac{18}{28} = \frac{9}{14} \qquad \frac{3}{4} \times \frac{7}{10} \quad \frac{21}{40}$$

$$\frac{3}{4} \times \frac{10}{11} \quad \frac{30}{44} = \frac{15}{22} \qquad \frac{3}{4} \times \frac{5}{9} \quad \frac{15}{36} = \frac{5}{12} \qquad \frac{3}{4} \times \frac{3}{8} \quad \frac{9}{32}$$

Developing Concepts Across the Grades

Topic	Prior Learning	Learning in Chapter 11	Later Learning
Add and Subtract Fractions	• Combine fractions of the same and different types Grade 4, Chapter 7	• Add and subtract fractions with like denominators • Investigate fractions with like denominators that sum to 1 Lessons 11.1–11.6	• Add and subtract mixed numbers with renaming Grade 6
Multiply Fractions	• Multiply whole numbers in the context of rectangular arrays Grade 4, Chapter 2	• Multiply fractions using an area model • Find a fraction of a set by multiplying a whole number by a fraction Lessons 11.7–11.9	• Multiply mixed numbers Grade 6
Measurement	• Relate labels on measuring tapes to points on a number line Grade 4, Chapter 7	• Add and subtract unlike things by finding a common group or unit, or by making measurement unit conversions Lesson 11.4	• Apply the distance formula • Change units within a system Grade 6

Chapter Planner

Lesson	Objectives	NCTM Standards	Vocabulary	Materials/Resources

CHAPTER 11 World Almanac For Kids • Vocabulary • Games • Challenge
Teacher Guide pp. 885A–885F, Student Handbook pp. 184–185, 194–198

1 **Adding and Subtracting Fractions with Like Denominators**

PACING 1 DAY

Teacher Guide
pp. 886–893

Lesson Activity Book
pp. 209–210

Student Handbook
Student Letter p. 183

- To add and subtract fractions with like denominators

1, 2, 6, 7, 8, 10

numerator
denominator
like denominators
improper fraction
mixed number

For the students:
- School-Home Connection TR: SHC41–SHC42
- TR: AM95
- scissors
- envelopes
- P85, E85, SR85

2 **More Adding and Subtracting Fractions with Like Denominators**

PACING 1 DAY

Teacher Guide
pp. 894–899

Lesson Activity Book
pp. 211–212

Student Handbook
Game p. 196
Review Model p. 186

- To add and subtract fractions with like denominators

1, 2, 6, 7, 8, 9, 10

like denominators
improper fraction
mixed number

For the students:
- TR: AM96–AM97
- pieces cut from TR: AM95 or fraction bars
- scissors
- index cards numbered 1–12
- P86, E86, SR86

3 **Stories about Adding and Subtracting Fractions**

PACING 1 DAY

Teacher Guide
pp. 900–905

Lesson Activity Book
pp. 213–214

Student Handbook
Explore p. 187

- To interpret and solve story problems involving addition and subtraction of fractions with like denominators
- To investigate fractions with like denominators that sum to 1

1, 2, 6, 7, 8, 9, 10

fractions that add to 1

For the students:
- pieces cut from TR: AM95–AM96 or fraction bars
- P87, E87, SR87

4 **Adding and Subtracting Unlike Things**

PACING 1 DAY

Teacher Guide
pp. 906–911

Lesson Activity Book
pp. 215–216

- To add and subtract unlike things by finding a common group or unit, or by making measurement unit conversions

1, 2, 4, 6, 7, 8, 9

common unit
unlike things

For the students:
- P88, E88, SR88

NCTM Standards 2000

1. Number and Operations
2. Algebra
3. Geometry
4. Measurement
5. Data Analysis and Probability
6. Problem Solving
7. Reasoning and Proof
8. Communication
9. Connections
10. Representation

Key

AG: Assessment Guide
E: Extension Book
LAB: Lesson Activity Book
P: Practice Book

SH: Student Handbook
SR: Spiral Review Book
TG: Teacher Guide
TR: Teacher Resource Book

MATH GLOSSARY in **Student Handbook** p. 266

Planner (continued)

Chapter Planner (continued)

Lesson	Objectives	NCTM Standards	Vocabulary	Materials/Resources
5 Adding and Subtracting Fractions with Unlike Denominators **PACING 1 DAY** Teacher Guide pp. 912–917 Lesson Activity Book pp. 217–218 Student Handbook Explore p. 188	• To add and subtract fractions with unlike denominators by finding equivalent fractions with a common denominator • To estimate sums and differences of mixed numbers	1, 2, 4, 6, 7, 8, 9	common denominator equivalent fractions unlike denominator	For the teacher: ▪ transparency of AM98 (optional) For the students: ▪ pattern blocks ▪ P89, E89, SR89 Music Connection: Musical Rhythm Teacher Guide p. 884
6 Stories with Fractions **PACING 1 DAY** Teacher Guide pp. 918–925 Lesson Activity Book pp. 219–220 Student Handbook Review Model p. 189	• To add and subtract fractions in the context of story problems	1, 4, 6, 7, 8, 9, 10	least common denominator	For the students: ▪ TR: AM99 ▪ scissors ▪ P90, E90, SR90
7 Using an Area Model to Multiply Fractions **PACING 1 DAY** Teacher Guide pp. 926–933 Lesson Activity Book pp. 221–222	• To multiply fractions using an area model	1, 4, 7, 8, 9, 10	area model	For the students: ▪ large squares of paper ▪ P91, E91, SR91
8 Using Other Models to Multiply Fractions **PACING 1 DAY** Teacher Guide pp. 934–941 Lesson Activity Book pp. 223–224 Student Handbook Explore p. 190 Review Model p. 191	• To multiply fractions using dot sketches and line intersections	1, 2, 6, 7, 8, 9, 10	dot sketch intersections	For the teacher: ▪ transparency of LAB p. 223 (optional) For the students: ▪ P92, E92, SR92
9 Fractions of Quantities **PACING 1 DAY** Teacher Guide pp. 942–947 Lesson Activity Book pp. 225–226 Student Handbook Game p. 197	• To find a fraction of a set by multiplying a whole number by a fraction	1, 6, 7, 8, 9	fraction of a set	For the students: ▪ TR: AM100, AM27 ▪ cards numbered 1–9 ▪ scissors ▪ P93, E93, SR93 Science Connection: Inside the Earth Teacher Guide p. 884
10 Stories about Multiplying Fractions **PACING 1 DAY** Teacher Guide pp. 948–953 Lesson Activity Book pp. 227–228	• To interpret and solve story problems that require multiplying fractions	1, 6, 7, 8, 9, 10	fraction of a fraction	For the students: ▪ P94, E94, SR94 Literature Connection: The Stock Market: Understanding and Applying Ratios, Decimals, Fractions, and Percentages Teacher Guide p. 884

Planner (continued)

Chapter Planner *(continued)*

Lesson	Objectives	NCTM Standards	Vocabulary	Materials/ Resources
11 **Problem Solving Strategy and Test Prep** PACING **1 DAY** **Teacher Guide** pp. 954–959 **Lesson Activity Book** pp. 229–230 **Student Handbook** Review Model pp. 192–193	• To practice the problem solving strategy *solve a simpler problem* • To articulate the steps and strategies used to solve problems • To prepare for standardized tests	1, 2, 6, 7, 8, 9		
CHAPTER 11 Assessment TG pp. 960–963, **LAB** pp. 231–232, **AG** pp. 89–92				**For the students:** ■ Chapter 11 Test pp. AG89–AG90

Games

Use the following games for skills practice and reinforcement of concepts.

Lessons 11.2 *Fraction Sums and Differences* provides an opportunity for students to add and subtract fractions with like denominators.

Lessons 11.6 ▶
Fraction Addition provides an opportunity for students to compute and compare sums of fractions.

Lessons 11.9 *Close or Closer* provides an opportunity for students to practice finding fractions of a set.

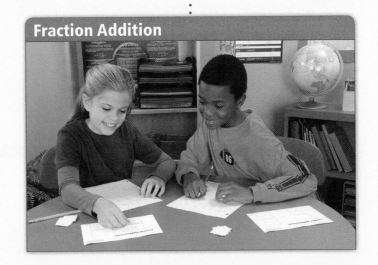
Fraction Addition

Planning Ahead

In **Lesson 11.1,** students need to cut out the fraction bars on AM95: Fraction Bars 1, and an envelope to store the fraction bars.

In **Lesson 11.2,** students will need to cut out the fraction bars on AM96: Fraction Bars 2. They also need the fraction bars from **Lesson 11.1** and AM97: *Fraction Sums and Differences* Game Board. Each pair of students will also need two sets of number cards from 1 to 12.

In **Lesson 11.5,** students will use pattern blocks.

In **Lesson 11.6,** students will need to cut out the number cards at the bottom of AM99: *Fraction Addition* Game.

In **Lesson 11.9,** students will need a set of number cards from 1 to 9 and AM27: Fraction Cards 1.

Developing Problem Solvers

Open-Ended Problem Solving

The Headline Story in the Daily Activities section of every lesson provides an open-ended problem for students to complete. For each story, there are many possible responses.

Headline Stories can be found on TG pages 887, 895, 901, 907, 913, 919, 927, 935, 943, and 949.

Leveled Problem Solving

Leveled Problem Solving provides an opportunity for students to apply learning from the lesson to a real-life situation. Problems are leveled by ability to allow students of all ability levels to become successful problem solvers. Each Leveled Problem Solving begins with a real-life scenario upon which three problems are built.

The levels of problems are:

❶ Basic Level	❷ On Level	❸ Above Level
students needing extra support	students working at grade level	students who are ready for more challenging problems

Leveled Problem Solving can be found on TG pages 893, 899, 905, 911, 917, 924, 932, 941, 947, and 953.

The World Almanac for Kids feature is designed to stimulate student interest in the math concepts they are about to learn. Students use data to solve problems and explain solutions. The Chapter 11 Project can be found on SH pages 184–185.

Write Math   **Reflect and Summarize the Lesson** poses a problem or question for students to think and write about. This feature can be found on TG pages 892, 898, 904, 910, 916, 923, 931, 940, 946, 952, and 956.

Other opportunities to write about math can be found on LAB pages 216, 218, 226, and 230.

Problem Solving Strategies

The focus of **Lesson 11.11** is the strategy, *solve a simpler problem.* However, students will use a variety of problem solving strategies as they work through the chapter. The chart below shows strategies that may be useful in completing each lesson.

Strategy	Lesson(s)	Description
Draw a Picture	11.1–11.5, 11.10	Sketch a picture to show a fraction story and draw a number line to solve a problem.
Look for a Pattern	11.8	Find patterns in multiplication of fractions.
Make a Model	11.1, 11.2, 11.7, 11.8	Use fraction bars to model a fraction story or play a game; make area models and dot models to show fraction multiplication; and use fraction machine to model finding fractions of a set.
✓ Solve a Simpler Problem	11.5, 11.6, 11.11	Use a common denominator to add and subtract fractions with unlike denominators.
Use Logical Reasoning	11.3, 11.4, 11.5, 11.6	Find fractions that sum to 1; find a common unit when adding or subtracting unlike things; estimate fraction sums and differences; and interpret fraction stories.
Write an Equation	11.1–11.4, 11.8	Write a number sentence to describe a fraction story and connect multiplication models to number sentences.

Meeting the Needs of All Learners

Differentiated Instruction

Extra Support	Activities for All	Enrichment
Intervention Activities TG pp. 893, 899, 905, 911, 917, 924, 932, 941, 947, 953	**Practice Book** pp. P85–P94	**Extension Activities** TG pp. 893, 899, 905, 911, 917, 924, 932, 941, 947, 953
	Spiral Review Book pp. SR85–SR94	**Extension Book** pp. E85–E94
	LAB Challenge LAB pp. 210, 212, 214, 216, 218, 220, 222, 224, 226, 228	**LAB Challenge** LAB pp. 210, 212, 214, 216, 218, 220, 222, 224, 226, 228
Lesson Notes **Basic Level** TG pp. 890, 892, 896, 897, 904, 916, 921, 931, 938, 945, 951	**Lesson Notes** **On Level** TG pp. 890, 916, 951, 952	**Lesson Notes** **Above Level** TG p. 952
Leveled Problem Solving **Basic Level** TG pp. 893, 899, 905, 911, 917, 924, 932, 941, 947, 953	**Leveled Problem Solving** **On Level** TG pp. 893, 899, 905, 911, 917, 924, 932, 941, 947, 953	**Leveled Problem Solving** **Above Level** TG pp. 893, 899, 905, 911, 917, 924, 932, 941, 947, 953

English Language Learners ELL

Suggestions for addressing the needs of students learning English as a second language are included in the Developing Mathematical Language section at the beginning of most lessons.

ELL activities for this chapter can be found on TG pages 887, 895, 901, 907, 913, 919, 927, 935, 943, and 949.

The Multi-Age Classroom

Grade 4	• Students on this level should be able to complete the lessons in Chapter 11 but might need some additional practice with key concepts and skills. • Give students more practice with fractions.	See Grade 5, Intervention Activities, Lessons 11.1–11.10. See Grade 4, Lessons 7.1–7.11.
Grade 5	• Students on this level should be able to complete the lessons in Chapter 11 with minimal adjustments.	See Grade 5, Practice pages P85–P94.
Grade 6	• Students on this level should be able to complete the lessons in Chapter 11 and to extend concepts and skills related to fractions. • Give students extended work with multiplying fractions.	See Grade 5, Extension pages E85–E94.

Cross Curricular Connections

Science Connection

Math Concept: multiplying fractions and whole numbers

Inside the Earth

Show students a diagram of Earth's layers. Share how the Earth is a sphere with a radius of about 6,400 kilometers. If we were to dig a hole to its center, we would have to dig through the crust—which varies from about 5 kilometers to about 40 kilometers, the mantle, the outer core and halfway through the inner core.

Have students compute the thickness of each layer by multiplying each fraction by 6,400 km. inner core = 1,280 km; outer core = 2,240 km; mantle = 2,880 km

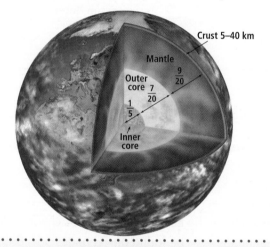

Crust 5–40 km

Mantle $\frac{9}{20}$

Outer core $\frac{7}{20}$

$\frac{1}{5}$

Inner core

Lesson 11.9

Music Connection

Math Concept: adding fractions with unlike denominators

Musical Rhythm

- Show students these musical notes.

Whole Note 4 beats Half Note 2 beats Eighth Note $\frac{1}{2}$ beat Quarter Note 1 beat Sixteenth Note $\frac{1}{4}$ beat

- Tell students that in $\frac{4}{4}$ time ("four-four time"), each measure gets 4 beats and the quarter note is one beat. Tell students that a vertical bar separates adjacent measures.

- Have students create four measures of rhythm, using each note at least once. Have volunteers demonstrate their rhythms by tapping on a desk or table.

Lesson 11.5

Literature Connection

Math Concept: fractions

The Stock Market: Understanding and Applying Ratios, Decimals, Fractions, and Percentages
By Orli Zuravicky

Students learn about ratios, decimals, fractions and percentages as they learn about some of the different numbers used in the stock market and what they represent.

Lesson 11.10

School-Home Connection

A reproducible copy of the School-Home Connection letter in English and in Spanish can be found in the *Teacher Resource Book,* pages SHC41–SHC44.

Encourage students to play *Clear the Board,* found on the School-Home Connection page, with a family member. Students will work with the concept of subtracting fractions in **Lessons 11.1–11.5.**

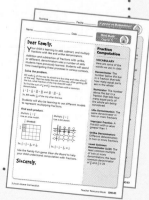

Assessment Options

There are many opportunities in *Think Math!* to assess students' understanding of concepts, skills, and problem solving. Learning Goals for Chapter 11 are provided below. The assessment options provide opportunities to evaluate whether or not students have retained learning from prior experiences. Choose the forms of assessment that best meet the needs of your students.

Chapter 11 Learning Goals

	Learning Goals	Lesson Number
11-A	Add and subtract fractions with like denominators	11.1–11.3
11-B	Add and subtract fractions with unlike denominators	11.4–11.6
11-C	Multiply fractions and identify a fraction of a set	11.7–11.10
11-D	Apply problem solving strategies such as *solve a simpler problem* to solve problems	11.11

✔ Informal Assessment

Ongoing Assessment
Provides insight into students' thinking to guide instruction (TG pp. 889, 897, 904, 920, 921)

Reflect and Summarize the Lesson
Checks understanding of lesson concepts (TG pp. 892, 898, 904, 910, 916, 923, 931, 940, 946, 952, 956)

Snapshot Assessment
Mental Math and Quick Write
Offers a quick observation of students' progress on chapter concepts and skills (TG pp. 960–961)

Performance Assessment
Provides quarterly assessment of Chapters 8–11 concepts using real-life situations
Assessment Guide
pp. AG219–AG224

✔ Formal Assessment

Standardized Test Prep
Problem Solving Test Prep
Prepares students for standardized tests
Lesson Activity Book p. 230 (TG p. 957)

Chapter 11 Review/Assessment
Reviews and assesses students' understanding of the chapter
Lesson Activity Book pp. 231–232 (TG p. 962)

Chapter 11 Test
Assesses the chapter concepts and skills
Assessment Guide
Form A pp. AG89–AG90
Form B pp. AG91–AG92

Benchmark 3 Assessment
Provides quarterly assessment of Chapters 8–11 concepts and skills
Assessment Guide
Benchmark 3A pp. AG93–AG100
Benchmark 3B pp. AG101–AG108

World Almanac for Kids

Use the World Almanac for Kids feature, *Joy Ride,* found on pp. 184–185 of the **Student Handbook,** to provide students with an opportunity to practice using their problem solving skills by solving real world problems.

FACT·ACTIVITY 1

1 $\frac{2}{48}$

2 $\frac{46}{48}$

3 $\frac{15}{48}$

4 $\frac{36}{48}$

5 7 minutes

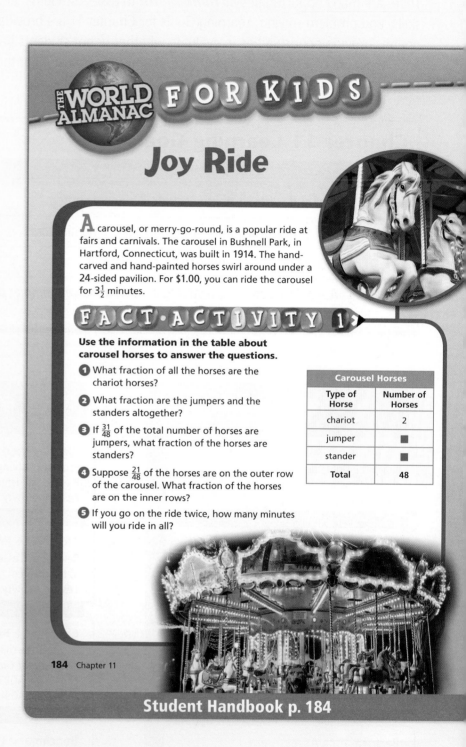

THE **WORLD ALMANAC** **FOR KIDS**

Joy Ride

A carousel, or merry-go-round, is a popular ride at fairs and carnivals. The carousel in Bushnell Park, in Hartford, Connecticut, was built in 1914. The hand-carved and hand-painted horses swirl around under a 24-sided pavilion. For $1.00, you can ride the carousel for $3\frac{1}{2}$ minutes.

FACT·ACTIVITY 1

Use the information in the table about carousel horses to answer the questions.

1 What fraction of all the horses are the chariot horses?

2 What fraction are the jumpers and the standers altogether?

3 If $\frac{31}{48}$ of the total number of horses are jumpers, what fraction of the horses are standers?

4 Suppose $\frac{21}{48}$ of the horses are on the outer row of the carousel. What fraction of the horses are on the inner rows?

5 If you go on the ride twice, how many minutes will you ride in all?

Carousel Horses	
Type of Horse	Number of Horses
chariot	2
jumper	■
stander	■
Total	48

184 Chapter 11

Student Handbook p. 184

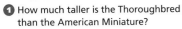

Our fascination with horses does not stop with carousel horses. Real horses can be much greater in size and weight than carousel horses. There are more than 200 breeds of horses in the world. The chart compares average heights and weights of different adult horse breeds.

① How much taller is the Thoroughbred than the American Miniature?

② Suppose a young Arabian foal gained $\frac{3}{4}$ lb, $\frac{7}{8}$ lb, and $\frac{15}{16}$ lb in 3 consecutive days. Find the total weight gain in the 3 days.

③ Which horse is $\frac{1}{4}$ the weight of a Thoroughbred?

Average Size of Horse Breeds		
Clydesdale	6 ft	1,800 lb
Thoroughbred	$5\frac{1}{3}$ ft	1,000 lb
Arabian	5 ft	900 lb
American Miniature	$2\frac{5}{6}$ ft	250 lb

CHAPTER PROJECT

A horse's size is often measured in hands. To measure by hands, one hand is placed on the ground and the other directly above it. The process is repeated by moving upward to the horse's shoulders. Work with a partner. How many hands tall are you? Use hands to estimate your height.

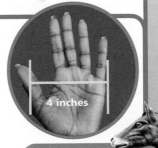

4 inches

- Have a partner trace your outline.
- Let your body length be equal to one unit. Use hands to measure the length of your body based on the outline.
- If your body length is about 14 hand-lengths long, then a hand represents $\frac{1}{14}$ of your body length.
- Use this measure to estimate body lengths of objects in the classroom. Display the results on a poster and share with your class.

ALMANAC Fact

Horses are thought to be related to a prehistoric animal called Hyracotherium that lived 50 million years ago and was about the size of a fox!

Student Handbook p. 185

FACT•ACTIVITY 2

① $5\frac{1}{3} - 2\frac{5}{6} = 2\frac{3}{6}$, or $2\frac{1}{2}$ feet

② $\frac{3}{4} + \frac{7}{8} + \frac{15}{16} = \frac{41}{16}$ lb, or $2\frac{9}{16}$ lb

③ American Miniature

CHAPTER PROJECT

Possible student response:

hand $= \frac{1}{14}$ body length

Sample objects:

Height of desk: $\frac{8}{14}$ body length

Length of book: $\frac{3}{14}$ body length

Length of table: $\frac{7}{14}$, or $\frac{1}{2}$ body length

Vocabulary

To reinforce vocabulary concepts, invite students to complete the vocabulary activities on pp. 194–195 of the **Student Handbook.** Encourage students to record their answers in their math journals.

Many responses are possible.

13 Possible answer: In order to add two *fractions*, both *fractions* must have the same *denominator*. First find equivalent *fractions* for each *fraction* and make sure that they all have the same *denominator*. Then add the *numerators* of the equivalent *fractions* to find the *numerator* of the sum. The *denominator* of the sum is the same as the *denominator* of the equivalent *fractions*.

14 Possible answer: First, subtract the *fraction* parts of the mixed numbers. Since the *denominators* are the same, equivalent *fractions* do not need to be found. Write the same *denominator* in the *denominator* of the *fraction* part of the answer and write the difference between the *numerators* as the *numerator* of the *fraction* part of the answer. Finally, subtract the whole numbers and write the difference between them to the left of the *fraction* part of the answer.

Chapter 11 | Vocabulary

Choose the best vocabulary term from Word List A for each sentence.

1 If several fractions represent length in inches, they have a(n) __?__. common unit

2 The product of two fractions is called a(n) __?__. fraction of a fraction

3 Two fractions that have the same denominator are fractions with a(n) __?__. common denominator

4 A number that has a whole number and a fraction is a(n) __?__. mixed number

5 If a fraction is greater than 1, it is called a(n) __?__. improper fraction

6 Two fractions that have the same value are __?__. equivalent fractions

7 The number below the bar of a fraction is the __?__. denominator

8 The number above the bar of a fraction is the __?__. numerator

9 The places where two lines cross in a dot sketch are called the __?__. intersections

10 A(n) __?__ is a rectangle in which the lengths of the sides represent the factors in a multiplication problem. area model

Word List A

area model
common denominator
common unit
denominator
dot sketch
equivalent fractions
fraction of a fraction
fraction of a set
improper fraction
intersections
least common denominator
mixed number
numerator
unlike denominators

Complete each analogy using the best term from Word List B.

11 Less than one is to proper fraction as greater than one is to __?__. mixed number

12 North America is to the equator as __?__ is to the fraction bar. numerator

Word List B

area model
denominator
mixed number
numerator

💬 Talk Math

Discuss with a partner what you have just learned about fractions. Use the vocabulary terms *numerator*, *denominator*, and *fraction*.

13 How can you add two fractions with unlike denominators?

14 How can you subtract mixed numbers with like denominators?

194 Chapter 11

Student Handbook p. 194

Word Definition Map

15 Create a word definition map for the word *mixed number*.

A What is it?

B What is it like?

C What are some examples?

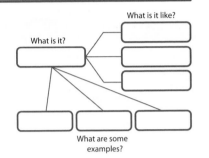

What is it?

What is it like?

What are some examples?

Tree Diagram

16 Create a tree diagram for the concept of *multiplying fractions*. Use what you know and what you have learned about multiplication and fractions.

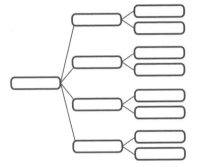

What's in a Word?

INTERSECTIONS *Intersections* are crossroads. A crossroad is the point where two or more roads cross each other. When you stand in a crossroad, you are standing on two roads at the same time. Line *intersections* are used to model multiplication of whole numbers and of fractions. The point where the lines cross—the *intersection*—is the solution to the problem. The solution is part of both lines, in much the same way as a person standing in a crossroad is part of both roads.

Chapter 11   **195**

Student Handbook p. 195

---

15 Many answers are possible. One example is provided.

What is it like?

the sum of a whole number and a fraction

What is it?

mixed number

measures and parts of measures

another way to write an improper fraction

$4\frac{1}{5}$ $2\frac{1}{4}$ $\frac{3}{2} = 1\frac{1}{2}$

What are some examples?

16 Many answers are possible. One example is provided.

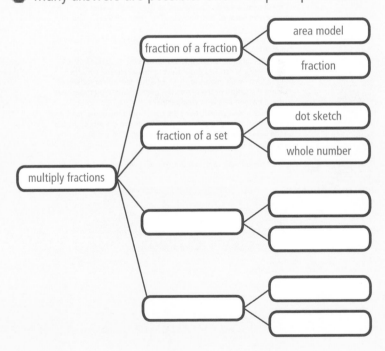

fraction of a fraction

area model

fraction

fraction of a set

dot sketch

whole number

multiply fractions

Games

Fraction Sums and Differences, in **Lesson 11.2** provides an opportunity for students to add and subtract fractions with like denominators. *Close or Closer,* in **Lesson 11.9** provides an opportunity for students to practice finding fractions of a set. These games can be found on pp. 196–197 of the *Student Handbook.*

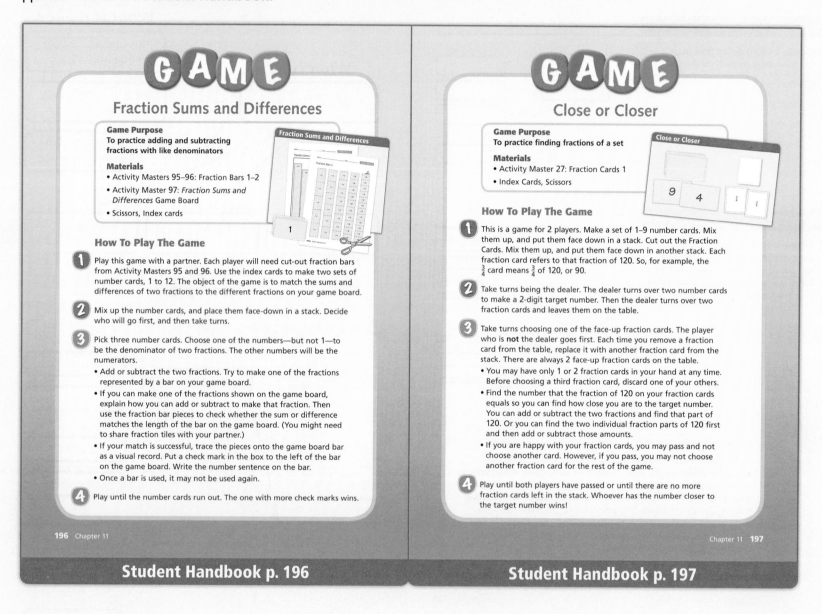

Fraction Sums and Differences

Game Purpose
To practice adding and subtracting fractions with like denominators

Materials
- Activity Masters 95–96: Fraction Bars 1–2
- Activity Master 97: *Fraction Sums and Differences* Game Board
- Scissors, Index cards

How To Play The Game

1 Play this game with a partner. Each player will need cut-out fraction bars from Activity Masters 95 and 96. Use the index cards to make two sets of number cards, 1 to 12. The object of the game is to match the sums and differences of two fractions to the different fractions on your game board.

2 Mix up the number cards, and place them face-down in a stack. Decide who will go first, and then take turns.

3 Pick three number cards. Choose one of the numbers—but not 1—to be the denominator of two fractions. The other numbers will be the numerators.

- Add or subtract the two fractions. Try to make one of the fractions represented by a bar on your game board.
- If you can make one of the fractions shown on the game board, explain how you can add or subtract to make that fraction. Then use the fraction bar pieces to check whether the sum or difference matches the length of the bar on the game board. (You might need to share fraction tiles with your partner.)
- If your match is successful, trace the pieces onto the game board bar as a visual record. Put a check mark in the box to the left of the bar on the game board. Write the number sentence on the bar.
- Once a bar is used, it may not be used again.

4 Play until the number cards run out. The one with more check marks wins.

196 Chapter 11

Student Handbook p. 196

Close or Closer

Game Purpose
To practice finding fractions of a set

Materials
- Activity Master 27: Fraction Cards 1
- Index Cards, Scissors

How To Play The Game

1 This is a game for 2 players. Make a set of 1–9 number cards. Mix them up, and put them face down in a stack. Cut out the Fraction Cards. Mix them up, and put them face down in another stack. Each fraction card refers to that fraction of 120. So, for example, the $\frac{3}{4}$ card means $\frac{3}{4}$ of 120, or 90.

2 Take turns being the dealer. The dealer turns over two number cards to make a 2-digit target number. Then the dealer turns over two fraction cards and leaves them on the table.

3 Take turns choosing one of the face-up fraction cards. The player who is **not** the dealer goes first. Each time you remove a fraction card from the table, replace it with another fraction card from the stack. There are always 2 face-up fraction cards on the table.

- You may have only 1 or 2 fraction cards in your hand at any time. Before choosing a third fraction card, discard one of your others.
- Find the number that the fraction of 120 on your fraction cards equals so you can find how close you are to the target number. You can add or subtract the two fractions and find that part of 120. Or you can find the two individual fraction parts of 120 first and then add or subtract those amounts.
- If you are happy with your fraction cards, you may pass and not choose another card. However, if you pass, you may not choose another fraction card for the rest of the game.

4 Play until both players have passed or until there are no more fraction cards left in the stack. Whoever has the number closer to the target number wins!

Chapter 11 197

Student Handbook p. 197

Challenge

The Challenge activity *Fractions of Areas* challenges students to find the fraction of a square represented by the various color sections. This activity can be found on p. 198 of the *Student Handbook.*

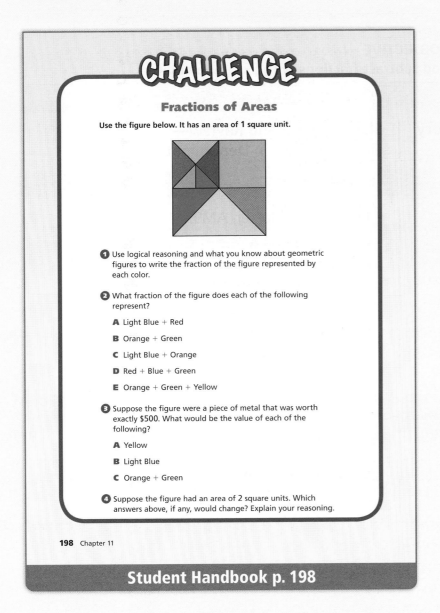

CHALLENGE

Fractions of Areas

Use the figure below. It has an area of **1** square unit.

❶ Use logical reasoning and what you know about geometric figures to write the fraction of the figure represented by each color.

❷ What fraction of the figure does each of the following represent?

A Light Blue + Red

B Orange + Green

C Light Blue + Orange

D Red + Blue + Green

E Orange + Green + Yellow

❸ Suppose the figure were a piece of metal that was worth exactly $500. What would be the value of each of the following?

A Yellow

B Light Blue

C Orange + Green

❹ Suppose the figure had an area of 2 square units. Which answers above, if any, would change? Explain your reasoning.

198 Chapter 11

Student Handbook p. 198

❶ light blue $= \frac{1}{16}$, purple $= \frac{1}{16}$, blue $= \frac{1}{32}$, light purple $= \frac{1}{32}$, red $= \frac{1}{16}$, orange $= \frac{1}{4}$, gray $= \frac{1}{8}$, yellow $= \frac{1}{4}$, green $= \frac{1}{8}$

❷ A. $\frac{2}{16}$ or $\frac{1}{8}$

B. $\frac{3}{8}$

C. $\frac{5}{16}$

D. $\frac{7}{32}$

E. $\frac{5}{8}$

❸ A. $125

B. $31.25

C. $187.50

❹ None of the answers would change; Possible explanation: In Problem 2, each color would still be the same fractional part of the whole. In Problem 3, since each color would still be the same fractional part of the whole, the value of each color would remain the same.

Lesson 1 Adding and Subtracting Fractions with Like Denominators

NCTM Standards 1, 2, 6, 7, 8, 10

Lesson Planner

STUDENT OBJECTIVE ·
- To add and subtract fractions with like denominators

1 | Daily Activities (TG p. 887)

Open-Ended Problem Solving/Headline Story	Skills Practice and Review— Finding Common Denominators

2 | Teach and Practice (TG pp. 888–892)

Ⓐ **Reading the Student Letter** (TG p. 888)

Ⓑ **Adding and Subtracting Like Things** (TG p. 889)

Ⓒ **Adding and Subtracting Fractions with Like Denominators** (TG pp. 890–891)

Ⓓ **Working with Fractions with Like Denominators** (TG p. 892)

MATERIALS
- TR: Activity Master, AM95
- scissors
- envelopes
- 📖 LAB pp. 209–210
- 📖 SH p. 183

3 | Differentiated Instruction (TG p. 893)

Leveled Problem Solving (TG p. 893)	Practice Book P85
Intervention Activity (TG p. 893)	Extension Book E85
Extension Activity (TG p. 893)	Spiral Review Book SR85

Lesson Notes

About the Lesson

One can only add or subtract *like* things: it makes no sense to add 5 inches and 8 minutes. Even when the numbers don't have an explicit context, addition and subtraction require that the numbers "measure" like quantities. We don't think of 4 tens plus 3 ones as 7 "somethings," but as 43, which is to say 43 *ones*. The same is true for adding or subtracting fractions.

When the denominators are the same (i.e., when it is like working with minutes and minutes or inches and inches), we can just add or subtract the numerators. This understanding decreases the chances that students will try to add or subtract the denominators, a common error when students first encounter fraction arithmetic on paper.

Use with Lesson Activity Book pp. 209–210.

Developing Mathematical Language

Vocabulary: numerator, denominator, like denominators, improper fraction, mixed number

To make 4 equal jumps from 0 to 12 on a number line, each jump must be $\frac{12}{4}$ (that is, 3) units long; to jump from 0 to 12 in 8 equal jumps, each jump must be $\frac{12}{8}$ (or $1\frac{1}{2}$) units long; to make this trip in 24 jumps, each jump must be $\frac{12}{24}$ (or $\frac{1}{2}$) unit long. The fractions, themselves, are numbers—in this example, the numbers $\frac{12}{4}$, $\frac{12}{8}$, $\frac{12}{24}$ represent lengths. The way we *write* fractions describes the division of one whole number by another (in this example, dividing the distance 12 by 4, 8, or 24). The fraction is a number, but so are the two parts of the way we write it. To avoid ambiguity when talking about how we *write* a fraction—so that we don't use the word "number" to mean three different things—we use the special names *numerator* (number above the line) and *denominator* (number below the line).

Familiarize students with the terms *numerator* and *denominator*.

Beginning Display several fractions and have students name the number in the *numerator* and *denominator* of each.

Intermediate Tell students the numbers for a *numerator* and a *denominator*. Have them write the fraction on paper.

Advanced Ask students to explain the differences between the *numerator* and the *denominator* of a fraction.

Open-Ended Problem Solving

Encourage students to use common fractions in responding to this Headline Story.

 Headline Story

> **To say how much time something took, Danisha began using fractions of an hour instead of minutes. What might she say and how many minutes might she mean?**

Possible responses: "I'll be there in three-quarters of an hour!" means in 45 minutes. One-tenth of an hour is 6 minutes. Two-thirds of an hour is 40 minutes. One and a half hours is 90 minutes.

Skills Practice and Review

Finding Common Denominators

Tell your students that you want to know which of two refrigerators is heavier. One fridge weighs $\frac{2}{3}$ of a ton and one weighs $\frac{9}{15}$ of a ton. Have students use dot sketches to find a common denominator for the two measurements. Start with a dot sketch for either of the fractions and draw equivalent fractions until the total number of dots is divisible by the *other* fraction's denominator.

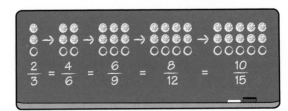

$$\frac{2}{3} = \frac{4}{6} = \frac{6}{9} = \frac{8}{12} = \frac{10}{15}$$

Once students have found a common denominator, ask them to compare the two fractions. Here are other fractions you might use.

$$\frac{5}{9}, \frac{2}{3} \qquad \frac{3}{4}, \frac{1}{3} \qquad \frac{1}{2}, \frac{5}{6} \qquad \frac{11}{15}, \frac{4}{5} \qquad \frac{5}{9}, \frac{11}{18}$$

individuals or whole class

5 MIN

NCTM Standards 1, 2, 7, 8

Ⓐ Reading the Student Letter

Purpose To introduce the content of the chapter

Introduce The Student Letter is designed to spur interest and curiosity. Have students read and discuss the letter. If you have already done the Skills Practice and Review activity, your students will have a recent experience with the dot sketches. If not, you might do the problem below.

Problem What do you get when you add 10 fifteenths and 9 fifteenths? What is the difference between 10 fifteenths and 9 fifteenths?

The letter asks students to compare two fractions with unlike denominators, but then reminds them of how to use dot sketches to make equivalent fractions with a common denominator. Students should use the dot sketches on the letter to answer the questions above.

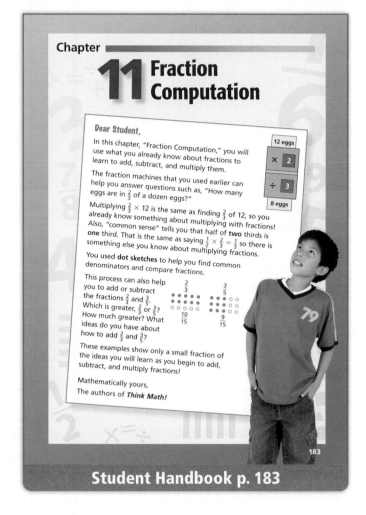

Student Handbook p. 183

B Adding and Subtracting Like Things

NCTM Standards 1, 2, 6, 7, 8

Purpose To prepare for adding and subtracting fractions with like denominators

Introduce Acknowledge to students that this exercise may seem "too young" to them at first, but say that it will prepare them for adding and subtracting fractions in the next activity. Explain that you will say a problem, and that students should pay particular attention to the units in each problem and use those units in giving their answers.

 ### Talk Math

❷ 6 pennies plus 3 pennies is how many pennies? 9 pennies

❷ 6 inches plus 3 inches is how many inches? 9 inches

❷ 6 twelfths plus 3 twelfths is how many twelfths? 9 twelfths

❷ If Jon ate 3 eighths of an 8-slice pizza, and Tanya ate 5 eighths, who ate more? How do you know? Tanya ate more. Five eighths is 2 more eighths than 3 eighths.

Problem Is it possible to add or subtract unlike things, such as inches and minutes?

Students should reason that one cannot add unlike things because there is no unit that includes both of them. That is, 2 inches + 3 minutes cannot equal 5 of anything. Even when the kinds of quantities can be added—such as 6 inches + 3 feet—we can't simply add the *numbers* unless the units are the same: 6 inches + 3 feet can be 42 inches, $3\frac{1}{2}$ feet, or just 3'6", but cannot be 9 of anything.

Tell students that the same is true for adding and subtracting fractions—we cannot just add the numerators unless the fractions are of the same type (the same denominator). Adding and subtracting fractions once they have the same denominator works just like adding and subtracting whole numbers. Students will see this in the next activity.

✓ Ongoing Assessment

- The main point of this lesson is for students to see that the same rules hold for adding and subtracting fractions as for adding other kinds of quantities—first you make sure you are working with like things.

- Keep an eye out for students who seem to recognize that "like things" means the same fractional part (i.e., the same denominator), and for those who need more help making this connection.

Materials

- For each student: AM95, scissors, envelope

NCTM Standards 1, 2, 7, 8, 10

(C) Adding and Subtracting Fractions with Like Denominators

Purpose To model addition and subtraction of fractions with like denominators using fraction bars

Introduce Have students cut out the bars from AM95: Fraction Bars 1, cutting around the outside of each bar and through the bars along the dotted lines. Then ask students to choose one fractional piece and figure out how many of those pieces make up the whole bar. (It does not matter, at this point, which of the smaller pieces they choose.) They might do this by matching up various-sized pieces to the whole bar and concluding, for example, that the whole bar is equivalent to 12 of the smallest pieces and that each of these pieces is $\frac{1}{12}$ of the whole bar.

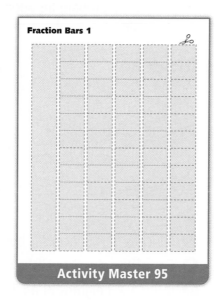

Fraction Bars 1

Activity Master 95

Differentiated Instruction

Basic Level/On Level Some students may find it helpful to label their fraction bars. They might label each individual twelfth on the front of the bar and then label the back with the equivalent fraction for the entire piece (for example, $\frac{1}{6}$ on the back of the piece that shows two separate twelfths on the front).

Task Have students use their fraction bar pieces to model story problems like the ones below.

Ask students to solve the problems with the bars, and then sketch a picture to explain their solution. Also have students write a number sentence to describe each problem. Students can rely on their pictures and numbers sentences when they talk about their solutions as a class.

❶ I wasn't sure how much ribbon I needed to make our decorations, so I bought a foot of ribbon. It turned out that I needed $\frac{5}{12}$ of a foot for making one decoration and $\frac{3}{12}$ of a foot for making another one. What fraction of a foot of ribbon did I need for making both? $\frac{5}{12} + \frac{3}{12} = \frac{8}{12} = \frac{2}{3}$ of a foot

❷ I measured a book that is close to 7 inches, or $\frac{7}{12}$ of a foot. Another book measured one foot. As a fraction of a foot, what is the difference in the two lengths? $\frac{12}{12} - \frac{7}{12} = \frac{5}{12}$ of a foot

❸ I measured one shoe that is close to 8 inches, or $\frac{8}{12}$ of a foot, and another shoe that is close to 6 inches, or $\frac{6}{12}$ of a foot. In fractions of a foot, what is the length of the two shoes lined up end-to-end? $\frac{8}{12} + \frac{6}{12} = \frac{14}{12} = 1\frac{2}{12} = 1\frac{1}{6}$ of a foot

As students discuss the solution to Problem 3, you may want to discuss the term "improper fraction". The term "improper fraction" is in such common use that students need to know what it refers to. But there is *nothing* "improper" about such fractions. In fact, mathematicians often leave results in this "improper" form, rather than converting to mixed numbers. Remember that 3.5, $3\frac{1}{2}$, and $\frac{7}{2}$ are all the same number, just different ways of *writing* it. Though common school usage calls $3\frac{1}{2}$ a mixed number and $\frac{1}{2}$ a fraction, as if they were different *kinds* of numbers, we'd never call 3.5 and 0.5 different kinds of numbers.

Have students place their fraction bars into an envelope so that they can use them again in future lessons.

Use with Lesson Activity Book pp. 209–210.

Extend Have your students order the answers to the story problems by placing them on a number line. If you have time, ask them to add other numbers to the number line, such as $2\frac{12}{12}$ (that is, 3).

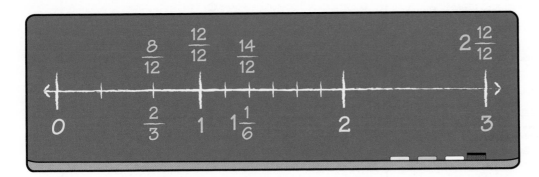

Working with Fractions with Like Denominators LAB pp. 209–210

individuals 👤 🕐 **20 MIN**

Purpose To add and subtract fraction with like denominators

NCTM Standards 1, 2, 7, 10

Lesson Activity Book p. 209

Name _____ Date _____

Chapter 11
Lesson 1 **Adding and Subtracting Fractions with Like Denominators**
NCTM Standards 1, 2, 7, 10

Complete the sentences with number words.

① twelve apples + eight apples = _____ twenty apples

② eight-eighths + three-eighths = _____ eleven-eighths

③ seven-fourths − four-fourths = _____ three-fourths

Shade the bars to show the sums. Complete the number sentences. Change improper fractions to mixed numbers. ▭ = 1

④ ▭ + ▭ = ▭

$\frac{2}{5} + \frac{3}{5} = \boxed{\frac{5}{5}} = \boxed{1}$

⑤ ▭ + ▭ = ▭

$\frac{5}{6} + \frac{3}{6} = \boxed{\frac{8}{6}} = \boxed{1\frac{2}{6}}$ or $1\frac{1}{3}$

⑥ ▭ + ▭ = ▭

$\frac{4}{7} + \frac{2}{7} = \boxed{\frac{6}{7}}$

Use the pictures to complete the number sentences. ▭ = 1

⑦ ▭ $\frac{5}{6} - \frac{2}{6} = \boxed{\frac{3}{6}}$ or $\frac{1}{2}$

⑧ ▭ $\frac{6}{8} - \frac{3}{8} = \boxed{\frac{3}{8}}$

11 × 19 **CCIX** two hundred nine **209**

ABOUT THE PAGE NUMBER 209 is divisible by the sum of its digits. 209: 2 + 0 + 9 = 11; 209 ÷ 11 = 19. This makes it a Harshad number.

Lesson Activity Book p. 210

Complete the number sentences.

⑨ $\frac{7}{17} + \frac{8}{17} = \boxed{\frac{15}{17}}$

⑩ $\frac{15}{25} - \frac{9}{25} = \boxed{\frac{6}{25}}$

⑪ $\frac{50}{32} - \frac{29}{32} = \boxed{\frac{21}{32}}$

⑫ $\frac{4}{16} + \boxed{\frac{9}{16}} = \frac{13}{16}$

⑬ $\frac{33}{70} + \frac{39}{70} = \boxed{\frac{72}{70}}$, or $1\frac{2}{70}$

⑭ $\boxed{\frac{27}{47}} - \frac{9}{47} = \frac{18}{47}$

⑮ Choose one of the number sentences above. Write it and three related addition and subtraction sentences.

$\frac{7}{17} + \frac{8}{17} = \frac{15}{17}$ Answers will vary. $\frac{15}{17} - \frac{7}{17} = \frac{8}{17}$

$\frac{8}{17} + \frac{7}{17} = \frac{15}{17}$ One possibility is shown. $\frac{15}{17} - \frac{8}{17} = \frac{7}{17}$

⑯ Challenge

$\frac{18}{98} + \frac{9}{98} + \frac{5}{98} + \frac{17}{98} = \boxed{\frac{49}{98}}$

Write an equivalent fraction for the sum. $\boxed{\frac{1}{2}}$

Accept other equivalent fractions.

210 two hundred ten **CCX** △ 2 × 3 × 5 × 7

ABOUT THE PAGE NUMBER 210 is a triangular number. It is a Harshad number. 210 = 1 + 2 + 3 + 4 + ... + 17 + 18 + 19 + 20. It is the product of the first 4 primes: = 2 × 3 × 5 × 7

Teaching Notes for LAB page 209

Students use number words and then pictures of fraction bars to add and subtract fractions with like denominators. It is mathematically acceptable to leave answers as improper fractions. If your state tests require that students simplify all fractions, ask them to do so on the page.

Differentiated Instruction Basic Level If you see students adding the denominators in Problems 4–6, ask them to read the number sentences orally. This will remind them that they are adding like things, and therefore, the unit of the sum is the same as the unit of the addends.

Teaching Notes for LAB page 210

Students complete number sentences (without pictures) to add and subtract fractions with like denominators, and then create a family of related addition and subtraction sentences using one of the completed sentences.

Concept Alert The variety of types of number sentences (missing sums, addends, and so on) reminds students that adding and subtracting fractions with like denominators is the same as adding and subtracting whole numbers.

Challenge Problem Students complete a number sentence with four addends and write an equivalent fraction for the sum.

Reflect and Summarize the Lesson

 Write Math

Draw a picture and write a number sentence for this fraction story. Jake and Erin ordered a large pizza. Jake ate $\frac{3}{12}$ of the pizza. Erin ate $\frac{5}{12}$ of the pizza. How much of the pizza did they eat in all?

$\frac{8}{12}$, or $\frac{2}{3}$ of the pizza; check students' drawings; $\frac{3}{12} + \frac{5}{12} = \frac{8}{12}$, or $\frac{2}{3}$.

Leveled Problem Solving

Daria ate $\frac{1}{12}$ of a pizza, Steve ate $\frac{7}{12}$ of it, and Mia ate $\frac{1}{12}$ of it.

❶ Basic Level

How much of the pizza did Daria and Steve eat in all? Explain.

$\frac{2}{3}$; $\frac{1}{12} + \frac{7}{12} = \frac{8}{12}$, and $\frac{8}{12} = \frac{2}{3}$

❷ On Level

How much more of the pizza did Steve eat than Daria? Explain.

$\frac{1}{2}$ more; $\frac{7}{12} - \frac{1}{12} = \frac{6}{12}$, and $\frac{6}{12} = \frac{1}{2}$

❸ Above Level

How much more of the pizza did Steve eat than what both Daria and Mia ate? $\frac{5}{12}$ more; $\frac{7}{12} - \left(\frac{1}{12} + \frac{1}{12}\right) = \frac{5}{12}$

Intervention

Activity Say the Denominator

Write a problem, such as "3 apples + 1 apple = ■," on the board. Ask students to complete it aloud together: "3 apples plus 1 apple equals 4 apples." Then write a related fraction addition problem, such as $\frac{3}{10} + \frac{1}{10}$, on the board. Ask students to complete it aloud together, "3 tenths plus 1 tenth equals 4 tenths." Have a student write and simplify the answer on the board. $\frac{4}{10} = \frac{2}{5}$ Repeat with other fraction addition and subtraction problems.

Practice

Adding and Subtracting Fractions with Like Denominators

Shade the bars to show the sums. Complete the number sentences. Change improper fractions to mixed numbers.

$\frac{4}{8} + \frac{5}{8} = \frac{9}{8} = 1\frac{1}{8}$

$\frac{2}{6} + \frac{4}{6} = \frac{6}{6} = 1$

Use the pictures to complete the number sentences.

$\frac{6}{7} - \frac{3}{7} = \frac{3}{7}$

$\frac{4}{5} - \frac{2}{5} = \frac{2}{5}$

Test Prep

The base of a parallelogram is two times its height. If the base is 12 centimeters, what is the area? Explain.

72 sq cm; the formula for the area of a parallelogram is $A = b \times h$. The height is 6 cm, so $A = 12 \times 6 = 72$ sq cm.

Practice P85

Extension

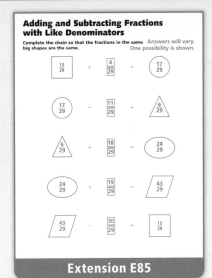

Adding and Subtracting Fractions with Like Denominators

Complete the chain so that the fractions in the same big shapes are the same. Answers will vary. One possibility is shown.

Extension E85

Spiral Review

Spiral Review Book page SR85 provides review of the following previously learned skills and concepts:

- using division to solve problems involving whole numbers
- relating pounds and kilograms

You may wish to have students work with partners to complete the page.

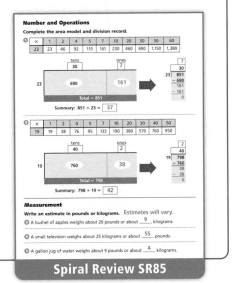

Spiral Review SR85

Extension Activity
Make a Magic Square

Show students this magic square.

4	9	2
3	5	7
8	1	6

Remind them it is a magic square because the numbers in all the rows, columns, and diagonals add up to the same number, which is 15. Challenge pairs of students to make a magic square using fractions. Some students might discover that they can use the numbers in the magic square above as numerators, creating fractions with like denominators.

More Adding and Subtracting Fractions with Like Denominators

NCTM Standards 1, 2, 6, 7, 8, 9, 10

Lesson Planner

STUDENT OBJECTIVE
- To add and subtract fractions with like denominators

1 Daily Activities (TG p. 895)

Open-Ended Problem Solving/Headline Story	Skills Practice and Review— Naming Common Denominators

2 Teach and Practice (TG pp. 896–898)

	MATERIALS
(A) **Playing a Game: *Fraction Sums and Differences*** (TG p. 896) (B) **Adding and Subtracting Fractions with Like Denominators** (TG p. 897)	• TR: Activity Masters, AM96–AM97 • bars cut from TR: AM95 or fraction bars • scissors • index cards numbered 1–12 • 📖 LAB pp. 211–212 • 📖 SH p. 186, 196

3 Differentiated Instruction (TG p. 899)

Leveled Problem Solving (TG p. 899)	Practice Book P86
Intervention Activity (TG p. 899)	Extension Book E86
Extension Activity (TG p. 899)	Spiral Review Book SR86

Lesson Notes

About the Lesson

Students continue to add and subtract fractions with like denominators, modeling these computations with fraction bars.

Use with Lesson Activity Book pp. 211–212.

Developing Mathematical Language

Vocabulary: like denominators, improper fraction, mixed number

A *mixed number* consists of a whole number and a fraction. Mathematically, the *mixed number* represents the sum of the whole number and the fraction in much the same way the number 46 represents the sum $40 + 6$.

Tell students that we can express a number in different ways, depending on how we are using it. The *improper fraction* $\frac{3}{2}$ can show that 3 cookies are split between 2 people. The number $1\frac{1}{2}$ shows how many cookies each person gets. Since $\frac{3}{2} = \frac{1}{2} + \frac{1}{2} + \frac{1}{2}$, we know that $\frac{3}{2} = 1 + \frac{1}{2} = 1\frac{1}{2}$. The reason we can add $\frac{1}{2} + \frac{1}{2} + \frac{1}{2}$, is because of the *like denominators*.

Familiarize students with the terms *like denominators, improper fraction,* and *mixed number.*

Beginning Tell students that the word *like* has different meanings. *Like* means "enjoy" in the question, "Does Mary like movies?" In the term, *like denominators, like* means "the same."

Intermediate Ask students to write two fractions with *like denominators* on paper and explain their choice of fractions.

Advanced Ask students to explain how they can tell whether a fraction is an *improper fraction.* Challenge them to write two different improper fractions with *like denominators.*

Open-Ended Problem Solving

Students should consider the "improper" fractions that might have been in Samantha's list in order to respond to this Headline Story.

 Headline Story

> Samantha made a list of "improper" fractions that, when rewritten as mixed numbers, were all between 3 and 4, and had a fractional part with a numerator of 1. What can you say about the improper fractions on her list?

Possible responses: We can list mixed numbers like $3\frac{1}{2}$, $3\frac{1}{3}$, $3\frac{1}{4}$, $3\frac{1}{5}$, $3\frac{1}{6}$, and so on, and figure out the improper fractions from that list. The numerators of the improper fractions are 7, 10, 13, 16, and keep skipping by 3. If the denominator of the improper fraction is odd, then its numerator is even. If the denominator of the improper fraction is even, then its numerator is odd.

Skills Practice and Review

Naming Common Denominators

Call out pairs of denominators and ask students to name at least two common denominators. Possible answers are given.

5 and 3 15, 30	2 and 6 6, 12	6 and 9 18, 36, 54
4 and 5 20, 40	4 and 6 12, 24	7 and 6 42, 84

Then give students a context for comparing fractions, and use fractions with unlike denominators. For example, you might tell them that two students are comparing their heights and that one of them is $4\frac{3}{4}$ feet tall and the other is $4\frac{5}{6}$ feet tall.

pairs

30 MIN

Materials

- For each student: AM96–AM97, pieces cut from AM95 or fraction bars, scissors, cards numbered 1–12

NCTM Standards 1, 2, 7, 8, 10

Differentiated Instruction

Basic Level If you have students who need support converting fraction sums and differences to their equivalent fractions, you might help them write equivalent fractions (with the denominators 2 through 12) on the fraction bars of the game board before they begin to play the game.

A Playing a Game: *Fraction Sums and Differences*

Purpose To practice adding and subtracting fractions with like denominators

Goal The object of the game, *Fraction Sums and Differences,* is for each student to match the sums and differences of fraction bars of varied lengths on their individual game boards. The player who matches the most sums and differences to bars wins.

Prepare Materials Give each student AM96: Fraction Bars 2 and have them cut out the fraction bars. Also give each student his or her cut-out fraction bars from the previous lesson and AM97: *Fraction Sums and Differences* Game Board. Each pair of students will need two sets of cards numbered 1 to 12. These cards should be placed face down in a stack. Students should have enough time to play multiple games during the time period.

Student Handbook p. 196

How to Play

❶ One player picks three number cards. The player chooses one of these numbers (but not the number 1) to be the denominator for both fractions; the other two numbers become the numerators of the two fractions.

❷ The player then adds or subtracts the two fractions, trying to generate one of the fractions represented by a bar on the game board.

❸ If the player can make one of the fractions shown on the game board, the player must explain how they can add or subtract to make that fraction, and then use the fraction bar pieces to check that the sum or difference matches the length of the bar on the game board. (Players may sometimes need to share their fraction bars.) If the match is successful, the player traces the pieces onto the game board bar as a visual record, puts a check mark in the box to the left of the bar on the game board, and writes the number sentence on the bar.

❹ Once a bar has been used, it may not be used again.

❺ Players take turns, and play continues until the number cards run out. At that point, the player who has the most check marks wins.

Activity Master 96

Activity Master 97

Use with Lesson Activity Book pp. 211–212.

Adding and Subtracting Fractions with Like Denominators LAB pp. 211–212

Purpose To add and subtract fractions with like denominators

NCTM Standards 1, 2, 6, 7, 9

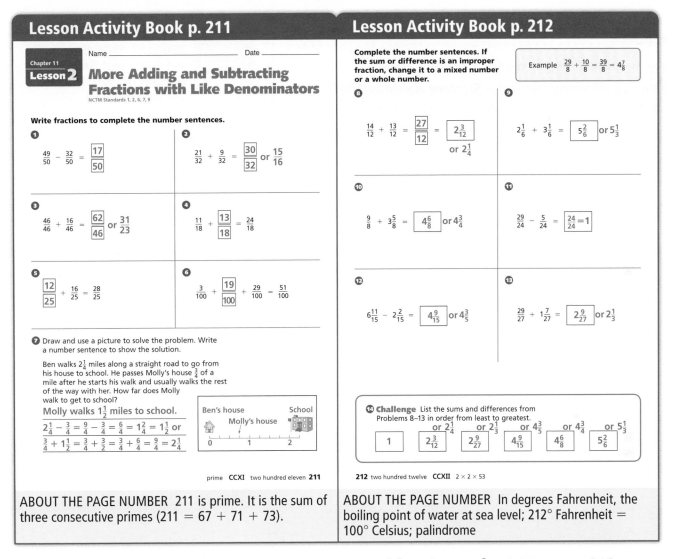

Lesson Activity Book p. 211

Chapter 11
Lesson 2 **More Adding and Subtracting Fractions with Like Denominators**
NCTM Standards 1, 2, 6, 7, 9

Write fractions to complete the number sentences.

1 $\frac{49}{50} - \frac{32}{50} = \frac{17}{50}$

2 $\frac{21}{32} + \frac{9}{32} = \frac{30}{32}$ or $\frac{15}{16}$

3 $\frac{46}{46} + \frac{16}{46} = \frac{62}{46}$ or $\frac{31}{23}$

4 $\frac{11}{18} + \frac{13}{18} = \frac{24}{18}$

5 $\frac{12}{25} + \frac{16}{25} = \frac{28}{25}$

6 $\frac{3}{100} + \frac{19}{100} + \frac{29}{100} = \frac{51}{100}$

7 Draw and use a picture to solve the problem. Write a number sentence to show the solution.

Ben walks $2\frac{1}{4}$ miles along a straight road to go from his house to school. He passes Molly's house $\frac{3}{4}$ of a mile after he starts his walk and usually walks the rest of the way with her. How far does Molly walk to get to school?

Molly walks $1\frac{1}{2}$ miles to school.

$2\frac{1}{4} - \frac{3}{4} = \frac{9}{4} - \frac{3}{4} = \frac{6}{4} = 1\frac{2}{4} = 1\frac{1}{2}$ or

$\frac{3}{4} + 1\frac{1}{2} = \frac{3}{4} + \frac{3}{2} = \frac{3}{4} + \frac{6}{4} = \frac{9}{4} = 2\frac{1}{4}$

Ben's house   School
🏠 Molly's house 🏫
0   1   2

prime **CCXI** two hundred eleven **211**

Lesson Activity Book p. 212

Complete the number sentences. If the sum or difference is an improper fraction, change it to a mixed number or a whole number.

Example $\frac{29}{8} + \frac{10}{8} = \frac{39}{8} = 4\frac{7}{8}$

8 $\frac{14}{12} + \frac{13}{12} = \frac{27}{12} = 2\frac{3}{12}$ or $2\frac{1}{4}$

9 $2\frac{1}{6} + 3\frac{1}{6} = 5\frac{2}{6}$ or $5\frac{1}{3}$

10 $\frac{9}{8} + 3\frac{5}{8} = 4\frac{6}{8}$ or $4\frac{3}{4}$

11 $\frac{29}{24} - \frac{5}{24} = \frac{24}{24} = 1$

12 $6\frac{11}{15} - 2\frac{2}{15} = 4\frac{9}{15}$ or $4\frac{3}{5}$

13 $\frac{29}{27} + 1\frac{7}{27} = 2\frac{9}{27}$ or $2\frac{1}{3}$

14 Challenge List the sums and differences from Problems 8–13 in order from least to greatest.

| | | | or $2\frac{1}{4}$ | or $2\frac{1}{3}$ | or $4\frac{3}{5}$ | or $4\frac{3}{4}$ | or $5\frac{1}{3}$ |

| 1 | $2\frac{3}{12}$ | $2\frac{9}{27}$ | $4\frac{9}{15}$ | $4\frac{6}{8}$ | $5\frac{2}{6}$ |

212 two hundred twelve **CCXII** $2 \times 2 \times 53$

ABOUT THE PAGE NUMBER 211 is prime. It is the sum of three consecutive primes (211 = 67 + 71 + 73).

ABOUT THE PAGE NUMBER In degrees Fahrenheit, the boiling point of water at sea level; 212° Fahrenheit = 100° Celsius; palindrome

Teaching Notes for LAB page 211
Students add and subtract fractions with like denominators. They draw and use a picture to help solve the problem at the bottom of the page. For example, students could use tick marks to indicate quarters of a mile.

Differentiated Instruction Basic Level As in the previous lesson, ask any students who add or subtract the denominator when finding a sum or difference to read the number sentence out loud. This should redirect their attention to the connection between adding and subtracting like objects and adding and subtracting fractions with like denominators.

Teaching Notes for LAB page 212
Students complete number sentences for addition and subtraction of improper fractions, mixed numbers, and a combination of these ways of writing numbers.

✔**Ongoing Assessment** While they are not required to do so, you might ask some students to simplify fractions, so that you can evaluate this ability.

Challenge Problem Students order fractions from least to greatest. Some students may write equivalent fractions to help them compare and order various fractions.

Write Math

Complete the two number sentences in the box. Explain how you found the sum and difference. $3\frac{11}{15} + 1\frac{4}{15} = 4\frac{15}{15}$, or $4 + 1 = 5$; $3\frac{11}{15} - 1\frac{4}{15} = 2\frac{7}{15}$ to find the sum I add the whole-number parts of the mixed numbers and then add the numerators of the two fractions. To find the difference I subtract the whole-number parts of the mixed numbers and then subtract the numerators of the two fractions.

$$3\frac{11}{15} + 1\frac{4}{15} = \blacksquare$$

$$3\frac{11}{15} - 1\frac{4}{15} = \blacksquare$$

Review Model

Refer students to Review Model: Adding and Subtracting Fractions with Like Denominators in the *Student Handbook* to see how to find the sums and differences of fractions with like denominators.

✔ **Check for Understanding**

❶ $\frac{6}{8}$, or $\frac{3}{4}$

❷ $\frac{6}{18}$, or $\frac{1}{3}$

❸ $\frac{15}{9}$, or $1\frac{6}{9}$, or $1\frac{2}{3}$

❹ $4\frac{1}{3}$

❺ $15\frac{4}{4}$, or 16

❻ $\frac{15}{15}$, or 1

❼ $4\frac{10}{6}$, or $5\frac{4}{6}$, or $5\frac{2}{3}$

❽ $3\frac{6}{12}$, or $3\frac{1}{2}$

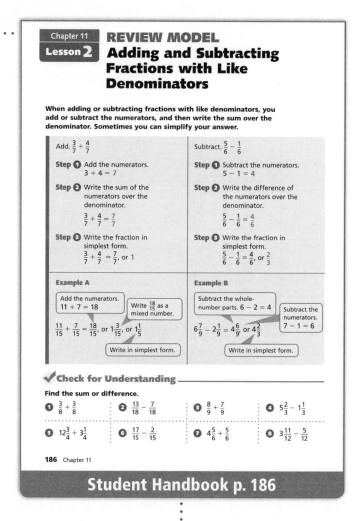

Student Handbook p. 186

Leveled Problem Solving

Isa has $7\frac{11}{12}$ yards of ribbon. She gives $4\frac{5}{12}$ yards to Dale and $2\frac{1}{12}$ yards to Anita.

❶ Basic Level

How much ribbon does she give away? Explain. $6\frac{1}{2}$ yd; $4\frac{5}{12} + 2\frac{1}{12} = 6\frac{6}{12} = 6\frac{1}{2}$

❷ On Level

How many more yards of ribbon does Isa give to Dale than to Anita? Explain. $2\frac{1}{3}$ yd; $4\frac{5}{12} - 2\frac{1}{12} = 2\frac{4}{12} = 2\frac{1}{3}$

❸ Above Level

Judd needs $1\frac{7}{12}$ yards of ribbon. Can Isa give him this ribbon from the ribbon she has left? Explain. No, she has only $1\frac{5}{12}$ yards of ribbon left. $4\frac{5}{12} + 2\frac{1}{12} = 6\frac{6}{12}$ and $7\frac{11}{12} - 6\frac{6}{12} = 1\frac{5}{12}$

Intervention

Activity Stepped Addition of Mixed Numbers

Give students two fractions with like denominators that they can use to write an addition sentence. For example: $\frac{3}{20} + \frac{7}{20} = \frac{10}{20} = \frac{1}{2}$. Then have students insert whole numbers in front of each given fraction to create a new addition sentence, such as $3\frac{3}{20} + 1\frac{7}{20} = \blacksquare$. $4\frac{10}{20} = 4\frac{1}{2}$ Have partners trade papers and check each other's answers. Repeat the activity with other fraction problems.

Practice

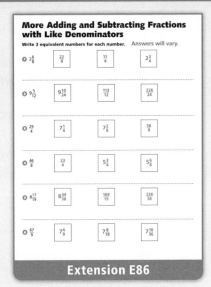

More Adding and Subtracting Fractions with Like Denominators

Write fractions to complete the number sentences.

Practice P86

Extension

More Adding and Subtracting Fractions with Like Denominators

Write 3 equivalent numbers for each number. Answers will vary.

Extension E86

Spiral Review

Spiral Review Book page SR86 provides review of the following previously learned skills and concepts:

- determining angle measures using relationships among angles formed when a line intersects a pair of parallel lines
- applying the problem solving strategy *draw a picture*

You may wish to have students work with partners to complete the page.

Geometry

Write the measure of each angle.

① m∠a = 65°
② m∠b = 65°
③ m∠c = 115°
④ m∠d = 115°
⑤ m∠e = 65°   ⑥ m∠f = 65°   ⑦ m∠g = 115°

Problem Solving
Use a strategy and solve.

⑧ Twenty students from a class are standing in line. One-fourth of the class is behind Martin. One-half of the class is in front of Nan. How many students are between Martin and Nan?
3 students; numbers 12, 13, and 14 counting from the front

⑨ Curtis and Sammy live 5 miles apart on the same road. They leave their houses at the same time and walk toward each other. If Curtis walks at 3 miles per hour and Sammy walks at 4 miles per hour, how far apart will they be in $\frac{1}{2}$ hour? Explain.
$1\frac{1}{2}$ miles; Possible explanation: in $\frac{1}{2}$ hr, Curtis will walk $1\frac{1}{2}$ miles, Sammy will walk 2 miles. $1\frac{1}{2} + 2 = 3\frac{1}{2}$, $5 - 3\frac{1}{2} = 1\frac{1}{2}$

⑩ Eight friends want to make the least number of phone calls so that each friend talks to every other one. How many phone calls would be needed?
28 phone calls

Spiral Review SR86

Extension Activity
Let Me Count the Ways

Challenge pairs of students to think of as many different equivalent ways of writing a given mixed number, such as $3\frac{1}{4}$, using denominators less than 100. Display lists so students can compare their work. Ask students to describe any patterns they used in making their lists. $\frac{13}{4}$, $3\frac{2}{8}$, $\frac{26}{8}$, $3\frac{4}{16}$, $\frac{52}{16}$, $3\frac{8}{32}$, $\frac{104}{32}$, $3\frac{16}{64}$, $\frac{208}{64}$

Lesson 3 Stories About Adding and Subtracting Fractions

NCTM Standards 1, 2, 6, 7, 8, 9, 10

Lesson Planner

STUDENT OBJECTIVES
- To interpret and solve story problems involving addition and subtraction of fractions with like denominators
- To investigate fractions with like denominators that sum to 1

1 Daily Activities (TG p. 901)

| Open-Ended Problem Solving/Headline Story | Skills Practice and Review— Changing Improper Fractions to Whole Numbers and Mixed Numbers |

2 Teach and Practice (TG pp. 902–904)

	MATERIALS
(A) **Exploring Situations with Fractions** (TG p. 902)	• pieces cut from TR: AM95 and AM96 or fraction bars
(B) **Finding Fractions that Sum to 1** (TG p. 903)	• 📖 LAB pp. 213–214
(C) **Solving Problems Involving Fractions** (TG p. 904)	• 📖 SH p. 187

3 Differentiated Instruction (TG p. 905)

Leveled Problem Solving (TG p. 905)	Practice Book P87
Intervention Activity (TG p. 905)	Extension Book E87
Extension Activity (TG p. 905)	Spiral Review Book SR87

Lesson Notes

About the Lesson

Students explore word problems that require adding and subtracting fractions. They also investigate fractions with like denominators that sum to 1 and look for patterns in the numerators and denominators of the addends.

Use with Lesson Activity Book pp. 213–214.

Developing Mathematical Language

Vocabulary: fractions that add to one

Students might understand the abstract notion of $\frac{5}{12} + \frac{7}{12} = \frac{12}{12} = 1$ by relating it to a familiar measure, such as a dozen eggs. They should be able to recognize that since 5 eggs are $\frac{5}{12}$ of a dozen and 7 eggs are $\frac{7}{12}$ of a dozen, $\frac{5}{12} + \frac{7}{12}$ is 12 eggs, which is 1 dozen eggs. Relate other denominators to other familiar measures, such as days of the week, quarts in a gallon, and feet in a yard.

Familiarize students with the term *fractions that add to one.*

Beginning Put together fraction bars for $\frac{2}{5}$ and $\frac{3}{5}$ to show *fractions that add to 1.* Record on the board $\frac{2}{5} + \frac{3}{5} = \frac{5}{5}$ = 1. Have students use fraction bars to model other *fractions that add to one.*

Intermediate Have students choose one denominator from 4 to 10 and use it to list on paper all possible fractions between 0 and 1. Then have students draw lines connecting *fractions that add to one.*

Advanced Ask students to explain how they know they have two *fractions that add to one.*

---

1 | Daily Activities

Open-Ended Problem Solving

Encourage students to draw pictures or use fraction bars to help them respond to this Headline Story. You can add challenge by asking for the fewest or most measurements, or the fewest or most measuring cups used.

 Headline Story

Our set of measuring cups has the following sizes: one-fourth cup, one-third cup, one-half cup, and one cup. Find at least 6 ways to measure $3\frac{3}{4}$ cups of flour.

Possible responses: 9 one-third cups + 3 one-fourth cups
3 cups + 1 one-half cup + 1 one-quarter cup
1 cup + 4 one-half cups + 3 one-quarter cups
15 one-quarter cups
4 cups − 1 one-quarter cup

Skills Practice and Review

Changing Improper Fractions to Whole Numbers and Mixed Numbers

Building off of the Headline Story, tell students that you need a certain amount of flour for a recipe. Write it as an improper fraction, and have them rename it as a whole or mixed number. To provide practice in listening to and writing fractions, have students say the mixed numbers out loud in addition to writing them down. If any students seem stuck, remind them to think first about how many wholes there are and then how many fractional pieces remain.

$\frac{6}{2}$	$\frac{11}{3}$	$\frac{15}{7}$	$\frac{7}{2}$	$\frac{13}{4}$	$\frac{29}{5}$	$\frac{9}{2}$
3	$3\frac{2}{3}$	$2\frac{1}{7}$	$3\frac{1}{2}$	$3\frac{1}{4}$	$5\frac{4}{5}$	$4\frac{1}{2}$

15 MIN

Materials
- For each student: pieces cut from AM95 and AM96 or fraction bars

NCTM Standards 1, 2, 6, 7, 8

(A) Exploring Situations with Fractions

Purpose To add and subtract mixed numbers

Introduce For this activity, students will use Explore: Fraction Stories and the fraction bars they cut from AM95 and AM96. Explain to students that they will use the fraction bars to model adding or subtracting of the fraction parts of the mixed numbers in the problems on the Explore page.

Task Have students complete Explore: Fraction Stories independently or with a partner. Students should use and sketch pictures of their fraction bars to record any work that will help them to share their solution process during the following discussion.

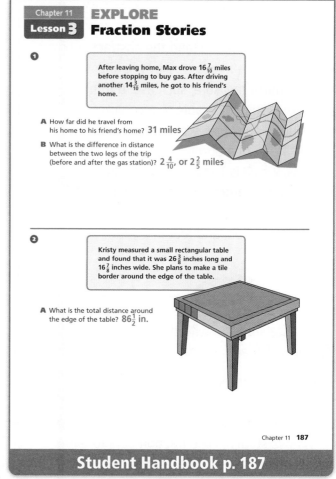

Chapter 11
Lesson 3

EXPLORE
Fraction Stories

❶ After leaving home, Max drove $16\frac{7}{10}$ miles before stopping to buy gas. After driving another $14\frac{3}{10}$ miles, he got to his friend's home.

A How far did he travel from his home to his friend's home? 31 miles

B What is the difference in distance between the two legs of the trip (before and after the gas station)? $2\frac{4}{10}$, or $2\frac{2}{5}$ miles

❷ Kristy measured a small rectangular table and found that it was $26\frac{3}{8}$ inches long and $16\frac{7}{8}$ inches wide. She plans to make a tile border around the edge of the table.

A What is the total distance around the edge of the table? $86\frac{1}{2}$ in.

Chapter 11 **187**

Student Handbook p. 187

 Talk Math

❓ How did you find the distance from Max's house to his friend's house? I added the two distances. To do this, I first added the whole-number parts of these distances and then I added the fractional parts of these distances. I ended up with $30 + \frac{10}{10}$, or $30 + 1$, which equals 31.

❓ How did you find the difference in distance between the two legs of Max's trip? I compared the two legs of the trip. I knew there was more than 2 miles difference because from $14\frac{3}{10}$ to just $16\frac{3}{10}$ is already 2 miles, and then from $16\frac{3}{10}$ to $16\frac{7}{10}$ is another $\frac{4}{10}$ mile, so from $14\frac{3}{10}$ to $16\frac{7}{10}$ is $2\frac{4}{10}$ miles. (Or, $16\frac{3}{10}$ is 2 miles more than $14\frac{3}{10}$, and $16\frac{7}{10}$ is even greater than that. How much greater? another $\frac{4}{10}$ mile; $16\frac{7}{10} - 14\frac{3}{10} = 2\frac{4}{10}$)

❓ How did you find the perimeter of the table? I doubled each of the given lengths of the table, using the perimeter formula $P = 2a + 2b$. Since $26\frac{3}{8} + 26\frac{3}{8} = 52\frac{6}{8}$ and $16\frac{7}{8} + 16\frac{7}{8} = 32\frac{14}{8} = 33\frac{6}{8}$, the perimeter is $52\frac{6}{8} + 33\frac{6}{8} = 85\frac{12}{8} = 86\frac{4}{8} = 86\frac{1}{2}$.

B **Finding Fractions that Sum to 1**

whole class   **10 MIN**

Materials
• For each student: pieces cut from AM95–AM96 or fraction bars

NCTM Standards 1, 7, 8

Purpose To find fractions that sum to 1

Introduce Students again use their fraction bars to add fractions. You might do this as a silent activity.

Task Write a few pairs of fractions, such as the ones below, whose sum is 1. Then, after you have written the first addend of the next pair, silently hand the chalk to a student who seems to have caught on to the pattern, to record the second addend. Continue with more pairs so that many students get a chance to participate. (Alternatively, do the activity out loud: explain that you will write a fraction and that students should name a fraction to add to it so that the sum of the two fractions is 1.)

$\frac{1}{8}$	$\frac{7}{8}$
$\frac{2}{5}$	$\frac{3}{5}$
$\frac{3}{7}$	$\frac{4}{7}$
$\frac{8}{11}$	$\frac{3}{11}$
$\frac{5}{16}$	$\frac{11}{16}$
. . .	. . .

Talk Math

❓ What can you add to $\frac{53}{60}$ to make a sum of 1? You can add $\frac{7}{60}$.

❓ What general patterns do you notice about the pairs of fractions that sum to 1? The sum of their numerators always equals the denominator. You can subtract the numerator of one fraction from its denominator to get the numerator of the other fraction.

❓ Will $\frac{5}{12} + \frac{6}{12}$ equal 1? How can you tell? No, it won't equal 1. The sum of the numerators is not 12. $\frac{6}{12} + \frac{6}{12} = 1$

Solving Problems Involving Fractions LAB pp. 213–214

Purpose To add and subtract fractions with like denominators

NCTM Standards 1, 6, 7, 9, 10

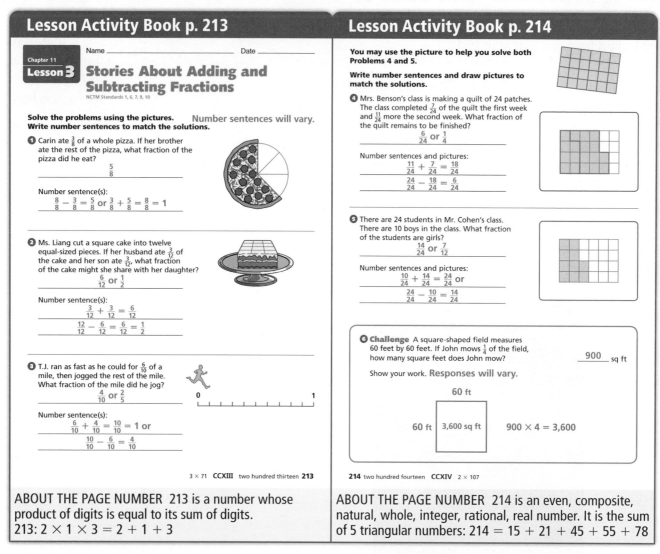

Lesson Activity Book p. 213

Chapter 11
Lesson **3** **Stories About Adding and Subtracting Fractions**
NCTM Standards 1, 6, 7, 9, 10

Name _____ Date _____

Solve the problems using the pictures.   Number sentences will vary.
Write number sentences to match the solutions.

❶ Carin ate $\frac{3}{8}$ of a whole pizza. If her brother ate the rest of the pizza, what fraction of the pizza did he eat?
$\frac{5}{8}$

Number sentence(s):
$\frac{8}{8} - \frac{3}{8} = \frac{5}{8}$ or $\frac{3}{8} + \frac{5}{8} = \frac{8}{8} = 1$

❷ Ms. Liang cut a square cake into twelve equal-sized pieces. If her husband ate $\frac{3}{12}$ of the cake and her son ate $\frac{3}{12}$, what fraction of the cake might she share with her daughter?
$\frac{6}{12}$ or $\frac{1}{2}$

Number sentence(s):
$\frac{3}{12} + \frac{3}{12} = \frac{6}{12}$
$\frac{12}{12} - \frac{6}{12} = \frac{6}{12} = \frac{1}{2}$

❸ T.J. ran as fast as he could for $\frac{6}{10}$ of a mile, then jogged the rest of the mile. What fraction of the mile did he jog?
$\frac{4}{10}$ or $\frac{2}{5}$

Number sentence(s):
$\frac{6}{10} + \frac{4}{10} = \frac{10}{10} = 1$ or
$\frac{10}{10} - \frac{6}{10} = \frac{4}{10}$

0 |||||||||| 1

3 × 71 CCXIII two hundred thirteen **213**

Lesson Activity Book p. 214

You may use the picture to help you solve both Problems 4 and 5.

Write number sentences and draw pictures to match the solutions.

❹ Mrs. Benson's class is making a quilt of 24 patches. The class completed $\frac{7}{24}$ of the quilt the first week and $\frac{11}{24}$ more the second week. What fraction of the quilt remains to be finished?
$\frac{6}{24}$ or $\frac{1}{4}$

Number sentences and pictures:
$\frac{11}{24} + \frac{7}{24} = \frac{18}{24}$
$\frac{24}{24} - \frac{18}{24} = \frac{6}{24}$

❺ There are 24 students in Mr. Cohen's class. There are 10 boys in the class. What fraction of the students are girls?
$\frac{14}{24}$ or $\frac{7}{12}$

Number sentences and pictures:
$\frac{10}{24} + \frac{14}{24} = \frac{24}{24}$ or
$\frac{24}{24} - \frac{10}{24} = \frac{14}{24}$

❻ **Challenge** A square-shaped field measures 60 feet by 60 feet. If John mows $\frac{1}{4}$ of the field, how many square feet does John mow?
_900_ sq ft

Show your work. **Responses will vary.**

60 ft
60 ft 3,600 sq ft   900 × 4 = 3,600

214 two hundred fourteen CCXIV 2 × 107

ABOUT THE PAGE NUMBER 213 is a number whose product of digits is equal to its sum of digits.
213: $2 \times 1 \times 3 = 2 + 1 + 3$

ABOUT THE PAGE NUMBER 214 is an even, composite, natural, whole, integer, rational, real number. It is the sum of 5 triangular numbers: $214 = 15 + 21 + 45 + 55 + 78$

Teaching Notes for LAB page 213

Students solve problems using addition, subtraction, or both, and write number sentences to match the stories and their solutions. Problem 2 requires both addition and subtraction. Some students might write two number sentences; others might add the fractions mentally and then record only the subtraction step. Either way of recording their work is appropriate.

Differentiated Instruction Basic Level Some students may benefit from using their fraction bars to model the situations on this page.

Teaching Notes for LAB page 214

Students solve subtraction story problems involving fractions with a larger denominator.

✓**Ongoing Assessment** This is the third lesson on adding and subtracting fractions with like denominators. Therefore, this page may work well as a quick assessment of your students' ability to solve word problems with pictures and write number sentences to show the operations and solutions.

Challenge Problem Students solve an area problem and multiply by $\frac{1}{4}$ (or divide by 4).

Reflect and Summarize the Lesson

 Write Math

Draw a picture to solve these problems. Then, write number sentences to match the solutions. Alex walked $1\frac{3}{10}$ miles from his home to Nick's house and then he walked $2\frac{7}{10}$ miles with Nick to the park. How far did Alex walk from his home to the park? 4 miles; $1\frac{3}{10} + 2\frac{7}{10} = 3\frac{10}{10}$, or 4; check students' drawings. How much farther did Alex walk with Nick than he walked alone? $1\frac{2}{5}$ miles; $2\frac{7}{10} - 1\frac{3}{10} = 1\frac{4}{10}$, or $1\frac{2}{5}$; check students' drawings.

Use with Lesson Activity Book pp. 213–214.

Leveled Problem Solving

Sunil lends $\frac{3}{16}$ of his CD collection to Lee and $\frac{7}{16}$ of his collection to Tamara.

❶ Basic Level

What fraction of Sunil's collection is left after lending to Lee? Explain. $\frac{16}{16} - \frac{3}{16} = \frac{13}{16}$. $\frac{16}{16}$ is Sunil's total collection, and $\frac{3}{16}$ is the part he lends to Lee.

❷ On Level

What fraction of Sunil's collection is left after lending to both Lee and Tamara? Explain. $\frac{16}{16} - \frac{10}{16} = \frac{6}{16} = \frac{3}{8}$, $\frac{3}{16} + \frac{7}{16} = \frac{10}{16}$ is the part he lent. $\frac{16}{16}$ is Sunil's total collection. The difference between $\frac{16}{16}$ and $\frac{10}{16}$ shows what part is left.

❸ Above Level

Can Sunil now lend $\frac{7}{16}$ of his collection to Sam? Explain. No; only $\frac{6}{16}$ remains, and $\frac{6}{16} < \frac{7}{16}$.

Intervention	Practice	Extension

Activity Counting on Fractions

Have students use graph paper to draw a number line that represents fractions they add or subtract. Each grid line will represent one unit of the fraction. Write a fraction on the board, have students draw a number line for the denominator, and then have them place a dot on it to represent the fraction. Tell students to "count on" to determine the fraction they can add to it to have two fractions whose sum is 1.

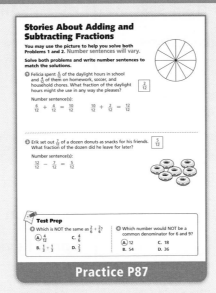

Practice P87

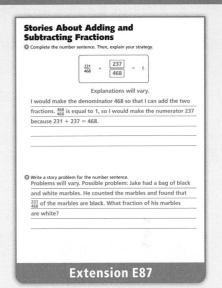

Extension E87

Spiral Review

Spiral Review Book page SR87 provides review of the following previously learned skills and concepts:

- finding the value of an expression when the value of x is given
- determining the median, mode, and range of data

You may wish to have students work with partners to complete the page.

Extension Activity
More than Two Mixed Numbers

Have students work in small groups. Ask each group to choose a denominator. Then ask each student in the group to write a mixed number using that denominator. Have students share their mixed numbers and add them. Invite students to share their addition strategies with other groups.

Algebra
Complete the sentence.

❶ If x = 3, then 2x + 5 = __11__	❷ If x = 2, then 3x − 1 = __5__
❸ If x = 1, then 8x + 4 = __12__	❹ If x = 6, then 3x + 2 = __20__
❺ If x = 5, then 5x + 5 = __30__	❻ If x = 3, then 4x − 7 = __5__
❼ If x = 9, then 3x + 1 = __28__	❽ If x = 10, then 4x − 2 = __38__
❾ If 3x − 1 = 14, then x = __5__	❿ If 4x + 2 = 26, then x = __6__
⓫ If 2x − 7 = 3, then x = __5__	⓬ If 7x − 1 = 13, then x = __2__
⓭ If 8x + 1 = 25, then x = __3__	⓮ If 10x + 2 = 22, then x = __2__
⓯ If 4x − 1 = 27, then x = __7__	⓰ If 11x + 6 = 61, then x = __5__

Data Analysis and Probability
For 17–19, use the line plot.

HIGH SCHOOL BASKETBALL TEAM HEIGHTS (IN INCHES)

⓱ What is the range of heights? 12 inches
⓲ What is the mode height? 76 inches
⓳ What is the median height? 74 inches

Spiral Review SR87

Lesson 4 Adding and Subtracting Unlike Things

NCTM Standards 1, 2, 4, 6, 7, 8, 9

Lesson Planner

STUDENT OBJECTIVE ···
- To add and subtract unlike things by finding a common group or unit, or by making measurement unit conversions

1 | Daily Activities (TG p. 907)

Open-Ended Problem Solving/Headline Story	Skills Practice and Review—Changing Mixed Numbers to Improper Fractions

2 | Teach and Practice (TG pp. 908–910)

	MATERIALS
Ⓐ **Adding Apples and Oranges** (TG p. 908)	• 📖 LAB pp. 215–216
Ⓑ **Adding and Subtracting Unlike Things** (TG p. 909)	
Ⓒ **Checking the Reasonableness of Converted Sums and Differences** (TG p. 910)	

3 | Differentiated Instruction (TG p. 911)

Leveled Problem Solving (TG p. 911)	Practice Book P88
Intervention Activity (TG p. 911)	Extension Book E88
Extension Activity (TG p. 911)	Spiral Review Book SR88

Lesson Notes

About the Lesson

Students revisit the important idea that one cannot add or subtract unless one can find an inclusive group, or common unit, for the sum or difference. For example, in combining inches and feet, we cannot simply add the numbers. To solve the problem, we must first change at least one of the numbers, by converting the number of feet to a number of inches, or the number of inches to a number of feet (or both to numbers of yards, centimeters, miles, etc.). For the same reason,

we need common denominators to add or subtract fractions with unlike denominators. The focus on finding a common unit is meant to help students attach meaning to the process and avoid the procedural error of adding or subtracting the denominators (as they do the numerators) when adding or subtracting fractions.

Use with Lesson Activity Book pp. 215–216.

Developing Mathematical Language

Vocabulary: common unit, unlike things

In order to add quantities, is necessary to have a *common unit.* For example, to add coins, it is helpful to use the *common unit* of cents. The sum or the value of the coins is quite different if there are 3 pennies, 1 dime, 2 nickels or 3 quarters. Some measurements are given in more than one unit of measure, such as 5 feet 2 inches. To add 3 inches to that measurement, we add the 3 inches only to the 2 inches part. The sum becomes 5 feet 5 inches.

Stress that *unlike things* cannot be combined without first deciding upon a *common unit.*

Familiarize students with the terms *common unit* and *unlike things.*

Beginning Review the word *common,* as meaning the same or alike. Show students several classroom items, such as pen, pencil, and crayons. Discuss how they are *unlike things.* Then guide students to make the connection that the items form a *common unit* because they are all things with which you can write.

Intermediate Ask students to identify two *unlike things* in the classroom and a possible *common unit* for the two items.

Advanced Name an item, such as a type of food. Have students name an *unlike thing.* Challenge students to name a *common unit* for the two items.

1 | Daily Activities

Open-Ended Problem Solving

Encourage students to find more than one possible answer.

 Headline Story

Margaret found a common denominator of 24 when she added two fractions. What might the denominators of the fractions she was adding have been?

Possible responses: The denominators could be 6 and 4. (However, for sixths and fourths there is a smaller common denominator that you could use: 12.) If the denominators were 8 and 3, then 24 would be the smallest common denominator. They could be 6 and 24, or they could be 8 and 12.

To extend this Headline Story, you might ask students if either of the denominators could be greater than 24. (Yes, if the fraction is not yet in simplest form.)

Skills Practice and Review

Changing Mixed Numbers to Improper Fractions

Tell students that the measurements for a recipe you are using are written as improper fractions, but that you need them renamed as a whole or mixed numbers to help you select your measuring tools. To provide practice in listening to and writing fractions, have students say the mixed numbers out loud in addition to writing them down.

If students need help, remind them to think first about how many wholes there are and then how many fractional pieces remain.

$1\frac{1}{4}$ $\frac{5}{4}$	$2\frac{2}{3}$ $\frac{8}{3}$	$2\frac{1}{6}$ $\frac{13}{6}$	$3\frac{1}{4}$ $\frac{13}{4}$
$2\frac{3}{4}$ $\frac{11}{4}$	$3\frac{2}{5}$ $\frac{17}{5}$	$4\frac{3}{4}$ $\frac{19}{4}$	$5\frac{1}{10}$ $\frac{51}{10}$
$5\frac{3}{8}$ $\frac{43}{8}$	$4\frac{5}{6}$ $\frac{29}{6}$	$6\frac{1}{9}$ $\frac{55}{9}$	$7\frac{3}{7}$ $\frac{52}{7}$

2 | Teach and Practice

whole class **10 MIN**

A Adding Apples and Oranges

NCTM Standards 1, 4, 6, 7, 8, 9

Purpose To add and subtract unlike things by finding a common unit

Introduce Ask students if they have heard of the expression, "That's like comparing apples and oranges!" Then ask them to explain the expression or to guess what they think it might mean. Help students to realize that since apples and oranges are two different units, they cannot be directly compared. Students naturally understand this and convey this understanding in their language and logic, but they still need to see that it applies equally well in the new arithmetic of fractions that they are learning. To help students make the connection, ask for the answer to 12 apples + 18 oranges. 30 pieces of fruit This conversion to a "common denominator" of fruit instead of apples or oranges when comparing or adding unlike things applies to fractions with unlike denominators. We can add "numerators"—numbers that enumerate how many—only when the units are the same.

Task **Have students add or subtract unlike things by finding a common unit.** Pose problems similar to the following ones and have students respond by finding the common unit that allows adding or subtracting the two unlike things.

- The school store sold pencils in small packs of 6 and larger packs of 12. Janice bought 3 small packs, and Jason bought 2 large packs. Who bought more? The question, as stated, is ambiguous (more of what?). Janice bought more packs, and Jason bought more pencils. To answer the question in a sensible way, one must settle on a single common unit—pencils or packs—to compare.

- Tyler gets paid by the hour to rake leaves. He raked for 3 hours on Saturday, and for 90 minutes on Sunday. How many hours did he rake that weekend? $4\frac{1}{2}$ hours

- One jump rope measures 5 feet and another measures 48 inches. What is the total length of both ropes? 9 feet, or 108 inches

- Jonathan spent 60 minutes on his reading homework. He had a total of 2 hours to work on his homework. How much time did he have left for homework other than reading? 1 hour, or 60 minutes

- Mandie poured 250 mL of juice into her glass from a 1L bottle. How much juice was left? 750 mL, or $\frac{3}{4}$L

Use with Lesson Activity Book pp. 215–216.

B Adding and Subtracting Unlike Things LAB pp. 215–216

individuals

30 MIN

Purpose To add and subtract unlike things to prepare for adding and subtracting unlike fractions

NCTM Standards 1, 2, 4, 6, 7

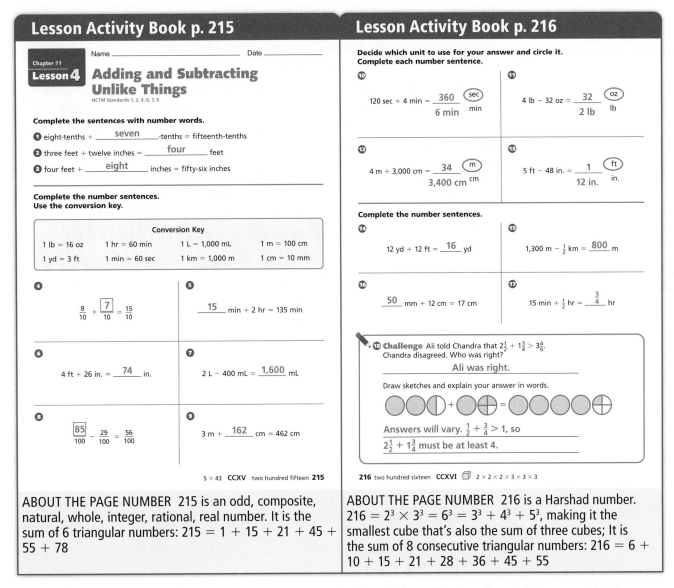

Lesson Activity Book p. 215

Chapter 11
Lesson 4
Adding and Subtracting Unlike Things
NCTM Standards 1, 2, 4, 6, 7, 9

Complete the sentences with number words.

❶ eight-tenths + ___seven___-tenths = fifteenth-tenths

❷ three feet + twelve inches = ___four___ feet

❸ four feet + ___eight___ inches = fifty-six inches

Complete the number sentences.
Use the conversion key.

Conversion Key			
1 lb = 16 oz	1 hr = 60 min	1 L = 1,000 mL	1 m = 100 cm
1 yd = 3 ft	1 min = 60 sec	1 km = 1,000 m	1 cm = 10 mm

❹ $\frac{8}{10} + \boxed{\frac{7}{10}} = \frac{15}{10}$

❺ ___15___ min + 2 hr = 135 min

❻ 4 ft + 26 in. = ___74___ in.

❼ 2 L − 400 mL = ___1,600___ mL

❽ $\boxed{\frac{85}{100}} - \frac{29}{100} = \frac{56}{100}$

❾ 3 m + ___162___ cm = 462 cm

5 × 43   CCXV   two hundred fifteen   **215**

Lesson Activity Book p. 216

Decide which unit to use for your answer and circle it.
Complete each number sentence.

❿ 120 sec + 4 min = ___360___ $\frac{\text{(sec)}}{6\text{ min}}$ min

⓫ 4 lb − 32 oz = ___32___ $\frac{\text{(oz)}}{2\text{ lb}}$ lb

⓬ 4 m + 3,000 cm = ___34___ $\frac{\text{(m)}}{3,400\text{ cm}}$ cm

⓭ 5 ft − 48 in. = ___1___ $\frac{\text{(ft)}}{12\text{ in.}}$ in.

Complete the number sentences.

⓮ 12 yd + 12 ft = ___16___ yd

⓯ 1,300 m − $\frac{1}{2}$ km = ___800___ m

⓰ ___50___ mm + 12 cm = 17 cm

⓱ 15 min + $\frac{1}{2}$ hr = ___$\frac{3}{4}$___ hr

⓲ **Challenge** Ali told Chandra that $2\frac{1}{2} + 1\frac{3}{4} > 3\frac{4}{6}$. Chandra disagreed. Who was right?

___Ali was right.___

Draw sketches and explain your answer in words.

Answers will vary. $\frac{1}{2} + \frac{3}{4} > 1$, so $2\frac{1}{2} + 1\frac{3}{4}$ must be at least 4.

216   two hundred sixteen   CCXVI $2 \times 2 \times 2 \times 3 \times 3 \times 3$

ABOUT THE PAGE NUMBER 215 is an odd, composite, natural, whole, integer, rational, real number. It is the sum of 6 triangular numbers: $215 = 1 + 15 + 21 + 45 + 55 + 78$

ABOUT THE PAGE NUMBER 216 is a Harshad number. $216 = 2^3 \times 3^3 = 6^3 = 3^3 + 4^3 + 5^3$, making it the smallest cube that's also the sum of three cubes; It is the sum of 8 consecutive triangular numbers: $216 = 6 + 10 + 15 + 21 + 28 + 36 + 45 + 55$

Teaching Notes for LAB page 215

Students use the context of measurement to add and subtract unlike things to prepare for doing the same in the context of fractions in the next lesson. A unit conversion key is given to help students complete both LAB pages. Some students may find it helpful to write converted numbers above or below the number sentences. Problem 1 and Problem 4 is the same to remind students about the necessity of using common units when dealing with unlike things.

Teaching Notes for LAB page 216

Students choose the unit to use for the sum or difference of unlike things, and then perform the necessary conversions.

Challenge Problem Students explain with sketches and words how they know a sum of mixed numbers is greater than (and not equal to) a given mixed number.

C Checking the Reasonableness of Converted Sums and Differences

Purpose To check the reasonableness of converted sums and differences

Introduce Explain to students that, when they need to convert to a common unit before performing a calculation (for example, when adding or subtracting unlike things), this introduces a new opportunity for making a mistake. Therefore, it is important to check the reasonableness of the conversions, or of the answer after performing the calculation.

Task Even though some of your students may not have completed Problems 10–17 on the LAB page, ask them to check some answers that you will write for those problems. You might tell them that some of the sums and differences you will write are incorrect, and students should identify and correct them.

10 120 seconds + 4 minutes = 360 seconds = 60 minutes Your students may notice the error (60 minutes) and justify the correct conversion (6 minutes) by explaining the conversion of 120 seconds to 2 minutes. Others may notice the error in the final conversions (360 seconds does not equal 60 minutes).

11 4 pounds − 32 ounces = 2 pounds = 32 ounces Once students agree that 2 pounds is a correct answer and 32 ounces is also correct, ask them to justify the answers and explain their solution strategies. Again, some may talk about the conversions of the 4 pounds or 32 ounces, while others may talk about the differences (2 pounds = 32 ounces). Be sure to point out that although the differences convert correctly, it is still important to check for accuracy of the subtraction.

12 4 meters + 3,000 centimeters = 3,040 centimeters = 34 meters Some students may explain that 4 m = 400 cm (not 40 cm), and so the sum should be 3,400 cm, not 3,040 cm. Others may see 3,000 cm as 30 meters and realize that the sum of 34 meters is correct. But since 3,040 cm is not equal to 34 meters, the centimeters answer is incorrect.

13 5 feet − 48 inches = 1 inch = 12 feet The units were reversed: 12 inches = 1 foot

Reflect and Summarize the Lesson

Write Math

Write the following problem on the board. Ask students to check the answer and explain whether the answer you have written is correct or incorrect. If the answer is incorrect, have them give the correct answer.

> 10 feet - 6 inches = 4 feet

The answer is incorrect because you can't subtract the number of inches from the number of feet without first writing the feet as inches or the inches as feet. 10 feet = 120 inches, so 10 feet − 6 inches = 120 inches − 6 inches = 114 inches. Or, 6 inches = $\frac{1}{2}$ foot, so 10 feet − 6 inches = 10 feet − $\frac{1}{2}$ foot = $9\frac{1}{2}$ feet.

Leveled Problem Solving

Alisha practiced flute for 30 minutes on Monday and for $1\frac{1}{4}$ hour on Tuesday.

❶ Basic Level

How can you find the total number of hours she practiced on Monday and Tuesday? Explain. Make the units both hours; change 30 min to $\frac{1}{2}$ hr; the units must be the same to add them.

❷ On Level

For how many minutes did she practice on Monday and Tuesday? Explain. 105 min; $1\frac{1}{4}$ hr = $(60 + 15)$ min = 75 min, $75 + 30 = 105$

❸ Above Level

Alisha was supposed to practice for 100 minutes on Tuesday. How many minutes did she skip? Explain. 25 min; 100 min − $1\frac{1}{4}$ hr = 100 min − 75 min = 25 min

---

Intervention

Activity Conversions

Write on the board an addition problem that requires one unit to be converted, such as 6 feet + 24 inches. Have students identify the larger unit. feet Then have students find the sum converting to the larger unit. 8 feet Then ask them to find the sum converting to the smaller unit. 96 inches Students should realize that the answers are equivalent measures. Repeat, finding the difference between the two measurements for both units.

Practice

Adding and Subtracting Unlike Things

Conversion Key

| 1 lb = 16 oz | 1 hr = 60 min | 1 L = 1,000 mL | 1 m = 100 cm |
| 1 yd = 3 ft | 1 min = 60 sec | 1 km = 1,000 m | 1 cm = 10 mm |

Complete the number sentences using the conversion key above.

❶ 8 yd + 15 ft = __13__ yd   ❷ 3 lb − 14 oz = __34__ oz

❸ __4__ m + 12 cm = 412 cm   ❹ 2 hr − __80__ min = 40 min

❺ 144 in. − 2 yd = __72__ in.   ❻ 12 m + 4,000 cm = __5,200__ cm

❼ __3__ hr + 120 min = 300 min   ❽ 3,000 mL − 1 L = __2__ L

Test Prep

❾ Jewell has 40 feet of fencing to put around a garden. What are the dimensions of the garden with the largest possible area? Explain.

10 ft × 10 ft; Possible explanation: the largest area will be a square. If the total length of fencing is 40 ft, then each side of the square will be 40 ft ÷ 4 = 10 ft.

Practice P88

Extension

Adding and Subtracting Unlike Things

Complete each number sentence with three different units.

❶ 42 m + 100 cm = __43__ m   ❷ 7 ft + 24 in. = __108__ in.
= __4,300__ cm   = __9__ ft
= __43,000__ mm   = __3__ yd

❸ 5 km − 2,000 m = __300,000__ cm   ❹ 480 min − 6 hr = __2__ hr
= __3,000__ m   = __120__ min
= __3__ km   = __7,200__ sec

❺ 87 yd − 93 ft = __56__ yd   ❻ 1,020 sec − 5 min = __720__ sec
= __168__ ft   = __12__ min
= __2,016__ in.   = __1__ hr

Extension E88

Spiral Review

Spiral Review Book page SR88 provides review of the following previously learned skills and concepts:

- using rounding to estimate decimals to the nearest whole number, tenth, or hundredth
- applying the problem solving strategy *guess and check*

You may wish to have students work with partners to complete the page.

Number and Operations

Round to the nearest whole number.

❶ 8.9 ⇨ __9__   ❷ 15.3 ⇨ __15__   ❸ 102.33 ⇨ __102__

❹ 257.91 ⇨ __258__   ❺ 39.55 ⇨ __40__   ❻ 1,801.18 ⇨ __1,801__

❼ 77.60 ⇨ __78__   ❽ 325.49 ⇨ __325__   ❾ 401.01 ⇨ __401__

Round to the nearest tenth.

❿ 1.26 ⇨ __1.3__   ⓫ 51.41 ⇨ __51.4__   ⓬ 17.822 ⇨ __17.8__

⓭ 409.751 ⇨ __409.8__   ⓮ 66.093 ⇨ __66.1__   ⓯ 858.392 ⇨ __858.4__

Round to the nearest hundredth.

⓰ 2.435 ⇨ __2.44__   ⓱ 1.083 ⇨ __1.08__   ⓲ 36.221 ⇨ __36.22__

⓳ 7.197 ⇨ __7.20__   ⓴ 40.366 ⇨ __40.37__   ㉑ 19.191 ⇨ __19.19__

Problem Solving

Use a strategy and solve.

㉒ Jerome opens his math textbook. The sum of the page numbers is 49. Their product is 600. At which two pages is Jerome looking? pages 24 and 25

㉓ Dwayne's father is 24 years older than Dwayne. Together, their ages add to 42. How old is Dwayne? 9 years old

㉔ Alison, Sherry, and Marisol bought some books at the mall. They spent a total of $35. If Sherry spent twice as much as Alison, and Alison spent twice as much as Marisol, how much did each girl spend? Marisol: $5, Alison: $10, Sherry: $20

Spiral Review SR88

Extension Activity
In a Heartbeat

Have students time how many seconds it takes for their heart to beat 100 times. Then have them compute how many seconds, minutes, and hours it would take for their hearts to beat 10,000 times at that rate.

Possible answer: 100 heartbeats in 90 seconds; 10,000 heartbeats in 9,000 seconds = 150 minutes = 2 hours 30 minutes

Lesson 5 · Adding and Subtracting Fractions with Unlike Denominators

NCTM Standards 1, 2, 4, 6, 7, 8, 9

Lesson Planner

STUDENT OBJECTIVES
- To add and subtract fractions with unlike denominators by finding equivalent fractions with a common denominator
- To estimate sums and differences of mixed numbers

1 Daily Activities (TG p. 913)

Open-Ended Problem solving/Headline Story	Skills Practice and Review— Changing Improper Fractions to Mixed Numbers

2 Teach and Practice (TG pp. 914–916)

	MATERIALS
(A) **Estimating Sums and Differences** (TG p. 914)	• transparency of AM98 (optional)
(B) **Adding and Subtracting with Unlike Denominators** (TG p. 915)	• pattern blocks
(C) **Finding Common Denominators** (TG p. 916)	• 📖 LAB pp. 217–218
	• 📖 SH p. 188

3 Differentiated Instruction (TG p. 917)

Leveled Problem Solving (TG p. 917)	Practice Book P89
Intervention Activity (TG p. 917)	Extension Book E89
Extension Activity (TG p. 917)	Spiral Review Book SR89
Music Connection (TG p. 884)	

Lesson Notes

About the Lesson

Students first use their knowledge of equivalent fractions and rounding to estimate sums and differences of fractions with unlike denominators. They then determine common denominators in contexts such as minutes and dozens. For example, to find the sum of $\frac{1}{2}$ hour and $\frac{1}{3}$ hour, students might add $\frac{30}{60}$ and $\frac{20}{60}$, taking the denominator from the context rather than using a smaller common denominator like 6.

About the Mathematics

Fractional notation can lead students to think of a fraction as two numbers rather than as one. Then, when students see a plus sign between fractions they just add everything in sight. This chapter's focus aims to attach meaning to fractional notation. Students are less apt to add halves and thirds to get fifths if they continue to focus on the meaning. To know how to add halves and thirds, students must see the importance of finding a new fraction from which one can build both halves and thirds.

Use with Lesson Activity Book pp. 217–218.

Developing Mathematical Language

Vocabulary: common denominator, equivalent fractions, unlike denominators

Relate common units to fractions with a *common denominator* and unlike things to fractions with *unlike denominators*. Understanding how to rename fractions as *equivalent fractions* allows students to determine whether two fractions with *unlike denominators* are equivalent. If two fractions are equivalent, it is possible to rename each fraction to a *common denominator* with the same numerator.

Familiarize students with the terms *common denominator* and *unlike denominators*.

Beginning Display several fractions with common and unlike denominators. Point to pairs of fractions. Ask students to tell whether they have a *common denominator* or *unlike denominators*.

Intermediate Write a fraction on the board. Ask a volunteer to write another fraction with a *common denominator*. Ask another volunteer to write a fraction with an *unlike denominator*.

Advanced Have each student write a fraction on paper. Then you write a fraction on the board. Ask students, one by one, whether the two fractions share a *common denominator* or have *unlike denominators*.

Open-Ended Problem Solving

After students consider some responses to this Headline Story, ask them whether Jake could ever finish his licorice if he continued to eat only half of the remaining licorice. no

 Headline Story

Jake had $2\frac{1}{2}$ feet of licorice. He ate half of it and wrote down how much was left. Then, he ate half of the remaining licorice and wrote down how much was left. He continued to do this as he ate his licorice.

Possible responses: After he ate half of it, $1\frac{1}{4}$ (or $\frac{5}{4}$) feet remained. The next time, $\frac{5}{8}$ feet remained. Then $\frac{5}{16}$ feet were left. The denominator keeps doubling, but the numerator is always 5. Or, half of $2 + \frac{1}{2}$ is $1 + \frac{1}{4}$, then half of that is $\frac{1}{2} + \frac{1}{8}$, and half of that is $\frac{1}{4} + \frac{1}{16}$, and so on . . .

Skills Practice and Review

Changing Improper Fractions to Mixed Numbers

Tell students that measurements were kept for the number of yards students were able to throw a ball in gym class. The problem is that the measurements were recorded as improper fractions, and you need them renamed as whole or mixed numbers. To provide practice in listening to and writing fractions, have students say the mixed numbers out loud in addition to writing them.

$2\frac{5}{6}$ $\frac{17}{6}$	$3\frac{4}{9}$ $\frac{31}{9}$	$4\frac{7}{8}$ $\frac{39}{8}$	$2\frac{9}{10}$ $\frac{29}{10}$
$6\frac{4}{5}$ $\frac{34}{5}$	$4\frac{8}{9}$ $\frac{44}{9}$	$5\frac{3}{4}$ $\frac{23}{4}$	$6\frac{11}{12}$ $\frac{83}{12}$
$4\frac{5}{8}$ $\frac{37}{8}$	$7\frac{6}{7}$ $\frac{55}{7}$	$8\frac{10}{11}$ $\frac{98}{11}$	$9\frac{7}{12}$ $\frac{115}{12}$

individuals
or pairs

15 MIN

A Estimating Sums and Differences

NCTM Standards 1, 4, 6, 7, 8

Purpose To estimate the sums and differences of problems involving fractions with unlike denominators

Introduce For this activity, students will use Explore: Estimating Sums and Differences. Tell students that they should not be doing any precise calculations on this page. Instead, they should practice getting good, quick estimates for the answers to problems involving addition or subtraction of fractions with unlike denominators.

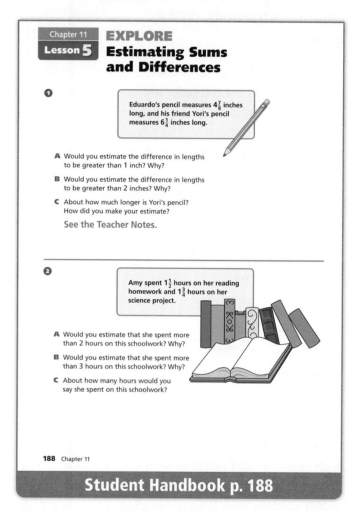

Chapter 11
Lesson 5
**EXPLORE
Estimating Sums and Differences**

❶ Eduardo's pencil measures $4\frac{7}{8}$ inches long, and his friend Yori's pencil measures $6\frac{1}{4}$ inches long.

A Would you estimate the difference in lengths to be greater than 1 inch? Why?

B Would you estimate the difference in lengths to be greater than 2 inches? Why?

C About how much longer is Yori's pencil? How did you make your estimate?

See the Teacher Notes.

❷ Amy spent $1\frac{1}{2}$ hours on her reading homework and $1\frac{3}{4}$ hours on her science project.

A Would you estimate that she spent more than 2 hours on this schoolwork? Why?

B Would you estimate that she spent more than 3 hours on this schoolwork? Why?

C About how many hours would you say she spent on this schoolwork?

188 Chapter 11

Student Handbook p. 188

Teacher Story

❝Several of my students sketched number lines to help them make estimates on Explore: Estimating Sums and Differences. For the top of the page, it helped students to see that there was a whole number and a little on each end between the two measurements. For the bottom of the page, they made a mark at $1\frac{1}{2}$ on the number line and then counted on from there.❞

Task Have students complete **Explore: Estimating Sums and Differences independently or in pairs.** Although the problems on the page contain fractions with unlike denominators, students' knowledge of equivalent fractions will help them answer the estimation questions.

Talk Math

❓ Would you estimate the difference in the lengths of Edouardo's and Yori's pencils to be greater than 1 inch? Why? Yes. I rounded the two measurements to the nearest whole number and then compared them. One measurement is a little less than 5 inches and the other is a little more than 6 inches, so that's a difference of more than 1 inch.

❓ Would you estimate the difference in pencil lengths to be greater than 2 inches? Why? No; $4\frac{7}{8}$ is close to 5 and subtracting 5 from $6\frac{1}{4}$ is less than 2.

❓ About how much longer is Yori's pencil than Edouardo's? Students should see that the difference in lengths is somewhere between 1 and 2 inches. Accept any estimates within this range.

❓ About how many hours did Amy spend on her schoolwork? Students should see that she spent between 3 and 4 hours on her schoolwork since $\frac{1}{2} + \frac{3}{4}$ is greater than 1. They may estimate between 3 and $3\frac{1}{2}$ hours. Some may even give the exact answer, $3\frac{1}{4}$, as they are likely to find it easy to combine halves and fourths.

Adding and Subtracting with Unlike Denominators

Purpose To add fractions with unlike denominators

Introduce Some students may already have ideas about finding a common denominator to add fractions with unlike denominators. For others, this idea will be completely new. Tell them that this activity gives them a way of using common denominators in the familiar contexts of time, dozens, and pattern blocks.

Problem What is $\frac{1}{2} + \frac{1}{3}$?

Display the first problem on AM98: What is $\frac{1}{2} + \frac{1}{3}$? or sketch a similar picture on the board. Read the first problem aloud and ask students for ideas. Students are likely to answer that $\frac{1}{2}$ hour + $\frac{1}{3}$ hour is 30 minutes + 20 minutes, or 50 minutes, but they may need some prompting to write the minutes as a fraction of an hour, $\frac{50}{60}$.

Now reveal the second problem (or sketch a dozen eggs) and read the problem. Again, students may begin by figuring out that half of a dozen eggs is 6 eggs and a third of a dozen eggs is 4 eggs to give the answer as 10 eggs. They may need your help to record the fraction of a dozen as $\frac{10}{12}$.

You may want to let students explore the third problem with pattern blocks, or you might demonstrate the problem by holding up a yellow hexagon, covering half of it with a red trapezoid, and covering another third of it with a blue rhombus. Show students a green triangle block and ask how it might be used to solve the problem. Students might reason that six triangles completely cover a hexagon, so each one represents a sixth. The red trapezoid and blue rhombus, together, cover all but $\frac{1}{6}$ of the hexagon, so they must cover $\frac{5}{6}$ of it. Or, students might see that three triangles (three sixths) cover a trapezoid, and that two triangles (two sixths) cover a rhombus. Therefore, covering $\frac{1}{2}$ and $\frac{1}{3}$ of the hexagon is the same as covering $\frac{5}{6}$ of it.

💬 **Talk Math**

❷ What is $\frac{1}{2} + \frac{1}{3}$? If students have not already simplified the first two answers ($\frac{50}{60}$ and $\frac{10}{12}$), have them do so now. They should see that all of the answers on the page are equivalent to $\frac{5}{6}$ and that the sum of $\frac{1}{2}$ and $\frac{1}{3}$ is $\frac{5}{6}$.

❷ We found $\frac{1}{2} + \frac{1}{3}$ in three different situations. Using fractions, can you write number sentences that match each of the situations?

$\frac{30}{60} + \frac{20}{60} = \frac{50}{60}$ (60 minutes in an hour)

$\frac{6}{12} + \frac{4}{12} = \frac{10}{12}$ (12 eggs in a dozen)

$\frac{3}{6} + \frac{2}{6} = \frac{5}{6}$ (6 triangle blocks cover a hexagon block)

In each case, using the context provided, students found a common denominator so that they could add the fractions $\frac{1}{2}$ and $\frac{1}{3}$.

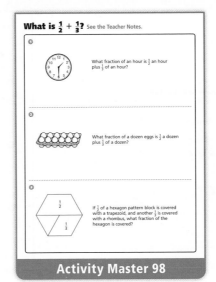

What is $\frac{1}{2} + \frac{1}{3}$? See the Teacher Notes.

What fraction of an hour is $\frac{1}{2}$ an hour plus $\frac{1}{3}$ of an hour?

What fraction of a dozen eggs is $\frac{1}{2}$ a dozen plus $\frac{1}{3}$ of a dozen?

If $\frac{1}{2}$ of a hexagon pattern block is covered with a trapezoid, and another $\frac{1}{3}$ is covered with a rhombus, what fraction of the hexagon is covered?

Activity Master 98

Materials
- For the teacher: transparency of AM98 (optional)
- For each student: pattern blocks

NCTM Standards 1, 6, 7, 8, 9

C Finding Common Denominators LAB pp. 217–218

Purpose To add and subtract fractions with unlike denominators

NCTM Standards 1, 2, 4, 6, 7, 8, 9

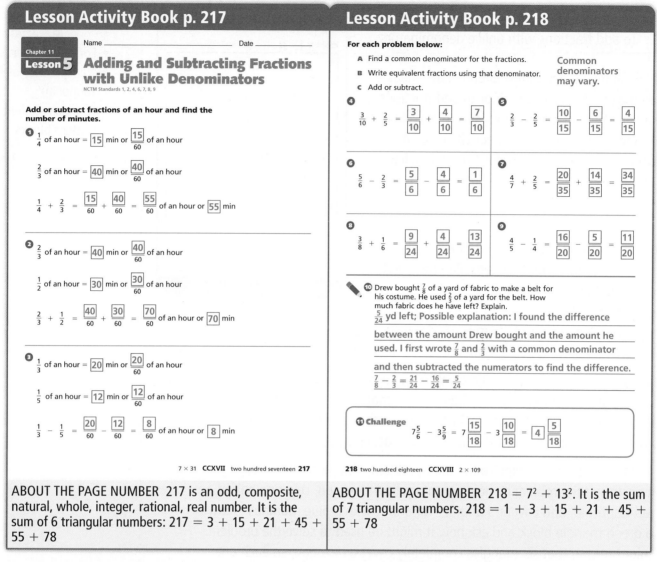

Lesson Activity Book p. 217

Chapter 11
Lesson 5

Adding and Subtracting Fractions with Unlike Denominators
NCTM Standards 1, 2, 4, 6, 7, 8, 9

Add or subtract fractions of an hour and find the number of minutes.

1 $\frac{1}{4}$ of an hour = $\boxed{15}$ min or $\frac{\boxed{15}}{60}$ of an hour

$\frac{2}{3}$ of an hour = $\boxed{40}$ min or $\frac{\boxed{40}}{60}$ of an hour

$\frac{1}{4} + \frac{2}{3} = \frac{\boxed{15}}{60} + \frac{\boxed{40}}{60} = \frac{\boxed{55}}{60}$ of an hour or $\boxed{55}$ min

2 $\frac{2}{3}$ of an hour = $\boxed{40}$ min or $\frac{\boxed{40}}{60}$ of an hour

$\frac{1}{2}$ of an hour = $\boxed{30}$ min or $\frac{\boxed{30}}{60}$ of an hour

$\frac{2}{3} + \frac{1}{2} = \frac{\boxed{40}}{60} + \frac{\boxed{30}}{60} = \frac{\boxed{70}}{60}$ of an hour or $\boxed{70}$ min

3 $\frac{1}{3}$ of an hour = $\boxed{20}$ min or $\frac{\boxed{20}}{60}$ of an hour

$\frac{1}{5}$ of an hour = $\boxed{12}$ min or $\frac{\boxed{12}}{60}$ of an hour

$\frac{1}{3} - \frac{1}{5} = \frac{\boxed{20}}{60} - \frac{\boxed{12}}{60} = \frac{\boxed{8}}{60}$ of an hour or $\boxed{8}$ min

7 × 31 CCXVII two hundred seventeen **217**

Lesson Activity Book p. 218

For each problem below:

A Find a common denominator for the fractions.

B Write equivalent fractions using that denominator.

C Add or subtract.

Common denominators may vary.

4 $\frac{3}{10} + \frac{2}{5} = \frac{\boxed{3}}{\boxed{10}} + \frac{\boxed{4}}{\boxed{10}} = \frac{\boxed{7}}{\boxed{10}}$

5 $\frac{2}{3} - \frac{2}{5} = \frac{\boxed{10}}{\boxed{15}} - \frac{\boxed{6}}{\boxed{15}} = \frac{\boxed{4}}{\boxed{15}}$

6 $\frac{5}{6} - \frac{2}{3} = \frac{\boxed{5}}{\boxed{6}} - \frac{\boxed{4}}{\boxed{6}} = \frac{\boxed{1}}{\boxed{6}}$

7 $\frac{4}{7} + \frac{2}{5} = \frac{\boxed{20}}{\boxed{35}} + \frac{\boxed{14}}{\boxed{35}} = \frac{\boxed{34}}{\boxed{35}}$

8 $\frac{3}{8} + \frac{1}{6} = \frac{\boxed{9}}{\boxed{24}} + \frac{\boxed{4}}{\boxed{24}} = \frac{\boxed{13}}{\boxed{24}}$

9 $\frac{4}{5} - \frac{1}{4} = \frac{\boxed{16}}{\boxed{20}} - \frac{\boxed{5}}{\boxed{20}} = \frac{\boxed{11}}{\boxed{20}}$

10 Drew bought $\frac{7}{8}$ of a yard of fabric to make a belt for his costume. He used $\frac{2}{3}$ of a yard for the belt. How much fabric does he have left? Explain.

$\frac{5}{24}$ yd left; Possible explanation: I found the difference between the amount Drew bought and the amount he used. I first wrote $\frac{7}{8}$ and $\frac{2}{3}$ with a common denominator and then subtracted the numerators to find the difference.

$\frac{7}{8} - \frac{2}{3} = \frac{21}{24} - \frac{16}{24} = \frac{5}{24}$

11 Challenge $7\frac{5}{6} - 3\frac{5}{9} = 7\frac{\boxed{15}}{18} - 3\frac{\boxed{10}}{18} = \boxed{4}\frac{\boxed{5}}{18}$

218 two hundred eighteen CCXVIII 2 × 109

ABOUT THE PAGE NUMBER 217 is an odd, composite, natural, whole, integer, rational, real number. It is the sum of 6 triangular numbers: 217 = 3 + 15 + 21 + 45 + 55 + 78

ABOUT THE PAGE NUMBER 218 = 7^2 + 13^2. It is the sum of 7 triangular numbers. 218 = 1 + 3 + 15 + 21 + 45 + 55 + 78

Teaching Notes for LAB page 217

Students convert minutes to fractions of hours, add or subtract the fractions, and then convert the sum or difference back to minutes. Within this context, students do not need a special procedure for finding a common denominator, as the context provides it (60).

Teaching Notes for LAB page 218

Students find common denominators for fractions with unlike denominators.

Differentiated Instruction Basic Level/On Level
Some students may wish to draw dot sketches to find common denominators.

Challenge Problem Students subtract mixed numbers with unlike denominators.

Reflect and Summarize the Lesson

Write Math

Write the following problem on the board. Ask students to use what they know about equivalent fractions to help them estimate an answer to the problem. Students should see that the difference in lengths is between 2 and 3 feet. Accept any estimates within this range.

> Rebecca's jump rope is $8\frac{1}{4}$ feet long and her friend Sarah's jump rope is $5\frac{3}{4}$ feet long. About how much longer is Rebecca's jump rope? How did you make your estimate?

Leveled Problem Solving

Cleo has two lengths of fabric. The red fabric is $2\frac{3}{4}$ yards and the yellow fabric is $4\frac{1}{3}$ yards.

❶ Basic Level

Does Cleo have 2 yards more yellow fabric than red fabric? Explain. No; $2\frac{3}{4}$ rounds to 3, and $4\frac{1}{3}$ rounds to 4. $4 - 3 = 1$

❷ On Level

About how much fabric does she have in all? Explain. About 7 yd; $2\frac{3}{4}$ rounds to 3, and $4\frac{1}{3}$ rounds to 4. $3 + 4 = 7$

❸ Above Level

Cleo uses $1\frac{2}{3}$ yards each of the red and yellow fabric. About how much fabric does she have left? Explain. About 3 yd; if you round to the nearest whole number: $2\frac{3}{4} - 1\frac{2}{3} \rightarrow 3 - 2 = 1$ and $4\frac{1}{3} - 1\frac{2}{3} \rightarrow 4 - 2 = 2$; $1 + 2 = 3$

Intervention	Practice	Extension

Activity Finding Common Denominators

Have several students work an addition problem involving fractions with unlike denominators at the board, such as $\frac{2}{3} + \frac{1}{5}$. Guide students to multiply the unlike denominators to find a common denominator. $3 \times 5 = 15$ Then have students write equivalent fractions using that denominator. $\frac{10}{15} + \frac{3}{15}$ Watch for students who forget to change the numerator. Repeat with other fractions, using subtraction.

Adding and Subtracting Fractions with Unlike Denominators

Add or subtract fractions of an hour and find the number of minutes.

① $\frac{1}{2}$ of an hour = 30 min, or $\frac{30}{60}$ of an hour

$\frac{1}{3}$ of an hour = 20 min, or $\frac{20}{60}$ of an hour

$\frac{1}{2} - \frac{1}{3} = \frac{30}{60} - \frac{20}{60} = \frac{10}{60}$ of an hour, or 10 min

② $\frac{3}{4}$ of an hour = 45 min, or $\frac{45}{60}$ of an hour

$\frac{2}{3}$ of an hour = 40 min, or $\frac{40}{60}$ of an hour

$\frac{3}{4} + \frac{2}{3} = \frac{45}{60} + \frac{40}{60} = \frac{85}{60}$ of an hour, or 85 min

Test Prep

② Josie has a rectangular piece of paper that is 8 inches by 10 inches. She cuts the rectangle into two congruent triangles. What is the area of each triangle? Explain.

40 sq in.; Possible explanation: the area of the rectangle is 8 in. × 10 in., or 80 sq in. So, the area of each triangle is 80 sq in. ÷ 2, or 40 sq in.

Practice P89

Adding and Subtracting Fractions with Unlike Denominators

Find a common denominator in order to add the fractions.   Common denominators may vary.

① $\frac{2}{3} + \frac{5}{6} + \frac{1}{2} = \frac{4}{6} + \frac{5}{6} + \frac{3}{6} = \frac{12}{6}$

② $\frac{7}{8} + \frac{3}{4} + \frac{1}{6} = \frac{21}{24} + \frac{18}{24} + \frac{4}{24} = \frac{43}{24}$

③ $\frac{1}{2} + \frac{1}{3} + \frac{3}{5} = \frac{15}{30} + \frac{10}{30} + \frac{18}{30} = \frac{43}{30}$

Find a common denominator for the fractions in order to subtract the numbers.   Common denominators may vary.

④ $5\frac{1}{3} - 3\frac{1}{5} = 5\frac{5}{15} - 3\frac{3}{15} = 2\frac{2}{15}$

⑤ $6\frac{1}{4} - 4\frac{3}{8} = 6\frac{2}{8} - 4\frac{3}{8} = 5\frac{10}{8} - 4\frac{3}{8} = 1\frac{7}{8}$

Extension E89

Spiral Review

Spiral Review Book page SR89 provides review of the following previously learned skills and concepts:

- using algebraic notation to describe patterns in input-output tables
- finding equivalent capacity measurements

You may wish to have students work with partners to complete the page.

Algebra

Complete the table. Then write the rule for the relationship between the sets of data.

① $y = x + 2$ ② $y = x - 4$ ③ $y = 2x + 1$ ④ $y = x + 2$

⑤ $y = 3x$ ⑥ $y = 2x - 4$ ⑦ $y = x + 3$ ⑧ $y = x - 7$

Measurement

Write the equivalent measure.

⑨ 18 cups = $4\frac{1}{2}$ quarts   ⑩ 2 gallon = 16 pints

⑪ $2\frac{1}{2}$ quarts = 10 cups   ⑫ 9 pints = 18 cups

⑬ $3\frac{1}{2}$ gallons = 14 quarts   ⑭ $2\frac{1}{2}$ pints = 5 cups

Spiral Review SR89

Extension Activity
Common Denominator Shortcut

Write several fractions having unlike denominators on the board, such as $\frac{1}{2}, \frac{5}{9}, \frac{7}{12}, \frac{1}{15}$. Have students work in pairs to find common denominators for all possible pairs of fractions. Challenge students to discover a shortcut, if possible. Possible answers: for $\frac{1}{2}$ and $\frac{5}{9}$, 18; for $\frac{1}{2}$ and $\frac{7}{12}$, 12; for $\frac{1}{2}$ and $\frac{1}{15}$, 30; for $\frac{5}{9}$ and $\frac{7}{12}$, 36; for $\frac{5}{9}$ and $\frac{1}{15}$, 45; for $\frac{1}{15}$ and $\frac{7}{12}$, 60

Lesson 6 Stories with Fractions

NCTM Standards 1, 4, 6, 7, 8, 9, 10

Lesson Planner

STUDENT OBJECTIVE ·······································
- To add and subtract fractions in the context of story problems

1 Daily Activities (TG p. 919)

Open-Ended Problem Solving/Headline Story	Skills Practice and Review— Adding Mixed Numbers or Improper Fractions

2 Teach and Practice (TG pp. 920–923)

	MATERIALS
Ⓐ **Contexts for Adding and Subtracting Fractions** (TG p. 920)	• TR: Activity Master, AM99
Ⓑ **Solving Story Problems Involving Fractions** (TG p. 921)	• scissors • 📖 LAB pp. 219–220
Ⓒ **Playing a Game: *Fraction Addition*** (TG p. 922)	• 📖 SH p. 189

3 Differentiated Instruction (TG p. 924)

Leveled Problem Solving (TG p. 924)	Practice Book P90
Intervention Activity (TG p. 924)	Extension Book E90
Extension Activity (TG p. 924)	Spiral Review Book SR90

Lesson Notes

About the Lesson

Students continue to practice adding and subtracting fractions, this time figuring out which fractions to add or subtract by using their reading and reasoning skills to interpret mathematical stories. This lesson also emphasizes pairs of fractions that sum to 1.

The purpose of learning about fractions is *not,* for the most part, to survive everyday life, but to develop one's mathematical understanding in ways that will be essential in further mathematical study. Fractions are typically only used for measurements, and

arithmetic with fractions is very uncommon. To measure competently with an inch ruler, we need to be able to recognize halves, quarters, eighths, and sixteenths; to find the middle of things, we may have to know how to cut numbers like $5\frac{1}{2}$ in half. But "everyday life" does not call for adding $\frac{1}{4} + \frac{2}{3}$. Even when we double a recipe, we tend to—and may even *have* to because of the measuring tools—measure the specified quantity twice, rather than performing the arithmetic first and then measuring.

Use with Lesson Activity Book pp. 219–220.

Developing Mathematical Language

Vocabulary: least common denominator

The *least common denominator* (LCD) is the least common multiple of two or more denominators. By now, students can identify common denominators. Some students might need help in understanding the word *least*. Tell students it means "smallest in value." Show students pairs of fractions with common denominators, and point out that only one can be the *least common denominator*.

Familiarize students with the term *least common denominator*.

Beginning Talk about the meaning of the word *least*. Tell students it means "smallest in value." Write several numbers on the board, and have students point to the least number.

Intermediate Show equivalent pairs of fractions with common denominators, such as $\frac{12}{40}$ and $\frac{10}{40}$, or $\frac{6}{20}$ and $\frac{5}{20}$. Have students point to the pair with the *least common denominator*.

Advanced Have students write a sentence explaining what the *least common denominator* of two fractions is.

Open-Ended Problem Solving

Ask students what they can say about the situation described in this Headline Story. Watch for misinterpretations of the story: some students, when they see two numbers, are tempted to try finding their sum or difference. This problem uses the numbers quite differently.

 Headline Story

> Gavin had ____ marbles. He gave Luke $\frac{1}{3}$ of his marbles and then gave Briana $\frac{1}{2}$ of the marbles he had left. How many marbles do each of them have?

Possible responses: Gavin had to have a multiple of 3 for his number of marbles or he could not give away a third of his marbles. If he has 9 marbles, he gave away 3 to Luke. Then there would be 6 left and he'd give 3 to Briana. If Gavin had 12 marbles, Luke would get 4, Briana would get 4 marbles, and Gavin would have 4 left.

Skills Practice and Review

Adding Mixed Numbers or Improper Fractions

Give students paired addition problems, one with two mixed numbers and one with their equivalent improper fractions. Have students choose which of the pair they want to solve at their desks, and have students demonstrate both options at the board. Encourage students to experiment with both ways to add. Begin with problems that have like denominators and then move to some that have different denominators.

$$2\frac{2}{3} + 3\frac{2}{3} \qquad 5 + \frac{4}{3} = 6\frac{1}{3} \quad \text{and} \quad \frac{8}{3} + \frac{11}{3} = \frac{19}{3}$$

$$5\frac{3}{5} + 2\frac{4}{5} \qquad 7 + \frac{7}{5} = 8\frac{2}{5} \quad \text{and} \quad \frac{28}{5} + \frac{14}{5} = \frac{42}{5}$$

$$1\frac{3}{7} + 2\frac{4}{7} \qquad 3 + \frac{7}{7} = 4 \quad \text{and} \quad \frac{10}{7} + \frac{18}{7} = \frac{28}{7}$$

A Contexts for Adding and Subtracting Fractions

whole class   **10 MIN**

NCTM Standards 1, 4, 6, 7, 8, 9, 10

Purpose To find contexts where fractions are used in everyday life

Introduce Ask students to think of contexts where we could use fractions. They may come up with situations like measuring cooking ingredients, sewing, or measuring distances.

Possible Discussion

You might specifically discuss which fractions often come up in everyday life and which don't. In fact, only a limited number of fractions are commonly used—halves and quarters are used the most; eighths, sixteenths, tenths, and hundredths less often; thirds in some contexts; fifths rarely; and other fractions almost never.

Task **Have students write number sentences to match the contexts they generate for using fractions.** After students have come up with a few contexts for using fractions, ask them to elaborate on the contexts to describe a situation precisely enough to match it with a number sentence. For example, students might elaborate on the context of cooking by describing adding $\frac{3}{4}$ of a cup of oil and $\frac{3}{4}$ of a cup of water. A matching number sentence would be $\frac{3}{4} + \frac{3}{4} = \frac{6}{4} = 1\frac{1}{2}$ cups of liquid.

To solve the addition and subtraction sentences that they generate, your students may have various strategies for finding a common denominator. Encourage them to share strategies that they have developed in previous lessons, such as using equivalent fractions or drawing dot sketches.

> I need $\frac{1}{3}$ of a yard of fabric for a scarf and $2\frac{1}{2}$ more yards for a matching shirt. $\frac{1}{3} + 2\frac{1}{2} = 2\frac{5}{6}$
>
> A town is $4\frac{1}{2}$ miles away and we've already traveled $2\frac{3}{4}$ miles. $4\frac{1}{2} - 2\frac{3}{4} = 1\frac{3}{4}$
>
> Jason has a rope that is $3\frac{1}{2}$ feet long, while Kera's rope is $4\frac{1}{2}$ feet long. $3\frac{1}{2} + 4\frac{1}{2} = 8$ or $4\frac{1}{2} - 3\frac{1}{2} = 1$

✔ Ongoing Assessment

- Watch for students who are still adding fractions by adding the numerators and denominators. This familiar error tends to occur more often when students are given "rules" for adding fractions without understanding what that addition means and why the common denominator is necessary. Remind these students to use dot sketches to help visualize the fractions, find a common denominator, and then to use what they know about adding like things to add fractions with like denominators.

Solving Story Problems Involving Fractions LAB pp. 219–220

individuals

25 MIN

Purpose To identify addition and subtraction situations, and complete addition and subtraction problems involving fractions with unlike denominators

NCTM Standards 1, 2, 4, 6, 7, 9

Lesson Activity Book p. 219

Chapter 11
Lesson 6 **Stories with Fractions**
NCTM Standards 1, 2, 4, 6, 7, 9

Name _____ Date _____

1 Keffie and Danny were painting a mural at school. They need to make a special color, so they mixed $4\frac{1}{2}$ pints of blue paint, $2\frac{1}{6}$ pints of white paint, and $\frac{2}{3}$ of a pint of green paint.

Write a number sentence to show how many pints of their special color they had.

$4\frac{3}{6} + 2\frac{1}{6} + \frac{4}{6} = 6\frac{8}{6} = 7\frac{2}{6} =$
$7\frac{1}{3}$ pints

2 Jake ran five-sixths of a mile. Shayne ran three-fourths of a mile.

Who ran farther? Jake or Shayne?
$\frac{5}{6} = \frac{10}{12}$ $\frac{3}{4} = \frac{9}{12}$

Jake ran farther.

Write a number sentence to show the difference between the two distances.
$\frac{10}{12} - \frac{9}{12} = \frac{1}{12}$ of a mile

3 Michaela spent two-thirds of her allowance on a magazine. She spent one-fourth of her allowance on candy.

Write a number sentence to show the fraction of her allowance that she spent on both items.
$\frac{2}{3} + \frac{1}{4} = \frac{8}{12} + \frac{3}{12} = \frac{11}{12}$

Write a number sentence to show the fraction of her allowance she has left.
$\frac{12}{12} - \frac{11}{12} = \frac{1}{12}$ or $\frac{11}{12} + \frac{1}{12} = \frac{12}{12}$
She has $\frac{1}{12}$ of her allowance left.

4 Two-sevenths of the students in Sammy's class were at band practice. One-fourth of the students were at chorus practice.

Are there more students at band practice or at chorus practice?
$\frac{2}{7} = \frac{8}{28}$ $\frac{1}{4} = \frac{7}{28}$
More students are at band practice.

What fraction of the class is out of the room?
$\frac{8}{28} + \frac{7}{28} = \frac{15}{28}$

Write a number sentence to show the fraction of the class that is still in the room.
$\frac{28}{28} - \frac{15}{28} = \frac{13}{28}$

3 × 73 **CCXIX** two hundred nineteen **219**

ABOUT THE PAGE NUMBER 219 is the sum of 9 consecutive triangular numbers. 219 = 3 + 6 + 10 + 15 + 21 + 28 + 36 + 45 + 55

Lesson Activity Book p. 220

5 Joseph and Derek had a goal to collect twenty-four used books for the school book sale. In the first week Joseph collected 9 books and Derek collected 8 books.

What fraction of the goal has **Joseph** collected so far?
$\frac{9}{24}$ or $\frac{3}{8}$

What fraction of the goal has **Derek** collected so far?
$\frac{8}{24}$ or $\frac{1}{3}$

Write a number sentence to show the fraction of the goal that remains.
$\frac{24}{24} - \frac{17}{24} = \frac{7}{24}$

6 One day, Ahmad spent five-sixths of an hour on his homework and practiced piano for three-fifths of an hour.

How many minutes did he spend on homework?
50 minutes

How many minutes did he spend on piano?
36 minutes

Write a number sentence to show how many minutes he worked in all.
50 + 36 = 86 minutes

Write a number sentence to show how many hours he worked.
$\frac{50}{60} + \frac{36}{60} = \frac{86}{60} = 1\frac{26}{60}$ or $1\frac{13}{30}$ hr

7 Tifani braided yarn until she had a rope that was five-sixths of a yard long. Then Danisha braided another three-fourths of a yard onto the end of Tifani's rope.

How many yards long is the rope now?
$\frac{5}{6} + \frac{3}{4} = \frac{10}{12} + \frac{9}{12} = \frac{19}{12}$ or $1\frac{7}{12}$ yd

How many inches did Tifani braid?
30 in.

How many inches did Danisha braid?
27 in.

Write a number sentence to show how many more inches they have to braid to have a rope 5 feet long.
12 × 5 = 60   60 − 57 = 3 in.

8 **Challenge** Ani had fewer than 25 marbles. She dropped one-fifth of them behind the sofa and hid three-fourths of them in her brother's room. She put the rest in her room.

Could Ani have started with 12 marbles?
no

How many marbles did Ani have to start with?
20

How many are in her room?
1

220 two hundred twenty **CCXX** 2 × 2 × 5 × 11

ABOUT THE PAGE NUMBER 220 is divisible by the sum of its digits, so is a Harshad number. It is the sum of four consecutive primes (220 = 47 + 53 + 59 + 61). It is a tetrahedral number, the sum of the first ten triangular numbers.

Teaching Notes for LAB page 219

Depending on your class and their facility with word problems, you may want to work the first problem together. Remind students to read carefully and think about the situation before setting up a computation, and to check back and make sure that their answers make sense. Provide scratch paper for students to make sketches to help them find common denominators.

Differentiated Instruction **Basic Level** If students are still depending on dot sketches to find equivalent fractions, you might encourage them to predict how many dots their sketch will have before they complete it. Asking for this prediction may show them that they don't need to draw everything.

Teaching Notes for LAB page 220

Students work independently to complete word problems involving addition or subtraction of fractions. You might have students check their answers with a neighbor and discuss any differences in approaches or answers that they find.

✓Ongoing Assessment Observe your students to see who can find common denominators independently. If students are not finding the least common denominator, you may want to suggest that they find a smaller number that the denominators of both fractions will divide.

Challenge Problem Students figure out how large a set of objects might be by finding a common denominator.

Use with Lesson Activity Book pp. 219–220.

Chapter 11 • Lesson 6   **921**

pairs

 15 MIN

Materials

- For each student: AM99, scissors

NCTM Standards 1, 6, 7, 9

Teacher Story

"My class had a discussion around students' strategies in placing their cards in the boxes to make fractions. To get a high sum, students tried to place small numbers in the denominators and larger numbers as numerators. Still, since students don't know all four of the numbers before having to place each one, they couldn't always generate the largest possible sum with their given numbers, even using this strategy. I had my students play this game for many days, and some began evaluating their choices after they knew all four cards to see if they made good placements."

 Playing a Game: *Fraction Addition*

Purpose To compute and compare sums of fractions

Goal The object of the game, *Fraction Addition,* is to accumulate the greatest number of points by generating larger sums of two fractions than the other player.

Prepare Materials Each player needs to cut off the bottom of AM99: *Fraction Addition* Game and cut out the number cards. Each player retains the top of the page as their own individual game board.

How to Play

❶ Players shuffle their number cards and stack them in a stack face down.

❷ Players alternate turning over the top card from their stacks and placing each card in one of the four boxes of their game board until they have each made 2 fractions.

❸ Players use scratch paper to find common denominators and write equivalent fractions.

❹ Both players announce their sums and compare them. If necessary, they must find common denominators to compare the sums.

❺ The player with the greater sum receives a point.

❻ Players continue to make fractions, compare sums, and keep tallies for their wins. Play continues as time allows or until one player reaches 7 points.

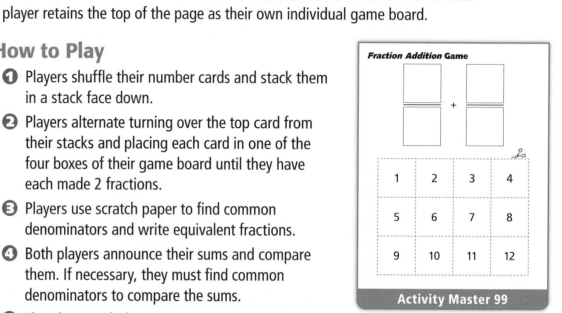

Fraction Addition Game

1	2	3	4
5	6	7	8
9	10	11	12

Activity Master 99

Extend After students have played the game once, you might offer variations on the game, such as aiming for the smallest sum instead of the largest one. As more of a challenge, you might suggest that the player whose sum is closest to a particular number, such as 2, gets a point.

Reflect and Summarize the Lesson

Write Math

Write a problem that involves adding or subtracting fractions with unlike denominators. Then explain how you would solve your problem. Problems will vary. Possible problem: To make banana muffins, Joel uses $\frac{1}{2}$ cup of white flour and $\frac{3}{4}$ cup of whole-wheat flour. How many cups of flour does he use? I need to find the sum of $\frac{1}{2}$ and $\frac{3}{4}$. First I write the numbers with a common denominator. Then I add the numerators and put the sum over the common denominator: $\frac{1}{2} + \frac{3}{4} = \frac{2}{4} + \frac{3}{4} = \frac{5}{4}$, or $1\frac{1}{4}$. So, Joel uses $\frac{5}{4}$, or $1\frac{1}{4}$ cups of flour.

Review Model

Refer students to Review Model: Adding and Subtracting Fractions with Unlike Denominators in the *Student Handbook* to see how to find the sums and differences of fractions with unlike denominators.

✔ **Check for Understanding**

❶ $\frac{5}{6}$

❷ $\frac{7}{18}$

❸ $5\frac{17}{12}$, or $6\frac{5}{12}$

❹ $4\frac{7}{15}$

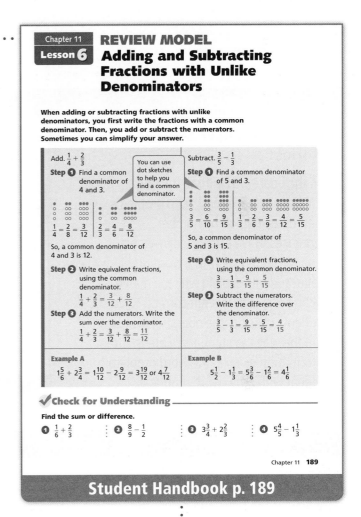

Student Handbook p. 189

Leveled Problem Solving

It is $\frac{2}{3}$ mile from Kirby to Rosetown and $\frac{3}{4}$ mile from Rosetown to Millton.

❶ Basic Level

What is the distance from Kirby to Millton through Rosetown? Explain. $1\frac{5}{12}$ mi; $\frac{2}{3} + \frac{3}{4} = 1\frac{5}{12}$

❷ On Level

How much farther is it from Rosetown to Millton than it is from Kirby to Rosetown? Explain. $\frac{1}{12}$ mi; $\frac{3}{4} - \frac{2}{3} = \frac{9}{12} - \frac{8}{12} = \frac{1}{12}$

❸ Above Level

What is the distance from Kirby to Millton through Rosetown and back again to Kirby? Explain. $2\frac{5}{6}$ mi; $\frac{3}{4} + \frac{2}{3} = \frac{9}{12} + \frac{8}{12} = \frac{17}{12} = 1\frac{5}{12}$, $1\frac{5}{12} + 1\frac{5}{12} = 2\frac{5}{6}$

| Intervention | Practice | Extension |

Activity Number Sentence Stories

On the board, write three fraction number sentences and word problems that match two of the number sentences. Have a volunteer match a number sentences with a word problem. Have students explain why the match is correct or why it is not correct. Have students consider the operation used and the way the numbers relate to the information given in the word problem. Repeat with other word problems.

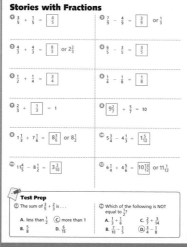

Practice P90

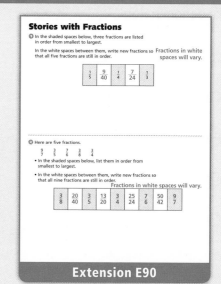

Extension E90

Spiral Review

Spiral Review Book page SR90 provides review of the following previously learned skills and concepts:

- connecting models for perimeter and area with their respective formulas and finding the perimeter and area of the figures
- applying the problem solving strategy *act it out*

You may wish to have students work with partners to complete the page.

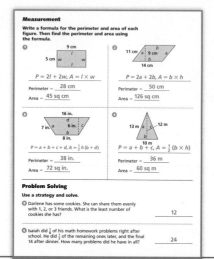

Spiral Review SR90

Extension Activity
Fraction Stories

Have each student toss a number cube four times. Tell students to use the first two numbers to write a fraction, and then use the second two numbers to write a different fraction. Then ask each student to write a story problem using the two fractions.

Have pairs of students trade problems and solve. Encourage students to share their problems in small groups.

Teacher's Notes 🍎

Daily Notes . . .

Quick Notes

More Ideas

Lesson 7 Using an Area Model to Multiply Fractions

NCTM Standards 1, 4, 7, 8, 9, 10

Lesson Planner

STUDENT OBJECTIVE ·······················
- To multiply fractions using an area model

1 Daily Activities (TG p. 927)

Open-Ended Problem Solving/Headline Story	Skills Practice and Review— Subtracting Mixed Numbers or Improper Fractions

2 Teach and Practice (TG pp. 928–931)

	MATERIALS
(A) **Finding the Area of a Rectangle** (TG p. 928)	• large squares of paper
(B) **Folding Paper to Find Fractional Area** (TG pp. 929–930)	• 📖 LAB pp. 221–222
(C) **Multiplying Fractions** (TG p. 931)	

3 Differentiated Instruction (TG p. 932)

Leveled Problem Solving (TG p. 932)	Practice Book P91
Intervention Activity (TG p. 932)	Extension Book E91
Extension Activity (TG p. 932)	Spiral Review Book SR91

Lesson Notes

About the Lesson

Students begin their study of multiplication of fractions using the familiar context of area, which shows how multiplying fractions is just like multiplying whole numbers, and gives students a model for visualizing the size of the fractional factors of their products. The area model for fraction multiplication starts with a square of area 1, marks the width and height according to the two fractions that will be multiplied, and sees into what fractional pieces this carves the area. (This and subsequent lessons on multiplying fractions may go beyond your state's standards. The ideas in these lessons are accessible to fifth graders and prepare them well for work in later grades.)

About the Mathematics

Just as adding and subtracting fractions have the same meaning as adding and subtracting whole numbers, multiplying fractions also has the same meaning and works the same way as whole-number multiplication. Just as 3×4 can mean "the area of a rectangle whose width is 3 units and whose height is 4 units," $\frac{1}{3} \times \frac{1}{4}$ can mean "the area of a rectangle whose width is $\frac{1}{3}$ of a unit and whose height is $\frac{1}{4}$ of a unit."

Use with Lesson Activity Book pp. 221–222.

Developing Mathematical Language

Vocabulary: area model

Students are already familiar with the concept of an *area model* from their work with whole-number multiplication. A reminder of the whole-number *area model* and how it works should help students relate it to multiplication of fractions. The only difference between a whole-number and a fraction *area model* is that the fraction *area model* uses only a fraction of the rectangle.

Familiarize students with the term *area model*.

Beginning Draw on the board an *area model* for a whole-number multiplication such as $3 \times 4 = 12$. Have students name the multiplication sentence that the *area model* represents.

Intermediate Have students draw an *area model* for a whole-number multiplication, such as $3 \times 5 = 15$.

Advanced Have students explain how an *area model* represents whole-number multiplication.

Open-Ended Problem Solving

Present the Headline Story. Ask students if such fractions can even exist. If so, ask them to find some. Also ask if there are patterns or methods that can help to find more such fractions.

 Headline Story

Wanted: two fractions with different denominators. Their sum must be 1.

Possible responses: $\frac{1}{3} + \frac{4}{6}$, or $\frac{10}{12} + \frac{1}{6}$, or $\frac{2}{10} + \frac{4}{5}$. You can find two fractions with the *same* denominator whose sum is 1, and change one of the fractions to an equivalent fraction with a different denominator.

Skills Practice and Review

Subtracting Mixed Numbers or Improper Fractions

Give students paired subtraction problems with mixed numbers in one, and the same numbers as improper fractions in the other. Let students choose which to solve at their desks. Encourage trying both ways, and choose students to demonstrate both on the board. Begin with like denominators; then, as appropriate, try unlike denominators.

$$3\frac{2}{3} - 2\frac{2}{3} \quad 1 \quad \text{and} \quad \frac{11}{3} - \frac{8}{3} \quad \frac{3}{3} = 1$$

$$2\frac{4}{7} - 1\frac{3}{7} \quad 1\frac{1}{7} \quad \text{and} \quad \frac{18}{7} - \frac{10}{7} \quad \frac{8}{7}$$

$$5\frac{3}{5} - 2\frac{4}{5} \quad 5\frac{3}{5} - 2\frac{3}{5} = 3, \text{ so } 5\frac{3}{5} - 2\frac{4}{5} = 2\frac{4}{5} \text{ and } \frac{28}{5} - \frac{14}{5} \quad \frac{14}{5}$$

whole class **5 MIN**

NCTM Standards 1, 4, 7, 8, 10

(A) Finding the Area of a Rectangle

Purpose To review the process of finding the area of a rectangle

Introduce Begin by asking students to recall the formula for the area of a rectangle. They might describe the method (multiply width times height), state a rule (area equals base times height), or recite a formula:

$A = b \times h.$

Task **Have students find the area of a rectangle.** Sketch a rectangle on the board and label it with a base (width) and a height. Choose fairly small numbers for the base and height so that you'll be able to show the individual square units of the area.

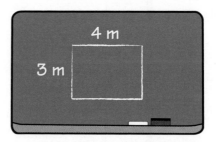

Students know that they can multiply these two dimensions to find the area: in this example, 12 square meters. Remind students why the formula works by drawing the lines that subdivide the rectangle into rows and columns of unit squares.

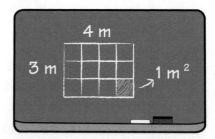

Practice If time permits, have volunteers come to the board and show similar examples to illustrate the process for finding the area of a rectangle.

Use with Lesson Activity Book pp. 221–222.

Folding Paper to Find Fractional Area

 whole class **20 MIN**

Materials
- For each student: 3 large paper squares

NCTM Standards 1, 4, 7, 8, 10

Purpose To use an area model to begin multiplying fractions

Introduce Building from the previous activity, tell students that they will now use what they know to find the area of part of a rectangle. Give each student 3 paper squares, and ask them to think of each one as a square meter. To check students' understanding, ask for the dimensions of each square, given that the area is one square meter. Students should reason that the width and height are both 1 meter since 1 meter × 1 meter = 1 square meter.

Task **Have students fold one paper square in half and shade one of the two resulting rectangles.** Sketch the situation on the board, and ask students for the dimensions (base and height in "meters") and area of the shaded part. Record their responses with a matching multiplication sentence.

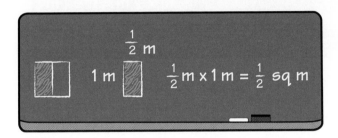

Task **Using a second square, have students fold it in half, and then in half again, perpendicular to the first fold. Have them open up the paper and shade one of the resulting squares.** Again, sketch the situation on the board, and ask students for the dimensions and area of the shaded part, recording their responses as before.

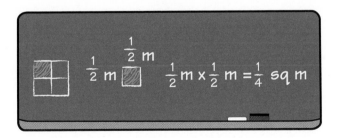

Teacher Story

"Some of my students had already been exposed to multiplying fractions and learned what they called a trick: multiply the numerators and the denominators to get the product. In this lesson they saw why the trick works.

I have a rule in my class that you can't use a "trick" unless you can say or show *why* it works. Several students actually got permission to use "the trick" because they were able to say things like, "You multiply the denominators because that tells you how many sections the paper will be divided into" and "You multiply the numerators because that tells how many sections you'll count.""

Task Have students fold the third paper square into fourths *in one direction.* (One way to describe this is to ask students to fold the square in half, and then in half again to make a long, thin strip.) **Then ask them to fold the square in half in the *other* direction. Have them open up the paper and shade a rectangle containing three small pieces in a row.**

Sketch the shaded part on the board, and ask for its base and height measurements, and for its area. If students are unsure, you may need to help them with questions about the area of one small piece ($\frac{1}{8}$ sq m) and how that relates to the area of the entire shaded region (3 small pieces, so $\frac{3}{8}$ sq m). Record the reasoning as before.

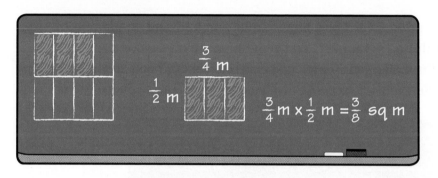

Concept Alert

Some students may notice that the products are always smaller than (or equal to) either of the factors, which is the opposite of how multiplication with whole-number factors works. You might encourage these students to use this fact as a check of their work or to consider why it is the case.

Use with Lesson Activity Book pp. 221–222.

Purpose To use an area model to multiply fractions

NCTM Standards 1, 6, 9, 10

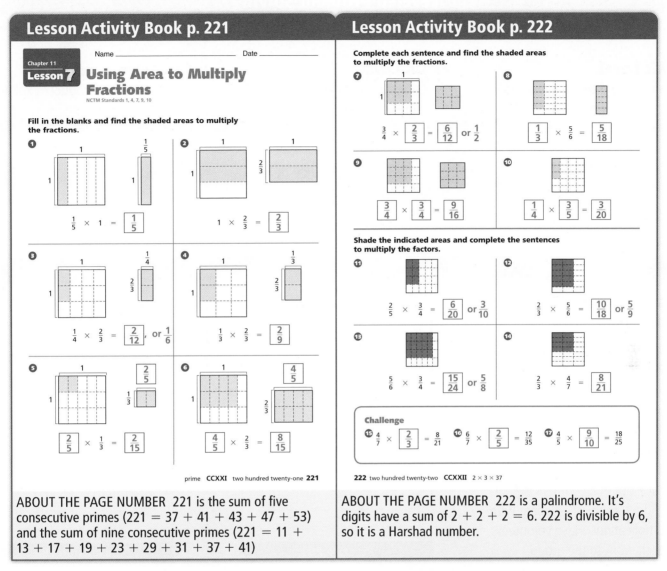

Lesson Activity Book p. 221

Lesson Activity Book p. 222

ABOUT THE PAGE NUMBER 221 is the sum of five consecutive primes (221 = 37 + 41 + 43 + 47 + 53) and the sum of nine consecutive primes (221 = 11 + 13 + 17 + 19 + 23 + 29 + 31 + 37 + 41)

ABOUT THE PAGE NUMBER 222 is a palindrome. It's digits have a sum of 2 + 2 + 2 = 6. 222 is divisible by 6, so it is a Harshad number.

Teaching Notes for LAB page 221

This page is similar to Activity B. Students use pictures to help find the dimensions and area of each shaded piece.

Differentiated Instruction **Basic Level** Some students may need more direction to complete the problems. For example they may need prompts like these: "The width (length) has been folded into ■ pieces, so each piece is ■ of the width (length). There are ■ equal small pieces in the folded square, so each piece is ■ of the area."

Teaching Notes for LAB page 222

Students continue finding areas by multiplying fractions. All of the original squares on this page are one square unit, although this is not labeled after Problem 7. Once students get to Problem 10, the shaded rectangle is no longer drawn separately from the main square.

Challenge Problem Students find missing factors in multiplication problems involving fractions. They can either draw their own pictures or use patterns to fill in the blanks.

Reflect and Summarize the Lesson

 Write Math

Explain how you can shade part of a square to help you find
$\frac{3}{4} \times \frac{1}{3}$. Possible answer: You can divide the paper into four equal parts one way and 3 equal parts the other way. To shade $\frac{3}{4}$ of $\frac{1}{3}$, you could shade 3 parts in the first row. $\frac{3}{4} \times \frac{1}{3} = \frac{3}{12}$, or $\frac{1}{4}$

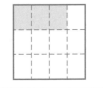

Leveled Problem Solving

Marisol is using an area model to multiply $\frac{3}{4}$ and $\frac{1}{2}$.

❶ Basic Level

How can she divide a square to represent the problem? Divide a square into 4 equal rows and 2 equal columns; 4 rows and 2 columns represent the denominators in the two fractions.

❷ On Level

Can you use an area model to represent the product? Explain. Yes; divide a square into 4 rows and 2 columns, and shade 3 rows and 1 column. The overlap is the product.

❸ Above Level

What is the product? Explain. $\frac{3}{8}$; 3 out of 8 parts of the area model are shaded.

Intervention	Practice	Extension

Activity Counter Multiplication

Provide fraction multiplication problems and counters. Write on the board $\frac{1}{2} \times \frac{2}{3}$. Have students multiply the denominators to find the number of counters needed, 6. Have students find half of those counters, 3, and then $\frac{2}{3}$ of the half, or 2. Guide students to see that 2 out of 6 counters is $\frac{2}{6}$, or $\frac{1}{3}$. The product, then, is $\frac{1}{3}$. Repeat with other multiplications. Have volunteers explain their work to the group.

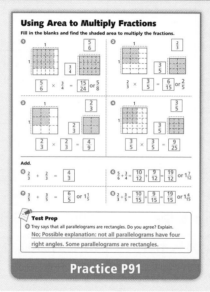

Practice P91

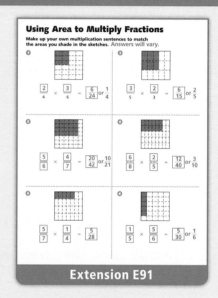

Extension E91

Spiral Review

Spiral Review Book page SR91 provides review of the following previously learned skills and concepts:

- recognizing that a fraction is equivalent to a given fraction
- investigating the features of Cross Number Puzzles

You may wish to have students work with partners to complete the page.

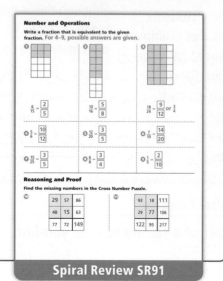

Spiral Review SR91

Extension Activity Mystery Factors

Have pairs of students create a fraction multiplication sentence. Then have them rewrite the sentence on a separate sheet of paper, leaving an answer blank in place of one of the factors. Have them trade papers with another pair of students to solve.

Teacher's Notes 🍎

Daily Notes . . .

Quick Notes

More Ideas

Lesson 8 Using Other Models to Multiply Fractions

NCTM Standards 1, 2, 6, 7, 8, 9, 10

Lesson Planner

STUDENT OBJECTIVE
- To multiply fractions using dot sketches and line intersections

1 Daily Activities (TG p. 935)

Open-Ended Problem Solving/Headline Story	Skills Practice and Review—Adding and Subtracting Fractions Greater than 1

2 Teach and Practice (TG pp. 936–940)

	MATERIALS
(A) **Exploring Multiplication with Fractions** (TG pp. 936–937)	• transparency of LAB p. 223 (optional)
(B) **Multiplying Fractions** (TG p. 938)	• LAB pp. 223–224
(C) **Finding Patterns in Multiplication of Fractions** (TG p. 939)	• SH pp. 190–191

3 Differentiated Instruction (TG p. 941)

Leveled Problem Solving (TG p. 941)	Practice Book P92
Intervention Activity (TG p. 941)	Extension Book E92
Extension Activity (TG p. 941)	Spiral Review Book SR92

Lesson Notes

About the Lesson

In the previous lesson, students used drawings of rectangles separated into arrays of equal-sized pieces to model the multiplication of fractions. These pictures are a good introduction to multiplying fractions because they help students to see the similarities between multiplying fractions and multiplying whole numbers, and help them to make sense of the resulting products. However, this kind of picture can be difficult to draw well, and if the drawing is inaccurate, it can also be difficult to interpret. In this lesson, students use an alternative model that is easier to draw: dot sketches. The dot sketches are like those used in earlier grades of *Think Math!* for multiplication of whole numbers.

About the Mathematics

As early as first grade of *Think Math!*, students see that finding the number of *combinations* uses multiplication. In this lesson, the exact same idea is extended from multiplying whole numbers to multiplying fractions.

  Use with Lesson Activity Book pp. 223–224.

Developing Mathematical Language

Vocabulary: dot sketch, intersections

Show students *dot sketches* that represent different whole-number multiplication problems. Point out that the dots are at the *intersections* of lines. Some students will relate *intersections* to street *intersections*. In fact, streets represent lines, and *intersections* are where they cross.

Encourage students to compare the *dot sketch* to the area model used in the previous lesson. Explain that the *dot sketch* is another model for the same types of multiplication problems they have been doing.

Familiarize students with the terms *dot sketch* and *intersections.*

Beginning On the board, draw several lines that intersect. Have students point out each of the *intersections.*

Intermediate Have students name street *intersections* with which they are familiar. Ask them to describe the *intersections;* for example, "There is an *intersection* at Main Street and Avenue A"; "Main Street crosses Avenue A at the *intersection.*"

Advanced Have students explain how a *dot sketch* and *intersections* can show multiplication.

Open-Ended Problem Solving

Ask students what they can say about the number of stuffed animals Caroline gave to her sister and brother.

 Headline Story

> Caroline had a collection of ____ stuffed animals, but decided to give a fourth of her collection to her younger sister. Then she decided to give half of the remaining animals to her baby brother.

Possible responses: Caroline's collection must be a multiple of 4 or she wouldn't be able to give a fourth to her sister. But not all multiples of 4 will allow her to divide the remaining animals in half for her brother. For example, 4 does not work but 8 does; 12 doesn't work, while 16 does; and so on. Multiples of 8 seem to work.

Skills Practice and Review

Adding and Subtracting Fractions Greater than 1

Give problems in which students add or subtract one mixed number and one improper fraction. Students may convert the mixed number to an improper fraction or vice versa, or they may handle the problem some other way. Choose students to demonstrate the various options. Begin with like denominators.

$$\frac{19}{4} + 1\frac{3}{4}$$

$$\frac{19}{4} + \frac{7}{4} = \frac{26}{4} \text{ or } 4\frac{3}{4} + 1\frac{3}{4} = 5\frac{6}{4} = 6\frac{2}{4} \text{ or}$$

$$1 + \frac{22}{4} = 1 + 5\frac{2}{4} = 6\frac{2}{4}$$

$$5\frac{3}{7} - \frac{18}{7} \qquad \frac{38}{7} - \frac{18}{7} = \frac{20}{7} \text{ or } 5\frac{3}{7} - 2\frac{4}{7} = 4\frac{10}{7} - 2\frac{4}{7} = 2\frac{6}{7}$$

pairs 15 MIN

Ⓐ Exploring Multiplication with Fractions

Purpose To use a dot model to multiply fractions

Introduce Students will use Explore: Combinations. You might remind students of the line intersection model they have used in earlier grades to model the number of possible pairings of items from two sets before having them complete the page. (See Possible Discussion.)

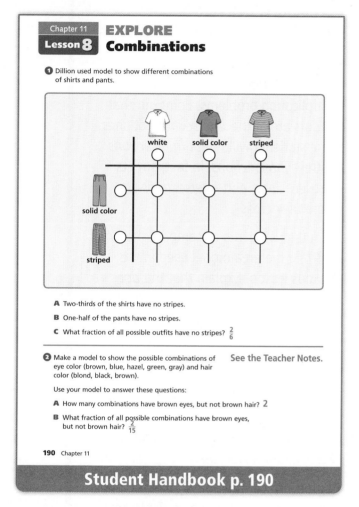

Chapter 11
Lesson 8
EXPLORE
Combinations

❶ Dillion used model to show different combinations of shirts and pants.

white   solid color   striped

solid color

striped

A Two-thirds of the shirts have no stripes.

B One-half of the pants have no stripes.

C What fraction of all possible outfits have no stripes? $\frac{2}{6}$

❷ Make a model to show the possible combinations of eye color (brown, blue, hazel, green, gray) and hair color (blond, black, brown).   See the Teacher Notes.

Use your model to answer these questions:

A How many combinations have brown eyes, but not brown hair? 2

B What fraction of all possible combinations have brown eyes, but not brown hair? $\frac{2}{15}$

190 Chapter 11

Student Handbook p. 190

Possible Discussion

If students don't remember that multiplication is used for finding the total number of possible pairings of items from two sets, you might relate the intersecting lines from pictures like the one below to the multiplication symbol: ×, which is itself composed of two crossing lines.

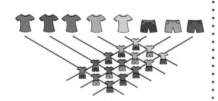

Task Have students complete Explore: Combinations with a partner.

Some students may realize that they can solve the problems by multiplying fractions. Other students may use the dot model to figure out the resulting fraction without performing the multiplication. Either way is fine at this point, but as you discuss the page with your students, attach number sentences to their responses so that they understand how the model connects to multiplication of fractions.

💬 **Talk Math**

❓ How many outfits have no stripes? Justify your answer with the dot model. 2; there are 2 intersections formed by lines extending from the pants and shirts without stripes.

❓ How many possible outfits are there? Justify your answer with the dot model. 6; there are 6 intersections formed by lines extending from the 2 shorts and 3 shirts.

❓ What fraction of all possible outfits have no stripes? Justify your answer with the dot model. $\frac{2}{6}$, or $\frac{1}{3}$; since 2 of the 6 possible outfits have no stripes, $\frac{2}{6}$ of the possible outfits have no stripes.

Use with Lesson Activity Book pp. 223–224.

Share Help students to see that, just as these intersection models can represent multiplication of whole numbers, they can also represent multiplication of fractions. For example, in Problem 1 from Explore: Combinations, the fraction of shirts without stripes × the fraction of pants without stripes = the fraction of outfits without stripes: $\frac{1}{2} \times \frac{2}{3} = \frac{2}{6}$.

Connect this model to the area model students used in **Lesson 11.7** to help them see that both models show $\frac{2}{3} \times \frac{1}{2} = \frac{2}{6}$.

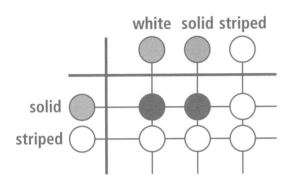 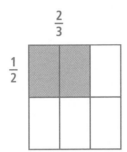

$$\frac{2}{3} \times \frac{1}{2} = \frac{2}{6}$$

Talk Math

❓ What did your model for the possible combinations of eye and hair color look like? Students' models may look different depending on the order in which they listed the eye and hair colors.

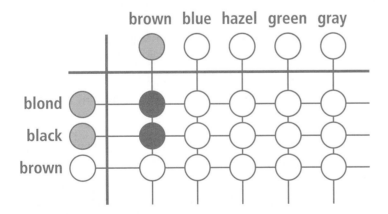

❓ How many combinations have brown eyes, but not brown hair? 2

❓ What fraction of all possible combinations have brown eyes, but not brown hair? Justify your answer with the dot model. $\frac{2}{15}$. There are 2 combinations of brown eyes with not-brown hair out of a total of 15 possible combinations.

❓ What number sentence can be used to find the fraction of all possible combinations of brown eyes with not-brown hair? $\frac{1}{5} \times \frac{2}{3} = \frac{2}{15}$

Purpose To use dot sketches to multiply fractions

NCTM Standards 1, 7, 10

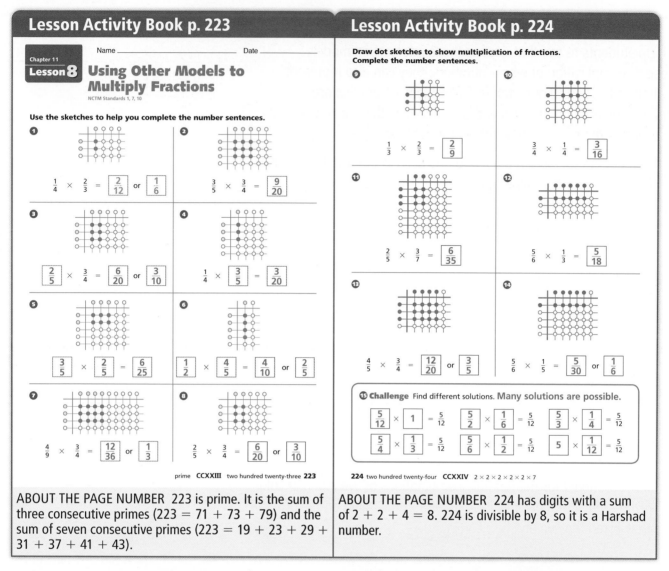

Teaching Notes for LAB page 223

The problems on this page are similar to those from the previous activity, so most students should be able to complete the page independently. The page provides dot sketches for students to use to help them complete the multiplication sentence below each sketch.

You may want to point out that for Problems 6–8, the products can be written in a simpler form as the product was in Problem 1.

Differentiated Instruction Basic Level If any students are unsure how to draw or interpret the dot sketches, you may wish to work with them in a small group.

Teaching Notes for LAB page 224

Students draw their own sketches, if they wish, to help them complete multiplication sentences with fractions. They also encounter some products on this page that can be written in a simpler form.

Concept Alert Some of your students may be able to find patterns in the problems on this page that will lead them to think more deeply about multiplying fractions. For example, students may notice that when the numerator of one factor is the same as the denominator of the other factor, they are actually multiplying and dividing by the same number, and so the effects cancel each other out.

Challenge Problem Students find as many pairs of factors as they can that result in a product of $\frac{5}{12}$.

Finding Patterns in Multiplication of Fractions

Purpose To find a pattern in fraction multiplication

Introduce Ask students if they have found a way to predict the product of two fractions just by looking at the factors, and without drawing a dot model or area model. Some students may already have noticed that the numerator of the product is the product of the numerators of the factors, and the denominator of the product is the product of the denominators of the factors. The rest of this activity will clarify this pattern for students who may not have noticed it.

Task Have students look for patterns in the multiplication problems on the LAB page 223. If possible, put up a transparency of the LAB page to help your class see the patterns described during the discussion.

Talk Math

❷ **What pattern do you notice in the numerators? Why does this pattern make sense?** Since you color every place where the lines from two shaded dots intersect, it's just multiplying those two numbers (the numerators). Multiplication gives you the total number of intersections where there are shaded dots.

❷ **What pattern do you notice in the denominators? Why does this pattern make sense?** The total number of intersections is the product of the two denominators because one denominator is expressed as the number of lines in one direction, and the other as the number of lines that intersect them.

Materials
• For the teacher: transparency of LAB page 223 (optional)

NCTM Standards 2, 7, 8, 9

Possible Discussion

Although it's critical for students to see the patterns in multiplication of fractions that result in a simple computational technique—multiply the numerators to get the numerator of the product, multiply the denominators to get the denominator of the product—conversations like these may lead students to search for similar patterns in addition and subtraction of fractions. You may even have an outbreak of students adding numerators and denominators to find the sum of two fractions when they had not done so before! This is one reason that addition and subtraction problems continue to appear in other parts of these lessons.

Reflect and Summarize the Lesson

Write Math

Explain how you could use a dot sketch to find $\frac{1}{3} \times \frac{3}{4}$. Possible explanation: I would draw three dots with one shaded across the top of the diagram and four dots with 3 shaded along the left side of the diagram. Then I would shade the dots where the top shaded dots and the left shaded dots intersect. That would show that $\frac{1}{3} \times \frac{3}{4} = \frac{3}{12}$, or $\frac{1}{4}$.

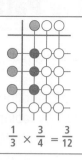

$$\frac{1}{3} \times \frac{3}{4} = \frac{3}{12}$$

Review Model

Refer students to Review Model: Multiplying Fractions in the *Student Handbook* to see how to find the product of two fractions.

✔ Check for Understanding

❶ $\frac{2}{20}$, or $\frac{1}{10}$

❷ $\frac{3}{8}$

❸ $\frac{15}{48}$, or $\frac{5}{16}$

❹ $\frac{3}{30}$, or $\frac{1}{10}$

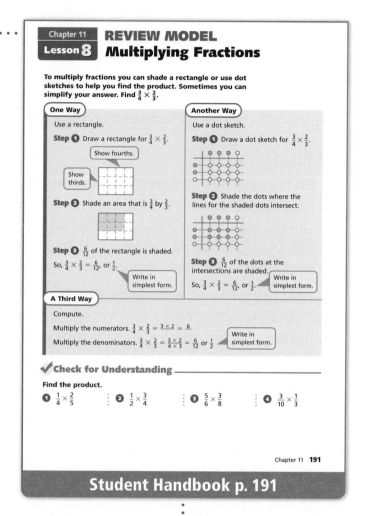

Student Handbook p. 191

Use with Lesson Activity Book pp. 223–224.

3 | Differentiated Instruction

Leveled Problem Solving

Mikel is using a dot sketch to multiply $\frac{4}{5} \times \frac{2}{3}$.

❶ Basic Level

How many dots are shaded across the top and down left side? Explain. 4 of 5 dots across the top, 2 of 3 dots down the left side; $\frac{4}{5}$ is 4 of 5 dots, $\frac{2}{3}$ is 2 of 3 dots.

❷ On Level

How many intersections are shaded in all? Explain. 8 intersections; 4 columns of 2 rows each will be shaded.

❸ Above Level

What is the product? Explain.
$$\frac{8}{15}; \frac{4}{5} \times \frac{2}{3} = \frac{4 \times 2}{5 \times 3} = \frac{8}{15}$$

Intervention	Practice	Extension

Activity Dot Sketch Puzzles

Guide students to create dot sketches for finding the product of two fractions. Have them cut the inside (product) array from the outside part (top and side, the factors). Collect the two parts from each student, and hand them out randomly so each pair of students receives two outside parts and two inside parts. Have the pairs of students determine the fractions used to create the inside parts and the product that the outside parts would generate.

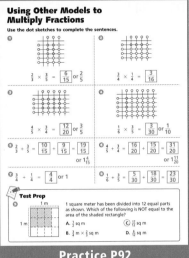

Practice P92

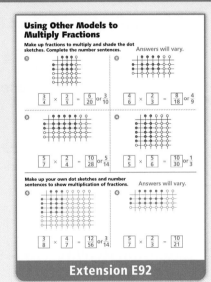

Extension E92

Spiral Review

Spiral Review Book page SR92 provides review of the following previously learned skills and concepts:

- making an organized list of all combinations of coins totaling 22 cents and 26 cents.

- applying the problem solving strategy *solve a simpler problem*

You may wish to have students work with partners to complete the page.

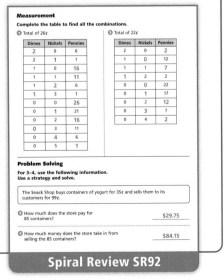

Spiral Review SR92

Extension Activity
Manufacturing Factors

Ask each student to choose a number between 1 and 100 that is a multiple of 2, 3, 4, or 5. Then have pairs of students use the two numbers they chose to create a proper fraction. Tell students that this is their target product. Have partners work together to write pairs of factors whose product is their target product. Give them a time limit to write as many problems as they can.

Use with Lesson Activity Book pp. 223–224.

Lesson 9 Fractions of Quantities

NCTM Standards 1, 6, 7, 8, 9

Lesson Planner

STUDENT OBJECTIVE
- To find a fraction of a set by multiplying a whole number by a fraction

1 | Daily Activities (TG p. 943)

Open-Ended Problem Solving/Headline Story	Skills Practice and Review— Multiplying Fractions

2 | Teach and Practice (TG pp. 944–946)

MATERIALS

Ⓐ **Exploring Fractions of a Set** (TG p. 944)

Ⓑ **Finding Fractions of a Set** (TG p. 945)

Ⓒ **Playing a Game: *Close or Closer*** (TG p. 946)

- TR: Activity Masters, AM100, AM27
- cards numbered 1–9
- scissors
- 📖 LAB pp. 225–226
- 📖 SH p. 197

3 | Differentiated Instruction (TG p. 947)

Leveled Problem Solving (TG p. 947)	Practice Book P93
Intervention Activity (TG p. 947)	Extension Book E93
Extension Activity (TG p. 947)	Spiral Review Book SR93
Science Connection (TG p. 884)	

Lesson Notes

About the Lesson

This lesson reminds students of an idea presented in **Chapter 4**: that certain kinds of fraction arithmetic require two operations on the integers that comprise the fraction—multiplication and division—and that the fraction notation tells us exactly what to multiply and divide by. The model of a "fraction machine" is reintroduced as a function machine that performs these two operations on an input (one operation on the input itself and the other on the result of the first operation). Students learn that finding a fraction of a number is exactly the same as multiplying the fraction machine's fraction by an input number. For example, students see that $\frac{2}{3}$ of 9 is the same as $\frac{2}{3} \times 9$.

Use with Lesson Activity Book pp. 225–226.

Developing Mathematical Language

Vocabulary: fraction of a set

Most students can relate to half of a set and have been doing so for several years. Students have also used fractions as a two-step function machine into which a whole number is input, multiplied by the numerator, and divided by the denominator. Build from the concept with which your students seem most comfortable.

Some students might not be familiar with the term *set,* however. Tell them that *set* is another word for *group.* A set often implies that the items in the group are alike or similar. And a set, like a group, is represented by whole numbers of items.

Familiarize students with the term *fraction of a set.*

Beginning Discuss the term *fraction of a set* as meaning "part of a set." Show a set of 8 crayons. Then place 4 of the crayons on a sheet of paper. Explain that half of the set of crayons is on the paper.

Intermediate Have students name items that are part of a set, such as crayons in a box, jigsaw puzzle pieces, and so on.

Advanced Show several fraction multiplication problems on the board. Include problems in which both factors are fractions, both factors are whole numbers, and one factor is a whole number and the other is a fraction. Have students circle each that could represent a *fraction of a set.*

Open-Ended Problem Solving

Ask students what they can say about this situation.

 Headline Story

I multiplied two fractions with different denominators. Then I added those same two fractions. What can you say about these activities?

Possible responses: I think it's easier to multiply because you can just multiply the numerators, and multiply the denominators. When you add the fractions, you can't just add the numerators; you have to convert these fractions to equivalent ones with a common denominator first. Usually, when you multiply the fractions, the product is less than the sum of those two fractions. But if you use two improper fractions, the sum might be less than the product. Here's an example: $\frac{8}{2} \times \frac{6}{3} = 8$ and $\frac{8}{2} + \frac{6}{3} = 6$. Sometimes the denominator of both the product and the sum will be the same.

 MENTAL MATH

Skills Practice and Review

Multiplying Fractions

Write a multiplication expression like $\frac{3}{4} \times \frac{5}{6}$, and ask students to find its value. $\frac{15}{24}$ Then ask if the product is in simplest form. If the product isn't in simplest form, ask students to simplify it. Its simplest form is $\frac{5}{8}$. Continue with other expressions that use $\frac{3}{4}$ as the multiplier.

$\frac{3}{4} \times \frac{1}{4}$ $\frac{3}{16}$	$\frac{3}{4} \times \frac{1}{9}$ $\frac{3}{36} = \frac{1}{12}$	$\frac{3}{4} \times \frac{4}{5}$ $\frac{12}{20} = \frac{3}{5}$
$\frac{3}{4} \times \frac{7}{8}$ $\frac{21}{32}$	$\frac{3}{4} \times \frac{6}{7}$ $\frac{18}{28} = \frac{9}{14}$	$\frac{3}{4} \times \frac{7}{10}$ $\frac{21}{40}$
$\frac{3}{4} \times \frac{10}{11}$ $\frac{30}{44} = \frac{15}{22}$	$\frac{3}{4} \times \frac{5}{9}$ $\frac{15}{36} = \frac{5}{12}$	$\frac{3}{4} \times \frac{3}{8}$ $\frac{9}{32}$

2 | Teach and Practice

individuals or
whole class

15 MIN

Materials

- For each student:
  AM100

NCTM Standards 1, 6, 7, 8

A Exploring Fractions of a Set

Purpose To begin finding fractions of a set

Introduce Give students AM100: Fractions of a Dozen and ask them to explain the machines on the page. Students should remember these machines from **Chapter 4.** The top of the machine indicates a multiplier and the bottom of the machine indicates a divisor. Tell students that these machines will help them to complete the problems on this page.

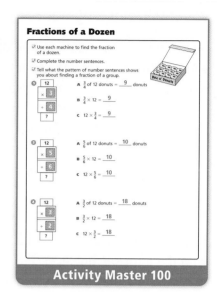

Activity Master 100

Concept Alert

Although a fraction performs two operations on the integers that comprise it, it is still a number, just like 12 is a number. The first expression in each group of number sentences is meant to reinforce this idea since it is read "three-fourths of 12" and does not contain a prescribed computation. To further emphasize the fact that fractions are numbers, you might also point out that just as $\frac{3}{4}$ is midway between $\frac{1}{2}$ and 1 on a number line, $\frac{3}{4}$ of 12 is midway between $\frac{1}{2}$ of 12 and 12 on a number line.

Task Have students complete AM100: Fractions of a Dozen.

Once students have completed the page, discuss the machines' connection with the groups of corresponding number sentences. Students should be able to say something about the numerator of a fraction indicating multiplication, and the denominator of a fraction indicating division. You might use the following questions to guide the discussion.

💬 Talk Math

❓ How did you complete Problem 1? I multiplied 12 by 3, and then divided the result by 4. Or, I divided 12 by 4 to find a quarter of 12, and then multiplied the result by 3.

❓ Where is the fraction in the number sentences represented in the machine? The two steps of the machine represent the fraction in the number sentences.

❓ How could you check that your answer makes sense? For Problem 1, I figured out that a quarter of 12 is 3, and 3 of those is 9. For Problem 2, I figured out that $\frac{5}{6}$ is a bit less than 1, so $\frac{5}{6}$ of 12 should be less than 12, but not by much. For Problem 3, I knew that $\frac{3}{2}$ is equivalent to $1\frac{1}{2}$, so I just added $\frac{1}{2}$ of 12, or 6, to 12 to get 18.

Possible Discussion

In Problem 3 on AM100, students may be surprised to find that a fraction of the number is larger than the number. You might point out to students that since the fraction asked for is greater than 1, the answer must be larger than the original whole.

Finding Fractions of a Set LAB pp. 225–226

individuals

20 MIN

Purpose To find a fraction of a set by multiplying a fraction by a whole number

NCTM Standards 1, 6, 7, 8, 9

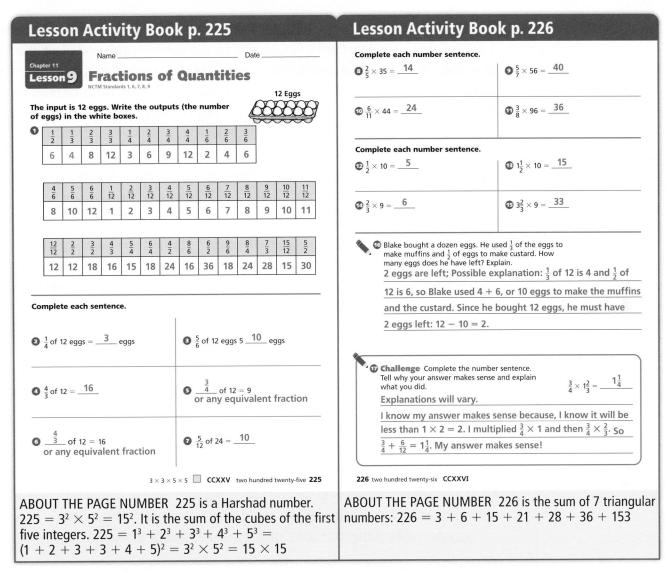

Lesson Activity Book p. 225

Name _____ Date _____

Chapter 11 Lesson 9 **Fractions of Quantities**
NCTM Standards 1, 6, 7, 8, 9

12 Eggs

The input is 12 eggs. Write the outputs (the number of eggs) in the white boxes.

1

$\frac{1}{2}$	$\frac{1}{3}$	$\frac{2}{3}$	$\frac{3}{3}$	$\frac{1}{4}$	$\frac{2}{4}$	$\frac{3}{4}$	$\frac{4}{4}$	$\frac{1}{6}$	$\frac{2}{6}$	$\frac{3}{6}$
6	4	8	12	3	6	9	12	2	4	6

$\frac{4}{6}$	$\frac{5}{6}$	$\frac{6}{6}$	$\frac{1}{12}$	$\frac{2}{12}$	$\frac{3}{12}$	$\frac{4}{12}$	$\frac{5}{12}$	$\frac{6}{12}$	$\frac{7}{12}$	$\frac{8}{12}$	$\frac{9}{12}$	$\frac{10}{12}$	$\frac{11}{12}$
8	10	12	1	2	3	4	5	6	7	8	9	10	11

$\frac{12}{12}$	$\frac{2}{2}$	$\frac{3}{2}$	$\frac{4}{3}$	$\frac{5}{4}$	$\frac{6}{4}$	$\frac{4}{2}$	$\frac{8}{6}$	$\frac{6}{2}$	$\frac{9}{6}$	$\frac{8}{4}$	$\frac{7}{3}$	$\frac{15}{12}$	$\frac{5}{2}$
12	12	18	16	15	18	24	16	36	18	24	28	15	30

Complete each sentence.

2 $\frac{1}{4}$ of 12 eggs = ___3___ eggs

3 $\frac{5}{6}$ of 12 eggs 5 ___10___ eggs

4 $\frac{4}{3}$ of 12 = ___16___

5 $\frac{3}{4}$ of 12 = 9
or any equivalent fraction

6 $\frac{4}{3}$ of 12 = 16
or any equivalent fraction

7 $\frac{5}{12}$ of 24 = ___10___

$3 \times 3 \times 5 \times 5$ ☐ **CCXXV** two hundred twenty-five **225**

ABOUT THE PAGE NUMBER 225 is a Harshad number. $225 = 3^2 \times 5^2 = 15^2$. It is the sum of the cubes of the first five integers. $225 = 1^3 + 2^3 + 3^3 + 4^3 + 5^3 = (1 + 2 + 3 + 3 + 4 + 5)^2 = 3^2 \times 5^2 = 15 \times 15$

Lesson Activity Book p. 226

Complete each number sentence.

8 $\frac{2}{5} \times 35 = $ ___14___

9 $\frac{5}{7} \times 56 = $ ___40___

10 $\frac{6}{11} \times 44 = $ ___24___

11 $\frac{3}{8} \times 96 = $ ___36___

Complete each number sentence.

12 $\frac{1}{2} \times 10 = $ ___5___

13 $1\frac{1}{2} \times 10 = $ ___15___

14 $\frac{2}{3} \times 9 = $ ___6___

15 $3\frac{2}{3} \times 9 = $ ___33___

16 Blake bought a dozen eggs. He used $\frac{1}{3}$ of the eggs to make muffins and $\frac{1}{2}$ of eggs to make custard. How many eggs does he have left? Explain.
2 eggs are left; Possible explanation: $\frac{1}{3}$ of 12 is 4 and $\frac{1}{2}$ of 12 is 6, so Blake used 4 + 6, or 10 eggs to make the muffins and the custard. Since he bought 12 eggs, he must have 2 eggs left: 12 − 10 = 2.

17 Challenge Complete the number sentence. Tell why your answer makes sense and explain what you did.

$\frac{3}{4} \times 1\frac{2}{3} = $ $1\frac{1}{4}$

Explanations will vary.
I know my answer makes sense because, I know it will be less than $1 \times 2 = 2$. I multiplied $\frac{3}{4} \times 1$ and then $\frac{3}{4} \times \frac{2}{3}$. So $\frac{3}{4} + \frac{6}{12} = 1\frac{1}{4}$. My answer makes sense!

226 two hundred twenty-six **CCXXVI**

ABOUT THE PAGE NUMBER 226 is the sum of 7 triangular numbers: $226 = 3 + 6 + 15 + 21 + 28 + 36 + 153$

Teaching Notes for LAB page 225

Students find many fractions of a dozen eggs by completing a table, and they then use numbers from the table in number sentences.

Differentiated Instruction Basic Level Some students may continue to find the imagery of the fraction machine helpful for the problems on the LAB page, and they may draw a rectangle around the fraction to resemble a machine and write the number to be multiplied as an input. After doing this for some time, most students will become comfortable just dividing and multiplying as the machine would, without the extra graphics.

Teaching Notes for LAB page 226

Students multiply fractions by whole numbers. Problems 12–15 challenge students to transition from multiplying a fraction by a whole number to multiplying a mixed number by a whole number. Problems 12 and 13 are related, as are Problems 14 and 15.

Challenge Problem Students multiply a fraction by a mixed number, justify the solution, and explain the strategy used.

Ⓒ Playing a Game: *Close or Closer*

Materials
• For each pair of students: cards numbered 1–9, AM27, scissors

NCTM Standards 1, 6, 7, 9

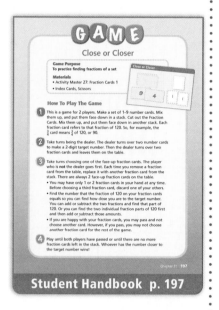

Student Handbook p. 197

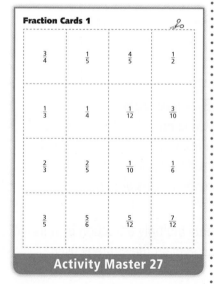

Activity Master 27

Purpose To practice finding fractions of a set

Goal The object of the game, *Close or Closer,* is to use one or more fraction cards to get a sum or difference as close to a target number as possible.

Prepare Materials Each pair of students will need a set of cards numbered 1–9 and AM27: Fraction Cards. Players shuffle the number cards and place them in a face down stack, and then cut the cards from AM27: Fraction Cards 1, shuffle them, and place them in a face down stack. Explain that the fraction cards all refer to the designated fraction of 120. So, for example, the $\frac{3}{4}$ card means $\frac{3}{4}$ of 120, or 90.

How to Play

❶ Players take turns being the dealer. The dealer turns over two number cards to generate a two-digit target number, and then turns over two fraction cards and leaves them on the table.

❷ Players alternate choosing one of the fraction cards. The non-dealer chooses first. After choosing a fraction card, the player picks another fraction card from the stack to place on the table so that there are again 2 cards on the table.

❸ Players may only have 1 or 2 fraction cards in their hand at any time, so if they choose a third fraction card, they must discard one of their cards into a separate discard stack.

❹ Each player should figure out the number that the fraction of 120 on their fraction cards equals in order to determine how close they are to their target number. (Students can first add or subtract the two fractions they have and find that part of 120 or they can find the two individual fraction parts of 120 first and then add or subtract those amounts.)

❺ If a player is satisfied with the fraction cards they have in their hand, they may pass and not choose another card. However, once a player passes, they may not pick another fraction card for the duration of the game.

❻ Play ends when both players have passed or when there are no more fraction cards left in the stack.

❼ The player whose fractions get them the closest to the target number when play ends wins. If both players are an equal distance from the target number, they both win.

Variation To make this game more challenging, players might hide the fraction cards they choose so that the other player doesn't know how close their opponent is to the target number. Also, by hiding their fraction cards, the opponent may not remember if a card they need has already been played or not.

Reflect and Summarize the Lesson

Write Math

Explain how you would find the number of eggs in $\frac{2}{3}$ of a dozen. Possible explanation: I would find $\frac{2}{3} \times 12$. I could think about a fraction machine and find $2 \times 12 = 24$ and then $24 \div 3 = 8$, so there are 8 eggs in $\frac{2}{3}$ of a dozen.

3 | Differentiated Instruction

Ruby has some marbles.

❶ Basic Level

She has 1 blue, 3 green, and 8 red marbles. What fraction of all the marbles are the blue and green marbles? Explain. $\frac{1}{3}$; $1 + 3 + 8 = 12$, $\frac{1}{12} + \frac{3}{12} = \frac{4}{12} = \frac{1}{3}$

❷ On Level

If she has 12 marbles and makes two piles of $\frac{1}{4}$ and $\frac{4}{6}$ of them, how many marbles would be in these piles? Explain. 11; $\frac{1}{4} \times 12 = 3$, $\frac{4}{6} \times 12 = 8$, $3 + 8 = 11$

❸ Above Level

She can separate them into sixths and into fourths. How many marbles could she start with? Explain. Any multiple of 12; 12 is the least number that can be separated into both sixths and fourths.

Intervention	Practice	Extension

Activity Counter Sets

Give students fraction-of-a-set problems and counters. Have them represent each whole number with that many counters. Then have them group the counters according to the denominator and gather the number of groups according to the numerator. That is their product. Select students to present solutions to the class.

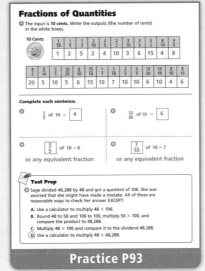

Practice P93

Extension E93

Spiral Review

Spiral Review Book page SR93 provides review of the following previously learned skills and concepts:

- using area models and puzzles to solve 2-digit multiplication problems.
- using and applying transformations

You may wish to have students work with partners to complete the page.

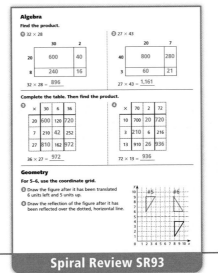

Spiral Review SR93

Extension Activity
Multiplying Mixed Numbers

Have students modify a dot sketch to determine how to multiply a mixed number by a fraction. The number $2\frac{1}{3}$, for example, can be represented by 7 rows grouped by threes. So, 3 rows + 3 rows + 1 row are shaded to represent $2\frac{1}{3}$. Watch for opportunities to connect to the distributive property.

Lesson 10 Stories about Multiplying Fractions

NCTM Standards 1, 6, 7, 8, 9, 10

Lesson Planner

STUDENT OBJECTIVE ···
- To interpret and solve story problems that require multiplying fractions

1 Daily Activities (TG p. 949)

Open-Ended Problem Solving/Headline Story	Skills Practice and Review—Many Common Denominators

2 Teach and Practice (TG pp. 950–952)

Ⓐ Exploring the Sizes of Products (TG p. 950)

Ⓑ Solving Problems Using Multiplication of Fractions (TG p. 951)

Ⓒ Using a Number Line to Solve a Problem (TG p. 952)

MATERIALS
- 📖 LAB pp. 227–228

3 Differentiated Instruction (TG p. 953)

Leveled Problem Solving (TG p. 953)	Practice Book P94
Intervention Activity (TG p. 953)	Extension Book E94
Extension Activity (TG p. 953)	Spiral Review Book SR94
Literature Connection (TG p. 884)	

Lesson Notes

About the Lesson

The stories in this lesson present realistic measurement situations that require multiplying fractions. Students must interpret the situation described in the problem, set up the necessary computation, perform it, and then check that their answer makes sense.

About the Mathematics

Your students' mathematics is beginning to grow beyond what is required for everyday situations. While we encounter fractions virtually every day, these situations generally don't involve arithmetic with fractions. Therefore, word problems involving adding, subtracting, or multiplying fractions with unlike denominators are often contrived. Even doubling or

halving recipes—which *is* an example of multiplying fractions—is not typically accomplished by formally performing the arithmetic separately from measuring the ingredients. Still, such arithmetic of fractions is one of the important stepping-stones to algebra.

Multiplication of fractions also brings some surprises with it. For example, unlike the multiplication of positive integers, the product of fractions can be smaller than the factors.

Developing Mathematical Language

Vocabulary: **fraction of a fraction**

Remind students that they have multiplied fractions by fractions to find a *fraction of a fraction*. Some students might relate the term *fraction of a set* to *fraction of a fraction*. Point out that instead of starting with a set or group of items as in a *fraction of a set*, applications for finding a *fraction of a fraction* often start with a part of a measure.

Familiarize students with the term *fraction of a fraction*.

Beginning Draw a rectangle on the board. Have a volunteer shade half of it and ask what the rectangle now shows. $\frac{1}{2}$ Have another volunteer now shade one third of the shaded part of the rectangle.

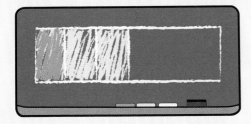

Write on the board $\frac{1}{3}$ of $\frac{1}{2}$ is a *fraction of a fraction*.

Intermediate Have students make two columns on paper and write *Fraction of a Set* at the top of one column and *Fraction of a Fraction* at the top of the other. Then ask them to write two examples in each column.

Advanced Have students describe the difference between a fraction of a set and a *fraction of a fraction*.

Open-Ended Problem Solving

Have students fill in the table to respond to this Headline Story. Make sure that the fractions they use make sense with the problem. For example, using a fraction greater than 1 doesn't make sense.

 Headline Story

Oh, no! Someone ate some of our cookies! Fill in the table with different fractions and the number of cookies eaten.

Possible entries: (Other fractions are possible.)

Beginning Number of Cookies	Fraction Eaten	Number of Cookies Eaten
48	$\frac{1}{2}$	24
48	$\frac{3}{4}$	36
48	$\frac{3}{12}$	12

Skills Practice and Review

Many Common Denominators

This may be done as a silent activity. Have students write any common denominator for the 2 given denominators. If they notice the smallest common denominator, have them put a star next to it.

3 and 4: 12*, 24, 120, 36, 480, ...   5 and 4: 200, 40, 20*, 60, ...

2 and 3: 6*, 18, 36, 24, 60, ...   6 and 9: 54, 36, 72, 18*, ...

4 and 6: 24, 12*, 120, 36, 72, ...   5 and 3: 15*, 30, 45, 60, ...

whole class **10 MIN**

NCTM Standards 7, 8, 9

Ⓐ Exploring the Sizes of Products

Purpose To compare the size of the product to the size of the factors in multiplication sentences involving fractions

Introduce Ask students if they think the product is greater than, equal to, or less than the factors in multiplication sentences. It is common to believe that multiplication always "makes things bigger." This activity helps to clarify when this is the case and when it is not.

Concept Alert

While we can compare the factors and product of multiplication problems in a context-free situation, we cannot make such comparisons in context. For example, it doesn't make sense to compare lengths (factors) and area (product). Comparing 3 inches of length and 2 square inches of area is just impossible! It does, however, still make sense to compare lengths multiplied by a whole number so that two lengths end up being compared.

Problem Is the product greater than, equal to, or less than the factors in multiplication sentences?

Use the following questions to help students consider this problem. These questions help students to see that, depending on the factors, the product could be greater than, equal to, or less than the factors in a multiplication situation.

💬 **Talk Math**

❓ Can you think of a multiplication sentence where the product is greater than both of the factors? Yes; any sentence where two whole numbers greater than 1 are multiplied will work.

❓ Can you think of a multiplication sentence where the product is equal to either of the factors? Yes; when a number is multiplied by 1 the product is equal to that number, and when a number is multiplied by 0, the product is also 0.

❓ Can you think of a multiplication sentence where the product is less than both of the factors? Yes; any sentence with two fractions less than 1 will work.

❓ Can you think of a multiplication sentence where the factors are both fractions and the product is the same as one of the factors? Yes; any sentence with a fraction equivalent to 0 or 1 will work.

❓ Can you think of a multiplication sentence where the factors are both fractions and the product is greater than both of the factors? This may be a challenge for your students, but help them to see that any sentence with two fractions greater than 1 will work.

Use with Lesson Activity Book pp. 227–228.

B Solving Problems Using Multiplication of Fractions LAB pp. 227–228

individuals 30 MIN

Purpose To interpret situations and solve story problems involving multiplication of fractions

NCTM Standards 1, 6, 7, 9, 10

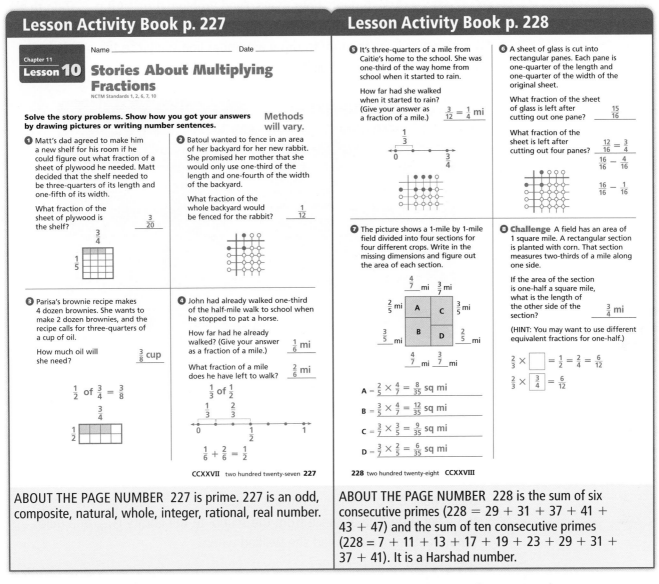

Lesson Activity Book p. 227

ABOUT THE PAGE NUMBER 227 is prime. 227 is an odd, composite, natural, whole, integer, rational, real number.

Lesson Activity Book p. 228

ABOUT THE PAGE NUMBER 228 is the sum of six consecutive primes ($228 = 29 + 31 + 37 + 41 + 43 + 47$) and the sum of ten consecutive primes ($228 = 7 + 11 + 13 + 17 + 19 + 23 + 29 + 31 + 37 + 41$). It is a Harshad number.

Teaching Notes for LAB page 227

Students interpret situations and solve story problems that involve multiplication of fractions. They should draw a picture or write a number sentence to explain their solution process. You might do the first problem as a class, asking volunteers to show or describe how they might solve the problem. If sketching and dividing the rectangle proves too difficult, suggest drawing an intersecting line model (as students used in **Lesson 10.8**).

Differentiated Instruction Basic Level/On Level
Students who make occasional computational errors might check their answers with dot sketches.

Teaching Notes for LAB page 228

The story problems on this LAB page are a bit more complex, often requiring more than one operation. Again, students draw pictures or write number sentences to explain their solutions. You might encourage students to work with a partner to share ideas and strategies.

Possible Discussion Students' drawings can be deceptively different, but still be correct. For example, both of these pictures show half of $\frac{2}{3}$.

Challenge Problem Students find a missing fractional factor.

C Using a Number Line to Solve a Problem

Materials
- For each student: completed LAB p. 227

NCTM Standards 1, 6, 7, 8, 10

Purpose To use a number line to solve problems involving fraction multiplication

Introduce Ask students how they solved Problem 4 on LAB p. 227. In this problem, students need to consider a fractional part of a fractional length. Someone may have thought to draw a number line similar to the one below. If not, you may want to draw it as a visual model.

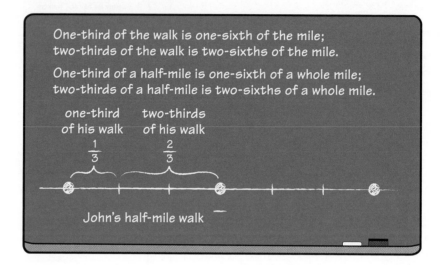

One-third of the walk is one-sixth of the mile; two-thirds of the walk is two-sixths of the mile.

One-third of a half-mile is one-sixth of a whole mile; two-thirds of a half-mile is two-sixths of a whole mile.

one-third of his walk $\frac{1}{3}$ two-thirds of his walk $\frac{2}{3}$

John's half-mile walk

This picture shows a mile, with John's half-mile walk labeled. It also shows $\frac{1}{3}$ of that half-mile walk, and that he has $\frac{2}{3}$ of his walk left. The diagram helps to show that $\frac{1}{3}$ of that half-mile walk is $\frac{1}{6}$ of a mile.

Differentiated Instruction

On Level/Above Level You may want to ask pairs of students to work together to suggest and then solve problems similar to the ones on LAB page 227.

Practice Ask students to try some related problems, such as the ones below, or to make up some of their own problems.

- Betsy walked $\frac{1}{2}$ of the way from the school to the library when she stopped to tie her shoe. The distance from the school to the library is $\frac{6}{10}$ of a mile. What fraction of a mile had she walked when she stopped to tie her shoe? Half of 6 tenths is 3 tenths. $\frac{1}{2} \times \frac{6}{10} = \frac{6}{20} = \frac{3}{10}$

- The library is $1\frac{1}{2}$ miles from Bryan's house. Bryan takes a bus $\frac{2}{3}$ of the way and then he walks the rest of the way. What fraction of a mile does he walk? He takes the bus $\frac{2}{3}$ of the way, so he walks $\frac{1}{3}$ of the way. $\frac{1}{3}$ of $1\frac{1}{2}$ is $\frac{1}{2}$. $\frac{1}{3} \times 1\frac{1}{2}$ mile $= \frac{1}{2}$ mile

Reflect and Summarize the Lesson

✏ Write Math

Explain how you would solve this problem. Then show the solution. I would find $\frac{1}{2} \times \frac{3}{4}$, which is $\frac{3}{8}$. So, she walked $\frac{3}{8}$ miles before stopping to rest.

Samantha lives $\frac{3}{4}$ mile from the park. She walked one-half of the way to the park and then stopped to rest. How far had she walked?

3 | Differentiated Instruction

Leveled Problem Solving

Devin is hiking a trail that is $\frac{7}{8}$ mile long.

❶ Basic Level

He stops to rest at a halfway mark. How far has he hiked? Explain. $\frac{7}{16}$ mi; $\frac{7}{8} \times \frac{1}{2} = \frac{7}{16}$

❷ On Level

He hikes $\frac{2}{3}$ of the trail and stops to rest. How far has he hiked? Explain. $\frac{7}{12}$ mi; $\frac{7}{8} \times \frac{2}{3} = \frac{14}{24} = \frac{7}{12}$

❸ Above Level

He hikes $\frac{2}{5}$ of the trail and stops to rest. How far is it to the end of the trail? Explain. $\frac{21}{40}$ mi; $\frac{5}{5} - \frac{2}{5} = \frac{3}{5}$, $\frac{3}{5} \times \frac{7}{8} = \frac{21}{40}$

Intervention

Activity Match the Problem

Write the following on the board, and have students copy it.

> Mrs. Hall left __?__ of a pizza on the table. Her son ate __?__ of it. How much of the entire pizza did her son eat?

Have students fill in the blanks with fractions and solve. Collect papers, and write only the solutions on the board. Read a problem aloud. Have students match it to the solution.

Practice

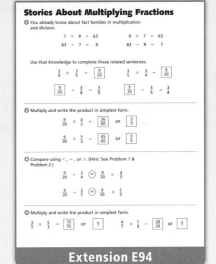

Practice P94

Extension

Extension E94

Spiral Review

Spiral Review Book page SR94 provides review of the following previously learned skills and concepts:

- finding factors of a number
- constructing a pictograph

You may wish to have students work with partners to complete the page.

Spiral Review SR94

Extension Activity
Finding Special Products

In the Extension for Lesson 10, students have found that the product of a fraction and its inverse is 1. Have students look for patterns to determine how to find two fractions whose product is 2. Students will discover that the product of a fraction and double its inverse is 2; for example, $\frac{2}{3} \times \frac{3 \times 2}{2} = 2$.

Lesson 11 Problem Solving Strategy and Test Prep

NCTM Standards 1, 2, 6, 7, 8, 9

Lesson Planner

STUDENT OBJECTIVES ....
- To practice the problem solving strategy *solve a simpler problem*
- To articulate the steps and strategies used to solve problems
- To prepare for standardized tests

Problem Solving Strategy:
Solve a Simpler Problem (TG pp. 955–956, 958–959)

MATERIALS

Ⓐ **Discussing the Problem Solving Strategy: Solve a Simpler Problem** (TG p. 955)

Ⓑ **Solving Problems by Applying the Strategy** (TG p. 956)

- 📖 LAB p. 229
- 📖 SH pp. 192–193

Problem Solving Test Prep (TG p. 957)

Ⓒ **Getting Ready for Standardized Tests** (TG p. 957)

- 📖 LAB p. 230

Lesson Notes

About Problem Solving

Problem Solving Strategy: Solve a Simpler Problem

In this last lesson of the chapter, students use the strategy *solve a simpler problem* to solve problems that require computation with fractions. They find common denominators to simplify adding, subtracting, and comparing fractions with unlike denominators.

Skills Practice and Review

Renaming fractions

Write each proper fraction, improper fraction, or mixed number on the board. Ask students to rename them—orally or in writing—in other equivalent forms. Use some that can be simplified as well as some that are already in their simplest form. You might invite students to make up some to follow these.

$$\frac{4}{3} \quad 1\frac{1}{3}, \frac{8}{6}, 1\frac{2}{6} \cdots \qquad \frac{9}{45} \quad \frac{3}{15}, \frac{1}{5}, \frac{6}{30} \cdots$$

$$\frac{30}{90} \quad \frac{3}{9}, \frac{1}{3}, \frac{100}{300} \cdots \qquad 4\frac{12}{18} \quad 4\frac{2}{3}, \frac{42}{9}, 4\frac{6}{9} \cdots$$

$$2\frac{8}{16} \quad \frac{5}{2}, 2\frac{2}{4}, \frac{15}{6} \cdots \qquad \frac{14}{5} \quad 2\frac{4}{5}, \frac{28}{10}, 2\frac{8}{10} \cdots$$

Use with Lesson Activity Book pp. 229–230.

Problem Solving Strategy

A Discussing the Problem Solving Strategy: Solve a Simpler Problem

whole class   15 MIN

NCTM Standards 1, 2, 6, 7, 8, 9

Purpose To share strategies for solving problems and focus on the problem solving strategy, *solve a simpler problem*

Introduce Remind students that throughout this chapter they have been using the strategy *solve a simpler problem* to help them solve problems as they have written equivalent fractions with common denominators to add and subtract fractions with unlike denominators.

Record the following problem on the board or on a blank transparency. Ask a volunteer to read the problem. Then have the students begin working on the problem.

Problem Aaron planted $\frac{3}{4}$ of his garden with tomato plants and $\frac{1}{8}$ of his garden with carrots. What fraction of his garden is planted?

Share Have students share their strategies for solving the problem. Students will likely suggest writing equivalent fractions with a common denominator for the two fractions in the problem.

Talk Math

❓ How would you solve this problem? Possible answer: I would find the sum of $\frac{3}{4}$ and $\frac{1}{8}$.

❓ How would you find the sum? First would find a common denominator for 4 and 8. That could be 8. Then I would write $\frac{3}{4}$ as the equivalent fraction $\frac{6}{8}$ and find the sum of the two fractions: $\frac{1}{8} + \frac{6}{8} = \frac{7}{8}$.

❓ Could you use another number as the common denominator of the two fractions? Explain. Yes; I could use lots of different numbers that are multiples of both 4 and 8, such as 16 or 32. For 16, I would rewrite the fractions as $\frac{2}{16}$ and $\frac{12}{16}$: $\frac{2}{16} + \frac{12}{16} = \frac{14}{16}$, or $\frac{7}{8}$.

❓ How would you find the part of the garden that is NOT planted? I would solve the number sentence $\frac{7}{8} + \underline{?} = 1$. The missing addend is $\frac{1}{8}$, so $\frac{1}{8}$ of the garden is NOT planted.

Solving Problems by Applying the Strategy LAB p. 229

Purpose To practice the problem solving strategy, *solve a simpler problem*

Teaching Notes for LAB page 229

Have students look at the first problem on LAB page 229 and, if available, put up a transparency of the page. Give students a few minutes to work on the first problem. Then have students share their strategies for solving the problem. If students don't suggest it, show how to use the problem solving strategy *solve a simpler problem* to solve the problem. You may want to ask questions like these to guide the discussion.

 ### Read to Understand

What do you know from reading this problem? Joshua spent $\frac{2}{10}$ of his allowance by Monday and $\frac{3}{5}$ of it by Wednesday.

What do you need to find out? the fraction of his allowance that he spend between Monday and Wednesday

 ### Plan

How can you solve this problem? You can *solve a simpler problem* by finding common denominators for the two fractions and then subtracting one from the other.

 ### Solve

How might you find a simpler problem? $\frac{2}{10}$ is equivalent to $\frac{1}{5}$, so you can subtract $\frac{3}{5} - \frac{1}{5} = \frac{2}{5}$. Or, write equivalent fractions with 10 as the common denominator: $\frac{3}{5} = \frac{6}{10}$, so $\frac{6}{10} - \frac{2}{10} = \frac{4}{10}$, or $\frac{2}{5}$.

So, Joshua spent $\frac{2}{5}$ of his allowance between Monday and Wednesday.

Check

Look back at the original problem. Does your answer make sense? How do you know?

Allow students to work independently or with a partner to solve the other problems on the page. When most students have completed the page, you might ask a couple of students to describe the specific strategies they used to solve the problems.

Lesson Activity Book p. 229

Name _____ Date _____

Chapter 11
Lesson 11 **Problem Solving Strategy**
Solve a Simpler Problem
NCTM Standards 1, 2, 6

Understand
Plan
Solve
Check

Solve each problem.

1 Joshua had spent two-tenths of his allowance by Monday. By Wednesday, he had spent a total of three-fifths of it. What fraction of his allowance did he spend between Monday and Wednesday?
$\frac{3}{5} - \frac{2}{10} = \frac{3}{5} - \frac{1}{5} = \frac{2}{5}$
He spent $\frac{2}{5}$ of his allowance
between Monday and
Wednesday.

2 Jayne walked a third of the way home from school, which brought her to the library. Then she walked a little farther to her friend's house. If Jane's friend lives four-sevenths of the way home from school, what fraction of Jane's walk is between the library and her friend's house?
$\frac{1}{3} + ? = \frac{4}{7}$ $\frac{7}{21} + \frac{5}{21} = \frac{12}{21}$
$\frac{5}{12}$ of Jane's walk home from
school is between the library
and her friend's house.

3 Ariel spent $\frac{3}{4}$ of an hour doing homework, Brad spent $\frac{5}{6}$ of an hour doing homework and Carla spent $\frac{2}{3}$ of an hour doing homework. List the children in order from the one who spent the most time to the one who spent the least time doing homework.
Brad, Ariel, Carla

4 Marti bought $\frac{3}{4}$ of a pound of green grapes and $\frac{7}{8}$ of a pound of red grapes. How many pounds of grapes did she buy?
$\frac{13}{8}$, or $1\frac{5}{8}$ pounds

CCXXIX two hundred twenty-nine **229**

ABOUT THE PAGE NUMBER 229 is prime. 229 is the smallest prime that remains prime when added to its reverse.

Reflect and Summarize the Lesson

 Write Math

How can using the strategy *solve a simpler problem* help you solve a problem involving the addition or subtraction of fractions? Possible answer: You can find a common denominator for the fractions, rewrite the fractions as equivalent fractions with the common denominator, and then subtract one fraction from the other.

C) Getting Ready for Standardized Tests LAB p. 230

 individuals

 20 MIN

NCTM Standards 1, 2, 6, 7, 8, 9, 10

Purpose To prepare students for standardized tests

Lesson Activity Book p. 230

Problem Solving Test Prep

Choose the correct answer.

1 Colleen's plant is $3\frac{1}{2}$ inches tall. It grows an average of $2\frac{1}{2}$ inches per week. How tall is it after 5 weeks?

A. 17 inches   C. $15\frac{1}{2}$ inches

B. 16 inches   D. $14\frac{1}{2}$ inches

2 Diagonals from the same vertex cut a polygon into triangles. How many triangles can be made from the diagonals of a 20-sided polygon?

A. 15   C. 17

B. 16   D. 18

3 A photograph is $\frac{5}{6}$ foot wide and $\frac{1}{2}$ foot high. How much greater is the photograph's width than its height?

A. 3 inches   C. 5 inches

B. 4 inches   D. 6 inches

4 Which relationship is shown by the data in the table?

x	3	5	7	8	14
y	5	9	13	15	27

A. $y = x + 3$

B. $y = x + 4$

C. $y = 2x - 1$

D. $y = 2x + 1$

Show What You Know

Solve each problem. Explain your answer.

5 Use the grid. Draw the result of rotating triangle A 90° counterclockwise around the dot. Then explain how you could show that the image of triangle A is congruent to triangle B.

Show that a translation of the image will exactly cover triangle B.

6 Pedro is making packages of pens and pencils for the school store. He has 48 pens and 60 pencils. Each package will have the same number of items. Each package will have only pens or only pencils. In how many different ways can he make the packages? If Pedro puts the greatest number of pens and pencils in each package, how many packages can he make in all?

6 different ways; packages of 1, 2, 3, 4, 6, or 12 items; 9 packages in all; 12 pens or 12 pencils in each package → 4 packages of pens and 5 packages of pencils

230 two hundred thirty   CCXXX

ABOUT THE PAGE NUMBER 230 is a Harshad number. It is the sum of 5 consecutive triangular numbers: $230 = 28 + 36 + 45 + 55 + 66$

Teaching Notes for LAB page 230

The test items on this page are written in the same style and arranged in the same format as those on many state assessments. The page is cumulative and is designed for students to apply a variety of problem solving strategies including *solve a simpler problem, write an equation,* and *look for a pattern.* Have students share the strategies they use.

The Item Analysis Chart below highlights one of the possible strategies that may be used for each item.

Show What You Know

Written Response

Direct students' attention to Problems 5 and 6. Explain that they must decide how to solve the problems. Then have students write an explanation of how they know their answer is correct. To provide more space for students to communicate their thinking about these problems, you may wish to have them write their responses and explanations on a separate sheet of paper. Use the Scoring Rubric below to evaluate their understanding.

Item Analysis Chart

Item	Strategy
1	Write an equation
2	Look for a pattern
3	Draw a picture, write an equation
4	Look for a pattern
5	Act it out
6	Solve a simpler problem; draw a picture

Scoring Rubric

2	• Demonstrates complete understanding of the problem and chooses an appropriate strategy to determine the solution.
1	• Demonstrates a partial understanding of the problem and chooses a strategy that does not lead to a complete and accurate solution.
0	• Demonstrates little understanding of the problem and shows little evidence of using any strategy to determine a solution.

Review Model

Refer students to the Problem Solving Strategy Review Model: Solve a Simpler Problem in the *Student Handbook* pp. 192–193 to review a model of the four steps they can use with problem solving strategy, *solve a simpler problem*.

Additional problem solving practice is also provided.

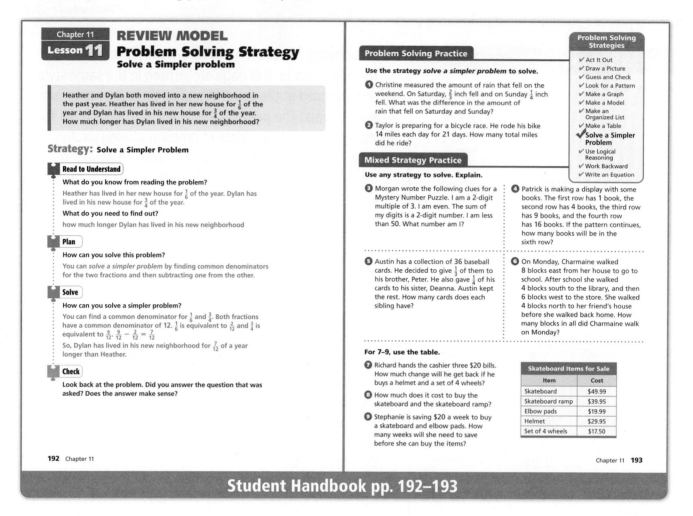

Student Handbook pp. 192–193

Task Have students read the problem at the top of the Review Model page. Then discuss.

Talk Math

? For how many months did each person live in the new neighborhood? Explain.
Heather: 2 months; Dylan: 9 months; Possible explanation: There are 12 months in a year. $\frac{1}{6}$ of 12 is 2 and $\frac{3}{4}$ of 12 is 9.

? How could you use what you know about the number of months each person lived in the new neighborhood to find how much longer Dylan lived in his new neighborhood? Possible answer: Dylan lived in the neighborhood for 7 months longer than Heather. 7 months is $\frac{7}{12}$ of a year.

Use with Lesson Activity Book pp. 229–230.

❶ $\frac{5}{12}$ inch; Possible explanation: You can use the strategy *solve a simpler problem* by finding a common denominator for the two fractions and then subtracting. $\frac{2}{3}$ is equivalent to $\frac{8}{12}$ and $\frac{1}{4}$ is equivalent to $\frac{3}{12}$. If you subtract $\frac{3}{12}$ inch from $\frac{8}{12}$ inch you get $\frac{5}{12}$ inch.

❷ 294 miles; Possible explanation: You can use the strategy *solve a simpler problem.* Multiply 14 by 20 and then make an adjustment by adding another 14. $14 \times 20 = 280$; $280 + 14 = 294$

Mixed Strategy Practice

❸ 48; Possible explanation: You can use *guess and check* to solve. You can use the first clue to make a systematic list of guesses for the number and then continue to check with each clue to see if the numbers still fit the clues.

❹ 36 books; Possible explanation: You can *look for a pattern* to solve. The second row has 3 more books than the first row. The third row has 5 more books than the second row, and the fourth row has 7 more books than the third row. If the pattern continues, the fifth row will have 25 books which is 9 more books than the fourth row, and the sixth row will have 11 more books than the fifth row, or 36 books.

❺ Austin, 15 baseball cards; Peter, 12 baseball cards; Deanna, 9 baseball cards; Possible explanation: You can *draw a picture* to solve. You can draw 36 baseball cards and divide them into twelfths. Austin gave $\frac{1}{3}$, or $\frac{4}{12}$, to Peter and $\frac{1}{4}$, or $\frac{3}{12}$, to Deanna. $\frac{4}{12}$ of 36 is 12 and $\frac{3}{12}$ of 36 is 9. If you add 12 and 9 you get 21. Then subtract 21 from 36 to find how many cards Austin has. He has 15 cards.

❻ 24 blocks; Possible explanation: You can *draw a picture* to solve.

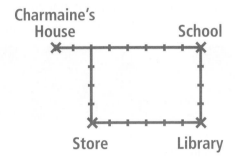

❼ $12.55; You can use the strategy *write an equation* to solve. If you add together $29.95, the amount of the helmet, and $17.50, the amount for a set of 4 wheels, you get $47.45. $29.95 + $17.50 = $47.45. Three $20 bills is $60. Subtract $47.45 from $60 and the result is $12.55. $60.00 − $47.45 = $12.55.

❽ $89.94; You can use the strategy *write an equation* to solve. $49.99 + $39.95 = $89.94.

❾ 4 weeks; You can use the strategy *write an equation* to solve. The cost of the skateboard and elbow pads is $49.99 + $19.99 = $69.98. Since $20 \times 4 = $80, Stephanie will have enough money in 4 weeks to buy the skateboard and elbow pads.

Fraction Computation

NCTM Standards 1, 3, 4, 6, 7, 9, 10

Purpose To provide students with an opportunity to demonstrate understanding of Chapter 11 concepts and skills

MATERIALS

- LAB pp. 231–232
- Chapter 11 Test
  (Assessment Guide
  pp. AG89–AG90)

Chapter 11 Learning Goals and Assessment Options

These learning goals are assessed in many ways throughout the chapter. The chart below correlates each learning goal to specific formal and informal assessment options.

	Learning Goals	Lesson Number	Snapshot Assessment	Chapter Review Item Numbers	Chapter Test Item Numbers
				LAB pp. 231–232	Assessment Guide pp. AG89–AG90
11–A	Add and subtract fractions with like denominators	11.1–11.3	1, 2	1–5	1, 2, 3, 6
11-B	Add and subtract fractions with unlike denominators	11.4–11.6	3, 4–6	6–13	4, 5, 7, 8
11-C	Multiply fractions and identify a fraction of a set	11.7–11.10	7–9	14–21	9–14
11-D	Apply problem solving strategies such as *solve a simpler problem* to solve problems	11.11	10	22	15

📷 Snapshot Assessment

The following Mental Math and Quick Write questions and tasks provide a quick, informal assessment of students' understanding of Chapter 11 concepts, skills, and problem solving strategies.

whole class   **10 MIN**

Mental Math This oral assessment uses mental math strategies and can be used with the whole class.

❶ To add or subtract fractions, the fractions must have _____ denominators. common or like

Add:

- $\frac{2}{5} + \frac{1}{5}$ $\frac{3}{5}$
- $\frac{1}{9} + \frac{4}{9}$ $\frac{5}{9}$
- $\frac{4}{5} + \frac{1}{5}$ $\frac{5}{5}$ or 1
- $\frac{5}{6} + \frac{2}{6}$ $\frac{7}{6}$ or $1\frac{1}{6}$

(Learning Goal 11-A)

❷ To subtract fractions with like denominators, you subtract the _____ to find the difference and the _____ remains the same. numerators; denominator

Subtract:

- $\frac{4}{5} - \frac{2}{5}$ $\frac{2}{5}$
- $\frac{5}{8} - \frac{2}{8}$ $\frac{3}{8}$
- $\frac{8}{9} - \frac{1}{9}$ $\frac{7}{9}$
- $\frac{13}{7} - \frac{5}{7}$ $\frac{8}{7}$ or $1\frac{1}{7}$

(Learning Goal 11-A)

❸ If you need to add or subtract fractions with unlike denominators, you must first find their _common_ denominator before you can add or subtract.

You can find a common denominator by finding a common _multiple_ of the original denominators.
(Learning Goal 11-B)

❹ Arithmetic is usually easiest if you find the _least_ _common_ multiple of the two denominators.

Give a common multiple of the two denominators:
- $\frac{1}{2}$ and $\frac{3}{4}$ 4, (8, 12, and so on)
- $\frac{2}{3}$ and $\frac{1}{6}$ 6, (12, 18, and so on)
- $\frac{1}{3}$ and $\frac{3}{4}$ 12, (24, 36, and so on)
- $\frac{4}{7}$ and $\frac{1}{2}$ 14, (28, 42, and so on)

(Learning Goal 11-B)

Quick Write This informal written assessment can be administered to small groups or the whole class. Read each question and have the students record responses on their write-on boards. Encourage students to listen and think about the questions before responding.

❺ Find the missing numerator to make an equivalent fraction, then solve:
- $\frac{2}{3} = \frac{?}{6}$ 4
- $\frac{1}{2} = \frac{?}{8}$ 4
- $\frac{3}{5} = \frac{?}{10}$ 6
- $\frac{3}{4} = \frac{?}{8}$ 6
- $\frac{1}{2} = \frac{?}{6}$ 3
- $\frac{1}{2} = \frac{?}{10}$ 5

(Learning Goal 11-B)

❻ Find a common denominator and solve:
- $\frac{3}{7} + \frac{8}{9} = \frac{83}{63}$ or $1\frac{20}{63}$
- $\frac{4}{5} - \frac{2}{4} = \frac{6}{20}$ or $\frac{3}{10}$
- $\frac{5}{8} - \frac{3}{8} = \frac{2}{8}$ or $\frac{1}{4}$

(Learning Goal 11-B)

❼ The after-school art club had 16 students. Exactly $\frac{3}{4}$ of them enjoy watercolor painting. How many students is that? Explain how you find your answer. 12 students; Possible explanation: I know $\frac{1}{4}$ of 16 is 4, so $\frac{3}{4}$ of 16 would be 3 groups of 4, or 12.
(Learning Goal 11-C)

❽ Use any model you would like to solve:
- $\frac{1}{3} \times \frac{2}{3} = ?$ $\frac{2}{9}$
- $\frac{1}{2} \times \frac{3}{4} = ?$ $\frac{3}{8}$
- $7 \times \frac{1}{3} = ?$ $\frac{7}{3}$ or $2\frac{1}{3}$

(Learning Goal 11-C)

❾ When you multiply two fractions that are between 0 and 1, is the product smaller than or larger than either fraction? smaller than
(Learning Goal 11-C)

❿ Mrs. White served $\frac{1}{2}$ of the 24 people in the cafeteria pizza and then served $\frac{1}{3}$ of the remaining people hamburgers. How many people in the cafeteria have already been served? Explain how you find your answers. 16 people have been served. Possible explanation: $\frac{1}{2}$ of 24 is 12, 12 people remain, $\frac{1}{3}$ of the remaining 12 is 4, add together the 12 people who had pizza and the 4 people who had hamburgers to get 16 people served.
(Learning Goal 11-D)

Formal Assessment

Chapter Review/Assessment The Chapter 11 Review/Assessment on *Lesson Activity Book* pages 231–232 assesses students' understanding of addition and subtraction of fractions with like and unlike denominators and multiplication of fractions. Students should be able to complete these pages independently.

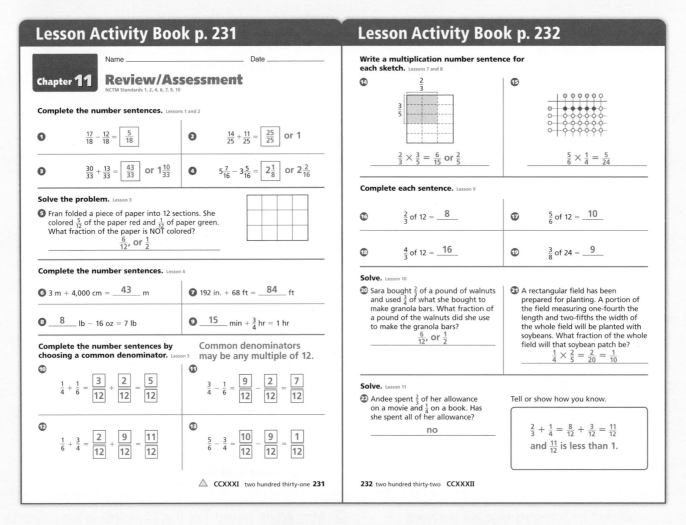

Lesson Activity Book p. 231

Name _____ Date _____

Chapter **11** **Review/Assessment**
NCTM Standards 1, 2, 4, 6, 7, 9, 10

Complete the number sentences. Lessons 1 and 2

1 $\frac{17}{18} - \frac{12}{18} = \boxed{\frac{5}{18}}$

2 $\frac{14}{25} + \frac{11}{25} = \boxed{\frac{25}{25}}$ or 1

3 $\frac{30}{33} + \frac{13}{33} = \boxed{\frac{43}{33}}$ or $1\frac{10}{33}$

4 $5\frac{7}{16} - 3\frac{5}{16} = \boxed{2\frac{1}{8}}$ or $2\frac{2}{16}$

Solve the problem. Lesson 3

5 Fran folded a piece of paper into 12 sections. She colored $\frac{5}{12}$ of the paper red and $\frac{1}{12}$ of paper green. What fraction of the paper is NOT colored?
$\frac{6}{12}$, or $\frac{1}{2}$

Complete the number sentences. Lesson 4

6 3 m + 4,000 cm = ____43____ m

7 192 in. + 68 ft = ____84____ ft

8 ___8___ lb − 16 oz = 7 lb

9 ___15___ min + $\frac{3}{4}$ hr = 1 hr

Complete the number sentences by choosing a common denominator. Lesson 5

Common denominators may be any multiple of 12.

10 $\frac{1}{4} + \frac{1}{6} = \boxed{\frac{3}{12}} + \boxed{\frac{2}{12}} = \boxed{\frac{5}{12}}$

11 $\frac{3}{4} - \frac{1}{6} = \boxed{\frac{9}{12}} - \boxed{\frac{2}{12}} = \boxed{\frac{7}{12}}$

12 $\frac{1}{6} + \frac{3}{4} = \boxed{\frac{2}{12}} + \boxed{\frac{9}{12}} = \boxed{\frac{11}{12}}$

13 $\frac{5}{6} - \frac{3}{4} = \boxed{\frac{10}{12}} - \boxed{\frac{9}{12}} = \boxed{\frac{1}{12}}$

△ CCXXXI two hundred thirty-one **231**

Lesson Activity Book p. 232

Write a multiplication number sentence for each sketch. Lessons 7 and 8

14
$\frac{2}{3} \times \frac{3}{5} = \frac{6}{15}$ or $\frac{2}{5}$

15
$\frac{5}{6} \times \frac{1}{4} = \frac{5}{24}$

Complete each sentence. Lesson 9

16 $\frac{2}{3}$ of 12 = ___8___

17 $\frac{5}{6}$ of 12 = ___10___

18 $\frac{4}{3}$ of 12 = ___16___

19 $\frac{3}{8}$ of 24 = ___9___

Solve. Lesson 10

20 Sara bought $\frac{2}{3}$ of a pound of walnuts and used $\frac{3}{4}$ of what she bought to make granola bars. What fraction of a pound of the walnuts did she use to make the granola bars?
$\frac{6}{12}$, or $\frac{1}{2}$

21 A rectangular field has been prepared for planting. A portion of the field measuring one-fourth the length and two-fifths the width of the whole field will be planted with soybeans. What fraction of the whole field will that soybean patch be?
$\frac{1}{4} \times \frac{2}{5} = \frac{2}{20} = \frac{1}{10}$

Solve. Lesson 11

22 Andee spent $\frac{2}{3}$ of her allowance on a movie and $\frac{1}{4}$ on a book. Has she spent all of her allowance?
no

Tell or show how you know.
$\frac{2}{3} + \frac{1}{4} = \frac{8}{12} + \frac{3}{12} = \frac{11}{12}$
and $\frac{11}{12}$ is less than 1.

232 two hundred thirty-two CCXXXII

Extra Support Students who have difficulty with items on the Chapter 11 Review/Assessment may need review of the lesson where development of the concept was provided. You can use the Intervention Activity to increase students' understanding before the Chapter Test is given.

Chapter Test Use the Chapter 11 Test in the *Assessment Guide* to assess concepts, skills, and problem solving from the chapter and to prepare students for standardized tests. The Chapter Test and other test items are also available online.

Chapter Notes

Quick Notes

More Ideas

Three-Dimensional Geometry

About the Chapter

In this chapter, students use what they already know from their work with two-dimensional figures to explore characteristics of three-dimensional figures. They build a variety of interesting and unusual three-dimensional figures and learn to describe and use important attributes of these figures to classify and sort them.

Describing Three-Dimensional Figures

Students extend their understanding of the attributes of two-dimensional figures to three-dimensional figures by cutting out and assembling nets. As students have success assembling a figure they will become curious and will make guesses about the three-dimensional figure the next two-dimensional net will make. Students will sharpen their descriptions as they compare their three-dimensional figures with the ones other students are building.

Classifying Three-Dimensional Figures

Once the class has built all the three-dimensional figures, they will have an interesting, collection of figures to explore and sort. As they use different attributes to classify the figures, they explore relationships among the *faces, edges,* and *vertices.* The ability to observe and classify figures lays the groundwork for the further development of geometric reasoning.

face   edge   vertex

Measuring Three-Dimensional Figures

While two-dimensional figures are measured in terms of perimeter and area, three-dimensional figures are measured in terms of surface area and volume. Working with their collection of three-dimensional figures, students explore ways to measure three-dimensional figures, building a strong connection to the formulas for calculating these measures.

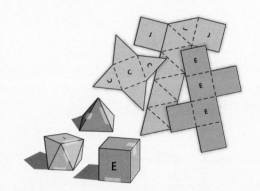

Developing Concepts Across the Grades

Topic	Prior Learning	Learning in Chapter 12	Later Learning
Three-Dimensional Figures	• Describe the attributes of prisms and pyramids Grade 4, Chapter 11	• Classify three-dimensional figures by their attributes • Distinguish cone, cylinders, and spheres from polyhedra Lessons 12.2, 12.3	• Draw different views of three-dimensional figures Grade 6
Nets and Surface Area	• Estimate and find the areas of the faces of prisms with rectangular faces Grade 4, Chapter 11	• Connect shapes in two-dimensional nets to faces on three-dimensional figures • Compute the total area of a net by first computing the area of each shape in the net Lessons 12.1, 12.6–12.8	• Use formulas to find surface areas Grade 6
Volume	• Find the volume of three-dimensional figures by building them out of inch cubes Grade 4, Chapter 11	• Use the formula *volume = base area × height* to find the volume of rectangular and triangular prisms Lessons 12.4, 12.5, 12.8	• Find the volume of pyramids and cylinders Grade 6

Chapter Planner

Lesson	Objectives	NCTM Standards	Vocabulary	Materials/ Resources

CHAPTER 12 World Almanac For Kids • Vocabulary • Games • Challenge
Teacher Guide 971A–971F, Student Handbook pp. 200–201, 212–216

1 **Transforming Two-Dimensional Nets into Three-Dimensional Figures**

Teacher Guide pp. 972–981
Lesson Activity Book pp. 233–234
Student Handbook
 Student Letter p. 199

- To connect shapes in nets to faces on three-dimensional figures
- To investigate features—such as number, shape, and position of faces—on a three-dimensional figure

3, 6, 7, 8, 9, 10

edges

faces

vertices

For the teacher:
- nets from TR: AM101–AM126
- scissors, tape

For the students:
- School-Home Connection TR: SHC45–SHC46
- nets from TR: AM101–AM126
- scissors, tape
- P95, E95, SR95

Social Studies Connection:
The Golden Rectangle
Teacher Guide p. 970

2 **Describing Three-Dimensional Figures**

Teacher Guide pp. 982–989
Lesson Activity Book pp. 235–236
Student Handbook
 Explore p. 202
 Review Model p. 203

- To classify three-dimensional figures by their attributes
- To describe and count the number of the faces, vertices, and edges of a three-dimensional figures

2, 3, 6, 7, 8, 9, 10

congruent

edges

parallel faces

perpendicular faces

vertices

For the teacher:
- class set of three-dimensional figures

For the students:
- P96, E96, SR96

3 **Sorting Three-Dimensional Figures**

Teacher Guide pp. 990–999
Lesson Activity Book pp. 237–238
Student Handbook
 Review Model p. 204

- To differentiate between polyhedra and other three-dimensional figures
- To define prisms and pyramids
- To distinguish cones, cylinders, and spheres from polyhedra

3, 7, 8, 9, 10

base

cone

cylinder

polyhedron

prism

pyramid

sphere

For the teacher:
- class set of three-dimensional figures
- models of sphere, cylinder, and cone

For the students:
- TR: AM127
- P97, E97, SR97

Literature Connection:
Mummy Math:
An Adventure in Geometry

4 **Volume of Rectangular Prisms**

Teacher Guide pp. 1000–1007
Lesson Activity Book pp. 239–240
Student Handbook
 Explore p. 205

- To connect models for the area of rectangles and the volume of rectangular prisms with their formulas and to use the formulas
- To use appropriate units to measure length, area, and volume

1, 3, 4, 6, 7, 8, 9, 10

base

height

length

width

cubic units

square units

volume

For the teacher:
- Figures B and E
- one-inch cubes

For the students:
- TR: AM128
- one-inch cubes
- P98, E98, SR98

NCTM Standards 2000
1. Number and Operations
2. Algebra
3. Geometry
4. Measurement
5. Data Analysis and Probability
6. Problem Solving
7. Reasoning and Proof
8. Communication
9. Connections
10. Representation

Key
AG: Assessment Guide
E: Extension Book
LAB: Lesson Activity Book
P: Practice Book
SH: Student Handbook
SR: Spiral Review Book
TG: Teacher Guide
TR: Teacher Resource Book

MATH GLOSSARY in **Student Handbook** p. 266

Planner (continued)

Chapter Planner *(continued)*

Lesson	Objectives	NCTM Standards	Vocabulary	Materials/Resources
5 **Volume of Prisms** PACING **1** DAY **Teacher Guide** pp. 1008–1017 **Lesson Activity Book** pp. 241–242 **Student Handbook** Explore p. 206 Review Model p. 207	• To relate the volumes of a triangular prism and a rectangular prism • To use the formula *volume = base area × height* to find the volume of rectangular and triangular prisms	1, 3, 4, 7, 8, 9, 10	rectangular prism triangular prism volume	**For the teacher:** ■ Figures B, L, O and S from the class set **For the students:** ■ one-inch cubes ■ P99, E99, SR99 **Science Connection:** **Shark Tanks** **Teacher Guide** p. 970
6 **Areas of Nets** PACING **1** DAY **Teacher Guide** pp. 1018–1025 **Lesson Activity Book** pp. 243–244 **Student Handbook** Explore p. 208 Game p. 214	• To compute the total area of a net by first computing the area of each shape in the net • To use formulas to find the areas of rectangles and triangles	1, 3, 4, 6, 7, 8, 9, 10	area of a net	**For the teacher:** ■ Figures C and J from the class set **For the students:** ■ cubes ■ coins ■ scratch paper ■ TR: AM129–AM131 ■ P100, E100, SR100
7 **Surface Area of Polyhedra** PACING **1** DAY **Teacher Guide** pp. 1026–1033 **Lesson Activity Book** pp. 245–246 **Student Handbook** Game p. 215 Review Model p. 209	• To find the surface areas of polyhedra • To explore how the surface area of a rectangle or triangle changes when the dimensions are doubled	1, 3, 4, 7, 8, 9, 10	surface area	**For the teacher:** ■ TR: AM132 ■ Figure C from the class set **For the students:** ■ cubes ■ coins ■ scratch paper ■ P101, E101, SR101
8 **Comparing Volume and Surface Area** PACING **1** DAY **Teacher Guide** pp. 1034–1041 **Lesson Activity Book** pp. 247–248	• To explore how volume and surface area of a prism change when the dimensions are doubled • To solve problems involving volume and surface area	1, 3, 4, 6, 7, 8, 9, 10	surface area volume	**For the teacher:** ■ nets from TR: AM129–AM131 ■ Figures B and E ■ rulers **For the students:** ■ TR: AM129–AM131 ■ P102, E102, SR102

Planner *(continued)*

Chapter Planner (continued)

Lesson	Objectives	NCTM Standards	Vocabulary	Materials/Resources
9 **Problem Solving Strategy and Test Prep** PACING 1 DAY **Teacher Guide** pp. 1042–1047 **Lesson Activity Book** pp. 249–250 **Student Handbook** Review Model pp. 210–211	• To practice the problem solving strategy *guess and check* • To articulate the steps and strategies used to solve problems • To prepare for standardized tests	1, 2, 3, 4, 6, 7, 8, 9, 10		**For the teacher:** ■ blank transparency (optional) **For the students:** ■ calculators
CHAPTER 12 Assessment TG pp. 1048–1051, **LAB** pp. 251–252, **AG** pp. AG109–AG112				■ **For the students:** ■ Chapter 12 Test pp. AG109–AG110

Planning Ahead

In **Lesson 12.1,** students will build three-dimensional figures from AM101–AM126. This set of figures will be used throughout the chapter.

In **Lesson 12.5** and in the Intervention or Extension Activities in **Lessons 12.4** and **12.7** students use one-inch cubes.

In **Lesson 12.6,** students will play *Volume Builder* in pairs. Each pair of students will need a coin, cubes, and scratch paper to record their scores.

In **Lesson 12.7,** students will play *Surface Area Builder* in pairs. Each pair of students will need a coin, cubes, and scratch paper to record their scores.

Games

Use the following games for skills practice and reinforcement of concepts.

Lesson 12.6 ▶
Volume Builder provides an opportunity for students to practice estimating and finding the volume of a rectangular prism.

Volume Builder

Lesson 12.7 *Surface Area Builder* provides an opportunity for students to practice estimating and finding the surface area of a rectangular prism.

Developing Problem Solvers

Open-Ended Problem Solving

The Headline Story in the Daily Activities section provides an open-ended situation where students can pose and solve problems. For each story, there are many possible responses. Headline Stories can be found on TG pages 973, 983, 991, 1001, 1009, 1019, 1027, and 1035.

Headline Story

WORLD ALMANAC FOR KIDS

The World Almanac for Kids feature is designed to stimulate student interest in the math concepts they are about to learn. Students use data to solve problems and explain solutions. The Chapter 12 Project can be found on SH pages 200–201.

Leveled Problem Solving

Leveled Problem Solving provides an opportunity for students to apply learning from the lesson to a real-life situation. Problems are leveled by ability to allow students of all ability levels to become successful problem solvers. Each Leveled Problem Solving begins with a real-life scenario upon which three problems are built.

The levels of problems are:

❶ Basic Level	❷ On Level	❸ Above Level
students needing extra support	students working at grade level	students who are ready for more challenging problems

Leveled Problem Solving can be found on TG pages 980, 989, 998, 1007, 1016, 1024, 1033, and 1041.

Write Math

Reflect and Summarize the Lesson poses a problem or question for students to think and write about. This feature can be found on TG pages 979, 988, 997, 1006, 1015, 1023, 1032, 1040, and 1044.

Other opportunities to write about math can be found on LAB pages 234, 235, 236, 238, 240, 244, 246, 248, and 250.

Problem Solving Strategies

The focus of **Lesson 12.9** is the strategy *guess and check*. However, students will use a variety of problem solving strategies as they work through the chapter. The chart below shows strategies that may be useful in completing each lesson.

Strategy	Lesson(s)	Description
✓ Guess and Check	12.9	Find the length of the edge of a cube when volume is given.
Look for a Pattern	12.1, 12.2, 12.8	Find patterns in the faces of three-dimensional figures; in the number of faces, vertices, and edges; and in how the surface area and volume of a prism changes when the dimensions are doubled.
Make a Model	12.1, 12.4, 12.6, 12.7	Use nets to make models of three-dimensional figures, build a pictured structure with cubes, and build prisms with cubes.
Make an Organized List	12.9	List guesses and checks to determine length of the edge of a cube when the volume is given.
Solve a Simpler Problem	12.4	Use cubes to build models of prisms to help determine the formula for the volume of a prism, relate the areas of the shapes on a net to the surface area on a polyhedron, and relate the volume of a triangular prism to the volume of a rectangular prism.
Use Logical Reasoning	12.1–12.9	Use logical reasoning to describe and classify three-dimensional figures by their attributes, and determine formulas for volume and surface area.

Meeting the Needs of All Learners

Differentiated Instruction		
Extra Support	**On Level**	**Enrichment**
Intervention Activities TG pp. 980, 989, 998, 1007, 1016, 1024, 1033, 1041	**Practice Book** pp. P95–P102	**Extension Activities** TG pp. 980, 989, 998, 1007, 1016, 1024, 1033, 1041
	Spiral Review Book pp. SR95–SR102	**Extension Book** pp. E95–E102
	LAB Challenge LAB pp. 234, 236, 238, 240, 242, 244, 246, 248	**LAB Challenge** LAB pp. 234, 236, 238, 240, 242, 244, 246, 248
Lesson Notes Basic Level TG pp. 978, 996	**Lesson Notes On Level** TG p. 1003	**Lesson Notes Above Level** TG pp. 1003, 1022, 1038
Leveled Problem Solving Basic Level TG pp. 980, 989, 998, 1007, 1016, 1024, 1033, 1041	**Leveled Problem Solving On Level** TG pp. 980, 989, 998, 1007, 1016, 1024, 1033, 1041	**Leveled Problem Solving Above Level** TG pp. 980, 989, 998, 1007, 1016, 1024, 1033, 1041

English Language Learners

Suggestions for addressing the needs of students learning English as a second language are included in the Developing Mathematical Language section at the beginning of most lessons.

ELL activities for this chapter can be found on TG pages 973, 983, 991, 1001, 1009, 1019, 1027, and 1035.

The Multi-Age Classroom

Grade 4	• Students on this level should be able to complete the lessons in Chapter 12 but might need some additional practice with key concepts and skills. • Give students more practice with three-dimensional figures.	See Grade 5, Intervention Activities, Lessons 12.1–12.8. See Grade 4, Lessons 11.1–11.6.
Grade 5	• Students on this level should be able to complete the lessons in Chapter 12 with minimal adjustments.	See Grade 5, Practice pages P95–P102.
Grade 6	• Students on this level should be able to complete the lessons in Chapter 12 and to extend concepts and skills related to three-dimensional geometry. • Give students extended work with volume and surface area.	See Grade 5, Extension pages E95–E102.

Cross Curricular Connections

Science Connection

Math Concept: volume and weight

Shark Tanks

Share the following information with the class.

- An aquarium has a 135,000-gallon shark tank.
- Water weighs approximately 8.3 pounds per gallon.
- A cubic foot of water weighs approximately 62.4 pounds.
- Have students figure out approximately how much the water in the aquarium's shark tank weighs. approximately 1,120,500 pounds: 135,000 × 8.3
- Ask student to calculate about how many cubic feet of water there are in the aquarium's shark tank. approximately 17,957 cubic feet of water: 1,120,500 ÷ 62.4
- You may wish to have students research other aquariums' shark tanks and apply the same reasoning to determine the weight of the tank's water and its volume in cubic feet.

Lesson 12.5

Social Studies Connection

Math Concept: two-dimensional shapes

The Golden Rectangle

Tell students that the golden rectangle, or golden ratio, has been known for at least 2,000 years. It represents a rectangle that many people believe is particularly pleasing to the eye.

In a golden rectangle, the length is approximately 1.6 times the width. Golden rectangles can be seen in architecture (for example, many people believe the United Nations building in New York City was built using the golden ratio as a guiding principle), and much art and design.

- Have students construct several golden rectangles, each with the same ratio of sides but different lengths and widths, and then cut out the rectangles.
- Have students measure and cut a square from their rectangle so that a rectangle is left. That rectangle will also be a golden rectangle.

Lesson 12.1

Literature Connection

Math Concept: Geometry

Mummy Math: An Adventure in Geometry
By Cindy Neuschwander
Illustrated by Bryan Langdo

As students learn to sort their three-dimensional geometric figures into pyramids and prisms, they will enjoy Matt and Bibi's adventure inside an ancient pyramid. The twins must use their knowledge about geometric figures to locate the pharaoh's burial chamber and the way out.

Lesson 12.3

School-Home Connection

A reproducible copy of the School-Home Connection letter in English and in Spanish can be found in the **Teacher Resource Book**, pages SHC45-SHC48.

Encourage students to play *Three-Dimensional Tic-Tac-Toe,* found on the School-Home Connection page, with a family member. Students will work with the concept of three-dimensional figures in **Lessons 12.1** through **12.9.**

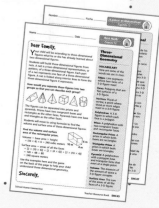

Assessment Options

There are many opportunities in *Think Math!* to assess students understanding of concepts, skills, and problem solving. Learning Goals for Chapter 12 are provided below. The assessment options provide opportunities to evaluate whether or not students have retained learning from prior experiences. Choose the forms of assessment that best meet the needs of your students.

Chapter 12 Learning Goals

	Learning Goals	Lesson Number
12-A	Identify and classify three-dimensional figures by their attributes, including faces, vertices, and edges	12.1–12.3
12-B	Find the volume of a triangular or rectangular prism and identify the appropriate unit of measure for volume	12.4, 12.5, 12.8
12-C	Find the surface area of a prism or pyramid and identify the appropriate unit of measure for surface area	12.6–12.8
12-D	Apply problem solving strategies such as *guess and check* to solve problems	12.9

✓ Informal Assessment

Ongoing Assessment
Provides insight into students' thinking to guide instruction (TG pp. 978, 986, 994, 996, 1002, 1012, 1014, 1020, 1028, 1030, 1036)

Reflect and Summarize the Lesson
Checks understanding of lesson concepts (TG pp. 979, 988, 997, 1006, 1015, 1023, 1032, 1040, 1044)

Snapshot Assessment
Mental Math and **Quick Write**
Offers a quick observation of students' progress on chapters concepts and skills (TG pp. 1048–1049)

Performance Assessment
Provides quarterly assessment of Chapters 12–15 concepts using real-life situations
Assessment Guide
pp. AG225–AG230

✓ Formal Assessment

Standardized Test Prep
Problem Solving Test Prep
Prepares students for standardized tests
Lesson Activity Book p. 250 (TG p. 1045)

Chapter 12 Review/Assessment
Reviews and assesses students' understanding of the chapter
Lesson Activity Book pp. 251–252 (TG p. 1050)

Chapter 12 Test
Assesses the chapter concepts and skills
Assessment Guide
Form A pp. AG109–AG110
Form B pp. AG111–AG112

Benchmark 4 Assessment
Provides quarterly assessment of Chapters 12–15 concepts and skills
Assessment Guide
Benchmark 4A pp. AG125–AG132
Benchmark 4B pp. AG133–AG140

World Almanac for Kids

Use the World Almanac for Kids feature, *Building a Birdhouse,* found on pp. 200–201 of the **Student Handbook,** to provide students with an opportunity to practice using their problem solving skills by solving real world problems.

FACT•ACTIVITY 1

❶ Possible answers: Birdhouse A: rectangle, trapezoid, square; Birdhouse B: triangle, rectangle; Birdhouse C: triangle, rectangle

❷ Possible answers: In Birdhouse A, the squares appear to be congruent and the two trapezoids on the sides of the birdhouse appear to be congruent. In Birdhouse B, the roof has 2 triangles that appear to be congruent and 3 rectangles that appear to be congruent. The base of the birdhouse has 4 rectangular sides that appear to be congruent and 2 smaller rectangular sides that appear to be congruent. In Birdhouse C, the four rectangular sides of the base appear to be congruent, the 2 smaller sides of the base appear to be congruent, and the four triangles on the roof appear to be congruent.

❸ Possible answers: Birdhouse A is a prism; Birdhouse B is made of a rectangular prism and has a triangular prism for the roof; Birdhouse C is made of a rectangular prism and has a square pyramid for the roof; Birdhouse D has a cylinder on the bottom with a cone for the roof.

❹ Roof B: 5 faces, 6 vertices, 9 edges; Roof C: 5 faces, 5 vertices, 8 edges

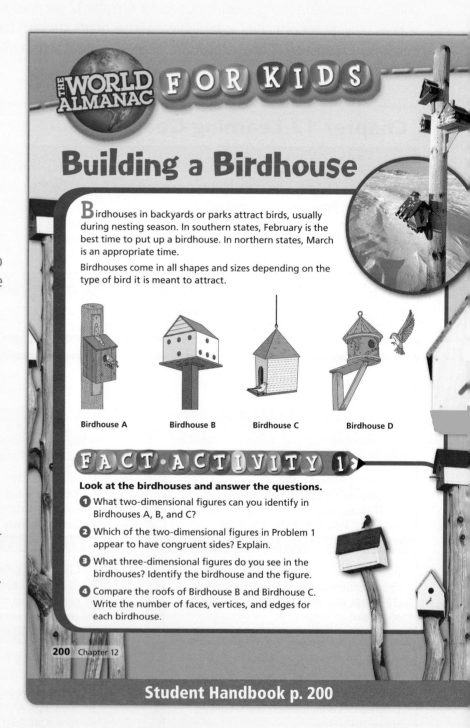

THE WORLD ALMANAC FOR KIDS

Building a Birdhouse

Birdhouses in backyards or parks attract birds, usually during nesting season. In southern states, February is the best time to put up a birdhouse. In northern states, March is an appropriate time.

Birdhouses come in all shapes and sizes depending on the type of bird it is meant to attract.

Birdhouse A   Birdhouse B   Birdhouse C   Birdhouse D

FACT•ACTIVITY 1:

Look at the birdhouses and answer the questions.

❶ What two-dimensional figures can you identify in Birdhouses A, B, and C?

❷ Which of the two-dimensional figures in Problem 1 appear to have congruent sides? Explain.

❸ What three-dimensional figures do you see in the birdhouses? Identify the birdhouse and the figure.

❹ Compare the roofs of Birdhouse B and Birdhouse C. Write the number of faces, vertices, and edges for each birdhouse.

200 Chapter 12

Student Handbook p. 200

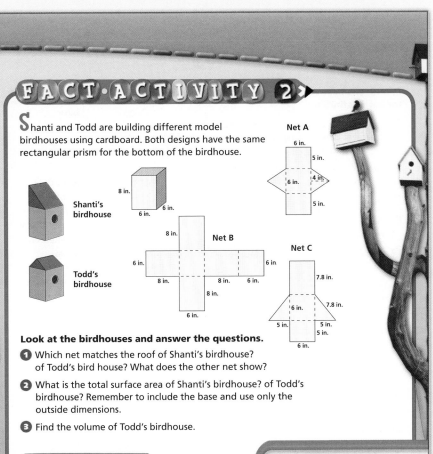

FACT·ACTIVITY 2

S hanti and Todd are building different model birdhouses using cardboard. Both designs have the same rectangular prism for the bottom of the birdhouse.

Net A

6 in.
5 in.
6 in. | 4 in.
6 in.
5 in.

8 in.
Shanti's birdhouse
6 in.
6 in.

8 in.
Net B
6 in. | 6 in.
8 in. | 8 in. | 6 in.
8 in.
6 in.

Net C
7.8 in.
6 in. | 7.8 in.
5 in. | 5 in.
6 in.

Todd's birdhouse

Look at the birdhouses and answer the questions.

❶ Which net matches the roof of Shanti's birdhouse? of Todd's bird house? What does the other net show?

❷ What is the total surface area of Shanti's birdhouse? of Todd's birdhouse? Remember to include the base and use only the outside dimensions.

❸ Find the volume of Todd's birdhouse.

CHAPTER PROJECT

You are going to design a birdhouse and then make a model which is half its actual size.

- Sketch a three-dimensional model and label its sides with measurements. Then draw a net with each side half of the given dimensions in the drawing.
- Trace the net on manila cardboard, cut it out, then fold and tape the sides together. Decorate your model.
- Find the surface area of the model.

FACT·ACTIVITY 2

❶ Shanti: Net C; Todd: Net A; Net B is the net of the bottom or base of both birdhouses.

❷ Shanti: $106.8 + 228 = 334.8 \approx 335$ sq in.; Todd: $84 + 228 = 312$ sq in.

❸ Volume of Todd's birdhouse roof:
$(\frac{1}{2} \times 6 \times 4) \times 6 = 72$;
bottom: $(6 \times 6) \times 8 = 288$;
Volume $= 72 + 288 = 360$ cu in.

CHAPTER PROJECT

Possible answer:

The design can be as simple as a rectangular prism. The possible model shown is a pyramid.

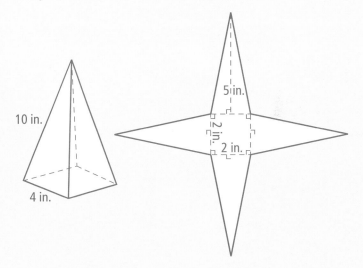

Model surface area:

$(2 \times 2) + 4 (\frac{1}{2} \times 2 \times 5) = 24$ sq

To reinforce vocabulary concepts, invite students to complete the vocabulary activities on pp. 212–213 of the **Student Handbook.** Encourage students to record their answers in their math journals.

Many responses are possible.

⓫ Possible response: A cone has one *base* that is a circle. A cylinder has two parallel *bases,* both of which are congruent circles.

⓬ Possible response: First, find the area of the triangular *base* and then multiply that by the *height* of the prism. For a triangular prism, the *height* is the length of the rectangular *face.*

⓭ Possible response: For a triangular prism, first find the area of each triangular *base* by multiplying $\frac{1}{2}$ *base* × *height.* Next, find the area of each rectangular face by multiplying length × width. Then add the areas, *base* + *base* + *face* + *face* + *face,* to find the surface area of the prism. For a rectangular prism, find the area of each *base* (length × width) and the area of each remaining *face* (length × width). Then add those areas to find the surface area of the prism.

Chapter 12 Vocabulary

Choose the best vocabulary term from Word List A for each definition.

Word List A

base
congruent
cubic units
edges
faces
height
length
parallel faces
perpendicular
polyhedron
prism
pyramid
square units
surface area
vertices
volume
width

❶ A(n) __?__ is a three-dimensional figure that has two congruent polygon-shaped bases and other faces that are all rectangles. **prism**

❷ The __?__ is the sum of the areas of all the surfaces of a three-dimensional figure. **surface area**

❸ Area is measured using __?__. **square units**

❹ The __?__ of a three-dimensional figure are line segments formed when two faces meet. **edges**

❺ The polygons that are flat surfaces of a three-dimensional figure are its __?__. **faces**

❻ The __?__ of a three-dimensional figure are the points where three or more of its edges intersect. **vertices**

❼ A three-dimensional figure with flat faces that are polygons is called a(n) __?__. **polyhedron**

❽ A(n) __?__ is a three-dimensional figure with a polygon base and faces that are triangles that meet at a common vertex. **pyramid**

Complete each analogy using the best term from Word List B.

Word List B

base
cone
sphere
volume

❾ Cylinder is to __?__ as prism is to pyramid. **cone**

❿ Banana is to banana peel as __?__ is to surface area. **volume**

Talk Math

Discuss with a partner what you have learned about three-dimensional figures. Use the vocabulary terms *base, faces,* and *height.*

⓫ How can you tell the difference between a cone and a cylinder?

⓬ How can you find the volume of a triangular prism?

⓭ How can you find the surface area of a prism?

212 Chapter 12

Student Handbook p. 212

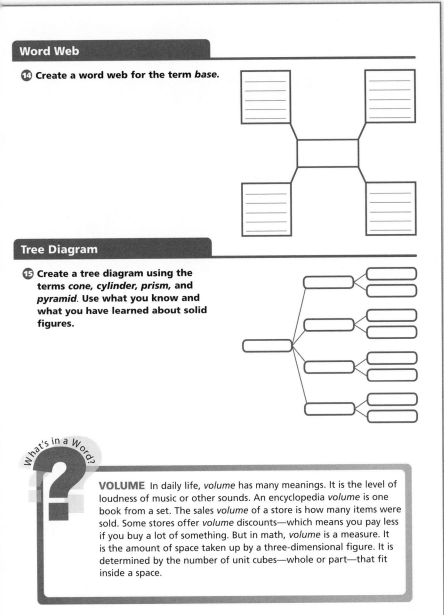

Word Web

14 Create a word web for the term *base*.

Tree Diagram

15 Create a tree diagram using the terms *cone, cylinder, prism,* and *pyramid*. Use what you know and what you have learned about solid figures.

What's in a Word?

VOLUME In daily life, *volume* has many meanings. It is the level of loudness of music or other sounds. An encyclopedia *volume* is one book from a set. The sales *volume* of a store is how many items were sold. Some stores offer *volume* discounts—which means you pay less if you buy a lot of something. But in math, *volume* is a measure. It is the amount of space taken up by a three-dimensional figure. It is determined by the number of unit cubes—whole or part—that fit inside a space.

Chapter 12 **213**

Student Handbook p. 213

14 Many answers are possible. One example is provided.

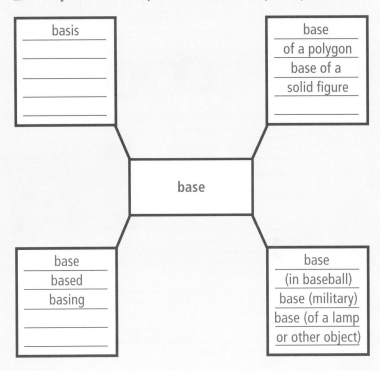

15 Many answers are possible. One example is provided.

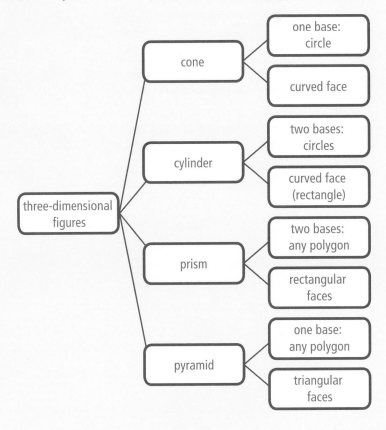

Games

Volume Builder in **Lesson 12.6** provides an opportunity for students to practice estimating and finding the volume of a rectangular prism. *Surface Area Builder* in **Lesson 12.7** provides an opportunity for students to practice estimating and finding the surface area of a rectangular prism. These games can be found on pp. 214–215 of the ***Student Handbook.***

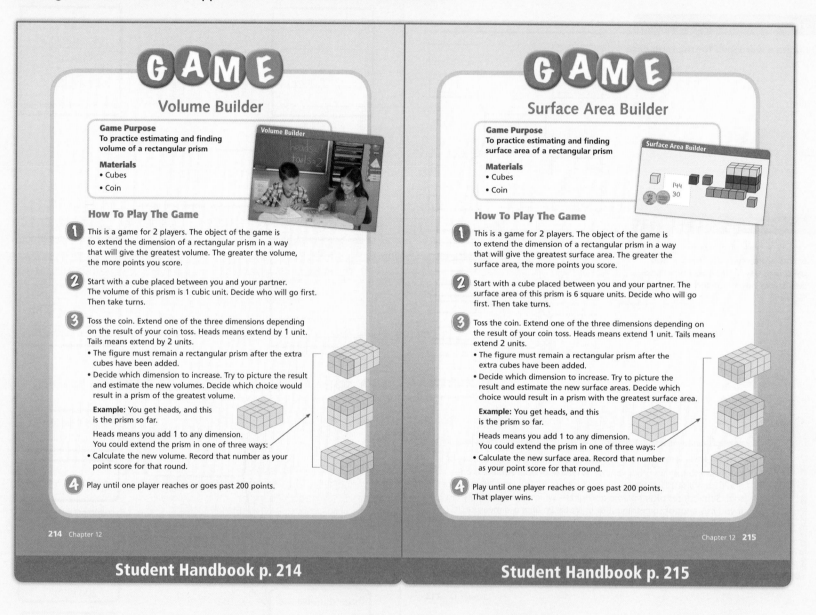

GAME

Volume Builder

Game Purpose
To practice estimating and finding volume of a rectangular prism

Materials
• Cubes
• Coin

How To Play The Game

1 This is a game for 2 players. The object of the game is to extend the dimension of a rectangular prism in a way that will give the greatest volume. The greater the volume, the more points you score.

2 Start with a cube placed between you and your partner. The volume of this prism is 1 cubic unit. Decide who will go first. Then take turns.

3 Toss the coin. Extend one of the three dimensions depending on the result of your coin toss. Heads means extend by 1 unit. Tails means extend by 2 units.

• The figure must remain a rectangular prism after the extra cubes have been added.

• Decide which dimension to increase. Try to picture the result and estimate the new volumes. Decide which choice would result in a prism of the greatest volume.

Example: You get heads, and this is the prism so far.

Heads means you add 1 to any dimension. You could extend the prism in one of three ways:

• Calculate the new volume. Record that number as your point score for that round.

4 Play until one player reaches or goes past 200 points.

214 Chapter 12

Student Handbook p. 214

GAME

Surface Area Builder

Game Purpose
To practice estimating and finding surface area of a rectangular prism

Materials
• Cubes
• Coin

How To Play The Game

1 This is a game for 2 players. The object of the game is to extend the dimension of a rectangular prism in a way that will give the greatest surface area. The greater the surface area, the more points you score.

2 Start with a cube placed between you and your partner. The surface area of this prism is 6 square units. Decide who will go first. Then take turns.

3 Toss the coin. Extend one of the three dimensions depending on the result of your coin toss. Heads means extend 1 unit. Tails means extend 2 units.

• The figure must remain a rectangular prism after the extra cubes have been added.

• Decide which dimension to increase. Try to picture the result and estimate the new surface areas. Decide which choice would result in a prism with the greatest surface area.

Example: You get heads, and this is the prism so far.

Heads means you add 1 to any dimension. You could extend the prism in one of three ways:

• Calculate the new surface area. Record that number as your point score for that round.

4 Play until one player reaches or goes past 200 points. That player wins.

Chapter 12 215

Student Handbook p. 215

Challenge

The Challenge activity *The Ever Changing Volume* challenges students to experiment to find the dimensions of a box with the greatest area. This activity can be found on p. 216 of the *Student Handbook.*

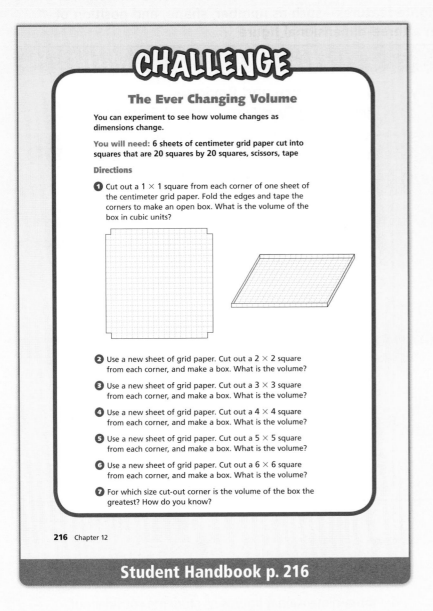

Student Handbook p. 216

❶ 18 × 18 × 1 = 324 cubic units

❷ 16 × 16 × 2 = 512 cubic units

❸ 14 × 14 × 3 = 588 cubic units

❹ 12 × 12 × 4 = 576 cubic units

❺ 10 × 10 × 5 = 500 cubic units

❻ 8 × 8 × 6 = 384 cubic units

❼ 3 × 3; Possible answer: boxes made from sheets with cut-out corners smaller than 3 × 3 have less volume. Boxes made from sheets with cut-out corners greater than 3 × 3 have less volume. So, it makes sense that a cut-out corner of 3 × 3 will give a box with the greatest volume.

Lesson Planner

STUDENT OBJECTIVES
- To connect shapes in nets to faces on three-dimensional figures
- To investigate features—such as number, shape, and position of faces—on a three-dimensional figure

1 Daily Activities (TG p. 973)

| Open-Ended Problem Solving/Headline Story | Skills Practice and Review— Reviewing Two-Dimensional Figures |

2 Teach and Practice (TG pp. 974–979)

	MATERIALS
(A) **Reading the Student Letter** (TG pp. 974–975)	• TR: Activity Masters, AM101–AM126
(B) **Making Three-Dimensional Figures** (TG pp. 976–977)	• scissors
(C) **Describing Faces** (TG p. 978)	• tape
(D) **Relating Two-Dimensional Nets and Three-Dimensional Figures** (TG p. 979)	• 📖 LAB pp. 233–234 • 📖 SH p. 199

3 Differentiated Instruction (TG p. 980)

Leveled Problem Solving (TG p. 980)	Practice Book P95
Intervention Activity (TG p. 980)	Extension Book E95
Extension Activity (TG p. 980)	Spiral Review Book SR95
Social Studies Connection (TG p. 970)	

Lesson Notes

About the Lesson

In this first lesson, students fold two-dimensional "nets" to construct three-dimensional figures whose faces are all polygons. Other three-dimensional figures, like the cone, cylinder, and sphere, do not have polygons as faces. Three-dimensional figures whose faces are all polygons have a special name: polyhedra (or polyhedrons). Students will use the three-dimensional figures they have made throughout the chapter. This lesson focuses on the faces of the three-dimensional figures as students consider not only the shapes of the faces, but other characteristics such as congruence, parallelism, and perpendicularity. The process of creating the nets themselves and the curiosity, comparison, and discussions that follow naturally as students cut, fold, and see the three-dimensional figures take shape all contribute to the learning that students will do in this and later lessons.

Developing Mathematical Language

Vocabulary: edges, faces, vertices

The purpose of specialized vocabulary is to clarify, not complicate, communication. The word "sides" was clear when we were talking only about two-dimensional figures. But when we casually talk about the "sides" of a cube, we probably mean the squares, not the line segments (which are the "sides" of the squares). In a room, the walls meet at a corner, but the word corner also refers to the point at which walls and floor meet. In three-dimensional geometry, we select new vocabulary that has only one meaning: *faces, edges,* and *vertices.*

Review the terms *faces, edges,* and *vertices* with students.

Beginning On the board, list the vocabulary terms, and draw a cube. Have students take turns pointing to a part of the cube and identifying the corresponding term.

Intermediate Show students two-dimensional and three-dimensional figures. Have students work in small groups to list and define the vocabulary terms that apply to two-dimensional figures, and then list and define the terms that apply to three-dimensional figures.

Advanced Have students work in small groups. One student secretly chooses a term from the vocabulary list. The other students in the group take turns asking yes or no questions until they correctly identify the secret term.

Open-Ended Problem Solving

Encourage students to picture the situation, and come up with good questions. How long might the ant's first edge be? Does the answer depend on which corner the ant starts at? What is the longest/shortest total trip? What is the longest three-segment trip?

 Headline Story

> **A cereal box measures 10 in. by 7 in. by $2\frac{1}{2}$ in. An ant starts at one corner of the box and crawls along the edges of the box. She never wanders away from the edges and never walks along an edge that she's already been on. After a while, she stops and rests at a corner. What can you say?**

Possible responses: The shortest walk she could have taken is $2\frac{1}{2}$ inches. Her very first edge could have been $2\frac{1}{2}$ inches, 7 inches, or 10 inches. The box has 12 edges, but she can't walk along all of them.

Skills Practice and Review

Reviewing Two-Dimensional Figures

Show one of the uncut AM101–AM126 Nets A–Z and ask students how many different faces appear in the net. If students answer with the total number of faces, mention that some of them are congruent—the same as others—and you are asking how many *different* faces there are. Net C, for example, has 5 faces, but four of them are congruent, so it has only two different faces. Net A has four faces, all triangles, but two are congruent, so it has only three different faces.

Continue discussing the shapes on various nets, so that students review vocabulary such as: triangle, square, non-square rectangle, non-rectangular parallelogram, trapezoid, pentagon, and congruent.

A Reading the Student Letter

NCTM Standards 3, 6, 7, 8, 9, 10

Purpose To explore the relationship between two-dimensional nets and three-dimensional figures and to introduce volume and surface area of three-dimensional figures

Introduce Have students read the Student Letter and briefly consider the questions. As students offer tentative answers, ask for enough clarity to make sure you and the class understand what they are saying, but don't worry about greater precision or correct answers. Students will learn much more about how two-dimensional nets and three-dimensional figures are related and about the volume and surface area of three-dimensional figures in future lessons in this chapter. This letter is designed to spur their interest and curiosity.

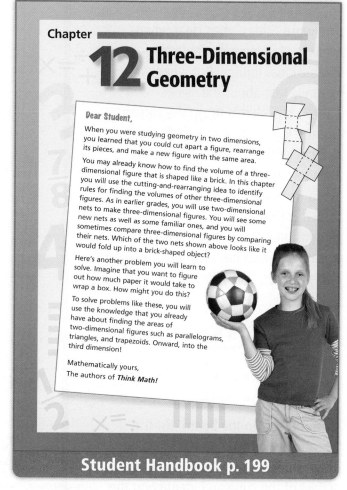

Student Handbook p. 199

Task Have students work with partners to try to describe as precisely and thoroughly as they can, the differences between the two nets, and the differences they might expect to see between the **two three-dimensional figures made from the nets.** Encourage them to think about the shapes of faces, how many of each kind, how many total...

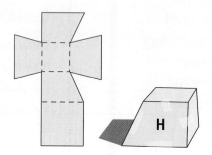

Talk Math After students have had an opportunity to discuss with their partners, follow with a class discussion.

❷ How are these two nets the same? How are they different? Possible answer: Each net is made of six polygons, which will become six faces of the three-dimensional figure when we fold it up. One net's faces are all rectangles. We think that will be shaped like a brick when it is folded. The other net has two squares, one smaller than the other, and four trapezoids. Two of the trapezoids look like they might be congruent. We couldn't picture anything it could be, but it certainly can't be a regular brick because not all of the angles are right angles.

Part of the reason for having unusual shapes in the Student Letter and the next activity is to build curiosity, and also to provide some contrast with the shapes children need to learn to identify. One cannot completely understand what a prism is without seeing things that are almost prisms, but not quite.

B **Making Three-Dimensional Figures**

Materials

- For the teacher: one of the nets from AM101–AM126 on cardstock (partly cut out to use for the demonstration), scissors, tape
- For each student: one of the nets from AM101–AM126 on cardstock, scissors, tape

NCTM Standards 3, 7, 8, 10

Purpose To assemble a three-dimensional figure from a two-dimensional net

Introduce It can be useful for everyone for you to review the process of cutting out nets, folding them, and taping the edges to make three-dimensional figures. The demonstration goes best if your own demonstration net is already partly cut out leaving one or two "tight" corners yet to cut.

As you cut, fold, and tape the net to form a three-dimensional figure, share these tips with your students as you demonstrate:

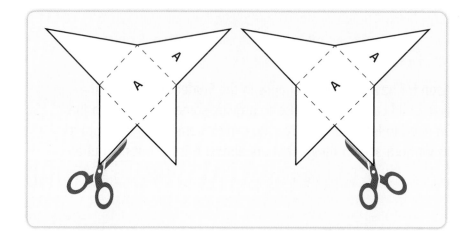

- To cut "tight" angles neatly, don't try to turn the scissors at the inside corner of the angle; cut toward the vertex along both sides of the angle.
- To make neat folds, it is often helpful to place the fold line of the net over the straight edge of a desk or counter and press to make an initial crease. Creasing against a ruler is also helpful.
- Tape neatly, so that the figure is easy to recognize. Small pieces of tape often work best.
- Taping can sometimes be hard, especially with the final edges, when one can't get one's fingers inside the figure to push against the tape to make it secure. Sometimes a pencil tucked in at an open vertex will help. Also, not all edges need to be taped, as long as the three-dimensional figure stays together and is neat enough to describe.
- Each student will receive a net that will likely be different from everyone else's.
- Each page contains a large net to cut out and fold, and a small copy that will be used on the LAB page (Activity D). Have students write their names by the small copy so that they can keep track of which one is theirs. The small versions do not need to be cut out exactly and should be kept flat, not folded. Students do not need to write their names on the three-dimensional figures, as they will belong to a class collection.
- Students should cut along the solid lines and fold along the dashed lines, just as you did.
- Students should fold so that the letter label stays on the outside, making the three-dimensional figures easy to refer to.

Use with Lesson Activity Book pp. 233–234.

Give each student one of the cardstock Activity Masters AM101–AM126 Nets A–Z and scissors. They can share the tape.

Task **Ask students to cut out the nets and assemble their three-dimensional figures.** Those who finish early can do a second three-dimensional figure. The class will need one of each of the twenty-six three-dimensional figure in its collection—that is, one three-dimensional figure from each net supplied. It does not matter if some three-dimensional figures are duplicated.

Talk Math As the students are cutting, and before they fold and tape to make their three-dimensional figures, you may want to circulate and ask individuals questions such as these.

❷ What two-dimensional figures are in your net? Answers will vary, depending on the net.

❷ Which figures in your net appear to be congruent? Answers will vary, depending on the net.

❷ What do you think your three-dimensional figure will look like? Answers will vary, depending on the net.

This discussion will be continued in Activity C when students relate the two-dimensional figures in the nets to the faces on the three-dimensional figures they have made.

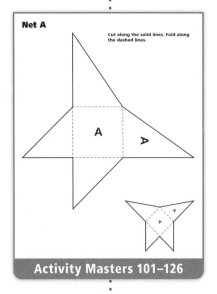

Net A

Cut along the solid lines. Fold along the dashed lines.

Activity Masters 101–126

Materials

- For each student: the solid he or she assembled in Activity B

NCTM Standards 3, 7, 8, 10

 Ongoing Assessment

- Do students correctly identify the number, shape, and position of the faces on a three-dimensional figure?

Differentiated Instruction

Basic Level To check for understanding of parallel and perpendicular, a quick game of Simon says may be useful.

C Describing Faces

Purpose To determine the number, shape, and position of faces in a three-dimensional figure

Introduce Three-dimensional figures can be described in many ways, and the next few lessons will be devoted to the features that can be described. In this activity, students will focus on the number, type, and positioning of *faces* (the squares, triangles, or other polygons that "surround" the insides of a three-dimensional figure). In the next lesson, students will count *edges* (the seams along which two faces meet at a fold line were taped), and *vertices* (the "corners" where more than two faces meet at a point). This vocabulary may be familiar to many students, but probably bears review. Students generally learn new vocabulary fastest when it is just used in context. (See Developing Mathematical Language for a note on these terms.)

Task **Approach the teaching of the word *face* by asking students to raise their three-dimensional figure in the air if it has at least one triangular *face*.** Context should make it clear what *face* refers to. Continue with other shapes such as parallelograms and trapezoids, each time re-using the term *face* as if they already understand (and many will, as this term has been encountered in earlier grades). You might say something like, "Hold up your three-dimensional figure if it appears to have at least one rectangular face." (Using the word "appears" acknowledges that we agree on the characteristics we're looking for, but that the actual figures may not be those shapes due to imprecision in construction, or even in the original drawings.)

Ask students to hold up three-dimensional figures that appear to have congruent faces (naming specific kinds of congruent faces if you'd like).

Ask for a show of three-dimensional figures that have at least one pair of faces that appear to be perpendicular to each other.

Finally, ask students to hold up three-dimensional figures that appear to have at least one pair of parallel faces. Students might try setting various faces of their three-dimensional figures on a flat surface to see if another face appears level, a "test" for parallel faces that they have likely performed in earlier grades.

🗨 Talk Math

❷ Using your hands, what do two faces that are perpendicular look like? One hand meets the other hand at a right angle where the two hands touch.

❷ Using your hands, what do two faces that are parallel look like? Explain how you know. The two hands are held the same distance apart; Possible answer: The two faces look like they are always the same distance apart and that is the definition of parallel.

For the next activity, students will need their small copies of the nets, but not the three-dimensional figures, so collect the figures now for use in later lessons.

Use with Lesson Activity Book pp. 233–234.

Relating Two-Dimensional Nets and Three-Dimensional Figures LAB pp. 233–234

Purpose To describe the faces of a three-dimensional figure

NCTM Standards 3, 7, 8, 9, 10

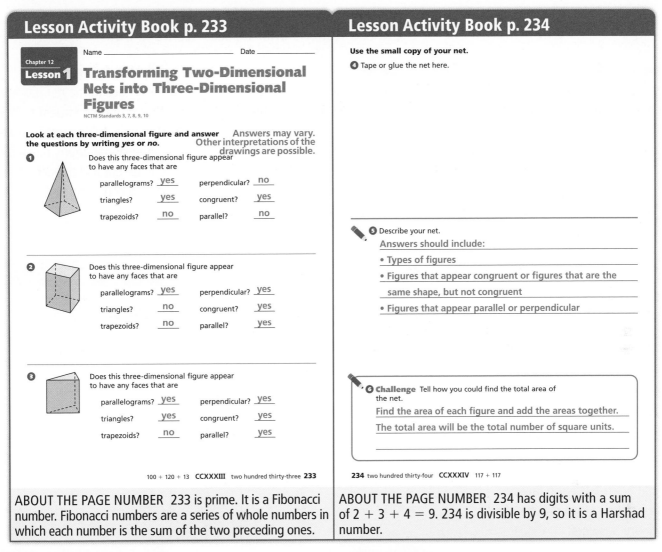

Lesson Activity Book p. 233

Name _____ Date _____

Chapter 12
Lesson 1 **Transforming Two-Dimensional Nets into Three-Dimensional Figures**
NCTM Standards 3, 7, 8, 9, 10

Look at each three-dimensional figure and answer the questions by writing *yes* or *no*.
Answers may vary. Other interpretations of the drawings are possible.

1 Does this three-dimensional figure appear to have any faces that are

parallelograms? yes   perpendicular? no

triangles? yes   congruent? yes

trapezoids? no   parallel? no

2 Does this three-dimensional figure appear to have any faces that are

parallelograms? yes   perpendicular? yes

triangles? no   congruent? yes

trapezoids? no   parallel? yes

3 Does this three-dimensional figure appear to have any faces that are

parallelograms? yes   perpendicular? yes

triangles? yes   congruent? yes

trapezoids? no   parallel? yes

100 + 120 + 13   CCXXXIII   two hundred thirty-three **233**

Lesson Activity Book p. 234

Use the small copy of your net.

4 Tape or glue the net here.

5 Describe your net.
Answers should include:
• Types of figures
• Figures that appear congruent or figures that are the same shape, but not congruent
• Figures that appear parallel or perpendicular

6 Challenge Tell how you could find the total area of the net.
Find the area of each figure and add the areas together.
The total area will be the total number of square units.

234 two hundred thirty-four   CCXXXIV   117 + 117

ABOUT THE PAGE NUMBER 233 is prime. It is a Fibonacci number. Fibonacci numbers are a series of whole numbers in which each number is the sum of the two preceding ones.

ABOUT THE PAGE NUMBER 234 has digits with a sum of 2 + 3 + 4 = 9. 234 is divisible by 9, so it is a Harshad number.

Teaching Notes for LAB page 233

Have students work on the LAB pages independently.

On LAB page 233, students look at pictures of three-dimensional figures to determine features of their faces. Drawings of three-dimensional figures are subject to viewer interpretation, and students may come up with different answers, particularly when trying to decide if the three-dimensional figures have any perpendicular or parallel faces.

Teaching Notes for LAB page 234

Students will need their small copies of the nets for this page.

Students describe their nets. They've written descriptions like these in earlier years, but each year's goal is to increase the detail of description and the precision and clarity of language. Encourage students to write not only what types of figures make up their net, but also how many of them, and whatever other features they think may help someone distinguish their net from other nets.

Challenge Problem The challenge problem asks students to think about finding the total area of a net.

Reflect and Summarize the Lesson

Write Math

How are the figures in a net related to the faces in a three-dimensional figure? Possible answer: A net is a pattern that can be folded to make a three-dimensional figure. The figures in the net are the faces of the three-dimensional figure.

Leveled Problem Solving

Mary is creating a three-dimensional figure from a net. Her net will fold into one of the three-dimensional figures we have built.

❶ Basic Level

Every face in the net is a triangle. Which three-dimensional figure could she be building? Figure F, M, or T

❷ On Level

The net has exactly two congruent scalene triangles. Which three-dimensional figure could she be building? Figure O or S

❸ Above Level

Every face in the net has another face that is congruent to it. When the net is folded into a three-dimensional figure, these faces will be parallel to each other. Which could she be building? Figure B, D, E, Q, or X.

Intervention	Practice	Extension

Intervention

Activity Parallels

Have each student choose a figure from the class set of three-dimensional figures. Then have students chose two faces of the figure and use the palms of their hands to show the relationship between the two faces. Ask students to record their answers to these questions: What is the name of the three-dimensional figure? Are the faces you chose parallel? Have groups of students share answers.

Practice

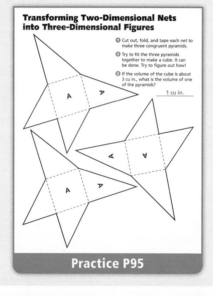

Practice P95

Extension

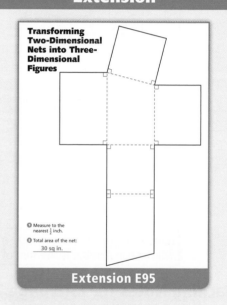

Extension E95

Spiral Review

Spiral Review Book page SR95 provides review of the following previously learned skills and concepts:

• finding the area of triangles and trapezoids

• using data in a table to find mode, median, and mean

You may wish to have students work with partners to complete the page.

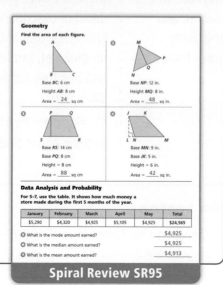

Spiral Review SR95

Extension Activity
Faces, Edges, and Vertices

Give each small group several of the three-dimensional figures made by the class.

Challenge each group to sort their figures into two groups. Have each group record the rule that they used to sort the figures.

Encourage them use at least one of the terms faces, edges, or vertices in the sorting rule.

Teacher's Notes 🍎

Daily Notes . . .

Quick Notes

More Ideas

Lesson 2 Describing Three-Dimensional Figures

NCTM Standards 2, 3, 6, 7, 8, 9, 10

Lesson Planner

STUDENT OBJECTIVES
- To classify three-dimensional figures by their attributes
- To describe and count the number of the faces, vertices, and edges of a three-dimensional figure

1 Daily Activities (TG p. 983)

Open-Ended Problem Solving/Headline Story	Skills Practice and Review— Describing the Shapes of Faces

2 Teach and Practice (TG pp. 984–988)

	MATERIALS
Ⓐ **Exploring Features of Three Dimensional Figures** (TG pp. 984–985)	• class set of three-dimensional figures from Lesson 12.1
Ⓑ **Describing Faces, Vertices, and Edges** (TG p. 986)	• 📖 LAB pp. 235–236
Ⓒ **Counting Faces, Vertices, and Edges** (TG p. 987)	• 📖 SH pp. 202–203

3 Differentiated Instruction (TG p. 989)

Leveled Problem Solving (TG p. 989)	Practice Book P96
Intervention Activity (TG p. 989)	Extension Book E96
Extension Activity (TG p. 989)	Spiral Review Book SR96

Lesson Notes

About the Lesson

In this lesson, students look more closely at specific three-dimensional figures and attributes such as congruent, parallel, and perpendicular faces, vertices, and edges. These observations will help them categorize and define polyhedrons in the next lesson.

Developing Mathematical Language

Vocabulary: congruent, edges, parallel faces, perpendicular faces, vertices

In this lesson, students will count *edges* and *vertices.* Some students may tumble the three-dimensional figure in their hands and lose track of what they have already counted. Show them how to hold the figure by opposite *vertices* or opposite *edges.* They can then rotate their wrists rather than the figure to count all the parts.

Students will examine *faces,* determining whether two *faces* are *congruent* (the same size and shape). Students will also examine the relative positions of *faces.* Have them compare *perpendicular faces* to the right angles of a desk. Have them check for *parallel faces* by resting the three-dimensional figure on a flat surface and looking for other faces that are level.

Review the terms *edges* and *vertices* with students.

Beginning Have students point to *edges* and *vertices* they see in the room, such as the *edge* and corner of the teacher's desk or of the door. Have them identify the shapes of the faces.

Intermediate Have students list familiar objects that have *edges* and *vertices.* Have them describe the *edges* and *vertices* of each. Have them identify the shapes of the *faces.*

Advanced Challenge students to identify familiar objects that have no *edges* or *vertices.*

1 Daily Activities

Open-Ended Problem Solving

Hold up two three-dimensional figures of similar size (from the classroom set). Read the Headline Story to the students. Encourage them to find more than one way to solve the problem.

 Headline Story

Suppose you have two three-dimensional figures of similar size. How might you decide which required more paper to build?

Possible responses: Measure the faces and find their areas. Unfold and compare the sizes of the faces. Weigh them and compare weights (take any tape off first). Unfold and place the nets on top of each other.

Skills Practice and Review

Describing the Shapes of Faces

Distribute the class set of three-dimensional figures to students. Keeping the pace lively and fun, pick students and ask questions like these.

- How many triangular (or trapezoidal or parallelogram-shaped) faces does your figure have?
- Are any of the faces parallelograms (or triangles)?
- How many *differently* shaped faces make up your figure?
- Do any of the faces appear to be congruent?
- Do any faces appear to be similar?

Or, you might try involving all students at once by asking, Who has a three-dimensional figure

- with at least two different faces?
- with only parallelogram-shaped faces?
- that appears to have at least 2 congruent faces?
- with a vertex at which *four* faces meet?

small groups 20 MIN

A Exploring Features of Three-Dimensional Figures

Materials

• For the teacher: class set of three-dimensional figures from Lesson 12.1

NCTM Standards 3, 6, 7, 8, 9, 10

Purpose To classify three-dimensional figures by their attributes

Introduce Split your class into small groups and give each group a copy of Explore: Three-Dimensional Figure Search. On this page, students will work together to find the three-dimensional figures that match each set of attributes. You might have each group work with only a subset of the three-dimensional figures at a time. For instance, you could split the three-dimensional figures into two sets and have half the groups work with one set and half with the other. You could also have each group work with a few three-dimensional figures at a time, rotating through stations or trading sets. Students need not look at all the three-dimensional figures.

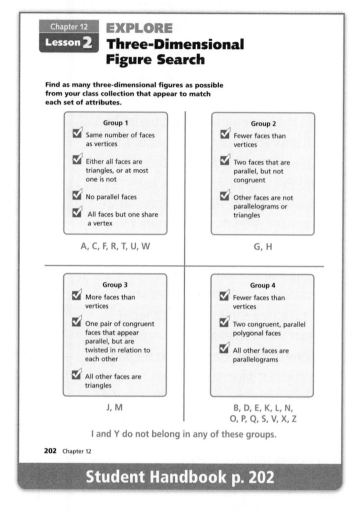

Student Handbook p. 202

Before beginning the task, hold up one of the three-dimensional figures and have volunteers first describe the faces of the three-dimensional figure, then the vertices of the three-dimensional figure, and finally the edges of the three-dimensional figure. This discussion will help ensure that students understand the meanings of these words before they begin the task.

Task **Have students work in small groups to complete Explore: Three-Dimensional Figure Search.** In this task they work together to find the three-dimensional figures that match each of the four sets of attributes listed on the page.

After students have completed the Explore page, use their results to place the three-dimensional figures into four groups as described on the page. At your option, you might label each group with an index card—1, 2, 3, and 4. Although some students may recognize the three-dimensional figures in Group 1 as pyramids and Group 4 as prisms, the focus here is seeing the similarities and differences according to attributes. The three-dimensional figures in Group 2 are like pyramids, with their "top part" cut off. Students don't need names for these "truncated pyramids" or the three-dimensional figures in

Use with Lesson Activity Book pp. 235–236.

Group 3 (called "antiprisms"). (Students who do the extension page in **Lesson 12.3** will be introduced to the term antiprism, but just as a way of referring to these interesting objects.)

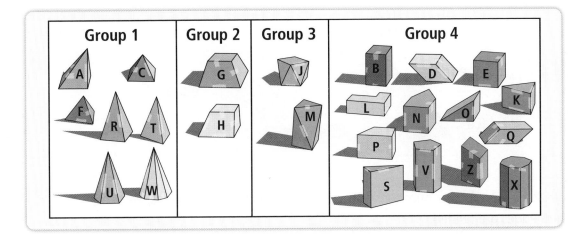

🗨 **Talk Math** Ask questions similar to the following to help students to see similarities and differences. Encourage them to hold up specific three-dimensional figures and point out the attributes, rather than respond by reading the attributes from the page. Although there are many possible responses, a few examples are provided

❷ What is the same about the three-dimensional figures in Groups 2 and 4? Possible answer: They have one pair of faces that seem parallel and then some other faces. **What attributes are different?** Possible answer: The faces that look parallel are not congruent for the three-dimensional figures in Group 2. The other faces on the three-dimensional figures in Group 2 are trapezoids. Group 4 has at least one pair of "congruent" parallel faces, and the other faces are parallelograms (usually rectangles).

❷ Compare the three-dimensional figures in Group 3 with those in Group 4. Possible answer: The three-dimensional figures in both groups have pairs of faces that seem parallel and congruent. In Group 3, the other faces are triangles. In Group 4 the other faces are parallelograms.

❷ How are the three-dimensional figures in Group 1 different from those in Group 4? Possible answer: The three-dimensional figures in Group 1 have no parallel faces, but the three-dimensional figures in Group 4 have at least one pair of parallel faces.

❷ Compare the three-dimensional figures in Group 1 with the three-dimensional figures in Group 3. Possible answer: Both are made mostly of triangles. The three-dimensional figures in Group 1 have as many triangles as there are edges around the base, and all the triangles meet at the same one point at the top. The side faces of the three-dimensional figures in Group 3 have twice as many triangles as there are edges around the base.

Use with Lesson Activity Book pp. 235–236

Teacher Story

❝Sometimes my students lose track of which faces, vertices, or edges they already counted on their three-dimensional figures. I suggested that they use a marker or highlighter to mark each face (or vertex or edge) as they count. This really seemed to help!

I also found that, to count vertices, students found it helpful to set the three-dimensional figure flat on the table, or even on their hand, and *first* count the vertices that were touching that table, then count the rest. That helped them organize their counting. This even seemed to help some visualize the three-dimensional figure well enough to count vertices mentally!❞

B Describing Faces, Vertices, and Edges

- For the teacher: class set of three-dimensional figures from Lesson 12.1

NCTM Standards 3, 7, 8, 9, 10

Purpose To describe the faces, vertices, and edges of three-dimensional figures

Introduce Display the class set of three-dimensional figures from **Lesson 12.1.** Begin by reviewing the terms face, edge, and vertex by asking a volunteer to choose a three-dimensional figure, and point to one of its faces, one of its edges, and one of its vertices.

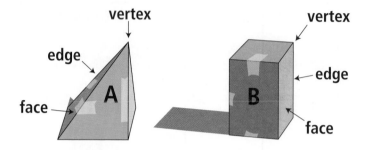

 **✓Ongoing Assessment**

- Do students correctly use the terms edge and face when referring to three-dimensional figures?

💬 **Talk Math** Ask questions such as these to focus on how faces, vertices, and edges are related.

❓ Describe edges in terms of faces. The edges are the lines along which the faces meet.

❓ Describe vertices in terms of faces. The vertices are the places where more than two faces meet at a point.

Task Ask volunteers to count the number of faces, vertices, and edges on three-dimensional figures as you hold them up. You may want to make a chart on the board to display the information.

Three-Dimensional Figure	Number of Faces	Number of Vertices	Number of Edges
A	5	5	8
B	6	8	12
C	5	5	8
D	6	8	12
E	6	8	12
F	4	4	6

Use with Lesson Activity Book pp. 235–236.

NCTM Standards 2, 3, 7, 8, 9, 10

Purpose To count the number of faces, vertices, and edges on a three-dimensional figure

---

Lesson Activity Book p. 235

Name _____ Date _____

Chapter 12
Lesson 2 **Describing Three-Dimensional Figures**
NCTM Standards 2, 3, 7, 8, 9, 10

❶ Choose a three-dimensional figure and record its letter here: _____

Describe the faces of your three-dimensional figure and tell if any faces appear to be *congruent, parallel,* or *perpendicular.*
Answers will vary.

❷ Complete the chart to show how many faces, vertices, and edges your three-dimensional figure has. **Answers will vary.**

Faces	
Vertices	
Edges	

Add the number of faces and vertices:

F + V = _____

From that sum, subtract the number of edges:

F + V − E = __2__

CCXXXV two hundred thirty-five **235**

Lesson Activity Book p. 236

❸ Find out what other students got as their answer for Problem 2. Are you surprised? Based on what you find out, write a sentence or two stating a possible conclusion about polyhedra.

When you add together the number of faces and vertices

and subtract the number of edges, you always get 2.

❹ Pick any prism. Choose one vertex of that prism. Count how many faces meet at that vertex.

A Is there any vertex of that prism at which a *different* number of faces meet?   no

B Would your answer be different if you chose a prism with a different base? Explain why.   no

A prism always has 3 faces meeting at each vertex.

❺ Pick any pyramid that has one non-triangular face. Choose one vertex of that pyramid. Count how many faces meet at that vertex.

A Is there any vertex of that pyramid at which a *different* number of faces meet?   yes

B Would your answer be different if you chose a pyramid with a different non-triangular base? Explain why.   no

For most of these, three faces meet at every vertex

but one.

❻ **Challenge** Sketch one of the three-dimensional figures you used on this page.
Sketches will vary.

236 two hundred thirty-six CCXXXVI 118 + 118

ABOUT THE PAGE NUMBER 235 is the sum of three consecutive primes (235 = 73 + 79 + 83) and the sum of 3 consecutive triangular numbers: (235 = 66 + 78 + 91)

ABOUT THE PAGE NUMBER The product of the digits (2 × 3 × 6 = 36) of 236 is the reverse of the sum of its prime factors (2 + 2 + 59 = 63).

Teaching Notes for LAB page 235

Students should work independently.

Each student will need a three-dimensional figure from the class collection.

Encourage students to be very specific when describing the faces of their three-dimensional figures. You might suggest they say how many of each kind of face there are and also the number of vertices and edges. Students might also describe how many faces meet at each vertex.

After writing the description of the three-dimensional figure's faces, students find the number of faces, plus the number of vertices, minus the number of edges.

Teaching Notes for LAB page 236

In Problem 3, students compare their results with the results obtained by other students. It may surprise students to learn that although they have very different answers for the *numbers* of faces, vertices, and edges on their three-dimensional figures, the computation F + V − E will always be 2, no matter what the polyhedron is. They are then asked to draw a conclusion from what they've observed. Well-written answers may include: what they did (counted vertices, faces, edges, performed a particular computation); what they observed (the inputs vary, but the results don't vary); and a general statement (maybe this is true for all polyhedrons).

Problems 4 and 5 ask students to make a generalization about the number of faces that meet at any vertex of a prism or a pyramid. You may want to suggest to some students that they investigate the "other" polyhedra and see what is true of them.

Challenge Problem The Challenge Problem asks students to try to sketch a three dimensional figure. This is a *very* difficult task for most people.

Write Math

Describe edges and vertices in terms of the faces of a three-dimensional figure.
The edges are the lines along which the faces meet. The vertices are the places where more than two faces meet at a point.

Review Model

Refer students to Review Model: Faces, Vertices and Edges in the *Student Handbook* to see how to identify and count the faces, vertices, and edges on a three-dimensional figure.

✔ Check for Understanding

Three-Dimensional Figure	Number of Faces	Number of Vertices	Number of Edges
❶	6	8	12
❷	4	4	6
❸	8	12	18
❹	7	7	12

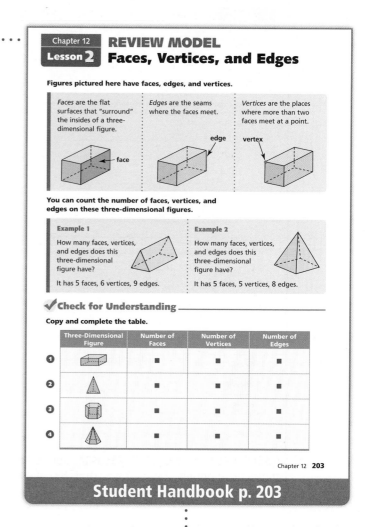

Student Handbook p. 203

Use with Lesson Activity Book pp. 235–236.

Leveled Problem Solving

Henri counts the number of faces and vertices on a three-dimensional figure from the class set. The three-dimensional figure has just one pentagonal face.

❶ Basic Level

How many faces does the three-dimensional figure have? Explain. 6 faces; 1 pentagon + 5 triangles = 6 faces

❷ On Level

How many vertices does the three-dimensional figure have? Explain. 6 vertices; 5 vertices for each vertex of the pentagon and 1 vertex where the triangles meet

❸ Above Level

Can you find the number of edges without counting them? Yes; F − E + V = 2; 12 − E = 2; E = 10

Intervention

Activity Edges

Have small groups use pencils to represent the edges of three-dimensional figures. Have one student create a two-dimensional figure. Then have the group discuss how many more pencils would be needed to complete a pyramid with that base. Then have them find the total number of pencils needed for all the edges of the pyramid.

Practice

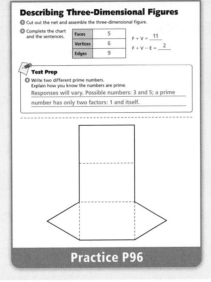

Practice P96

Extension

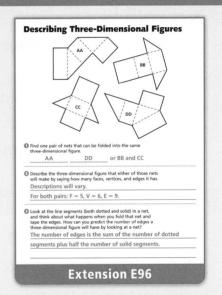

Extension E96

Spiral Review

Spiral Review Book page SR96 provides review of the following previously learned skills and concepts:

- using vertical records to find products of 2-digit factors
- applying problem solving strategy *look for a pattern*

You may wish to have students work with partners to complete the page.

Spiral Review SR96

Extension Activity
Faces and Vertices

Have students try to find three-dimensional figures from the class set that have more faces than vertices. Then challenge students to create another one like these, but with a pentagon or hexagon as the base.

Figures J and M both have more faces than vertices.

Students might construct the new polyhedron using toothpicks for short edges and or coffee stirrers for longer edges, and using marshmallows or gumdrops for the vertices.

Lesson 3 Sorting Three-Dimensional Figures

NCTM Standards 3, 7, 8, 9, 10

Lesson Planner

STUDENT OBJECTIVES
- To differentiate between polyhedra and other three-dimensional figures
- To define prisms and pyramids
- To distinguish cones, cylinders, and spheres from polyhedra

1 Daily Activities (TG p. 991)

Open-Ended Problem Solving/Headline Story	Skills Practice and Review— The Product of Three Numbers

2 Teach and Practice (TG pp. 992–997)

	MATERIALS
(A) **Sorting Three-Dimensional Figures** (TG pp. 992–993)	• TR: Activity Master, AM127
(B) **Defining Three-Dimensional Figures** (TG pp. 994–995)	• class set of three-dimensional figures from Lesson 12.1
(C) **Describing Three-Dimensional Figures** (TG p. 996)	• models of sphere, cylinder, and cone • 📖 LAB pp. 237–238 • 📖 SH p. 204

3 Differentiated Instruction (TG p. 998)

Leveled Problem Solving (TG p. 998)	Practice Book P97
Intervention Activity (TG p. 998)	Extension Book E97
Extension Activity (TG p. 998)	Spiral Review Book SR97
Literature Connection (TG p. 970)	

Lesson Notes

About the Lesson

In this lesson, students classify and define prisms, pyramids, cones, cylinders, and spheres based on their attributes. They distinguish between three-dimensional figures that are polyhedra and those that are not.

About the Mathematics

Though this lesson deals primarily with pyramids, prisms, cones, cylinders, and spheres, you can easily conceive of a wide variety of three-dimensional figures that do not fit into any of these categories.

We don't provide names for the many unfamiliar three-dimensional figures that students find in this lesson; one purpose of the lesson is to foster conversation about the various characteristics of these figures, conversation that could be cut short if names replaced the descriptions.

These three-dimensional figures give students opportunities to compare several kinds of figures that have two congruent and parallel "bases." Prisms have parallelograms (including rectangles) for all their remaining faces. Three-dimensional figures that are not prisms might have faces that are; triangles (Figures J and M) or trapezoids (Figure I) or even pentagons (Figure Y). Learning to analyze and compare is mathematically important. Correct vocabulary helps people communicate what they have analyzed.

Use with Lesson Activity Book pp. 237–238.

Developing Mathematical Language

Vocabulary: base, cone, cylinder, polyhedron, prism, pyramid, sphere

In this lesson, students describe *cylinders, cones, spheres, pyramids,* and *prisms* according to their attributes.

Polyhedron is the correct term for any three-dimensional figure whose faces are polygons. Students will need to distinguish between *polyhedra* and other solids that are not *polyhedra.*

Base is used in more than one way in mathematics. In two-dimensional geometry, it one of the parallel segments (or the length of that segment) in a parallelogram or trapezoid, or one side of a triangle. The definition of the *base* of a *polyhedron* is the face that determines the specific type of *prism* or *pyramid.*

Review the terms *base, cone, cylinder, prism,* and *pyramid* with students.

Beginning Select several *prisms* and *pyramids* from the class collection of three-dimensional figures. Have students point to each *base* and then name the polygon that identifies its shape.

Intermediate Have students identify common objects in the shape of a *cone, cylinder, prism,* and *pyramid.* Have them name the shape of the *base* or bases.

Advanced Have small groups discuss the similarities of *cones* and *pyramids* and of *cylinders* and *prisms.* Then have them discuss the similarities of *cones* and *cylinders* and of *prisms* and *pyramids.*

---

1 | Daily Activities

Open-Ended Problem Solving

Read the Headline Story to the students. Encourage students to use a model to find creative ways to answer the question.

 Headline Story

> A three-dimensional figure has 6 rectangular faces. Two edges are 1 inch long, two are 2 inches long, and one is 3 inches long. What can you figure out without measuring anything else?

Possible responses: All together, there are twelve edges: four are 1 in. long, four are 2 in. long, and four are 3 in. long. Two faces are 1 in. × 2 in., two are 1 in. × 3 in., and two are 2 in. × 3 in.

Skills Practice and Review

The Product of Three Numbers

In this quick drill, give students problems in which they must find the product of three numbers. This is a precursor to finding volume in the next lesson. You might give the problem orally and then call on a student at random to provide the answer.

This activity can be especially good practice if, by picking a useful order for the factors, students can simplify the multiplication. Choose problems that allow your students to find clever methods. Have students share their strategies as they solve the problems. Here are some suggested problems.

5 × 7 × 2 70	2 × 9 × 5 90	2 × 7 × 3 42
2 × 8 × 5 80	3 × 6 × 2 36	2 × 7 × 5 70
5 × 9 × 2 90	4 × 9 × 5 180	2 × 6 × 5 60
5 × 7 × 4 140	3 × 7 × 2 42	5 × 9 × 4 180

whole class **15 MIN**

Materials

- For the teacher: class set of three-dimensional figures from Lesson 12.1; models of sphere, cylinder, and cone

NCTM Standards 3, 7, 8, 9, 10

A Sorting Three-Dimensional Figures

Purpose To classify three-dimensional figures as pyramids, prisms, other polyhedra, and non-polyhedra

Introduce This initial activity helps students refresh their knowledge of pyramids, prisms, and other three-dimensional figures (including ones that are not polyhedra) from previous grades.

In the Task below, students will sort three-dimensional figures by identifying their attributes. Before they begin this sorting, group together a pyramid (such as Figure C), a prism (such as Figure B), a sphere, a cone, and a cylinder and ask students to briefly tell how these three-dimensional figures are alike and how they are different. Collectively, your students are likely to have names for all of these three-dimensional figures; if not, identify the ones they miss. Look for them to bring out at least the following ideas:

- All are three-dimensional figures.
- Spheres, cones, and cylinders are different from the others because they have no straight edges—they are not *polyhedra.* Your students might connect this term to *polygon. Poly* means "many." Polygons have many angles; polyhedra have many (polygon-shaped) faces.

Then to this group of five three-dimensional figures add the remaining polyhedra from the class collection (one each of Figures A–Z).

Concept Alert

Drawings of cones and cylinders *do* have "straight edges," but the three-dimensional objects themselves do not. It is more common in earlier grades, but some students still get distracted by this perception. This is especially important to remember on tests, which typically use pictures, rather than objects, as part of their questions.

Talk Math Give students a chance to investigate a few of the three-dimensional figures by posing these questions.

❓ Which of the three-dimensional figures do *not* have faces that are polygons? cylinder, cone, and sphere

❓ Which of the three-dimensional figures can be set so that one face lies flat on the table and another face is completely level at the top, parallel to the table top? Possible answer: all the prisms, some of the other polyhedra, and the cylinder

You might ask students to pick out some of the three-dimensional figures that they described in the answer to the question above. For some three-dimensional figures, the top will be level no matter how the three-dimensional figure is set on the table. For others, it depends how you place them: there may be only one position, or more than one, such that the top is parallel with the table. Some three-dimensional figures cannot lie on the table in any position and have a "level top." Looking for level tops is, for some students, the easiest way to test for parallel faces.

Task Invite students to help you sort all the three-dimensional figures into four categories: *Pyramids, Prisms, Other Polyhedra,* and *Non-polyhedral Three-Dimensional Figures.* You might designate these categories with labeled index cards or yarn circles. As the three-dimensional figures are sorted encourage discussion about how the three-dimensional figures in a given category are similar and how they are different. Begin with pyramids.

Use with Lesson Activity Book pp. 237–238.

- **Pyramids (Figures A, C, F, R, T, U, W):** Have students make one group of all the three-dimensional figures whose faces are polygons that don't have a level top in *any* position. Of the three-dimensional figures your class created, all the ones that have no parallel faces happen to be *pyramids:* one face can be any polygon, and the remaining faces are all triangles that meet at a single point. (See Developing Mathematical Language for more about *bases.*) You might want to ask what polygons form the bases of the various pyramids.

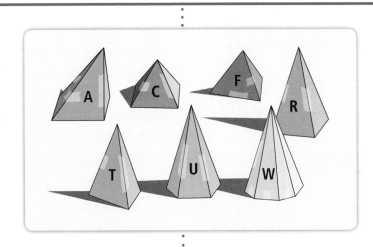

- **Prisms (Figures B, D, E, K, L, N, O, P, Q, S, V, X, Z):** The other three-dimensional figures in the class collection whose faces are polygons all *can* have a level top (parallel top and bottom) in at least one position. Ask students to find a way to set them on the table so that the parallel tops and bottoms are also *congruent* faces (the same size and shape) and all other faces are parallelograms. These congruent "top" and "bottom" faces are known as the *bases.* If all other faces are parallelograms (including rectangles and squares), the three-dimensional figure is called a *prism.* You might also note that the bases of a prism are always oriented in the same direction.

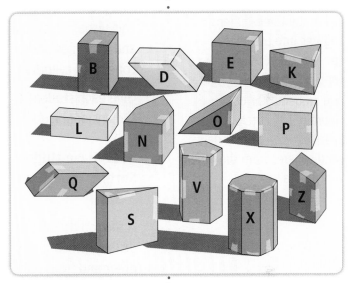

- **Other Polyhedra (Figures G, H, I, J, M, Y):** Some of these have parallel bases that are the same shape but different sizes, and they look a bit like pyramids with their tops cut off (Figures G and H). Two others (Figures J and M) have "side faces" that are all triangles, and their congruent bases are twisted with respect to one another. Figure I has congruent bases that are twisted with respect to each other, but the "side faces" are trapezoids. Figure Y is made entirely of pentagons and is ball-like without being a sphere.

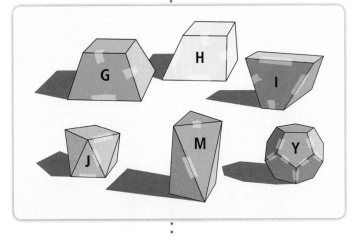

- **Non-polyhedral Figures (Models of cone, cylinder, sphere):** The cone, cylinder, and sphere belong in this group.

If possible, leave the three-dimensional figures in these groups for use during the next two activities.

In the next activity, students will use the examples in each category to define each type of three-dimensional figure more specifically.

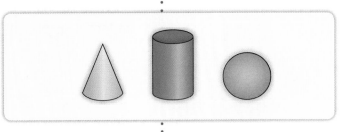

B Defining Three-Dimensional Figures

Purpose To distinguish cones, cylinders, and spheres from each other and from polyhedra

Introduce Begin by asking students to try this "thought experiment." Ask them to picture in their minds a rectangular prism with square bases. Now imagine that the square bases change to pentagons. You might hold up Figure V as an example. Then to hexagons . . . to octagons (Figure X) . . . to 20-sided bases . . . to 100-sided bases . . . to bases with a trillion sides! Ask a volunteer to describe how the three-dimensional figure would look. (It would look like a cylinder.)

Try a similar thought experiment beginning with a square pyramid (perhaps using Figure R as an example) then a pentagonal pyramid (Figure U), an octagonal pyramid (Figure W), and so on, with increasing numbers of sides until it begins to resemble a cone.

This visualization may help students see the similarities between cones and pyramids and between cylinders and prisms, but students will not define cones and cylinders mathematically at this point.

Give each student a copy of Activity Master 127: Sorting Three-Dimensional Figures.

Task Have students complete Activity Master 127: Sorting Three-Dimensional Figures together as a class.

Although the attributes listed help students to distinguish *cones, cylinders,* and *spheres* from each other and from polyhedra, students would need more sophisticated ideas and terms to define these three-dimensional figures.

You may wish to hold up the model of a sphere to help students visualize the second attribute listed for a sphere, "All points on its surface are the same distance from a single point." Students will have to imagine the point inside the ball. The idea of all points being the same distance from one central point is something students have seen before. On a flat surface, the circle is the only figure whose every point is the same distance from one central point. In three dimensions, the only such figure is the sphere. Students often see Figure Y as "ball-like" because it somewhat resembles a soccer-ball. Some may be able to picture that the vertices of this object are farther from its center than are the midpoints of its faces.

Materials

- For the teacher: class set of three-dimensional figures from Lesson 12.1; models of sphere, cone, and cylinder
- For each student: AM127

NCTM Standards 3, 7, 8, 9, 10

Ongoing Assessment

- Do students correctly sort all of the three-dimensional figures into pyramids, prisms, other polyhedra, and non-polyhedral figures?
- Do students correctly identify the differences between cones, cylinders, and spheres from the other polyhedra?

Sorting Three-Dimensional Figures

A ____ cylinder
  ☑ It has two parallel, congruent circular bases.
  ☑ It has another curved surface.

B ____ cone
  ☑ It has one circular base.
  ☑ It has another curved surface.

C ____ sphere
  ☑ It has no bases, edges, or vertices.
  ☑ All points on its surface are the same distance from a single point.

Polyhedra

D ____ pyramid
  ☑ One face may be any polygon, and all other faces are triangles.
  ☑ All faces but one share a vertex.
  ☑ It has the same number of vertices as faces.

E ____ prism
  ☑ It has two parallel, congruent, polygonal faces.
  ☑ All other faces are parallelograms.
  ☑ It has more vertices than faces.

Activity Master 127

Use with Lesson Activity Book pp. 237–238.

💬 **Talk Math**   After students match the attributes in Part D to the examples of pyramids and the attributes in Part E to prisms, ask the following questions.

❷ In a pyramid, how does the number of vertices compare to the number of faces? All the pyramids have the same number of vertices as faces.

❷ How would you define a pyramid? Possible answer: I would use the attributes on the activity master: one face may be any polygon, and all other faces are triangles, all of which meet at one vertex; it has the same number of vertices as faces.

❷ In a prism, how does the number of vertices compare to the number of faces? All the prisms have more vertices than faces.

❷ Are there three-dimensional figures that are not prisms that also have more vertices than faces? Explain. Yes; Figures G and H are not prisms but have more vertices than faces.

❷ How would you define a prism? Possible answer: I would use the attributes on the activity master: It has two parallel, congruent, polygonal faces; all other faces are parallelograms.

Possible Discussion

The attribute of having more vertices than faces is *not unique to prisms.* It is also true for Figures G and H in the "other polyhedrons" group, but it is *always true* for prisms. You may want to mention to your students that another way of saying this is that all prisms have this feature, but not all three-dimensional figures that have this feature are prisms.

Concept Alert

If necessary, remind students that although prisms *often* have rectangular faces (ignoring the bases), those "side faces" do not have to be rectangles, as long as they are at least parallelograms. Figure D is an example of a rectangular prism (or square prism) that has square bases and nonrectangular parallelograms for the other four faces.

Purpose To use attributes to describe three-dimensional figures

NCTM Standards 3, 7, 8, 9, 10

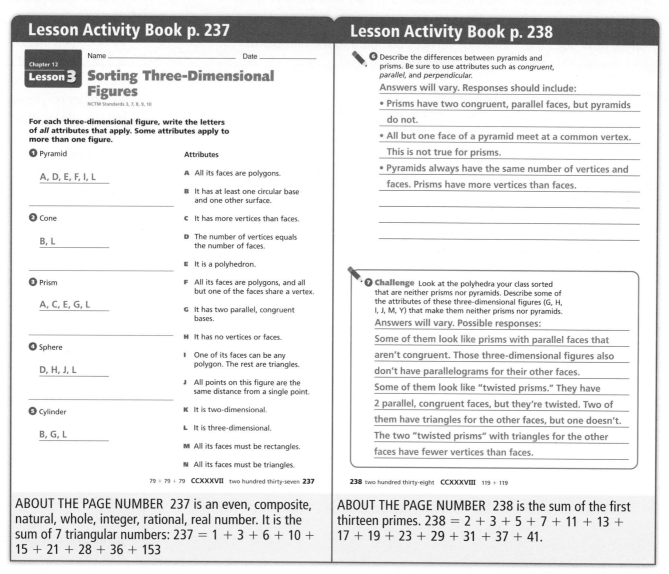

Lesson Activity Book p. 237

Name _____ Date _____

Chapter 12
Lesson 3 **Sorting Three-Dimensional Figures**
NCTM Standards 3, 7, 8, 9, 10

For each three-dimensional figure, write the letters of *all* attributes that apply. Some attributes apply to more than one figure.

1 Pyramid

A, D, E, F, I, L

2 Cone

B, L

3 Prism

A, C, E, G, L

4 Sphere

D, H, J, L

5 Cylinder

B, G, L

Attributes

A All its faces are polygons.

B It has at least one circular base and one other surface.

C It has more vertices than faces.

D The number of vertices equals the number of faces.

E It is a polyhedron.

F All its faces are polygons, and all but one of the faces share a vertex.

G It has two parallel, congruent bases.

H It has no vertices or faces.

I One of its faces can be any polygon. The rest are triangles.

J All points on this figure are the same distance from a single point.

K It is two-dimensional.

L It is three-dimensional.

M All its faces must be rectangles.

N All its faces must be triangles.

79 + 79 + 79 **CCXXXVII** two hundred thirty-seven **237**

ABOUT THE PAGE NUMBER 237 is an even, composite, natural, whole, integer, rational, real number. It is the sum of 7 triangular numbers: 237 = 1 + 3 + 6 + 10 + 15 + 21 + 28 + 36 + 153

Lesson Activity Book p. 238

6 Describe the differences between pyramids and prisms. Be sure to use attributes such as *congruent*, *parallel*, and *perpendicular*.

Answers will vary. Responses should include:

• Prisms have two congruent, parallel faces, but pyramids do not.

• All but one face of a pyramid meet at a common vertex. This is not true for prisms.

• Pyramids always have the same number of vertices and faces. Prisms have more vertices than faces.

7 Challenge Look at the polyhedra your class sorted that are neither prisms nor pyramids. Describe some of the attributes of these three-dimensional figures (G, H, I, J, M, Y) that make them neither prisms nor pyramids.

Answers will vary. Possible responses:

Some of them look like prisms with parallel faces that aren't congruent. Those three-dimensional figures also don't have parallelograms for their other faces.

Some of them look like "twisted prisms." They have 2 parallel, congruent faces, but they're twisted. Two of them have triangles for the other faces, but one doesn't. The two "twisted prisms" with triangles for the other faces have fewer vertices than faces.

238 two hundred thirty-eight **CCXXXVIII** 119 + 119

ABOUT THE PAGE NUMBER 238 is the sum of the first thirteen primes. 238 = 2 + 3 + 5 + 7 + 11 + 13 + 17 + 19 + 23 + 29 + 31 + 37 + 41.

Teaching Notes for LAB page 237

Have students work on the LAB pages independently or in pairs. Some students may benefit from referring to their completed Activity Master: 127 or the sorted three-dimensional figures.

On LAB page 237, students identify attributes of specific three-dimensional figures.

Some students may generalize the idea of "vertex" to conclude that a cone has the same number of vertices as faces and put down attribute D for the cone. Although a cone does have a "point," the terms vertex and edge are used to describe polyhedrons and not three-dimensional figures with curved surfaces. To avoid confusion, use "point" or "apex" when referring to a cone.

Teaching Notes for LAB page 238

On this page, students are asked to differentiate between pyramids and prisms by stating specific attributes such as congruent, parallel, and perpendicular faces.

Challenge Problem The challenge problem asks students to describe some of the attributes of the polyhedra that are neither prisms nor pyramids.

Ongoing Assessment The LAB pages provide an opportunity to assess students' ability to differentiate between different types of three-dimensional figures and match the correct terms to the defining attributes. Some students may need to rely on concrete examples, while others can identify the figures by envisioning the shapes with the desired attributes.

Differentiated Instruction Basic Level As students are working on the LAB pages, watch for any students who seem unsure of the meanings of any of the attributes. If necessary, support them by choosing three-dimensional figures and pointing to congruent faces, vertices, edges, and so on.

Reflect and Summarize the Lesson

Write Math

How are a cylinder and a prism alike? How are they different? Possible answer: Both a cylinder and a prism have bases that are parallel and congruent. A cylinder has circular bases and a curved surface, while a prism has polygons as bases with all other faces flat.

Review Model . . . .

Refer students to Review Model: Classifying Three-Dimensional Figures in the *Student Handbook* to see how to classify a three-dimensional figure as a polyhedron or not a polyhedron and how to identify prisms and pyramids.

✔ Check for Understanding

❶ other polyhedron

❷ pyramid

❸ not a polyhedron

❹ prism

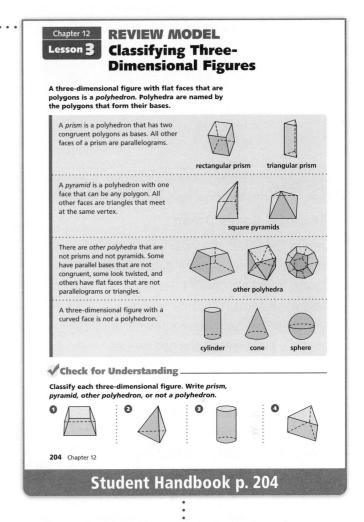

Leveled Problem Solving

A circus tent top is shaped like a pyramid. It has 10 isosceles triangles whose sides are 130 feet, 130 feet, and 80 feet.

❶ Basic Level

What is the length of one edge of the base? Explain. 80 feet; the bases of the isosceles triangles make an edge with the base of the pyramid.

❷ On Level

What is the perimeter of the base of the pyramid? Explain. 800 feet; the base of each isosceles triangle is 80 feet, which is the length of one edge of the base. There are 10 triangles, so the face of the base has 10 sides. 80 × 10 = 800

❸ Above Level

There is rope along each edge of the pyramid. How much rope is used? Explain.
2,100 ft; 10 × 130 ft for edges between triangles, 10 × 80 ft for pyramid base. (10 × 130) + (10 × 80) = 1,300 + 800 = 2,100

Intervention

Activity Bases Down

Display the pyramids and prisms from the class set of three-dimensional figures from **Lesson 12.1**. Have pairs of students record the visible face shapes of each. Have students compare and contrast the two groups of three-dimensional figures.

Then randomly distribute the pyramids and prisms to pairs of students. Have each pair stand the figure on its base. Have students verify that each figure is correctly placed on its base.

Practice

Sorting Three-Dimensional Figures

❶ Cut out each net and fold it along the dotted lines to make a three-dimensional figure.

❷ Fit these two figures together (by matching two congruent faces together, one from each figure) to make a new figure.

See what new figures you can make.

How many ways can you combine these to make a prism? How many ways can you combine them to make a pyramid?

Part 1

Part 2

Practice P97

Extension

Sorting Three-Dimensional Figures

Find the 6 polyhedra in your class collection that are neither *prisms* nor *pyramids*. Use them to help you complete the page.

❶ Find the 2 three-dimensional figures that have all the following attributes and write their letters on the lines below.
☑ two parallel, polygonal faces that are not congruent
☑ other faces are not parallelograms or triangles
☑ more vertices than faces
G   H

❷ Three-dimensional Figures J and M may be called *antiprisms*. Write some attributes that describe both of these shapes. Possible answers are given.
☑ One pair of congruent, parallel faces are twisted in relation to each other.

☑ All the other faces are triangles.

☑ They both have fewer vertices than faces.

Extension E97

Spiral Review

Spiral Review Book page SR97 provides review of the following previously learned skills and concepts:

- using the pattern of square number differences to find products related to square numbers
- using reasoning to find decimal sums

You may wish to have students work with partners to complete the page.

Algebra
Complete the multiplication.

❶ 12 × 12 = 144 ❖ 11 × 13 = _143_

❷ 22 × 22 = 484 ❖ 21 × 23 = _483_

❸ 15² = 225 ❖ 14 × 16 = _224_

❹ 29 × 29 = _841_ ❖ 28 × 30 = _840_

❺ 53² = _2,809_ ❖ 52 × 54 = _2,808_

❻ 50² = 2,500 ❖ (50 − 1)(50 + 1) = _2,499_

❼ 65 × 65 = _4,225_ ❖ (65 − 1)(65 + 1) = _4,224_

Reasoning and Proof
Complete the number sentences.

❶ 9 + 3.5 = _12.5_   ❼ 7 + 4.3 = _11.3_   ❹ 4 + 2.7 = _6.7_
9.4 + 3 = _12.4_   7.3 + 4 = _11.3_   4.7 + 2 = _6.7_
9.4 + 3.5 = _12.9_   7.3 + 4.3 = _11.6_   4.7 + 2.7 = _7.4_
94 + 35 = _129_   73 + 43 = _116_   47 + 27 = _74_
0.94 + 0.35 = _1.29_   0.73 + 0.43 = _1.16_   0.47 + 0.27 = _0.74_

⑪ 1 + 8.2 = _9.2_   ❻ 6 + 5.3 = _11.3_   ❹ 4.6 + 8 = _12.6_
1.6 + 8 = _9.6_   6.9 + 5 = _11.9_   4 + 8.6 = _12.6_
1.6 + 8.2 = _9.8_   6.9 + 5.3 = _12.2_   4.6 + 8.6 = _13.2_
16 + 82 = _98_   69 + 53 = _122_   46 + 86 = _132_
0.16 + 0.82 = _0.98_   0.69 + 0.53 = _1.22_   0.46 + 0.86 = _1.32_

Spiral Review SR97

Extension Activity
Guess My Three-Dimensional Figure

Give each student a prism, a pyramid, a cone, or a cylinder. Have students write the name of the three-dimensional figure, the number of its faces, edges, and vertices, and the shapes of its faces.

Then have students play "Guess My Three-Dimensional Figure." They take turns asking *yes* or *no* questions to identify the three-dimensional figure and the shape of its base or bases.

Teacher's Notes 🍎

Daily Notes . . .

Quick Notes

More Ideas

Volume of Rectangular Prisms

NCTM Standards 1, 3, 4, 6, 7, 8, 9, 10

Lesson Planner

STUDENT OBJECTIVES
STUDENT OBJECTIVES
- To connect models for the area of rectangles and the volume of rectangular prisms with their formulas and to use the formulas
- To use appropriate units to measure length, area, and volume

1 Daily Activities (TG p. 1001)

Open-Ended Problem Solving/Headline Story	Skills Practice and Review— Describing Parallel, Perpendicular, and Congruent Faces

2 Teach and Practice (TG pp. 1002–1006)

MATERIALS

Ⓐ **Building Three-Dimensional Structures** (TG pp. 1002–1003)

Ⓑ **Finding Volume of Rectangular Prisms** (TG pp. 1004–1005)

Ⓒ **Finding Area of Rectangles and Volume of Rectangular Prisms** (TG p. 1006)

- Figures B and E from the class set
- TR: Activity Master, AM128
- one-inch cubes
- 📖 LAB pp. 239–240
- 📖 SH p. 205

3 Differentiated Instruction (TG p. 1007)

Leveled Problem Solving (TG p. 1007)	Practice Book P98
Intervention Activity (TG p. 1007)	Extension Book E98
Extension Activity (TG p. 1007)	Spiral Review Book SR98

Lesson Notes

About the Lesson

Students come to understand volume as the amount of space contained within the boundaries of a three-dimensional figure. Then, extending their understanding of why multiplying the two dimensions of a rectangle, *base length* × *height,* gives its area, students find the volume of a three-dimensional rectangular figure (rectangular prism) by multiplying its base *area* × height.

About the Mathematics

There is no *mathematical* distinction between volume and capacity—both refer to the amount of "space" within a three-dimensional region—but we tend to use these terms in different contexts. In general usage, capacity refers to the amount of a substance (such as air or water) that the object can contain; volume refers to the amount of space the object itself takes up. Each paper polyhedron in the class collection is the *surface* of a three-dimensional figure—the *boundary* of a three-dimensional region. In fact, the mathematical definitions of the three-dimensional figures—sphere, cone, cylinder, prism, pyramid, and so on—refer to the *surfaces:* the hollow shells, not the contents, of these regions.

Use with Lesson Activity Book pp. 239–240.

Developing Mathematical Language

Vocabulary: <u>base</u>, <u>height</u>, <u>length</u>, <u>width</u>, <u>cubic units</u>, <u>square units</u>, <u>volume</u>

Students connect finding the area of a polygon in *square units* to finding the area of a *base* of a polyhedron. To determine the *volume* of a prism (in *cubic units*), one must multiply the area of the *base* times the *height* of the prism, measured perpendicular to the *base.* Obviously, the use of *base* and *height* in both two and three dimensions can provide challenges for students, so connections to concrete objects such as square tiles, inch cubes, and models of three-dimensional polyhedra are important.

Review the terms *length, width,* and *height* with students.

Beginning Have students name objects in the classroom that have *length, width,* and *height.* Have students point to the *length, width,* and *height* of each object they name.

Intermediate Give pairs of students some cubes. Have one student give dimensions for the *length, width,* and *height* of a rectangular prism while the other creates that prism with the cubes.

Advanced Demonstrate how to draw a rectangular prism by drawing two rectangles diagonally apart from one another, connecting the corresponding vertices, and erasing parts of hidden lines to make them dashed rules. Then have students draw a rectangular prism

Open-Ended Problem Solving

Read the Headline Story to the students. Encourage them to think of creative ways to describe the polyhedron.

 Headline Story

Imagine a polyhedron that is neither a prism nor a pyramid. Describe how it might look.

Possible responses: It could look like a prism, but with bases that are not congruent. It could look like a "twisted prism," or like a pyramid, but without a "point" at the top.

Skills Practice and Review

Describing Parallel, Perpendicular, and Congruent Faces

Distribute the class set of figures to students. Keep the pace lively and involve all students by asking, Who has a three-dimensional figure with

- at least two faces perpendicular to each other?
- only one pair of parallel faces?
- no parallel faces?
- no perpendicular faces?
- no congruent faces?
- only one pair of congruent faces?
- more vertices than faces?
- more than 12 edges?
- parallel faces that are "twisted" with respect to each other?

If time permits, ask volunteers to answer these questions.

- How many pairs of parallel triangular faces does your three-dimensional figure have?
- Which faces are perpendicular to another face?
- Which faces are perpendicular to a different-shaped face?
- Which faces are parallel to each other?

pairs · 15 MIN

Materials
- For each pair: AM128 and about 20 one-inch cubes

NCTM Standards 3, 4, 6, 7, 8, 9, 10

✔ **Ongoing Assessment**

- Do students add the area of each level of a three-dimensional figure together to find the volume?

A Building Three-Dimensional Structures

Purpose To use cubes to model finding the volume of a structure and to determine the appropriate units for measuring length, area, and volume

Introduce Write the measurement terms length, area, and volume on the board.

Ask students to tell what they know about these terms, and to suggest when they might measure length, when they might measure area, and when they might measure volume.

Give each pair of students Activity Master 128: Structures and Layers, Explore: Measuring Three-Dimensional Structures, and about 20 one-inch cubes. They will also need a piece of paper to draw their sketches.

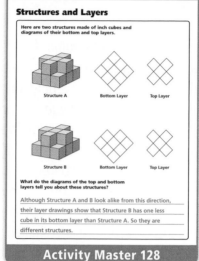

Activity Master 128

Task Have partners work together to solve the problems on AM128 and the Explore page. After they have had time to complete the problems, discuss the problems and answers.

On AM128, students should note that both structures look alike and that it is only by looking at the bottom layer of each structure that you can tell that Structure A had one more cube than Structure B.

On the Explore page, students will find that it takes 19 cubes to build the structure (Problem 1). Help them understand that the 19 one-inch cubes represent the measurement of the structure's volume, or how much space it occupies. Each inch cube has the volume "one cubic inch," so the volume of the structure is 19 cubic inches. Ask students, "If you built a structure with 24 of the same cubes, what would the volume be?" 24 cubic inches

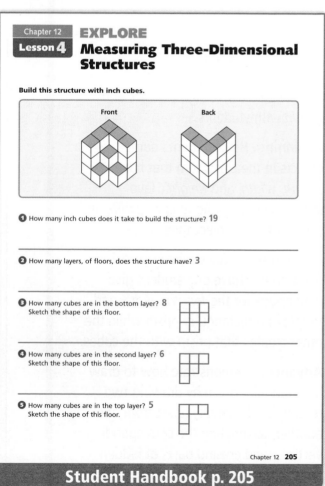

Student Handbook p. 205

As students discuss Problems 3, 4, and 5 about the number of cubes in each layer, you might sketch the "floor plan" of each layer on the board. One way to do this is to draw a tic-tac-toe frame, surround it with a square to form a 3-by-3 array, and then erase the extra squares that are not part of that floor.

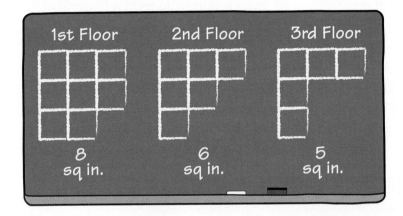

We can sensibly ask about the area of each floor. The middle floor has an area of 6 square inches.

Talk Math To help clarify the use of linear measure (inches, centimeters, miles, and so on), square measure (square inches, square centimeters, square miles and so on), and cubic measure (cubic inches, cubic centimeters, and so on), ask these questions.

❷ What are some examples of units of length? Possible answers: inches, feet, centimeters, miles, kilometers

❷ Why don't we use square yards or square meters to measure length? When we measure length, we measure only one direction or dimension. A square unit covers two dimensions, or area.

❷ Why do we use square units (like square inches) to measure area? We're measuring in two directions. A square has two directions, or two dimensions—length and width.

❷ Why do we measure the space inside a building or other three-dimensional figure in cubic units? You have to measure in three directions—length, width, and height. A cube has those three dimensions.

❷ What are the names of units that you would use to measure volume? cubic centimeters, cubic inches, cubic feet, cubic meters

Differentiated Instruction

On Level/Above Level Some students may enjoy recording volumes as "units cubed." They know that the exponent 2 means "squared" and may have written areas as units squared. Although we say "square inches, square miles, cubic centimeters, cubic inches" and so on, the notation requires the exponent to be placed after the unit, not the number. For example, 4 sq yd may be recorded as 4 yd^2. It is important not to confuse this notation with 4^2 yd—which *sounds* more like "four square yards," but has a very different meaning! The latter is a way of writing "16 yards"—4 squared is 16, and the "yards" remains just "yards." By contrast, the notation 4 yd^2 leaves the 4 alone and shows that the yard is squared, giving a square yard.

Materials

• For the teacher: Figures B and E, one-inch cubes

NCTM Standards 1, 3, 4, 7, 8, 9, 10

B **Finding Volume of Rectangular Prisms**

Purpose To use cubes to model finding the volume of a prism

Introduce We compute volume by comparing to a unit volume (a cubic centimeter, a cubic inch, a cubic foot, a cubic yard, or some other usefully-sized cube), just as we compute area by comparing to a unit area (a square inch, a square centimeter, a square mile, and so on).

Hold up Figure B and pose this question: How many cubic inches (one-inch cubes) do you think would fit inside Figure B? Invite a student to build a figure like Figure B from one-inch cubes and see how many it takes. Repeat this for Figure E.

Problem **How can we find the volume of a prism without counting all the cubes?** Demonstrate the construction of the rectangular prism below with cubes. Explain to students that just as we compute the area of a rectangle by seeing how many squares fit in one row and then multiplying by the number of rows,

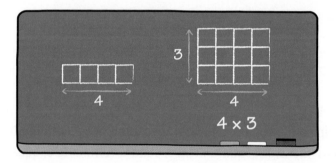

we compute the volume of a rectangular three-dimensional figure by seeing how many cubes fit in one layer, and then multiplying by the number of layers. The number of cubes that fit in one layer (the volume of a prism that has a height of just one unit) is the same as the number of squares in the base (the area of the base).

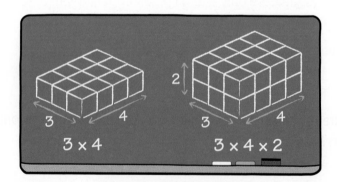

💬 **Talk Math** You may want to ask questions such as these to guide the discussion about finding the volume of a rectangular prism.

❷ How do you compute the area of the floor of a rectangular prism without counting the squares one by one? Measure the two dimensions along the base—length and width—and multiply.

❷ What is the formula for finding the area of a rectangle? *area = length × width* or *area = base × height*

❷ How many one-inch cubes can be placed on a floor of a rectangular prism with an area 12 square inches? 12 cubes How much volume do those cubes represent? 12 cubic inches

Refer students to the model of the rectangular prism built with cubes.

❷ How many layers are in the model? 2

❷ How do you compute the model's volume without counting all the cubes? Multiply the height—that is, the number of layers—by the number of cubes on the base layer. That is, *area of the base × height,* or 3 × 4 × 2.

❷ What is a formula for finding the volume of a prism? *volume = area of the base × height* or *volume = length × width × height*

💬 **Talk Math** To give students additional experience selecting appropriate units of measure for volume, ask the questions below.

❷ What unit of measure would you use to measure the volume of a swimming pool—cubic millimeters, cubic kilometers, cubic inches, or cubic feet? cubic feet

❷ What unit of measure would you use to measure the volume of a shoebox—cubic meters, cubic kilometers, cubic inches, or cubic feet? cubic inches

❷ What unit of measure would you use to measure the volume of an empty cylindrical coffee can—cubic centimeters, cubic kilometers, cubic yards, or cubic feet? cubic centimeters

Possible Discussion

Briefly point out the similarity between the height of the building (in this case, the number of layers of inch cubes) and the height measurement of its rectangular base. Students may recall that the height of a rectangle is the perpendicular distance from the base to the top. The height of a building is the perpendicular distance from its base to the top.

Finding Area of Rectangles and Volume of Rectangular Prisms LAB pp. 239–240

individuals 20 MIN

Purpose To find the area and volume of rectangular prisms

NCTM Standards 1, 3, 4, 7, 8, 9, 10

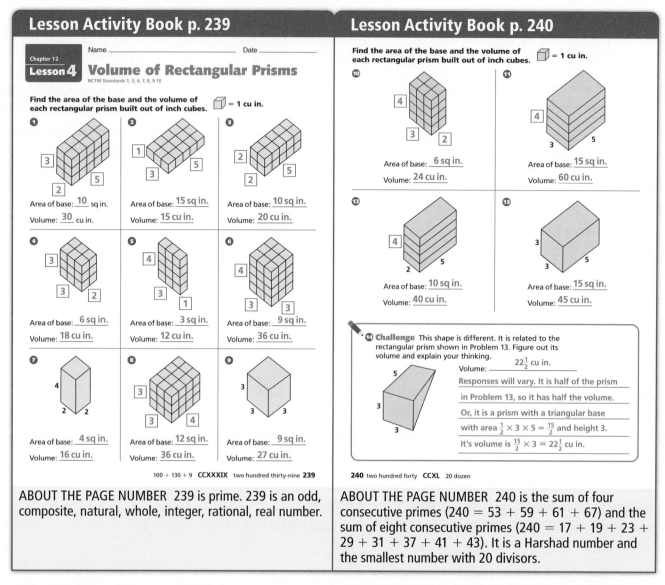

Teaching Notes for LAB page 239

Students practice and extend the ideas that they began to learn during Activities A and B. Most problems show buildings in which the unit cubes are clearly visible, as in the diagrams in Activity B. Students must find the dimensions by looking at the picture. They then use that information to compute the area of the base, and the volume of the three-dimensional figure.

Problems 7 and 9 (on page 239) and Problem 13 (on page 240) show the dimensions because the unit cubes are not visible.

Teaching Notes for LAB page 240

Problems 11 and 12 give the dimensions of the base and show the building "in layers" as a way of indicating the height, showing that the volume is height times the area of the base.

Challenge Problem The challenge problem shows a non-rectangular shape. Just as the triangle's area is half the area of the rectangle (or parallelogram) that has the same base and height, this figure's volume is half of the volume of a rectangular building with the same dimensions.

Reflect and Summarize the Lesson

 Write Math

Elizabeth built a rectangular prism out of one-inch cubes. The bottom layer covered a rectangle that was 4 cubes wide and 5 cubes long. Then she put two more layers the same size on top of the first layer. How can you find the volume of the prism she built without counting the cubes one-by-one? Possible answer: You can multiply the area of the base by the height: 3 inches × 5 inches × 3 inches = 45 cubic inches.

3 | Differentiated Instruction

Leveled Problem Solving

Jamal covers a rectangle with 2 rows of 10 one-inch cubes. Then he stacks identical layers to make a prism.

❶ Basic Level
How many cubes does Jamal use to create 3 layers? Explain.
60 cubes; $2 \times 10 \times 3 = 60$

❷ On Level
If Jamal's prism is 8 inches tall, what is its volume? Explain.
160 in.³; $2 \times 10 \times 8 = 160$

❸ Above Level
Jamal stacks cubes until he has a square face on the longer side of base. The prism has more than 50 cubes. What is its volume? Explain. 200 in.³; $10 \times 10 \times 2 = 200$

Intervention	Practice	Extension

Intervention

Activity Building Blocks

Give each group several cubes. Assign one student in each group to be the builder. Another student gives the dimensions of a rectangular base, while the builder represents it with cubes. The builder then uses the remaining cubes to build the prism as high as possible. The other students check the dimensions of the prism and multiply them. Then they find the volume of the prism. Have students switch roles and repeat the activity.

Practice

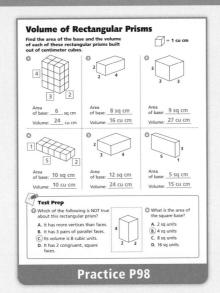

Practice P98

Extension

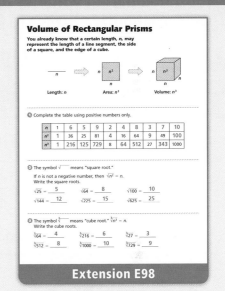

Extension E98

Spiral Review

Spiral Review Book page SR98 provides review of the following previously learned skills and concepts:

- multiplying fractions using an area model
- comparing customary and metric units of capacity

You may wish to have students work with partners to complete the page.

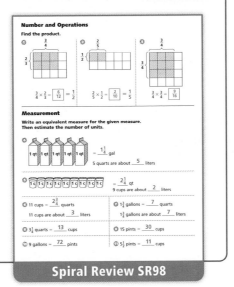

Spiral Review SR98

Extension Activity
What's My Size?

Have each student choose the dimensions of a prism and calculate its volume. Have students ask yes or no questions until they guess the volume of the leader's prism. Then have them continue asking questions until they guess the correct dimensions.

Encourage students to discover the shortcut of dividing the volume by the area of the base to find the height.

Lesson 5 Volume of Prisms

NCTM Standards 1, 3, 4, 7, 8, 9, 10

Lesson Planner

STUDENT OBJECTIVES

- To relate the volumes of a triangular prism and a rectangular prism
- To use the formula *volume = base area × height* to find the volume of rectangular and triangular prisms

1 Daily Activities (TG p. 1009)

Open-Ended Problem Solving/Headline Story	Skills Practice and Review—Describing Edges

2 Teach and Practice (TG pp. 1010–1015)

Ⓐ **Finding Volumes of Prisms** (TG pp. 1010–1011)

Ⓑ **Comparing Volumes of Rectangular and Triangular Prisms** (TG pp. 1012–1013)

Ⓒ **Finding Volumes of Triangular Prisms** (TG p. 1014)

MATERIALS

- Figures B, L, O, and S from the class set
- one-inch cubes
- 📖 LAB pp. 241–242
- 📖 SH pp. 206–207

3 Differentiated Instruction (TG p. 1016)

Leveled Problem Solving (TG p. 1016)

Intervention Activity (TG p. 1016)

Extension Activity (TG p. 1016)

Science Connection (TG p. 970)

Practice Book P99

Extension Book E99

Spiral Review Book SR99

Lesson Notes

About the Lesson

Students have used two congruent paper triangles to make a parallelogram, and so have seen why the triangle's area is half that of the parallelogram. In this lesson, students connect this idea to finding the volume of a triangular prism. Once they realize that two congruent triangular prisms can form a rectangular prism, they can compute the volume of the rectangular prism (by first finding the area of a rectangular face and then multiplying by the prism's height) and then halve the result. They find that this is equivalent to computing the area of the triangular base and multiplying by the prism's height.

 Use with Lesson Activity Book pp. 241–242.

Developing Mathematical Language

Vocabulary: rectangular prism, triangular prism, volume

Discuss how the shape of a base defines a prism. A *rectangular prism* has two congruent parallel bases that are rectangles. When all of the faces of a *rectangular prism* are rectangles, any of its faces can be considered a base. The only way a *triangular prism* can satisfy "all other (non-base) faces are parallelograms" is for the bases to be the triangular faces. You may want to use the other prisms (triangular, K, O, S: rectangular (including square), B, D, E, Q; pentagonal, N, V; hexagonal, L; trapezoidal, P; octagonal, X) to practice this idea of naming prisms after their base.

Review the terms *rectangular prism* and *triangular prism* with students.

Beginning Display prisms from the class set of three-dimensional figures. Have students select all the prisms with a rectangular or triangular base.

Intermediate Display prisms from the class set of three-dimensional figures. Have students pick out first the *triangular prisms* and then the *rectangular prisms*.

Advanced Have pairs of students make a chart like the one below.

Prism	faces	vertices	edges
Triangular	5	6	9
Rectangular	6	8	12

Have one student give a clue, such as, "The number of edges is twice the number of faces." The other student uses the chart to identify the prism.

Open-Ended Problem Solving

Draw this table on the board and read the Headline Story to the students. If your class needs help getting started, you might ask whether $2 \times 2 \times 2$ is halfway between $1 \times 1 \times 1$ and $3 \times 3 \times 3$.

 Headline Story

Complete this table that shows the edge lengths and volumes of some cubes. Without computing the volume of a 2.5 × 2.5 × 2.5 cube, say whether it will be closer to 2 × 2 × 2, or 3 × 3 × 3, or halfway between the two. Explain.

Edge (in.)	Volume (in.³)
1	1
2	8
3	

Possible responses: 2 is halfway between 1 and 3, but the volume of a 2-inch cube is 8, *much* closer to 1 than to 27. 2.5 is halfway between 2 and 3, so, I think the volume of a 2.5-inch cube will be closer to the volume of a 2-inch cube than to a 3-inch cube.

Skills Practice and Review

Describing Edges

Distribute the three-dimensional figures from the class set to students. Ask: Who has a three-dimensional figure with

- at least two edges connecting perpendicular faces?
- no edges along which perpendicular faces meet?
- fewer edges than vertices? (No one)
- more edges than vertices? (Everyone)
- more edges than faces? (Everyone)
- at least one pair of perpendicular edges?

pairs

15 MIN

Materials

- For the teacher: Figures B, L, O, and S from the class set
- For each pair: about 20 one-inch cubes

NCTM Standards 1, 3, 4, 7, 8, 9, 10

A Finding Volumes of Prisms

Purpose To use the formula *volume = area of the base × height* to find the volume of rectangular and triangular prisms

Introduce Each pair of students needs a copy of Explore: Volume of Prisms and about 20 one-inch cubes. The diagrams on the page show the dimensions of Figures B, L, and O (or S) from the class set.

Before students begin working on the Explore page, hold up Figures O and S and ask students what they notice about these three-dimensional figures. Students may already have noticed that nets for Figures O and S looked different but formed the same three-dimensional figures. If no one has mentioned this before, you might ask any students who have these nets to show them and then compare the prisms.

Task Have pairs of students work on Explore: Volume of Prisms. Display all four prisms—B, L, O, and S—where students can see them or come to take a closer look while they are completing the Explore page. Students are asked to model Prisms B and L with cubes; they cannot, of course, model Triangular Prisms O or S. Have students select and use an appropriate unit to measure the volumes of the prisms and find out which prism, B or L, has the greater volume.

Chapter 12 EXPLORE
Lesson 5 Volume of Prisms

Use the information in each diagram to predict how many inch cubes you will need to build the prism. Build each with cubes and record the volume.

Prism B
Base: 2 in.
2 in.

Prism L
1 in.
1 in.
Base:
2 in.
1 in.
3 in.

Height of Prism: 3 in.
How many cubes? 12
What is the volume? 12 cu in.

Height of Prism: 1 in.
How many cubes? 4
What is the volume? 4 cu in.

Use the information in the diagram or Figures O and S from the class collection.

How might you find the volume of a triangular prism?
Possible answer: Multiply the three dimensions to find the volume of a brick of this size, and then take half. Or, multiply the base area by the height

2 in.
Height of Prism: 3 in.
3 in.

206 Chapter 12

Student Handbook p. 206

💬 **Talk Math** After your students have had a few minutes to complete the Explore page, ask questions like these.

❷ Do you need to use cubes to find the volumes of Prisms B and L? No; the dimensions of the prisms are given, so you can calculate the volumes using the formula *volume = base area × height.* You can use the cubes to check your predictions or your computations.

❷ What is the area of the base of Prism B? 4 sq in. What is its volume? 12 cu in.

❷ What is the area of the base of Prism L? 4 sq in. What is its volume? 4 cu in.

❷ Which prism, B or L, has the greater volume? Prism B

❷ It does not say to use cubes to build Prism O or S. Is there a way to build Prism O or S with cubes? no

❷ What is the area of the triangular base of Prism O or S? Explain how you found this area. 3 sq in.; I used the formula for the area of a triangle: *Area = $\frac{1}{2}$ × base length × height.*

❷ How might you find the volume of a triangular prism? Possible answer: I know the volume for a square or rectangular prism is *volume = base area × height.* It should work the same for a triangular prism.

Students will continue to investigate how to find the volume of a triangular prism during the next activity.

B Comparing Volumes of Rectangular and Triangular Prisms

Purpose To extend the formula for finding the area of a triangle to finding the volume of a triangular prism

Introduce Show students Prisms O and S and discuss what they already know about these prisms from the previous activity (They are congruent triangular prisms). Show them different ways of how they can put these together to form a "brick," or rectangular prism.

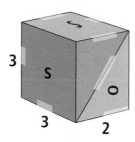 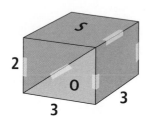 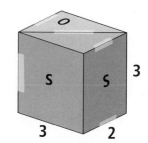

✓ Ongoing Assessment

- Do students understand the relationship between the volume of a rectangular prism and the volume of the two triangular prisms that make it?

- Do students accurately compute the volume of rectangular and triangular prisms?

Ask your students how they would find the volume of these rectangular prisms. Most will remember from their work in **Lesson 12.4** that they can find the area of the base (*length* × *width*) and then multiply by the height of the prism to find its volume.

Task **Have students find the volume of the prism in each of the three orientations.**

Show each orientation and have students confirm that the volume of the rectangular prism is 18 cubic inches by multiplying the base area times the height.

 Talk Math Separate the two prisms and ask this question.

❷ What is the volume of one of these triangular prisms? How do you know?
9 cu in.; Possible answer: Since the triangular prisms are congruent and two of them have a volume of 18 cu in., each of them must have a volume of 9 cu in.

Use with Lesson Activity Book pp. 241–242.

Talk Math Put either Prism O or Prism S aside and set the other one on its (triangular) base. Ask these questions.

❷ Is this prism "sitting" on its base? How do you know? Yes; the top and bottom of the prism are level and the other faces are parallelograms.

❷ How would you describe the base of this prism? It's a right triangle.

❷ What is the formula for finding the area of a triangle? *Area* $= \frac{1}{2} \times$ *base length* $\times$ *height*

❷ What is the base area of this prism? 3 sq in. $(\frac{1}{2} \times 3 \times 2)$

❷ What is the height of this prism? 3 in.

❷ What volume do you get if you multiply the base area times the height? 9 cu in. (3 sq in. $\times$ 3 in.)

❷ Is that the same volume that we found earlier by thinking about the triangular prism as half of a rectangular prism? yes

If time permits, repeat this activity, assigning different dimensions to the triangular prism and finding its volume in two ways:

• by finding the area of the rectangular solid that could be formed by putting the two triangular prisms together, then dividing by 2;

• by multiplying the base area of the prism times the height of the prism.

Concept Alert

Some students might see or set a triangular prism on one of its rectangular faces and consider that a "base" of the prism. Remind students that a prism's bases have to be congruent and parallel.

Finding Volumes of Triangular Prisms LAB pp. 241–242

Purpose To find the volumes of triangular prisms

NCTM Standards 1, 3, 4, 7, 8, 9, 10

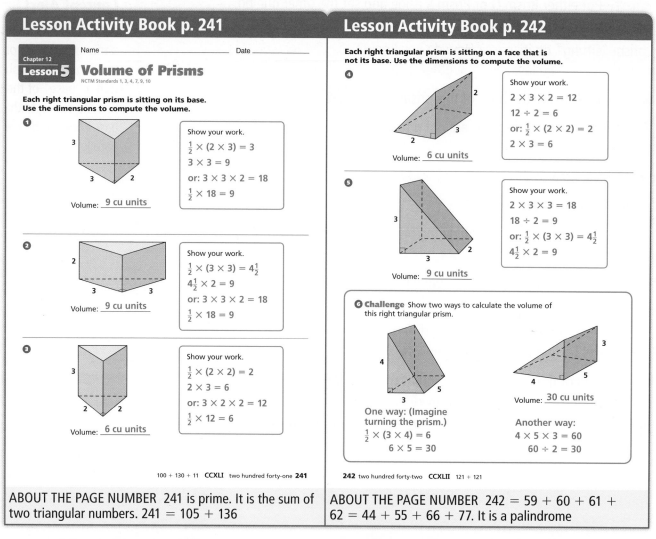

ABOUT THE PAGE NUMBER 241 is prime. It is the sum of two triangular numbers. 241 = 105 + 136

ABOUT THE PAGE NUMBER 242 = 59 + 60 + 61 + 62 = 44 + 55 + 66 + 77. It is a palindrome

Teaching Notes for LAB page 241

On this page, students may compute the areas of triangular bases and then find the volumes of triangular prisms or may treat these as halves of rectangular prisms and find the volume that way.

The dimensions of the triangular base and the height of each prism are given, so students may use the formula *volume = base area × height.*

✔**Ongoing Assessment** These LAB pages provide an opportunity to informally assess your students' ability to find the areas of two-dimensional figures and the volumes of three-dimensional prisms.

Teaching Notes for LAB page 242

On this page, the triangular prisms each sit on a rectangular face with the dimensions given. Students may compute the volume of a rectangular prism that would be made from two such triangular prisms and then halve the volume to find the volume of the one triangular prism. They could also imagine turning the prism so that it is sitting on a triangular base and use the formula *volume = base area × height.*

Challenge Problem The Challenge Problem asks students to compute the volume of a triangular prism two different ways.

Reflect and Summarize the Lesson

 Write Math

How is the volume of a triangular prism related to the volume of a rectangular prism with the same length, width, and height? The volume of a triangular prism is one half the volume of a rectangular prism with the same length, width, and height.

Review Model . . . .

Refer students to Review Model: Volume of a Prism in the *Student Handbook* to see how to find the volume of a prism.

✔ Check for Understanding

❶ 40 cu ft

❷ 54 cu m

❸ 9 cu cm

❹ $37\frac{1}{2}$ cu yd

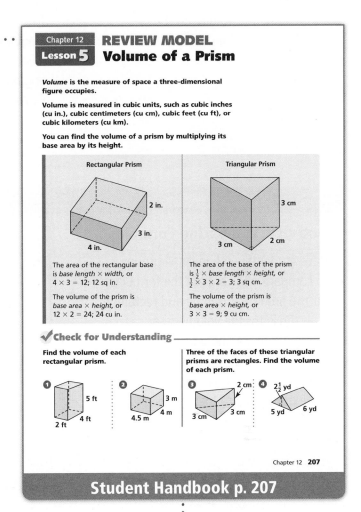

Student Handbook p. 207

Leveled Problem Solving

A triangular cheese wedge has a height of 5 inches. The base of the wedge is a right triangle with a 4-inch base length and a 3-inch height.

❶ Basic Level

What is the volume of the cheese? Explain. 30 in.³; $V = \frac{1}{2} \times 3 \times 4 \times 5 = 30$

❷ On Level

The cheese wedge was made by diagonally cutting a rectangular prism. What is the volume of the original rectangular prism? Explain. 60 in.³; it is twice that of the cheese wedge: $2(\frac{1}{2} \times 3 \times 4 \times 5) = 3 \times 4 \times 5 = 60$.

❸ Above Level

If, instead, the wedge was 3 inches high and the height of the triangular base was 5 inches, would the volume of the prism be different? Explain. no; $\frac{1}{2} \times 3 \times 4 \times 5 = 30 = \frac{1}{2} \times 5 \times 4 \times 3$

| Intervention | Practice | Extension |

Activity Comparing Formulas

Have students work in small groups to compare and contrast the formulas for the area of a triangle and rectangle with those for the volume of a triangular prism and a rectangular prism. Encourage students to make a table or draw pictures to help them. Have groups share their work.

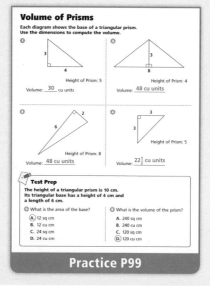

Practice P99

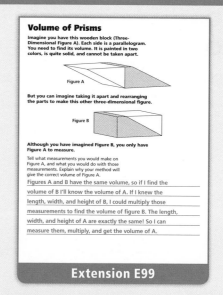

Extension E99

Spiral Review

Spiral Review Book page SR99 provides a review of the following previously learned skills and concepts:

- finding the perimeter of parallelograms
- applying the problem solving strategy *act it out*

You may wish to have students work with partners to complete the page.

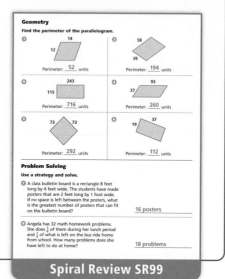

Spiral Review SR99

Extension Activity
Find the Height

Have students work in small groups. Have one student say the height of the base of a triangular prism. Have another student say the base length of the triangular prism. Then have all students in the group work together to determine the height of the prism if its volume is 200 cubic units.

Teacher's Notes 🍎

Daily Notes . . .

Quick Notes

More Ideas

Lesson 6 · Areas of Nets

NCTM Standards 1, 3, 4, 6, 7, 8, 9, 10

Lesson Planner

STUDENT OBJECTIVES
- To compute the total area of a net by first computing the area of each shape in the net
- To use formulas to find the areas of rectangles and triangles

1 Daily Activities (TG p. 1019)

Open-Ended Problem Solving/Headline Story	Skills Practice and Review— Finding Area

2 Teach and Practice (TG pp. 1020–1023)

	MATERIALS
(A) **Figuring Out How Much Paper Was Used** (TG pp. 1020–1021) (B) **Finding the Area of a Net** (TG p. 1022) (C) **Playing a Game: Volume Builder** (TG p. 1023)	• Figures C and J from the class set • TR: Activity Masters, AM129–AM131 • rulers • cubes • coins • scratch paper • 📖 LAB pp. 243–244 • 📖 SH pp. 208, 214

3 Differentiated Instruction (TG p. 1024)

Leveled Problem Solving (TG p. 1024)	Practice Book P100
Intervention Activity (TG p. 1024)	Extension Book E100
Extension Activity (TG p. 1024)	Spiral Review Book SR100

Lesson Notes

About the Lesson

Students apply their knowledge about areas of two-dimensional figures to finding the surface area of three-dimensional figures. In most cases, the measurements suggest exact computations of this total area, but in some cases approximation is appropriate.

Developing Mathematical Language

Vocabulary: area of a net

It is hard to define *area* in a precise way and still keep the idea clear and intuitively sensible for students. In this lesson, we give *"surface area"* meaning by treating it as "how much paper is used up" in making a particular figure. But paper isn't area: it has thickness, and so it is really three-dimensional, as is everything that we can see.

The two pictures below feel like they "use up" very different amounts of paper, yet they have the same area.

It is fine, and probably necessary at this stage, to leave students with an informal understanding of area.

Familiarize students with the term *area of a net*.

Beginning Show students Net B—cut out. Explain that the *area of the net* is the sum of the areas of all the shapes that make up the net. Ask them how many areas of figures make up the *area of the net?* 6

Intermediate Show students Net B and Net C—both cut out. Explain that the paper represents the *area of the net*. Ask them which net they think has the greater area (uses more paper) and how they could check.

Advanced Show students Net B. Have them describe to a partner how they would find the *area of this net*.

Open-Ended Problem Solving

Read the Headline Story to the students. If students are not sure how to begin to answer the question, you might want to suggest that they draw nets on grid paper.

 Headline Story

Heidi and Peng each built a rectangular prism. They do not look the same, but Heidi tells Peng that they will have the same volume. Can you think of some dimensions for the figures that make them look different but have the same volume?

Possible responses: $1 \times 2 \times 6 = 12$ cu units and $3 \times 2 \times 2 = 12$ cu units; $2 \times 3 \times 6 = 36$ cu units and $3 \times 3 \times 4 = 36$ cu units.

Skills Practice and Review

Finding Area

Sketch the three figures on the board and ask students for the formulas for the areas.

Point to a figure, give the measurements shown in the chart, and have a student give the missing measurement. Repeat problems with different numbers.

Figure	Area	Base Length	Height
rectangle	12 sq in.	4 in.	3 in.
parallelogram	56 sq mi	14 mi	4 mi
parallelogram	56 sq ft	14 ft	4 ft
triangle	56 sq ft	4 ft	28 ft

individuals   20 MIN

Ⓐ **Figuring Out How Much Paper Was Used**

Materials
- For the teacher: Figures C and J from the class set
- For each student: ruler

NCTM Standards 1, 3, 4, 6, 7, 8, 9, 10

Purpose To find the area of a net

Introduce Hold up a three-dimensional figure— Figure J is good for this purpose, but any three-dimensional figure will do— and pose this question: "How could we figure out how much paper was used in creating this three-dimensional figure?"

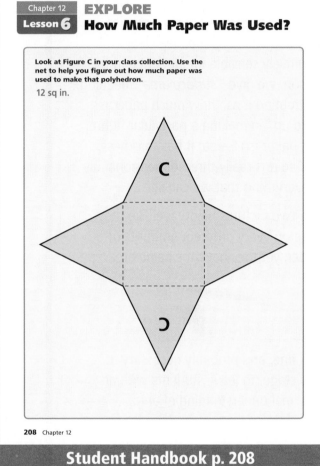

Student Handbook p. 208

✔**Ongoing Assessment**
- Do students understand that surface area is the sum of the areas of all the faces in a three-dimensional figure?

You might ask your students if a net of the three-dimensional figure might help. If they don't connect the idea of *how much paper* to area, remind them that they know how to figure out the area of each part of the net; together, all those areas tell how much paper was used. Another name for this total area is the *surface area* of the three-dimensional figure (because it is the area of the surface of the three-dimensional figure).

Show Figure C and tell students that they will be figuring out how much paper was used to make it. Each student will need a copy of Explore: How Much Paper Was Used? and a ruler.

Use with Lesson Activity Book pp. 243–244.

Task Have students work independently on **Explore: How Much Paper Was Used?** Encourage them to record the measurements and calculations right on the net. As they work, watch to be sure that they are measuring the *height*, not one of the sides, of each triangle (as shown below).

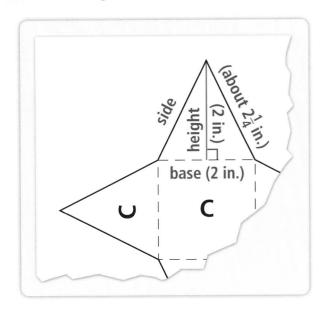

Talk Math After students have had a chance to find the total area of the net ask these questions.

❓ How much paper was used? 12 sq in.

❓ How did you figure that out? Possible answer: I broke the problem down into simpler problems, finding the areas of the 4 triangles and the square, and summing them to find the area of the entire net.

❓ Did anyone think of a shortcut for finding the area? Explain why your shortcut works. Possible answer: I multiplied the area of one of the triangles by 4. The triangles are congruent, so they have the same area.

Teacher Story

❝I found that some students enjoyed this exploratory challenge after they completed the Explore page. I asked them to cut the net of Figure C so that the parts can be rearranged to form a rectangle with the same total area (12 sq in.). Here are two ways.

1) Cut off the four triangles, and join pairs of them to make parallelograms. Then cut and rearrange one (or both) of these parallelograms and reassemble all the pieces to make a 6-by-2 rectangle.

2) Leave two opposite triangles attached to the base square. Cut the other two triangles in half symmetrically, and tape those halves to the attached triangles to "straighten out the slant" and form a rectangle. ❞

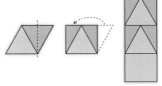

Concept Alert

Some students will feel that more paper is "used up" in making each triangle in Net C (on the Explore page) than in making a rectangle that contains just two square inches, because it appears that more paper is wasted. However, the two shapes use the same amount of paper.

Purpose To find the area of a net

NCTM Standards 1, 3, 4, 6, 7, 8, 9, 10

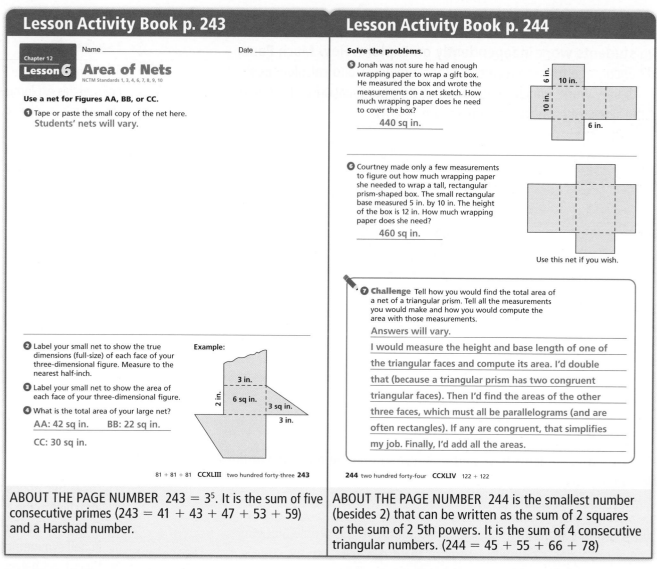

Lesson Activity Book p. 243

Name _____ Date _____

Chapter 12
Lesson 6 **Area of Nets**
NCTM Standards 1, 3, 4, 6, 7, 8, 9, 10

Use a net for Figures AA, BB, or CC.

❶ Tape or paste the small copy of the net here.
Students' nets will vary.

❷ Label your small net to show the true dimensions (full-size) of each face of your three-dimensional figure. Measure to the nearest half-inch.

❸ Label your small net to show the area of each face of your three-dimensional figure.

❹ What is the total area of your large net?
AA: 42 sq in.   BB: 22 sq in.
CC: 30 sq in.

Example:

3 in.
6 sq in.
2 in.
3 sq in.
3 in.
3 in.

81 + 81 + 81   CCXLIII   two hundred forty-three **243**

ABOUT THE PAGE NUMBER $243 = 3^5$. It is the sum of five consecutive primes ($243 = 41 + 43 + 47 + 53 + 59$) and a Harshad number.

Lesson Activity Book p. 244

Solve the problems.

❺ Jonah was not sure he had enough wrapping paper to wrap a gift box. He measured the box and wrote the measurements on a net sketch. How much wrapping paper does he need to cover the box?
440 sq in.

6 in.   10 in.
10 in.
6 in.

❻ Courtney made only a few measurements to figure out how much wrapping paper she needed to wrap a tall, rectangular prism-shaped box. The small rectangular base measured 5 in. by 10 in. The height of the box is 12 in. How much wrapping paper does she need?
460 sq in.

Use this net if you wish.

❼ **Challenge** Tell how you would find the total area of a net of a triangular prism. Tell all the measurements you would make and how you would compute the area with those measurements.
Answers will vary.
I would measure the height and base length of one of the triangular faces and compute its area. I'd double that (because a triangular prism has two congruent triangular faces). Then I'd find the areas of the other three faces, which must all be parallelograms (and are often rectangles). If any are congruent, that simplifies my job. Finally, I'd add all the areas.

244 two hundred forty-four   CCXLIV   122 + 122

ABOUT THE PAGE NUMBER 244 is the smallest number (besides 2) that can be written as the sum of 2 squares or the sum of 2 5th powers. It is the sum of 4 consecutive triangular numbers. ($244 = 45 + 55 + 66 + 78$)

Teaching Notes for LAB page 243

Each student will need a ruler and one of the Activity Masters 129–131: Nets AA, BB, CC. Students make their measurements on the larger net and record them on the smaller copy, which they will attach to the LAB page.

Have students write their names on the back of the large nets and save them, unfolded, for **Lesson 12.8.**

The calculations for AM131: Net CC are a bit more challenging than the others, but should be reasonable for most students.

Differentiated Instruction **Above Level** Some students using Net CC (for a trapezoidal prism) might find it interesting, or even helpful, to think about the area of their trapezoids this way. To find the area, they need to halve the sum of the base lengths and then multiply by the height. Because that height is 2, the multiplying by 2 and halving cancel each other out (they "undo" each other). Therefore, in this case, the area is just the sum of the base lengths!

Teaching Notes for LAB page 244

Students solve story problems by finding the surface area of various boxes Students should use appropriate units to measure the area of each face of the net.

Challenge Problem The Challenge Problem asks students to describe the process for finding the total area of a net of a triangular prism.

Playing a Game: *Volume Builder*

Purpose To practice estimating and finding volumes of a rectangular prism

Goal The object of the game, *Volume Builder,* is for players to extend the dimension of a given rectangular prism in a way that will give the greatest volume. The greater the volume of the prism, the more points the player scores. The winner is the player with the most points when play ends.

Materials
• For each pair: cubes, a coin, scratch paper

NCTM Standards 1, 3, 4, 6, 7, 8, 9, 10

Prepare Materials Students play in pairs. Each pair needs a coin, cubes, and scratch paper to record their scores. Write this on the board.

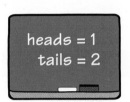

heads = 1
tails = 2

Student Handbook p. 214

How to Play

❶ Play starts with a cube placed between the players. The volume of this prism is 1 cubic unit.

❷ At a player's turn, the player tosses a coin and extends one of the three dimensions of the rectangular prism by 1 or 2 (depending on the coin toss), putting the appropriate cubes in place. The figure must remain a rectangular prism after the extra blocks have been added. A player decides which dimension to increase by picturing the result and estimating the new volumes in order to decide which choice would result in a prism of greatest volume.

For example, a player who got heads could extend this prism in one of the three ways shown at the right.

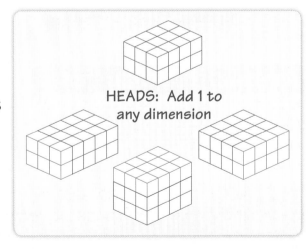

HEADS: Add 1 to any dimension

❸ Have students use appropriate units to measure the new volume, and record that number as their point score for that round.

❹ Players alternate turns until one player's reaches or exceeds 200 points and wins.

Reflect and Summarize the Lesson

 Write Math

Explain how you would find the total area of a net of a rectangular prism. Possible explanation: I would measure the base lengths and the heights of the six rectangular faces and find the area of each face. Then I would add together all the areas to find the total area of the net. Answers might give more efficient techniques.

Leveled Problem Solving

Donna is calculating the area of a net for a rectangular prism.

❶ Basic Level

What is the greatest number of different areas to compute? Explain. 3; the net for a rectangular prism has two of each possible rectangle.

❷ On Level

What formula should Donna use to compute the area of each shape on the net? Explain. *Area = length × width*; each face of a rectangular prism is a rectangle, so Donna should use the formula for the area of a rectangle.

❸ Above Level

The dimensions of the different rectangles are 3 inches by 4 inches, 3 inches by 5 inches, and 4 inches by 5 inches. What is the total area of the net? Explain. 94 in.²; 2 × (3 × 4) + 2 × (3 × 5) + 2 × (4 × 5) = 94

Intervention	Practice	Extension

Intervention

Activity Net Area

Have students use rectangular prisms. Have them trace each face of the prism on grid paper and lightly shade each face. Next, have them determine the area of each face by finding the number of shaded squares for each face. Then have them find the area of the net by finding the sum of the areas of the faces.

Practice

Area of Nets
The answers are given. Write questions to match.

Answers	Questions
❶ Find the height of this two-dimensional figure and the length of its base, and then multiply those two numbers.	How do you find the area of a parallelogram?
❷ Find the areas of all the faces and then add them up.	How do you find the total area of a net? or How do you find the surface area of a solid?
❸ It is a three-dimensional figure with a base that could be any polygon. All the other faces are triangles that meet at a common vertex.	What is a pyramid?
❹ Find the height of this three-dimensional figure, and find the length and width of the rectangular base. Multiply those three numbers.	How do you find the volume of a rectangular prism?
❺ Measure the base and height of this two-dimensional figure, multiply those two numbers, and then take half the result.	How do you find the area of a triangle?

Test Prep
❻ How many edges does a rectangular prism have? Explain what an edge of a prism is.
12 edges; An edge of a prism is where two faces of the prism meet.

Practice P100

Extension

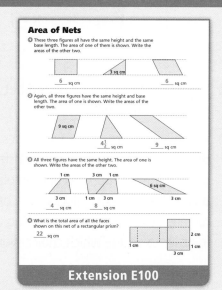

Area of Nets

❶ These three figures all have the same height and the same base length. The area of one of them is shown. Write the areas of the other two.

❷ Again, all three figures have the same height and base length. The area of one is shown. Write the areas of the other two.

❸ All three figures have the same height. The area of one is shown. Write the areas of the other two.

❹ What is the total area of all the faces shown on this net of a rectangular prism?

Extension E100

Spiral Review

Spiral Review Book page SR100 provides review of the following previously learned skills and concepts:

• using division to solve problems involving whole numbers

• analyzing data in a line plot to determine range, mode, and median

You may wish to have students work with partners to complete the page.

Number and Operations
Solve the problem. Tell what to do with the remainder. *Write the remainder; show the remainder as a decimal, or show the remainder as a fraction.*

❶ How many 15-inch pieces of wood can be made from a piece of lumber that is 110 inches long?
7 pieces of wood; ignore the remainder.

❷ The Math Club members collected $143.75 by washing cars. They washed 25 cars. How much did they charge for each car?
$5.75 per car; show the remainder as a decimal.

❸ A large cooler holds 130 ounces of juice. If the juice is used to fill 20 identical cups, how many ounces will be in each cup?
6 1/2 ounces; show the remainder as a fraction.

❹ Each shipping carton holds 6 canisters of popcorn. How many cartons can be filled if there are 75 canisters of popcorn?
12 cartons; ignore the remainder.

Data Analysis and Probability
For 5–7, use the line plot.

STUDENTS READING LAST MONTH

❺ What is the range of books read?
6

❻ What is the mode number of books read?
5

❼ What is the median number of books read?
4

Spiral Review SR100

Extension Activity
Matching Nets

Provide small groups with several of the three-dimensional figures and copies of the corresponding nets from AM101–AM126.

Have the groups match nets to their corresponding three-dimensional figures. After matching the nets with the figures, have them exchange the set of figures and nets with another group.

Teacher's Notes 🍎

Daily Notes . . .

Quick Notes

More Ideas

Lesson 7 Surface Area of Polyhedra

NCTM Standards 1, 3, 4, 7, 8, 9, 10

Lesson Planner

STUDENT OBJECTIVES
- To find the surface areas of polyhedra
- To explore how the surface area of a rectangle or triangle changes when the dimensions are doubled

1 | Daily Activities (TG p. 1027)

Open-Ended Problem Solving/Headline Story	Skills Practice and Review—Finding Volume

2 | Teach and Practice (TG pp. 1028–1032)

	MATERIALS
(A) **Defining Surface Area** (TG p. 1028)	• TR: Activity Master, AM132
(B) **Finding Shortcuts for Calculating Surface Area** (TG p. 1029)	• Figure C from the class set
(C) **Finding Surface Area** (TG p. 1030)	• cubes
(D) **Playing a Game: *Surface Area Builder*** (TG p. 1031)	• coins
	• scratch paper
	• 📖 LAB pp. 245–246
	• 📖 SH p. 209

3 | Differentiated Instruction (TG p. 1033)

Leveled Problem Solving (TG p. 1033)	Practice Book P101
Intervention Activity (TG p. 1033)	Extension Book E101
Extension Activity (TG p. 1033)	Spiral Review Book SR101

Lesson Notes

About the Lesson

In this lesson, students connect finding the total area of a net (**Lesson 12.6**) with finding the *surface area* of a three-dimensional figure: the area that forms (or covers) the surface of a three-dimensional figure. Students also begin investigating the effect of scale on area. What happens to the area of a polygon when you double all the dimensions? What happens to the surface area of a polyhedron when you double all the dimensions? Some students may also choose to investigate the effect of scale on volume in this lesson and in **Lesson 12.8.**

Developing Mathematical Language

Vocabulary: surface area

Surface area is the area of the surface of the three-dimensional figure. In the case of a polyhedron, it is the total area of all the faces that make up that surface.

The *surface area* of a three-dimensional figure and the area of its net are the same, but the images are different. Students will need to recognize the terms in order to answer questions about them. You can help them translate between the two ideas by giving students a net and associating finding its area with finding the *surface area* of the three-dimensional figure and vice versa. Over time, this will reduce students' dependence on nets.

Review the term *surface area* with students.

Beginning Show students a three-dimensional figure. Have them describe the shapes in the net of the three-dimensional figure.

Intermediate Give small groups of students a set of nets from AM101–AM126 and their corresponding three-dimensional figures from the class set. Have students match the nets to the three-dimensional figures.

Advanced Have students work in small groups to compute the area of one of the nets from AM101–AM126. Then have them identify the corresponding three-dimensional figures in the class set. Have them discuss how the area of the net compares with the *surface area* of the three-dimensional figure.

Open-Ended Problem Solving

Read the Headline Story to the students. You may want to encourage them to organize the information in a table.

 Headline Story

What whole-number dimensions would you use to make a rectangular cardboard box with a volume of 24 cu ft using as little cardboard as possible?

A 2 ft by 3 ft by 4 ft box uses the least amount of cardboard.

Skills Practice and Review

Finding Volume

Sketch the two three-dimensional figures on the board and ask students for the formulas for the volumes.

Point to a three-dimensional figures, give the measurements shown in the chart, and have a student give the missing measurement. Repeat problems with different numbers.

Three-Dimensional Figures	Volume	Height	Area of Base
Triangular prism	24 cu in.	4 in.	6 sq in.
Rectangular prism	1,000 cu cm	10 cm	100 sq cm
Rectangular prism	72 cu in.		Possible dimensions: $8 \times 9 \times 1, 6 \times 6 \times 2, \ldots$

Materials

- For the teacher: AM132, Figure C from the class set

NCTM Standards 1, 3, 4, 7, 8, 9, 10

A Defining Surface Area

Purpose To relate the total area of a net and the surface area of the three-dimensional figure made from that net

Introduce You will need a cut out Net C from Activity Master 132: Surface Area and Figure C from the classroom set. Ask how Net C is related to Figure C. Students will likely mention that if you fold up and tape Net C you will have a three-dimensional figure—just like Figure C from the classroom set.

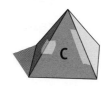

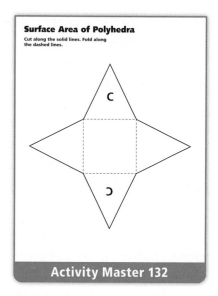

Surface Area of Polyhedra

Cut along the solid lines. Fold along the dashed lines.

Activity Master 132

Concept Alert

Some students may need time to make the connection between areas of nets and surface area. Such students may benefit from seeing un-taped nets repeatedly folded up (to show the resulting three-dimensional figure) and unfolded (to show that the net represents the surface area of the three-dimensional figure).

Problem **How would you find the total area of all the faces on Figure C?** Encourage students to discuss the answer to this question.

Talk Math You may want to use the questions below to guide the discussion.

❓ How would you find the total area of the net? I would find the area of each face. Then I would add the areas of the five faces together to find the total area of the net.

❓ How would you find the total area of all the faces on Figure C? It is the same as the total area of the net. So, I would find the area of the net that can be folded into the three-dimensional figure.

Fold Net C around Figure C to show that finding the area of a net is the same as finding the area of the polyhedron's surface. (The net won't fit precisely because of the thickness of paper and the additional space taken up by the tape, but it should be close enough.)

✔ **Ongoing Assessment**

- Do students correctly identify a net with a three-dimensional figure?
- Do students correctly identify a three-dimensional figure with its corresponding net?

If students are not familiar with the term *surface area,* explain to them that the area of a polyhedron's surface is simply called its *surface area.* A point to emphasize is that although students may find it easier to use the net when measuring the dimensions of the faces and keeping track of their work, they are also computing the *total surface area of the three-dimensional figure.*

Finding Shortcuts for Calculating Surface Area

Purpose To suggest a shortcut for finding the surface area of a polyhedron with two or more congruent faces

Introduce Hold up Figure C (or a different figure that has two or more congruent faces). Have a volunteer identify the faces that are congruent.

Task **Ask students what they might do, other than judging by eye, to check if faces are congruent.** Note that an actual *proof* cannot rely on measuring, as measurement is approximate, but, at this level, suggesting measurement of sides and angles indicates that students recognize that they need more confirmation than eyeballing the shape and size. Students might also suggest tracing one figure and seeing if the other fits the trace.

Talk Math You may want to use the questions below to continue the discussion.

❓ How could you do a quick check to see if the edges of the three-dimensional figure are perpendicular? Possible answer: I could use the corner of a piece of paper or a protractor.

❓ Can you think of a shortcut for finding the area of nets? Possible answer: If you know certain faces are congruent, you don't need to keep computing their areas. You can use multiplication instead. For example, because a cube has 6 congruent faces, you can multiply the area of one face by 6.

Materials
• For the teacher: Figure C from the class set

NCTM Standards 1, 3, 4, 7, 8, 9, 10

Concept Alert

When recording a multiple-step process, students may incorrectly use equals signs. For example, in calculating the surface area of the figure below, a student might think . . .

"I see four triangles. The area of one of them is $\frac{1}{2}(4 \times 2)$, or 4, and then I add on the three others, which gives me 16, and then I add on the area of the square, which gives me 20."

That person might write that sequence of steps like this:
$\frac{1}{2}(4 \times 2) = 4 + 4 + 4 + 4 = 16 + 4 = 20$

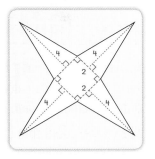

The thinking is correct. Yet, it is not a mathematically correct statement. Correctly used, the equals sign signals equal quantities. To address this in class, you might suggest writing each step as a separate number sentence.

$\frac{1}{2}(4 \times 2) = 4$
$4 \times 4 = 16$
$16 + 4 = 20$

Finding Surface Area LAB pp. 245–246

 individuals 20 MIN

Purpose To find the surface area of a polyhedron and to explore how the area of a rectangle or a triangle quadruples when its dimensions are doubled

NCTM Standards 1, 3, 4, 7, 8, 9, 10

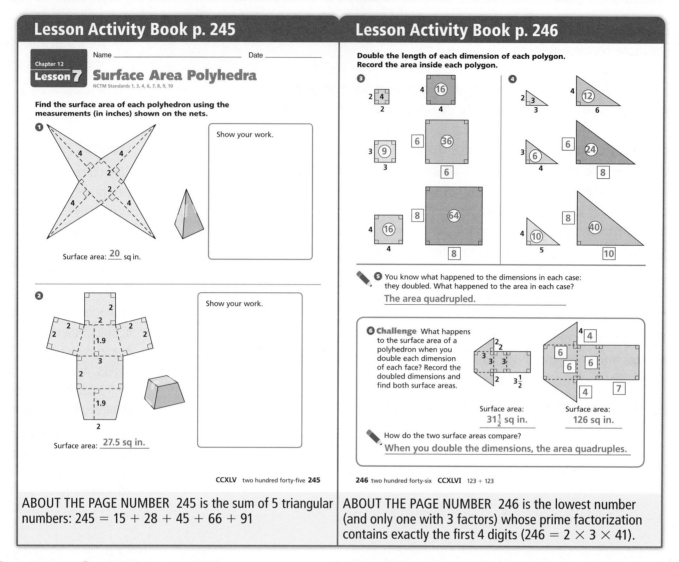

ABOUT THE PAGE NUMBER 245 is the sum of 5 triangular numbers: 245 = 15 + 28 + 45 + 66 + 91

ABOUT THE PAGE NUMBER 246 is the lowest number (and only one with 3 factors) whose prime factorization contains exactly the first 4 digits (246 = 2 × 3 × 41).

Teaching Notes for LAB page 245

On this page, students calculate surface areas of polyhedra using measurements given on nets.

It is likely (and good) that students will do much of the computation mentally. You might occasionally ask students to tell you orally how they got the numbers they recorded.

✔**Ongoing Assessment** LAB page 245 provides an opportunity for you to observe your students' recall and use of the area formulas for parallelograms, triangles, and trapezoids as they calculate surface areas of polyhedra.

Teaching Notes for LAB page 246

On this page, students double the dimensions of squares and triangles to see the effect on area. When dimensions are doubled, area is quadrupled. (More generally, when a two-dimensional figure's dimensions are multiplied by n, the area is multiplied by n^2.)

Challenge Problem The challenge problem asks students to double the dimensions of each face of a polyhedron (using a net) to see the effect on surface area. As the surface area is just the sum of all the individual areas of the faces, it, too, quadruples when the dimensions double. Students will extend this idea of scaling dimensions (multiplying all dimensions by the same number) to volume in **Lesson 12.8**.

D **Playing a Game:** *Surface Area Builder*

Purpose To practice estimating and finding surface area of a rectangular prism

Goal The object of the game, *Surface Area Builder,* is for players to extend the dimension of a given rectangular prism in a way that will give the greatest surface area. The greater the surface area of the prism, the more points the player scores. The winner is the player with the most points when play ends. This game is very similar to *Volume Builder* in **Lesson 12.6.**

Prepare Materials Students play in pairs. Each pair needs a coin, cubes, and scratch paper to record their scores. Write this on the board.

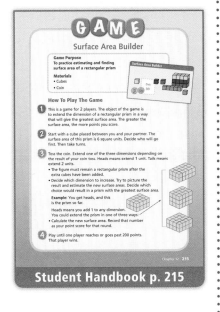
Student Handbook p. 215

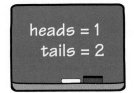
heads = 1
tails = 2

How to Play

1 Play starts with a cube placed between the players. The surface area of this prism is 6 square units.

2 At a player's turn, the player tosses a coin and extends one of the three dimensions of the rectangular prism by 1 or 2 (depending on the coin toss), putting the appropriate cubes in place. The figure must remain a rectangular prism after the extra blocks have been added. A player decides which dimension to increase by picturing the result and estimating the new surface areas in order to decide which choice would result in a prism of greatest surface area.

For example, a player who got heads could extend this prism in one of the three ways shown at the right.

3 Players then calculate the new surface area, and record that number as their point score for that round.

4 Players alternate turns until one player's score reaches or exceeds 200 points and wins.

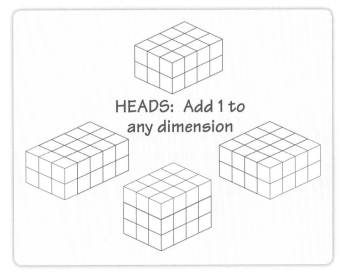
HEADS: Add 1 to any dimension

Materials
• For each pair: cubes, a coin, scratch paper

NCTM Standards 1, 3, 4, 6, 7, 8, 9, 10

Concept Alert

Students may fully understand the difference between volume and surface area, and yet mix up the two as they play this game, solely because they've played a similar game before using volume.

Be alert, watching for this slip, but where you see the slip, try just asking which game the kids are playing "volume" or "surface area." Perhaps, they'll notice the slip by themselves.

In some cases, students may genuinely have the two concepts confused, but this is less common.

Write Math How does this total area of a net relate to the surface area of the prism you could make from the net? *Possible answer: they're the same.*

Review Model . . . .

Refer students to Review Model: Surface Area in the *Student Handbook* to see how to use a net of a three-dimensional figure to help you find the surface area of the three-dimensional figure.

✔ Check for Understanding

❶ 72 sq ft

❷ 48 sq cm

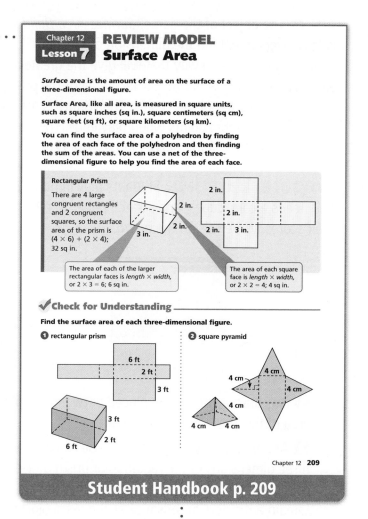

Student Handbook p. 209

3 | Differentiated Instruction

Leveled Problem Solving

Each edge of Zeb's cube is 5 inches long.

❶ Basic Level

The surface area is 150 square inches. What is the surface area of a cube whose sides are 10 inches long? Explain. 600 in.²; since 10 is twice 5, multiply 150 by 2², or 4.

❷ On Level

Zeb calculated the surface area as 125 square inches. What mistake did he make? Explain and correct his error. Zeb calculated volume $(5 \times 5 \times 5 = 125$ cu. in.). Surface area = area of a face $(5 \times 5$ sq. in.) $\times$ the number of faces (6) = 150 sq. in.

❸ Above Level

How many times greater is the surface area of a cube if the sides are tripled? Explain. 9 times greater; the surface area increases by a factor of 3².

Intervention	Practice	Extension

Activity Surface Area and Volume

Have students work in pairs to determine the surface area and volume of a 1-inch cube. Have them do the same for a 2-inch cube and for cubes up through a 9-inch cube.

Ask pairs to organize their data in a table. Have them answer the question, "Which increases faster—surface area or volume?"

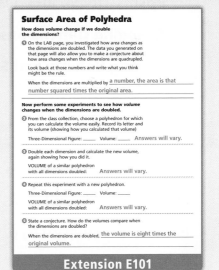

Practice P101

Extension E101

Extension Activity
Sum Surface Area!

Have students work in pairs. Give each pair 24 cubes. Challenge them to use the cubes to build a rectangular prism with the greatest "exposed" surface area. (The base of the prism is not exposed.) Tell students that they do not have to use all of the cubes.

Have each pair explain to the class how to compute the exposed surface area of their prism. The greatest exposed surface area would be for a prism 1-by-1-by-24; exposed surface area = 97 in.² if it stands vertically, like a tower.

Spiral Review

Spiral Review Book page SR101 provides review of the following previously learned skills and concepts:

- identifying prime and composite numbers
- applying the problem solving strategy *solve a simpler problem*

You may wish to have students work with partners to complete the page.

Spiral Review SR101

Lesson 8 Comparing Volume and Surface Area

NCTM Standards 1, 3, 4, 6, 7, 8, 9, 10

Lesson Planner

STUDENT OBJECTIVES
- To explore how volume and surface area of a prism change when the dimensions are doubled
- To solve problems involving volume and surface area

1 | Daily Activities (TG p. 1035)

| Open-Ended Problem Solving/Headline Story | Skills Practice and Review—Volumes of Cubes |

2 | Teach and Practice (TG pp. 1036–1040)

Ⓐ Comparing Volume and Surface Area of Prisms (TG pp. 1036–1037)

Ⓑ Changing Dimensions (TG pp. 1038–1039)

Ⓒ Solving Volume and Surface Area Problems (TG p. 1040)

MATERIALS
- one of the nets from TR: Activity Masters, AM129–AM131 and the polyhedron it makes
- calculators
- Figures B and E from the class set
- rulers
- 📖 LAB pp. 247–248

3 | Differentiated Instruction (TG p. 1041)

Leveled Problem Solving (TG p. 1041)	Practice Book P102
Intervention Activity (TG p. 1041)	Extension Book E102
Extension Activity (TG p. 1041)	Spiral Review Book SR102

Lesson Notes

About the Lesson

In this lesson, students solidify their understanding of the measurements of surface area and volume. They fold and unfold a net to represent the difference between the two-dimensional measurement of area and the three-dimensional measurement of volume. They also solve story problems involving both measurements and continue to investigate the effect of scale—in particular, doubling the dimensions—on area and volume.

About the Mathematics

On the LAB page in **Lesson 12.7**, students began investigating the effect of scaling (in this case,

doubling the dimensions) on the areas of polygons. A change of scale multiplies all the dimensions by the same factor. The dimensions could double or triple or quadruple, or they could be halved, or multiplied by $\frac{1}{3}$. If an object is two-dimensional, then *both* its dimensions are multiplied by that factor. In their experiments, students discover that doubling the dimensions multiplies the area by 4.

In Activity B, students see that doubling the dimensions multiplies the *volume* by 8. Seeing that these things are true may be an appealing surprise, but *why* are they true? That is genuinely important.

Use with Lesson Activity Book pp. 247–248.

Developing Mathematical Language

Vocabulary: surface area, volume

In this lesson students compare the measurements of *volume* and *surface area.* You may recall a similar comparison of area and perimeter of two-dimensional figures: area is the two-dimensional measure of the space "inside" the figure, and perimeter is a one-dimensional measurement of the figure's boundary. With three-dimensional figures, students have learned that volume is the three-dimensional measurement of the space inside the figure and that *surface area* is the two-dimensional measurement of the figure's boundary.

Review the terms *volume* and *surface area* with students.

Beginning Show students Figure B from the class set. Discuss how to find the *volume* of the three-dimensional figure. Then remove the tape and show the flattened net. Discuss how to find the *surface area* of the three-dimensional figure.

Intermediate Show students Figure B from the class set. Have students describe the difference between *volume* and *surface area* of a three-dimensional figure.

Advanced Show students Figure B from the class set. Have pairs of students describe to each other how to find the *volume* and *surface area* of the three-dimensional figure and then find the two measurements.

Open-Ended Problem Solving

Read the puzzle to students. You might encourage students to talk about ways to solve the puzzle and to record the puzzle in symbolic notation and to ask themselves whether the puzzle has any solutions that are not whole numbers.

 Headline Story

> **I thought of a number, added 4 to it, and multiplied that total by 5. The result was a two-digit number whose tens digit is 6.**

Possible responses: $5 \times (n + 4)$; the story tells us that after multiplying by 5, we get a number that is in the 60s. If that number is 60 or 65, then before multiplying by 5 we had 12 or 13. The "*n*" by itself, is 4 less than that; it could be 8 or 9. Would 8.5 also work? No, but 8.4 would!

Skills Practice and Review

Volumes of Cubes

Ask students to recall both the features of a cube and also the way to compute the volume of a cube. Pose the following questions and allow students time to perform the multiplication on their calculators.

If the length of the edge of a cube is

- 2 units, what is its volume? $2 \times 2 \times 2 = 8$; 8 cubic units
- 10 units, what is its volume? 1,000 cubic units
- 4 units, what is its volume? $4 \times 4 \times 4 = 64$; 64 cubic units
- 6 units, what is its volume? $6 \times 6 \times 6 = 216$; 216 cubic units

Now mention that another way to talk about finding the volume of a cube is to say you are "cubing" the edge length. Continue by asking students to cube various edge lengths. In **Lesson 12.9,** students will work backward from volumes of cubes to find edge lengths.

2 | Teach and Practice

whole class 10 MIN

Materials

- For the teacher: one of the nets from TR: AM129–AM131 and the polyhedron it makes
- For each student: TR: AM129–AM131 from Lesson 12.6

NCTM Standards 1, 3, 4, 6, 7, 8, 9, 10

Ongoing Assessment

- Do students understand the difference between surface area and volume?

A Comparing Volume and Surface Area of Prisms

Purpose To distinguish between the volume and surface area of a prism

Introduce Have your students get out their nets from **Lesson 12.6**—Activity Masters 129–131: Nets AA, BB, CC—or provide them with new ones to cut out. Instruct them to fold along the dotted lines, but not tape the edges, to make the polyhedra. You will also need a copy of one of these same three nets and the (completed and taped) polyhedron that it makes.

Begin by asking your students to imagine the net as a model, or a smaller version of an unfolded box that needs all the outside surfaces painted.

Talk Math Without using the specific terminology "surface area" or even "total area," ask students these questions.

? How can you figure out the area that needs to be painted? Measure each face, figure out its area, and add all the areas together.

? What kind of units do you use for the answer? Correct answers include the generic "square units" as well as more specific responses like square inches, square feet, square miles, square meters. Answers that do not specify that the units are *square* units (that is, answers like inches, feet, centimeters, yards, and so on) are not correct.

Show how your net "wraps around" the three-dimensional figure, and, gesturing to show you are referring to the entire surface of the three-dimensional figure, ask what that area is called. If students have not yet spontaneously used the term "surface area" in their responses, use it in context, perhaps saying something like when we're measuring the *volume* of a three-dimensional figure, we're measuring the amount of space *inside* it. The *surface* of the three-dimensional figure is a two-dimensional figure, like the net, wrapped around that inside space. The surface area of the three-dimensional figure is the same as the total area of the net.

Task **Now hold up your taped polyhedron. Ask your students to close up their nets. Then ask how we can find the measure of the space inside the box?** With the aim of eliciting students' understanding of volume and its associated terminology, you might begin by noting that we can find the length of the edges of this box. We can find the area of the faces of the box.

Talk Math Then ask these questions.

❓ What do we call the measure of the *space inside* the box? volume

❓ How can we measure that volume? Possible answers: We can fill the box with cubic units—centimeters, inches, or feet, according to the size of the box—or we can measure the area of the base and multiply by the box's height.

❓ What kind of units do we use for measuring volume? Volume is measured in *cubic* units.

Have students select and use an appropriate unit to measure the volume of their net, and then have them find out which net has the greatest volume.

Ask a few volunteers to show on their three-dimensional figures where they would make these measurements. Make sure the class sees all three three-dimensional figures. For Nets AA and BB, rectangular prisms, any base may be considered the base of the prism. The height may be any perpendicular edge. For Net CC, a trapezoidal prism, the trapezoid is its defining base, and the two base lengths and base heights are needed to find its area. The height of the prism is any edge perpendicular to the trapezoidal base.

Share Conclude by asking students to show, using their net, the difference between volume and surface area, and the difference between the calculations they perform to determine these quantities. Be sure the following ideas come up in the discussion:

- Surface area is the size (or amount) of the boundary that surrounds a three-dimensional figure. Volume is the size or amount of space inside the closed boundary of that three-dimensional figure. At your discretion, and depending on your class, you might want to draw attention to how these ideas relate to perimeter and area of two-dimensional figures. Perimeter is a measurement of the boundary; area is a measurement of the space inside that closed boundary.

- You can calculate surface area by making measurements on the net or on the faces of the three-dimensional figure itself. One way to measure volume of a prism is to find the area of the base that defines the prism— the polygon that gives the prism its name (triangular, rectangular, pentagonal, trapezoidal, etc.)—and multiply that area by the height of the prism. The number of cubes that can sit *on* the base matches the number of squares that fit in the base. So, the height of the prism says how many layers of that many cubes there are.

- Students can open and close their nets as they distinguish surface area from volume: Open it up to think about finding the "area of the surface," or surface area; close it up to think about finding the volume of the prism.

Understanding Volume: Selecting Appropriate Units

Students may need to gain more familiarity with selecting appropriate units of measure for volume. Ask the questions below.

- What unit of measure would you use to measure the volume of a cereal box— cubic meters, cubic feet, cubic miles, or cubic inches? cubic inches

- What unit of measure would you use to measure the volume of a gymnasium —cubic meters, cubic centimeters, cubic miles, or cubic inches? cubic meters

- What unit of measure would you use to measure the volume of a sphere that was about the size of Earth— cubic meters, cubic feet, cubic miles, or cubic inches? cubic miles

Encourage students to name other things for which volume could be measured. Then have students discuss what units of measure they would use to measure the volume of them.

Materials
- For the teacher: Figures B and E from the class set, ruler

NCTM Standards 1, 3, 4, 6, 7, 8, 9, 10

Differentiated Instruction

Above Level If your students actually fold and tape eight copies of Prisms B and E, they can assemble the eight copies and create a single prism in which each dimension is doubled. Some students might find it interesting to try this experiment with 8 copies of other prisms. Even triangular prisms can be assembled to create a similar triangular prism with twice the dimensions, and the task can be an interesting challenge for visually and manually adept students. Even though the property about volume—doubling the dimension multiplies the volume by 8—applies to all three-dimensional figures, other three-dimensional figures cannot, in general be assembled in the same way as rectangular and triangular prism can, to show that.

B Changing Dimensions

Purpose To explore how the volume and surface area of a prism change when the dimensions are doubled

Introduce Ask students to talk about models—small replicas of larger objects—that they have seen. Some students may own or have seen model cars, train sets, or dollhouses. If no one mentions it, remark that architects make intricate scale models of buildings before constructing the actual buildings. You might ask if anyone knows what a "scale model" is. (Each dimension of the model is a fixed fraction of the real measurement of the full-scale object or building.) Your students may be familiar with the scale on a map, another example of a "scale drawing" of the real thing, in which a small measurement, like a centimeter, may stand for many miles in the real world.

Task **Show your students Figure B and ask them to imagine that it is a model of one room of a dollhouse. Hold the prism on one of its non-square bases and have a volunteer use a ruler to help you measure the base length and width: 2 in. by 3 in. and then the height: 2 in.** Record the dimensions on the board.

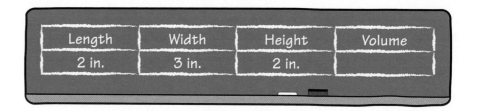

Length	Width	Height	Volume
2 in.	3 in.	2 in.	

Talk Math Ask questions such as these.

- What is the volume of this prism? 12 cu in.

- Could we have used a different face as the base to find the volume of this prism? Explain. Yes. The volume of a rectangular prism may be computed using any face as the base. If we used the 2 in. by 2 in. face as the base, then the height is 3 in., and the volume is still 12 cu in.

- Suppose I double each of the dimensions. What will the volume of the larger prism be? 4 in. by 6 in. by 4 in. produces a volume of 96 cu in.

- Does doubling the dimensions double the volume? No; the volume is now 8 times what it was before.

Practice Follow the same procedure with Figure E. Once again, doubling the dimensions multiplies the volume by 8.

Task **Present this new problem to students. What happens to the surface area when we double the dimensions?** Ask students to suggest a way of computing the surface area of Figure B. If they don't think of organizing their approach to take advantage of the congruent faces, you might ask how many faces of each type the figure has.

Talk Math Ask questions such as these.

❷ What is the surface area of this prism? Explain how you find the surface area. 32 sq in. The prism has four congruent faces that measure 2 in. by 3 in. and two other congruent faces that measure 2 in. by 2 in. So, the surface area is 4 × 6 sq in. + 2 × 4 sq in., or 32 sq in. in all.

❷ Suppose I double each of the dimensions. What will the surface area of the larger prism be? Explain. Now the four congruent faces measure 4 in. by 6 in. and the other two congruent faces measure 4 in. by 4 in. Each face has quadrupled in area, so the new surface area is 128 sq in.

❷ Did the surface area double like the dimensions? No; the surface area is 4 times what it was before.

Practice At your discretion, review this problem with Figure E.

Extend Have the class consider how surface area changes when you *triple* the dimensions. You might also invite your students to investigate this effect on other prisms at some later time.

Solving Volume and Surface Area Problems LAB pp. 247–248

 individuals **25 MIN**

Purpose To solve problems involving volume and surface area

NCTM Standards 1, 3, 4, 6, 7, 8, 9, 10

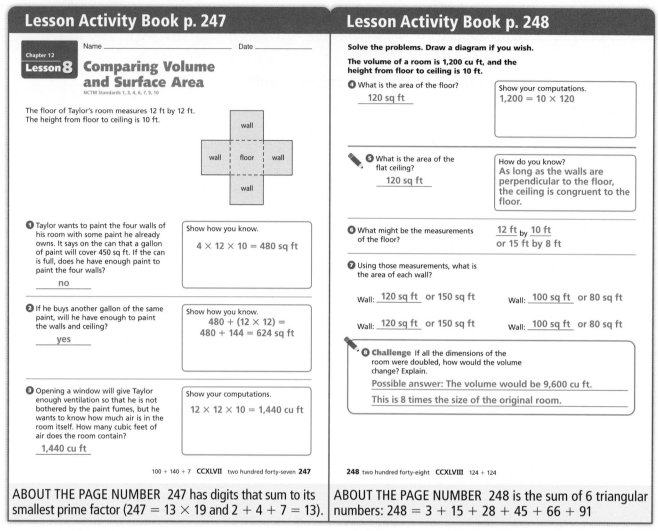

Lesson Activity Book p. 247

Name _____ Date _____

Chapter 12
Lesson 8 **Comparing Volume and Surface Area**
NCTM Standards 1, 3, 4, 6, 7, 9, 10

The floor of Taylor's room measures 12 ft by 12 ft. The height from floor to ceiling is 10 ft.

wall

wall | floor | wall

wall

❶ Taylor wants to paint the four walls of his room with some paint he already owns. It says on the can that a gallon of paint will cover 450 sq ft. If the can is full, does he have enough paint to paint the four walls?

___no___

Show how you know.
$4 \times 12 \times 10 = 480$ sq ft

❷ If he buys another gallon of the same paint, will he have enough to paint the walls and ceiling?

___yes___

Show how you know.
$480 + (12 \times 12) =$
$480 + 144 = 624$ sq ft

❸ Opening a window will give Taylor enough ventilation so that he is not bothered by the paint fumes, but he wants to know how much air is in the room itself. How many cubic feet of air does the room contain?

___1,440 cu ft___

Show your computations.
$12 \times 12 \times 10 = 1,440$ cu ft

100 + 140 + 7   **CCXLVII**   two hundred forty-seven **247**

Lesson Activity Book p. 248

Solve the problems. Draw a diagram if you wish.

The volume of a room is 1,200 cu ft, and the height from floor to ceiling is 10 ft.

❹ What is the area of the floor?

___120 sq ft___

Show your computations.
$1,200 = 10 \times 120$

❺ What is the area of the flat ceiling?

___120 sq ft___

How do you know?
As long as the walls are perpendicular to the floor, the ceiling is congruent to the floor.

❻ What might be the measurements of the floor?

12 ft by 10 ft
or 15 ft by 8 ft

❼ Using those measurements, what is the area of each wall?

Wall: __120 sq ft__ or 150 sq ft   Wall: __100 sq ft__ or 80 sq ft

Wall: __120 sq ft__ or 150 sq ft   Wall: __100 sq ft__ or 80 sq ft

❽ **Challenge** If all the dimensions of the room were doubled, how would the volume change? Explain.

Possible answer: The volume would be 9,600 cu ft.

This is 8 times the size of the original room.

248 two hundred forty-eight   **CCXLVIII**   124 + 124

ABOUT THE PAGE NUMBER 247 has digits that sum to its smallest prime factor (247 = 13 × 19 and 2 + 4 + 7 = 13).

ABOUT THE PAGE NUMBER 248 is the sum of 6 triangular numbers: 248 = 3 + 15 + 28 + 45 + 66 + 91

Teaching Notes for LAB page 247
Students may work independently or in pairs. This page challenges them to solve three related story problems, two involving area and the last involving volume. Some dimensions are given, but students must use reasoning to figure out some others. For example, they are told the floor dimensions and the height of a room, but not the dimensions of the walls. They are also not told the dimensions of the ceiling, but must reason that if the walls are rectangular and the ceiling is flat, then the ceiling's dimensions will be the same as the floor.

Teaching Notes for LAB page 248
On this page, students encounter a multi-step story problem involving area and volume. They are given the volume and height of a room and must figure out other dimensions and areas.

Students need to use reasonable dimensions in Problem 6. You might accept 20 ft by 6 ft or 24 ft by 5 ft, even though these dimensions describe a very narrow room.

Challenge Problem The challenge problem asks students to double dimensions to find a new volume.

Reflect and Summarize the Lesson

Write Math

How do the volume and the surface area of a prism change when the dimensions are doubled? Give an example. Use pictures, words or numbers to explain your answer.

When the dimensions of a prism are doubled, the volume of the prism is 8 times greater and the surface area is 4 times greater. The smaller prism is 1 in. by 2 in. by 3 in., has a volume of 6 cu in., and a surface area of 22 sq in. The larger prism is 2 in. by 4 in. by 6 in., has a volume of 48 cu in., and a surface area of 88 sq in.

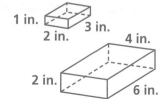

Use with Lesson Activity Book pp. 247–248.

3 | Differentiated Instruction

Leveled Problem Solving

Jill's pup tent has a surface area of 81 square feet and a volume of 36 cubic feet.

① Basic Level

How could Jill find the surface area and volume of a tent with dimensions that are double those of her tent? Explain. *Multiply the surface area of her tent by 4; multiply the volume of her tent by 8.*

② On Level

What are the surface area and volume of a tent with dimensions that are double those of Jill's tent? Explain. *SA = 324 ft², V = 288 ft³; SA: 81 × 4 = 324, V: 36 × 8 = 288*

③ Above Level

What are the surface area and volume of tent whose dimensions are triple those of Jill's tent? Explain. *729 ft², 972 ft³; triple means to multiply by 3. SA: 3 × 3 × 81 = 729; V: 3 × 3 × 3 × 36 = 972*

Intervention	Practice	Extension

Activity Doubling

Give students grid paper and the dimensions of a rectangular prism, such as 2-by-3-by-4 units. Ask them to draw each of the 6 faces of the prism and compute the total surface area. Then ask them to double the dimensions and draw the faces of the new prism, and find the surface area. Ask them to explain why doubling the dimensions quadruples the surface area.

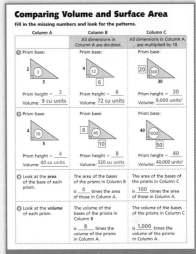

Practice P102

Extension E102

Spiral Review

Spiral Review Book page SR102 provides review of the following previously learned skills and concepts:

- identifying rules for input-output tables
- classifying quadrilaterals according to attributes such as congruent parts and perpendicular and parallel lines

You may wish to have students work with partners to complete the page.

Spiral Review SR102

Extension Activity
Just One Dimension

Have students work in small groups. Ask them to compute the surface area and volume of a cube. Then have them double just one dimension of the cube and compute the new surface area and volume. Have them repeat the process with two more cubes of different sizes, record their results in a table, and look for any patterns. Ask each group to present their findings to the class.

Problem Solving Strategy and Test Prep

NCTM Standards 1, 2, 3, 4, 6, 7, 8, 9, 10

Lesson Planner

STUDENT OBJECTIVES
- To practice the problem solving strategy *guess and check*
- To articulate the steps and strategies used to solve problems
- To prepare for standardized tests

Problem Solving Strategy:
Guess and Check (TG pp. 1042–1043)

MATERIALS

(A) **Discussing the Problem Solving Strategy: Guess and Check** (TG p. 1042)

(B) **Solving Problems by Applying the Strategy** (TG p. 1043)

- blank transparency (optional)
- calculators
- 📖 LAB p. 249
- 📖 SH pp. 210–211

Problem Solving Test Prep (TG p. 1044)

(C) **Getting Ready for Standardized Tests** (TG p. 1044)

- 📖 LAB p. 250

Lesson Notes

About Problem Solving

Problem Solving Strategy: Guess and Check

This lesson poses a challenge to students: find the edge length of a cube when the volume is not a "perfect cube" (a whole number cubed). For example, students find that the edge length of a cube with a volume of 1,000 cubic units is 10, because 10^3 = 10 × 10 × 10 = 1,000. What then, is the edge length of a cube with a volume of 500 cubic units? Is it 5 units? Is it 7 or 8, or somewhere between 7 and 8? Students use their knowledge of decimal numbers and the strategy *guess and check* to get close to target volumes.

This lesson also assesses students' knowledge of critical attributes of three-dimensional figures (such as congruence, parallelism, and perpendicularity of faces) and their ability to calculate volume and surface area.

Skills Practice and Review

MENTAL MATH

Edge Lengths of Cubes

This activity is an introduction to Activity B in this lesson. Students will each need a calculator and will cube edge lengths to get volumes. They will then begin with the volume of a cube and try to determine its edge length. Have students record their answer in a chart like the one below.

Length of Edge	Volume
4 units	4 × 4 × 4 = 64; 64 cu units
6 units	6 × 6 × 6 = 216; 216 cu units
5.2 units	5.2 × 5.2 × 5.2 = 140.608; 140.608 cu units
2 units	8 cu units
3 units	27 cu units
10 units	1,000 cu units
	500 cu units

For the final problem in the table, have students test whatever answer they give by multiplying. They will investigate this further in Activity B.

Problem Solving Strategy

A Discussing the Problem Solving Strategy: Guess and Check

whole class 15 MIN

Materials
• For the teacher: blank transparency (optional)

NCTM Standards 1, 2, 3, 4, 6, 7, 8, 9, 10

Purpose To share strategies for solving problems and focus on the problem solving strategy, *guess and check*

Introduce Before posing the problem below, review how to find the area of a square. Students should be able to say that you multiply the length of the side by itself, or square the length of the side. Write the formula on the board.

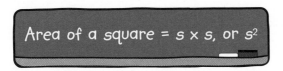

Area of a square = $s \times s$, or s^2

Present the following problem on the board or transparency. Ask a volunteer to read the problem. Then have the students solve it independently.

Problem Joel wants to plant a square vegetable garden with an area of 30 square feet. About how long should he make each side of his garden?

Share After students have worked for a while, have them share their strategies for solving the problem. Some students will probably suggest *guessing and checking* numbers for the length of a side until they find a number multiplied by itself that gives a product close to 30.

Students will see quickly that 5^2 is less than 30, but that 6^2 is too much, and so they must try lengths between 5 and 6. Tell students that they don't need an exact answer, but the *best answer* they can find. An organized list can help them record and keep track of the results of their guesses.

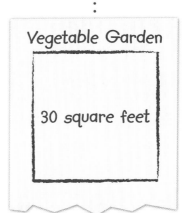

Vegetable Garden

30 square feet

Talk Math Ask questions like these to guide the discussion.

❓ How did you decide what length to guess? Possible answer: I started by thinking of whole numbers that when I squared them were close to 30.

❓ How do you know that the length should be between 5 feet and 6 feet? 5^2 is less than 30, and 6^2 is greater than 30, so the length of the side must be between 5 feet and 6 feet.

❓ About how long is the side? Possible answer: Answers will vary depending on how many decimal places are used. 5.48 feet is an appropriate answer.

Solving Problems by Applying the Strategy LAB p. 249

Purpose To practice the problem solving strategy, *guess and check*

NCTM Standards 1, 2, 3, 4, 6, 7, 8, 9, 10

Teaching Notes for LAB page 249

If you have not already done the Skills Practice and Review activity, do it now to begin this activity. Then have students read Problem 1 on LAB page 249 and explain the table headings. Tell them that *n* represents an edge length that they might try and n^3 represents the volume: $n^3 = n \times n \times n$. Have students share their strategies for solving the problem. Students will most likely suggest using the problem solving strategy *guess and check*. You may want to ask questions like these to guide the discussion:

Read to Understand

What do you know from reading the problem? Hope has a cube-shaped box that has a volume of 500 cubic units. What do you need to find out? the edge length of Hope's cube-shaped box

Plan

How can you solve this problem? I can *guess and check* by trying different numbers for the length, and keeping track of whether the numbers give a volume that is greater than or less than the target volume of 500 cubic units.

Solve

How might you guess and check to solve the problem? Try an edge length and multiply it by itself three times. If the volume is less than the target volume, increase the guess. If the volume is greater than the target volume, decrease the guess.

Check

Look back at the original problem. Did you answer the question that was asked? Does your answer make sense? How do you know?

Students will likely discover fairly quickly that 7^3 is less than 500 and that 8^3 is greater than 500. They will then need to try lengths between the 7 and 8. Remind students that they are not looking for an exact answer, but the *best answer* they can find.

Lesson Activity Book p. 249

Chapter 12 Lesson 9 **Problem Solving Strategy**
Guess and Check
NCTM Standards 1, 2, 3, 4, 6, 7, 8, 9, 10

Understand / Plan / Solve / Check

You may use a calculator and the tables to help you solve the problems.

❶ Hope has a cube-shaped box. Its volume is 500 cubic units. About how many units long is each edge? Record the actual numbers that students supply. These are examples.

❷ The volume of a large ice cube is 100 cubic centimeters. What is the approximate length of one edge? Examples are shown. Entries will vary.

Edge n	Volume n³	> or < Target Volume	Edge n	Volume n³	> or < Target Volume
5	125	< 500	4	64	< 100
7	343	< 500	5	125	> 100
8	512	> 500	4.5	91.125	< 100
7.5	421.875	< 500	4.75	107.171875	> 100
7.75	465.484375	< 500	4.65	100.544625	> 100
7.9	493.039	< 500			○ 100
7.93	498.677257	< 500			○ 100
7.95	502.459875	> 500			○ 100
7.94	500.566184	> 500			○ 100
7.937	499.999006	< 500			○ 100

83 + 83 + 83 **CCXLIX** two hundred forty-nine **249**

ABOUT THE PAGE NUMBER 249 is the sum of 7 triangular numbers: 249 = 1 + 3 + 15 + 28 + 45 + 66 + 91.

Reflect and Summarize the Lesson

Write Math

How can you use the strategy *guess and check* to help you find the length of the edge of a cube when you know the volume of the cube? Possible answer: I can guess a length for the edge, and then cube that length to find the volume of a cube with that edge length. Then I can adjust the length I chose—by either increasing or decreasing the number depending on how the volume I got relates to the volume I am looking for—and check my second guess. I can keep guessing and checking until I find an edge length that will give a volume close to the volume I am looking for.

Problem Solving Test Prep

C Getting Ready for Standardized Tests LAB p. 250

individuals · 20 MIN

Purpose To prepare students for standardized tests

NCTM Standards 1, 6

Lesson Activity Book p. 250

Problem Solving Test Prep

1 Henry, Jamie, and Sam are three friends. Their ages are consecutive numbers. The product of their ages is 2,145 more than the sum of their ages. Sam is the oldest. How old is Sam?

A. 12
B. 13
C. 14 ✓
D. 15

2 The surface area of a cube is 150 square inches. What is the volume of the cube?

A. 150 cubic inches
B. 125 cubic inches ✓
C. 100 cubic inches
D. 75 cubic inches

Show What You Know

Solve each problem. Explain your answer.

3 Darla has a square beach towel that measures 96 inches on each side. She folds it in half, then folds it in half again, and finally folds it in half again. What is the area that the folded towel would cover? Explain how you solved the problem.

8 square feet, or 1,152 square inches; possible explanation: convert 96 inches to 8 feet, and then find the area of the towel in square feet: $8 \times 8 =$ 64 square feet. Divide 64 by 2, then by 2 again, and finally by 2 again to find the final area, 8 square feet.
(8 sq ft × 144 sq in. per square foot = 1,152 sq in.)

4 Students in the architecture club are using cubes to build a model of an apartment house. Each cube represents one room. Every outside wall of a cube will have one window. If the students use 27 cubes, what is the least number of windows that is possible? What is the greatest? Explain how you solved the problem.

The least number of windows is 36 if they build the house in the shape of a cube. Each of the 4 sides of the building will have 9 windows. The greatest number is 108 if they stack one cube on top of another. Each side will have 27 windows: $4 \times 27 = 108$.

250 two hundred fifty   CCL

ABOUT THE PAGE NUMBER 250 is the smallest multi-digit number such that the sum of the squares of its prime factors equals the sum of the squares of its digits.

Teaching Notes for LAB page 250

The test items on this page are written in the same style and arranged in the same format as those on many state assessments. The page is cumulative and is designed for students to apply a variety of problem-solving strategies including *write an equation, draw a picture,* and *guess and check.* Students might share the strategies they use.

The Item Analysis Chart indicates one of the possible strategies that may be used for each test item.

Show What You Know

Written Response

Direct students' attention to Problems 3 and 4. Explain that they must decide how to solve the problems. Then have students write an explanation of how they know their answer is correct. To provide more space for students to communicate their thinking about these problems, you may wish to have them write their explanations on a separate sheet of paper. Use the Scoring Rubric below to evaluate their understanding.

Item Analysis Chart

Item	Strategy
1	Guess and check
2	Write an equation
3	Draw a picture
4	Make a model

Scoring Rubric

2	• Demonstrates complete understanding of the problem and chooses an appropriate strategy to determine the solution
1	• Demonstrates a partial understanding of the problem and chooses a strategy that does not lead to a complete and accurate solution
0	• Demonstrates little understanding of the problem and shows little evidence of using any strategy to determine a solution

---

Review Model

Refer students to the Problem Solving Strategy Review Model: Guess and Check in the **Student Handbook** pp. 210–211 to review a model of the four steps they can use with problem solving strategy, *guess and check.*

Additional problem solving practice is also provided.

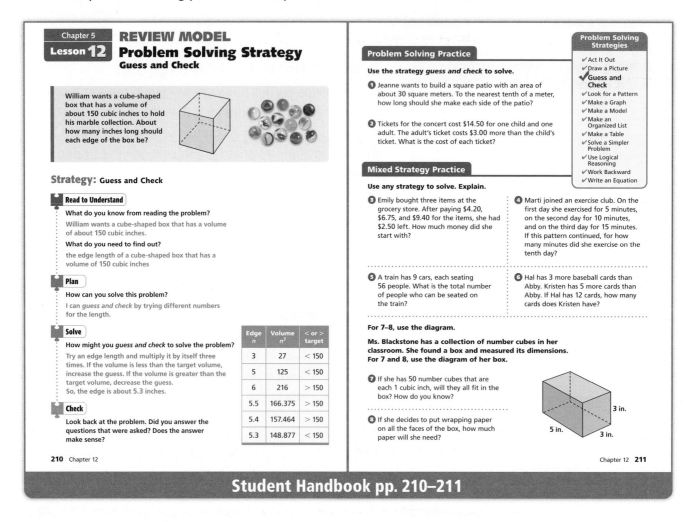

Student Handbook pp. 210–211

Task Have students read the problem at the top of the Review Model page. Then discuss.

Talk Math

❓ If you know the edge length is between 5 and 6 inches, how might you estimate the tenths place of the edge length measure? Possible answer: When I found the cubes of 5 and 6, I found that 150 was closer to the cube of 5 than to the cube of 6. So I estimated that the tenths digit was between 1 and 5.

❓ William won a big bag of marbles that increased the amount of room he needed to 1,200 cubic inches. If William wanted a new cube-shaped box, what would the edge lengths of the new box have to be? 10.6; Possible explanation: 1,200 cu. in. is 8 times 150 cu. in. I know that when dimensions double, the volume increases by a factor of 8. Since the volume increased by a factor of 8, the new box needs edge lengths that are twice as long. $5.3 \times 2 = 10.6$ in.

1 5.5 meters; Possible explanation: Using the strategy *guess and check,* I found that the patio is between 5 and 6 meters in width and length. I squared 5.1, 5.2, 5.3, 5.4, 5.5, and 5.6 and saw that 5.5 squared is the closest area to 30 square meters.

2 Adult: $8.75, Child: $5.75; Possible explanation: Using the strategy *guess and check* I guessed a price for a child's ticket, added $3 to the price I chose for the child's ticket to find the price of an adult ticket, and then found the sum of the two prices. Then, I adjusted the price of the child's ticket based on whether the sum was greater than or less than $14.50. I recorded my guesses in a table like this.

Child's Ticket	Adult's Ticket	Total cost	< or > $14.50
$3.00	$6.00	$9.00	<
$5.00	$8.00	$13.00	<
$6.00	$9.00	$15.00	>
$5.75	$8.75	$14.50	just right

3 $22.85; Possible explanation: Using the strategy *work backward,* I found the starting amount of money by adding the money that remained to the money she spent. $2.50 + $9.40 + $6.75 + $4.20 = $22.85

4 50 minutes; Possible explanation: Using the strategy *find a pattern,* I saw that every day Marti increased her time by 5 minutes, so by following the pattern I found that on the tenth day she exercised 50 minutes.

5 504 people; Possible explanation: Using the strategy *solve a simpler problem,* I first solved for the number of people in 3 cars, $3 \times 56 = 168$ people. Then I multiplied that number by 3 to find the total number of people in 9 cars, $9 \times 168 = 504$ people.

6 14 cards; Possible explanation: Using the strategy *work backward,* I found that since Abby has 3 fewer cards than Hal, she has $12 - 3 = 9$ cards. Kristen has 5 more cards than Abby, so since Abby has 9 cards, Kristen has $9 + 5 = 14$ cards.

7 No; Possible explanation: Using the strategy *act it out,* I found the volume of the box was 45 cubic inches. This volume was less than 50 cubic inches, which was the amount of space the 50 number cubes needed.

8 78 square inches; Possible explanation: By using the strategy *draw a picture,* I drew diagrams of all the faces of the box and labeled their dimensions. I calculated the area of each face and then added them all together, finding the surface area of the entire box.

Three-Dimensional Geometry

NCTM Standards 1, 3, 4, 6, 7, 9, 10

Purpose To provide students with an opportunity to demonstrate understanding of Chapter 12 concepts and skills

MATERIALS

- LAB pp. 251–252
- Chapter 12 Test (Assessment Guide pp. AG109–AG110)

Chapter 12 Learning Goals and Assessment Options

These learning goals are assessed in many ways throughout the chapter. The chart below correlates each learning goal to specific formal and informal assessment options.

	Learning Goals	Lesson Number	Snapshot Assessment	Chapter Review Item Numbers	Chapter Test Item Numbers
				LAB pp. 251–252	Assessment Guide pp. AG109–AG110
12-A	Identify and classify three-dimensional figures by their attributes, including faces, vertices, and edges	12.1–12.3	1, 5	1–7	1–8
12-B	Find the volume of a triangular or rectangular prism and identify the appropriate unit of measurement for volume	12.4, 12.5, 12.8	2, 6	8–9	9–12
12-C	Find the surface area of a prism or pyramid and identify the appropriate unit of measure for surface area	12.6–12.8	3, 4, 7	11, 12	13
12-D	Apply problem solving strategies such as *guess and check* to solve problems	12.9	8	13, 14	14–16

📷 Snapshot Assessment

The following Mental Math and Quick Write questions and tasks provide a quick, informal assessment of students' understanding of Chapter 12 concepts, skills, and problem solving strategies.

whole class · 10 MIN

Mental Math This oral assessment uses mental math strategies and can be used with the whole class.

❶ If you took a three-dimensional cardboard box and cut it along some of its edges so you could open it up, and lay it flat, the resulting net will be made up of only rectangles. How many? 6

Each fold line between each section would be called an _____ if it were still the three-dimensional box. edge

Each section would be called a _____ if it were still a three-dimensional box. face

What would we call the place where more than two faces meet at a point? vertex
(Learning Goal 12-A)

❷ What is the formula for finding the area of a rectangle? *Area = length × width* or *Area = base × height*

What is the formula for finding the volume of a rectangular prism? Volume = area of the base × height (or volume = length × width × height)

A rectangular prism has a length of 4 cubes, a width of 3 cubes, and a height of 5 cubes. What is the volume? 60 cubic units
(Learning Goal 12-B)

❸ What do we call the amount or size of the boundary that surrounds a three-dimensional figure? surface area How might a net of a prism help you find the surface area of the prism? Answers may vary; possible answer: you could find the area of each face, then add all areas together to find the total surface area.
(Learning Goal 12-C)

❹ The area of just one face of a cube is 4 square meters. What is the total surface area of the whole cube? Explain how you find your answer. 24 square meters; I know a cube has 6 congruent faces, so I multiply the area of one face by 6 to find the total surface area.

A triangular pyramid has 4 congruent faces. The total surface area is 16 square inches. What is the area of just one face? 4 square inches
(Learning Goal 12-C)

Quick Write This informal written assessment can be administered to small groups or the whole class. Read each question and have the students record responses on their write-on boards. Encourage students to listen and think about the questions before responding.

❺ What three-dimensional figure has:
- rectangular faces, 8 vertices, 12 edges? rectangular prism
- 4 triangular faces, 4 vertices, 6 edges? triangular pyramid
- Name some three-dimensional figures that are not polyhedra. cylinder, cone, sphere
- Which three-dimensional figures can be set so that one face lies flat on a table, and another face is completely level on top, parallel to the table top and the other faces are parallelograms? prisms
- A polyhedron with a single base that is a polygon and all other faces are triangles is called a <u>pyramid</u>.
- In a pyramid, the point where the triangular faces meet is called the <u>vertex</u>.
- Is a cylinder a polyhedron? Why or why not? no, because the circular base is not a polygon
(Learning Goal 12-A)

❻ Find the volume for each rectangular prism:
- length 4 ft, width 3 ft, height 2 ft 24 cu ft
- length 2.5 m, width 2 m, height 3.2 m 16 cu m
Find the volume for each triangular prism:
- triangular base: length 4 cm, height 4 cm; height of prism: 3 cm 24 cu cm
- triangular base: length 6 yd., height 3 yd.; height of prism: 4.5 yd. 40.5 cu yd
- If just the length of a rectangular prism is doubled, what will happen to the volume? It will also double.
- If just the height of a rectangular prism is cut in half, then what will happen to its volume? It will be half of the original volume.
- The volume of a triangular prism was reported as 15 cubic grams; is this reasonable? Why or why not? no, because grams measure mass, not length, width, or height
(Learning Goal 12-B)

❼ Find the total surface area of a rectangular prism whose front face area is 16 sq cm, the left side face area is 12 sq cm, and the bottom face area is 48 sq cm. Show or explain how you find the answer. 152 square cm; (front) 16 + (back) 16 + (left side) 12 + (right side) 12 + (bottom) 48 + (top) 48 = 152 square cm
(Learning Goal 12-C)

❽ Jennifer wants to wrap a gift. The box measures 12 in. long, 8 in. wide, and 3 in. high. She has a roll of wrapping paper which is 500 square inches. Can she wrap the whole package with that paper? Show your work to explain your answer. Yes; she needs 312 square inches of wrapping paper since that is the surface area of the box. She will have 2 faces with areas of 12 × 8, or 96 square inches, 2 faces with areas of 8 × 3, or 24 square inches, and two faces with areas of 12 × 3, or 36 square inches each. 96 + 96 + 24 + 24 + 36 + 36 = 312, so the total surface area is 312 square inches.
(Learning Goal 12-D)

Formal Assessment

Chapter Review/Assessment The Chapter 12 Review/Assessment on *Lesson Activity Book* pages 251–252 assesses students' understanding of attributes of three-dimensional figures, how to find the volume and surface of three-dimensional figures, and problem solving. Students should be able to complete these pages independently.

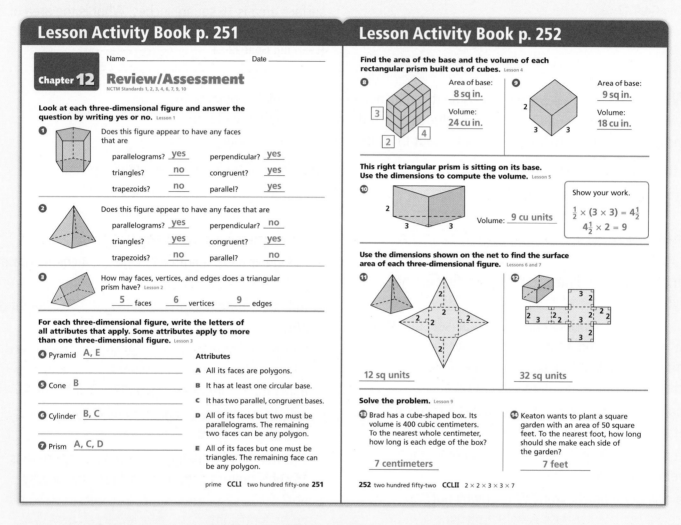

Lesson Activity Book p. 251

Name _____ Date _____

Chapter 12 **Review/Assessment**
NCTM Standards 1, 2, 3, 4, 6, 7, 9, 10

Look at each three-dimensional figure and answer the question by writing yes or no. Lesson 1

❶ Does this figure appear to have any faces that are

parallelograms? **yes**   perpendicular? **yes**

triangles? **no**   congruent? **yes**

trapezoids? **no**   parallel? **yes**

❷ Does this figure appear to have any faces that are

parallelograms? **yes**   perpendicular? **no**

triangles? **yes**   congruent? **yes**

trapezoids? **no**   parallel? **no**

❸ How may faces, vertices, and edges does a triangular prism have? Lesson 2

5 faces   **6** vertices   **9** edges

For each three-dimensional figure, write the letters of all attributes that apply. Some attributes apply to more than one three-dimensional figure. Lesson 3

❹ Pyramid **A, E**

❺ Cone **B**

❻ Cylinder **B, C**

❼ Prism **A, C, D**

Attributes

A All its faces are polygons.

B It has at least one circular base.

C It has two parallel, congruent bases.

D All of its faces but two must be parallelograms. The remaining two faces can be any polygon.

E All of its faces but one must be triangles. The remaining face can be any polygon.

prime **CCLI** two hundred fifty-one **251**

Lesson Activity Book p. 252

Find the area of the base and the volume of each rectangular prism built out of cubes. Lesson 4

❽ Area of base: **8 sq in.**   Volume: **24 cu in.**

❾ Area of base: **9 sq in.**   Volume: **18 cu in.**

This right triangular prism is sitting on its base. Use the dimensions to compute the volume. Lesson 5

❿ Volume: **9 cu units**

Show your work.
$\frac{1}{2} \times (3 \times 3) = 4\frac{1}{2}$
$4\frac{1}{2} \times 2 = 9$

Use the dimensions shown on the net to find the surface area of each three-dimensional figure. Lessons 6 and 7

⓫ **12 sq units**

⓬ **32 sq units**

Solve the problem. Lesson 9

⓭ Brad has a cube-shaped box. Its volume is 400 cubic centimeters. To the nearest whole centimeter, how long is each edge of the box?

7 centimeters

⓮ Keaton wants to plant a square garden with an area of 50 square feet. To the nearest foot, how long should she make each side of the garden?

7 feet

252 two hundred fifty-two **CCLII** $2 \times 2 \times 3 \times 3 \times 7$

Extra Support Students who have difficulty with items on the Chapter 12 Review/Assessment may need review of the lesson where development of the concept was provided. You can use the Intervention Activity to increase students' understanding before the Chapter Test is given.

Chapter Test Use the Chapter 12 Test in the *Assessment Guide* to assess concepts, skills, and problem solving from the chapter and to prepare students for standardized tests. The Chapter Test and other test items are also available online.

Chapter Notes

Quick Notes

More Ideas

_____
_____
_____
_____
_____
_____
_____
_____
_____
_____
_____
_____
_____
_____
_____
_____
_____
_____
_____
_____
_____
_____
_____

Fun with Algebra

About the Chapter

In this chapter, students see algebraic notation as a language: a shorthand way to record relationships, a more convenient way to write what they would otherwise say in words.

Students have been thinking algebraically throughout the year. Generalizations such as stating a rule that the output is always twice the input require algebraic reasoning. We don't need to know a quantity for the input to understand the situation. That's what algebra is all about.

Students revisit some algebraic themes they already know and understand: to "undo" addition you subtract, and to "undo" multiplication you divide; if you have two weights that balance (that is, the two weights are equal), removing the same amount from each side will keep them in balance. The lessons in this chapter pay more attention to visual and symbolic representations of these themes than students have seen.

Visual Representations Diagrams, such as bags with an unknown number of marbles or rectangular areas with unknown dimensions, provide a more concrete sense to an abstract, verbal description of a situation. Making a connection between a diagram and a mathematical relationship it illustrates is an important part of being able to use the diagram to solve problems. The image of balancing weights is a powerful one for students and adults alike: imagining unknown quantities as different kinds of blocks (for balance scales) or shapes hanging from a mobile allows one to focus on the relationships among those quantities without getting distracted by the abstraction of letters.

Symbolic Representations At a certain point, however, drawing a shape and using a letter are not very different. When finding the weight of a star shape on a mobile, whether students write $\star = 5$ or $S = 5$, the level of abstraction required is the same. Both are a shorthand for "the star weighs 5 units," but $S = 5$ is easier to write and so a simpler and more efficient record.

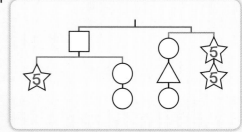

Developing Concepts Across the Grades

Topic	Prior Learning	Learning in Chapter 13	Later Learning
Visual Representations	• Use pictures of bags and counters to describe the steps in a number puzzle Grade 4, Chapter 14	• Recognize and create balanced mobiles • Use diagrams to illustrate mathematical relationships Lessons 13.1–13.3, 13.6	• Relate graphs and equations Grade 6
Symbolic Representations	• Read and write symbols that describe the steps in a number puzzle Grade 4, Chapter 14	• Use words, diagrams, and shorthand to describe calculations • Use algebraic shorthand as a tool for recording relationships Lessons 13.3, 13.4, 13.6, 13.7	• Match problem situations and expressions • Create problem situations for equations Grade 6
Solve Equations	• Find the value of x in number sentences Grade 4, Chapter 14	• Solve simple equations Lessons 13.3, 13.4, 13.7	• Solve equations with integers and rational numbers Grade 6

CHAPTER 13 World Almanac For Kids • Vocabulary • Games • Challenge
Teacher Guide pp. 1059A–1059F, Student Handbook pp. 218–219, 228–232

1

Introducing Mobiles

PACING 1 DAY

Teacher Guide
pp. 1060–1067
Lesson Activity Book
pp. 253–254
Student Handbook
Student Letter p. 217

- To recognize and create balanced mobiles

1, 2, 7, 8, 9, 10

mobile

For the teacher:
- transparency of AM133 (optional)
- completed mobile

For the students:
- School-Home Connection TR: SHC49–SHC50
- wire hangers, twist ties or pipe cleaners, small plastic bags, small objects of equal weight
- P103, E103, SR103

2

Balancing Mobiles

PACING 1 DAY

Teacher Guide
pp. 1068–1075
Lesson Activity Book
pp. 255–256
Student Handbook
Explore p. 220

- To solve mobile puzzles that involve several unknown quantities

1, 2, 7, 8, 9

balance

For the teacher:
- transparency of AM134 (optional)

For the students:
- TR: AM134
- P104, E104, SR104

3

Equations for Mobiles

PACING 1 DAY

Teacher Guide
pp. 1076–1083
Lesson Activity Book
pp. 257–258
Student Handbook
Review Model p. 221

- To solve puzzles about the relationships among several unknown quantities
- To use algebraic shorthand as a tool for recording relationships

1, 2, 7, 8, 9

equation

For the teacher:
- transparency of AM135 (optional)

For the students:
- TR: AM136
- P105, E105, SR105

Literature Connection:
A Gebra Named AL
Teacher Guide p. 1058

4

Balance Puzzles

PACING 1 DAY

Teacher Guide
pp. 1084–1093
Lesson Activity Book
pp. 259–260
Student Handbook
Explore p. 222
Game p.230
Review Model p. 223

- To solve simple equations

1, 2, 7, 8, 9, 10

balance scale

For the teacher:
- transparencies of AM137–AM138 (optional)

For the students:
- TR: AM137–AM138
- paper clips
- P106, E106, SR106

5

Number Tricks

PACING 1 DAY

Teacher Guide
pp. 1094–1101
Lesson Activity Book
pp. 261–262

- To explore and explain number tricks
- To use words, diagrams, and shorthand to describe calculations on "the number you picked"

1, 2, 6, 7, 8, 9, 10

variable

For the teacher:
- transparency of AM139 (optional)

For the students:
- P107, E107, SR107

NCTM Standards 2000
1. Number and Operations
2. Algebra
3. Geometry
4. Measurement
5. Data Analysis and Probability
6. Problem Solving
7. Reasoning and Proof
8. Communication
9. Connections
10. Representation

Key
AG: Assessment Guide
E: Extension Book
LAB: Lesson Activity Book
P: Practice Book
SH: Student Handbook
SR: Spiral Review Book
TG: Teacher Guide
TR: Teacher Resource Book

MATH GLOSSARY in **Student Handbook** p. 266

Planner (continued)

Lesson	Objectives	NCTM Standards	Vocabulary	Materials/ Resources
6 **Making Diagrams** PACING 1 DAY **Teacher Guide** pp. 1102–1109 **Lesson Activity Book** pp. 263–264 **Student Handbook** Game p. 231 Review Model p. 224	• To select and use diagrams to illustrate mathematical relationships • To connect diagrams and algebraic expressions	2, 8, 9, 10	describing situations with diagrams	**For the students:** ■ TR: AM140 ■ counters in two colors ■ number cubes in different colors ■ P108, E108, SR108 **Science Connection:** **Levers and Fulcrums Teacher Guide** p. 1058
7 **Equations for Stories** PACING 1 DAY **Teacher Guide** pp. 1110–1117 **Lesson Activity Book** pp. 265–266 **Student Handbook** Review Model p. 225	• To find a rule for a situation in a story problem • To record and use such a rule using algebraic notation	1, 2, 6, 7, 8, 9	describing situations with equations	**For the teacher:** ■ transparency of AM141 (optional) **For the students:** ■ TR: AM141 ■ P109, E109, SR109 **Art History Connection:** **Inventor of the Mobile Teacher Guide** p. 1058
8 **Problem Solving Strategy and Test Prep** PACING 1 DAY **Teacher Guide** pp. 1118–1123 **Lesson Activity Book** pp. 267–268 **Student Handbook** Review Model pp. 226–227	• To practice the problem solving strategy *work backward* • To articulate the steps and strategies used to solve problems • To prepare for standardized tests	1, 2, 5, 6, 7, 8, 9, 10		

CHAPTER 13 Assessment
TG pp. 1124–1127, **LAB** pp. 269–270, **AG** pp. 113–116

For the students:
■ Chapter 13 Test pp. AG113–AG114

Games....

Use the following games for skills practice and reinforcement of concepts.

Lesson 13.4 ▶

The Balance Puzzle provides an opportunity for students to relate balance puzzles to equations and to solve the puzzles.

The Balance Puzzle

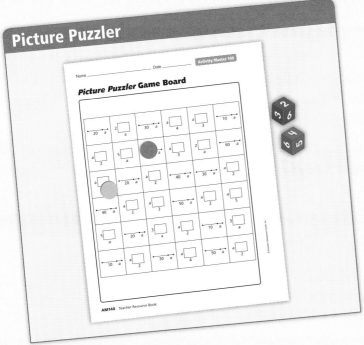

Picture Puzzler

◀ **Lesson 13.6** *Picture Puzzler* provides and opportunity for students to select diagrams to match given sums or products.

Planning Ahead

In **Lesson 13.1,** students use wire hangers, twist ties or pipe cleaners, small plastic bags, and small objects of equal weight to make mobiles. They use a number cube in the Extension Activity.

In **Lesson 13.4,** students will be playing *The Balance Puzzle.* Each pair of students will need AM137: *The Balance Puzzle* Scale and Spinner, a set of game pieces from AM138: *The Balance Puzzle*

Game Pieces, a pencil, and a paper clip. A balance scale is used in the ELL activity.

In **Lesson 13.6,** students will be playing *Picture Puzzler.* Each pair of students will need AM140: *Picture Puzzler* Game Board, 20 counters in two colors, and 2 number cubes in different colors.

Developing Problem Solvers

Open-Ended Problem Solving

The Headline Story in the Daily Activities section of every lesson provides an open-ended problem for students to complete. For each story there are many possible responses.

Headline Stories can be found on TG pages 1061, 1069, 1077, 1085, 1095, 1103, and 1111.

Headline Story

Leveled Problem Solving

Leveled Problem Solving provides an opportunity for students to apply learning from the lesson to a real-life situation. Problems are leveled by ability to allow students of all ability levels to become successful problem solvers. Each Leveled Problem Solving begins with a real-life scenario upon which three problems are built.

The levels of problems are:

1 Basic Level	**2** On Level	**3** Above Level
students needing extra support	students working at grade level	students who are ready for more challenging problems

Leveled Problem Solving can be found on TG pages 1066, 1074, 1083, 1093, 1101, 1109, and 1116.

THE WORLD ALMANAC FOR KIDS

The World Almanac for Kids feature is designed to stimulate student interest for the math concepts they are about to learn. Students use data to solve problems and explain solutions. The Chapter 13 Project can be found on SH pages 218–219.

Write Math — Reflect and Summarize the Lesson poses a

problem or question for students to think and write about. This feature can be found on TG pages 1065, 1073, 1082, 1092, 1100, 1108, 1115, and 1120.

Other opportunities to write about math can be found on LAB pages 255, 262, 265, 266, and 268.

Problem Solving Strategies

The focus of **Lesson 12.8** is the strategy *work backward.* However, students will use a variety of problem solving strategies as they work through the chapter. The chart below shows strategies that may be useful in completing each lesson.

Strategy	Lesson(s)	Description
Act It Out	13.1	Make a mobile by balancing the weights of the shapes on each arm.
Draw a Picture	13.5, 13.6	Use "bag and dot" representation to solve number tricks and draw diagrams to represent situations and to solve problems.
Make a Model	13.1, 13.4	Use a mobile or a balance scale to model a balanced equation.
Make a Table	13.3, 13.5	Record the weights of shapes in a mobile given different total weights and show how words, diagrams, shorthand, and numbers are related.
Use Logical Reasoning	13.2, 13.3, 13.4	Find the weights of shapes on a mobile and solve equations.
✓ **Work Backward**	13.2, 13.5	Find the weights of the shapes on a mobile when given the total weight and find the value of a variable given the result of the calculations.
Write an Equation	13.3–13.5, 13.7, 13.8	Write an equation to describe a mobile or a balance scale and to solve a number trick or to solve a problem.

Meeting the Needs of All Learners

Differentiated Instruction

Extra Support	Activities for All	Enrichment
Intervention Activities TG pp. 1066, 1074, 1083, 1093, 1101, 1109, 1116	**Practice Book** pp. P103–P109	**Extension Activities** TG pp. 1066, 1074, 1083, 1093, 1101, 1109, 1116
	Spiral Review Book pp. SR103–SR109	**Extension Book** pp. E103–E109
	LAB Challenge LAB pp. 254, 256, 258, 260, 262, 264, 266	**LAB Challenge** LAB pp. 254, 256, 258, 260, 262, 264, 266
Lesson Notes **Basic Level** TG pp. 1081, 1086	**Lesson Notes** **On Level** TG p. 1086	**Lesson Notes** **Above Level** TG p. 1105
Leveled Problem Solving **Basic Level** TG pp. 1066, 1074, 1083, 1093, 1101, 1109, 1116	**Leveled Problem Solving** **On Level** TG pp. 1066, 1074, 1083, 1093, 1101, 1109, 1116	**Leveled Problem Solving** **Above Level** TG pp. 1066, 1074, 1083, 1093, 1101, 1109, 1116

English Language Learners

Suggestions for addressing the needs of students learning English as a second language are included in the Developing Mathematical Language section at the beginning of most lessons.

ELL activities for this chapter can be found on TG pages 1061, 1069, 1077, 1085, 1095, 1103, and 1111.

The Multi-Age Classroom

Grade 4	• Students on this level should be able to complete the lessons in Chapter 13 but might need some additional practice with key concepts and skills. • Give students more practice with variables.	See Grade 5, Intervention Activities, Lessons 13.1–13.7. See Grade 4, Lessons 14.1–14.4.
Grade 5	• Students on this level should be able to complete the lessons in Chapter 13 with minimal adjustments.	See Grade 5, Practice pages P103–P109.
Grade 6	• Students on this level should be able to complete the lessons in Chapter 13 and to extend concepts and skills related to solving equations. • Give students extended work with equations.	See Grade 5, Extension pages E103–E109.

Cross Curricular Connections

Science Connection

Math Concept: diagrams and algebraic expressions

Levers and Fulcrums

• Tell students that a lever is a simple machine that makes work easier. Common examples of levers are teeter-totters, or seesaws, crowbars, and rowboat oars.

• Show students this diagram of a simple lever.

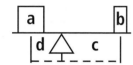

• Explain that a lever consists of a bar or board that rests or pivots on a fulcrum. If a and b represent the weights of the objects and c and d represent the distance from the fulcrum to the center of their respective weights, then $a \times d = b \times c$ makes the board balance.

• Have students toss a number cube labeled 1 to 6 to get values for a, b, and c. Then have them solve for d.

• Next, have students toss a number cube labeled 1 to 6 to get values for a, c, and d. Then have them solve for b.

Lesson 13.6

Art History Connection

Math Concept: algebraic notation

Inventor of the Mobile

• Tell students that Alexander Calder is thought to be the artist who made the first mobile.

• Show students the following table of important dates in Calder's life.

LIFE EVENTS OF ALEXANDER CALDER	
Event	**Year**
Born	1898
Graduated from technical school	1919
Entered art school	1923
Graduated from art school	1926
Died	1976

• Have students write an equation to determine Calder's age when he graduated from technical school, when he graduated from art school, and when he died. Possible answer: $1898 + n = 1919$, $1898 + n = 1926$, $1898 + n = 1976$

Lesson 13.7

Literature Connection

Math Concept: equations

A Gebra Named Al
By Wendy Isdell

This is a delightful book about a girl named Julie with a problem with mathematics. This book teaches and reemphasizes the concept of order of operations and other mathematical facts in a whimsical setting.

Lesson 13.3

School-Home Connection

A reproducible copy of the School-Home Connection letter in English and in Spanish can be found in the *Teacher Resource Book,* pages SHC49–SHC52.

Encourage students to play *Balance,* found on the School-Home Connection page, with a family member. Students will work with the mobiles in **Lessons 13.1, 13.2** and **13.3.**

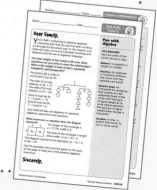

There are many opportunities in *Think Math!* to assess students' understanding of concepts, skills and problem solving. Learning Goals for Chapter 13 are provided below. The assessment options provide opportunities to evaluate whether or not students have retained learning from prior experiences. Choose the forms of assessment that best meet the needs of your students.

Chapter 13 Learning Goals

	Learning Goals	Lesson Number
13-A	Use models to demonstrate and write equal equations	13.1–13.4
13-B	Use a diagram to describe a mathematical relationship to help solve a problem	13.6
13-C	Identify and write an equation to describe a mathematical relationship to help solve a problem	13.3, 13.7
13-D	Apply problem solving strategies such as *work backward* to solve problems	13.5, 13.8

✔ Informal Assessment

Ongoing Assessment
Provides insight into students' thinking to guide instruction (TG pp. 1073, 1081, 1097, 1114)

Reflect and Summarize the Lesson
Checks understanding of lesson concepts (TG pp. 1065, 1073, 1082, 1092, 1100, 1108, 1115, 1120)

Snapshot Assessment
Mental Math and **Quick Write**
Offers a quick observation of students' progress on chapter concepts and skills (TG pp. 1124–1125)

Performance Assessment
Provides quarterly assessment of Chapters 12–15 concepts using real-life situations
Assessment Guide
pp. AG225–AG230

✔ Formal Assessment

Standardized Test Prep
Problem Solving Test Prep
Prepares students for standardized tests
Lesson Activity Book p. 268 (TG p. 1121)

Chapter 13 Review/Assessment
Reviews and assesses students' understanding of the chapter
Lesson Activity Book pp. 269–270 (TG p. 1126)

Chapter 13 Test
Assesses the chapters concepts and skills
Assessment Guide
Form A pp. AG113–AG114
Form B pp. AG115–AG116

Benchmark 4 Assessment
Provides quarterly assessment of Chapters 12–15 concepts and skills
Assessment Guide
Benchmark 4A pp. AG125–AG132
Benchmark 4B pp. AG133–AG140

World Almanac for Kids

Use the World Almanac for Kids feature, *Balancing Act,* found on pp. 218–219 of the **Student Handbook,** to provide students with an opportunity to practice using their problem solving skills by solving real world problems.

FACT•ACTIVITY 1

❶ 12 ounces

❷ 3 more juggling balls
$(6 + 6 + 3 = 3 + 3 + 3 + 3 + 3)$

❸ Possible answer: left: 2 balls and 1 club balance with right: 1 club and 1 hat

❹ The *b* represents a juggling ball.

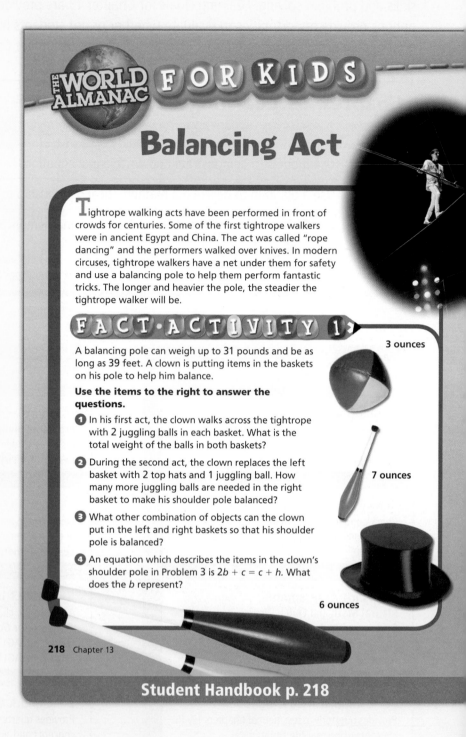

THE WORLD ALMANAC FOR KIDS

Balancing Act

Tightrope walking acts have been performed in front of crowds for centuries. Some of the first tightrope walkers were in ancient Egypt and China. The act was called "rope dancing" and the performers walked over knives. In modern circuses, tightrope walkers have a net under them for safety and use a balancing pole to help them perform fantastic tricks. The longer and heavier the pole, the steadier the tightrope walker will be.

FACT•ACTIVITY 1

A balancing pole can weigh up to 31 pounds and be as long as 39 feet. A clown is putting items in the baskets on his pole to help him balance.

Use the items to the right to answer the questions.

❶ In his first act, the clown walks across the tightrope with 2 juggling balls in each basket. What is the total weight of the balls in both baskets?

❷ During the second act, the clown replaces the left basket with 2 top hats and 1 juggling ball. How many more juggling balls are needed in the right basket to make his shoulder pole balanced?

❸ What other combination of objects can the clown put in the left and right baskets so that his shoulder pole is balanced?

❹ An equation which describes the items in the clown's shoulder pole in Problem 3 is $2b + c = c + h$. What does the *b* represent?

3 ounces

7 ounces

6 ounces

218   Chapter 13

Student Handbook p. 218

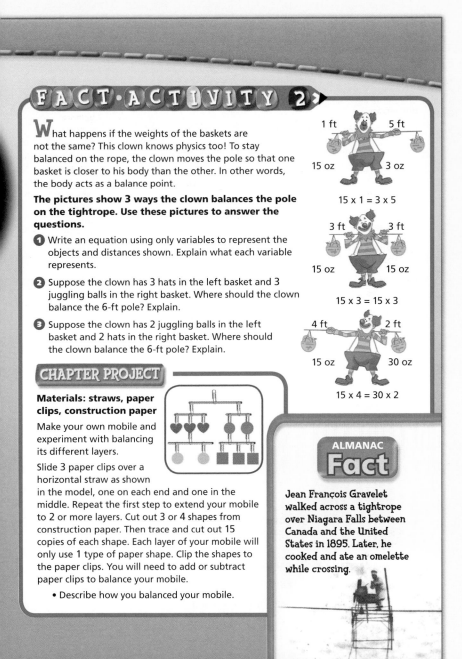

FACT · ACTIVITY 2

What happens if the weights of the baskets are not the same? This clown knows physics too! To stay balanced on the rope, the clown moves the pole so that one basket is closer to his body than the other. In other words, the body acts as a balance point.

The pictures show 3 ways the clown balances the pole on the tightrope. Use these pictures to answer the questions.

❶ Write an equation using only variables to represent the objects and distances shown. Explain what each variable represents.

❷ Suppose the clown has 3 hats in the left basket and 3 juggling balls in the right basket. Where should the clown balance the 6-ft pole? Explain.

❸ Suppose the clown has 2 juggling balls in the left basket and 2 hats in the right basket. Where should the clown balance the 6-ft pole? Explain.

CHAPTER PROJECT

Materials: straws, paper clips, construction paper

Make your own mobile and experiment with balancing its different layers.

Slide 3 paper clips over a horizontal straw as shown in the model, one on each end and one in the middle. Repeat the first step to extend your mobile to 2 or more layers. Cut out 3 or 4 shapes from construction paper. Then trace and cut out 15 copies of each shape. Each layer of your mobile will only use 1 type of paper shape. Clip the shapes to the paper clips. You will need to add or subtract paper clips to balance your mobile.

• Describe how you balanced your mobile.

1 ft   5 ft
15 oz   3 oz

$15 \times 1 = 3 \times 5$

3 ft   3 ft
15 oz   15 oz

$15 \times 3 = 15 \times 3$

4 ft   2 ft
15 oz   30 oz

$15 \times 4 = 30 \times 2$

ALMANAC
Fact

Jean François Gravelet walked across a tightrope over Niagara Falls between Canada and the United States in 1895. Later, he cooked and ate an omelette while crossing.

Student Handbook p. 219

FACT · ACTIVITY 2

❶ Possible answer: $lx = ry$; l represents the left basket weight, r represents the right basket weight, x represents the distance from the body to the left basket, y represents the distance from the body to the right basket

❷ 4 feet from the right basket; Possible explanation: I used guess and check. Since $18x = 9y$, then $x = 2$ ft from the left basket, and $y = 4$ ft from the right basket

❸ 4 feet from the left basket; Possible explanation: I used guess and check. Since $6x = 12y$, then $x = 4$ ft from the left basket, and $y = 2$ ft from the right basket.

CHAPTER PROJECT

Check students' mobiles

Possible answer: I had to add 3 paper clips to one side for the mobile to balance.

Vocabulary

To reinforce vocabulary concepts, invite students to complete the vocabulary activities on pp. 228–229 of the *Student Handbook.* Encourage students to record their answers in their math journals.

Many responses are possible.

⑩ Possible response: If one side of a mobile is heavier than the other side, it becomes lopsided and does not move freely. If one side of an *equation* has more value than the other side, then the sides are not *balanced,* and it is not a true *equation.* When the correct value replaces the variable, then the *equation balances* and is a true *equation.*

⑪ Possible response: If one side of the *balance* scale is heavier than the other side, it becomes lopsided, and then you know that the two sides do not weigh the same. If one side of an *equation* has more value than the other side, then the sides are not *balanced,* and it is not a true *equation.* When the correct value replaces the *variable,* then the *equation balances* and is a true *equation.*

⑫ Possible response: First look for the part of the diagram that represents the *variable.* If there are 4 bags, for example, then the *variable* is represented by the bags. The number of bags is the number that the *variable* is multiplied by. If there is only one bag and a number is added to or subtracted from it, then that is what is written on one side of the *equation.* On the other side of the *equation* is the amount that is equal to the number and the *variable.* The *equation* will *balance* when the correct number replaces the *variable.*

Chapter 13 Vocabulary

Choose the best vocabulary term from Word List A for each definition.

① Word List A

- balance
- balance scale
- describing situations with diagrams
- describing situations with equations
- equation
- mobile
- variable

① Art with hanging parts that move easily is called a(n) __?__. **mobile**

② To __?__ a mobile, both sides of an arm must have the same weight. **balance**

③ An algebraic or numerical sentence that shows two quantities are equal is a(n) __?__. **equation**

④ A(n) __?__ has two pans and pivots freely on a fulcrum to compare weights. **balance scale**

⑤ A letter or symbol that stands for one or more values is called a(n) __?__. **variable**

⑥ When you use algebra to represent word problems, you are __?__. **describing situations with equations**

⑦ When you use pictures to solve word problems, you are __?__. **describing situations with diagrams**

Complete each analogy using the best term from Word List B.

Word List B

- balance scale
- equation
- mobile
- variable

⑧ Seat is to seesaw as pan is to __?__. **balance scale**

⑨ Word is to sentence as __?__ is to equation. **variable**

Talk Math

Use the vocabulary terms *equation, balance,* and *variable* to discuss with a partner what you have just learned about algebra.

⑩ How are a mobile and an equation alike?

⑪ How are a balance scale and an equation alike?

⑫ How can you write an equation from a diagram?

228 Chapter 13

Student Handbook p. 228

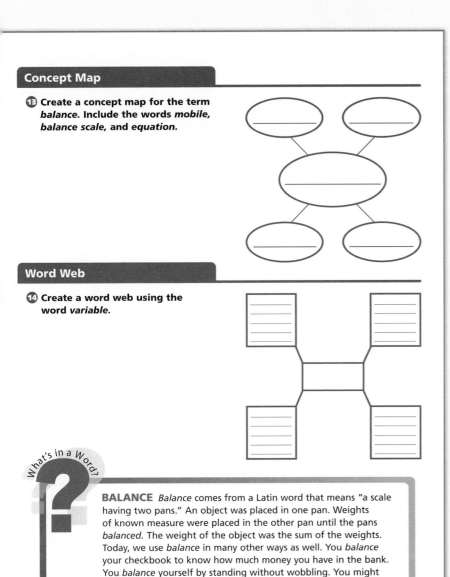

Concept Map

13 **Create a concept map for the term** *balance.* **Include the words** *mobile,* *balance scale,* **and** *equation.*

Word Web

14 **Create a word web using the word** *variable.*

What's in a Word?

BALANCE *Balance* comes from a Latin word that means "a scale having two pans." An object was placed in one pan. Weights of known measure were placed in the other pan until the pans *balanced.* The weight of the object was the sum of the weights. Today, we use *balance* in many other ways as well. You *balance* your checkbook to know how much money you have in the bank. You *balance* yourself by standing without wobbling. You might use a *balance* beam in gym class. A *balanced* meal has just the right number of elements.

Chapter 13 **229**

Student Handbook p. 229

13 Many answers are possible. One example is provided.

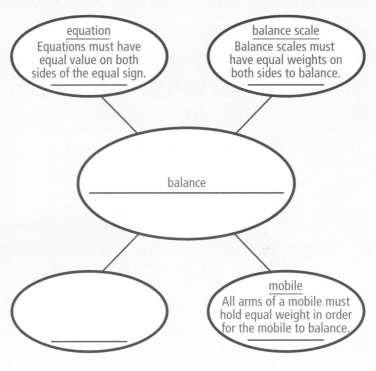

14 Many answers are possible. One example is provided.

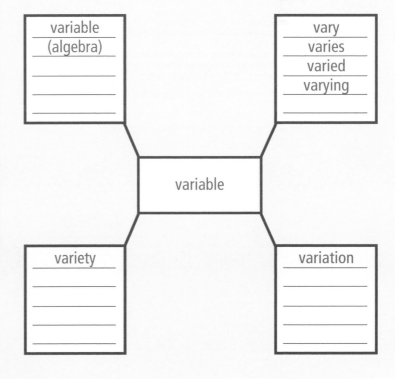

The *Balance Puzzle* in **Lesson 13.4** provides an opportunity for students to relate puzzles to equations and to solve the puzzles. *Picture Puzzler* in **Lesson 13.6** provides an opportunity for students to select diagrams to match given sums or products. These games can be found on pp. 230-231 of the *Student Handbook.*

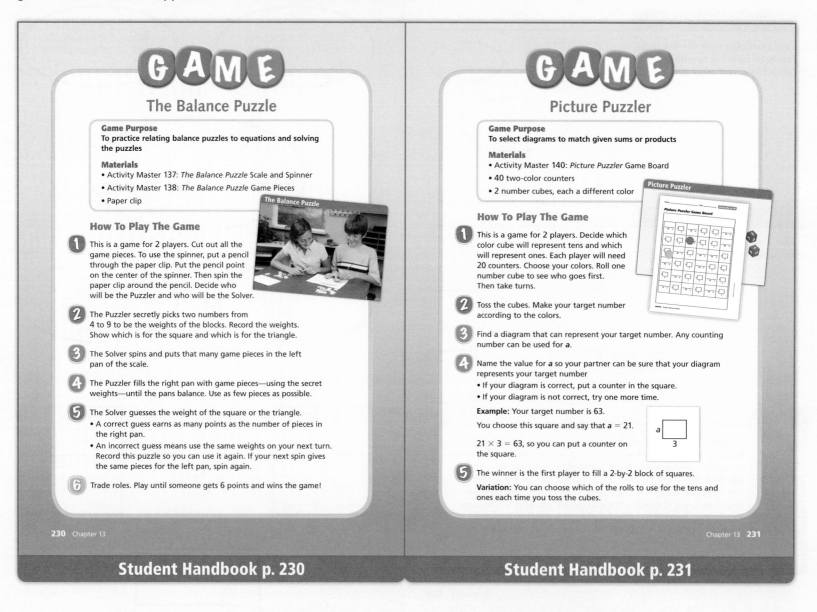

GAME

The Balance Puzzle

Game Purpose
To practice relating balance puzzles to equations and solving the puzzles

Materials
• Activity Master 137: *The Balance Puzzle* Scale and Spinner
• Activity Master 138: *The Balance Puzzle* Game Pieces
• Paper clip

How To Play The Game

1 This is a game for 2 players. Cut out all the game pieces. To use the spinner, put a pencil through the paper clip. Put the pencil point on the center of the spinner. Then spin the paper clip around the pencil. Decide who will be the Puzzler and who will be the Solver.

2 The Puzzler secretly picks two numbers from 4 to 9 to be the weights of the blocks. Record the weights. Show which is for the square and which is for the triangle.

3 The Solver spins and puts that many game pieces in the left pan of the scale.

4 The Puzzler fills the right pan with game pieces—using the secret weights—until the pans balance. Use as few pieces as possible.

5 The Solver guesses the weight of the square or the triangle.
• A correct guess earns as many points as the number of pieces in the right pan.
• An incorrect guess means use the same weights on your next turn. Record this puzzle so you can use it again. If your next spin gives the same pieces for the left pan, spin again.

6 Trade roles. Play until someone gets 6 points and wins the game!

GAME

Picture Puzzler

Game Purpose
To select diagrams to match given sums or products

Materials
• Activity Master 140: *Picture Puzzler* Game Board
• 40 two-color counters
• 2 number cubes, each a different color

How To Play The Game

1 This is a game for 2 players. Decide which color cube will represent tens and which will represent ones. Each player will need 20 counters. Choose your colors. Roll one number cube to see who goes first. Then take turns.

2 Toss the cubes. Make your target number according to the colors.

3 Find a diagram that can represent your target number. Any counting number can be used for *a*.

4 Name the value for *a* so your partner can be sure that your diagram represents your target number
• If your diagram is correct, put a counter in the square.
• If your diagram is not correct, try one more time.

Example: Your target number is 63.

You choose this square and say that *a* = 21.

$21 \times 3 = 63$, so you can put a counter on the square.

5 The winner is the first player to fill a 2-by-2 block of squares.

Variation: You can choose which of the rolls to use for the tens and ones each time you toss the cubes.

Challenge

The Challenge activity *Balance Please!* challenges students to find weights for the shapes on a mobile to make it balance. This activity can be found on p. 232 of the ***Student Handbook.***

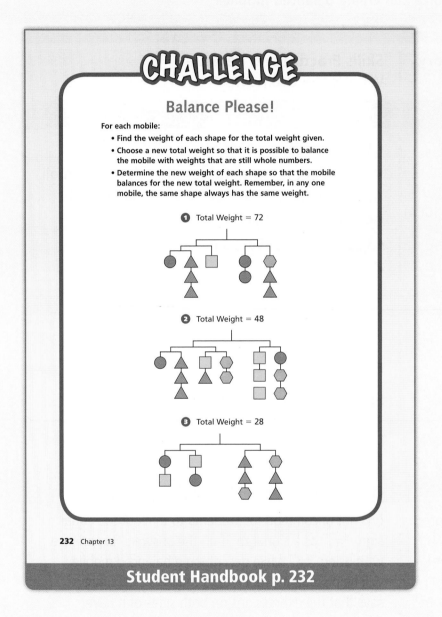

❶ For total weight = 72: $C = 9$, $T = 3$, $S = 18$, $H = 12$; possible new weight: 144; then $C = 18$, $T = 6$, $S = 36$, $H = 24$

❷ For total weight = 48: $C = 6$, $T = 2$, $S = 4$, $H = 3$; Possible new weight: 96; then $C = 12$, $T = 4$, $S = 8$, $H = 6$

❸ Possible answers: for total weight = 28: $C = 6$, $S = 1$, $T = 2$, $H = 3$; possible new weight: 56; then $C = 12$, $S = 2$, $T = 4$, $H = 6$

Lesson 1 Introducing Mobiles

NCTM Standards 1, 2, 7, 8, 9, 10

Lesson Planner

STUDENT OBJECTIVE ·
- To recognize and create balanced mobiles

1 Daily Activities (TG p. 1061)

Open-Ended Problem Solving/Headline Story	Skills Practice and Review— What's the Unknown?

2 Teach and Practice (TG pp. 1062–1065)

	MATERIALS
Ⓐ **Reading the Student Letter** (TG p. 1062)	• transparency of AM133
Ⓑ **Making a Mobile** (TG p. 1063)	• wire hangers, twist ties or pipe cleaners, small plastic bags, small objects of equal weight
Ⓒ **Determining Balance in Mobiles** (TG p. 1064)	• completed mobile
Ⓓ **Balanced and Unbalanced Mobiles** (TG p. 1065)	• 📖 LAB pp. 253–254
	• 📖 SH p. 217

3 Differentiated Instruction (TG p. 1066)

Leveled Problem Solving (TG p. 1066)	Practice Book P103
Intervention Activity (TG p. 1066)	Extension Book E103
Extension Activity (TG p. 1066)	Spiral Review Book SR103

Lesson Notes

About the Lesson

This lesson presents a balanced mobile as a model for demonstrating equality. In order for a mobile to be balanced, each arm must have the same total weight on each end. In future lessons, this idea will extend to using equations to describe equalities shown in mobiles and other balances and then extend to solving equations.

About the Mathematics

It is not uncommon for students to think of the equal sign, "=," as a signal to "find the answer." Experience with using "=" while describing a balanced mobile will help students understand that this sign simply says that the expressions on both sides of it have the same value. This understanding of "=" will help students handle equations. They find that they must manipulate the two expressions (on both sides of the sign), keeping in mind that these expressions have the same value.

Developing Mathematical Language

Vocabulary: mobile

The word *mobile* is not a mathematical term; it is just used in this chapter to help students understand the meaning of equations. Knowing the English language meaning of the word *mobile* is all that is needed for students to understand the lesson.

Familiarize students with the term *mobile.*

Beginning Have students create a simple *mobile* with coat hangers. Use the word *mobile* each time a hanger is placed on the *mobile.*

Intermediate Tell students that the word *mobile* has more than one meaning in English. It is both a naming word, or noun, that names a type of art and a describing word. As a describing word, it means "can be moved." Students might be familiar with the term "*mobile* phone," in which the word *mobile* is an adjective. Have students describe a *mobile* they might create.

Advanced Tell students that the word *mobile* is both a noun, or a thing, and an adjective, or a word that describes another word. As an adjective, *mobile* means to be "able to be moved." Have students write a few sentences explaining how the adjective *mobile* fits the noun *mobile.*

Open-Ended Problem Solving

Suggest that students sketch possibilities on paper or dry erase boards. Emphasize that they may estimate the angle measurements, taking care to notice whether the angles are acute, obtuse, or right.

 Headline Story

None of the other angles in quadrilateral *ABCD* are larger than ∠*B*. ∠*A* and ∠*C* are congruent, and ∠*D* is a right angle. What can you say?

Possible responses: Quadrilateral *ABCD* could be a rectangle; then all of the angles would be 90°. ∠*B* cannot be acute, because if it was, then ∠*D* will be larger than it. If ∠*B* is a right angle, *ABCD* has to be a rectangle. If angle ∠*B* measures 110°, then ∠*B* and ∠*D* together measure 200°, and ∠*A* and ∠*C* have to measure 80° each so that the total for all four angles is 360°. This is how *ABCD* could look.

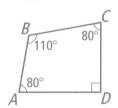

Skills Practice and Review

What's the Unknown?

Review understanding and solving algebraic equations and solving for the unknown with students by asking them to figure out the value of the letter (variable) in equations such as those below.

Write examples on the board one at a time. If necessary, you might prompt students by asking, for the first example, "10 times what number equals 150?"

$10N = 150$	$2A = 36$	$5B = 100$	$12C = 144$
$4 + D = 11$	$100 - E = 83$	$F + 29 = 50$	$G - 46 = 79$

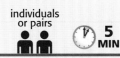 individuals or pairs 5 MIN

Materials
- For the teacher: completed mobile used in Activity B or commercially made mobile

NCTM Standards 1, 2, 7, 8, 9

Ⓐ Reading the Student Letter

Purpose To introduce mobiles and the content of the chapter

Introduce If you have already constructed your own mobile as an example for Activity B, hold it up or display it for the class to see. Alternatively or additionally, show a commercially made mobile. Encourage students to share what they know about mobiles and related words such as *mobile* (movable) and *mobile home* (large, transportable house trailer).

Have students look at the Student Letter. You might allow students to work with partners or individually to find the total weight of the balanced mobile pictured in the letter.

Task **Have students discuss the mobile pictured on the Student Letter and begin to connect parts of a balanced mobile to equal weights or quantities.**

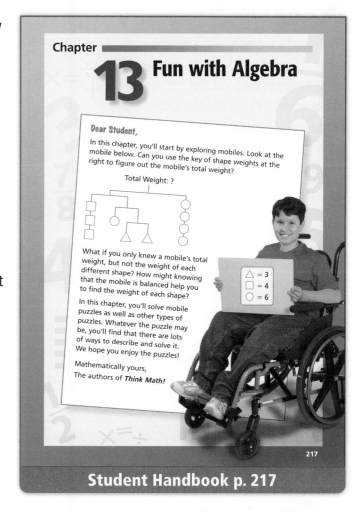

Student Handbook p. 217

💬 **Talk Math**

❷ What is the total weight of the balanced mobile pictured in the letter? 48

❷ Starting at the top of the mobile, look at the arm at the top of the mobile. What is the weight on the right end of the arm at the top of the mobile? 24

❷ The letter states that the mobile is balanced. What do you think that tells you about the weight on the left arm of the mobile? It must also equal 24.

❷ The letter asks you to think about finding the weight of each shape on a mobile if you know the mobile's total weight. Look at the arm with two triangles on the right end and a circle on the left end. Is the weight of two triangles equal to the weight of the circle? yes

❷ Look at the top arm on the left side of the mobile. Is the weight of three squares equal to the weight of a circle and two triangles on the other side? yes

Use with Lesson Activity Book pp. 253–254.

Making a Mobile

Purpose To make mobiles in order to connect the idea of balance with equality

Introduce If you like, show students a completed mobile.

You might choose to have each group use different objects or all use the same kind. Small manipulatives or small sticky note pads placed in the plastic bags work well.

Task Tell students that each group will create a balanced mobile from three hangers, three small bags, and a number of small objects.

Tell students that they may make holes near the top of the bags and use the twist ties or pipe cleaners to attach the bags to the hangers. If any students are puzzled as to why they have three rather than four bags, tell them that this is the challenge of the activity: to find out how they can make the mobile balanced using exactly three bags and three hangers. (A hanger is needed on both sides of the top hanger to equalize the weight before the objects are added to the bags.)

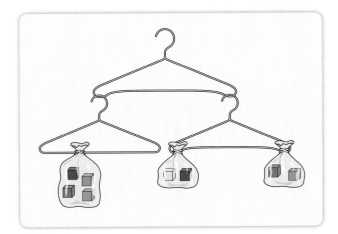

Share When the groups have completed their mobiles, briefly ask each group to show their mobile and state the number of equally weighted objects placed on each side of the mobile. Students will find that there must always be an even number of objects on the side of the mobile with only one bag.

Materials
- For the teacher: completed mobile
- For each group of students: 3 wire hangers, 3 twist ties or pipe cleaners, 3 small plastic bags, several small objects of equal weight

NCTM Standards 8, 10

Teacher Story

"I found it helpful to bend two of the wire hangers down at each end (the top one and the one that holds two bags) so that the other hangers or bags don't slide into the middle. I showed this to my class before they began to construct theirs."

Determining Balance in Mobiles

Materials
- For the teacher:
  transparency of AM133
  (optional)

NCTM Standards 1, 2, 7, 8, 9

Purpose To learn that in order for a mobile to be balanced, each of its arms must be balanced

Introduce Project the transparency of AM133: Balanced and Unbalanced Mobiles or sketch Mobile A on the board.

Balanced and Unbalanced Mobiles

Activity Master 133

Problem **Is each arm of Mobile A on AM133 balanced? Find the missing weights or the total weight for each mobile.**

💬 **Talk Math**

❓ Look at the first (top) arm of Mobile A that has a total weight of 12. Is the arm balanced? yes

❓ How do you know it's balanced? There is exactly half the total weight, or 6 on each side of the mobile.

❓ Look at the second arm of Mobile A on the right side. Is this arm balanced? no

❓ What makes a mobile a balanced mobile? Each of its arms must be balanced.

Work through the other mobile diagrams, asking volunteers to supply the missing information. Conclude by asking students to recall which mobile diagrams are balanced B and C and which are unbalanced A and D.

Purpose To recognize and create balanced mobiles

NCTM Standards 1, 2, 7, 9, 10

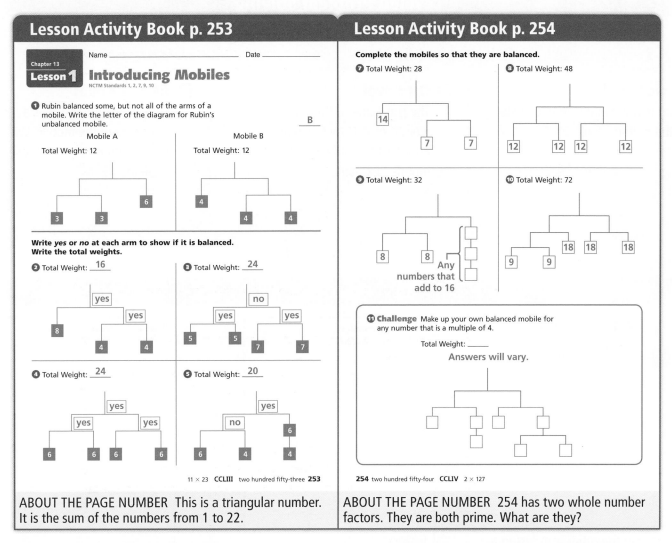

Teaching Notes for LAB page 253
In Problems 2–5, students first determine whether each arm of each mobile is balanced, and then find the total weight of each mobile.

Teaching Notes for LAB page 254
The total weight of each mobile is given and students supply the individual weights in order to balance the mobiles.

Challenge Problem Students are challenged to complete a mobile diagram, supplying both the total weight and the individual weights.

Reflect and Summarize the Lesson

Write Math

Maria made a mobile that balanced. On the right side she hung one small plastic bag with 12 cubes. On the left side she hung two small plastic bags with the same number of cubes in each of these bags. How many cubes did she put in each of the plastic bags on the left? Explain how you know. 6 cubes in each plastic bag; Possible explanation: For the mobile to balance, the number of cubes on the left must be equal to the number on the right. 6 + 6 = 12; so there are 6 cubes in each bag on the left.

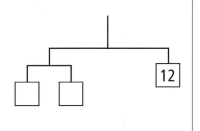

Leveled Problem Solving

Tony's mobile has 1 arm. The total weight of the balanced mobile is 16.

❶ Basic Level

What is the weight on each side of the mobile? Explain. 8; the mobile is balanced, so each side of the arm must have half the weight. Half of 16 is 8.

❷ On Level

The right side of the arm has a weight of 2. How much must be added to this side to balance the mobile? Explain. 6; each side must have half the weight, or a weight of 8. A weight of 6 must be added to the right side for a total of 8.

❸ Above Level

Suppose another arm is added to each side of the mobile. What is the weight on each of those arms? Explain. 4; each side of the top arm must have half the total weight, or 8. Each side of the other arms must have half of 8, or 4.

Intervention	Practice	Extension

Activity Symbol Balance

Display these symbol equalities.

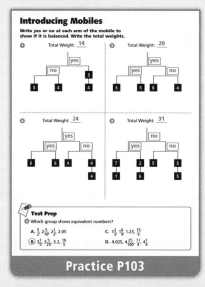

Tell students that the total weight for a mobile must equal the rectangle. Have a volunteer draw one arm of the mobile. one square Ask another volunteer draw the other arm, using a different shape. two triangles Repeat for other total weights.

Practice P103

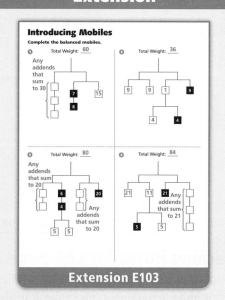

Extension E103

Spiral Review

Spiral Review Book page SR103 provides review of the following previously learned skills and concepts:

- writing rules for input-output pairs
- classifying three-dimensional figures by their attributes

You may wish to have students work with partners to complete the page.

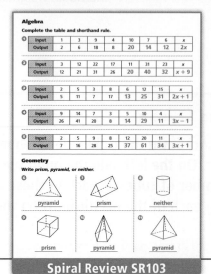

Spiral Review SR103

Extension Activity
What's the Weight?

Have students work in pairs. Each partner rolls a number cube once to determine the weights of two shapes for a mobile; for example, star = 3 and circle = 6. Have students use the shapes to create a drawing of two different mobiles: one balanced and one unbalanced. Tell students to identify the total weight and explain why it is balanced on the balanced mobile. Then have them tell why the unbalanced mobile is not balanced and explain how to make it balance. Repeat several times.

Teacher's Notes

Daily Notes . . .

Quick Notes

More Ideas

Lesson 2 Balancing Mobiles

NCTM Standards 1, 2, 7, 8, 9

Lesson Planner

STUDENT OBJECTIVE ·
- To solve mobile puzzles that involve several unknown quantities

1 | Daily Activities (TG p. 1069)

| Open-Ended Problem Solving/Headline Story | Skills Practice and Review— What's the Unknown? |

2 | Teach and Practice (TG pp. 1070–1073)

	MATERIALS
Ⓐ **Balancing Mobiles** (TG pp. 1070–1071)	• TR: Activity Master, AM134
Ⓑ **Solving Mobile Puzzles** (TG p. 1072)	• transparency of AM134
Ⓒ **More Mobile Puzzles** (TG p. 1073)	• 📖 LAB pp. 255–256
	• 📖 SH p. 220

3 | Differentiated Instruction (TG p. 1074)

Leveled Problem Solving (TG p. 1074)	Practice Book P104
Intervention Activity (TG p. 1074)	Extension Book E104
Extension Activity (TG p. 1074)	Spiral Review Book SR104

Lesson Notes

About the Lesson

Using balancing mobile puzzles as a context, this lesson introduces the ideas and thinking required to solve equations. Shapes of different weights hang on arms in such a way that the two ends of the arm must weigh the same to balance. Therefore, each side of the arm is a half of the total weight of the arm. Students must reason logically to solve the puzzles.

Use with Lesson Activity Book pp. 255–256.

Developing Mathematical Language

Vocabulary: balance

As students work with mobiles, discuss how they need to *balance* the mobiles so that they can move freely. Point out that a mobile that does not *balance* droops to one side. Point out other examples of *balance;* for example, people must *balance* their body weight to stand and walk or to stand on one foot. To *balance* an equation is fundamental to manipulating and solving equations. If students understand the concept of *balancing,* it will lay the groundwork for more advanced work in algebra.

Familiarize students with the term *balance.*

Beginning Demonstrate showing how to *balance* a ruler on your finger. Have each student *balance* a pencil or a ruler on his or her finger.

Intermediate Draw a seesaw on the board. Name an object in the classroom, such as a student desk, that you could put on one end of the seesaw. Then ask what could you do to *balance* the seesaw.

Advanced Have students focus on *balance* as a verb, to describe an action to *balance* a mobile.

Open-Ended Problem Solving

Give students a few minutes to think through the problem and then ask them to share their ideas.

 **Headline Story**

> **How can you find the number of minutes from the end of school today until 6 PM on the last day of the month?**

Possible responses: You need to know how many days there are until the end of the month, counting tomorrow as day 1. Multiply that by 24, the number of hours in a day. Add the number of hours between the end of school today and midnight, and 18 hours for midnight to 6 PM on the last day of the month (or subtract 6 if you counted the last day of the month itself). Multiply the result by 60 (and add any additional minutes needed, if school doesn't end on the hour).

Skills Practice and Review

What's the Unknown?

As in **Lesson 13.1,** review algebraic equations and solving for the unknown with students by asking them to figure out the value of the letter in each equation. Begin with expressions that require only one operation, and depending on your class, include some requiring two operations. Write examples such as these on the board.

$$15N = 225 \qquad A^2 = 144 \qquad 6B - 10 = 50$$
$$4C + 12 = 24 \qquad D^2 + 1 = 101 \qquad E^2 - 17 = 64$$

2 | Teach and Practice

NCTM Standards 1, 2, 7, 8, 9

A Balancing Mobiles

Purpose To develop strategies for finding individual weights on balanced mobiles

Introduce Read the top of the Explore: Balancing Mobiles with the class to be sure they understand how the mobiles balance. Each side of an arm must weigh the same. In the second example, a circle and two squares must balance the other circle and two squares. This example includes another level: one square must balance another square.

Task **Give students some time to work Mobiles A and B independently, and then discuss how students solved them.** In order to solve the problems, students must *work backward,* starting with the total weight and reasoning logically to figure out the weights of the pieces that add up to that total. Here are some examples of how students might reason to solve the sample puzzles:

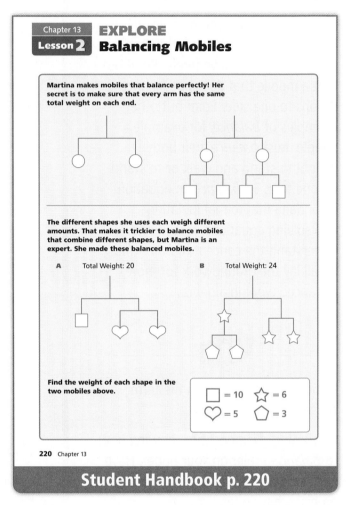

Student Handbook p. 220

- **Mobile A:** Because the two sides of the arm must be the same weight to balance, each side must be half of the total, so each is 10. The square is the only object on the left, so it must equal 10. The two hearts together weigh 10, so each must weigh half of that (since they're the same): each weighs 5.

- **Mobile B:** Each side of the arm must be half of the total weight, so each must be 12. Since the side with the two stars weighs 12, each star weighs 6. What about the other side? Well, it weighs 12 all together, and we know that the star weighs 6, so the two pentagons weigh 6 together, or 3 each.

Share Invite the class to give some suggestions about working with puzzles like these. If necessary, ask some of these guiding questions.

Talk Math

❷ **For Mobile B, why can't you start with the left side (the star and two pentagons)?** Possible answer: Since you don't know how much the star weighs, you can't figure out the weight of the pentagons.

❷ **So what's a good way to begin?** Possible answer: Look for a side of an arm that doesn't have any objects hanging in the middle.

Emphasize that it is important to look at both sides of an arm first to decide where to begin.

❷ **How do you find the weight of a particular side?** Possible answer: It's half of the weight of both sides of an arm.

❷ **How do you use that to find the weight of a particular shape?** Possible answer: Look to see if there's a side with only that shape. Or, if the weights of all the other shapes are known, you can find the weight of a particular shape.

❷ **What should you do when you find one shape's weight?** Possible answer: Write that number inside the shape everywhere in the mobile.

B Solving Mobile Puzzles

Materials
- For the teacher: transparency of AM134
- For each pair of students: AM134

NCTM Standards 1, 2, 7, 9

Teacher Story

"I demonstrated for my students what I do to solve the puzzles. I write the halved numbers at each side of an arm and the weights inside or near each shape."

Total Weight: 36

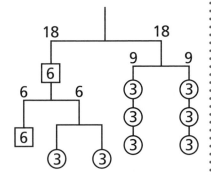

Purpose To find individual weights in balanced mobiles

Introduce Give students AM134: More Mobiles and let them work in pairs to solve them.

Problem **What are the weights for the shapes in the three mobiles on AM134?** These mobiles are similar to the ones from the previous activity, but they are a little more complex. Here are possible solutions, although students may take different paths to the same conclusions.

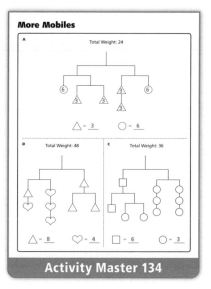

Activity Master 134

- **Mobile A:** Each side of an arm must be half the total weight, or 12. Then one one side only has a circle, which must be 6. Since two triangles balance a circle, they must both be 3.

- **Mobile B:** Each side must be half of 48, or 24. On the right, there are three triangles, so each must weigh 8. On the left side, each side of the arm must weigh 12. We already know the triangle is 8, so the heart must be 4. We can check by looking at the other side that has three hearts.

- **Mobile C:** The right side of the arm has six circles, which must weigh 18, so each circle weighs 3. Since two circles balance one square, the square must weigh 6.

You may want to share with your students the suggestion for solving a mobile puzzle that is mentioned in the Teacher Story at the left.

C **More Mobile Puzzles** LAB pp. 255–256

individuals **15 MIN**

Purpose To solve mobile puzzles

NCTM Standards 1, 2, 7, 8, 9

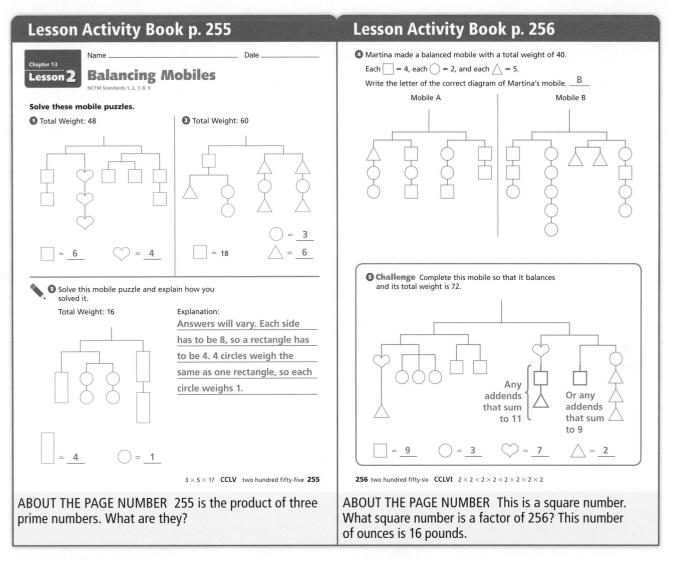

Lesson Activity Book p. 255

Chapter 13
Lesson 2 **Balancing Mobiles**
NCTM Standards 1, 2, 7, 8, 9

Name _____ Date _____

Solve these mobile puzzles.

1 Total Weight: 48

□ = 6   ♡ = 4

2 Total Weight: 60

□ = 18   ○ = 3   △ = 6

3 Solve this mobile puzzle and explain how you solved it.

Total Weight: 16

Explanation:
Answers will vary. Each side has to be 8, so a rectangle has to be 4. 4 circles weigh the same as one rectangle, so each circle weighs 1.

▯ = 4   ○ = 1

3 × 5 × 17   CCLV   two hundred fifty-five **255**

Lesson Activity Book p. 256

4 Martina made a balanced mobile with a total weight of 40.
Each □ = 4, each ○ = 2, and each △ = 5.
Write the letter of the correct diagram of Martina's mobile. __B__

Mobile A   Mobile B

5 Challenge Complete this mobile so that it balances and its total weight is 72.

Any addends that sum to 11   Or any addends that sum to 9

□ = 9   ○ = 3   ♡ = 7   △ = 2

256 two hundred fifty-six   CCLVI   2 × 2 × 2 × 2 × 2 × 2 × 2 × 2

ABOUT THE PAGE NUMBER 255 is the product of three prime numbers. What are they?

ABOUT THE PAGE NUMBER This is a square number. What square number is a factor of 256? This number of ounces is 16 pounds.

Teaching Notes for LAB page 255

Students continue to explore mobile problems that can be solved directly, one shape at a time. In Problem 3 students record how they solved the problem.

✓**Ongoing Assessment** To assess how well your students approach these puzzles, you might ask them to work independently on the LAB page. If you find most students are unsure of what to do, take extra time to review different solutions to these problems—reviewing the tips for solving these problems, as given in Activity A.

Teaching Notes for LAB page 256

On this page, students select a diagram for a balanced mobile of a specific total weight.

Challenge Problem This problem challenges students to complete a balanced mobile of a specific total weight. First they must determine the weight of each shape in order to complete the mobile.

Reflect and Summarize the Lesson

 Write Math

Glenn used three different shapes to make a balanced mobile that had a total weight of 24. Draw a sketch of a mobile he could have made. Tell the weight of each shape. Explain how you know that the mobile you drew is balanced. A possible mobile is shown. I know it is balanced because the numbers on the shapes on each side of an arm are equal.

Total Weight: 24

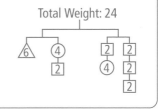

Leveled Problem Solving

A mobile has a total weight of 30. Circles weigh 5, squares weigh 10, and triangles weigh 3.

❶ Basic Level

The mobile has only two different shapes. If only circles are on one side, can it be balanced? Explain. Yes; 3 circles = 15, 1 square + 1 circle = 10 + 5 = 15.

❷ On Level

The mobile has three different shapes. One side has a circle and a square. Can the mobile be balanced using only triangles on the other side? Explain. Yes; use 5 triangles, $5 \times 3 = 15$.

❸ Above Level

The mobile has only two different shapes. If only squares are on one side, can it be balanced? Explain. No; each side must weigh 15. There is no way to make 15 using only squares.

Intervention

Activity Symbol Puzzles

Display this table of symbols.

◣ = 2	▣ = 6
● = 3	★ = 8

Direct pairs of students to make a puzzle with a total of either 20 or 24. Ask them to verify that their puzzles balance. Then erase the table. Have students copy their puzzles and exchange with another pair to solve.

Practice

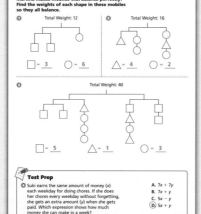

Practice P104

Extension

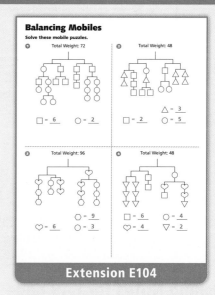

Extension E104

Spiral Review

Spiral Review Book page SR104 provides review of the following previously learned skills and concepts:

- solving problems that involve division
- selecting and using appropriate units and formulas to measure length, perimeter, and area

You may wish to have students work with partners to complete the page.

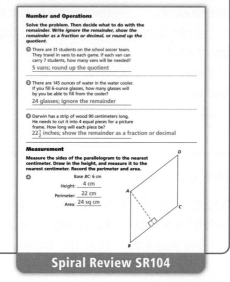

Spiral Review SR104

Extension Activity
Make a Puzzle

Have students work in pairs to create a mobile puzzle using at least three shapes. As they create the mobile, they should include the amounts in each shape. (This will be the key for checking later on.) After they have created the mobile, have them copy it with the shapes only and the total at the top. Have pairs trade puzzles and solve.

Teacher's Notes 🍎

Daily Notes . . .

Quick Notes

More Ideas

_____

_____

_____

_____

_____

_____

_____

_____

_____

_____

_____

_____

_____

_____

_____

_____

_____

_____

_____

_____

_____

Lesson 3 Equations for Mobiles

NCTM Standards 1, 2, 7, 8, 9

Lesson Planner

STUDENT OBJECTIVES
- To solve puzzles about the relationships among several unknown quantities
- To use algebraic shorthand as a tool for recording relationships

1 Daily Activities (TG p. 1077)

Open-Ended Problem Solving/Headline Story	Skills Practice and Review—Comparing Fractions

2 Teach and Practice (TG pp. 1078–1082)

(A) Finding Equations for Mobiles (TG pp. 1078–1079)

(B) Using Equations to Help Solve Mobile Puzzles (TG p. 1080)

(C) Describing Mobiles with Equations (TG p. 1081)

MATERIALS

- TR: Activity Master, AM136
- transparency of AM135 (optional)
- 📖 LAB pp. 257–258
- 📖 SH p. 221

3 Differentiated Instruction (TG p. 1083)

Leveled Problem Solving (TG p. 1083)

Intervention Activity (TG p. 1083)

Extension Activity (TG p. 1083)

Literature Connection (TG p. 1058)

Practice Book P105

Extension Book E105

Spiral Review Book SR105

Lesson Notes

About the Lesson

The strategies students use to solve mobile puzzles will become important strategies for solving equations. In this lesson, students write equations for mobile puzzles to record relationships described by the mobiles. While equations are used in this lesson merely for recording information and not as a way to solve puzzles, the process of recording information can help students in solving puzzles.

Use with Lesson Activity Book pp. 257–258.

Developing Mathematical Language

Vocabulary: equation

All the work with balancing mobiles comes together in balancing an *equation.* Instead of weights, students will balance numerical amounts. Tell students that the word *equation* stems from the word *equal,* meaning that one side is equal to the other side, and an *equation* must include an equal sign. An *equation* is shorthand notation for the balance of a mobile, and the equal sign is the center on which both sides balance.

Familiarize students with the term *equation.*

Beginning On the board, write and label an expression, 3×4, and an *equation,* $3 \times 4 = 12$. Write $6 \times 3 = \blacksquare$ on the board. Ask students what number would make it an *equation.*

Intermediate Write two addition and multiplication expressions on the board. Write two addition and multiplication equations on the board. Ask students to name each *equation.*

Advanced Write a multiplication sentence on the board with an incorrect answer, such as $8 \times 11 = 56$. Ask students to determine whether it is an *equation* and justify their responses.

---

1 | Daily Activities

Open-Ended Problem Solving

After allowing students a few minutes to think about the problem, ask them to share their ideas. Encourage them to record their suggestions using expressions with variables.

 Headline Story

> **Fran takes *S* steps when she walks a mile. How can you estimate the length of her step in feet? in inches?**

Possible responses: You need to know how many feet are in a mile (and how many inches are in a foot). There are 5,280 feet in a mile, so divide 5,280 by *S* to estimate the length of Fran's step in feet: $(5,280 \div S)$. Multiply that answer by 12 (since are 12 inches in a foot) to estimate the length in inches. You could also start with the number of inches in a mile $(5,280 \times 12 = 63,630)$ and divide that by *S* to find the length of Fran's step in inches: $63,630 \div S$.

Skills Practice and Review

Comparing Fractions

This activity will help prepare students for work with probability in **Chapter 14.** Students should explain how they know that the first fraction is less than, greater than, or equal to the second fraction. For example, for the first example shown, one student might convert $\frac{6}{100}$ to $\frac{3}{50}$ and another might convert $\frac{4}{50}$ to $\frac{8}{100}$.

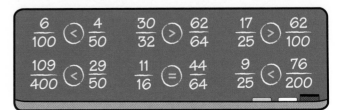

$$\frac{6}{100} \,\textcircled{<}\, \frac{4}{50} \qquad \frac{30}{32} \,\textcircled{>}\, \frac{62}{64} \qquad \frac{17}{25} \,\textcircled{>}\, \frac{62}{100}$$

$$\frac{109}{400} \,\textcircled{<}\, \frac{29}{50} \qquad \frac{11}{16} \,\textcircled{=}\, \frac{44}{64} \qquad \frac{9}{25} \,\textcircled{<}\, \frac{76}{200}$$

whole class   **10 MIN**

Materials
- For the teacher: transparency of AM135 (optional)

NCTM Standards 1, 2, 7, 8, 9

A Finding Equations for Mobiles

Purpose To use equations to describe relationships in mobiles

Introduce Project a transparency of AM135: Which Equations Describe This Mobile?, covering Problem 3. Ask students if it's possible to solve the mobile. The total weight is missing, so it's not possible.

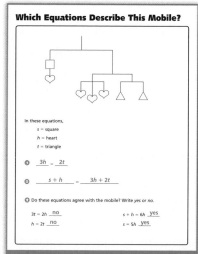

Which Equations Describe This Mobile?

In these equations,
s = square
h = heart
t = triangle

① 3h = 2t

② s + h = 3h + 2t

③ Do these equations agree with the mobile? Write yes or no.

3t = 2h no   s + h = 6h yes
h = 2t no   s = 5h yes

Activity Master 135

Task **Have the class solve the puzzle for a total weight of 24, 48, and 72.** Record the shapes' weights for one total weight, then record a different total weight and ask students to solve the puzzle again. Make the table and fill it in while solving the puzzle.

Total Weight	24	48	72
Heart's Weight	2	4	6
Square's Weight	10	20	30
Triangle's Weight	3	6	9

After the table is filled in, look at the relationships between the individual weights and the relationships between the individual weights and the total weights.

Ask students to look for relationships between the numbers in the table. Here are a few they may notice:

- The total weight is the heart's weight times 12.
- The total weight is the triangle's weight times 8.
- The weight of the square is 5 times greater than the heart's weight.

                                    Use with Lesson Activity Book pp. 257–258.

Now suggest recording some of the relationships in the mobile. Ask students to use the following shorthand: *s* for the square's weight, *h* for the heart's weight, and *t* for the triangle's weight.

Talk Math

❷ How could you describe the relationship between the heart's and triangle's weights on the right side of the mobile? Possible response: Three hearts balance (equal) two triangles.

❷ How could you write that as an equation? $3h = 2t$, or $2t = 3h$

❷ What equation describes the balance between the right and the left parts of the mobile? Possible response: $s + h = 3h + 2t$, or $s + h = h + h + h + t + t$

Now draw students' attention to the equations in Problem 3 and ask them to decide if each one agrees with the mobile. Depending on your class, you may wish show the following substitutions on your transparency to help students see the equivalences.

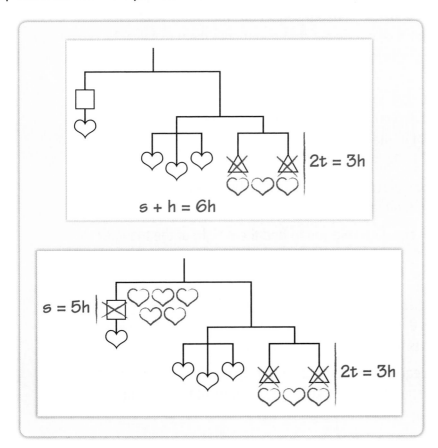

B **Using Equations to Help Solve Mobile Puzzles**

Materials

- For each student: AM136

NCTM Standards 1, 2, 7, 8, 9

Purpose To solve mobile puzzles using relationships recorded in the form of equations

Introduce Give students AM136: Mobiles and Equations to work on in pairs or individually. You might suggest using first letters of shape words for the corresponding weights, but other letters or symbols could also be used. Tell students that there are many different equations that they might write to describe parts of the mobiles, and that some of these equations might help them to solve the mobile puzzles.

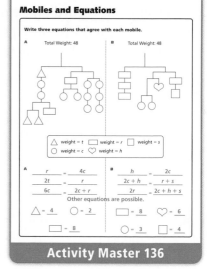

Activity Master 136

Concept Alert

Students are more likely to write the equation $3r = 2c + h + r + s$ than $2r = 2c + h + s$. As in Activity A, you might show this equivalence by crossing off a rectangle on each side of the mobile (making sure that students agree that doing so does not affect the mobile's balance).

Task After students have completed the page, have volunteers record various equations for both mobiles on the board.

You might spend time first asking students to find equations that are essentially the same, such as $r = 4c$ and $4c = r$. Next, ask volunteers to explain how they know each equation describes a part of the mobile. You might hear responses such as, "I know $r = 4c$ because the side of the arm with six circles has to balance the other side with a rectangle and two circles, so the rectangle must equal four circles." Now ask students to identify equations that show relationships between the weights of the shapes that might help them to solve the puzzles.

💬 **Talk Math**

❓ One equation that describes a part of Mobile A is $r = 4c$. How will this relationship help you to find the weight of the rectangle once you figure out the weight of the circle? Possible answer: You just multiply the weight of the circle by 4 to find the weight of the rectangle.

❓ Which equation describes the relationship between the weight of the rectangle and the triangle? $r = 2t$

❓ How will that equation help you to find the weight of the triangle? Possible answer: After I find the weight of the rectangle, I'll find a half of it and it will be the weight of the triangle.

Confirm with students that the triangle weights 4, the circle weighs 2, and the rectangle weighs 8 in Mobile A. Then, follow a similar process looking at the equations students found to describe Mobile B.

❓ How can the equation $r + s = 2c + h$ help you find the weights of the circle and the heart once you know the weights of the rectangle and the square? Possible answer: You know that $r + s = 12$, so $2c + h = 12$. You know that $2c = h$, and so $h + h = 12$ and $h = 6$, and then $c = 3$. Also, you can easily find r ($3r = 24$) and then s ($r + s = 12$).

Confirm with students that the rectangle weighs 8, the heart weighs 6, the circle weighs 3, and the square weighs 4 in Mobile B.

Use with **Lesson Activity Book** pp. 257–258.

individuals

20 MIN

Purpose To select, write, and use equations to help solve mobile puzzles

NCTM Standards 1, 2, 7, 8, 9

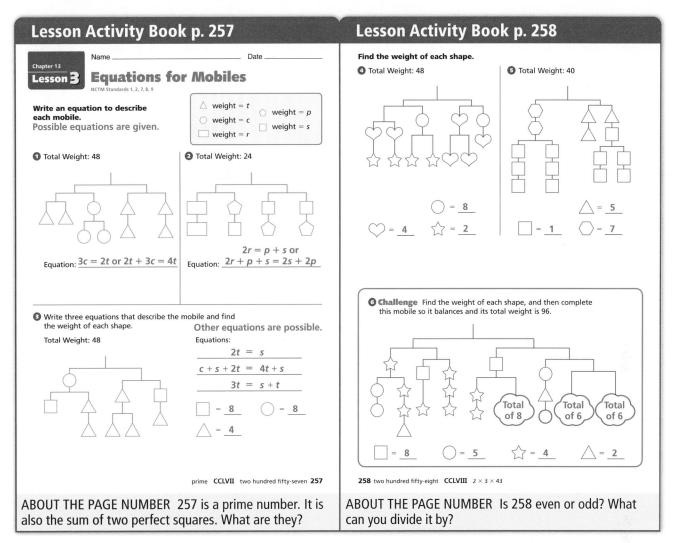

Lesson Activity Book p. 257

Chapter 13 Lesson 3 **Equations for Mobiles**
NCTM Standards 1, 2, 7, 8, 9

Name _____ Date _____

Write an equation to describe each mobile.
Possible equations are given.

△ weight = t   ◇ weight = p
○ weight = c   ☐ weight = s
☐ weight = r

❶ Total Weight: 48

❷ Total Weight: 24

Equation: $3c = 2t$ or $2t + 3c = 4t$

Equation: $2r = p + s$ or $2r + p + s = 2s + 2p$

❸ Write three equations that describe the mobile and find the weight of each shape.

Total Weight: 48

Other equations are possible.

Equations:
$$2t = s$$
$$c + s + 2t = 4t + s$$
$$3t = s + t$$

☐ = 8   ○ = 8
△ = 4

prime **CCLVII** two hundred fifty-seven **257**

Lesson Activity Book p. 258

Find the weight of each shape.

❹ Total Weight: 48

❺ Total Weight: 40

○ = 8
♡ = 4   ☆ = 2

△ = 5
☐ = 1   ⬡ = 7

❻ Challenge Find the weight of each shape, and then complete this mobile so it balances and its total weight is 96.

Total of 8   Total of 6   Total of 6

☐ = 8   ○ = 5   ☆ = 4   △ = 2

258 two hundred fifty-eight **CCLVIII** $2 \times 3 \times 43$

ABOUT THE PAGE NUMBER 257 is a prime number. It is also the sum of two perfect squares. What are they?

ABOUT THE PAGE NUMBER Is 258 even or odd? What can you divide it by?

Teaching Notes for LAB page 257

Students continue to solve mobile puzzles, finding matching equations or writing equations to describe the mobiles.

Differentiated Instruction **Basic Level** As students work on the puzzles, some may need extra help getting started. You might have these tips written out to guide students.

1. Look for the side of an arm that doesn't have any objects hanging in the middle.

2. Use the fact that each side of an arm must be half the total weight.

3. Keep halving the total weight until you get to a side with shapes of one kind.

Teaching Notes for LAB page 258

Students solve mobile puzzles. In doing so, they will use relationships among the shapes' weights. For example, for the mobile in Problem 4, they might use the fact that the weight of one circle equals that of two hearts, and for the mobile in Problem 5, they might use the fact that one triangle's weight equals the weight of five squares.

✔Ongoing Assessment As students are working on both LAB pages, make note of those that continue to need support to know where to begin in solving the puzzles.

Challenge Problem This problem challenges students to reconstruct and solve a complex, mobile puzzle.

Write Math

Write two equations that describe this mobile and find the weight of each shape. Explain. Equations may vary. Possible equations: $2s = c + 2t$, $c + 2t = s + 3t$, $2s + c + 2t = c + 5t + s$. Each equation describes the left and right sides of an arm of the mobile. For the mobile to balance, $2s = s + 3t = c + 2t = 12$, so $s = 6$, $t = 2$, and $c = 8$.

Total Weight: 48

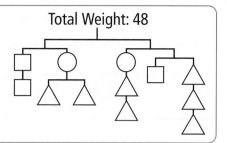

Review Model

Refer students to Review Model: Writing an Equation for a Mobile in the *Student Handbook* to see how to use algebraic shorthand (equations) as a tool for recording relationships shown in mobiles.

✔ Check for Understanding

① Equations will vary. Possible equations:
$1s = 2c$; $3t = 1s + 2c$; $4s = 3t + 1s + 2c$; $\triangle = 4$, $\bigcirc = 3$, $\square = 6$

② Equations will vary. Possible equations:
$2c = 3s$; $1t = 2c$; $2c + 3s = 1t + 2c$; $\triangle = 6$, $\bigcirc = 3$, $\square = 2$

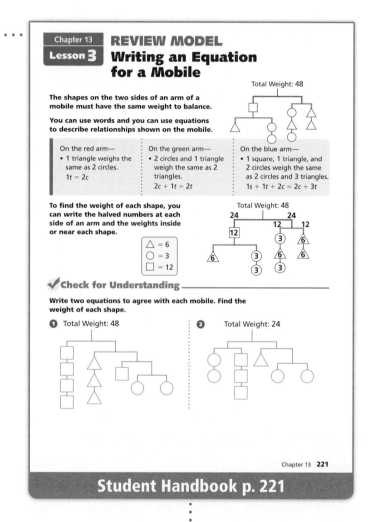

Chapter 13 **REVIEW MODEL**
Lesson 3 **Writing an Equation for a Mobile**

Total Weight: 48

The shapes on the two sides of an arm of a mobile must have the same weight to balance.

You can use words and you can use equations to describe relationships shown on the mobile.

On the red arm—	On the green arm—	On the blue arm—
• 1 triangle weighs the same as 2 circles. $1t = 2c$	• 2 circles and 1 triangle weigh the same as 2 triangles. $2c + 1t = 2t$	• 1 square, 1 triangle, and 2 circles weigh the same as 2 circles and 3 triangles. $1s + 1t + 2c = 2c + 3t$

To find the weight of each shape, you can write the halved numbers at each side of an arm and the weights inside or near each shape.

$\triangle = 6$
$\bigcirc = 3$
$\square = 12$

Total Weight: 48
24   24
12   12   12

✔ **Check for Understanding**

Write two equations to agree with each mobile. Find the weight of each shape.

① Total Weight: 48

② Total Weight: 24

Chapter 13 **221**

Student Handbook p. 221

3 | Differentiated Instruction

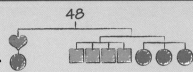

Emile drew this mobile.

❶ Basic Level
What equations describe the right side of his mobile? Explain $4s = 3c$, $4s = 12$, $3c = 12$; both sides of the arm must be equal. The whole arm is equal to 24, so each side is equal to 12.

❷ On Level
What is the weight of each shape? Explain $s = 3$, $c = 4$, $h = 20$; each side must add to 24, and each of the lower arms must sum to 12. $4s = 12$ and $3c = 12$, so $s = 3$ and $c = 4$. $h + 4 = 24$, so $h = 20$.

❸ Above Level
If the total weight for his mobile changes to 96, what are the weights of each shape? How do the new weights compare to original weights? $s = 6$, $c = 8$, and $h = 40$; the weight of each shape doubles because the total is doubled.

Intervention

Activity Mobile Equations

Ask pairs of students to draw a mobile with a total of 12 using two different shapes. At least one of the shapes should be repeated. Direct students to write an equation that describes the balanced mobile. Have each pair show and explain their balanced mobile to another pair of students.

Have partners repeat the activity for another total, such as 30 or 36.

Practice

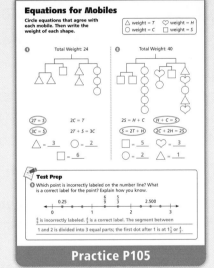

Practice P105

Extension

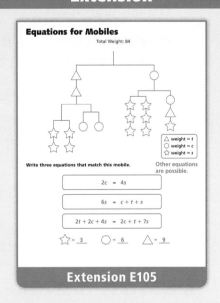

Extension E105

Spiral Review

Spiral Review Book page SR105 provides review of the following previously learned skills and concepts:

- recognizing that the sum of the angle measures in a triangle is 180 degrees
- applying the problem solving strategy *solve a simpler problem*

You may wish to have students work with partners to complete the page.

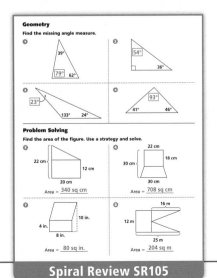

Spiral Review SR105

Extension Activity
Balance the Mobile

Display the mobile shown below. Have students find at least three different solutions for the mobile. The solution should include the total and the value of each weight.

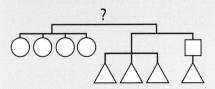

Sample solutions: Total 24, $t = 2$, $c = 3$, $s = 4$; Total 48, $t = 4$, $c = 6$, $s = 8$; Total 72, $t = 6$, $c = 9$, $s = 12$.

Lesson 4 Balance Puzzles

NCTM Standards 1, 2, 7, 8, 9, 10

Lesson Planner

STUDENT OBJECTIVE
- To solve simple equations

1 Daily Activities (TG p. 1085)

Open-Ended Problem Solving/Headline Story	Skills Practice and Review— Comparing Fractions

2 Teach and Practice (TG pp. 1086–1091)

Ⓐ **Exploring a Balance Puzzle** (TG p. 1086)

Ⓑ **Recording and Solving Balance Puzzles** (TG pp. 1087–1088)

Ⓒ **Playing a Game:** *The Balance Puzzle* (TG pp. 1089–1090)

Ⓓ **Solving Balance Puzzles** (TG p. 1091)

MATERIALS

- TR: Activity Masters, AM137–AM138
- transparencies of AM137–AM138 (optional)
- paper clips
- 📖 LAB pp. 259–260
- 📖 SH pp. 222–223, 230

3 Differentiated Instruction (TG p. 1093)

Leveled Problem Solving (TG p. 1093)	Practice Book P106
Intervention Activity (TG p. 1093)	Extension Book E106
Extension Activity (TG p. 1093)	Spiral Review Book SR106

Lesson Notes

About the Lesson

In this lesson, students are introduced to balance puzzles and use equations to describe and solve them. The idea of balance is familiar to students from the mobiles: for the balance, the weights on both sides must be equal. Working with balance puzzles and with equations that describe them, students use the fact that the balance (and an equality) remains if the same quantity is added or taken away from both sides.

About the Mathematics

Balance puzzles give students a concrete way of looking at algebraic equations: the pans must balance, so the weights on them must be equal. Students can see that if you remove the same weights from both pans, the pans remain balanced. By using equations to describe the balance puzzles, students translate the situations into more abstract mathematical representations, but now they can work with them easily. Adding the same quantities and taking away the same quantities from both parts of equations will become important steps that students will use for solving equations.

Developing Mathematical Language

Vocabulary: balance scale

Students might liken a *balance scale* to an upside-down mobile. Instead of hanging, the *balance scale* balances on a fulcrum that rests on a flat surface. You might also relate a *balance scale* to a seesaw or to a pan balance used in science class. The important idea of a *balance scale* is that it tells when weights on both sides of the scale are equal. When they are not equal, the balance tips to the heavier side. That image is useful in writing and solving equations.

Familiarize students with the term *balance scale*.

Beginning Show students a *balance scale* as is used in a science class or have students help you make a rough *balance scale* using common classroom objects.

Intermediate Discuss with students how a *balance scale* works to measure the weight of an object. The object to be measured is placed on one side, and weights are placed on the other. Have students tell when the scale would be in balance. when the weights equal the weight of the object

Advanced Have students decide whether a *balance scale* is more like a seesaw or more like a mobile and explain their choices.

Open-Ended Problem Solving

This problem is as much about recognizing what information is needed, and how to get it, as it is about recognizing the operations needed. You might need to explicitly ask, "What information do you need to get first?"

 Headline Story

> Suppose you have a brick. How can you find the weight of a cubic foot of bricks just like that one?

Possible responses: You need to weigh the brick, but you also need to know how many bricks fit in a cubic foot. You could measure the brick's sides and calculate its volume in cubic inches. There are $12 \times 12 \times 12$ cubic inches in a foot (1,728 cubic inches), so there are $1,728 \div$ (volume of one brick) in a cubic foot. Multiply that result by the weight of the brick.

Skills Practice and Review

Comparing Fractions

As in **Lesson 13.3**, this activity is intended to help prepare students for work with probability in **Chapter 14**. Students should explain how they know that the first fraction is less than, greater than, or equal to the second fraction.

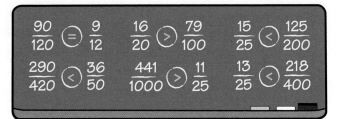

$$\frac{90}{120} \; \bigcirc\!= \; \frac{9}{12} \qquad \frac{16}{20} \; \bigcirc\!> \; \frac{79}{100} \qquad \frac{15}{25} \; \bigcirc\!< \; \frac{125}{200}$$

$$\frac{290}{420} \; \bigcirc\!< \; \frac{36}{50} \qquad \frac{441}{1000} \; \bigcirc\!> \; \frac{11}{25} \qquad \frac{13}{25} \; \bigcirc\!< \; \frac{218}{400}$$

pairs or whole class   ⏱ **10 MIN**

Materials
- For the teacher: transparencies of AM137–AM138 (optional)

NCTM Standards 1, 2, 7, 8, 9

Differentiated Instruction

Basic Level As in **Lesson 13.3,** some students may need to see the shapes crossed out on the puzzles in order to see what is left.

On Level As with the mobile puzzles, students may find it helpful to write values/ weights for the shapes in or near each one.

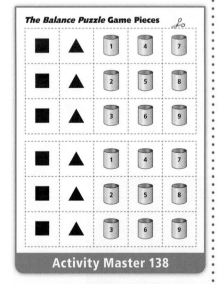

Activity Master 138

A Exploring a Balance Puzzle

Purpose To determine weights of objects in balance puzzles

Introduce Explore: Exploring Balance Puzzles presents students with a balance puzzle. Be sure students understand how a balance scale works—to balance, the two pans must each have the same total weight.

Task Have students work on the problems on the Explore page in pairs and then explain their strategies for finding the weights of the blocks. Ask them to show their reasoning using transparencies from the game board and game pieces (used in Activity C) on the overhead, or by drawing the puzzle on the board. Here are some possibilities:

- **Start by evaluating the total weight of the blocks with known weights.** In Problem 1, for example, if a △ weighs 3 ounces, then the left pan has 2 □s and 3 ounces and the right pan has 1 □ and 9 ounces. Removing 1 □ and 3 ounces from each pan will keep them balanced, leaving □ in the left pan and 6 ounces in the right. So 1 □ must weigh 6 ounces.

- **Start by simplifying the groups of objects in the pans while keeping the balance.** Take 1 □ from each of the pans, and the pans will still balance. Then, take 1 △ off of each of the pans. The pans will still balance, but now there will be only 1 □ on the left one and 2 △s on the right one, so the □ must weigh twice as much as a △—that's 6 ounces. You may also what to mention that □ = 2△ is a true equation for whatever value is given to □.

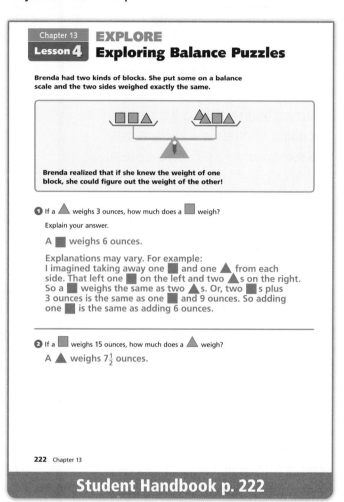

Chapter 13 EXPLORE
Lesson 4 Exploring Balance Puzzles

Brenda had two kinds of blocks. She put some on a balance scale and the two sides weighed exactly the same.

Brenda realized that if she knew the weight of one block, she could figure out the weight of the other!

❶ If a △ weighs 3 ounces, how much does a □ weigh? Explain your answer.

A □ weighs 6 ounces.

Explanations may vary. For example: I imagined taking away one □ and one △ from each side. That left one □ on the left and two △s on the right. So a □ weighs the same as two △s. Or, two □s plus 3 ounces is the same as one □ and 9 ounces. So adding one □ is the same as adding 6 ounces.

❷ If a □ weighs 15 ounces, how much does a △ weigh?

A △ weighs 7½ ounces.

222 Chapter 13

Student Handbook p. 222

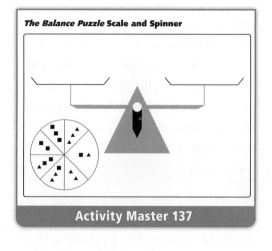

Activity Master 137

Recording and Solving Balance Puzzles

Purpose To describe balance puzzles with equations and to solve the puzzles

Introduce Tell the class that Brenda made another puzzle, this time using different blocks and a 3-ounce weight. Show them this puzzle.

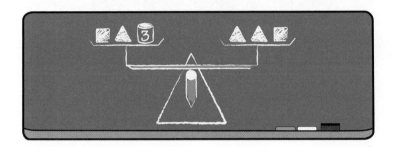

Task **Tell the students you want to record the puzzle before you move the pieces again, and ask for some suggestions about how to record it.** Some students will suggest just drawing the puzzle. If no student suggests using a shorthand notation, tell the class you think the puzzle looks sort of like an equation with a lot of things on both sides of the equals sign, and ask if anyone else can see it. Work with the class to arrive at an equation that represents the puzzle, like one of the following.

$$\blacksquare + \blacktriangle + 3 = \blacktriangle + \blacktriangle + \blacksquare$$
or
$$\blacksquare + \blacktriangle + 3 = 2\,\blacktriangle + \blacksquare$$

Students may also suggest writing equations with letters for the unknowns, such as these.

$$s + t + 3 = t + t + s$$
or
$$s + t + 3 = 2t + s$$

Ask students to find the weight of the triangle block.

Talk Math

❓ **What is one way that you could begin to solve the puzzle?** Possible answer: You could remove a triangle from each side. (If this suggestion is made, cross out the corresponding parts in either type of equation you have written on the board, as shown below.)

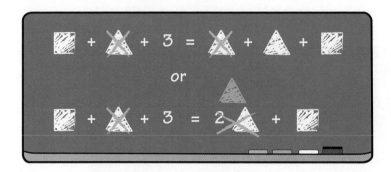

❓ **What is a different way that you could begin?** Remove a square from each side.

❓ **Will the balance remain if both a triangle and a square are removed from each side?** yes

❓ **Once you have removed both a triangle and a square from each side, what do you know?** The weight of the triangle is 3 ounces.

Extend If time allows, give students one more puzzle to try before moving on to the game. Have them write an equation to describe it, either with small shapes or letters for the unknowns, and find the weight of the square (4.5 oz) for this puzzle.

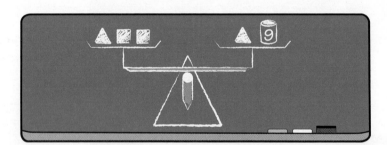

Use with Lesson Activity Book pp. 259–260.

Playing a Game: The Balance Puzzle

Purpose To practice relating balance puzzles to equations and solving the puzzles

Goal The object of the game, *The Balance Puzzle,* is to be the first player to reach 6 points.

Prepare Materials Each pair of students needs AM137: *The Balance Puzzle* Scale and Spinner and a set of game pieces from AM138: *The Balance Puzzle* Game Pieces: three squares, three triangles, and one of each numbered weights from 1 to 9. To make the spinner, players can hold a pencil tip at the center of the circle on the game board and spin a paper clip around the tip. Players decide who will be the Puzzler first, and who will be the Solver.

Materials
• For each pair of students: AM137–AM138, paper clip

NCTM Standards 1, 2, 7, 8, 9, 10

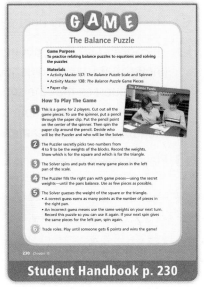

Student Handbook p. 230

How to Play

❶ The Puzzler secretly picks two numbers from 4 to 9 to be the weights of the blocks, and records both picks, noting which is for the square and which is for the triangle. They may both have the same weight!

❷ The Solver spins the spinner, and puts the pieces shown on the indicated space in the left pan of the balance puzzle. *(Note: If the Solver didn't guess a correct weight for the previous round and gets the same pieces, spin again.)*

❸ The Puzzler then fills the right pan using the remaining pieces so that, for the chosen weights, the pans will balance. The Puzzler should try to use as few pieces as possible!

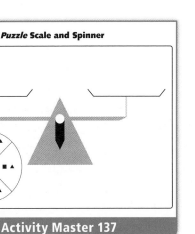

Activity Master 137

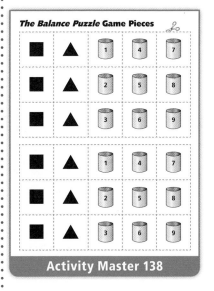

Activity Master 138

❹ The Solver now tries to find the weight of *either* kind of block, square or triangle. The Solver may guess, which sometimes is necessary.

   A   If the Solver is correct, the Solver scores points equal to the number of pieces in the right pan.

   B   If the Solver is not correct, the Solver will try again with the same weights in the next round. The Solver should record the original puzzle in this round—that information can still be used for the next round. (Also, if the Solver's next spin gives the same pieces for the left pan, the Solver should spin again.)

❺ Players trade roles and continue. The first player to reach 6 points wins!

Sample Round

❶ The Puzzler secretly chooses (and records) 5 for the square and 8 for the triangle.

❷ The Solver spins, gets a triangle and two squares (total of 18) and puts those pieces on the left pan of the balance scale.

❸ The Puzzler fills the right pan with a square, a 9, and a 4 (total of 18).

❹ The Solver can think about removing one square from each pan and then knows that triangle plus square equals 13. There are lots of possibilities, so Solver guesses that the square is 6. Guess is incorrect. Solver records the puzzle in order to be able to use the information in the next round when the Puzzler uses the same weights again.

❺ Players trade roles.

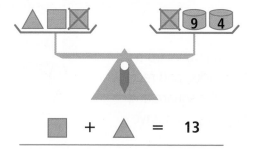

$$\blacksquare + \triangle = 13$$

    Use with Lesson Activity Book pp. 259–260.

individuals  15 MIN

Purpose To solve balance puzzles and use equations to describe puzzles

NCTM Standards 1, 2, 7, 9, 10

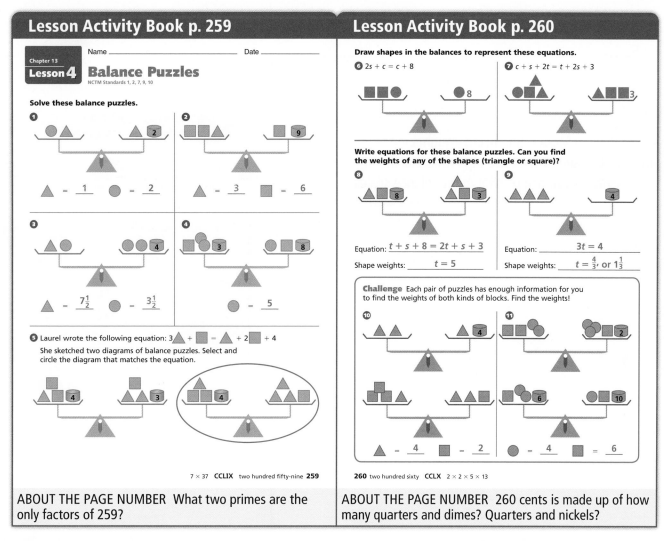

Lesson Activity Book p. 259

Chapter 13
Lesson 4 **Balance Puzzles**
NCTM Standards 1, 2, 7, 9, 10

Name _____ Date _____

Solve these balance puzzles.

1. △ = 1   ● = 2
2. △ = 3   ■ = 6
3. △ = 7½   ● = 3½
4. ● = 5

5. Laurel wrote the following equation: 3△ + ■ = △ + 2■ + 4
She sketched two diagrams of balance puzzles. Select and circle the diagram that matches the equation.

7 × 37 **CCLIX** two hundred fifty-nine **259**

ABOUT THE PAGE NUMBER What two primes are the only factors of 259?

Lesson Activity Book p. 260

Draw shapes in the balances to represent these equations.

6. 2s + c = c + 8
7. c + s + 2t = t + 2s + 3

Write equations for these balance puzzles. Can you find the weights of any of the shapes (triangle or square)?

8. Equation: t + s + 8 = 2t + s + 3
   Shape weights: t = 5
9. Equation: 3t = 4
   Shape weights: t = 4/3 or 1⅓

Challenge Each pair of puzzles has enough information for you to find the weights of both kinds of blocks. Find the weights!

10. △ = 4   ■ = 2
11. ● = 4   ■ = 6

260 two hundred sixty **CCLX** 2 × 2 × 5 × 13

ABOUT THE PAGE NUMBER 260 cents is made up of how many quarters and dimes? Quarters and nickels?

Teaching Notes for LAB page 259
This page includes several balance puzzles. For Problems 1–4, students solve for one of the blocks. For Problem 5, students select the balance puzzle that fits a given equation.

Teaching Notes for LAB page 260
Students create puzzles to fit given equations for Problems 6 and 7. For Problems 8 and 9, students write equations to match puzzles and find the weight of one block in each puzzle. Students may use shapes or letters to represent the unknowns in their equations.

Challenge Problem This challenge shows pairs of balances that students use to find the values for both kinds of blocks.

Write Math

Jennifer drew a balance puzzle that looked like this. Explain how you would find the weight of the square. Possible explanation: I could remove a triangle from each side. Then I know that the weight of 2 squares is 8. So, the weight of 1 square must be 4 ounces.

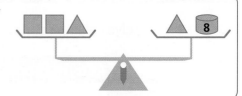

Review Model

Refer students to Review Model: Balancing Weights in the *Student Handbook* to see how to use algebraic shorthand (equations) to describe relationships shown on balance scales.

✔ **Check for Understanding**

❶ $3c + t + 2 = 2t + c + 2$, or $2c = t$

❷ $s + 2t + 8 = 2s + t + 6$, or $t + 8 = s + 6$, or $t + 2 = s$

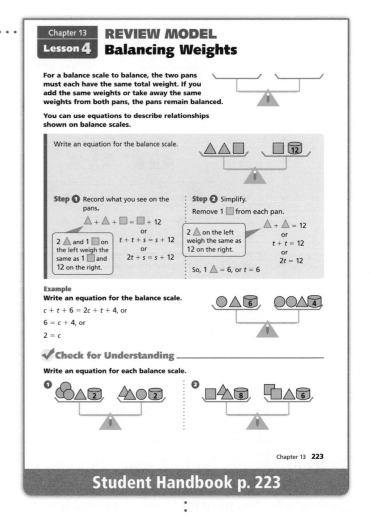

Student Handbook p. 223

3 | Differentiated Instruction

Leveled Problem Solving

A balance puzzle has two squares and a weight for 10 on the right pan.

❶ Basic Level

The left pan has two squares and a triangle. What is the weight of the triangle? Explain. 10; each side has two squares, so the triangle must weigh 10.

❷ On Level

The left pan has two squares and two triangles. Write an equation for the puzzle. What is the weight of the triangle? Explain. Possible answer: $2s + 2t = 2s + 10$; $t = 5$; since both sides have $2s$, then $2t = 10$. So, $t = 5$.

❸ Above Level

The left pan has two squares, three triangles and a weight of 4. What is the weight of the triangle? Explain. $t = 2$; $2s + 3t + 4 = 2s + 10$; $3t + 4 = 10$; $3t = 6$, so $t = 2$.

Intervention	Practice	Extension

Activity **Build a Puzzle**

Draw a balance puzzle with a triangle on the left pan and a weight of 8 on the right pan. Have students find the weight of the triangle. 8 Draw another triangle, and have students find the new weight of each triangle. 4

Then draw a square on both sides of the balance. Discuss that the weight of the triangles does not change.

Repeat with more triangles, squares, and other weights.

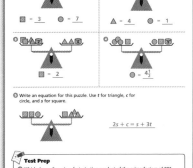

Practice P106

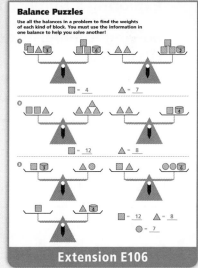

Extension E106

Spiral Review

Spiral Review Book page SR106 provides review of the following previously learned skills and concepts:

- determining the mode and range of data in a graph
- using the formula *volume = base area × height* to find the volume of rectangular and triangular prisms

You may wish to have students work with partners to complete the page.

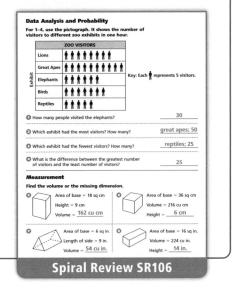

Spiral Review SR106

Extension Activity
Puzzle Roll

Have students draw three different balance puzzles using squares and triangles, with a circle to represent the weight. Tell them to leave all of the shapes blank. Then have them roll a number cube twice to make a 2-digit number. This number is the weight (circle). Encourage students to complete all three puzzles. They might need to assign a weight to one of the shapes in order to solve for the other shape.

Lesson 5 Number Tricks

NCTM Standards 1, 2, 6, 7, 8, 9, 10

Lesson Planner

STUDENT OBJECTIVES
- To explore and explain number tricks
- To use words, diagrams, and shorthand to describe calculations on "the number you picked"

1 Daily Activities (TG p. 1095)

| Open-Ended Problem Solving/Headline Story | Skills Practice and Review— Equivalent Fraction Chains |

2 Teach and Practice (TG pp. 1096–1100)

MATERIALS

(A) **Diagrams, Shorthand, and Numbers** (TG pp. 1096–1097)

(B) **Exploring a Number Trick** (TG pp. 1098–1099)

(C) **Solving Number Tricks and Problems** (TG p. 1100)

- transparency of AM139 (optional)
- 📖 LAB pp. 261–262

3 Differentiated Instruction (TG p. 1101)

Leveled Problem Solving (TG p. 1101)	Practice Book P107
Intervention Activity (TG p. 1101)	Extension Book E107
Extension Activity (TG p. 1101)	Spiral Review Book SR107

Lesson Notes

About the Lesson

This lesson brings back the "bag and dot" representation and algebraic notation that students used in **Chapter 1.** Students use words, diagrams, and shorthand to describe sets of calculations on "the number you thought of"—that is, on a variable—and work backward to find the value of that variable given the result of the calculations.

About the Mathematics

In Activity A in this lesson, students use reasoning that allows them to solve equations. This reasoning is rooted in their exploration of balance puzzles in the previous lesson: if two quantities are equal and you do the same thing to each quantity (for example, add 3, multiply by 6, subtract 4), the results are also equal.

Sometimes students employ this reasoning even when they are not using "=". It happens, for example, when students say something like "I know that 6 bags and 8 dots are 80, so 6 bags and 18 dots must be 90."

Use with Lesson Activity Book pp. 261–262.

Developing Mathematical Language

Vocabulary: variable

A *variable* is a letter or symbol that stands for one or more numbers. It represents an unknown quantity. *Variable* can be a confusing term. In solving an equation for a *variable,* the value does not vary—it is unknown. In later studies, students will encounter dependent and independent *variables* where the value of the dependent *variable* changes with the value of the independent *variable.* Also, students might write expressions to describe situations in which the *variable* could stand for different amounts; for example, "Ed is buying some tickets for $5 each. How much does he spend?" The number of dollars Ed spends can be described by the expression 5*n*, where *n* can take on different values.

Familiarize students with the term *variable.*

Beginning Display an equation or formula with a *variable.* Have students point to the *variable.*

Intermediate Ask students write an equation using a *variable,* such as *n.*

Advanced Have students write an addition or multiplication fact on paper. Ask them to replace one of the numbers with a *variable.* Then have them read their equations aloud as you write them on the board. Tell students to use the term *variable* as they read their equations. For example, 6 + *n* = 9 would be "6 plus the *variable n* equals 9."

Open-Ended Problem Solving

Suggest that students organize their responses in some way, for example, in a table.

 Headline Story

> **How many ways can Tom make a rectangle with a perimeter of 24 using square tiles? What is the least number of square tiles that Tom can use?**

Possible responses: He could have made a 6 by 6 square using 36 tiles. The two dimensions of the rectangle have to have a sum of 12. The square will have the largest area and the longest and narrowest rectangle will have the smallest area. Possible dimensions, and their areas, can be listed in a table. There are 6 different rectangles whose dimensions are whole numbers (if we consider a rectangle and that rectangle turned sideways as the same). A rectangle that is 1 tile by 11 tiles uses the least number of tiles. It uses 11 tiles.

Length	1	2	3	4	5	6
Width	11	10	9	8	7	6
Area	11	20	27	32	35	36

 MENTAL MATH

Skills Practice and Review

Equivalent Fraction Chains

The goal of this activity is to create chains of equivalent fractions. Fractions already in simplest form are likely to be easiest, so write some on the board that are, but also others that are not. Indicate how many equivalent fractions should be written for each, allowing for each student present to contribute to one chain. You might arrange this review as a silent activity and allow students to choose the chain to which they would like to add.

2 | Teach and Practice

A Diagrams, Shorthand, and Numbers

Materials
- For the teacher: transparency of AM139 (optional)

NCTM Standards 1, 2, 7, 8, 9, 10

Purpose To use diagrams and shorthand expressions to solve number tricks

Introduce Recite these steps for a number trick. Give students time between the steps to perform the operations.

Activity Master 139

❶ **Think of a number no greater than 10. (Write it down in case you forget it later).**

❷ **Add 3 to it.**

❸ **Multiply the result by 6.**

❹ **Subtract 10 from that.**

❺ **Divide the result by 2.**

❻ **Subtract 4.**

❼ **Divide by 3.**

The result should be the original number you picked!

Task Put a transparency of AM139: Number Trick Steps on the overhead or sketch the table below on the board. Repeat the number trick with a new number (in table below, 5), inviting a volunteer to write a number visibly on the table. Go through the steps, filling in the Numbers column.

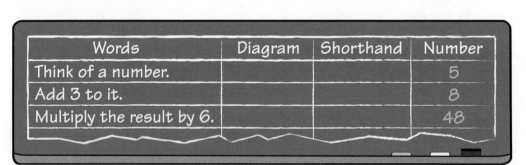

Words	Diagram	Shorthand	Number
Think of a number.			5
Add 3 to it.			8
Multiply the result by 6.			48

Why does this work? That's what the diagrams and shorthand columns can help you see. Complete the first row, using a bag to represent the number for the diagram column. Tell students that the bag can hold any number of marbles, for example, 5, as in the "number" column.

Practice Go through the puzzle again as a silent activity, offering the pen to students so they can supply the next diagram at each step. You may need to remind students that they can use dots for the three added marbles in the second step. When the class agrees on a diagram, translate it for the shorthand column. Students should catch on quickly to writing the shorthand. The completed table may look like this (your numbers, of course, may be different).

Words	Diagram	Shorthand	Number
Think of a number.	🜚	N	5
Add 3 to it.	🜚:	$N + 3$	8
Multiply the result by 6.	🜚:🜚:🜚:🜚:🜚:🜚:	$6N + 18$	48
Subtract 10 from that.	🜚:🜚:🜚:🜚 🜚 🜚	$6N + 8$	38
Divide the result by 2.	🜚:🜚 🜚.	$3N + 4$	19
Subtract 4.	🜚 🜚 🜚	$3N$	15
Divide by 3.	🜚	N	5

Extend Now erase your entries in the Number column but leave all of the diagrams and shorthand. Write 80 in the "Subtract 10 from that." row, and cover all the rows following that step.

Words	Diagram	Shorthand	Number
Subtract 10 from that.	🜚:🜚:🜚:🜚 🜚 🜚	$6N + 8$	80

💬 Talk Math

❓ What if you were doing the number trick and you stopped and had the volunteer tell you the result of the calculations up to this point? Could you figure out the original number using the strategy *work backward*? *(If students aren't sure how to begin, refer to the diagrams or shorthand. You have 6 bags and 8 dots right now, for a total of 80 dots. How can you figure out what's in a single bag?)* Possible answers:

- You could go backward through each step of the number trick, and as the last thing we did to get 80 was subtract 10, we would first add 10.

- I can just use the last shorthand to figure out that if $6N + 8$ is 80, then $6N$ must be 72, so N must be 12.

Teacher Story

❝Some students found it difficult to draw the bags and marbles in the space provided. I used this as a good opportunity to point out that while diagrams are helpful, they can be tedious to draw. I suggested they might write "🜚🜚🜚🜚🜚🜚 + 18" or even just "6🜚 + 18," taking the picture notation even closer to the letter shorthand. This also allowed students who were making up tricks on their own to represent numbers that required "removing marbles from the bags", which can be hard to represent with diagrams.❞

✔ Ongoing Assessment

As you introduce the number trick to students, take note of any who are making calculations on paper. Those students may be doing so for convenience, but you might later check their mental math skills and their fluency with multiplication facts.

B Exploring a Number Trick

NCTM Standards 1, 2, 7, 8, 9, 10

Purpose To investigate why a number trick works

Introduce Now have students try this new number trick, which is a little different than the ones they've tried before. Recite these 4 steps orally allowing time between steps for students to perform the operations.

❶ Think of a whole number and write it down.

❷ Also write down the next four counting numbers.

❸ Add all five numbers.

❹ Double the sum.

Tell students that if they give you their result, you will tell them what number they started with. You can immediately tell what number a student started with by dividing by 10 and subtracting 2. (For example, if a student got 360, you divide 360 by 10 (36) and subtract 2 (34). The number the student thought of was 34.) Demonstrate a few times that you can ask for a final result and instantly know the starting number.

Possible Discussion

As students work, look for ideas that may be worth sharing in a later discussion. Some, for example, may have made an input/output table, tried various input numbers, and looked for a pattern in the pairs of input and output numbers. Feel free to ask questions that help organize or focus students' attention. "How many bags are in the final result?" Or, "have you tried making a table of actual numbers?"

Task Write the four steps of the instructions on the board and tell students they need to figure out how the "magician"—in this case, you—figures out so quickly from the result what the starting number must have been.

> 1. Think of a whole number and write it down.
> 2. Also write down the next four counting numbers.
> 3. Add all five numbers.
> 4. Double the sum.

To help them get started, suggest that they could record each step of the trick and ask them to suggest a way of representing the "number" in the **Step 1:** "Think of a whole number and write it down." They might choose to represent it with a picture of a bag (⛅) or they might choose to call the number N (or any other letter).

To get students started with **Step 2**, ask them how they can represent the next counting number (⛅· or $N + 1$). Now, challenge them to finish representing the steps individually or in pairs and figure out how you found their starting numbers.

Use with Lesson Activity Book pp. 261–262.

Share When they seem ready, ask the class to share their ideas. Use pictures of bags or algebraic notation whenever it seems a particularly convenient way to record students' solutions or to help the class talk about them, but only when it truly helps.

- After **Step 3**, the bag and marbles image might look something like this.

- After **Step 4**, it might look like this.

We now have 10 bags of whatever amount the person first thought of (or that number times 10) and 20 extra marbles. Adding 20 marbles to that multiple of 10 still leaves a multiple of 10. (Aha! That's why the results all have a zero in the ones place!) If we know how many marbles are in this entire diagram, we can find out what's in one bag by subtracting the 20 extra marbles first (leaving just 10 bags), and then dividing by 10. We could also imagine dividing the whole thing by 10 (putting 1 bag and 2 marbles in each group) and then subtracting the two marbles to find out how much is in just one bag.

If we use algebraic notation and call the first number N, then the next four counting numbers are $(N + 1)$, $(N + 2)$, $(N + 3)$ and $(N + 4)$.

- After **Step 3**, the algebraic notation might look like this.

$$N + (N + 1) + (N + 2) + (N + 3) + (N + 4) =$$
$$N + N + N + N + N + 1 + 2 + 3 + 4 =$$
$$5N + 10$$

- Doubling $5N + 10$ gives $10N + 20$ after **Step 4.**

Again, we can divide by 10. If we imagine "dealing this out evenly" among 10 people, each gets an N and each gets a 2, or $N + 2$. Subtracting 2 gives us N, the original number.

Another way to picture dividing by 10 is to imagine evening out the groups by taking extra parts from some and adding them to others.

This gives each group $N + 2$ marbles: the middle value of the original group. Because all 10 groups are now the same, we can divide by 10 to find the number of marbles in one group.

Purpose To use diagrams and shorthand expressions to solve number tricks and story problems

NCTM Standards 1, 2, 6, 7, 8, 9, 10

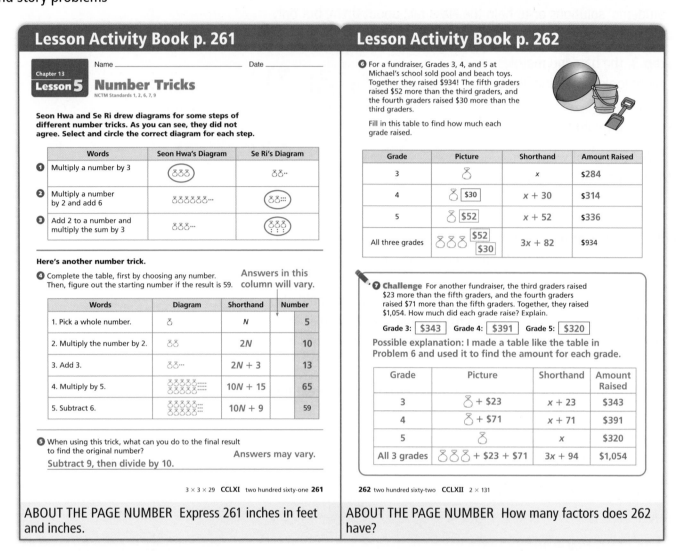

ABOUT THE PAGE NUMBER Express 261 inches in feet and inches.

ABOUT THE PAGE NUMBER How many factors does 262 have?

Teaching Notes for LAB page 261

Students may work with partners on this page. They begin by selecting the correct diagrams for steps in number tricks. In Problems 4 and 5, students represent the steps of a number trick and explain how the trick works.

Teacher Story "For Problem 5, I actually had a student who answered, "If you take off the ones digit, the answer is the other digit or digits." I thought about it and she was correct! As a class, we looked at other examples and related this to place value: $10N + 9 = N9$, where $N9$ is a two-digit number."

Teaching Notes for LAB page 262

This page presents a challenging story problem broken down into steps similar to the number tricks that students have already seen. Students must think backward to find the amount raised by individual grades, which make up the total amount raised.

Challenge Problem This problem is a repeat of Problem 6 but with different numbers and without the support of the shorthand and diagram table. Students must use their experience with Problem 6 to help them work through this one.

Reflect and Summarize the Lesson

 Write Math

Suppose this is a step in a Number Trick. Explain how you would use a diagram or algebraic shorthand to represent the step. Then tell what the starting number is if the ending number is 12. For a diagram, I would draw 2 bags and 6 dots. For algebraic shorthand, I would write $2N + 6$. If the ending number is 12, the starting number is 3.

Multiply a number by 2 and add 6.

3 | Differentiated Instruction

Leveled Problem Solving

Here are the steps in a Number Trick: (1) Think of a number. (2) Add it to the next counting number. (3) Multiply by 2.

❶ Basic Level
How could you represent step 2 using algebraic shorthand? Explain. $n + (n + 1) = 2n + 1$; n is the number, and $n + 1$ is the next counting number.

❷ On Level
If the ending number is 22, what is the starting number? 5; the last step could be represented by $4n + 2$; $4n + 2 = 22$, so $n = 5$.

❸ Above Level
One more step is added: Subtract the number. If the ending number is 26, what is the starting number? Explain. 8; the final steps would be $3n + 2 = 26$; $3n = 24$, so $n = 8$.

Intervention

Activity Start at the End

Work with students to make a number trick that starts with "Think of a number." Have students suggest two more steps to complete the number trick. At each step, have a volunteer draw a diagram or use algebraic shorthand to show the step.

Then give students an ending number, and have them find your starting number. Repeat several times.

Practice

Number Tricks

Maxie invented this number trick.

① Complete the chart, picking a starting number for yourself.

Words	Diagram	Shorthand	Number
Pick a number.	⌛	N	
Double it.	⌛⌛	2N	
Add 7.	⌛⌛·······	2N + 7	Answers in this column will vary.
Multiply by 3.	⌛⌛⦙⦙ ⌛⌛⦙⦙ ⌛⌛⦙⦙	6N + 21	
Subtract 11.	⌛⌛⦙⦙ ⌛⌛⦙ ⌛⌛	6N + 10	
Divide by 2.	⌛⌛⦙ ⌛	3N + 5	

② Barry said his final result was 26. Find his starting number, and explain how you found it.

His starting number was 7. Explanations may vary.

Possible explanation: I worked backward: 26 × 2 = 52; 52 + 11 = 63; 63 ÷ 3 = 21; 21 − 7 = 14; 14 ÷ 2 = 7

Test Prep

③ Carlos practices piano for 35 minutes every day. How much time will he spend practicing in the 31 days of May? Explain how you found your answer.

1,085 minutes; I multiplied 35 × 31. 35 × 30 = 1,050

1,050 + 35 = 1,085

Practice P107

Extension

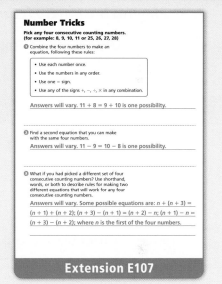

Number Tricks

Pick any four consecutive counting numbers. (for example: 8, 9, 10, 11 or 25, 26, 27, 28)

① Combine the four numbers to make an equation, following these rules:
- Use each number once.
- Use the numbers in any order.
- Use one = sign.
- Use any of the signs +, −, ÷, × in any combination.

Answers will vary. 11 + 8 = 9 + 10 is one possibility.

② Find a second equation that you can make with the same four numbers.

Answers will vary. 11 − 9 = 10 − 8 is one possibility.

③ What if you had picked a different set of four consecutive counting numbers? Use shorthand, words, or both to describe rules for making two different equations that will work for any four consecutive counting numbers.

Answers will vary. Some possible equations are: $n + (n + 3) = (n + 1) + (n + 2)$; $(n + 3) − (n + 1) = (n + 2) − n$; $(n + 1) − n = (n + 3) − (n + 2)$; where n is the first of the four numbers.

Extension E107

Spiral Review

Spiral Review Book page SR107 provides review of the following previously learned skills and concepts:
- using multiplication to solve problems involving 2- and 3-digit numbers
- using estimation and common sense to check the reasonableness of answers to problems with decimals

You may wish to have students work with partners to complete the page.

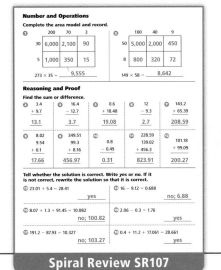

Number and Operations

Complete the area model and record.

	200	70	3
30	6,000	2,100	90
5	1,000	350	15

273 × 35 = _9,555_

	100	40	9
50	5,000	2,000	450
8	800	320	72

149 × 58 = _8,642_

Reasoning and Proof

Find the sum or difference.

④ 3.4 + 9.7 = 13.1

⑤ 16.4 − 12.7 = 3.7

⑥ 0.6 + 18.48 = 19.08

⑦ 12 − 9.3 = 2.7

⑧ 143.2 + 65.39 = 208.59

⑨ 8.02 9.54 + 0.1 = 17.66

⑩ 349.51 99.3 + 8.16 = 456.97

⑪ 0.8 − 0.49 = 0.31

⑫ 228.59 139.02 + 456.3 = 823.91

⑬ 101.18 + 99.09 = 200.27

Tell whether the solution is correct. Write yes or no. If it is not correct, rewrite the solution so that it is correct.

⑭ 23.01 + 5.4 = 28.41   yes

⑮ 16 − 9.12 = 0.688   no; 6.88

⑯ 8.07 + 1.3 + 91.45 = 10.082   no; 100.82

⑰ 2.06 − 0.3 = 1.76   yes

⑱ 191.2 − 87.93 = 10.327   no; 103.27

⑲ 0.4 + 11.2 + 17.061 = 28.661   yes

Spiral Review SR107

Extension Activity
Number Tricks

Have students work in pairs to make their own number tricks. Have them list three to five steps. Suggest that they include at least two different operations. Then direct pairs to use algebraic shorthand to represent the ending number. Have them practice finding the starting number by taking turns to find the starting number as one works through the steps with the ending number.

Then have pairs try out their number tricks with other pairs.

Lesson 6 Making Diagrams

NCTM Standards 2, 8, 9, 10

Lesson Planner

STUDENT OBJECTIVES
- To select and use diagrams to illustrate mathematical relationships
- To connect diagrams and algebraic expressions

1 Daily Activities (TG p. 1103)

Open-Ended Problem Solving/Headline Story	Skills Practice and Review—Solving Balance Puzzles

2 Teach and Practice (TG pp. 1104–1108)

MATERIALS

Ⓐ **Illustrating Situations** (TG pp. 1104–1105)

Ⓑ **Playing a Game: *Picture Puzzler*** (TG p. 1106)

Ⓒ **Using Diagrams to Represent Situations** (TG p. 1107)

- TR: Activity Master, AM140
- counters in two colors, number cubes in different colors
- 📖 LAB pp. 263–264
- 📖 SH pp. 224, 231

3 Differentiated Instruction (TG p. 1109)

Leveled Problem Solving (TG p. 1109)	Practice Book P108
Intervention Activity (TG p. 1109)	Extension Book E108
Extension Activity (TG p. 1109)	Spiral Review Book SR108
Science Connection (TG p. 1058)	

Lesson Notes

About the Lesson

Diagrams are useful tools in many mathematical situations. Students have been using diagrams for many years by now, but usually in concrete situations for which they know all the quantities needed to create the diagram. For situations in which one of those quantities is not known, diagrams must be flexible—and the person using the diagram must know they can't rely on relative sizes and lengths for figuring out unknowns. In this lesson, students work with diagrams that show both additive and multiplicative relationships between quantities, including some that are unknown quantities.

Developing Mathematical Language

Vocabulary: describing situations with diagrams

Students who still interpret all things literally might struggle with this lesson because *describing situations with diagrams* entails creating diagrams that are vague. Encourage literally-minded students to relax their literal interpretations. Some students might want to draw several different diagrams to represent one situation with various possibilities. Allow them to do this at first; but if they persist, point out how time-consuming it is and help them come up with a shorthand notation for their multiple diagrams.

Familiarize students with the phrase *describing situations with diagrams.*

Beginning Define the individual words in the phrase for students. Tell students that a *situation* is like a story and a *diagram* is a picture. Then have them practice saying the phrase, *describing situations with diagrams,* aloud with you.

Intermediate Draw a diagram on the board, such as one illustrating how to get from your classroom to the cafeteria. Have students tell whether you are *describing a situation with a diagram.*

Advanced Encourage students to name instances when they might be *describing situations with diagrams.* Possible answers: directing a person from one place to another; teaching someone to dance; showing someone how to build something.

Open-Ended Problem Solving

After students have had a chance to think about the strategies they might use to solve the problem, have them share their ideas.

 Headline Story

> Joelle loves riding horses. She weighs about 5 times as much as her favorite saddle and a tenth of what her horse weighs. If you know the total weight of Joelle, her saddle, and her horse, how can you find the weight of the saddle?

Possible response: As Joelle weighs 5 times as much as the saddle and the horse weighs ten times as much as she does, the horse weighs 50 times what the saddle weighs. So the horse, Joelle, and the saddle together weigh 56 times what the saddle alone weighs (50 for the horse, 5 for Joelle, and 1 for the saddle itself). Divide the combined weight by 56 to get the weight of the saddle.

Skills Practice and Review

Solving Balance Puzzles

Give students some balance puzzles and have them solve them. Use the transparencies of the *Balance Puzzle* (scale and spinner and game pieces) from **Lesson 13.4**. To be sure a puzzle is solvable, you might use only one type of shape. Or, if you use both types of shapes, be sure one shape (but not both) has the same number on each side.

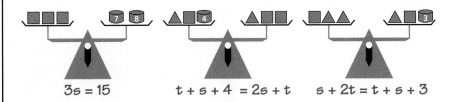

$3s = 15$ $t + s + 4 = 2s + t$ $s + 2t = t + s + 3$

whole class · 15 MIN

NCTM Standards 2, 8, 9, 10

Ⓐ Illustrating Situations

Purpose To use diagrams to represent situations

Introduce Remind students that they have seen and drawn many types of diagrams to represent mathematical situations. For example, ask someone to show a diagram to represent three rows of four. Students might draw an array as shown below or they might draw an area model.

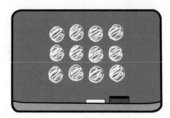

Now ask for a number sentence to describe the diagram. (One number sentence for this array is $3 \times 4 = 12$; other sentences of the same fact family are also possible.)

Task **Ask students for ideas about representing a situation when one of the values is not known. For example, how would you represent** *three rows of the same size?* We can't make an array, but we can still show what we do know, and use shorthand to represent what we don't.

Show any diagrams and expressions students create. Include examples such as these, if no student suggests them.

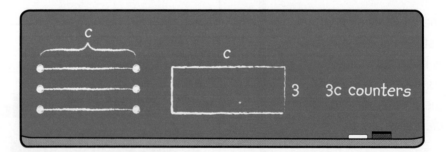

Next, introduce a part-part-whole situation with an unknown part. For example, ask students how they might represent *four more than before.* Students may think of the bag and dot representation, and/or the shorthand expression, $n + 4$.

Here are some other diagrams to show students if they don't come up with them on their own.

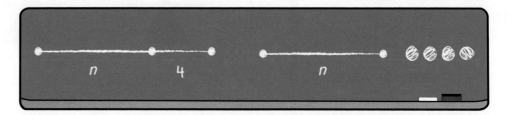

Use with Lesson Activity Book pp. 263–264.

Now challenge students to think of diagrams to represent a situation such as *add four to a number and multiply the result by 7.* Students may use a bag and dot representation or one of these.

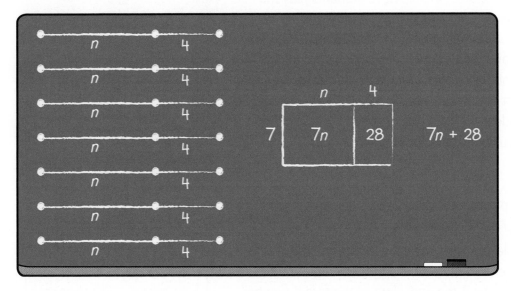

Practice Give stories such as the following and have students provide diagrams and expressions for them. You might also give a drawing or expression and have students make up a story to go with it.

- The students in gym class split into two teams to play whiffle ball. Each team had the same number of girls and the same number of boys. They each made a line with the ten girls on the left of their lines.

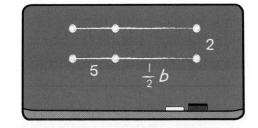

- When Carl made cookies, he put balls of dough on a cookie sheet. He could fit six cookies in each row. Jean moved the balls of dough on the cookie sheet closer together and added a few more balls of dough to each row.

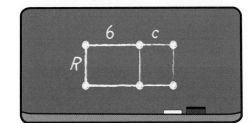

- A standard playing card is 5.7 cm wide. Harry lay out a deck of 52 playing cards, short sides touching, on the kitchen floor. He added a few more cards from another deck so the line of cards reached from wall to wall.

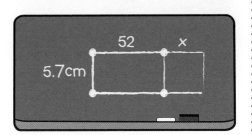

Use with Lesson Activity Book pp. 263–264.

Differentiated Instruction

Above Level Have pairs of students work together to make up stories and give a drawing or expression for the story.

Materials

- For each pair of students: AM140, 40 counters in two colors; 2 number cubes in different colors: for example, one blue and one green

NCTM Standards 2, 9, 10

Teacher Story

"All my number cubes were the same color, so I had students roll a single cube twice, recording their rolls. The first roll was the target number's tens digit and the second was the target number's ones digit.**"**

B Playing a Game: *Picture Puzzler*

Purpose To select diagrams to match given sums or products

Goal The object of the game, *Picture Puzzler,* is to be the first player to fill a 2-by-2 block of squares with counters.

Prepare Materials Have students play the game in pairs. Each student will need up to 20 counters of a single color (different colors for the two players), and the pair will need a game board (AM140) and two number cubes, one green and one blue (other colors can be substituted). To introduce the game, show students at least one example of tossing the number cube and selecting a space.

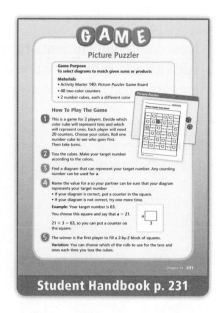
Student Handbook p. 231

How to Play

❶ Each player tosses one cube. The player with the higher number goes first.

❷ The player tosses the cubes to form a target number. The blue cube is the tens digit and the green cube is the ones digit of the target number.

❸ The player finds a diagram that can represent the target number. Any counting number can be used for *a*.

❹ The player must announce the value used for *a*. The other player should verify that the chosen diagram represents the target number.

❺ If the diagram correctly represents the target number, the player puts a counter in the square. If not, the player may try one more time.

❻ The first player to fill in a 2-by-2 block of squares wins.

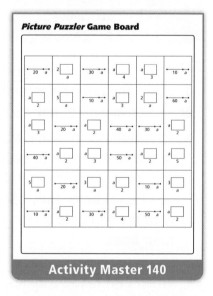
Activity Master 140

Variation Students may choose which of the rolls to use for the tens digit and which to use for the ones digit.

individuals  15 MIN

Purpose To use diagrams to represent situations and to connect diagrams with algebraic shorthand

NCTM Standards 2, 8, 10

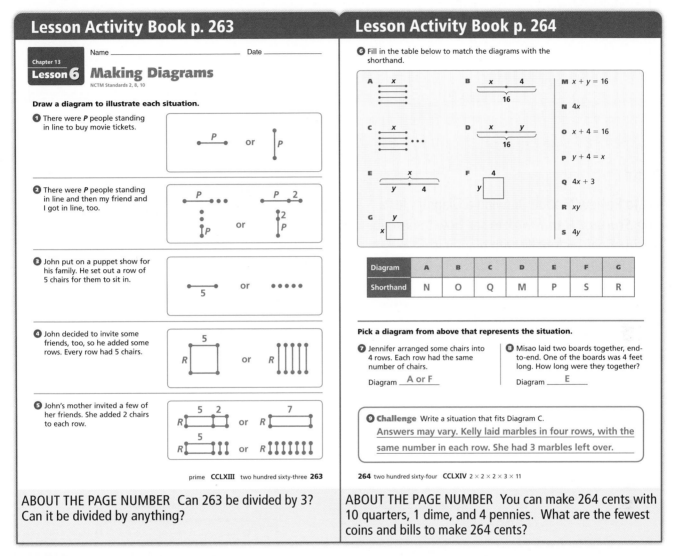

Lesson Activity Book p. 263

Name _____ Date _____

Chapter 13
Lesson 6 **Making Diagrams**
NCTM Standards 2, 8, 10

Draw a diagram to illustrate each situation.

1 There were *P* people standing in line to buy movie tickets.

2 There were *P* people standing in line and then my friend and I got in line, too.

3 John put on a puppet show for his family. He set out a row of 5 chairs for them to sit in.

4 John decided to invite some friends, too, so he added some rows. Every row had 5 chairs.

5 John's mother invited a few of her friends. She added 2 chairs to each row.

prime **CCLXIII** two hundred sixty-three **263**

Lesson Activity Book p. 264

G Fill in the table below to match the diagrams with the shorthand.

Diagram	A	B	C	D	E	F	G
Shorthand	N	O	Q	M	P	S	R

Pick a diagram from above that represents the situation.

7 Jennifer arranged some chairs into 4 rows. Each row had the same number of chairs.

Diagram ___A or F___

8 Misao laid two boards together, end-to-end. One of the boards was 4 feet long. How long were they together?

Diagram ___E___

9 Challenge Write a situation that fits Diagram C.
Answers may vary. Kelly laid marbles in four rows, with the same number in each row. She had 3 marbles left over.

264 two hundred sixty-four **CCLXIV** 2 × 2 × 2 × 3 × 11

ABOUT THE PAGE NUMBER Can 263 be divided by 3? Can it be divided by anything?

ABOUT THE PAGE NUMBER You can make 264 cents with 10 quarters, 1 dime, and 4 pennies. What are the fewest coins and bills to make 264 cents?

Teaching Notes for LAB page 263
Students draw diagrams to represent situations. Ask them to work independently and remind them that their diagrams will not necessarily be the same as those of others.

Teaching Notes for LAB page 264
On this page, students make connections between shorthand expressions, diagrams, and situations.

Challenge Problem Students are asked to write a situation to match a specific diagram.

Reflect and Summarize the Lesson

Write Math

Read the problem at the right. Draw a diagram to describe how long the two pieces were together. Explain your diagram.

Diagrams will vary. This is a possible diagram.
Possible explanation: The part of the segment labeled 2 represents the 2-foot piece of ribbon, the part labeled *x* represents the unknown length of the second piece of ribbon, and *y* represents the total length of the two pieces of ribbon placed end-to-end.

> Ashley placed two pieces of ribbon together end-to-end. One piece was 2 feet long. How long were the two pieces together?

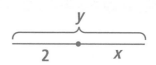

Review Model

Refer students to Review Model: Drawing a Diagram for a Situation in the *Student Handbook* to see how to describe mathematical situations pictorially with diagrams.

✓ Check for Understanding

Diagrams will vary. A possible diagram is shown for each.

1   8   *x*

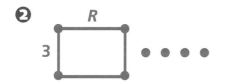

2   *R*
    3

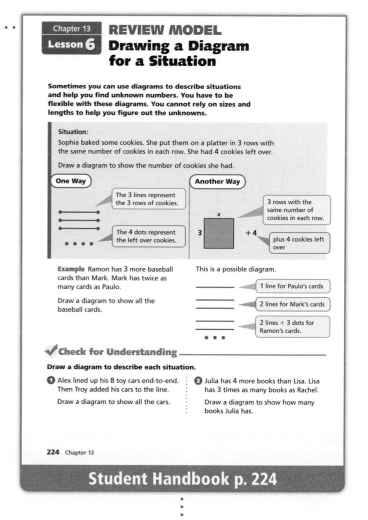

Student Handbook p. 224

3 | Differentiated Instruction

Leveled Problem Solving

Brady put 3 photos on each scrapbook page. Then he added some number of photos to each page.

❶ Basic Level

Draw a diagram to show the number of photos on one page. Explain your diagram. Diagrams may vary; one part is labeled 3 for the 3 photos. The other is labeled *p* for the added photos.

❷ On Level

Draw a diagram to show the number of photos on 4 pages. Explain your diagram. Diagrams may vary; one part is labeled 3 for the 3 photos. The other is labeled *p* for the added photos. Repeats 4 times for 4 pages.

❸ Above Level

He removes one photo from each page. Show the number of photos on a page if he doubles the number on each page. Explain. Diagrams may vary; one part is labeled 3 −1 photos. The other is labeled *p*. Repeat 2 times for doubling.

Intervention

Activity Diagram Cues

Have students work together to create a table that connects operations with possible diagrams. Have them draw diagrams to represent situations such as the following.

- A stack of books is increased by 3 books.
- Some marbles are added to a bag with 10 marbles.
- There are 8 students in each row in the class.

Practice

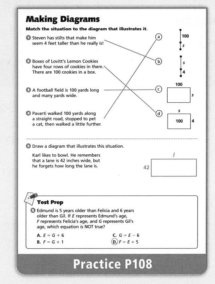

Practice P108

Extension

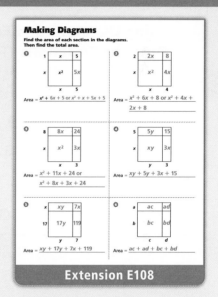

Extension E108

Spiral Review

Spiral Review Book page SR108 provides review of the following previously learned skills and concepts:

- adding and subtracting fractions with like denominators
- finding the surface area of polyhedra

You may wish to have students work with partners to complete the page.

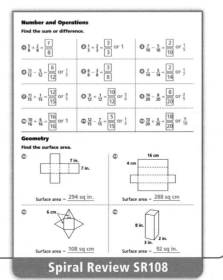

Spiral Review SR108

Extension Activity
Teamwork

Have students work together in small groups to create a number story about students on a team. The story should have two unknown amounts. After the story has been created, ask each student in the group to draw a diagram to represent the story. Then have students compare diagrams. Sample story: Only some of the players on a team wear a uniform to practice. The team practices with uniforms against non-uniforms. Two of the uniforms play with the non-uniforms so that sides are equal.

Lesson 7 Equations for Stories

NCTM Standards 1, 2, 6, 7, 8, 9

Lesson Planner

STUDENT OBJECTIVES
- To find a rule for a situation in a story problem
- To record and use such a rule using algebraic notation

1 Daily Activities (TG p. 1111)

Open-Ended Problem Solving/Headline Story	Skills Practice and Review—Solving Balance Puzzles

2 Teach and Practice (TG pp. 1112–1115)

(A) **Exploring a Situation** (TG p. 1112)

(B) **Extending the Problem** (TG p. 1113)

(C) **Using Diagrams and Equations to Describe Situations** (TG p. 1114)

MATERIALS
- TR: Activity Master, AM141
- transparency of AM141 (optional)
- 📖 LAB pp. 265–266
- 📖 SH p. 225

3 Differentiated Instruction (TG p. 1116)

Leveled Problem Solving (TG p. 1116)	Practice Book P109
Intervention Activity (TG p. 1116)	Extension Book E109
Extension Activity (TG p. 1116)	Spiral Review Book SR109
Art History Connection (TG p. 1058)	

Lesson Notes

About the Lesson

In this lesson, students describe situations using mathematical representations, both pictorially with diagrams and symbolically with equations. This is an important step in using algebra to solve real problems.

About the Mathematics

Many mathematical problems are about relationships among quantities. Such related quantities could be, for example, the length, width, and area of a rectangle; the ages of siblings; the prices of three kinds of food, the number of each kind that was purchased, and the total amount of money that was paid. If you know the rules that describe how quantities are related, then you can figure out the unknown quantity if you know the values of the other related quantities.

For example, the Game Show puzzle presents students with a situation where they need to find some unknown quantities: the number of correct and incorrect answers Vincent gave. If we only knew that he earns 3 points for a correct answer and loses 1 point for an incorrect answer, we could pick any counting numbers as values and figure out a score. But because the problem also tells us that he answered exactly 20 questions and earned 44 points, only one combination of correct and incorrect answers will work. Also, although there are two unknown quantities, we know how they are related: the number of correct questions plus the number of incorrect questions must sum to 20. So once we know how many questions he answered correctly, that relationship tells us how many questions he answered incorrectly.

Use with Lesson Activity Book pp. 265–266.

Developing Mathematical Language

Vocabulary: describing situations with equations

Describing situations with equations requires abstract thinking, and not all students are ready for this. Many will first need to describe situations with diagrams before *describing situations with equations,* and they will need prompts to write an equation from any information. *Describing situations with equations* will be mastered in a later grade.

Familiarize students with the phrase *describing situations with equations.*

Beginning Draw a diagram, and write a corresponding equation; for example, 3 stars and some more stars equal 5 stars.

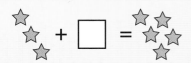

Show students how the drawing describes the equation. Ask pairs of students to say *describing situations with equations* aloud together.

Intermediate Have students write a sentence or brief paragraph explaining how *describing situations with equations* differs from describing situations with diagrams.

Advanced Have students compare, using their own words, *describing situations with equations* and describing situations with diagrams.

Open-Ended Problem Solving

After reading over the story, you may need to reassure students that two-dollar bills do exist! Also, students may forget about half-dollar and dollar coins, so you may need to remind them that there are six possible coins for the change.

 Headline Story

> **Sandy bought some things at the store and paid with a two-dollar bill. The change was five coins, but none of the coins had the same value as any other coin. What could the amount of Sandy's purchase have been?**

Possible responses: There are six coins: penny (P), nickel (N), dime (D), quarter (Q), half-dollar (H), and dollar ($). So, there is only one coin that is *not* used. The amount of her purchase could have been $0.10, $0.14, $0.19, $0.34, $0.59, or $1.09.

Skills Practice and Review

Solving Balance Puzzles

As in **Lesson 13.6,** give students some balance puzzles and have them solve them. Use the transparencies of the *Balance Puzzle* (scale and spinner and game pieces) from **Lesson 13.4.** Be sure a puzzle is solvable, Here are some examples.

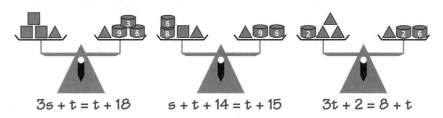

$3s + t = t + 18$ $\qquad$ $s + t + 14 = t + 15$ $\qquad$ $3t + 2 = 8 + t$

individuals or pairs

20 MIN

Materials

- For the teacher:
  transparency of AM141
  (optional)
- For each student:
  AM141

NCTM Standards 1, 2, 7, 8, 9

Concept Alert

Although it's useful for students to think about the different 'tools' they have for approaching a problem, it's also useful for them to understand that solving a problem is rarely a matter of picking one 'tool' to do the whole job. What's important is that they can think about problems in ways that make sense to them and help them figure out the answer. For example, as the class discusses problem-solving strategies, it's likely that a particular way of thinking about the problem will include elements of more than one strategy. For example, starting with the total of 44 points, figuring out how many right answers are needed to get at least that total, and then adding right and wrong answers to get to 20 questions and 44 points could be described as a combination of *working backward* and *guessing and checking.*

(A) Exploring a Situation

Purpose To solve a word problem using logical thinking

Introduce Put a transparency of AM141: The Game Show Puzzle on the overhead or write the problem on the board. The Game Show problem presents a puzzle for students to solve. Give them time to work individually or in pairs.

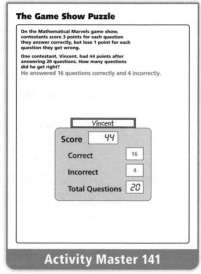

The Game Show Puzzle

On the Mathematical Marvels game show, contestants score 3 points for each question they answer correctly, but lose 1 point for each question they get wrong.

One contestant, Vincent, had 44 points after answering 20 questions. How many questions did he get right?
He answered 16 questions correctly and 4 incorrectly.

Vincent
Score 44
Correct 16
Incorrect 4
Total Questions 20

Activity Master 141

Task Ask the class to share their ideas and solutions for the puzzle. Even if students have not finished solving the puzzle, they may be able to explain the solution method they were using. Here are a few ways students may approach the puzzle.

- Calculate how many points Vincent would get if he answered *every* question correctly. He earns 3 points for every correct answer (3 × 20) and loses 1 point for every error (1 × 0, as he did not make any) so his total would have been 60 points. But we know he actually earned 44 points, so he must have answered some questions incorrectly. We can try other combinations in order, or strategically guess and check, moving higher or lower depending on the results: What if he got 19 right and 1 wrong? What if he got 17 right and 3 wrong? It won't take very many guesses to find the answer this way: 16 correct and 4 incorrect means that Vincent earned 16 × 3 points and lost 4 × 1, for a total of 44 points.

- Ask how getting one more answer wrong changes the score. Vincent wouldn't be able to *add* the 3 points that question is worth, but subtracts 1 instead; in other words, each wrong answer costs him 4 points. If he gets 20 right, he ends up with 60 total points; his score of 44 is 16 less than that, which means he gave 4 wrong answers.

- Build up to 44 points. 44 isn't divisible by 3. Fifteen right answers would earn 45 points, 1 point too much, so the remaining 5 questions must make Vincent lose exactly 1 point. One wrong answer will get us back to 44 points. Now we just need to work with the remaining 4 questions so that the points earned and lost cancel each other out. One correct answer will add 3, and three wrong answers will subtract 3, leaving exactly 44 points.

B Extending the Problem

NCTM Standards 1, 2, 7, 8, 9

Purpose To analyze relationships to solve word problems about The Game Show puzzle

Introduce Ask students to give a rule that describes the relationship between the total points and the number of correct answers and wrong answers for The Game Show puzzle. Then ask them for a shorthand version of that relationship (an equation) using *P, C,* and *W* for total *P*oints, *C*orrect, and *W*rong answers. One possibility is $P = 3C - W$.

Task **Have students use their equations to find the total points, the number of correct answers, or the number of wrong answers when the other two values are known. Ask students to explain what they did to get their solutions.**

- Arnie answered 20 questions, and gave 13 correct and 7 wrong answers. How many points did he get? 32; Possible explanations: Plugging in the values for *C* and *W* into the equation, you get $P = (3 \times 13) - 7$ so $P = 32$.

- Belinda answered 15 questions, and answered 13 of them correctly. How many points did she get? 37

- Chuck answered 20 questions, but he only got 9 right. How many points did he get? 16

- Darla answered 25 questions, and got 24 right! How many points did she get? 71

- Evan got 8 right. How many points did he get? We don't have enough information to find the total number of points. We need to know the total number of questions, or the number of questions answered incorrectly!

- Felicia got 35 points. She got 14 correct. How many did she get wrong? 7; Possible explanation: This time I didn't know *W,* so I put the other numbers into the equation: $35 = (14 \times 3) - W$, so $W = 7$.

- Genji got 25 points. She got 2 wrong. How many did she get right? 9; Possible explanation: $25 = 3C - 2$ so $C = 9$.

Point out that the equation they're using has three letters—three things you don't know. If you know two, you can find the other one.

individuals 👤 🕐 25 MIN

Purpose To represent situations with diagrams or equations

NCTM Standards 1, 2, 6, 7, 8. 9

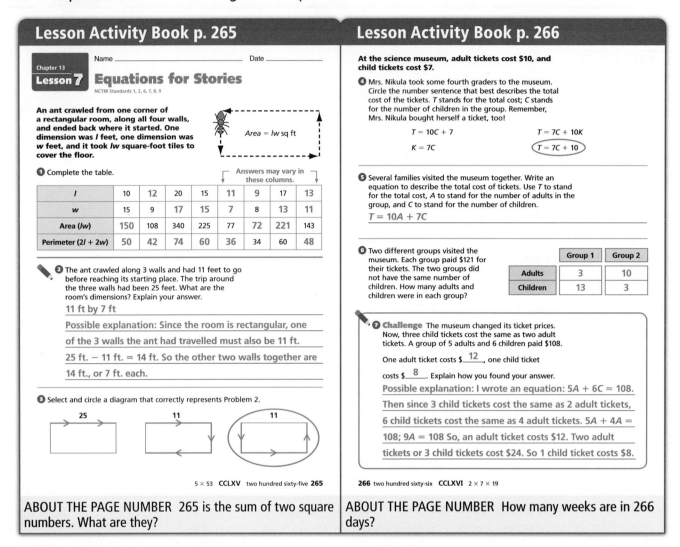

Lesson Activity Book p. 265

Name _____ Date _____

Chapter 13
Lesson 7 Equations for Stories
NCTM Standards 1, 2, 6, 7, 8, 9

An ant crawled from one corner of a rectangular room, along all four walls, and ended back where it started. One dimension was *l* feet, one dimension was *w* feet, and it took *lw* square-foot tiles to cover the floor.

Area = *lw* sq ft

① Complete the table.

⌐ Answers may vary in these columns. ¬

l	10	12	20	15	11	9	17	13
w	15	9	17	15	7	8	13	11
Area (*lw*)	150	108	340	225	77	72	221	143
Perimeter (2*l* + 2*w*)	50	42	74	60	36	34	60	48

② The ant crawled along 3 walls and had 11 feet to go before reaching its starting place. The trip around the three walls had been 25 feet. What are the room's dimensions? Explain your answer.

11 ft by 7 ft

Possible explanation: Since the room is rectangular, one of the 3 walls the ant had travelled must also be 11 ft.

25 ft. − 11 ft. = 14 ft. So the other two walls together are

14 ft., or 7 ft. each.

③ Select and circle a diagram that correctly represents Problem 2.

25   11   11

5 × 53 **CCLXV** two hundred sixty-five **265**

Lesson Activity Book p. 266

At the science museum, adult tickets cost $10, and child tickets cost $7.

④ Mrs. Nikula took some fourth graders to the museum. Circle the number sentence that best describes the total cost of the tickets. *T* stands for the total cost; *C* stands for the number of children in the group. Remember, Mrs. Nikula bought herself a ticket, too!

$T = 10C + 7$ $T = 7C + 10K$

$K = 7C$ $(T = 7C + 10)$

⑤ Several families visited the museum together. Write an equation to describe the total cost of tickets. Use *T* to stand for the total cost, *A* to stand for the number of adults in the group, and *C* to stand for the number of children.

$T = 10A + 7C$

⑥ Two different groups visited the museum. Each group paid $121 for their tickets. The two groups did not have the same number of children. How many adults and children were in each group?

	Group 1	Group 2
Adults	3	10
Children	13	3

⑦ Challenge The museum changed its ticket prices. Now, three child tickets cost the same as two adult tickets. A group of 5 adults and 6 children paid $108.

One adult ticket costs $ __12__, one child ticket

costs $ __8__. Explain how you found your answer.

Possible explanation: I wrote an equation: 5A + 6C = 108.

Then since 3 child tickets cost the same as 2 adult tickets,

6 child tickets cost the same as 4 adult tickets. 5A + 4A =

108; 9A = 108 So, an adult ticket costs $12. Two adult

tickets or 3 child tickets cost $24. So 1 child ticket costs $8.

266 two hundred sixty-six **CCLXVI** 2 × 7 × 19

ABOUT THE PAGE NUMBER 265 is the sum of two square numbers. What are they?

ABOUT THE PAGE NUMBER How many weeks are in 266 days?

Teaching Notes for LAB page 265

Students use diagrams and the relationships between the side lengths of a rectangle and its area and perimeter to solve problems.

✔**Ongoing Assessment** Ask students to work independently in order to assess students' facility using and differentiating between area and perimeter formulas.

Teaching Notes for LAB page 266

Students select, write, and use equations to help them solve problems.

Challenge Problem As in Problem 6, students must reason logically to solve a problem about the relationship between two unknown quantities.

Reflect and Summarize the Lesson

Write Math

Read the problem on the right. Write an equation to describe the total amount Sophia earned. Use *M* for the amount Sophia earned each time she mowed and *T* for the total amount she earned. Explain your **equation.** Possible equation: $T = 4M + 10$ Possible explanation: The equation shows that the total amount Sophia earned is 4 times the amount she earned for mowing plus the number of dollars she earned for planting flowers.

> Sophia mowed her neighbor's lawn 4 times in July. She also earned an extra $10 planting flowers.

Review Model

Refer students to Review Model: Writing an Equation for a Situation in the ***Student Handbook*** to see how to describe mathematical situations symbolically with equations.

✔ Check for Understanding

1 The total amount Marcus spent is $2 times the number of markers plus $6 times the number of notebooks. $t = 2m + 6n$

2 The total number of dimes Tami has is 3 times the number of dimes in each pocket plus 8. $t = 3p + 8$

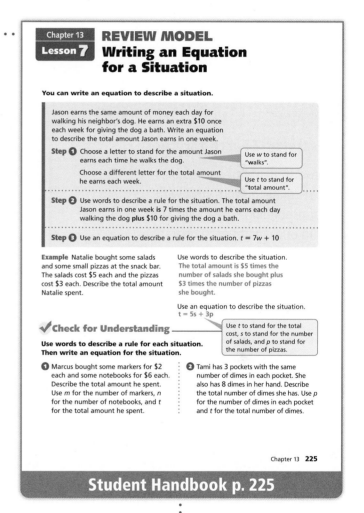

Student Handbook p. 225

Leveled Problem Solving

Natalia read 3 books in a detective series.
Each book has the same number of pages.

❶ Basic Level

What equation describes the total number of pages she read? Explain. Possible answer: $3s = t$; s stands for the number of pages in each book, so 3 times s is the total for 3 books.

❷ On Level

She also read a book by a different author. What equation describes the total number of pages she read? Explain. Possible answer: $3s + d = t$; $3s$ is the pages in the series, and d is the number of pages in the other book.

❸ Above Level

She also read a book that was 25 pages longer than the books in the series. What equation describes the total number of pages she read? Possible answer: $4s + 25 = t$; $3s + (s + 25) = 4s + 25$

| Intervention | Practice | Extension |

Activity Search for Cues

Have students create a table that connects word cues with corresponding operations. Start them with one cue for each operation.

Add	More than
Subtract	Less than
Multiply	Times as many
Divide	Put in equal groups

Provide problems to help them recognize additional cues.

Equations for Stories

Jackie went to the pet store to look at the iguanas and birds.

❶ She noticed the animals had 24 feet all together. Complete the table to show the possible combinations of birds and iguanas.

Birds	0	2	4	6	8	10	12
Iguanas	6	5	4	3	2	1	0

❷ If there are also 18 eyes, how many of each animal was there?   6 birds and 3 iguanas

On another day, there were B birds and I iguanas.

❸ Write an equation that gives the number of eyes, E, for the birds and iguanas. $E = 2B + 2I$ or $E = 2(B + I)$

❹ Write an equation that gives the number of feet, F. $F = 2B + 4I$ or $F = 2(B + 2I)$

Test Prep

❺ This rectangular prism is made of 1 cm cubes. What is its volume? Explain how you found the volume.

120 cu cm; I multiplied the length (6 cm) × the width (5 cm) × height (4 cm). 6 cm × 5 cm × 4 cm = 120 cu cm

Practice P109

Equations for Stories

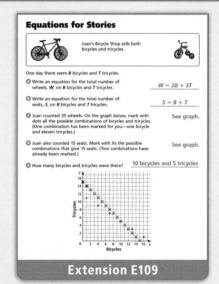

Juan's Bicycle Shop sells both bicycles and tricycles.

One day there were B bicycles and T tricycles.

❺ Write an equation for the total number of wheels, W, on B bicycles and T tricycles. $W = 2B + 3T$

❻ Write an equation for the total number of seats, S, on B bicycles and T tricycles. $S = B + T$

❼ Juan counted 35 wheels. On the graph below, mark with dots all the possible combinations of bicycles and tricycles. (One combination has been marked for you—one bicycle and eleven tricycles.)   See graph.

❽ Juan also counted 15 seats. Mark with Xs the possible combinations that give 15 seats. (Two combinations have already been marked.)   See graph.

❾ How many bicycles and tricycles were there?   10 bicycles and 5 tricycles

Extension E109

Spiral Review

Spiral Review Book page SR109 provides review of the following previously learned skills and concepts:

- using algebraic shorthand as a tool for recording relationships
- applying the problem solving strategy *guess and check*

You may wish to have students work with partners to complete the page.

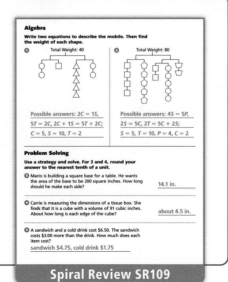

Algebra

Write two equations to describe the mobile. Then find the weight of each shape.

❶ Total Weight: 40

❷ Total Weight: 80

Possible answers: 2C = 1S, 5T = 2C, 2C + 1S = 5T + 2C; C = 5, S = 10, T = 2

Possible answers: 4S = 5P, 2S = 5C, 2T = 5C + 2S; S = 5, T = 10, P = 4, C = 2

Problem Solving

Use a strategy and solve. For 3 and 4, round your answer to the nearest tenth of a unit.

❸ Mario is building a square base for a table. He wants the area of the base to be 200 square inches. How long should he make each side?   14.1 in.

❹ Carrie is measuring the dimensions of a tissue box. She finds that it is a cube with a volume of 91 cubic inches. About how long is each edge of the cube?   about 4.5 in.

❺ A sandwich and a cold drink cost $6.50. The sandwich costs $3.00 more than the drink. How much does each item cost?   sandwich $4.75, cold drink $1.75

Spiral Review SR109

Extension Activity
Equations to Problems

Ask students to choose three of the following equations:

$$6x + 1 = 26$$
$$3y - 4 = 26$$
$$3(a + 2) = 21$$
$$6(c - 1) = 24$$
$$(w + 4) \div 2 = 8.$$

Have them write a problem that can be represented by each equation they chose.

Teacher's Notes 🍎

Daily Notes . . .

Quick Notes

More Ideas

Lesson 8 Problem Solving Strategy and Test Prep

NCTM Standards 1, 2, 5, 6, 7, 8, 9, 10

Lesson Planner

STUDENT OBJECTIVES
- To practice the problem solving strategy *work backward*
- To articulate the steps and strategies used to solve problems
- To prepare for standardized tests

Problem Solving Strategy:
Solve a Simpler Problem (TG pp. 1119–1120, 1122–1123)

MATERIALS

Ⓐ **Discussing the Problem Solving Strategy: Work Backward** (TG p. 1119)

Ⓑ **Solving Problems by Applying the Strategy** (TG p. 1120)

- LAB p. 267
- SH pp. 226–227

Problem Solving Test Prep (TG p. 1121)

Ⓒ **Getting Ready for Standardized Tests** (TG p. 1121)

- LAB p. 268

Lesson Notes

About Problem Solving

Problem Solving Strategy: Work Backward

In this final lesson of the chapter, students use their problem-solving skills to answer questions for which working backward is a very helpful strategy.

The LAB pages assess students' mastery of concepts and skills from this chapter, including connecting representations of mathematical situations and applying algebraic thinking.

Skills Practice and Review

MENTAL MATH

Fractions Greater Than, Less Than, and Equal to 1

This activity was introduced in Chapter 4, but is suggested here as a review to prepare for working with probability in the next chapter, **Chapter 14.** Start this table on the board:

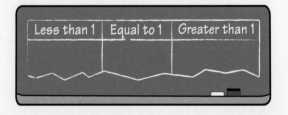

| Less than 1 | Equal to 1 | Greater than 1 |

Ask volunteers to think of fractions and list them in the appropriate categories. If one category is under-represented, you may want to specify the kind of fraction you'd like. Students who are successful at this have already generalized the rule: fractions greater than 1 have numerators larger than their denominators; those that are less than 1 have numerators smaller than their denominators; fractions whose numerators and denominators are the same are equal to 1.

Use with Lesson Activity Book pp. 267–268.

Problem Solving Strategy

(A) Discussing the Problem Solving Strategy: Work Backward

Purpose To share strategies for solving problems and focus on the problem solving strategy, *work backward*

Introduce Remind students that throughout this chapter they have been using the strategy *work backward* to help them solve problems as they figure out the weights of the shapes in a mobile when given the total weight and find the value of a variable given the result of the calculations.

Record the following problem on the board or on a blank transparency. Ask a volunteer to read the problem. Then have the students begin working on the problem.

Problem On Saturday, Rachel's plant was $\frac{5}{6}$ foot tall. It had grown $\frac{1}{4}$ foot from Thursday to Saturday. It had grown $\frac{1}{3}$ foot from Tuesday to Thursday. How tall was Rachel's plant on Tuesday?

Share Have students share their strategies for solving the problem. Students may suggest working backward from the height of the plant on Saturday to find the height on Tuesday.

💬 Talk Math

❷ What might you do to help you see the relationship between the heights on Tuesday, Thursday, and Saturday? You could draw a diagram to help you visualize the relationship.

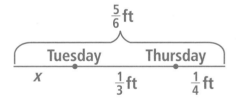

❷ How does the diagram help you know how to solve the problem? From the diagram I can see that if I subtract $\frac{1}{4}$ from $\frac{5}{6}$ I'll get the height on Thursday, and subtracting $\frac{1}{3}$ from that will give the height on Tuesday. $\frac{5}{6} - \frac{1}{4} = \frac{7}{12}$, so the plant was $\frac{7}{12}$ ft on Thursday. $\frac{7}{12} - \frac{1}{3} = \frac{1}{4}$, so the plant was $\frac{1}{4}$ ft high on Tuesday.

❷ Is there another way you could solve the problem? Possible answer: I could first add the amount the plant grew from Tuesday to Thursday to the amount it grew between Thursday and Saturday, and then subtract that sum from the height on Saturday. $\frac{3}{3} + \frac{1}{4} = \frac{7}{12}$ and $\frac{5}{6} - \frac{7}{12} = \frac{3}{12}$, or $\frac{1}{4}$.

Solving Problems by Applying the Strategy LAB p. 267

Purpose To practice the problem solving strategy, *work backward*

NCTM Standards 1, 2, 6, 7, 8, 9

Teaching Notes for LAB page 267

Have students look at the first problem on LAB page 267. Give students a few minutes to work on the problem. Then have students share their strategies for solving the problem. If students don't suggest it, show how to use the problem solving strategy *work backward* to solve the problem. Ask questions like these.

Read to Understand

What do you know from reading the problem? Vlad made up a number trick for Lecia. Lecia's result was 14.

What do you need to find out? Lecia's starting number

Plan

How can you solve this problem? You can work backward from the result to find the starting number.

Solve

How could you work backward? You can use Lecia's result and work backward through the list of steps, figuring out what she needed before she applied each step. Or, write an equation using, for example, *N* for the starting number, then work backward "undoing" the operations you'd do to *N* to get the final result.

- The last step is **divide by 3.** What do you do to undo that step? Multiply by 3: $14 \times 3 = 42$.

- The step before that is **subtract 12.** How do you undo that step? Add 12: $42 + 12 = 54$.

- The step before that is **multiply by 3.** How do you undo that step? Divide by 3: $54 \div 3 = 18$.

- The step before that is **add 10.** How do you undo that step? Subtract 10: $18 - 10 = 8$.

Check

Look back at the original problem. Does your answer make sense? How do you know? You can take your result and go forward through the number trick to be sure you get the same result Lecia got.

Lesson Activity Book p. 267

Name _____ Date _____

Chapter 13
Lesson 8

Problem Solving Strategy and Test Prep
Work Backward
NCTM Standards 1, 2, 5, 6, 7, 8, 9, 10

Understand
Plan
Solve
Check

❶ Vlad enjoyed inventing number tricks for his friends. He gave this one to Lecia.

- Pick a whole number.
- Add 10.
- Multiply by 3.
- Subtract 12.
- Divide by 3.
- Tell me your result, and I'll tell you your starting number

Lecia's result was 14. What was her starting number?   __8__

❷ Vlad has a younger brother, Sergi. Sergi is half the age of their sister, Katya. Katya is two years older than their sister, Sonya. Sonya is half Vlad's age. Vlad is 16. How old is Sergi?   __5__

❸ Abby, Belinda, Charles, and Ernie each brought some cars to Dante's house. They decided to make teams of their cars and have races. When they put the cars together, they noticed that Abby had one more car than Charles, Belinda had one more than Abby, Dante had one more than Belinda, and Ernie had one more than Dante! When they shared their cars, each friend had 5 cars for their team. How many cars did each of the friends have at first?

Abby: __4__ cars   Belinda: __5__ cars   Charles: __3__ cars

Dante: __6__ cars   Ernie: __7__ cars

3 × 89   **CCLXVII**   two hundred sixty-seven **267**

ABOUT THE PAGE NUMBER Express 267 inches as feet and inches.

Reflect and Summarize the Lesson

Write Math

How can using the strategy *work backward* help you solve a problem? Possible answer: By working backward you can begin with the result and undo the operations in the steps before the result to get the starting number.

(C) Getting Ready for Standardized Tests LAB p. 268

individuals · 30 MIN

Purpose To prepare students for standardized tests

NCTM Standards 1, 2, 5, 6, 7, 8, 9, 10

Lesson Activity Book p. 268

Problem Solving Test Prep

Choose the correct answer.

1 Kara had $\frac{1}{8}$ pound of sugar left after making a cake. She used $\frac{1}{4}$ pound of sugar for the batter and $\frac{1}{8}$ pound of sugar for the icing. How much sugar did Kara start with?

A. 1 pound   C. $\frac{1}{2}$ pound

B. $\frac{3}{4}$ pound   D. $\frac{3}{8}$ pound

2 Which is the only measure that is **not** one of the numbers in the set?

2, 2, 4, 4, 5, 6, 7, 8

A. mean   C. mode

B. range   D. median

3 Which product is shown by the model?

$$\frac{3}{4}$$

$$\frac{1}{3}$$

A. $\frac{1}{12}$ B. $\frac{1}{4}$ C. $\frac{1}{3}$ D. $\frac{3}{4}$

4 Marco's dog weighs 34 pounds. Since its birth, it has gained 33 pounds and lost 1 pound. How much did Marco's dog weigh when it was born?

A. 1 pound   C. 3 pounds

B. 2 pounds   D. 4 pounds

✎ Show What You Know

Solve each problem. Explain your answer.

5 The total weight of the mobile is 48 pounds. Write the shapes in order from lightest to heaviest.

Triangle, square, hexagon, circle;

Possible explanation: each side of

the top arm weighs 12 lb; it takes 6 triangles to equal 12 lb but only 4 squares, 3 hexagons, and 2 circles.

6 An amusement park charges $16 admission. Special rides are S dollars each. Write an equation to find the total cost, T, including W special rides. If you spent $30 in all and special rides cost $2 each, how could you use your equation to find the number of special rides you went on?

$T = 16 + WS$; Possible

explanation: the equation would

become 30 = 16 + 2W. Solve:

14 = 2W, W = 7. Check: 30 =

16 + 2(7), 30 = 16 + 14, 30 = 30.

268 two hundred sixty-eight   **CCLXVIII**   2 × 2 × 67

ABOUT THE PAGE NUMBER What is half of 268? How can you find the answer mentally?

Teaching Notes for LAB page 268

The test items on this page are written in the same style and arranged in the same format as those on many state assessments. The page is cumulative and is designed for students to apply a variety of problem solving strategies including *work backward, use logical reasoning, and draw a picture.* Have students share the strategies they use.

The Item Analysis Chart below highlights one of the possible strategies that may be used for each item.

Show What You Know

Written Response

Direct students' attention to Problems 5 and 6. Explain that they must decide how to solve the problems. Then have students write an explanation of how they know their answer is correct. To provide more space for students to communicate their thinking about these problems, you may wish to have them write their responses and explanations on a separate sheet of paper. Use the Scoring Rubric below to evaluate their understanding.

Item Analysis Chart

Item	Strategy
1	Work backward
2	Use logical reasoning
3	Draw a picture
4	Work backward
5	Guess and check; use logical reasoning
6	Guess and check, make a table

Scoring Rubric

2	• Demonstrates complete understanding of the problem and chooses an appropriate strategy to determine the solution
1	• Demonstrates a partial understanding of the problem and chooses a strategy that does not lead to a complete and accurate solution
0	• Demonstrates little understanding of the problem and shows little evidence of using any strategy to determine a solution

---

Refer students to the Problem Solving Strategy Review Model: Work Backward in the *Student Handbook* pp. 226–227 to review a model of the four steps they can use with problem solving strategy, *work backward.*

Additional problem solving practice is also provided.

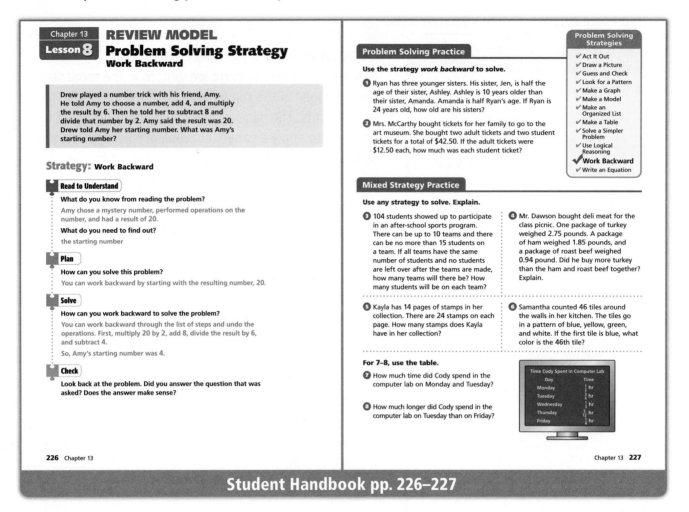

Student Handbook pp. 226–227

Task Have students read the problem at the top of the Review Model page. Then discuss.

Talk Math

❓ What operation can you use to undo addition? subtraction

❓ What operation can you use to undo subtraction? addition

❓ What operation can you use to undo multiplication? division

❓ What operation can you use to undo division? multiplication

❓ What would you do first to find Amy's starting number? Possible answer: Since the last step is "divide by 2", I would multiply Amy's final result by 2 to undo this step: 20 × 2 = 40.

Amanda is half Ryan's age, which is 24 ÷ 2, or 12 years old. Ashley is 10 years older than Amanda, which is 12 + 10, or 22 years old. Jen is half of Ashley's age, which is 22 ÷ 2, or 11 years old.

❷ $8.75; Possible explanation: You can use the strategy *work backward.* You know that Mrs. McCarthy spent a total of $42.50. Subtract the cost of two adult tickets from $42.50. $42.50 − ($12.50 + $12.50) = $17.50. Divide $17.50 by two, since she bought two student tickets. $17.50 ÷ 2 = $8.75

Mixed Strategy Practice

❸ 8 teams, 13 students; Possible explanation: You can use *guess and check* to solve. Students know that there can be up to 10 teams with no more than 15 students on a team. All teams have the same number of students and no students are left over. If you divide the 104 students by a number of students on each team, you can find the number of teams. You can guess and check with numbers starting at 15 looking for a remainder of 0. When 13 students are on each team, there are 8 teams and no students are left over.

❹ No; Possible explanation: You can *make a model* to solve. Students can use base-ten blocks to model the number of pounds of weight in the deli meat. You can combine the blocks representing the ham and roast beef. Combine 1 flat, 8 rods, and 5 units with 9 rods and 4 units. You get 1 flat, 17 rods, and 9 units. Trade 10 rods for 1 flat and then you have 2 flats, 7 rods, and 9 units. The ham and roast beef weigh a total of 2.79 pounds. 1.85 + 0.94 = 2.79. That is more than 2.75 pounds, the weight of the turkey.

	10	4
20	200	80
4	40	16

×	10	4	
20	200	80	280
4	40	16	56
	240	96	336

❻ yellow; Possible explanation: You can *look for a pattern* to solve. Every 4th tile will be white, so the 44th tile will be white. There are an additional 2 tiles and they will be blue and then yellow.

❼ $1\frac{1}{4}$ hr; Possible explanation: You can use the strategy *solve a simpler problem* to solve. You can find common denominators for the two fractions and then add them together. $\frac{1}{2} + \frac{3}{4}$ is the same as $\frac{2}{4} + \frac{3}{4}$. $\frac{2}{4} + \frac{3}{4} = \frac{5}{4}$, or $1\frac{1}{4}$

❽ $\frac{1}{2}$ hr; Possible explanation: You can use the strategy *write an equation* to solve. $\frac{3}{4} - \frac{1}{4} = \frac{2}{4}$, or $\frac{1}{2}$

Fun with Algebra

NCTM Standards 1, 3, 4, 6, 7, 9, 10

Purpose To provide students with an opportunity to demonstrate understanding of Chapter 13 concepts and skills

> **MATERIALS**
> • LAB pp. 269–270
> • Chapter 13 Test (Assessment Guide pp. AG113–AG114)

Chapter 13 Learning Goals and Assessment Options

These learning goals are assessed in many ways throughout the chapter. The chart below correlates each learning goal to specific formal and informal assessment options.

Learning Goals		Lesson Number	Snapshot Assessment	Chapter Review Item Numbers	Chapter Test Item Numbers
			Item Number	LAB pp. 269–270	Assessment Guide pp. AG113–AG114
13-A	Use models to demonstrate and write equal equations	13.1–13.4	1, 5	1–6	1–6
13-B	Use a diagram to describe a mathematical relationship to help solve a problem	13.6	2, 6	8	7, 8
13-C	Identify and write an equation to describe a mathematical relationship to help solve a problem	13.3, 13.7	3, 4, 7	1, 3, 9	9, 10
13-D	Apply problem solving strategies such as *work backward* to solve problems	13.5, 13.8	8	7, 10	11, 12

Snapshot Assessment

whole class — 10 MIN

The following Mental Math and Quick Write questions and tasks provide a quick, informal assessment of students' understanding of Chapter 13 concepts, skills, and problem solving strategies.

Mental Math This oral assessment uses mental math strategies and can be used with the whole class.

❶ Steven made a mobile that balanced. On the left side, he hung 3 small bags with the same number of cubes in each bag. On the right side, he hung two small bags with 6 cubes in each bag. Give an equation. $4 \times 3 = 6 \times 2$ Explain how you know. He needs 4 in each of 3 bags to get 12 on the left, since the right has 2 bags of 6, or 12.

• What would happen to the mobile if one bag was removed on the left? The right side would go down and the left side would go up because it would not be balanced.
(Learning Goal 13-A)

❷ • Each row has f chairs. How can we show 4 rows with the same number of chairs? $4f$ or $4 \times f$; also accept $f + f + f + f$

• Each row has n chairs + 2. How can we show 3 rows of the same number of chairs? $3(n + 2)$ or $3n + 6$; also accept $(n + 2) + (n + 2) + (n + 2)$

• Each row has g chairs − 1. How can we show 2 rows of the same number of chairs? $2(g - 1)$ or $2g - 2$; also accept $(g - 1) + (g - 1)$
(Learning Goal 13-B)

❸ You receive points for guessing letters in a mystery word. Let **P** stand for points, **C** for correct guesses, and **W** for wrong guesses. Each correct guess gets 3 points; each wrong guess takes away 1 point. What equation can be used to represent the points counted. Possible equation: $P = 3C - W$
(Learning Goal 13-C)

❹ Jack guessed the letters in a mystery word. He answered 25 questions, giving 20 correct answers (plus 3 points each), and 5 wrong answers (minus 1 point each). How many points does he get? (Use **P** for points.) 55 points; $P = (3 \times 20) - (1 \times 5) = 60 - 5 = 55$.
(Learning Goal 13-C)

Quick Write This informal written assessment can be administered to small groups or the whole class. Read each question and have the students record responses on their write-on boards. Encourage students to listen and think about the questions before responding.

❺ An unbalanced mobile has 3 circles on the left and 2 squares on the right. Each circle weighs 3 g and each square weighs 4 g. What could be added to balance the mobile? Explain your answer. Answers will vary; possible answer: add 1 more circle to the left for a total of 12 g on the left, and then add 1 more square to the right for a total of 12 g on the right.

- Write an equation for the balanced mobile above; let *c* stand for circles and *s* stand for squares.
  Answers will vary; possible answer: $4c = 3s$.
  (Learning Goal 13-A)

❻ Draw a diagram to describe this situation. Ken put two pieces of masking tape together end-to-end. One piece was 6 inches long. Explain your diagram.
Diagrams will vary; Possible diagram:

$$\underset{y}{\overset{6 \qquad x}{\rule{4cm}{0.4pt}}}$$

Possible explanation: The part labeled 6 represents the 6-inch piece of tape, the part labeled *x* represents the unknown length of the second piece, and *y* represents the total length of tape.
(Learning Goal 13-B)

❼ You receive points for guessing letters in a mystery word. For every correct letter you guess, you get 5 points. When you guess the wrong letter, you lose a point. Let **P** stand for points, let **C** stand for correct guesses, and let **W** stand for wrong guesses. Write an equation to show how to find the points earned.
Possible equation: $P = 5C - W$

- Now write an equation using the values to find the points Sean receives if he guesses the whole mystery word with 4 correct guesses and 12 wrong guesses. Then solve. $P = 5 \times 4 - 12$
  Sean received $20 - 12$, or 8 points.
  (Learning Goal 13-C)

❽ Sara has now finished $\frac{7}{8}$ of her project for school. Since yesterday, she completed $\frac{1}{4}$ of the project. The day before, she completed $\frac{1}{2}$ of the project. How far along was the project 2 days ago? Use pictures, numbers, or words to explain your answer.

$\frac{1}{8}$ of the project was done 2 days ago.

$\frac{7}{8} - \frac{1}{4} = \frac{7}{8} - \frac{2}{8} = \frac{5}{8}$ was done 1 day ago.

Then $\frac{5}{8} - \frac{1}{2} = \frac{5}{8} - \frac{4}{8} = \frac{1}{8}$ was completed 2 days ago.
(Learning Goal 13-D)

Chapter 13 ASSESSMENT

Formal Assessment

Chapter Review/Assessment The Chapter 13 Review/Assessment on *Lesson Activity Book* pages 269–270 assesses students' understanding of balancing weights, diagrams, and equations to show the relationships among unknown quantities and to solve problems. Students should be able to complete these pages independently.

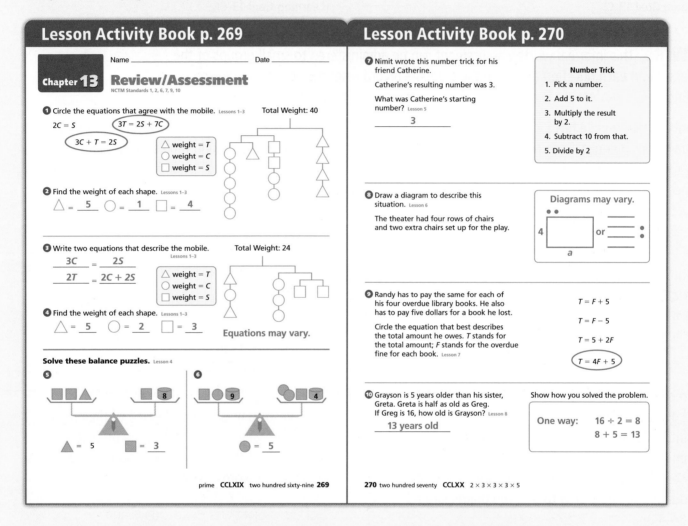

Extra Support Students who have difficulty with items on the Chapter 13 Review/Assessment may need review of the lesson where development of the concept was provided. You can use the Intervention Activity to increase students' understanding before the Chapter Test is given.

Chapter Test Use the Chapter 13 Test in the *Assessment Guide* to assess concepts, skills, and problem solving from the chapter and to prepare students for standardized tests. The Chapter Test and other test items are also available online.

Chapter Notes

Quick Notes

More Ideas

_____
_____
_____
_____
_____
_____
_____
_____
_____
_____
_____
_____
_____
_____
_____
_____
_____
_____
_____
_____
_____
_____

Big Idea Conduct probability experiments and collect, organize, display, and interpret data

Data and Probability

About the Chapter

In this chapter, students conduct experiments, developing their abilities to understand and reason about probability. They also continue their work with data from earlier years, gaining more experience collecting, organizing, displaying, and interpreting information.

Probability Experiments Questions about how likely something is come up every day. Students learn that there are two ways to determine probabilities—by gathering data from experiments and by analyzing possible outcomes. They experiment with objects such as coins and cards and see that the probabilities they assign to their results can help predict what is likely to happen over the long run. They come to see that the greater the number of trials in such an experiment, the closer the experimental probabilities are likely to be to the actual probabilities. Students also investigate sampling as a way to obtain information about a population and consider how scientists and TV networks use similar sampling techniques.

Data Collection, Display, and Interpretation Students are introduced to percents. They use percents to interpret results of experiments recorded in circle graphs.

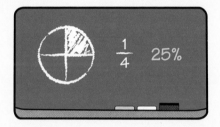

Developing Concepts Across the Grades

Topic	Prior Learning	Learning in Chapter 14	Later Learning
Probability	• Describe the probability of an event as impossible, unlikely, likely, or certain • Compare probabilities of events **Grade 4, Chapter 10**	• Determine all the possible outcomes of a probability experiment • Use the results of an experiment to make predictions **Lessons 14.1–14.6**	• Determine the probability for independent and dependent events • Use the Fundamental Counting Principal **Grade 6**
Graph Data	• Interpret bar graphs • Graph and analyze survey data **Grade 4, Chapter 10**	• Interpret data in circle graphs • Construct circle graphs **Lesson 14.6**	• Interpret box-and-whisker graphs • Construct circle graphs with degrees **Grade 6**
Fractions, Decimals, and Percents	• Express probability as a fraction **Grade 4, Chapter 10**	• Use fractions to describe the results of an experiment • Relate percents, fractions, and decimals **Lessons 14.1–14.6**	• Understand percents greater than 100% and less than 1% • Find percent of a number **Grade 6**

Chapter Planner

Lesson	Objectives	NCTM Standards	Vocabulary	Materials/Resources
CHAPTER 14 World Almanac For Kids • Vocabulary • Games • Challenge **Teacher Guide** pp. 1135A–1135F, **Student Handbook** pp. 234–235, 244–248				
1 **Conducting a Probability Experiment** PACING **1** DAY **Teacher Guide** pp. 1136–1143 **Lesson Activity Book** pp. 271–272 **Student Handbook** Student Letter p. 233 Explore p. 236	• To determine all possible outcomes of a probability experiment • To use fractions to describe experimental results	1, 5, 7, 8, 9	event outcome probability	**For the students:** ■ School-Home Connection TR: SHC53–SHC54 ■ TR: AM142 ■ scissors ■ red, blue, green, and yellow crayons ■ paper clips ■ coins ■ P110, E110, SR110 Literature Connection: **Do You Wanna Bet?** **Teacher Guide** p. 1134
2 **Finding Probabilities** PACING **1** DAY **Teacher Guide** pp. 1144–1153 **Lesson Activity Book** pp. 273–274 **Student Handbook** Game p. 246 Review Model p. 237	• To list possible outcomes and probabilities before conducting an experiment • To use experimental results to make predictions	5, 7, 8, 9	certain improbable probable	**For the teacher:** ■ transparency of AM145 (optional) ■ calculators **For the students:** ■ TR: AM143–AM144 ■ scissors ■ P111, E111, SR111
3 **Sampling Experiments** PACING **1** DAY **Teacher Guide** pp. 1154–1161 **Lesson Activity Book** pp. 275–276 **Student Handbook** Explore p. 238	• To use results of an experiment to make predictions • To use fractions to describe the results of an experiment	1, 5, 6, 7, 8, 9	sampling	**For the teacher:** ■ transparency of AM146 **For the students:** ■ opaque bags with red, blue, and green cubes ■ P112, E112, SR112
4 **Another Sampling Experiment** PACING **1** DAY **Teacher Guide** pp. 1162–1169 **Lesson Activity Book** pp. 277–278	• To use fractions to describe the results of an experiment • To choose a random sample from a population • To consider the size of a random sample	5, 7, 8, 9	population random sample	**For the teacher:** ■ transparency of AM147–AM148 (optional) ■ opaque bags with red, blue, and green cubes **For the students:** ■ TR: AM148 ■ numbered decahedra or TR: AM143 ■ P113, E113, SR113 Language Arts Connection: **Common Vowels** **Teacher Guide** p. 1134

NCTM Standards 2000
1. Number and Operations
2. Algebra
3. Geometry
4. Measurement
5. Data Analysis and Probability
6. Problem Solving
7. Reasoning and Proof
8. Communication
9. Connections
10. Representation

Key
AG: Assessment Guide
E: Extension Book
LAB: Lesson Activity Book
P: Practice Book
SH: Student Handbook
SR: Spiral Review Book
TG: Teacher Guide
TR: Teacher Resource Book

MATH GLOSSARY in **Student Handbook** p. 266

Planner (continued)

Chapter Planner (continued)

Lesson	Objectives	NCTM Standards	Vocabulary	Materials/ Resources
5 **Introducing Percents** PACING 1 DAY **Teacher Guide** pp. 1170–1177 **Lesson Activity Book** pp. 279–280 **Student Handbook** Game p. 247 Review Model p. 239	• To relate percents, fractions, and decimals	1, 7, 8, 9	**percent**	**For the students:** ■ TR: AM149–AM150 ■ scissors ■ P114, E114, SR114 **Science Connection:** **Caterpillar Anatomy Teacher Guide** p. 1134
6 **Circle Graphs** PACING 1 DAY **Teacher Guide** pp. 1178–1185 **Lesson Activity Book** pp. 281–282 **Student Handbook** Explore p. 240 Review Model p. 241	• To interpret data in circle graphs • To construct circle graphs	1, 5, 6, 7, 8, 9, 10	**sector**	**For the teacher:** ■ transparency of TR: AM151 (optional) **For the students:** ■ TR: AM151 ■ rulers ■ calculators ■ P115, E115, SR115
7 **Problem Solving Strategy and Test Prep** PACING 1 DAY **Teacher Guide** pp. 1186–1191 **Lesson Activity Book** pp. 283–284 **Student Handbook** Review Model pp. 242–243	• To practice the problem solving strategy *make a table* • To articulate the steps and strategies used to solve problems • To prepare for standardized tests	1, 5, 6, 7, 8, 9, 10		

CHAPTER 14 Assessment

TG pp. 1192–1195, **LAB** pp. 285–286, **AG** pp. AG117–AG120

For the students:
■ Chapter 14 Test pp. AG117–AG118

Games

Use the following games for skills practice and reinforcement of concepts.

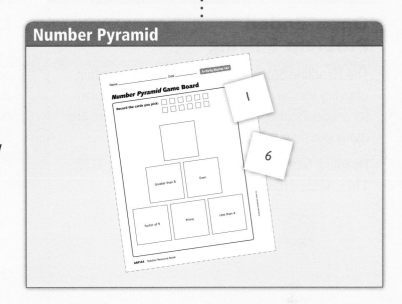

Number Pyramid

Lesson 14.2 ▶
Number Pyramid provides an opportunity for students to categorize numbers while generating a random data set.

Matching Quantities

◀ **Lesson 14.5** *Matching Quantities* provides an opportunity for students to convert between fractions, decimals, and percents.

Planning Ahead

In **Lesson 14.1**, each group of students needs AM142: Colors Spinner, scissors, a pencil, a paper clip, and crayons for coloring the sections of the spinner. For LAB page 271, each student will need two different coins.

In **Lesson 14.2**, students will be playing *Number Pyramid*. Each student will need AM144: *Number Pyramid* Game Board and AM143: Blank Cards. Students will write the numbers 1 through 12 on the blank cards and then cut them out.

In **Lesson 14.3**, each group of students needs an opaque bag of 4 red, 6 blue, and 2 green counters.

In **Lesson 14.4**, the teacher will need an opaque bag of 2 red, 3 blue, and 10 green counters. For LAB page 277, each student needs a numbered decahedron or a deck of cards labeled 0–9 to generate numbers for a random sample.

In **Lesson 14.5**, students will be playing *Matching Quantities*. Each pair of students will need AM149 and AM150: *Matching Quantities* Cards 1 and 2 and a pair of scissors to cut out the cards.

In **Lesson 14.6**, students will need a ruler, or other straightedge, and may need a calculator to help them make a circle graph.

Developing Problem Solvers

Open-Ended Problem Solving

The Headline Story in the Daily Activities section of every lesson provides an open-ended problem for students to complete. For each story there are many possible responses.

Headline Stories can be found on TG pages 1137, 1145, 1155, 1163, 1171, and 1179.

Headline Story

Leveled Problem Solving

Leveled Problem Solving provides an opportunity for students to apply learning from the lesson to a real-life situation. Problems are leveled by ability to allow students of all ability levels to become successful problem solvers. Each Leveled Problem Solving begins with a real-life scenario upon which three problems are built.

The levels of problems are:

❶ Basic Level	❷ On Level	❸ Above Level
students needing extra support	students working at grade level	students who are ready for more challenging problems.

Leveled Problem Solving can be found on TG pages 1143, 1152, 1160, 1168, 1177, and 1184.

 **FOR KIDS**

The World Almanac for Kids feature is designed to stimulate student interest for the math concepts they are about to learn. Students use data to solve problems and explain solutions. The Chapter 14 Project can be found on SH pages 234–235.

Write Math **Reflect and Summarize the Lesson** poses a problem or question for students to think and write about. This feature can be found on TG pages 1142, 1151, 1159, 1167, 1176, 1183, and 1188.

Other opportunities to write about math can be found on LAB pages 274, 275, 276, 278, 280, and 284.

Problem–Solving Strategies

The focus of **Lesson 14.7** is the strategy *make a table.* However, students will use a variety of problem solving strategies as they work through the chapter. The chart below shows strategies that may be useful in completing each lesson.

Strategy	Lesson(s)	Description
Act It Out	14.1, 14.2, 14.3, 14.4	Conduct probability experiments.
Make a Graph	14.6	Make a circle graph.
Make a Model	14.3, 14.4	Perform a sampling experiment.
✓ **Make a Table**	14.1, 14.2, 14.3, 14.4, 14.7	Organize data gathered in probability experiment, show various ways of classifying the numbers 1 through 12, record results of sampling experiment, and organize data gathered in a survey.
Solve a Simpler Problem	14.3, 14.4	Use results of a sampling experiment to make predictions about a total population.
Use Logical Reasoning	14.1, 14.2, 14.3, 14.4, 14.5, 14.6	Determine theoretical probabilities, use the results of a completed experiment to write questions and answers relating to the data, compare theoretical and experimental probabilities, interpret the results of sampling experiments in the context of probability, consider how large a sample should be to represent the population, connect percents, fractions, and decimals, and interpret data in circle graphs.

Meeting the Needs of All Learners

Differentiated Instruction

Extra Support	Activities for All	Enrichment
Intervention Activities TG pp. 1143, 1152, 1160, 1168, 1177, 1184	**Practice Book** pp. P110–P115	**Extension Activities** TG pp. 1143, 1152, 1160, 1168, 1177, 1184
	Spiral Review Book pp. SR110–SR115	**Extension Book** pp. E110–E115
	LAB Challenge LAB pp. 272, 274, 276, 278, 280, 282	**LAB Challenge** LAB pp. 272, 274, 276, 278, 280, 282
Lesson Notes **Basic Level** TG pp. 1142, 1146, 1159, 1173	**Lesson Notes** **On Level** TG pp. 1159, 1173	**Lesson Notes** **Above Level** TG p. 1181
Leveled Problem Solving **Basic Level** TG pp. 1143, 1152, 1160, 1168, 1177, 1184	**Leveled Problem Solving** **On Level** TG pp. 1143, 1152, 1160, 1168, 1177, 1184	**Leveled Problem Solving** **Above Level** TG pp. 1143, 1152, 1160, 1168, 1177, 1184

English Language Learners

Suggestions for addressing the needs of students learning English as a second language are included in the Developing Mathematical Language section at the beginning of most lessons.

ELL activities for this chapter can be found on TG pages 1137, 1145, 1155, 1163, 1171, and 1179.

The Multi-Age Classroom

Grade 4	• Students on this level should be able to complete the lessons in Chapter 14 but might need some additional practice with key concepts and skills. • Give students more practice with probability.	See Grade 5, Intervention Activities Lessons 14.1–14.6. See Grade 4, Lessons 10.1–10.5.
Grade 5	• Students on this level should be able to complete the lessons in Chapter 14 with minimal adjustments.	See Grade 5, Practice pages P110–P115.
Grade 6	• Students on this level should be able to complete the lessons in Chapter 14 and to extend concepts and skills related to probability and percent. • Give students extended work with probability and percents	See Grade 5, Extension pages E110–E115.

Cross Curricular Connections

Science Connection

Math Concept: relate fractions to percent

Caterpillar Anatomy

- Tell students that butterflies have 4 cycles: egg, larva, pupa, and adult. The larva is commonly called a caterpillar.

- A caterpillar has 14 segments that make up the head, thorax, and abdomen. Show students a diagram like this one.

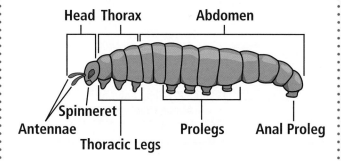

- Have students determine what percent of the abdominal segments have legs. 50%

Lesson 14.5

Language Arts Connection

Math Concept: make predictions

Common Vowels

- Remind students the English alphabet has consonants and vowels. Tell them that the 5 most common vowels are *a, e, i, o,* and *u.*

- Divide the class into groups. Have each group choose a paragraph from a story or history book. Ask them to keep a tally of the number of words that have each vowel. Students can organize their work in a chart like this one:

- Have students then count the number of words in the paragraph. In the far right column, have students write the fraction of tallied words to the total number of words.

Vowel	Tally	Total	Fraction
a			
e			
i			
o			
u			

- Compare fractions. Then combine all data from each group, and have students determine the resulting fractions.

Lesson 14.4

Literature Connection

Math Concept: probability

Do You Wanna Bet?
By Jean Cushman and Martha Weston

This book teaches students about a wide range of topics in probability through short stories about Danny and Brian. Each story is an independent part of a larger story, allowing this book to be used at various times throughout this chapter.

Lesson 14.1

Home-School Connection

A reproducible copy of the School-Home Connection letter in English and Spanish can be found in the *Teacher Resource Book* page SHC53–SHC56.

Encourage students to play *Race Course,* found on the School-Home Connection page, with a family member. Students will work with the concept of probability in **Lessons 14.1** and **14.2.**

Assessment Options

There are many opportunities in *Think Math!* to assess students' understanding of concepts, skills, and problem solving. Learning Goals for Chapter 14 are provided below. The assessment options provide opportunities to evaluate whether or not students have retained learning from prior experiences. Choose the forms of assessment that best meet the needs of your students.

Chapter 14 Learning Goals

	Learning Goals	Lesson Number
14-A	Summarize experimental data and use probability to make predictions	14.1, 14.2
14-B	Use sampling to obtain information about a population	14.3, 14.4
14-C	Relate percents, fractions, and decimals	14.5
14-D	Use percents to interpret and record experiment results with circle graphs	14.6
14-E	Apply problem solving strategies such as *make a table* to solve problems	14.7

✓ Informal Assessment

Ongoing Assessment
Provides insight into students' thinking to guide instruction (TG pp. 1147 and 1174)

Reflect and Summarize the Lesson
Checks understanding of lesson concepts (TG pp. 1142, 1151, 1159, 1167, 1176, 1183, and 1188)

Snapshot Assessment
Mental Math and **Quick Write**
Offers a quick observation of students' progress on chapter concepts and skills (TG pp. 1192–1193)

Performance Assessment
Provides quarterly assessment of Chapters 12–15 concepts using real-life situations
Assessment Guide
pp. AG225–AG230

✓ Formal Assessment

Standardized Test Prep
Problem Solving Test Prep
Prepares students for standardized tests
Lesson Activity Book p. 284 (TG p. 1189)

Chapter 14 Review/Assessment
Reviews and assesses students' understanding of the chapter
Lesson Activity Book pp. 285–286 (TG p. 1194)

Chapter 14 Test
Assesses the chapters concepts and skills
Assessment Guide
Form A pp. AG117–AG118
Form B pp. AG119–AG120

Benchmark 4 Assessment
Provides quarterly assessment of Chapters 12–15 concepts and skills
Assessment Guide
Benchmark 4A pp. AG125–AG132
Benchmark 4B pp. AG133–AG140

World Almanac for Kids

Use the World Almanac for Kids feature, *Probability and Data,* found on pp. 234–235 of the **Student Handbook,** to provide students with an opportunity to practice using their problem solving skills by solving real world problems.

FACT•ACTIVITY 1

❶ $\frac{1}{16}$; $\frac{2}{16}$, or $\frac{1}{8}$; 0

❷ $\frac{6}{16}$, or $\frac{3}{8}$

❸ $\frac{10}{16}$, or $\frac{5}{8}$

❹ $\frac{6}{16} + \frac{2}{16} = \frac{8}{16}$, or $\frac{1}{2}$

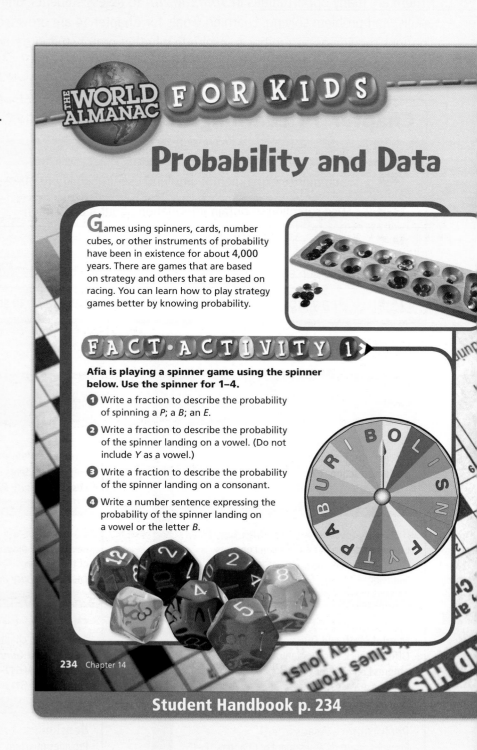

THE WORLD ALMANAC FOR KIDS

Probability and Data

Games using spinners, cards, number cubes, or other instruments of probability have been in existence for about 4,000 years. There are games that are based on strategy and others that are based on racing. You can learn how to play strategy games better by knowing probability.

FACT•ACTIVITY 1

Afia is playing a spinner game using the spinner below. Use the spinner for 1–4.

❶ Write a fraction to describe the probability of spinning a *P*; a *B*; an *E*.

❷ Write a fraction to describe the probability of the spinner landing on a vowel. (Do not include *Y* as a vowel.)

❸ Write a fraction to describe the probability of the spinner landing on a consonant.

❹ Write a number sentence expressing the probability of the spinner landing on a vowel or the letter *B*.

234 Chapter 14

Student Handbook p. 234

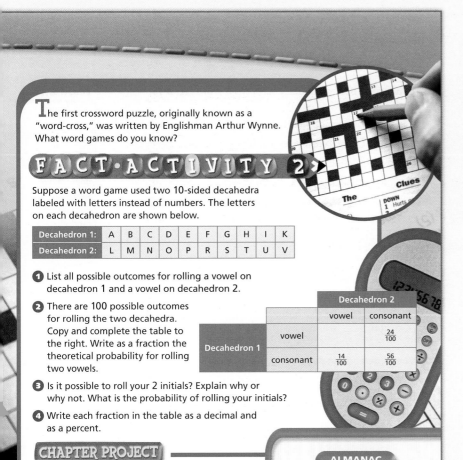

The first crossword puzzle, originally known as a "word-cross," was written by Englishman Arthur Wynne. What word games do you know?

FACT·ACTIVITY 2

Suppose a word game used two 10-sided decahedra labeled with letters instead of numbers. The letters on each decahedron are shown below.

| Decahedron 1: | A | B | C | D | E | F | G | H | I | K |
| Decahedron 2: | L | M | N | O | P | R | S | T | U | V |

❶ List all possible outcomes for rolling a vowel on decahedron 1 and a vowel on decahedron 2.

❷ There are 100 possible outcomes for rolling the two decahedra. Copy and complete the table to the right. Write as a fraction the theoretical probability for rolling two vowels.

	Decahedron 2	
Decahedron 1		vowel	consonant
	vowel		$\frac{24}{100}$
	consonant	$\frac{14}{100}$	$\frac{56}{100}$

❸ Is it possible to roll your 2 initials? Explain why or why not. What is the probability of rolling your initials?

❹ Write each fraction in the table as a decimal and as a percent.

CHAPTER PROJECT

Working in small groups, determine a question you would like your classmates to answer such as, "What is your favorite board game?" Other acceptable survey topics include word games or sports games.

Survey 20 people and make a poster to present your results. Use a circle graph to display the data. Using your results, write questions for other students to answer. Then make a prediction about the favorite game of a larger group of students (such as all 5th graders).

ALMANAC Fact

At the Elliott Avedon Museum and Archives of Games in Waterloo, Canada, visitors not only see exhibits about board games, but they also get to sit down and play the games. There are more than 5,000 objects and documents at the museum.

Student Handbook p. 235

FACT·ACTIVITY 2

❶ A-O, A-U, E-O, E-U, I-O, I-U

❷ $\frac{6}{100}$

❸ Possible answer: Yes; My initials are CP. There's only 1 way out of 100 to do it, so the probability is $\frac{1}{100}$.

❹ 0.06, 6%; 0.24, 24%; 0.14, 14%; .56, 56%

CHAPTER PROJECT

Possible answer:

A circle graph showing the results of 20 people surveyed:

- Game A: 10%
- Game B: 45%
- Game C: 25%
- Game D: 20%

Prediction: Most people prefer Game B.

Check students' graphs.

Vocabulary

To reinforce vocabulary concepts, invite students to complete the vocabulary activities on pp. 244–245 of the *Student Handbook.* Encourage students to record their answers in their math journals.

Many responses are possible.

13 Possible response: First, you have to know which of the possible *outcomes* are favorable. Do an experiment to find how many of the results are favorable *outcomes.* Then write a fraction in this form to represent the *probability*: $\frac{\text{number of results with favorable outcomes}}{\text{number of trials}}$. Simplify the fraction.

14 Possible response: Use a number cube. A number cube has 6 possible *outcomes.* If you want an *outcome* of 3, toss the number cube 50 times to see how many times it comes up 3. If it happens 6 out of 50 times, then the *probability* is $\frac{6}{50} = \frac{3}{25}$.

15 Possible response: The greater the number of trials, the more accurate the results and the closer we can expect the experimental *probability* to be to the theoretical *probability.* For example, if you want to know the *probability* of a particular outcome, like pulling a blue marble from a bag, but you do only one trial and the result is not a blue marble, you might predict that there are no blue marbles in the bag. If you do two trials with results of one blue and one not blue, then the experimental *probability* is, so far, $\frac{1}{2}$. The more trials you do, the closer you are likely to be to the theoretical probability.

Chapter 14 **Vocabulary**

Choose the best vocabulary term from Word List A for each sentence.

1 A set of outcomes is called a(n) __?__. **event**

2 A(n) __?__ outcome is one that is sure to happen. **certain**

3 A possible result of an experiment is called a(n) __?__. **outcome**

4 A(n) __?__ outcome is an unlikely outcome. **improbable**

5 A(n) __?__ experiment is an experiment used to make predictions about a population. **sampling**

6 The __?__ is the likelihood that an event will happen. **probability**

7 The __?__ is the full set in a sampling experiment. **population**

8 To tell the number of hundredths, you can use a(n) __?__. **percent**

9 A(n) __?__ is a part of a population. **sample**

10 Every member of a population has equal chance of being selected in a(n) __?__ selection. **random**

Word List A

probability
outcome
event
certain
probable
improbable
sampling
population
random
sample
percent

Complete each analogy using the best term from Word List B.

11 Part is to whole as __?__ is to population. **sample**

12 Yes is to no as __?__ is to impossible. **certain**

Word List B

certain
event
sample

Talk Math

Discuss with a partner what you have learned about probability. Use the vocabulary terms *outcome* and *probability*.

13 How can you use a fraction to describe the results of a probability experiment?

14 How can you use an experiment to make a prediction?

15 How does the number of trials affect the results of a probability experiment?

244 Chapter 14

Student Handbook p. 244

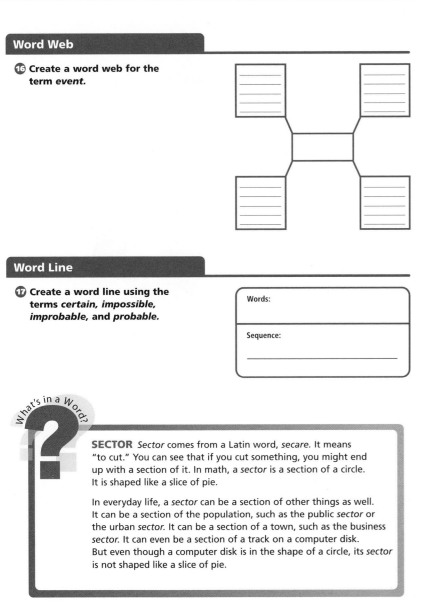

Word Web

16 Create a word web for the term *event*.

Word Line

17 Create a word line using the terms *certain*, *impossible*, *improbable*, and *probable*.

Words:

Sequence:

SECTOR *Sector* comes from a Latin word, *secare*. It means "to cut." You can see that if you cut something, you might end up with a section of it. In math, a *sector* is a section of a circle. It is shaped like a slice of pie.

In everyday life, a *sector* can be a section of other things as well. It can be a section of the population, such as the public *sector* or the urban *sector*. It can be a section of a town, such as the business *sector*. It can even be a section of a track on a computer disk. But even though a computer disk is in the shape of a circle, its *sector* is not shaped like a slice of pie.

Chapter 14 **245**

Student Handbook p. 245

---

16 Many answers are possible. One example is provided.

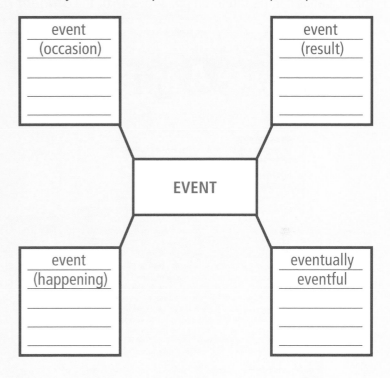

| event (occasion) | event (result) |
| EVENT |
| event (happening) | eventually eventful |

17

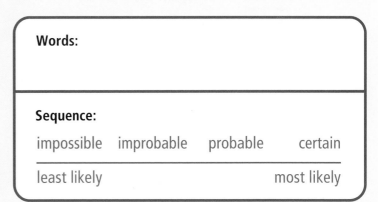

Words:

Sequence:

| impossible | improbable | probable | certain |
| least likely | | | most likely |

Games

Number Pyramid in **Lesson 14.2** provides an opportunity for students to categorize numbers while generating a random data set. *Matching Quantities* in **Lesson 14.5** provides an opportunity for students to convert between fractions, decimals, and percents. These games can be found on pp. 246–247 of the *Student Handbook.*

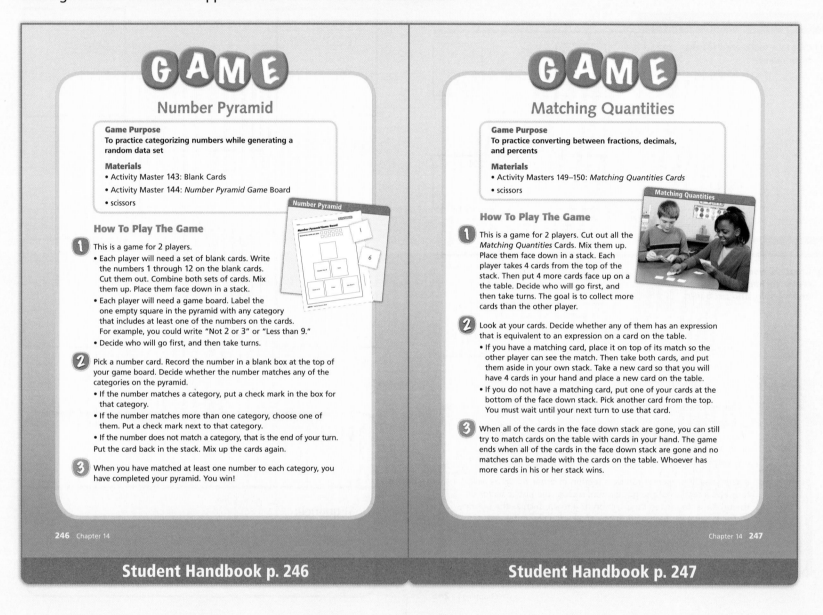

GAME

Number Pyramid

Game Purpose
To practice categorizing numbers while generating a random data set

Materials
• Activity Master 143: Blank Cards
• Activity Master 144: *Number Pyramid Game* Board
• scissors

How To Play The Game

1 This is a game for 2 players.
• Each player will need a set of blank cards. Write the numbers 1 through 12 on the blank cards. Cut them out. Combine both sets of cards. Mix them up. Place them face down in a stack.
• Each player will need a game board. Label the one empty square in the pyramid with any category that includes at least one of the numbers on the cards. For example, you could write "Not 2 or 3" or "Less than 9."
• Decide who will go first, and then take turns.

2 Pick a number card. Record the number in a blank box at the top of your game board. Decide whether the number matches any of the categories on the pyramid.
• If the number matches a category, put a check mark in the box for that category.
• If the number matches more than one category, choose one of them. Put a check mark next to that category.
• If the number does not match a category, that is the end of your turn. Put the card back in the stack. Mix up the cards again.

3 When you have matched at least one number to each category, you have completed your pyramid. You win!

246 Chapter 14

GAME

Matching Quantities

Game Purpose
To practice converting between fractions, decimals, and percents

Materials
• Activity Masters 149–150: *Matching Quantities Cards*
• scissors

How To Play The Game

1 This is a game for 2 players. Cut out all the *Matching Quantities* Cards. Mix them up. Place them face down in a stack. Each player takes 4 cards from the top of the stack. Then put 4 more cards face up on a the table. Decide who will go first, and then take turns. The goal is to collect more cards than the other player.

2 Look at your cards. Decide whether any of them has an expression that is equivalent to an expression on a card on the table.
• If you have a matching card, place it on top of its match so the other player can see the match. Then take both cards, and put them aside in your own stack. Take a new card so that you will have 4 cards in your hand and place a new card on the table.
• If you do not have a matching card, put one of your cards at the bottom of the face down stack. Pick another card from the top. You must wait until your next turn to use that card.

3 When all of the cards in the face down stack are gone, you can still try to match cards on the table with cards in your hand. The game ends when all of the cards in the face down stack are gone and no matches can be made with the cards on the table. Whoever has more cards in his or her stack wins.

Chapter 14 247

Student Handbook p. 246

Student Handbook p. 247

Challenge

The Challenge activity *Theoretical and Experimental Probabilities* challenges students to compare the experimental probabilities found by conducting an experiment with the theoretical probabilities found mathematically. This activity can be found on p. 248 of the *Student Handbook.*

Answers will vary. Check students' work; encourage students to explain their reasoning.

CHALLENGE

Theoretical and Experimental Probabilities

Try a probability experiment.

PART 1: Count the number of boys and girls in your class, including yourself. Tear a sheet of paper into the same number of pieces as the number of boys and girls. On each small piece of paper, write a B for each boy or a G for each girl in your class. Put the pieces into a bag.

- If you pick one paper, is it more likely to have a *B* or *G* on it?
- What is the probability that you will pick *B*? a *G*?

That is the theoretical probability. You know the number of boys and girls, and each paper has a fair chance of being chosen, so you can find this probability mathematically.

PART 2: Now pick 20 times. Record B or G for each pick. Put the paper back in the bag after each pick. Copy the table below. Keep a tally of your results.

Boy/Girl	Number of Picks	Totals
B		
G		

Write these two fractions.

$$\frac{\text{number of boys picked}}{\text{total number of picks}} \quad \text{and} \quad \frac{\text{number of girls picked}}{\text{total number of picks}}$$

Those are experimental probabilities.

- Do you think the experimental probabilities are close to the theoretical probabilities?

PART 3: Work in a group of 4 students. Each student should do the experiment 30 more times. Then, combine your results. Write the new experimental probabilities. The denominator of each fraction will be 200. That includes the 20 original trials plus the 30 more.

- How do the group's results compare to the theoretical probabilities?
- Did the experimental probabilities with 200 trials come closer to the theoretical probabilities than the experiment with 20 trials?

If you did 2,000 trials, the results would be very close to the theoretical probabilities. The greater the number of trials, the closer you will get.

248 Chapter 14

Student Handbook p. 248

Conducting a Probability Experiment

NCTM Standards 1, 5, 7, 8, 9

Lesson Planner

STUDENT OBJECTIVES
- To determine all possible outcomes of a probability experiment
- To use fractions to describe experimental results

1 Daily Activities (TG p. 1137)

Open-Ended Problem Solving/Headline Story	Skills Practice and Review— Finding Equivalent Fractions

2 Teach and Practice (TG pp. 1138–1142)

MATERIALS

(A) **Reading the Student Letter** (TG p. 1138)

(B) **Describing Probability** (TG p. 1139)

(C) **Making Predictions** (TG pp. 1140–1141)

(D) **Finding Probabilities** (TG p. 1142)

- TR: Activity Master, AM142
- scissors
- red, blue, green, and yellow crayons
- paper clips
- coins
- 📖 LAB pp. 271–272
- 📖 SH p. 233, 236

3 Differentiated Instruction (TG p. 1143)

Leveled Problem Solving (TG p. 1143)	Practice Book P110
Intervention Activity (TG p. 1143)	Extension Book E110
Extension Activity (TG p. 1143)	Spiral Review Book SR110
Literature Connection (TG p. 1134)	

Lesson Notes

About the Lesson

Students conduct experiments, list possible outcomes, and use fractions to describe the results. They also combine experimental results across the class, and use that larger sample to make predictions. Students will later see how sample size affects predictive value.

About the Mathematics

Probability is the measure of the likelihood of a particular event, expressed as a number from 0 to 1, where 0 means the event is never expected to occur and 1 means the event is always expectable. This wording is deliberate. While a coin *could* land on its edge, this outcome is never expected.

If all outcomes of a potential experiment are equally likely, then the probability of an event can be figured out theoretically (that is, without performing the experiment): it is the number of outcomes that are part of the event divided by the total number of equally likely possible outcomes. For example, the theoretical probability of a single number cube landing on "even" is $\frac{1}{2}$ since the event contains 3 outcomes (2, 4, or 6) of

(continued on page R5)

Developing Mathematical Language

Vocabulary: outcome, probability, event

In most *probability* experiments, we can list the possible *outcomes.* For example, if the experiment involves tossing a number cube, there are six possible *outcomes:* 1 through 6. Try to use *outcome* only to refer to what may happen in one trial of an experiment, and not to mean what actually did happen, which is how the word is used in casual English. An *event* is one or more *outcomes* that we are paying attention to. For example, if we cared only whether the number cube turned up odd or even, the six possible *outcomes* would be treated as two possible *events:* odd or even.

Probability is the measure of the likelihood of the occurrence of a particular *event.* The *probability* of an *event* is a number from 0 to 1, zero being the least probable.

Familiarize students with the terms *outcome* and *event.*

Beginning Demonstrate the *event* of tossing a number cube. Ask students to name one *outcome* they might expect.

Intermediate Have students describe a *probability* experiment and an *event* in the experiment. Then have them name one *outcome* that would mean the *event* occurred.

Advanced Have students explain the difference between an *outcome* and an *event.*

Open-Ended Problem Solving

This Headline Story helps to introduce probability to your students.

 Headline Story

> **Each day, 5 students put their names in a bag. One name is selected at random to take attendance. So far this week, a girl was chosen every day. Today is Friday, and 3 girls and 2 boys put their names into the bag. Is a boy or a girl more likely to be chosen today?**

Possible responses: Students might expect that because girls have been picked for so many days, it's not likely to happen again. Or, they might think that this week must be girls' week and so a girl will be picked again. But, since there is no reason to think that any one student is more likely to be picked than any other, and because there are more girls' than boys' names in the bag, it is actually more likely that a girl will be picked.

Skills Practice and Review

Finding Equivalent Fractions

Give students a simple, familiar fraction, like $\frac{1}{2}$ or $\frac{3}{4}$, and ask for an equivalent fraction. You might give fractions that can easily be made equivalent to a fraction with a denominator of 100, and especially request such fractions among the responses, as this will help students in their work with probability and percents in this chapter.

$$\frac{2}{5}: \frac{4}{10}, \frac{40}{100}, \frac{20}{50} \qquad \frac{1}{25}: \frac{10}{250}, \frac{2}{50}, \frac{4}{100} \qquad \frac{3}{2}: \frac{6}{4}, \frac{36}{24}, \frac{150}{100}$$

whole class · **5 MIN**

NCTM Standards 5, 8, 9

Ⓐ Reading the Student Letter

Purpose To introduce the content of the chapter

Introduce The Student Letter is designed to spur interest and curiosity. Have students read and discuss the letter. If they have already done the Headline Story, they may have already discussed the idea that the probability of an event does not change based on previous independent events. Still, students will likely continue to struggle with this counter-intuitive idea, and you may spend some time discussing their ideas about the chances of the coin described in the letter landing on heads yet again after 10, or even 50, heads in a row.

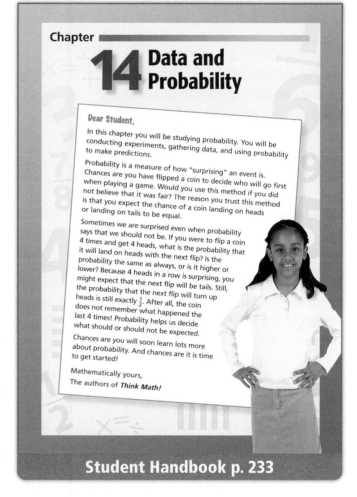

Chapter

14 Data and Probability

Dear Student,

In this chapter you will be studying probability. You will be conducting experiments, gathering data, and using probability to make predictions.

Probability is a measure of how "surprising" an event is. Chances are you have flipped a coin to decide who will go first when playing a game. Would you use this method if you did not believe that it was fair? The reason you trust this method is that you expect the chance of a coin landing on heads or landing on tails to be equal.

Sometimes we are surprised even when probability says that we should not be. If you were to flip a coin 4 times and get 4 heads, what is the probability that it will land on heads with the next flip? Is the probability the same as always, or is it higher or lower? Because 4 heads in a row is surprising, you might expect that the next flip will be tails. Still, the probability that the next flip will turn up heads is still exactly $\frac{1}{2}$. After all, the coin does not remember what happened the last 4 times! Probability helps us decide what should or should not be expected.

Chances are you will soon learn lots more about probability. And chances are it is time to get started!

Mathematically yours,
The authors of *Think Math!*

Student Handbook p. 233

Concept Alert

The words *likely* and *unlikely* are used in this lesson simply as transitional words, guiding students from their intuitions about probability to more specific descriptions of probabilities using fractions.

Two important ideas may come up in this discussion:

• What happens next in the experiment cannot depend on what happened before because the penny cannot "remember" what happened before.

• On the other hand, the more the experiment fails to fit the theory, the more likely it is that the theory simply does not apply in this case. Perhaps this is a trick penny!

Task Have students discuss the answer to the question "What is probability?" By having students share their thoughts about probability you will have a sense of their previous experience with it, as well as their misconceptions.

The letter begins to introduce the idea of probability. The situation of the coin flip described in the letter is an example of a quite common misconception. You might listen for students' use of words like *impossible* to describe events that are highly unlikely, but are not in fact impossible. You might point out to such students that the event is extremely unlikely or unexpected, but that it is not impossible, and then ask for an example of something impossible. (Students may disagree about what is truly impossible.)

Use with Lesson Activity Book pp. 271–272.

B **Describing Probability**

Purpose To introduce students to the measure of probability

Introduce Have students look at Explore: A Probability Experiment. Ask students what they notice about the spinner on the page. They should see that each color does not cover an equal sweep of the spinner. To emphasize this point, ask students if the spinner seems fair. Then, divide your class into 5 groups.

Task Have students **complete the Explore page to figure out how likely it is for the spinner to land on each color.** The size of the groups is unimportant, but it is important to have exactly 5 groups to produce a data set of numbers that are easy to work with in the next activity. Each group will need AM142: Colors Spinner, scissors, a pencil, a paper clip, and crayons for coloring the sections of the spinner the designated colors.

Once all of the groups have recorded their data from 20 spins discuss their results using questions like the following.

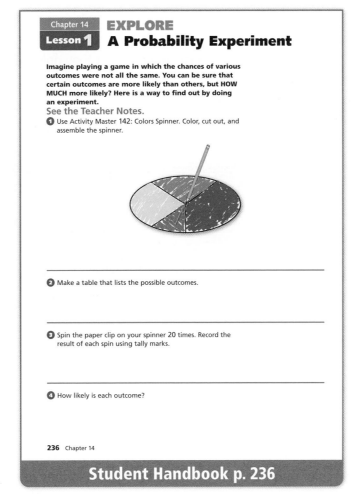

Chapter 14 **EXPLORE**
Lesson 1 **A Probability Experiment**

Imagine playing a game in which the chances of various outcomes were not all the same. You can be sure that certain outcomes are more likely than others, but HOW MUCH more likely? Here is a way to find out by doing an experiment.
See the Teacher Notes.
❶ Use Activity Master 142: Colors Spinner. Color, cut out, and assemble the spinner.

❷ Make a table that lists the possible outcomes.

❸ Spin the paper clip on your spinner 20 times. Record the result of each spin using tally marks.

❹ How likely is each outcome?

236 Chapter 14

Student Handbook p. 236

Materials
- For each group: AM142, scissors, paper clip, crayons

NCTM Standards 5, 7, 8, 9

Concept Alert

The possible events in an experiment depend on the purpose of the experiment. For example, if all we cared about when tossing a number cube was whether the result was even or odd, we should list only two possible events: even and odd. The possible *outcomes* depend only on the experiment, not on its purpose. The number cube experiment has six possible outcomes: 1 through 6.

💬 Talk Math

❓ What are the possible outcomes when you spin the spinner? red, yellow, green, and blue

❓ How many spins landed on blue? red? yellow? green? Answers will vary. Be sure that students realize that although the results vary, no result is "more correct" than any other.

❓ How could you use fractions to describe the results? Answers will vary. Possible answer: If a group had 12 of the 20 spins land on blue, they might record this result as $\frac{12}{20}$.

❓ How likely is each outcome? Theoretically blue is most likely, yellow is second most likely, green is third most likely, and red is the least likely.

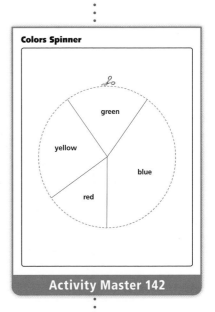

Colors Spinner

✂

green

yellow

blue

red

Activity Master 142

NCTM Standards 1, 5, 7, 8, 9

C Making Predictions

Purpose To use the combined results of an experiment to make predictions about future experimental trials

Introduce Explain that the more data points you have for an experiment, the closer your results will be to the actual probability for the events of that experiment. In experiments with few trials, one or two "unexpected" events can really make a big difference. For example, in the experiment with the spinner that students just conducted, if they only spin 3 times, at least one color would not appear at all! But after many spins, such a strange imbalance would be unexpected.

Sketch a table like the one below on the board or use a transparency.

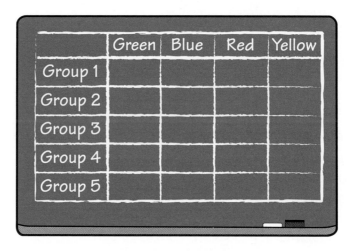

Concept Alert

Theoretical probability can be computed for the spinner experiment using the angles to figure out what fraction of the circle each sector takes up. In theory, those fractions predict the fraction of spins that would land on each color.

Here, we are determining the probabilities by experiment, rather than by theory. We rely on experimental results to predict the fraction of spins that would land on a certain color. As the number of trials increases, these experimental probabilities become more and more precise and reliable for prediction ("The Law of Large Numbers").

Task Have a student from each of the 5 groups in the previous activity report the number of times the spinner landed on each color. Ask students to report the results as the *number* of times it landed on each color rather than as the *fraction* of times so that you can total the numbers of landings on each color. As a check that all spins have been recorded, make sure that each row sums to 20.

Ask students to notice how many spins are now recorded in the entire table. Each of the 5 groups made 20 spins for a grand total of 100 spins. Then have students add the numbers in each column and record the fraction of spins (out of 100) that landed on each color. (For example, if 49 spins landed on blue, students should record $\frac{49}{100}$ below the column labeled blue.) The four fractions **must** add to $\frac{100}{100}$, or 1.

Use your total class results to discuss various probabilities, and then have students use these combined results to make predictions. Ask questions similar to these.

Talk Math

❷ What is the probability of landing on green? possible answer: $\frac{21}{100}$

❷ What is the probability of landing on green OR red? The answer should be the sum of the probability of each event, so a possible answer might be $\frac{21}{100} + \frac{15}{100} = \frac{36}{100}$.

❷ What is the probability of landing on any color but red? One way of figuring this out is to add up the probabilities of landing on the other three colors. Another way is to subtract the probability of landing on red from 1, leaving the probability of not landing on red.

❷ Based on this experiment, if you spin the spinner 200 times, how many times would you expect it to land on green? possible answer: about 42 times What fraction is that? $\frac{42}{200}$ or $\frac{21}{100}$—the same fraction as with 100 trials!

❷ If you were to spin this spinner 500 times, or even 1,000 times, what fraction of spins would you expect it to land on green? Again, I would expect the same fraction, $\frac{21}{100}$, since that is all I have to go on. However, the actual experiment would be expected to be more precise.

Purpose To conduct an experiment, list the possible outcomes, and find the likelihood of those outcomes

NCTM Standards 5, 7, 8, 9

Lesson Activity Book p. 271

Name _____ Date _____

Chapter 14
Lesson 1 **Conducting a Probability Experiment**
NCTM Standards 5, 7, 8, 9

A probability experiment: How many heads?

❶ If you flip one penny and one nickel at the same time, what are the possible outcomes?

	Penny	
	H	**T**
Nickel **h**	hH	hT
t	tH	tT

❷ Perform the experiment. Flip the two coins 20 times. Record the number of heads for each flip in the table below.

Results will vary.

Trial	1	2	3	4	5	6	7	8	9	10
Number of Heads										

Trial	11	12	13	14	15	16	17	18	19	20
Number of Heads										

❸ Use fractions to describe your results. **Results will vary.**

0 heads: □/20   1 head: □/□   2 heads: □/□

prime **CCLXXI** two hundred seventy-one **271**

ABOUT THE PAGE NUMBER 271 is part of a pair of twin primes. What number is the twin prime?

Lesson Activity Book p. 272

This table shows Alison's data for the same coin-flipping experiment.

Trial	1	2	3	4	5	6	7	8	9	10
Number of Heads	1	1	2	0	1	2	1	0	0	1

Trial	11	12	13	14	15	16	17	18	19	20
Number of Heads	1	1	1	2	0	1	0	1	1	2

Supply the missing question (Q) or answer (A).

❹ Q: What are the possible outcomes?   A: 2 heads, 1 head, 0 heads

❺ Q: How many times did Alison flip the coins?   A: 20 times

❻ Q: In what fraction of all the trials did the outcome "two heads" occur?   A: $\frac{4}{20}$ or $\frac{1}{5}$

❼ Q: In what fraction of the trials did the outcome "one head" occur?   A: $\frac{11}{20}$

Make up a question and corresponding answer of your own.

❽ Q: Questions will vary.   A: Answers will vary.

❾ **Challenge** Write a question about the data in the table above for which this number sentence would be a reasonable answer.
Q: In what fraction of all the trials did the outcome "two heads" or "zero heads" occur?   A: $\frac{4}{20} + \frac{5}{20} = \frac{9}{20}$

272 two hundred seventy-two **CCLXXII** $2 \times 2 \times 2 \times 2 \times 17$

ABOUT THE PAGE NUMBER 272 is a palindrome. This number of ounces is 17 pounds.

Teaching Notes for LAB page 271

Students will each need two different coins (e.g., penny and nickel) to perform the experiment on this page. They first record the possible outcomes of the experiment (Hh, Ht, Th, Tt, where the capital letter describes the penny and the small letter describes the nickel), and then they record their data in a table, writing fractions to describe the results of their experiment.

Differentiated Instruction Basic Level Some students may need to turn the coins to show different combinations of heads and tails to find the four possible outcomes.

Teaching Notes for LAB page 272

Students use the results of a completed experiment to write corresponding questions and answers relating to the data.

Concept Alert The numbers in the table for the completed experiment on this LAB page are roughly what theoretical probability would predict: 2 heads $\frac{1}{4}$ of the time; 1 head $\frac{1}{2}$ of the time (because this event includes two of the four possible outcomes); 0 heads $\frac{1}{4}$ of the time.

Challenge Problem Students write a question for which the sum of two probabilities is the answer.

Reflect and Summarize the Lesson

Write Math Kalista flipped a coin 10 times. The coin landed heads up 3 times. In what fraction of the trials did the outcome "tails" occur? Explain. $\frac{7}{10}$; If the coin landed heads up 3 of the 10 times, it must have landed tails up 7 times, or $\frac{7}{10}$ of the trials.

3 | Differentiated Instruction

Leveled Problem Solving

Ben tossed a 1–6 number cube 20 times.
An even number came up 12 times.

❶ Basic Level

In what fraction of the trials did an even outcome occur? Explain. $\frac{3}{5}$; it was even 12 times out of 20, so the probability is $\frac{12}{20}$, or $\frac{3}{5}$.

❷ On Level

In what fraction of the trials did an odd outcome occur? Explain. $\frac{2}{5}$; odd occurred 20 − 12, or 8 times, so the probability is $\frac{8}{20}$, or $\frac{2}{5}$.

❸ Above Level

What is the probability that an even outcome will occur the next time he tosses the number cube? Explain. $\frac{1}{2}$; an even outcome is just as likely as an odd outcome.

Intervention

Activity A New Spin on Spinners

Have students design a spinner with at least three colors. Tell them to color the spinners so that one color will be more likely than either of the other two. Collect the spinners and hold them up one at a time. For each spinner, ask which is the most likely outcome and the least likely outcome. If time permits, have students compare the spinners in action.

Practice

Conducting a Probability Experiment
The table shows the results of spinning an unequal color spinner.

Green	JHT I
Blue	JHT III
Red	IIII
Yellow	JHT II

❶ What are the possible outcomes? green, blue, red, yellow

❷ How many spins were made? 25

❸ Based on this experiment, write fractions to describe the probability of spinning:

Green $\frac{6}{25}$ Blue $\frac{8}{25}$ Red $\frac{4}{25}$ Yellow $\frac{7}{25}$

❹ Write a fraction (based on these results) to show the probability of spinning blue OR red. $\frac{12}{25}$

Test Prep

❺ The formula, or rule, $Volume = \frac{1}{2} \times (base\ length\ 1 + base\ length\ 2) \times height$ describes the process for finding:

A. the volume of a prism   C. the area of a trapezoid
B. the area of a triangle   D. the volume of a pyramid

❻ What is the area of this triangle?
(A) 6 sq m   C. 12 sq m
B. 7.5 sq m   D. 15 sq m

Practice P110

Extension

Conducting a Probability Experiment
You may have noticed that different groups had different results for the Colors Spinner experiment. No one result is "more correct" than another. When you consider the whole class's results, you get closer to what you might expect to happen.

❶ If the whole spinner is 1, write a fraction estimate for the area of each color section. If you want, you may cut up the spinner to compare the pieces. Fractions should be close to these.

Green $\frac{4}{20}$ Blue $\frac{8}{20}$ Red $\frac{2}{20}$ Yellow $\frac{6}{20}$

❷ Write fractions that describe your class's results for the probability experiment with the Colors Spinner. Results will vary.

Green _____ Blue _____ Red _____ Yellow _____

❸ Compare your answers to Problem 1 and Problem 2. How similar or different are they?

Answers will vary.

Extension E110

Spiral Review

Spiral Review Book page SR110 provides review of the following previously learned skills and concepts:

- connecting shapes in two-dimensional nets to faces
- applying the problem solving strategy *solve a simpler problem*

You may wish to have students work with partners to complete the page.

Geometry
Write the shape of the faces and the number of each shape that would be on a net of the three-dimensional figure.

❶ Shape of face triangle   Number of faces 4
❷ Shape of face square   Number of faces 6
❸ Shape of face triangle   Number of faces 2
Shape of face rectangle   Number of faces 3
❹ Shape of face triangle   Number of faces 5
Shape of face pentagon   Number of faces 1

Problem Solving

For 5–7, use the story. Use a strategy and solve.
On each school day, Garrett spends $3.00 on bus fare, $1.75 for lunch, and $0.75 for a snack.

❺ How much does Garrett spend in a month when there are 20 school days? $110.00

❻ How much more does Garrett spend in a month with 21 school days than in a month with 17 school days? $22.00

❼ Garrett's school year has 180 days. His parents have set aside $1,200 for his expenses. Have they set aside enough? If so, how much extra is there? If not, how much more is needed? yes; $210.00 extra

Spiral Review SR110

Extension Activity
Designing a Probability

Have students work in pairs. Give each student graph paper. Have each student write, on a separate sheet of paper, a fraction with a denominator from 5 to 12. Then have partners trade fractions. Each partner then designs a square dartboard for which the probability of the outcome of hitting red should result in the given fraction.

Lesson 2 Finding Probabilities

NCTM Standards 5, 7, 8, 9

Lesson Planner

STUDENT OBJECTIVES
- To list possible outcomes and probabilities before conducting an experiment
- To use experimental results to make predictions

1 | Daily Activities (TG p. 1145)

Open-Ended Problem Solving/Headline Story	Skills Practice and Review—Listing Possible Outcomes

2 | Teach and Practice (TG pp. 1146–1152)

	MATERIALS
(A) **Predicting Probability** (TG pp. 1146–1147)	• TR: Activity Masters, AM143–AM144
(B) **Playing a Game:** *Number Pyramid* (TG p. 1148)	• transparency of AM145 (optional)
(C) **Discussing the Experiment** (TG pp. 1149–1150)	• scissors
(D) **Finding Probabilities** (TG p. 1151)	• calculators
	• LAB pp. 273–274
	• SH p. 237, 246

3 | Differentiated Instruction (TG p. 1153)

Leveled Problem Solving (TG p. 1153)	Practice Book P111
Intervention Activity (TG p. 1153)	Extension Book E111
Extension Activity (TG p. 1153)	Spiral Review Book SR111

Lesson Notes

About the Lesson

Students classify the numbers 1 through 12 in various ways (e.g., as even, prime, or less than 4) and figure out the theoretical probability of specific events, like drawing an even number when drawing a random number from 1 to 12. They also perform the experiments in groups, write the results as fractions, and compare those results with theoretical probabilities. Finally, they combine the groups' results to get more reliable data for predictions about future trials.

About the Mathematics

When we can safely assume that all outcomes are equally likely, we can compute a theoretical probability by dividing the number of outcomes we are interested in (sometimes called "favorable outcomes") by the number of all possible outcomes. The probability of getting a 2 when rolling a number cube is $\frac{1}{6}$, as is the probability of getting a 5. What if we wanted to find the probability of getting a 2 *or* a 5? When the two events are entirely separate (we can't ever get a 2 and a 5 on the same roll), we *add* the probabilities of each event: $\frac{1}{6} + \frac{1}{6} = \frac{2}{6} = \frac{1}{3}$. The *event* we care about (getting a 2 or a 5) constitutes 2 of the 6 equally likely *outcomes.*

(continued on page R5)

Developing Mathematical Language

Vocabulary: certain, improbable, probable

Students have a tendency to think in terms of black and white—either/or. However, many events in our natural world fall into the gray area of being either *probable* or *improbable,* meaning the likelihood of an occurrence is neither *certain* nor impossible. Encourage students to think critically in this large gray area. Encourage them to justify their reasoning, especially whenever they say an event is *certain* or impossible.

Familiarize students with the terms *certain, improbable,* and *probable.*

Beginning On the board, write the terms *improbable* and *probable.* Have a student circle the parts of the words that are the same. Point out that the prefix *im-* means "not," so *improbable,* means "not *probable."*

Intermediate On the board write the terms *certain, improbable,* and *probable.* Have students name other words or phrases for each term. For example, for *certain,* students might say "definite," "for sure," "it will happen," "no doubt."

Advanced Make two columns on the board with the heads *probable* and *improbable.* Ask students to complete the list by naming *probable* and *improbable* events.

Open-Ended Problem Solving

Students should consider the theoretical probabilities of various outcomes of tossing number cubes in determining when each player receives a point. You might even have students play this game with their assigned point values during some free time during the day.

 Headline Story

> **Invent a game called "Mine/Yours" where both players toss a number cube at the same time, but only one of the players gets a point. Make the game as fair as possible.**

Possible responses: We could each claim certain sums. We can make a table and figure out all of the ways the different sums can happen—there are a total of 36 ways. One way to make it as fair as possible is for one player to get a point for tosses of 2, 3, 4, 5, and 6 (15 ways), the other player to get a point for tosses of 8, 9, 10, 11, and 12 (15 ways), and neither player to get a point for a toss of 7. Or, one player could get a point for even sums and the other could get a point for odd sums.

Skills Practice and Review

Listing Possible Outcomes

Have students imagine flipping a penny and a nickel and then listing all possible outcomes. Students may suggest recording in a table or with a sketch of intersecting lines to ensure listing all of the options.

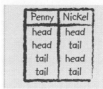 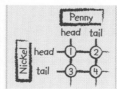

Then ask the class to imagine flipping a dime, a nickel, and a quarter and have them make a table of all the possible outcomes.

whole class   10 MIN

NCTM Standards 5, 7, 8, 9

A Predicting Probability

Purpose To determine theoretical probabilities

Introduce Ask students to imagine a small deck of cards with each of the numbers 1 to 12 on a card. Have students list all of the possible outcomes of picking one card at random, and ask if there is an equal likelihood of drawing any one of these cards. yes Then ask students for the probability of drawing a particular number, such as 7. Students should reason that because there is only one card with a 7 on it and there are 12 total cards that have an equal chance of being picked, the probability is one in twelve, or $\frac{1}{12}$.

Talk Math

❓ What is the probability of picking a card that is not a seven? Since we will pick a seven about $\frac{1}{12}$ of the time, we will pick another card $\frac{11}{12}$ of the time.

❓ What is the probability of picking a card that is greater than 6? There are 6 cards that are greater than six, and each of these cards has a $\frac{1}{12}$ chance of being picked (since there are a total of 12 possible cards). Therefore, we will pick a card that is greater than six about $\frac{6}{12}$, or $\frac{1}{2}$, of the time.

Task Have students determine the probability of various events.

Make a table with various ways of classifying the numbers 1 through 12 and ask for the probability of getting a card in that category and of getting a card that is not in that category. (Use the categories shown in the table below, which appear in the game in the next activity, and also allow students to suggest other possible events. For example, students might suggest square numbers or one-digit numbers.)

Event	Cards in the category defined by this event	Probability of this event	Probability of drawing a card not in that category
Less than 4	1, 2, 3	$\frac{3}{12}$ or $\frac{1}{4}$	$\frac{9}{12}$ or $\frac{3}{4}$
Even	2, 4, 6, 8, 10, 12	$\frac{6}{12}$ or $\frac{1}{2}$	$\frac{6}{12}$ or $\frac{1}{2}$
Greater than 8	9, 10, 11, 12	$\frac{4}{12}$ or $\frac{1}{3}$	$\frac{8}{12}$ or $\frac{2}{3}$
Prime	2, 3, 5, 7, 11	$\frac{5}{12}$	$\frac{7}{12}$
Factor of 9	1, 3, 9	$\frac{3}{12}$ or $\frac{1}{4}$	$\frac{9}{12}$ or $\frac{3}{4}$

Differentiated Instruction

Basic Level Students who say that the probability is "low" or "high" rather than attaching a specific value to the probability may have the correct *concept* and even know how to compute that probability, but simply not realize that asking for the probability *means* that you want a numeric answer. If prompting students with questions about whether the probability is, for example, $\frac{1}{2}$ or $\frac{1}{4}$ isn't sufficient, you may need to model the type of reasoning you want. For example, you might say that there is only 1 seven, and there are 12 cards, or that one of the 12 cards is a seven so $\frac{1}{12}$ of the cards are sevens. You might also remind students that this means that over the long run we can expect to pick a seven about $\frac{1}{12}$ of the time when we randomly select a card from the deck.

Share Now ask students to use these probabilities to predict how often they will get a particular result. Save their responses because students will actually conduct this experiment during the game in the next activity, and can then compare their predictions (based on theoretical probability) to the experimental probability.

💬 Talk Math

❷ If the probability of drawing a prime number is $\frac{5}{12}$, about how many times would you expect to draw a card with a prime number if you drew a card 120 times? about 50 (50 out of 120 draws is equivalent to $\frac{5}{12}$.) What if you drew 240 cards? about 100 (100 out of 240 draws is equivalent to $\frac{5}{12}$.)

❷ If you drew 100 times, about how many times would you expect to draw a card with an even number? about 50 because I would expect half of the draws to have an even number since half of the cards have an even number on them

pairs

10 MIN

B Playing a Game: *Number Pyramid*

Materials
• for each student:
  AM143–AM144, scissors

NCTM Standards 5, 8, 9

Purpose To practice categorizing numbers while generating a random data set

Goal The object of the game, *Number Pyramid,* is to match a number to all 6 categories on AM144: *Number Pyramid* Game Board.

Prepare the Materials Give each student AM144: *Number Pyramid* Game Board and AM143: Blank Cards. Have students write the numbers 1 through 12 on the blank cards and then cut them out. Pairs of students should then combine their number cards, shuffle them, and place them face down. Before beginning play, each student labels the one empty square on their game board (AM144) with any category that includes at least one of the numbers from 1 through 12. For example, students might write "Not 2 or 3" or "Less than 9."

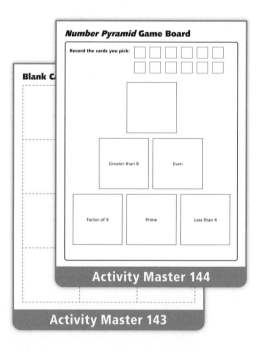

Student Handbook p. 246

Concept Alert

As a (non-coincidental!) byproduct of playing this game, if the students shuffle carefully each time, they are generating random data. By combining the data of each group in the next activity, your class should easily have over 100 data points, which they will then compare to the theoretical probabilities they determined in the previous activity. By combining data, a large enough data set will be created for students to see that the experimental probabilities are approaching the theoretical probabilities.

How to Play

❶ Players alternate picking a number card, recording the number at the top of their game board, replacing the card in the deck, and re-shuffling the cards.

❷ Each time a player selects a card, they should decide if it matches any of the categories on their game board. If the number matches more than one category the player must decide which category they would like to use it for. They then put a check beside that box or cover it with a game piece of some kind. If the number does not match any category, students should still record it at the top of the page, but that is the end of their turn.

Note: Students are likely to forget to record each number they draw, especially when they don't use that number to cover a square on the *Number Pyramid* Game Board. Give students frequent reminders to record their draws.

❸ When a player has matched at least one number to each category, they have completed their number pyramid, and they win. (Students might decide that each player should have the same number of turns. Once one player completes their pyramid, the other player may have one more turn if their first turn came after the winner's first turn. If students allow an equal number of turns, there may be more than one winner.)

Use with Lesson Activity Book pp. 273–274.

Discussing the Experiment

Purpose To find experimental probabilities and compare them to theoretical probabilities

Introduce Display AM145: Class Results or sketch a table similar to the one on the top of the page. Tell students that you want to record the number of times each of the numbers, 1 through 12, was drawn while they played the *Number Pyramid* game. Ask one student from each group to record their results in the chart. They should put a tally mark in the column for a number each time that number was drawn. A row is provided for a second game in case any students play the game more than once.

Materials
• For the teacher: transparency of AM145 (optional), calculator

NCTM Standards 5, 7, 8, 9

Task Have students record the experimental probabilities of each event on AM145. Students already found the theoretical probabilities in the first activity, so fill these in for your students. As you do this, ask each group to find their experimental probabilities for their particular game. Make sure students realize that they should be using all of the numbers they drew to do this, and not just the numbers that they matched to a particular category. Then have the class find the experimental probabilities of the combined data. This will help students to see that summarizing the results from the entire class will give a more valid prediction for future experiments.

Class Results

	1	2	3	4	5	6	7	8	9	10	11	12
Game 1 Card Numbers												
Game 2 Card Numbers												

Event	Theoretical Probability	Experimental Probability
Less than 4	$\frac{}{12}$	—
Even	$\frac{}{12}$	—
Greater than 8	$\frac{}{12}$	—
Prime	$\frac{}{12}$	—
Factor of 9	$\frac{}{12}$	—

Activity Master 145

💬 **Talk Math**

❷ Based on your *individual group's data*, what is the experimental probability of getting a number less than 4? How does this compare to the theoretical probability? Group data will show varying numbers of occurrences of the numbers 1, 2, and 3. If these numbers occurred, say 7 times out of 20 draws, the group's experimental results would suggest a probability of $\frac{7}{20}$. Since the theoretical probability of this event is $\frac{1}{4}$, more numbers less than 4 were actually drawn than theory predicts. (If the fractions are not easy to compare, have a volunteer convert them to decimals on a calculator.)

❷ Based on the *combined class data*, what is the experimental probability of getting a number less than 4? How does this compare to the theoretical probability? Possible answer: Comparisons of overall class experimental results to theoretical probability is done the same way. These results, because they involve a larger data set, are likely to be closer to theoretical probability.

❷ Are the experimental results of the entire class closer to the theoretical probability than the individual group's experimental results? In general, the answer will be yes.

Conclude by using the class's experimental probabilities to make predictions.

❷ About how many times would you expect to see a number greater than 8 if 100 draws were made? What about if there were 1,000 draws? Since the theoretical probability of getting a number greater than 8 is $\frac{1}{3}$, one might expect to get either 33 or 34 numbers greater than 8 after drawing a card 100 times. However, the experimental results do not have to match theoretical predictions exactly. In fact, in the case of 100 draws, one can't get exactly $\frac{1}{3}$ of them to be greater than 9 because that would require $33\frac{1}{3}$ cards to be greater than 8! With 1,000 draws, the experimental results should more closely match the prediction.

Use with Lesson Activity Book pp. 273–274.

individuals

20 MIN

Purpose To find theoretical and experimental probabilities, and then use them to make predictions

NCTM Standards 5, 7, 8, 9

Lesson Activity Book p. 273

Name _____ Date _____

Chapter 14
Lesson 2 **Finding Probabilities**
NCTM Standards 5, 7, 8, 9

Mika is going to draw 1 card at random from the following deck.

| 1 | 4 | 9 | 16 | 25 | 36 |

| 49 | 64 | 81 | 100 | 121 | 144 |

❶ For each event listed at the right, write a fraction to describe the probability of this event happening.

Event	Probability
a Number is less than 40	$\frac{6}{12}$, or $\frac{1}{2}$
b Units digit is 1 or 9	$\frac{5}{12}$
c Units digit is 2, 3, or 7	$\frac{0}{12}$, or 0
d Number is greater than 50	$\frac{5}{12}$
e Number is a multiple of 3	$\frac{4}{12}$, or $\frac{1}{3}$

❷ Make a deck of cards to match those above and conduct the experiment. Draw a card and record your result in the table below. Return the card to the deck and shuffle well. Repeat for a total of 20 draws. **Results will vary.**

Draw	1	2	3	4	5	6	7	8	9	10	11	12	13	14	15	16	17	18	19	20
Card Drawn																				

❸ Assign a probability for each event based on your experiment in Problem 2. **Results will vary.**

Event	Experimental Probability
a Number is less than 40	☐/20
b Units digit is 1 or 9	
c Units digit is 2, 3, or 7	
d Number is greater than 50	
e Number is a multiple of 3	

3 × 7 × 13 **CCLXXIII** two hundred seventy-three **273**

ABOUT THE PAGE NUMBER Is 273 inches more or less than 22 feet?

Lesson Activity Book p. 274

For another experiment, you will draw a card at random from a deck whose cards are numbered with the cubes of numbers from 1 to 10. Write the possible outcomes on these cards.

| 1 | 8 | 27 | 64 | 125 | 216 | 343 | 512 | 729 | 1,000 |

✏ ❹ Complete the following statements and give reasons that correspond to this experiment. **Answers will vary.**

a I am CERTAIN to draw _____ .

Why? _____

b The probability is greater than $\frac{1}{2}$ that I will draw _____ .

Why? _____

c The probability is less than $\frac{1}{2}$ that I will draw _____ .

Why? _____

d It is IMPOSSIBLE that I will draw _____ .

Why? _____

❺ Imagine that you conduct this experiment. Write 2 questions about the probability of some event occurring. Then answer your question. (One example is given.)

Q: What is the probability that I will draw an even number?   A: $\frac{5}{10}$, or $\frac{1}{2}$ **Answers will vary.**

Q: _____   A: _____

Q: _____   A: _____

✏ ❻ **Challenge** Look at LAB p. 273. How well did the predicted probabilities (Problem 1) match the experimental probabilities (Problem 2)? Explain why you think they did or did not match. **Answer will vary but should include the idea that 20 is a very small number of trials and could include unexpected results.**

274 two hundred seventy-four **CCLXXIV** 2 × 137

ABOUT THE PAGE NUMBER What 3-digit prime number is a factor of 274?

Teaching Notes for LAB page 273

Students find the probability of five events for a new deck of 12 cards. They then make a similar deck (using another copy of AM143) to conduct an experiment. They record their results of 20 trials and use fractions to describe the results of their experiment.

Teaching Notes for LAB page 274

Students make a deck of cards for the cubes of numbers from 1 through 10. You may need to remind students that cubing a number means finding the product that uses that number as a factor 3 times (that is, "6 cubed" means 6 × 6 × 6). They also complete statements about the probability of events for these numbers. For Problem 5, students do not need to conduct the experiment. They might write questions and answers based on theoretical probabilities.

Challenge Problem Students compare the theoretical probability and the experimental probability from LAB page 274.

Write Math

Cheryl has a deck of ten cards with these numbers: 1, 3, 5, 7, 9, 11, 13, 15, 17, 19. Cheryl will draw a card at random from the deck. Name an event for which there is a probability of $\frac{1}{2}$ that it will happen. Then name an event for which there is a probability of 1 that it will happen. Answers will vary. Possible answers: For a probability of $\frac{1}{2}$: the number is greater than 10; for a probability of 1: the number is odd.

Review Model . . . .

Refer students to Review Model: Finding Probability in the *Student Handbook* to see how to use a fraction to describe the probability of an event.

✔ **Check for Understanding**

❶ $\frac{2}{7}$

❷ $\frac{4}{7}$

❸ $\frac{2}{7}$

❹ $\frac{2}{5}$

❺ $\frac{4}{5}$

❻ $\frac{0}{5}$ or 0

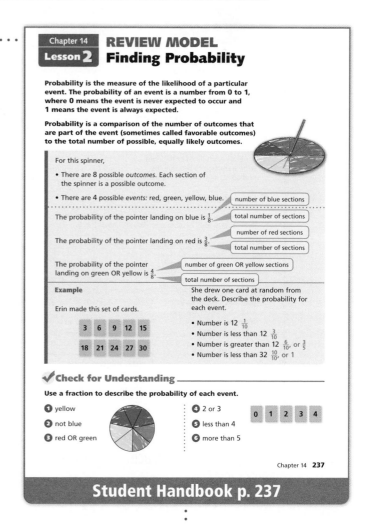

Student Handbook p. 237

Use with Lesson Activity Book pp. 273–274.

3 | Differentiated Instruction

Leveled Problem Solving

**Kristi has a stack of cards labeled 1 to 10.
She will pick a card at random from the stack.**

❶ Basic Level

Name an event with a probability of 0. Explain. Possible answer: picking a 12; picking anything besides a number from 1 to 10 is impossible.

❷ On Level

Name an event with a probability of $\frac{1}{2}$. Explain. Possible answer: any odd number between 1 and 10 (1, 3, 5, 7, 9); there are 5 odd numbers, so 5 out of 10 are odd.

❸ Above Level

Name an event with a probability of $\frac{4}{5}$. Explain. Possible answer: a number less than 9 or greater than 2 or that doesn't have 1 as a digit.

Intervention

Activity Compare Probabilities

Draw a number line on the board with a tick mark at each end and one tick mark in the middle. Label the tick marks from left to right: 0, $\frac{1}{2}$, 1.

Have each student think of two probability fractions, one improbable and the other probable. Then have each student graph his or her two probabilities on the number line. Help students use the concept of comparing fractions to compare likelihoods.

Practice

Finding Probabilities

Lena and four of her friends each drew a card at random from this deck 20 times. The table shows their results.

| 2 | 4 | 6 | 8 | 10 | 12 | 14 | 16 | 18 | 20 |

Results of Card Draw

List 4 possible events. Then use the table above to write a fraction that describes the probability of each of the events. Answers will vary.

	Event	Experimental Probability
❶	Even number	$\frac{100}{100}$
❷		
❸		
❹		

Test Prep

❶ If you draw a card from the deck above, what is the probability of drawing a card where the sum of the digits is odd? Explain how you know.

$\frac{1}{2}$; Possible explanation: The sum of the digits on five of the ten cards is odd, so the probability is $\frac{5}{10}$ or $\frac{1}{2}$.

Practice P111

Extension

Finding Probabilities

You will need to picture or make a deck of cards that consists of 25 cards numbered 0–25 with a red marker and 25 cards numbered 0–25 with a black marker.

❶ Suppose you draw a card at random from the deck. What is the probability that you will get _____? Write some events that might fit in that blank space, and then figure out the probability of getting that event. Some ideas are suggested below to get you started. Answers will vary.

	Events		Probability
1.	A number greater than 19	1.	$\frac{12}{52}$
2.	A red number	2.	$\frac{26}{52}$ or $\frac{1}{2}$
3.	A black odd number	3.	$\frac{13}{52}$
4.		4.	
5.		5.	
6.		6.	
7.		7.	
8.		8.	

❷ Think about performing a probability experiment using these cards. How many times do you think you would need to draw a card in order to get experimental results that are close to the probabilities you wrote in the table above? Explain why you chose that number.

Answers will vary.

100 draws might be okay, but 200, 500, or more is better.

Extension E111

Spiral Review

Spiral Review Book page SR111 provides review of the following previously learned skills and concepts:

• using division to solve problems

• determining the mean, median, mode, and range of data displayed in a table

You may wish to have students work with partners to complete the page.

Number and Operations

Divide. Show your work.

❶ 19⟌798 → 42
❷ 56⟌784 → 14
❸ 28⟌1,764 → 63
❹ 83⟌3,901 → 47

Probability and Data Analysis

For 5–9, use the survey results.

Fifty people were asked how many different phones they had.

Number of Phones	1	2	3	4	5
Number of People Responding	8	20	11	8	3

❺ What was the least number of phones any of the people said they had? — 1

❻ What was the greatest number of phones any of the people said they had? — 5

❼ What was the range of answers? — 4

❽ What was the median number of phones people had? — 2

❾ What was the mode number of phones? — 2

Spiral Review SR111

Extension Activity
The Probability Game

Have each student secretly write a number of coins, such as 3 pennies and 2 dimes. Then ask students to find the probability of randomly selecting each coin.

Assign partners. Each partner states either the number of coins or the number of different types of coins he or she has. Then partners take turns asking for the probability of selecting a particular coin. The winner is the first to identify the coins and how many of each there are.

Lesson 3 Sampling Experiments

NCTM Standards 1, 5, 6, 7, 8, 9

Lesson Planner

STUDENT OBJECTIVES
- To use results of an experiment to make predictions
- To use fractions to describe the results of an experiment

1 Daily Activities (TG p. 1155)

Open-Ended Problem Solving/Headline Story	Skills Practice and Review— Listing Possible Outcomes

2 Teach and Practice (TG pp. 1156–1159)

	MATERIALS
(A) **Solving a Mystery** (TG pp. 1156–1157)	• opaque bags—each with 4 red, 6 blue, and 2 green cubes
(B) **Making Predictions** (TG pp. 1157–1158)	• transparency of AM146 (optional)
(C) **Interpreting Results of a Sampling Experiment** (TG p. 1159)	• 📖 LAB pp. 275–276 • 📖 SH p. 238

3 Differentiated Instruction (TG p. 1160)

Leveled Problem Solving (TG p. 1160)	Practice Book P112
Intervention Activity (TG p. 1160)	Extension Book E112
Extension Activity (TG p. 1160)	Spiral Review Book SR112

Lesson Notes

About the Lesson

Students investigate sampling as a way to obtain information about an entire set of data (i.e., the population). They use their results to make predictions about the population, recognizing that they cannot find the size of the population or the size of any of the subgroups without additional information. By continuing to express the results of their experiments using fractions, students practice interpreting the results of their experiments in the context of probability.

Use with Lesson Activity Book pp. 275–276.

Developing Mathematical Language

Vocabulary: sampling

A *sampling* is a technique used to determine probabilities for different subsets within a whole set or to determine the size of a population. Conservationists use this method to estimate the size of a population of wildlife. They first capture and tag a few animals and then release them. After a short time, they capture a group of the same species and see what fraction is tagged. Suppose, for example, conservationists tagged and released 10 bears. Then if they recaptured 4 bears of which 2 were tagged, they could estimate that half of the population had been tagged and that region would have about 20 bears in it.

Familiarize students with the term *sampling.*

Beginning To help students understand *sampling,* discuss the word *sample.* Point out that a sample is just a small part of something. Students might be familiar with samples given out in grocery stores to introduce a new product. Discuss how a sample of a new type of cracker might be one cracker but that the product for purchase is a box of crackers.

Intermediate Describe several probability experiments, and have students discuss whether each involves *sampling.*

Advanced Have students write a brief paragraph about *sampling* and when it would be a useful method.

Open-Ended Problem Solving

Ask students what they can and cannot say about the marbles in the bag and how much certainty they can say it with.

 Headline Story

> **April's friend put marbles of three different colors in a bag without letting April know what colors or how many of each. April then took one marble out of the bag, recorded its color, and put it back. She repeated this activity several times. One-third of the marbles she took out were red.**

Possible responses: We don't know how many pulls she took, but it must have been a multiple of 3—she might have seen 2 reds out of 6 pulls. We don't know what the other two colors are or in what fraction of pulls they appeared. We don't know how many marbles are in the bag. We do know for sure that there is at least one red marble in the bag. It is possible that there is exactly one red marble and that April just happened to pull it out quite frequently.

Skills Practice and Review

Listing Possible Outcomes

As in the previous lesson, tell students to imagine rolling two number cubes. Call on students to list pairs of numbers that could be rolled. Ask for suggestions of ways to work systematically to ensure listing all the options. Students may suggest recording with a table or with a sketch of intersecting lines like this.

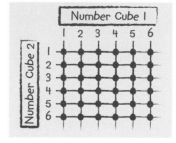

whole class 15 MIN

Materials
- For each group: opaque bag containing 4 red, 6 blue, and 2 green cubes

NCTM Standards 5, 7, 8, 9

(A) Solving a Mystery

Purpose To perform a sampling experiment

Introduce Divide the class into 5 groups of any size. Each group needs Explore: A Sampling Experiment and a bag of cubes that you have prepared. (The bag should be opaque and contain 4 red, 6 blue, and 2 green cubes, but students should not know the number of cubes of each color.) Make sure that students realize that every bag contains the exactly the same number of cubes of each color.

Read the top of the Explore page and the steps for performing the experiment together, and make sure students understand their task. You might ask why this process is called a "sampling experiment." (The experiment involves repeatedly taking samples from the bag to try to figure out what's in the bag.)

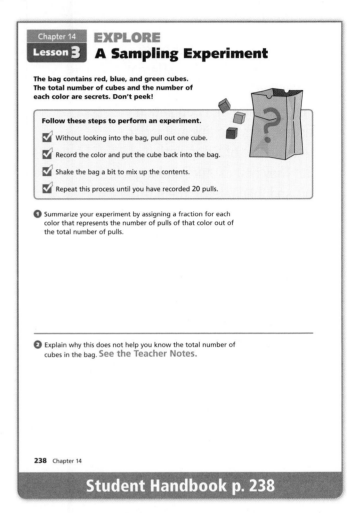

Student Handbook p. 238

Task Have each group complete Explore: A Sampling Experiment. As students are working, one person in each group should record the color of each pull. After all 20 pulls have been taken and recorded, a different group member should record the results for each color as a fraction of the total pulls.

Share Ask groups to share their results, and then have the class compare the results of each group. Your students have now had enough experience with probability experiments to not be surprised by a fair amount of variation after only 20 pulls. (You do not need to record the results on the board now. That will be done in the next activity.)

Use with Lesson Activity Book pp. 275–276.

Talk Math

❷ Why did different groups get different results? Possible answer: Just as two different groups tossing number cubes would get different tosses, different groups picking cubes from a bag would get different picks.

❷ Why can't this experiment help you know how many cubes are in the bag? You may find that you have some students who are not initially convinced that you can't know exactly how many cubes are in the bag from performing this type of experiment. If so, allow students to debate a bit and convince each other, but if necessary you might ask if it's possible to know that a cube you've pulled is one that you've pulled before. (No—that's why you don't know how many cubes there are in the bag.)

B Making Predictions

Purpose To interpret the results of a sampling experiment

Introduce Project a transparency of AM146: Class Results—Color Cubes or draw a similar table. As in previous lessons, tell students that they are going to combine the data of each group in order to generate a larger data set that should more closely approximate the actual distribution of color cubes in the bags.

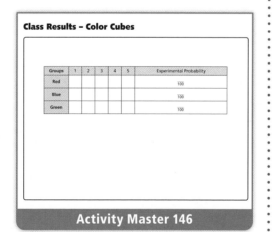

Class Results – Color Cubes

Groups	1	2	3	4	5	Experimental Probability
Red						$\frac{}{100}$
Blue						$\frac{}{100}$
Green						$\frac{}{100}$

Activity Master 146

Materials
- For the teacher: transparency of AM146 (optional)

NCTM Standards 5, 7, 8, 9

Task Ask for volunteers to record the **number of cubes of each color each group pulled (not the fraction of all pulls).** Ask students to do a quick check once all the groups' results are put into the table to ensure that the sum of each column is 20. Then, add across the rows and write a fraction that describes how many pulls (out of 100) were of that color. For example, if the groups drew 9, 8, 10, 12, and 8 blue cubes, you record $\frac{47}{100}$ in that row. Depending on your class, you may want to confirm that they understand these new fractions—they represent the total number of pulls for each color out of a class total of 100 pulls. You might once again have volunteers do a quick check to be sure that the 5 fractions add up to $\frac{100}{100}$, or 1.

Concept Alert

In approximating the number of times a certain event occurs when there are a given number of trials, students are practicing finding equivalent fractions using the number of trials as the denominators. Similarly, students might think of fraction machines to figure out the number of outcomes that would be expected if a certain fraction of the number of trials results in that event.

💬 **Talk Math** Now ask students to use the class's experimental results to make predictions about the colors of the cubes in the bags.

❷ If you knew there were 100 cubes in the bag, about how many would you predict are red? blue? green? Students should use their class experimental results to respond to this question. For example, if the combined class data indicates that 35 of the 100 total pulls resulted in red cubes, students might say that there were 35 red cubes in the bag.

❷ If you knew there were 200 cubes in the bag, about how many would you predict are red? blue? green? Students should again use their class experimental results. Since they found the fraction of pulls that resulted in a particular color when there were 100 pulls, they can double the number of pulls of each color when the number of pulls doubles. (In other words, they find an equivalent fraction with a denominator of 200.)

❷ If you knew there were only 10 cubes in the bag, about how many would you predict are red? blue? green? Again students use the class results to generate as close to an equivalent fraction as the experimental result using a denominator of 10. For example, if the combined class data indicates that 35 of the 100 total pulls resulted in red cubes, students might say there probably were 3 or 4 red cubes out of 10 in the bag.

Then show students the 4 red cubes in one of the bags and tell them this is all of the reds. Then look again at the class's experimental results.

❷ Now that you know there are exactly 4 red cubes in each bag, do you think there are more than, fewer than, or exactly 10 cubes in each bag? Why? This is a difficult question, and students will need help responding. Help them to see that they should compare their class's experimental results to the fraction $\frac{4}{10}$ to answer this question. If the experimental result is less than $\frac{4}{10}$, then students should expect there to be fewer than 4 red cubes for every 10 cubes in the bag and therefore predict that there are more than 10 cubes in the bag. Using similar reasoning, if the experimental result is more than $\frac{4}{10}$, students might expect that there are fewer than 10 cubes in the bag, and if the experimental result is nearly equivalent to $\frac{4}{10}$ students might expect that there are 10 cubes in the bag.

Now show students the 6 blue cubes, and again tell them this is all of the blues. This makes it obvious that there are more than 10 cubes because students know there are green cubes in the bag too.

❷ How do the number of green cubes compare to the numbers of blue and red cubes? Most likely, the experimental results will indicate that there should be fewer green cubes than either blue or red ones.

Reveal the remaining 2 green cubes.

❷ How do the experimental results match up with the actual fraction of each color of cubes in the bag: $\frac{1}{3}$ red, $\frac{1}{2}$ blue, and $\frac{1}{6}$ green? Answers will vary and will depend on the class's experimental results.

Use with Lesson Activity Book pp. 275–276.

Interpreting Results of a Sampling Experiment LAB pp. 275–276

Purpose To find experimental probabilities and use them to answer questions

NCTM Standards 1, 5, 6, 7, 8, 9

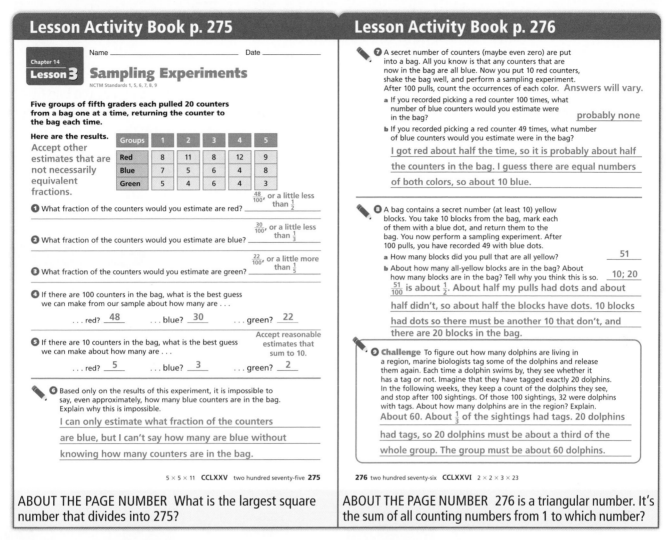

Lesson Activity Book p. 275

Name _____ Date _____

Chapter 14
Lesson 3 **Sampling Experiments**
NCTM Standards 1, 5, 6, 7, 8, 9

Five groups of fifth graders each pulled 20 counters from a bag one at a time, returning the counter to the bag each time.

Here are the results.
Accept other estimates that are not necessarily equivalent fractions.

Groups	1	2	3	4	5
Red	8	11	8	12	9
Blue	7	5	6	4	8
Green	5	4	6	4	3

❶ What fraction of the counters would you estimate are red? $\frac{48}{100}$, or a little less than $\frac{1}{2}$

❷ What fraction of the counters would you estimate are blue? $\frac{30}{100}$, or a little less than $\frac{1}{3}$

❸ What fraction of the counters would you estimate are green? $\frac{22}{100}$, or a little more than $\frac{1}{5}$

❹ If there are 100 counters in the bag, what is the best guess we can make from our sample about how many are . . .

. . . red? **48**   . . . blue? **30**   . . . green? **22**

❺ If there are 10 counters in the bag, what is the best guess we can make about how many are . . .

Accept reasonable estimates that sum to 10.

. . . red? **5**   . . . blue? **3**   . . . green? **2**

❻ Based only on the results of this experiment, it is impossible to say, even approximately, how many blue counters are in the bag. Explain why this is impossible.

I can only estimate what fraction of the counters are blue, but I can't say how many are blue without knowing how many counters are in the bag.

5 × 5 × 11 CCLXXV two hundred seventy-five **275**

ABOUT THE PAGE NUMBER What is the largest square number that divides into 275?

Lesson Activity Book p. 276

❼ A secret number of counters (maybe even zero) are put into a bag. All you know is that any counters that are now in the bag are all blue. Now you put 10 red counters, shake the bag well, and perform a sampling experiment. After 100 pulls, count the occurrences of each color. **Answers will vary.**

a If you recorded picking a red counter 100 times, what number of blue counters would you estimate were in the bag? **probably none**

b If you recorded picking a red counter 49 times, what number of blue counters would you estimate were in the bag?

I got red about half the time, so it is probably about half the counters in the bag. I guess there are equal numbers of both colors, so about 10 blue.

❽ A bag contains a secret number (at least 10) yellow blocks. You take 10 blocks from the bag, mark each of them with a blue dot, and return them to the bag. You now perform a sampling experiment. After 100 pulls, you have recorded 49 with blue dots.

a How many blocks did you pull that are all yellow? **51**

b About how many all-yellow blocks are in the bag? About how many blocks are in the bag? Tell why you think this is so. **10; 20**

$\frac{51}{100}$ is about $\frac{1}{2}$. About half my pulls had dots and about half didn't, so about half the blocks have dots. 10 blocks had dots so there must be another 10 that don't, and there are 20 blocks in the bag.

❾ **Challenge** To figure out how many dolphins are living in a region, marine biologists tag some of the dolphins and release them again. Each time a dolphin swims by, they see whether it has a tag or not. Imagine that they have tagged exactly 20 dolphins. In the following weeks, they keep a count of the dolphins they see, and stop after 100 sightings. Of those 100 sightings, 32 were dolphins with tags. About how many dolphins are in the region? Explain.

About 60. About $\frac{1}{3}$ of the sightings had tags. 20 dolphins had tags, so 20 dolphins must be about a third of the whole group. The group must be about 60 dolphins.

276 two hundred seventy-six CCLXXVI 2 × 2 × 3 × 23

ABOUT THE PAGE NUMBER 276 is a triangular number. It's the sum of all counting numbers from 1 to which number?

Teaching Notes for LAB page 275

Students answer questions using a table of data from a similar experiment to the one they conducted in Activity A. They record the results of the experiment as fractions and then use these results to make predictions.

Differentiated Instruction Basic Level/On Level

Some students may find it helpful to write the outcomes for all 100 pulls at the end of each row as was done during Activity B in the lesson.

Teaching Notes for LAB page 276

Students solve two problems that are similar to capture-recapture sampling techniques used by scientists. They use some of the information they are given to make predictions, and explain their reasoning.

Challenge Problem To solve the Challenge Problem, students need to determine that approximately $\frac{1}{3}$ of the dolphins were tagged. Therefore, 20 tagged dolphins are about $\frac{1}{3}$ of the population of about 60 dolphins.

Reflect and Summarize the Lesson

Write Math A bag has a secret number of red tiles. You add 10 blue tiles to the bag, shake the bag, and perform a sampling experiment. You take a tile from the bag, record its color, put it back, shake the bag, and pick another tile. You do this until you have record 100 pulls. If you pulled a blue tile 52 times, how many red tiles do you suppose were in the bag? Explain. 10 red tiles; I picked blue about half of the time so about half of the tiles are probably blue. There are 10 blue tiles, so there are about 10 red tiles.

Leveled Problem Solving

Lakesha samples a bag of red tiles and blue tiles. She replaces the tile each time.

❶ Basic Level

She samples the bag 40 times, and 20 tiles are red. About what fraction of the tiles are red? **Explain.** about $\frac{1}{2}$; 20 red out of 40 trials is $\frac{20}{40}$, or $\frac{1}{2}$.

❷ On Level

She samples the bag 48 times, and 16 tiles are red. About what fraction of the tiles are red? **Explain.** about $\frac{1}{3}$; 16 red out of 48 trials is $\frac{16}{48}$, or $\frac{1}{3}$.

❸ Above Level

She samples the bag 60 times, and 24 tiles are red. About what fraction of the tiles are blue? **Explain.** about $\frac{3}{5}$; $60 - 24 = 36$, so 36 were blue, 36 blue out of 60 trials is $\frac{36}{60}$, or $\frac{3}{5}$.

Intervention

Activity The Blind Sampling

Ask a volunteer to face away or close eyes while you secretly place a counter in several students' hands. Tell students to keep their counters hidden. Then ask the volunteer to randomly select a few students and record whether they have a counter. Have them use the information to determine the fraction of the students who have counters.

Practice

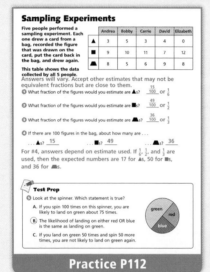

Practice P112

Extension

Sampling Experiments

The sampling experiments described on LAB page 276 are sometimes called the Capture-Recapture method. This method is one way scientists estimate the size of populations of animals.

As an experiment, Jake used this method to estimate the number of children in his neighborhood. On Tuesday, after school, he spent a half hour watching all the children who entered the toy shop near his school. Forty-one children entered. Jake knew them all, and wrote down their names. On Wednesday, he went back to the toy shop at the same time, and watched again. About the same number of children entered the store in the half-hour that he watched, but only ten of them were on his list.

❶ What estimate would you make, based on these numbers?
Only $\frac{1}{4}$ of the children were seen the day before, so the

41 "tagged" children must be about $\frac{1}{4}$ of the population.

There are about 160 children.

❷ Then Jake thought about it some more and decided his experiment might not be giving him reliable numbers. His first thought was that perhaps children who had gone one day might be less likely to go the very next day. If that is true, how should he change his estimate?

There are probably fewer than 160 children in the neighborhood.

❸ Then he wondered if there were many children who simply **never** go to the toy store. If there are, how should that change his estimate of the number of children in his community?
His experiment, if it was accurate, told him that about 160 children visit that store. If there are many children who don't go there, then the number of children in the community is greater than 160.

Extension E112

Spiral Review

Spiral Review Book page SR112 provides review of the following previously learned skills and concepts:

• selecting and using appropriate units to measure length and perimeter

• applying the problem solving strategy *work backward*

You may wish to have students work with partners to complete the page.

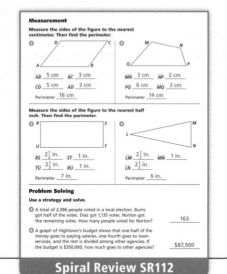

Spiral Review SR112

Extension Activity
What's My Word?

Have students think up a word and write each letter, including any repeated letters (such as the letter *B* in the word *BUBBLE*) of the word on a small square of paper. Then have students place the papers in a bag and challenge a partner to correctly guess the word after 20 or more trials. A trial is randomly taking a letter from the bag, recording it, and returning it.

Teacher's Notes 🍎

Daily Notes . . .

Quick Notes

More Ideas

Lesson 4 | Another Sampling Experiment

NCTM Standards 5, 7, 8, 9

Lesson Planner

STUDENT OBJECTIVES ·
- To use fractions to describe the results of an experiment
- To choose a random sample from a population
- To consider the size of a random sample

1 | Daily Activities (TG p. 1163)

Open-Ended Problem Solving/Headline Story	Skills Practice and Review— Rounding Decimals

2 | Teach and Practice (TG pp. 1164–1167)

Ⓐ How Many Looks Does it Take? (TG pp. 1164–1165)

Ⓑ Choosing a Random Sample (TG p. 1166)

Ⓒ Conducting a Random Sample Experiment (TG p. 1167)

MATERIALS

- opaque bag with 2 red, 3 blue, and 10 green cubes
- TR: Activity Master, AM148
- transparencies of AM147–AM148 (optional)
- numbered decahedra or TR: AM143
- 📖 LAB pp. 277–278

3 | Differentiated Instruction (TG p. 1168)

Leveled Problem Solving (TG p. 1168)	Practice Book P113
Intervention Activity (TG p. 1168)	Extension Book E113
Extension Activity (TG p. 1168)	Spiral Review Book SR113
Language Arts Connection (TG p. 1134)	

Lesson Notes

About the Lesson

In this lesson, students conduct another sampling experiment. They choose a random sample from a population and consider how large the sample should be to represent the population fairly well. Students also find and compare the experimental probabilities from a random sample to the fractions that describe the entire population, noting the effect of sample size on this comparison.

Use with Lesson Activity Book pp. 277–278.

Developing Mathematical Language

Vocabulary: population, random, sample

Students likely understand the term *random* from their everyday experiences. *Random* events are ones that don't have any logic to them. In the context of selecting a subset from a whole set in an experiment, *random* means that every member of the population has an equal chance of being selected as a member of a *sample*.

Familiarize students with the terms *population, random,* and *sample*.

Beginning Have a group of students stand up and be a *population*. Then select a *sample* from that *population*. Repeat with other collections or items, such as books or pencils.

Intermediate On the board, make a list of *populations* and a jumbled list of samples from each *population*. Have students match them by drawing a line between the *population* and its sample.

Advanced Have students explain different ways of choosing a *sample* from a *population*. Ask students to explain when a *sample* is a *random sample*.

Open-Ended Problem Solving

If we flip a penny, we expect that, over the long run, it will land on heads about half the time. But we don't know what to expect if we flip a shell or a bottle cap. Maybe landing open-side up and down are not equally likely. One way to find out is to perform an experiment, as Leo does in this Headline Story.

 Headline Story

Leo flipped a shell 100 times. It landed open-side up 73 times and open-side down 27 times. Shawna then flipped the shell 10 times and got 4 up and 6 down. Max is going to flip the shell one more time. Is it more likely to land open-side up or open-side down?

Possible responses: 10 trials is a very small number, so it's better to make a prediction based on 100 trials. It appears that it is more likely the shell will land open-side up.

Skills Practice and Review

Rounding Decimals

Write decimals on the board and ask students to round them to particular place values. You might ask students to both write the rounded numbers on the board and say them. Here are some examples: 0.462 (round to the nearest tenth, hundredth); 3.5672 (round to the nearest hundredth, one, tenth, thousandth)

| 0.462 | 0.5 | 0.46 | | 3.5672 | 3.57 | 4 | 3.6 | 3.567 |

whole class · **15 MIN**

Materials

- For the teacher: transparency of AM147 (optional), opaque bag with 2 red, 3 blue, and 10 green cubes

NCTM Standards 5, 7, 8, 9

A How Many Looks Does it Take?

Purpose To consider sample size in a sampling experiment

Introduce Ask students to imagine they want to know approximately what fraction of all fish in a pond are minnows. Have students suppose there are three kinds of fish in the pond, and tell them that we could use a different color cube to represent each type of fish. Then have them imagine scooping a net in the water and catching one fish at a time. Make sure they realize that after each scoop, we always put the fish back.

Project a transparency of AM147: Sampling Experiment 2—Color Cubes or copy the table on the board or chart paper. Tell students that red, green, and blue color cubes each represent a different type of fish, but that the number of cubes in the bag is a secret (just as we would not be able to know the exact number of fish in a pond).

Sampling Experiment 2 – Color Cubes

Pull	R	G	B	Experimental probability for each color
1				$R = \frac{1}{1}$ $G = \frac{1}{1}$ $B = \frac{1}{1}$
2				$R = \frac{}{2}$ $G = \frac{}{2}$ $B = \frac{}{2}$
3				$R = \frac{}{3}$ $G = \frac{}{3}$ $B = \frac{}{3}$
4				
5				
6				
7				
8				
9				
10				
11				
12				
13				
14				
15				
16				
17				
18				
19				
20				
21				
22				
23				
24				
25				

Activity Master 147

Task Have students list the possible outcomes of scooping one cube out of the bag. Then conduct the experiment by having a volunteer reach into the bag (without looking inside it) and pull out a cube. Record each pull with a dot in the appropriate column on AM147, and have students record the experimental probability for each color.

After a few pulls your table might look like this.

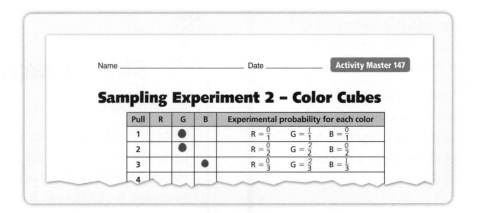

Name _____ Date _____ **Activity Master 147**

Sampling Experiment 2 – Color Cubes

Pull	R	G	B	Experimental probability for each color
1		●		$R = \frac{0}{1}$ $G = \frac{1}{1}$ $B = \frac{0}{1}$
2		●		$R = \frac{0}{2}$ $G = \frac{2}{2}$ $B = \frac{0}{2}$
3			●	$R = \frac{0}{3}$ $G = \frac{2}{3}$ $B = \frac{1}{3}$
4				

Use with Lesson Activity Book pp. 277–278.

Talk Math Use the following questions to help guide the activity.

❷ How many scoops have been made so far? Where do you indicate the number of scoops in the experimental probability? The denominator indicates the number of scoops that have been made so far. If only 2 scoops have been made so far, the denominator is 2. (If the fraction is in simplest form the denominator may not indicate the total number of trials.)

❷ How many of all the scoops so far have resulted in a green cube? How would you record this experimental result as a fraction? Possible answer: Three of the first 4 scoops have been green so the experimental result for green so far is $\frac{3}{4}$.

❷ Do you think we've scooped enough cubes to predict how many of each color are in the bag? Possible answer: We have not yet pulled a red cube and since we know there is one in the bag, we haven't scooped enough cubes yet.

❷ Do you think the 25 scoops you made were enough to make predictions from the results? Would a different number of trials have been better? Possible answer: Predictions can be made no matter how many scoops were made; the question is how many scoops are needed for the prediction to be a good estimate. While there is no special number of trials to use in an experiment, the greater the number of trials, the better the prediction tends to be. But a larger number of trials would have taken more time!

Share Reveal the number of each color cube in the bag and have students compare the experimental probabilities to the actual fractions for each color: $\frac{2}{15}$ red, $\frac{3}{15}$ blue, and $\frac{10}{15}$ green. Conclude this activity by asking students if they think the pairs of fractions would be closer to each other with a larger sample size. This will allow students to review the idea that more trials allows the experimental probability to more closely approach the theoretical probability.

B Choosing a Random Sample

Materials
- For the teacher:
  transparency of AM148
  (optional)
- For each student:
  AM148

NCTM Standards 5, 9

Possible Discussion

If you or your students are interested, you might research more about the use of diaries and TV meters for gathering data on TV viewing.

Purpose To introduce students to how random samples are generated

Introduce Ask students if they have ever wondered how TV networks decide whether to continue producing a show or to cancel it. You might ask if students think the networks ask the opinions of all 300 million people in the US. It will probably not surprise your students that only a sample of the population is surveyed. It may surprise them that fairly good estimates can be made that way.

Talk Math

❓ How might a sample of people in the US be chosen from the entire population? Students may have ideas about the use of computer data banks or phone books as sources of telephone numbers and addresses for contacting a random sample. But to make sure the people you contact are randomly selected is more difficult.

Littletown Data

List #	TV Preferences	List #	TV Preferences	List #	TV Preferences	List #	TV Preferences
0	D	25	C	50	N	75	A
1	N	26	A	51	D	76	C
2	C	27	N	52	A	77	C
3	C	28	C	53	C	78	C
4	B	29	D	54	C	79	N
5	D	30	C	55	A	80	A
6	D	31	B	56	C	81	B
7	N	32	D	57	C	82	C
8	N	33	A	58	B	83	N
9	D	34	C	59	A	84	A
10	N	35	N	60	N	85	D
11	B	36	C	61	C	86	C
12	A	37	N	62	N	87	C
13	B	38	A	63	A	88	N
14	C	39	N	64	B	89	N
15	N	40	D	65	D	90	N
16	N	41	N	66	C	91	C
17	A	42	D	67	A	92	N
18	C	43	A	68	N	93	D
19	N	44	B	69	B	94	A
20	C	45	C	70	A	95	N
21	B	46	A	71	C	96	C
22	D	47	C	72	C	97	D
23	C	48	C	73	A	98	N
24	D	49	A	74	A	99	N

Activity Master 148

Project a transparency of AM148: Littletown Data or give each student a copy. Tell students that they will use this data bank that shows the favorite TV shows (A, B, C, D, or N for "none") of a population of 100 people to select a random sample on the LAB pages for this lesson.

Problem How might you use this bank of data to select a random sample? (That is, how can this bank be used to ensure that each participant has an equal chance of being chosen?) There are many creative possibilities that your students may mention such as repeatedly closing their eyes and placing a finger on a number or cutting up the table into individual numbers and pulling some from a bag.

Students will explore one possible method of randomly selecting participants from this data bank on LAB pp. 277–278.

Conducting a Random Sample Experiment LAB pp. 277–278

individuals · 25 MIN

Purpose To simulate a random sampling experiment and interpret the results

NCTM Standards 5, 7, 8, 9

Lesson Activity Book p. 277

Name _____ Date _____

Chapter 14 Lesson 4 Another Sampling Experiment
NCTM Standards 5, 7, 8, 9

All 100 people in Littletown were asked to choose their favorite TV show (A, B, C, D, or N for "none"). You will use the Littletown data (on AM148: Littletown Data) to see how accurate an estimate you can get from a much smaller sample.

1 The Littletown data are arranged in a list to make it easy to choose a sample randomly. You will use a numbered decahedron to generate 20 sets of data points at random.

- ☑ Toss the decahedron to determine the tens digit of the data point you will choose.
- ☑ Toss the decahedron to determine the ones digit of the data point you will choose.
- ☑ Find this number in the data bank and note that participant's TV show preference.
- ☑ Record the list number and that person's preferred show in the table below.
- ☑ Repeat until you have recorded 20 different people and their shows. (If you get the same list number again, repeat the three steps above.)

Results will vary.

Person	1	2	3	4	5	6	7	8	9	10
List Number										
TV Show										

Person	11	12	13	14	15	16	17	18	19	20
List Number										
TV Show										

prime CCLXXVII two hundred seventy-seven **277**

ABOUT THE PAGE NUMBER How far is 277 from 300?

Lesson Activity Book p. 278

2 Record the fraction of the sample that watched each show.

Show A: ☐/20   Show B: ☐/☐   Show C: ☐/☐

Show D: ☐/☐   N (none): ☐/☐   Results will vary.

3 Because your sample was chosen randomly, it is reasonable to assume that your proportions are similar to those of the total population.

Why should you not expect the fractions for each show to be exactly the same in the sample as in the total population?
A sample gives some, but not all the population's data, so it is not necessarily exactly the same.

4 Now use the entire population of Littletown and find the fractions that watched each show.

Show A: $\frac{20}{100}$ or $\frac{1}{5}$ Show B: $\frac{10}{100}$ or $\frac{1}{10}$ Show C: $\frac{30}{100}$ or $\frac{3}{10}$

Show D: $\frac{15}{100}$ or $\frac{3}{20}$ N (none): $\frac{25}{100}$ or $\frac{1}{4}$

5 Challenge Why are samples surveyed? Why not survey the total population every time?
It might be too difficult or expensive to survey the total population. A well chosen sample is often good enough.

278 two hundred seventy-eight CCLXXVIII 2 × 139

ABOUT THE PAGE NUMBER 278 is the product of what two prime numbers?

Teaching Notes for LAB page 277

Students are presented with a real world sampling problem—sampling a population of 100 TV viewers' favorite TV shows. They need a copy of AM148: Littletown Data to select their sample using a numbered decahedron as their random generator. Demonstrate the procedure for randomly selecting the sample as you read over the directions as a class.

Teacher Story "I didn't have 10-sided numbered decahedron so my students made a deck of cards labeled 0–9 using AM143 and selected a card at random. This card indicated the tens digit. They then replaced it in the deck, shuffled the deck, and picked another card for the ones digit. That's how they generated their numbers."

Teaching Notes for LAB page 278

Students record the experimental results as the fractions of the sample that watched each show. They also determine results for the entire population, and compare them to the results from the smaller sample.

Challenge Problem This problem asks students why samples are used instead of entire populations when conducting an experiment.

Reflect and Summarize the Lesson

Write Math

Why are samples, rather than the total populations, used to survey a population?
Possible answer: It is often too difficult, too expensive, and sometimes impossible to survey a total population. A random sample usually gives an accurate enough result.

Leveled Problem Solving

There are about 3,000 students at the high school. Ricardo is conducting a survey about changing the school colors.

① Basic Level

He conducts the survey using his 10 best friends. Is that a random sample Explain. No; to be random, each person in the school should have the same probability of being chosen for the survey.

② On Level

Which is better, a random sample of 20 students or of 200 students? Explain. 200 students; a larger sample is more likely to more closely resemble the total population.

③ Above Level

If 7 of the first 10 students prefer red and gold, can you conclude that most students want red and gold? Explain. No; 10 is too small a sample, and it might not be a random sample.

Intervention

Activity My Word!

Have each student tally the letters in a word, such as *mathematics,* and then write a probability for each letter. Next, have students write a sentence using the word. Then have students write new probabilities for the same letters. Finally, have students complete a paragraph using the sentence and write new probabilities for the letters. Compare probabilities, and discuss why the paragraph is a better representation of the frequency of letters in our language.

Practice

Practice P113

Extension

Extension E113

Extension Activity
Three Questions Game

Give each student an opaque bag and two colors of tiles. Have students select 20 tiles and secretly keep track of how many of one color go into the bag. One student should pour the contents of one bag into a partner's bag. Students should take turns pulling tiles from the bag one at a time, recording, and returning tiles. At the end of any turn, a student can guess how many color tiles the partner put in. The student who guesses correctly with the fewest questions wins.

Spiral Review

Spiral Review Book page SR113 provides review of the following previously learned skills and concepts:

• adding and subtracting fractions with unlike denominators by finding equivalent fractions with a common denominator

• seeing that the sum of the angle measures in a quadrilateral is 360 degrees

You may wish to have students work with partners to complete the page.

Spiral Review SR113

Use with Lesson Activity Book pp. 277–278.

Teacher's Notes 🍎

Daily Notes . . .

Quick Notes

More Ideas

Lesson 5 Introducing Percents

NCTM Standards 1, 7, 8, 9

Lesson Planner

STUDENT OBJECTIVE ·
- To relate percents, fractions, and decimals

1 Daily Activities (TG p. 1171)

| Open-Ended Problem Solving/Headline Story | Skills Practice and Review—Rounding Decimals |

2 Teach and Practice (TG pp. 1172–1176)

	MATERIALS
Ⓐ **Examples of Percents in the Real World** (TG p. 1172)	• TR: Activity Masters, AM149–AM150
Ⓑ **Understanding the Meaning of Percents** (TG p. 1173)	• scissors
Ⓒ **Relating Fractions and Percents** (TG p. 1174)	• 📖 LAB pp. 279–280
Ⓓ **Playing a Game:** *Matching Quantities* (TG p. 1175)	• 📖 SH p. 239, 247

3 Differentiated Instruction (TG p. 1177)

Leveled Problem Solving (TG p. 1177)	Practice Book P114
Intervention Activity (TG p. 1177)	Extension Book E114
Extension Activity (TG p. 1177)	Spiral Review Book SR114
Science Connection (TG p. 1134)	

Lesson Notes

About the Lesson

Students have been studying probability in this chapter and describing results with fractions. Experimenters, however, often share their results using decimals or percents. In this lesson, students connect percents, fractions, and decimals. In **Lesson 14.6,** students will use fractions and percents to describe data represented in circle graphs.

Use with Lesson Activity Book pp. 279–280.

Developing Mathematical Language

Vocabulary: percent

The word *percent* gives a clue to its meaning: *percent* literally means "per hundred." So "fifty percent" means 50 per 100. Students might remember that "cent" means 100 by thinking about 100 cents in a dollar, 100 centimeters in a meter, or 100 years in a century. To understand better what the "per" means, you might relate it to other uses that students are familiar with, such as 50 miles per hour (i.e., 50 miles in an hour).

Familiarize students with the term *percent.*

Beginning Write some fractions, whole numbers, and *percents* on the board. As you point to each one, have students identify it.

Intermediate Write the term *percent* on the board. Underline *-cent* in the term, and make a connection between 100 cents in 1 dollar and *percent* meaning "per hundred."

Advanced Ask students to explain how the term *percent* might relate to 100 cents in 1 dollar and *percent* meaning "per hundred."

Open-Ended Problem Solving

Even though students have not yet discussed percents, they have had experience with them and likely know some of the more common ones such as 100%, 50%, 25%, and 75%.

 Headline Story

> We know that 100% is the whole amount and 50% is $\frac{1}{2}$ of it because 50 is half of 100. List some other fractions and percents that are equivalent.

Possible responses: 25% is half of 50%, and since half of $\frac{1}{2}$ is $\frac{1}{4}$, 25% must equal $\frac{1}{4}$. $\frac{3}{4}$ of 100 is 75 so 75% is equal to $\frac{3}{4}$. $\frac{1}{10}$ of 100 is 10, so that would be 10%.

Skills Practice and Review

Rounding Decimals

As in the previous activity, write decimals and ask students to round them to particular place values. You might either ask students to write the rounded numbers on the board, say them aloud, or both. Here are some examples: 1.896 (Round to the nearest one, hundredth, tenth); 18.705 (Round to the nearest hundredth, one, tenth, ten); 6.3333 (Round to the nearest thousandth, hundredth, tenth).

1.896	2	1.90	1.9	
18.705	18.71	19	18.7	20
6.3333	6.333	6.33	6.3	

whole class

5 MIN

NCTM Standards 8, 9

A Examples of Percents in the Real World

Purpose To introduce percents

Introduce Ask students what they already know about percents. They may have seen percents used to describe a score on schoolwork and will know that 90% is better than 70%. Most students will understand 100% and 50% in context, but not yet be able to generalize to know what 10% or 25% mean. Briefly discuss any other common uses that your students suggest.

Teacher Story

"I asked my students to bring in examples of percents used in print materials like magazines and newspapers. We made a bulletin board with all of the examples."

Task **Have students explain what the percents in the following situations mean.** The point of this discussion is to reveal how much students already know about percents so that you can use this understanding as an anchor for extending their knowledge when that is appropriate. For example, if they already associate 50% with $\frac{1}{2}$ then you can refer to that to help them see that 25% (which seems like it "ought" to be half of 50%) means $\frac{1}{4}$ since $\frac{1}{4}$ is half of $\frac{1}{2}$.

- **We won 50% of our games.**
- **The price is reduced by 25%.**
- **The t-shirt is made of 50% cotton and 50% polyester.**
- **The hot dogs are 100% beef.**

💬 **Talk Math**

❓ Just as fractions refer to a "whole," percents also refer to a "whole." What is the "whole" in each of these situations? 50% of the games refers to the whole number of games played. A price reduction of 25% is 25% of the original price. All the matter used to produce material for the t-shirt is the "whole" in the third situation. All food components used to make that hot dogs is the "whole" in the last situation.

❓ What percent of games were either lost or tied? Since 50% of the games were won, the other 50% (for a total of 100%—the whole) must have either been lost or tied.

Use with Lesson Activity Book pp. 279–280.

B   Understanding the Meaning of Percents

Purpose To understand the meaning of percents

Introduce Review the meaning of percent. Tell students that a percent is a part of 100 and may be written as a fraction with 100 as a denominator. This definition will help students to work with percents by using what they already know about fractions. Have students convert a few fractions with 100 as a denominator into percents to help them understand this definition. For example, $\frac{50}{100}$ is 50% and $\frac{23}{100}$ is 23%.

Problem **If a percent may be written as a fraction with 100 as the denominator, how do we find percent equivalents for fractions with denominators other than 100?**

Call up 5 students to stand and face the class, and ask 3 of them to raise their hands. Ask the class for the fraction that represents the number of students raising their hand? $\frac{3}{5}$ Then ask for suggestions of how to figure out what percent of the students are raising their hand. If no one has an idea, ask if there is a way to change $\frac{3}{5}$ to an equivalent fraction with a denominator of 100. Yes, $\frac{3}{5} = \frac{60}{100}$. Therefore, 60% of the students are raising their hand.

Repeat this activity for other fractions. For each fraction, call up a number (equal to the fraction's denominator) of students and have a number of them (equal to the fraction's numerator) raise their hand. For now, stick with fractions that are easily converted to hundredths. List the original fraction first, then the equivalent fractions that students give until there is one with 100 in the denominator. Then ask for the percent.

$\frac{5}{10}$ 50%	$\frac{1}{4}$ 25%	$\frac{3}{4}$ 75%	$\frac{1}{5}$ 20%	$\frac{3}{10}$ 30%

💬 Talk Math

❓ **What does 125% mean?** Possible answers: It is more than 100% so it must be more than one whole. Since a percent is equivalent to a fraction with a denominator of 100, 125% is equivalent to $\frac{125}{100}$, which is equivalent to $\frac{100}{100} + \frac{25}{100}$, or $1\frac{1}{4}$.

❓ **When might a fraction greater than 100 be used?** Possible answers: If there is extra credit on a test and you get everything right and the extra credit, your score may be greater than 100%. If a factory made more erasers than the previous year, they might achieve 125% of last year's production.

❓ **Would you ever see a shirt for 125% off?** No, because that would be more discounted than the cost of the shirt.

Extend Ask students how they would write a fraction that cannot easily be converted to an equivalent fraction with a denominator of 100 as a percent, such as $\frac{1}{3}$. Ask students if they remember what $\frac{1}{3}$ is as a decimal, or give them a calculator to find the decimal equivalent. Because this decimal repeats forever we can write it as $33\frac{1}{3}$ hundredths or $33\frac{1}{3}$% (or we could approximate it as 33.3%).

Use with Lesson Activity Book pp. 279–280.

Differentiated Instruction

Basic Level/On Level Some students may be unfamiliar with the symbol for percent, %. For clarity, you might just tell them this symbol is read "percent."

Relating Fractions and Percents LAB pp. 279–280

Purpose To convert between fractions, decimals, and percents

NCTM Standards 1, 7, 8, 9

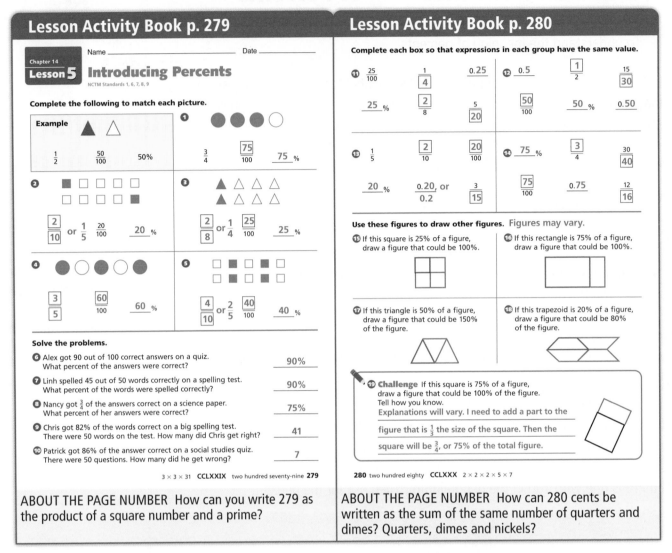

Teaching Notes for LAB page 279

Students match fractions, decimals, and percents to pictures representing fractions of sets. They then solve story problems involving the use of fractions and percents. These problems provide a context familiar to many students—scores on tests and schoolwork written as the percent of correctly completed tasks.

Teaching Notes for LAB page 280

Students write fractions, decimals, and percents with the same values and then use percents in the context of drawing proportional figures. Students may either add on to the figures that are already drawn on the page, or they may draw new figures.

✔ Ongoing Assessment Observe students' facility recognizing and writing equivalent fractions and decimals. Do they recognize that $0.5 = 0.50 = \frac{50}{100} = \frac{1}{2}$?

Challenge Problem Students tell and show how they add on to a figure that represents 75% to show a figure that represents 100%.

D **Playing a Game:** *Matching Quantities*

Purpose To practice converting between fractions, decimals, and percents

Goal The object of the game, *Matching Quantities,* is to collect more cards than your partner.

Prepare the Materials Give each pair of students AM149 and AM150: *Matching Quantities* Cards 1 and 2 and have them cut out the cards, shuffle them, and place them in a stack face down. Each partner should draw 4 cards from the top of the stack and then one player should place 4 cards face up in the middle of the table.

How to Play

❶ The first player looks at his or her cards to see if any of the cards has an expression that is equivalent to an expression on a card on the table.

- If the player has a matching card, the player places the card on top of its match so that the partner can see the match. Then the player takes both cards from the table, puts the cards in a separate stack and draws new cards to replace both the card in their hand and the card on the table that was matched.

- If the player does not have a matching card, he or she puts one of the cards in his or her hand at the bottom of the face down stack on the table and then picks a new card.

❷ When all of the cards in the face down stack are gone, players may still try to match cards on the table with cards in their hand. Play continues until all of the cards in the face down stack are gone and no matches can be made with the cards on the table.

❸ The player with more cards at the end of the game wins.

Extend If students are very comfortable converting between fractions, decimals, and percents, you might allow them to make a match by adding two of their cards. For example, students might match $\frac{1}{4}$ and 50% with the 0.75 card.

Materials
- For each pair:
  AM149–AM150, scissors

NCTM Standards 1

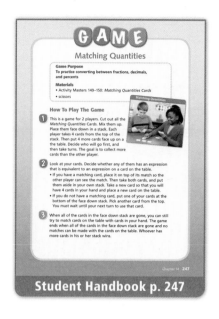

Student Handbook p. 247

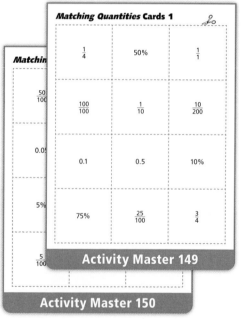

Activity Master 149

Activity Master 150

Reflect and Summarize the Lesson

Write Math

Anthony got 40 out of 50 answers correct on a math quiz. What percent of the answers were correct? Explain how you know. 80%; Possible explanation: 40 of 50 is $\frac{40}{50}$ which is equivalent to $\frac{80}{100}$, and $\frac{80}{100}$ is equivalent to 80%.

Review Model ....

Refer students to Review Model: Understanding Percent in the *Student Handbook* to see how to relate fractions, decimals, and percents.

✔ Check for Understanding

❶ 25%

❷ 60%

❸ 30%

❹ 100%

❺ 92%

❻ 25%

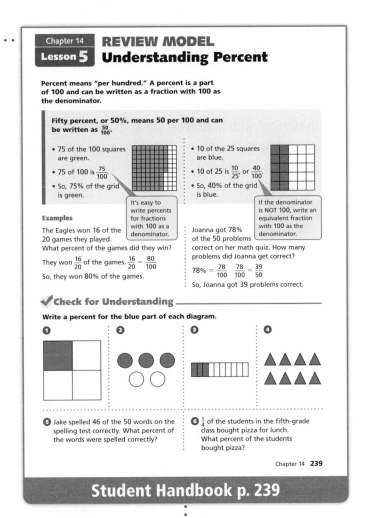

Student Handbook p. 239

Leveled Problem Solving

In a survey about favorite foods, 8 people named pizza as their favorite food.

❶ Basic Level
If 10 people were surveyed, what percent named pizza? Explain.
80%; 8 out of 10 is the same as 80 out of 100.

❷ On Level
If 25 people were surveyed, what percent named pizza? Explain.
32%; 8 out of 25 is the same as 32 out of 100.

❸ Above Level
Exactly 40% of the people surveyed named pizza. How many people were surveyed? Explain.
20 people; 40% is 40 in 100, or 4 in 10, which is the same as 8 in 20 people.

Intervention	Practice	Extension

Intervention

Activity Related Percents

Have students work in pairs to write related percents, such as 1% and 10%, 2% and 20%, 3% and 30%, and so on. Have partners generate related decimals and fractions. Suggest they use a table like this one:

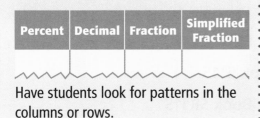

Percent	Decimal	Fraction	Simplified Fraction

Have students look for patterns in the columns or rows.

Practice

Introducing Percents

Make designs by shading in some of the hundredths. Record the fraction and percent for the shaded part of the large square.

Answers will vary.

Answers will vary.

Test Prep
One point is incorrectly labeled on the number line. Which point is it? Explain how you know what the label should be.

$\frac{1}{8}$; Possible explanation: The point should be labeled $\frac{1}{4}$ because it is $\frac{1}{4}$ of the distance between 0 and 1.

Practice P114

Extension

Introducing Percents

Fill in the missing parts of this table.

	50%	25%	10%	75%	5%
1 hour	30 min	15 min	6 min	45 min	3 min
1 yd and 4 in.	20 in.	10 in.	4 in.	30 in.	2 in.
5 dollars	$2.50	$1.25	$0.50	$3.75	$0.25

To solve this one correctly, you may have to think hard about which entries to fill in first.

	10%	40 %	15%	5 %	25 %
$25.00	$2.50	$10.00	$3.75	$1.25	$6.25
1 min	6 sec	24 sec	9 sec	3 sec	15 sec
10 ft	1 ft	4 ft	18 in.	6 in.	2½ ft

Extension E114

Spiral Review

Spiral Review Book page SR114 provides review of the following previously learned skills and concepts:

- selecting and using diagrams to illustrate mathematical relationships
- constructing a line plot for given data and then analyzing the data

You may wish to have students work with partners to complete the page.

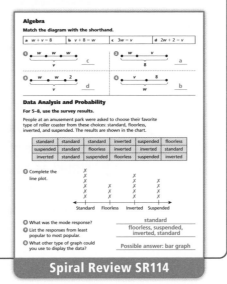

Spiral Review SR114

Extension Activity
Quick Numbers

Have students work in pairs. Have each partner write three different numbers—one as a fraction, one as a decimal, and one as a percent. Then have partners trade papers. Each partner works to be the first to represent each of the three numbers in all three forms (fraction, decimal, percent). The partner who is done first receives 1 point. Repeat until one partner is ahead by 2 points. After students have finished, discuss which numbers were easier or harder to write as percents.

Lesson 6 Circle Graphs

NCTM Standards 1, 5, 6, 7, 8, 9, 10

Lesson Planner

STUDENT OBJECTIVES
- To interpret data in circle graphs
- To construct circle graphs

1 Daily Activities (TG p. 1179)

Open-Ended Problem Solving/Headline Story	Skills Practice and Review— Converting Fractions to Percents and Rounding to the Nearest Hundredth

2 Teach and Practice (TG pp. 1180–1183)

	MATERIALS
Ⓐ **Reading a Circle Graph** (TG p. 1180) Ⓑ **Making a Circle Graph** (TG p. 1181) Ⓒ **Interpreting Circle Graphs** (TG p. 1182)	• TR: Activity Master, AM151 • transparency of AM151 (optional) • rulers • calculators • 📖 LAB pp. 281–282 • 📖 SH pp. 240–241

3 Differentiated Instruction (TG p. 1184)

Leveled Problem Solving (TG p. 1184)	Practice Book P115
Intervention Activity (TG p. 1184)	Extension Book E115
Extension Activity (TG p. 1184)	Spiral Review Book SR115

Lesson Notes

About the Lesson

In this lesson, students use what they learned about percents in the previous lesson to read and construct circle graphs. Students also review the measure of *mode,* or most frequently occurring value in a set of data, and see that there may be more than one mode.

About the Mathematics

Circle graphs, or pie charts, are commonly used to picture data when the mode, or most frequently occurring data value, is important. The mode is easily visible in such a representation, and therefore circle graphs are often used to show the results of a survey or vote. However, while they may be easy to read, circle graphs can be difficult to construct. Data stated as a fraction or percent must be thought of as fraction or percent of a circle and then converted into a number of degrees of angle measure.

Use with Lesson Activity Book pp. 281–282.

Developing Mathematical Language

Vocabulary: sector

Students will likely understand the meaning of the term *sector* when you use it in the context of describing the individual pie-shaped sections of circle graphs.

Familiarize students with the term *sector*.

Beginning Draw a circle on the board, Draw and point out a *sector* of the circle. Then ask students to go to the board and draw other *sectors* of the circle.

Intermediate Ask students to name some things that might be divided into *sectors*. Possible answers: pie, pizza, wheel, window

Advanced Draw a circle showing a *sector* on the board. Ask students to describe the *sector*.

Open-Ended Problem Solving

This Headline Story lends itself to a wide variety of responses, many of which are hardly mathematical. As always, encourage students to focus on the math in the story.

 Headline Story

> Ashlee felt strongly that recess should be held before lunch. How might a survey help her to convince the principal?

Possible responses: She could survey the students at the school to find out the percent of students who prefer recess before lunch. She might survey the teachers or parents as well. She would want a majority of people to agree with her, which would be more than 50%. She would also need to survey enough people for the principal to think the survey reflects the thinking of the school population. She might include students of different grade levels to make her sample more representative of the school population.

Skills Practice and Review

Converting Fractions to Percents and Rounding to the Nearest Hundredth

Materials
• calculator

Each student will need a calculator. List a few fractions on the board or ask students to provide them. Tell them you want to know what percent (rounded to the closest tenth of a percent) the fraction represents. If students are unsure how to figure this out with the calculator, remind them that they can convert the fractions to decimals. If necessary, tell them they can do this by dividing each numerator by its denominator. Since the first three digits to the right of the decimal point tell the number of thousandths, students should round the decimal to the nearest thousandth in order to find the percent.

NCTM Standards 5, 6, 7, 8, 9, 10

A Reading a Circle Graph

Purpose To introduce and interpret a circle graph

Introduce Have students look at Explore: A Circle Graph and ask students if they know what type of graph this is. Most students will have seen a graph like this before, but not all will know that they are called circle or pie graphs. If students seem unfamiliar with this type of graph, you might discuss when these graphs are typically used or look in an almanac or magazine to try to find some examples. These graphs are good for showing the mode of a data set, and are therefore often used to display the results of a survey or vote. (See About the Mathematics.)

Task Have students work individually to complete Explore: A Circle Graph.

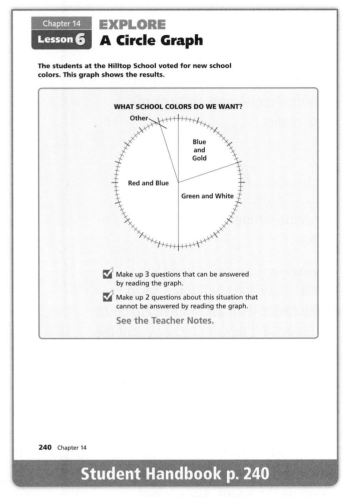

Chapter 14
Lesson 6

EXPLORE
A Circle Graph

The students at the Hilltop School voted for new school colors. This graph shows the results.

WHAT SCHOOL COLORS DO WE WANT?

Other
Blue and Gold
Red and Blue
Green and White

☑ Make up 3 questions that can be answered by reading the graph.

☑ Make up 2 questions about this situation that cannot be answered by reading the graph.

See the Teacher Notes.

240 Chapter 14

Student Handbook p. 240

💬 **Talk Math**

❓ What are some questions that can be answered by the graph, and what are the answers to those questions? Possible questions and answers: Which colors received the most votes? (red and blue) Which option received the fewest votes? (other) Does it appear that an equal number of students voted for red and blue as voted for something else? (No; it appears that fewer voted for red and blue.)

❓ What are some questions that cannot be answered by the graph? Possible questions: How many students voted? How many students voted for red and blue? Did everyone at the school get to vote?

❓ What is the mode response? Red and blue is the mode response.

Share Ask students to think about why the graph is drawn as a circle. Help them to see that each section can show a part, or a fraction, of a whole by taking up that fraction of the whole circle. On this Explore page, the whole is the student population of Hilltop School.

Use with Lesson Activity Book pp. 281–282.

Making a Circle Graph

individuals or whole class

15 MIN

Purpose To construct a circle graph by converting fractions to a percent of a circle

Introduce Give students AM151: School Lunch Favorites, a ruler, and a calculator. Have students read the introduction and ask if they know how many students answered the survey. (If you assume that each person was only allowed to make one choice, then you just sum the number of votes.)

Task **Complete AM151: School Lunch Favorites as a class.** If possible, display AM151 as a transparency and ask students how many small sections the tick marks have divided the circle into. A short thick line indicates every fifth tick mark, and a long thick line indicates every tenth tick mark to make counting 100 sections easier.

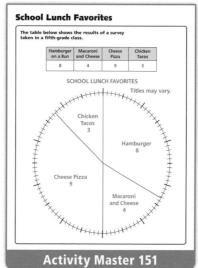

School Lunch Favorites

The table below shows the results of a survey taken in a fifth-grade class.

Hamburger on a Bun	Macaroni and Cheese	Cheese Pizza	Chicken Tacos
8	4	9	3

SCHOOL LUNCH FAVORITES   Titles may vary.

Chicken Tacos 3

Hamburger 8

Cheese Pizza 9

Macaroni and Cheese 4

Activity Master 151

Materials
- For the teacher: transparency of AM151 (optional)
- For each student: AM151, ruler, calculator

NCTM Standards 1, 6, 7, 9, 10

Then ask students for ideas of how to use tick marks on the circle to construct a circle graph of the data in the table. If students don't suggest it, mention writing fractions for the data in the table and converting the fractions to percents so that they can use the tick marks to represent that percent of the circle.

Since the denominator of the data will be 24, students may need to use calculators to convert the fractions to decimals. Once students figure out the percent of the circle to section off, they should draw a line to the center of the circle using a ruler. An initial radius has been drawn so students will only have to draw one line to make each section. Students should complete their graphs by labeling each sector with the appropriate name and number of votes and writing a title for the graph.

For example, 3 out of 24 people voted for chicken tacos, so $\frac{3}{24}$, or $\frac{1}{8}$, of students voted for chicken tacos. As a decimal, this is 0.125, which is 12.5%. Since each tick mark sections off 1% of the circle, students can move 12 and a half spaces away from the initial radius, draw another radius, and label this section "Chicken Tacos."

Differentiated Instruction

Above Level Some students may enjoy taking a survey of their classmates to find out their favorite school subject, favorite sport, or favorite Saturday activity. After compiling the data they can use a blank circle graph at the bottom of a new AM151 to make a circle graph of the data. Have students share their results.

Purpose To interpret data in a circle graph and to translate data into a circle graph

NCTM Standards 1, 5, 6, 7, 8, 9, 10

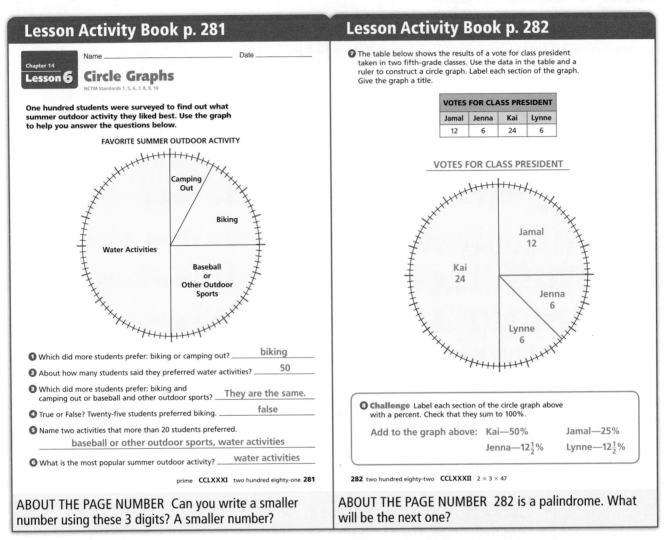

Lesson Activity Book p. 281

Name _____ Date _____

Chapter 14
Lesson 6 **Circle Graphs**
NCTM Standards 1, 5, 6, 7, 8, 9, 10

One hundred students were surveyed to find out what summer outdoor activity they liked best. Use the graph to help you answer the questions below.

FAVORITE SUMMER OUTDOOR ACTIVITY

Camping Out

Biking

Water Activities

Baseball or Other Outdoor Sports

❶ Which did more students prefer: biking or camping out? ____ biking

❷ About how many students said they preferred water activities? ____ 50

❸ Which did more students prefer: biking and camping out or baseball and other outdoor sports? ____ They are the same.

❹ True or False? Twenty-five students preferred biking. ____ false

❺ Name two activities that more than 20 students preferred.
baseball or other outdoor sports, water activities

❻ What is the most popular summer outdoor activity? ____ water activities

prime **CCLXXXI** two hundred eighty-one **281**

ABOUT THE PAGE NUMBER Can you write a smaller number using these 3 digits? A smaller number?

Lesson Activity Book p. 282

❼ The table below shows the results of a vote for class president taken in two fifth-grade classes. Use the data in the table and a ruler to construct a circle graph. Label each section of the graph. Give the graph a title.

VOTES FOR CLASS PRESIDENT			
Jamal	Jenna	Kai	Lynne
12	6	24	6

VOTES FOR CLASS PRESIDENT

Jamal 12

Kai 24

Jenna 6

Lynne 6

❽ **Challenge** Label each section of the circle graph above with a percent. Check that they sum to 100%.

Add to the graph above: Kai—50%   Jamal—25%
Jenna—12½%   Lynne—12½%

282 two hundred eighty-two **CCLXXXII** 2 × 3 × 47

ABOUT THE PAGE NUMBER 282 is a palindrome. What will be the next one?

Teaching Notes for LAB page 281

Students interpret a circle graph to answer questions. They must use information from the introduction and the graph.

For Problem 6, you may want to discuss the fact that the answer to this question is the mode response.

Teaching Notes for LAB page 282

Students need a ruler to construct the sections of a circle graph using data from a table. They finish the graph by appropriately labeling each sector and writing a title.

Challenge Problem This problem asks students to also label each sector of a circle graph with the percent of the circle it covers.

Concept Alert In the challenge, if students write 13% for Jenna and Lynne, they might notice that due to rounding the decimals to the nearest hundredth (percent), the sum of the percents in the graph sum to slightly more than 100.

Write Math

Jennifer surveyed 50 people to find out what fruit they liked best. She made this graph of the results. Which response is the mode? Explain how you can tell. Grapes is the mode response because the section of the graph for grapes is larger than any other section, so more students chose grapes than any other fruit.

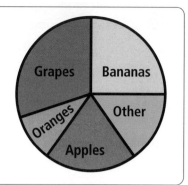

Review Model

Refer students to Review Model: Making Circle Graphs in the **Student Handbook** to see how to use percents to make a circle graph. Students will need a copy of the blank circle graph at the bottom of AM151 to complete this Review Model.

✓Check for Understanding

OUR FAVORITE VACATIONS

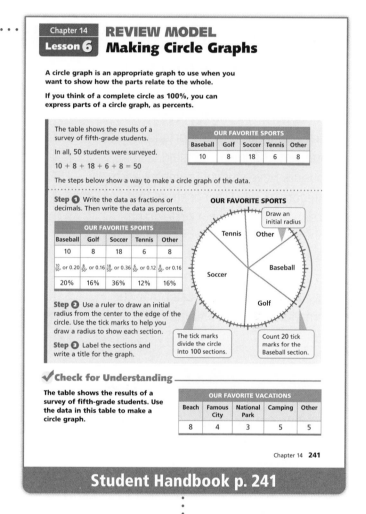

Student Handbook p. 241

Leveled Problem Solving

**Dion is making a circle graph for T-shirts sold on Saturday:
90 red, 150 blue, 36 pink, 9 orange, and 15 green.**

❶ Basic Level

What fraction of the circle
represents the blue T-shirts?
Explain. $\frac{1}{2}$; the total number of
T-shirts sold is 300, and $\frac{150}{300} = \frac{1}{2}$.

❷ On Level

What percent of the circle
represents the green T-shirts?
Explain. 5%; the total is 300,
and $\frac{15}{300} = \frac{5}{100}$.

❸ Above Level

Which color does he label 12%?
Explain. pink; the total is 300,
and $\frac{36}{300} = \frac{12}{100}$.

Intervention

Activity Compare Data to 25%

Draw on the board several circle graphs
for budgets, labeling the sectors with
such categories as transportation,
food, entertainment, clothing, and
housing. Have students compare each
category to 25%. Demonstrate that
to determine 25% on a circle graph,
you can place the corner of a paper at
the center of the circle. If the sector is
less than the corner, then the sector is
less than 25%. If it is greater than the
corner, then it is greater than 25%.

Practice

Circle Graphs

Sixty fifth graders were surveyed to find out their
favorite types of books to read. The results are
summarized in this graph.

❶ Which did more fifth graders prefer
to read about: sports or science?

science

FAVORITE TYPE OF BOOK

❷ True or false? About a third of the fifth
graders chose fiction as their favorite
reading material.

true

❸ About how many fifth graders preferred
to read about sports?

15

❹ About what fraction of the students preferred
reading about sports or history? $\frac{35}{100}$ or $\frac{7}{20}$

Test Prep

❺ Which of the following is NOT equivalent to $\frac{2}{8}$ of 360°?

Ⓐ $\frac{1}{4} \times 90°$ B. 90°   C. $\frac{4}{8} \times 180°$ D. $\frac{1}{4}$ of 360°

❻ Chris made a set of ten cards for multiples of 2 from 2 to 20. He drew one
card at random from the deck. What is the probability that he drew a card
that is a multiple of 3?

A. $\frac{2}{10}$ Ⓑ $\frac{3}{10}$ C. $\frac{4}{10}$ D. $\frac{5}{10}$

Practice P115

Extension

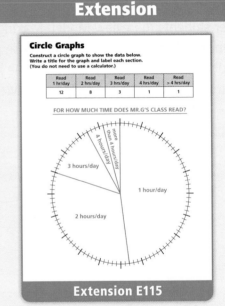

Circle Graphs

Construct a circle graph to show the data below.
Write a title for the graph and label each section.
(You do not need to use a calculator.)

Read 1 hr/day	Read 2 hrs/day	Read 3 hrs/day	Read 4 hrs/day	Read > 4 hrs/day
12	8	3	1	1

FOR HOW MUCH TIME DOES MR.G'S CLASS READ?

Extension E115

Spiral Review

Spiral Review Book page SR115 provides
review of the following previously learned
skills and concepts:

- subtracting decimals
- using formulas to find the areas of
  rectangles and triangles

You may wish to have students work with
partners to complete the page.

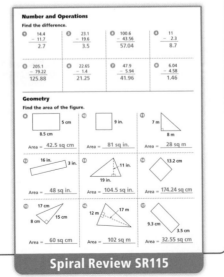

Number and Operations
Find the difference.

❶ 14.4 − 11.7 = 2.7   ❷ 23.1 − 19.6 = 3.5   ❸ 100.6 − 43.56 = 57.04   ❹ 11 − 2.3 = 8.7

❺ 205.1 − 79.22 = 125.88   ❻ 22.65 − 1.4 = 21.25   ❼ 47.9 − 5.94 = 41.96   ❽ 6.04 − 4.58 = 1.46

Geometry
Find the area of the figure.

❾ 5 cm, 8.5 cm   Area = 42.5 sq cm   ❿ 9 in.   Area = 81 in.   ⓫ 7 in., 8 m   Area = 28 sq m

⓬ 16 in., 3 in.   Area = 48 sq in.   ⓭ 11 in., 19 in.   Area = 104.5 sq in.   ⓮ 13.2 cm   Area = 174.24 sq cm

⓯ 17 cm, 8 cm, 15 cm   Area = 60 sq cm   ⓰ 12 m, 17 m   Area = 102 sq m   ⓱ 9.3 cm, 3.5 cm   Area = 32.55 sq cm

Spiral Review SR115

Extension Activity
Budgeting Time

Have students list the things they do
every day, such as sleeping, eating,
and attending school. Then have
them write the amount of time, to the
nearest hour, that they spend in each
activity. Finally, have them make a
circle graph for how they spend each
day. Have students work in pairs to
write a couple of sentences comparing
their graphs.

Use with Lesson Activity Book pp. 281–282.

Teacher's Notes 🍎

Daily Notes . . .

Quick Notes

More Ideas

Lesson 7 Problem Solving Strategy and Test Prep

NCTM Standards 1, 5, 6, 7, 8, 9, 10

Lesson Planner

STUDENT OBJECTIVES
- To practice the problem solving strategy *make a table*
- To articulate the steps and strategies used to solve problems
- To prepare for standardized tests

Problem Solving Strategy: **MATERIALS**
Solve a Simpler Problem (TG pp. 1187–1188, 1190–1191)

Ⓐ **Discussing the Problem Solving Strategy: Make a Table** (TG p. 1187)

Ⓑ **Solving Problems by Applying the Strategy** (TG p. 1188)

-  LAB p. 283
- SH pp. 242–243

 Problem Solving Test Prep (TG p. 1189)

Ⓒ **Getting Ready for Standardized Tests** (TG p. 1189)

- LAB p. 284

Lesson Notes

About Problem Solving

Problem Solving Strategy: Make a Table

In this last lesson of the chapter, students use the problem solving strategy *make a table* to analyze data about the birthdays of students in Mrs. Roger's class.

Students are also assessed on describing and predicting the results of probability experiments, and interpreting circle graphs.

MENTAL MATH Skills Practice and Review

Converting Fractions to Percents

Materials
- calculators

Each student will need a calculator. List a few fractions on the board or ask students to provide them. While students have likely memorized certain fraction/percent equivalences, such as $\frac{1}{2} = 50\%$ and $\frac{1}{4} = 25\%$, practicing with a calculator may help students to become more comfortable with others. If necessary, ask for volunteers to remind the class of the procedure for converting a fraction to a decimal and then rounding to name the percent. You might mention that it is not always necessary to round a percent to a whole number, but that it is a common practice.

Use with Lesson Activity Book pp. 283–284.

Problem Solving Strategy

A Discussing the Problem Solving Strategy: Make a Table

whole class   15 MIN

NCTM Standards 1, 5, 6, 7, 8, 9, 10

Purpose To share strategies for solving problems and focus on the problem solving strategy, *make a table*

Introduce Remind students that throughout this chapter they have been using the strategy *make a table* to help them collect and organize data in probability and sampling experiments.

Record the following problem on the board or on a blank transparency. Ask a volunteer to read the problem. Then have the students begin working on the problem.

Problem The students in Brad's fifth-grade class told their favorite sport to watch on TV. This is what they said:

Dudley - baseball, Carmen - soccer, Lee - gymnastics, Dylan - football, Thomas - baseball, Connor - soccer, Jordan - basketball, Julia - soccer, Ryan - baseball, Albert - soccer, Yolanda - football, Avery - soccer, LeAnn - soccer, Brittney - gymnastics, Rhonda - basketball, Grant - football, Ian - gymnastics, Emma - soccer, Kalista - basketball, Issac - football

Make a table to help you answer this question: What fraction of the class chose soccer?

Share Have students share the strategies for solving the problem. Students may suggest different ways of drawing a table to organize the data.

Talk Math

❓ **How does making a table help you answer the question?** A table helps you organize the data to make it easier to know how many people were surveyed, what sports they mentioned, and how many selected each sport.

❓ **How would you make the table?** Answers will vary. One table is shown.

Basketball	Football	Baseball	Soccer	Gymnastics
|||	||||	|||	~~||||~~ ||	|||

❓ **How many students were surveyed? Tell how you know.** 20 students were surveyed. There are 20 tally marks—one for each vote—in the table.

❓ **What fraction of the class chose soccer?** $\frac{7}{20}$

(B) Solving Problems by Applying the Strategy LAB p. 283

whole class 10 MIN

NCTM Standards 1, 5, 6, 7, 8, 9, 10

Purpose To practice the problem solving strategy, *make a table*

Teaching Notes for LAB page 283

Have students look at the problem on LAB page 283 and, if available, put up a transparency of the page. Give students a few minutes to think about how they will make a table to answer the questions. Then have students share their ideas. Since all four questions ask about the months, making a table which shows the number of students with birthdays in each month will probably be most helpful. You may want to ask questions like these to guide the discussion.

Read to Understand

What do you know from reading the problem? the names of the students in Mrs. Roger's class and their birthdays

What do you need to find out to answer Problem 2? the month with the least number of birthdays.

Plan

How can you solve this problem? You can make a table to organize the data.

How could you make a table? You could make a table of students' birthdays by month and use tally marks to indicate the number of students with birthdays in each month.

Solve

How might you use a table to solve the problem? Look for the month that has the least number of student birthdays. May is the only month with no birthdays, so May has the least number of birthdays.

Check

Look back at the original problem. Does your answer make sense? How do you know?

Allow students to work independently or with a partner to answer the other questions on the page. When most students have completed the page, you might ask a couple of students to explain how they answered the questions.

Lesson Activity Book p. 283

Name ____________ Date ____________

Chapter 14 Lesson 7

Problem Solving Strategy

Make a Table

NCTM Standards 1, 5, 7, 8, 10

Understand Plan Solve Check

This is an alphabetical list of students in Mrs. Roger's class and their birthdays.

Ali	June 20	Kenny	March 20	Nancy	August 5
Carlos	July 7	Kim	April 28	Owen	February 21
Deb	July 1	Laura	August 25	Rosa	April 4
Devin	January 2	Lorenzo	July 17	Sam	November 8
Fran	June 29	Marie	November 12	Trina	September 8
Glenn	March 20	Mimi	September 12	Wayne	October 25
Katherine	March 23	Moses	June 29	William	December 2

1. Make a table that will help you answer these questions.

Use the table you made to answer these questions.

2. Which month has the least number of birthdays? May

3. What fraction of the class has a birthday in July? $\frac{3}{21}$, or $\frac{1}{7}$

4. What fraction of the class has birthdays from January to December? $\frac{21}{21}$

5. What month has the most number of birthdays? March, June, July

Month	Number of Students
Jan	I
Feb	I
Mar	III
Apr	II
May	
Jun	III
Jul	III
Aug	II
Sep	II
Oct	I
Nov	II
Dec	I

Tables styles will vary.

prime CCLXXXIII two hundred eighty-three 283

ABOUT THE PAGE NUMBER You can multiply by 283 by multiplying by 200, 80, and 3.

Reflect and Summarize the Lesson

Write Math

How can using the strategy *make a table* help you solve a problem?
Possible answer: Making a table can help you organize the data in the best way for solving the problem.

C **Getting Ready for Standardized Tests** LAB p. 284

individuals

30 MIN

Purpose To prepare students for standardized tests

NCTM Standards 1, 2, 3, 4, 5, 6, 8

Lesson Activity Book p. 284

Problem Solving Test Prep

Choose the correct answer.

1 Which number makes the inequality true?

831,492 < ■ < 831,501

A. 831,520   C. 831,499
B. 831,502   D. 831,399

2 Which is the only description of the figure that is **not** correct?

A. parallelogram, rhombus
B. quadrilateral, parallelogram
C. quadrilateral, rhombus
D. parallelogram, trapezoid

3 Juice boxes are packed in groups of 3. What is the greatest number of groups that can be made from 583 juice boxes?

A. 193   C. 195
B. 194   D. 196

4 What is the area of the figure?

26 in.   24 in.
32 in.   10 in.

A. 240 sq in.   C. 768 sq in.
B. 260 sq in.   D. 832 sq in.

Show What You Know

Solve each problem. Explain your answer.

5 Ty tossed two 1–6 number cubes. He added the numbers. He started a table to show the probability of each outcome. Copy and complete the table.

Outcome	Probability
2	$\frac{1}{36}$
3	$\frac{2}{36}$
4	$\frac{3}{36}$

5: $\frac{4}{36}$; 6: $\frac{5}{36}$; 7: $\frac{6}{36}$; 8: $\frac{5}{36}$; 9: $\frac{4}{36}$;
10: $\frac{3}{36}$; 11: $\frac{2}{36}$; 12: $\frac{1}{36}$; Possible answer: use an addition table to find the total ways for each sum.

6 Copy and complete the table of all possible outcomes for this experiment: Toss a coin and a 1–6 number cube. Name an event that has a probability of exactly $\frac{1}{4}$.

Outcome	Probability
Heads, 1	$\frac{1}{12}$
Heads, 2	$\frac{1}{12}$
Heads, 3	$\frac{1}{12}$

(H,4), (H,5), (H,6), (T,1), (T,2), (T,3), (T,4), (T,5), (T,6); Possible answers: (Heads, even), (Heads, odd), (Tails, even), (Tails, odd), (Heads, prime)

284 two hundred eighty-four   **CCLXXXIV**   2 × 2 × 71

ABOUT THE PAGE NUMBER 284 is the product of a perfect square and a prime. What are they?

Teaching Notes for LAB page 284

The test items on this page are written in the same style and arranged in the same format as those on many state assessments. The page is cumulative and is designed for students to apply a variety of problem solving strategies including *make a table, use logical reasoning, and write an equation.* Have students share the strategies they use.

The Item Analysis Chart below highlights one of the possible strategies that may be used for each item.

Show What You Know

Written Response

Direct students' attention to Problems 5 and 6. Explain that they must decide how to solve the problems. Then have students write an explanation of how they know their answer is correct. To provide more space for students to communicate their thinking about these problems, you may wish to have them write their responses and explanations on a separate sheet of paper. Use the Scoring Rubric below to evaluate their understanding.

Item Analysis Chart

Item	Strategy
1	Use logical reasoning
2	Write an equation
3	Look for a pattern
4	Write an equation, use a formula
5	Make a table
6	Make a table

Scoring Rubric

2	• Demonstrates complete understanding of the problem and chooses an appropriate strategy to determine the solution
1	• Demonstrates a partial understanding of the problem and chooses a strategy that does not lead to a complete and accurate solution
0	• Demonstrates little understanding of the problem and shows little evidence of using any strategy to determine a solution

Review Model..

Refer students to the Problem Solving Strategy Review Model: Make a Table in the *Student Handbook* pp. 242–243 to review a model of the four steps they can use with problem solving strategy, *make a table.*

Additional problem solving practice is also provided.

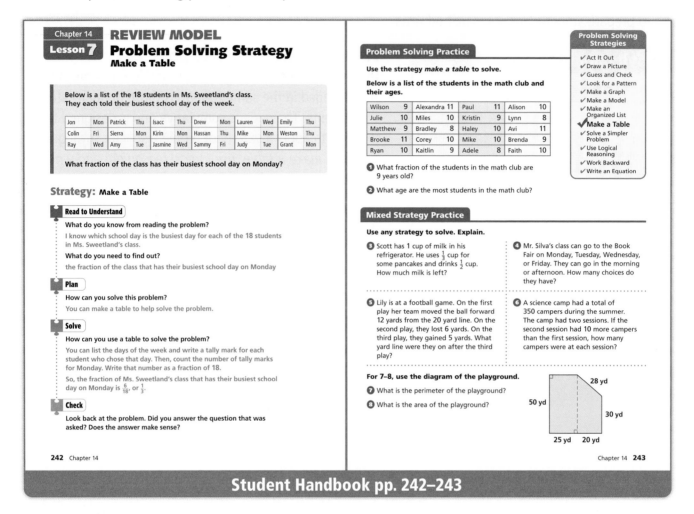

Task Have students read the problem at the top of the Review Model page. Then discuss.

Talk Math

❓ **Why is it helpful to organize the data by day of the week?** That will make it easier to find the number of students whose busiest day is Monday to answer the question.

❓ **What are three other questions you could answer by looking at the table you made?** Questions will vary. Possible questions: What fraction of the class has their busiest school day on Friday (or Tuesday, or Wednesday, or Thursday)? Which is the busiest school day for the most students? What fraction of the class has their busiest school day on Monday or Tuesday?

❶ $\frac{5}{20}$, or $\frac{1}{4}$; Possible explanation: You can use the strategy *make a table*. You can list the ages of the students in the math club (8 through 11) and then make a tally mark for each student who is that age. You can count the number of students who are age 9 and then write that number as a fraction over 20, the total number of students in the math club. The fraction $\frac{5}{20}$ can be simplified to $\frac{1}{4}$.

❷ 10 years old; Possible explanation: You can use the strategy *make a table.* You can use the table you made for Problem 1. Look to see which age has the most tally marks beside it.

❸ $\frac{1}{6}$ cup; Possible explanation: You can *solve a simpler problem* to solve. You can find common denominators for the two fractions and then add them together. $\frac{1}{3} + \frac{1}{2} = \frac{2}{6} + \frac{3}{6} = \frac{5}{6}$. You can then subtract $\frac{5}{6}$ from 1 cup of milk to find that there will be $\frac{1}{6}$ cup left.

❹ 8 choices: Possible explanation: You can use the strategy *make an organized list* to find the 8 choices.

Monday–morning

Monday–afternoon

Tuesday–morning

Tuesday–afternoon

Wednesday–morning

Wednesday–afternoon

Friday–morning

Friday–afternoon

❺ 31-yard line; Possible explanation: You can *draw a picture* to solve. You can draw a number line with the numbers 20 to 35 marked. Move forward and backward as the team moves the ball and see where the ball is after three plays.

❻ 170 for the 1st session, 180 for the 2nd session; Possible explanation: You can use *guess and check* to solve. Guess the number of campers at the first session. Add 10 to that number and find the sum. Then check to see if the sum of the two numbers is 350. Keep guessing and checking until the sum is 350.

❼ 178 yards; Possible explanation: You can *write an equation* to solve. To find the perimeter, you need to add the lengths of all the sides together: $50 + 25 + 20 + 30 + 28 + 25 = 178$.

❽ 2,050 square yards; Possible explanation: You can *solve a simpler problem* to solve. You can split the odd-shaped playground into polygons that have areas you know how to find. You can split the figure into a rectangle, and a trapezoid. Find the area of each polygon and then find the sum of the areas.

Data and Probability

NCTM Standards 1, 2, 5, 6, 7, 9, 10

Purpose To provide students with an opportunity to demonstrate understanding of Chapter 14 concepts and skills

MATERIALS
- LAB pp. 285–286
- Chapter 14 Test
  (Assessment Guide pp. AG117–AG118)

Chapter 14 Learning Goals and Assessment Options

These learning goals are assessed in many ways throughout the chapter. The chart below correlates each learning goal to specific formal and informal assessment options.

	Learning Goals	Lesson Number	Snapshot Assessment	Chapter Review Item Numbers	Chapter Test Item Numbers
			Item Number	LAB pp. 285–286	Assessment Guide pp. AG117–AG118
14-A	Summarize experimental data and use probability to make predictions	14.1, 14.2	1, 5	1–5	1–6
14-B	Use sampling to obtain information about a population	14.3, 14.4	2, 6	6–9	8–10
14-C	Relate percents, fractions, and decimals	14.5	3, 7, 8	10–15	11, 12
14-D	Use percents to interpret and record experiment results with circle graphs	14.6	4, 10	16–17	13–15
14-E	Apply problem solving strategies such as *make a table* to solve problems	14.7	9	18	7

Snapshot Assessment

The following Mental Math and Quick Write questions and tasks provide a quick, informal assessment of students' understanding of Chapter 14 concepts, skills, and problem solving strategies.

whole class 10 MIN

Mental Math This oral assessment uses mental math strategies and can be used with the whole class.

❶ You have a spinner with 6 equal parts; 2 parts are yellow, 1 part is blue, 1 part is red, 1 part is green, and 1 part is orange.
- What are the possible outcomes? yellow, blue, red, green, and orange
- What outcome is most likely to occur? yellow
- State the theoretical probability of spinning yellow as a fraction. $\frac{2}{6}$, or $\frac{1}{3}$
- State the theoretical probability of spinning blue as a fraction. $\frac{1}{6}$

(Learning Goal 14-A)

❷ Forty marbles colored blue, green, yellow, or red are in a brown bag. You do not know how many of each color are inside the bag. You draw only 20 of the marbles and record these results: 10 blue, 5 green, and 5 yellow. What conclusions can you make, based upon the results so far? Answers will vary; may include: there are twice as many blue as green or yellow; it is unlikely to draw red; the actual results are unknown until all marbles have been drawn. Accept all justifiable answers.

(Learning Goal 14-B)

❸ The probability of spinning blue on a spinner is $\frac{3}{4}$. What is the probability

- as a percent? 75%
- as a decimal? 0.75

   (Learning Goal 14-C)

❹ Half of a circle graph is labeled pizza, $\frac{1}{4}$ of the graph is labeled hamburgers, and $\frac{1}{4}$ of the graph is labeled salad bar.

- What percent of those surveyed chose pizza? 50%
- What percent chose salad bar? 25%

   (Learning Goal 14-D)

Quick Write This informal written assessment can be administered to small groups or the whole class. Read each question and have the students record responses on their write-on boards. Encourage students to listen and think about the questions before responding.

❺ Hank plans on tossing a cube, numbered from 1 to 6, 60 times.

- What is the theoretical probability he rolls an odd number on any roll? $\frac{1}{2}$
- What is the theoretical probability he rolls a 2 on any roll? $\frac{1}{6}$
- What is the theoretical probability he rolls a 4 or a 6 on any roll? $\frac{1}{3}$

He rolls the cube 60 times and records the results: 1 is rolled 7 times, 2 is rolled 12 times, 3 is rolled 11 times, 4 is rolled 9 times, 5 is rolled 9 times, and 6 is rolled 12 times. What numbers had experimental probabilities that were greater than their theoretical probabilities? 2, 3, and 6 occurred more often than expected.
(Learning Goal 14-A)

❻ Miss Hamlin's fifth graders wanted to survey the whole fifth grade to find out the favorite after school activity, but decided to take a sample.

Results of the sample were: 5 enjoy reading, 4 played a game, 7 get together with friends, 2 help neighbors, and 2 enjoy getting homework done. Based on the sample, how many out of 100 do you predict will choose reading? Write your answer as a fraction. $\frac{25}{100}$, or $\frac{1}{4}$
(Learning Goal 14-B)

❼ Robert takes a quiz and gets 8 out of 10 questions correct. What percent of the questions did he get correct? Explain how you got your answer. 80%; Possible explanation: $\frac{8}{10} = \frac{80}{100} = 80\%$
(Learning Goal 14-C)

❽ Anna got 42 out of 50 questions correct on a computer game. What percent of the answers were correct? Explain how you know. 84%; Possible explanation: $\frac{42}{50} = \frac{84}{100} = 84\%$

- What decimal shows 84%? 0.84

   (Learning Goal 14-C)

❾ Design a table to show this favorite color data: red, blue, green, green, red, red, blue, yellow, orange, blue, red, red. Answers will vary. Check to see that 5 red, 3 blue, 2 green, 1 yellow, and 1 orange are included, for a total of 12 responses.

- What fraction of the responses were red? How do you know? $\frac{5}{12}$, since 5 out of 12 responses were red
- What fraction were blue? $\frac{3}{12}$, or $\frac{1}{4}$

   (Learning Goal 14-E)

❿ A circle graph reports favorite games in the gym. $\frac{1}{4}$ of the graph is labeled dodgeball, $\frac{1}{4}$ of the graph is labeled line soccer, $\frac{1}{5}$ of the graph is labeled volleyball, and $\frac{3}{10}$ of the graph is labeled basketball.

- Which activity is the most favorite of those included? basketball
- How do you know? $\frac{3}{10}$ is greater than the other fractions in the graph
- Which games were favored equally? dodgeball and line soccer

   (Learning Goal 14-D)

Formal Assessment

Chapter Review/Assessment The Chapter 14 Review/Assessment on *Lesson Activity Book* pages 285–286 assesses students' understanding of data and probability.

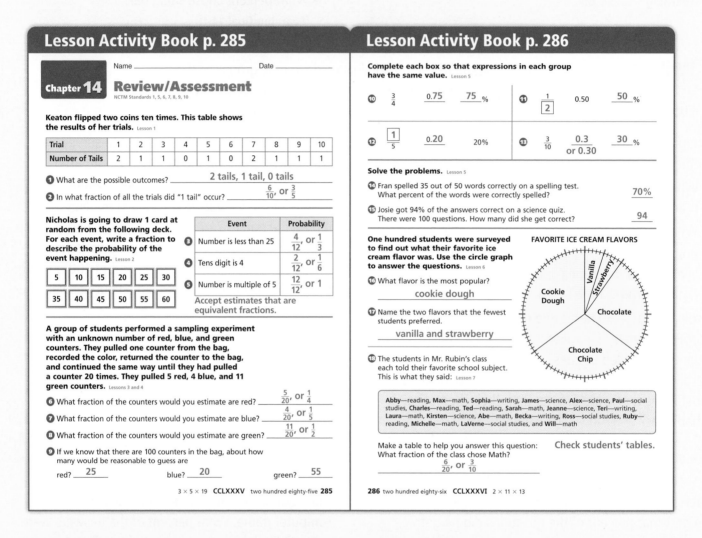

Lesson Activity Book p. 285

Name _____ Date _____

Chapter 14 Review/Assessment
NCTM Standards 1, 5, 6, 7, 8, 9, 10

Keaton flipped two coins ten times. This table shows the results of her trials. Lesson 1

Trial	1	2	3	4	5	6	7	8	9	10
Number of Tails	2	1	1	0	1	0	2	1	1	1

1 What are the possible outcomes? __2 tails, 1 tail, 0 tails__

2 In what fraction of all the trials did "1 tail" occur? $\frac{6}{10}$, or $\frac{3}{5}$

Nicholas is going to draw 1 card at random from the following deck. For each event, write a fraction to describe the probability of the event happening. Lesson 2

| 5 | 10 | 15 | 20 | 25 | 30 |
| 35 | 40 | 45 | 50 | 55 | 60 |

Event	Probability
3 Number is less than 25	$\frac{4}{12}$, or $\frac{1}{3}$
4 Tens digit is 4	$\frac{2}{12}$, or $\frac{1}{6}$
5 Number is multiple of 5	$\frac{12}{12}$, or 1

Accept estimates that are equivalent fractions.

A group of students performed a sampling experiment with an unknown number of red, blue, and green counters. They pulled one counter from the bag, recorded the color, returned the counter to the bag, and continued the same way until they had pulled a counter 20 times. They pulled 5 red, 4 blue, and 11 green counters. Lessons 3 and 4

6 What fraction of the counters would you estimate are red? $\frac{5}{20}$, or $\frac{1}{4}$

7 What fraction of the counters would you estimate are blue? $\frac{4}{20}$, or $\frac{1}{5}$

8 What fraction of the counters would you estimate are green? $\frac{11}{20}$, or $\frac{1}{2}$

9 If we know that there are 100 counters in the bag, about how many would be reasonable to guess are

red? __25__   blue? __20__   green? __55__

3 × 5 × 19 CCLXXXV two hundred eighty-five **285**

Lesson Activity Book p. 286

Complete each box so that expressions in each group have the same value. Lesson 5

10 $\frac{3}{4}$ __0.75__   __75__ %   **11** $\frac{1}{\boxed{2}}$ 0.50   __50__ %

12 $\frac{1}{5}$ __0.20__   20%   **13** $\frac{3}{10}$ 0.3 or 0.30   __30__ %

Solve the problems. Lesson 5

14 Fran spelled 35 out of 50 words correctly on a spelling test. What percent of the words were correctly spelled? __70%__

15 Josie got 94% of the answers correct on a science quiz. There were 100 questions. How many did she get correct? __94__

One hundred students were surveyed to find out what their favorite ice cream flavor was. Use the circle graph to answer the questions. Lesson 6

FAVORITE ICE CREAM FLAVORS

(circle graph: Vanilla, Strawberry, Chocolate, Chocolate Chip, Cookie Dough)

16 What flavor is the most popular?
__cookie dough__

17 Name the two flavors that the fewest students preferred.
__vanilla and strawberry__

18 The students in Mr. Rubin's class each told their favorite school subject. This is what they said: Lesson 7

Abby—reading, Max—math, Sophia—writing, James—science, Alex—science, Paul—social studies, Charles—reading, Ted—reading, Sarah—math, Jeanne—science, Teri—writing, Laura—math, Kirsten—science, Abe—math, Becka—writing, Ross—social studies, Ruby—reading, Michelle—math, LaVerne—social studies, and Will—math

Make a table to help you answer this question: **Check students' tables.**
What fraction of the class chose Math?
$\frac{6}{20}$, or $\frac{3}{10}$

286 two hundred eighty-six CCLXXXVI 2 × 11 × 13

Extra Support Students who have difficulty with items on the Chapter 14 Review/Assessment may need review of the lesson where development of the concept was provided. You can use the Intervention Activity to increase students' understanding before the Chapter Test is given.

Chapter Test Use the Chapter 14 Test in the *Assessment Guide* to assess concepts, skills, and problem solving from the chapter and to prepare students for standardized tests. The Chapter Test and other test items are also available online.

Chapter Notes

Quick Notes

More Ideas

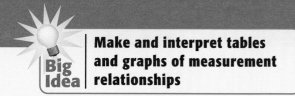

Graphing

About the Chapter

In this chapter, students work on a coordinate grid. They use grids to display data, plotting points that use two numbers, for example—a specified distance and time—as coordinates.

Graphing Relationships "Graphing" on the coordinate plane can show the relationship between two quantities or measures (which can each have various values). Often, these measures can be related by a mathematical rule. For example, the conversion of pints to cups can be expressed as the rule, *number of cups = 2 × number of pints*. To graph this relationship, we can collect some pairs of the same capacities expressed in cups and pints, and use these ordered pairs of numbers as the coordinates for points. If we know that the rule is true for any input (as we know it is in the case of cups and pints) and is a straight line, we can plot two points, connect them, and use the graph to get information about other input/output pairs.

Preparing The Coordinate Grid Setting up the coordinate grid on which a graph appears is an important skill. Students focus on labeling the axes and numbering each axis with an appropriate scale.

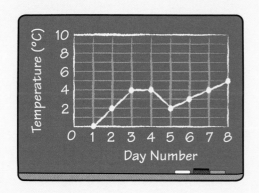

Developing Concepts Across the Grades

Topic	Prior Learning	Learning in Chapter 15	Later Learning
Coordinate Grid	• Identify points on a coordinate grid using ordered pairs of numbers **Grade 4, Chapter 12**	• Graph points on a coordinate grid • Investigate linear graphs using both positive and negative coordinates **Lessons 15.1, 15.2, 15.6**	• Graph linear relationships **Grade 6**
Measurement	• Convert between inches, feet, and yards • Convert between cups, pints, quarts, and gallons **Grade 4, Chapter 9**	• Review and practice conversions between measurement units **Lessons 15.2, 15.3**	• Convert and compare units between systems of measurement **Grade 6**
Functions	• Graph ordered pairs of numbers that are related to a rule **Grade 4, Chapter 12**	• Explore graphs of linear relationships • Make straight-line graphs of proportional relationships **Lessons 15.1, 15.4–15.6**	• Identify linear functions and nonlinear functions **Grade 6**

Chapter Planner

Lesson	Objectives	NCTM Standards	Vocabulary	Materials/Resources

CHAPTER 15 World Almanac For Kids • Vocabulary • Games • Challenge
Teacher Guide pp. 1203A–1203F, Student Handbook pp. 250–251, 258–262

1 Graphing Points

PACING 1 DAY

Teacher Guide
pp. 1204–1211
Lesson Activity Book
pp. 287–288
Student Handbook
Student Letter p. 249
Game p. 260

- To graph points on a coordinate grid
- To relate slope and rate of change

1, 3, 6, 7, 8, 9, 10

slope

rate

For the teacher:
- transparency of AM152 (optional)

For the students:
- School-Home Connection TR: SHC57–SHC58
- TR: AM153
- straightedges
- color pencils
- P116, E116, SR116

Literature Connection:
Natural Wonders of the World: Converting Distance Measurements to Metric Units
Teacher Guide p. 1202

2 Graphing Capacity Conversions

PACING 1 DAY

Teacher Guide
pp. 1212–1219
Lesson Activity Book
pp. 289–290
Student Handbook
Review Model p. 252

- To make straight-line graphs of proportional relationships
- To review the relationships among cups, pints, quarts, and gallons

2, 3, 4, 5, 6, 7, 8, 9, 10

converting measurements

coordinate grid

For the teacher:
- transparencies of AM154–AM155 (optional)
- straightedges

For the students:
- TR: AM155–AM156
- straightedges
- P117, E117, SR117

3 Changing the Scale of Graphs

PACING 1 DAY

Teacher Guide
pp. 1220–1229
Lesson Activity Book
pp. 291–292
Student Handbook
Explore p. 253
Review Model p. 254

- To vary the scale of graphs in order to better display data
- To further explore graphs of linear relationships
- To review and practice conversions between measurement units

2, 3, 4, 5, 6, 7, 8, 9, 10

interval

scale

For the teacher:
- transparency of AM157 (optional)

For the students:
- TR: AM157
- straightedges
- P118, E118, SR118

4 Graphing Change Over Time

PACING 1 DAY

Teacher Guide
pp. 1230–1237
Lesson Activity Book
pp. 293–294
Student Handbook
Explore p. 255

- To understand the proportional relationship between distance and time when the speed is constant

2, 3, 4, 5, 6, 7, 8, 9, 10

miles per hour

speed

For the teacher:
- transparency of AM34 (optional)
- straightedges

For the students:
- P119, E119, SR119

Science Connection:
Animal Speed
Teacher Guide p. 1202

NCTM Standards 2000
1. Number and Operations
2. Algebra
3. Geometry
4. Measurement
5. Data Analysis and Probability
6. Problem Solving
7. Reasoning and Proof
8. Communication
9. Connections
10. Representation

Key
AG: Assessment Guide
E: Extension Book
LAB: Lesson Activity Book
P: Practice Book
SH: Student Handbook
SR: Spiral Review Book
TG: Teacher Guide
TR: Teacher Resource Book

MATH GLOSSARY in **Student Handbook** p. 266

Planner *(continued)*

Chapter Planner *(continued)*

Lesson	Objectives	NCTM Standards	Vocabulary	Materials/ Resources
5 Graphing the Story of a Trip PACING 1 DAY **Teacher Guide** pp. 1238–1245 **Lesson Activity Book** pp. 295–296 **Student Handbook** Game p. 261	• To graph distances traveled over different time intervals • To interpret story problems and graphs about speed, distance, and time	2, 3, 4, 5, 6, 7, 8, 9, 10	constant speed steepness	**For the teacher:** ▪ transparency of AM159 (optional) **For the students:** ▪ TR: AM158, AM160–AM162 ▪ straightedges ▪ color pencils ▪ scissors ▪ P120, E120, SR120
6 Graphing Temperature Conversions PACING 1 DAY **Teacher Guide** pp. 1246–1251 **Lesson Activity Book** pp. 297–298	• To further investigate linear graphs, using both positive and negative coordinates • To review the Celsius and Fahrenheit systems for measuring temperature	1, 2, 3, 7, 8, 9, 10	conversion rule conversion graph	**For the teacher:** ▪ transparency of AM163 (optional) **For the students:** ▪ P121, E121, SR121 **Social Studies Connection: Temperature Extremes Teacher Guide** p. 1202
7 Problem Solving Strategy and Test Prep PACING 1 DAY **Teacher Guide** pp. 1252–1257 **Lesson Activity Book** pp. 299–300 **Student Handbook** Review Model pp. 256–257	• To practice the problem solving strategy *make a table* • To articulate the steps and strategies used to solve problems • To prepare for standardized tests	1, 2, 6, 7, 8, 10		
Chapter 15 Assessment **TG** pp. 1258–1261, **LAB** pp. 301–302, **AG** pp. AG121–AG124				**For the students:** ▪ Chapter 15 Test pp. AG121–AG122

Games

Use the following games for skills practice
and reinforcement of concepts.

Lesson 15.1 ▶

Graphing Tic-Tac-Toe provides an opportunity
for students to recognize when points on a
coordinate grid lie along a straight line.

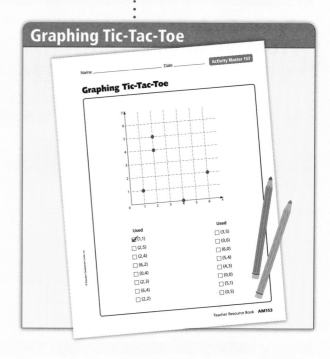

◀ **Lesson 15.5** *The Great Race* provides an
opportunity for students to plot points to show time
and the related distance traveled.

Planning Ahead

In **Lesson 15.1,** students will be playing *Graphing Tic-Tac-Toe.*
Each pair of students will need AM153: *Graphing Tic-Tac-Toe* and
2 color pencils.

For the Review Model in **Lesson 15.2,** students will each need
two copies of AM154: Conversion Graph I to make graphs for the
problems at the bottom of the page.

For the Review Model in **Lesson 15.3,** students will each need
two copies of AM157: Conversion Graph III to make graphs for
the problems at the bottom of the page.

In **Lessons 15.2, 15.3, 15.4,** and **15.5** students will use
straightedges to help them verify that points on a graph lie along
a straight line.

In **Lesson 15.5,** students will be playing *The Great Race.* Each
pair of students will need AM160: *The Great Race* Game Board,
AM161: *The Great Race* Time Card, AM162: *The Great Race*
Distance Cards, 2 color pencils, a straightedge, and scissors.

Developing Problem Solvers

Open-Ended Problem Solving

The Headline Story in the Daily Activities section of every lesson provides an open-ended problem for students to complete. For each story there are many possible responses.

Headline Stories can be found on TG pages 1205, 1213, 1221, 1231, 1239, and 1247.

Headline Story

Leveled Problem Solving

Leveled Problem Solving provides an opportunity for students to apply learning from the lesson to a real-life situation. Problems are leveled by ability to allow students of all ability levels to become successful problem solvers. Each Leveled Problem Solving begins with a real-life scenario upon which three problems are built.

The levels of problems are:

❶ Basic Level	❷ On Level	❸ Above Level
students needing extra support	students working at grade level	students who are ready for more challenging problems

Leveled Problem Solving can be found on TG pages 1210, 1219, 1228, 1237, 1244, and 1251.

THE WORLD ALMANAC FOR KIDS

The World Almanac for Kids feature is designed to stimulate student interest for the math concepts they are about to learn. Students use data to solve problems and explain solutions. The Chapter 15 Project can be found on SH pages 250–251.

Write Math

Reflect and Summarize the Lesson poses a problem or question for students to think and write about. This feature can be found on TG pages 1209, 1218, 1227, 1236, 1243, 1250, and 1254.

Other opportunities to write about math can be found on LAB pages 288, 289, 292, 295, 296, 298, and 300.

Problem Solving Strategies

The focus of **Lesson 15.7** is the strategy *make a table.* However, students will use a variety of problem solving strategies as they work through the chapter. The chart below shows strategies that may be useful in completing each lesson.

Strategy	Lesson(s)	Description
Draw a Picture	15.7	Draw the next picture in a sequence.
Look for a Pattern	15.1, 15.7	Identify a rule for a pattern of squares shown on a graph and predict the number of squares in Picture *N* of a sequence.
Make a Graph	15.1, 15.2, 15.3, 15.4, 15.5, 15.6	Make a straight-line graph to show a constant rate of change, measurement conversions, and to help determine a pattern in a sequence of squares and show distance traveled over different time intervals.
✓ **Make a Table**	15.1, 15.2, 15.3, 15.4, 15.6, 15.7	Show constant relationships between two units including measurement conversions and show relationships among the pictures in a sequence.
Use Logical Reasoning	15.1, 15.2, 15.3, 15.4, 15.5, 15.6, 15.7	Interpret a straight-line graph as showing a constant rate of change; noticing that the steeper the line, the faster the rate of change; determine an appropriate scale for a graph; interpret story problems and graphs about measurement conversions and speed, distance, and time.

Meeting the Needs of All Learners

Differentiated Instruction

Extra Support	On Level	Enrichment
Intervention Activities TG pp. 1210, 1219, 1228, 1237, 1244, 1251	Practice Book pp. P116–P121	Extension Activities TG pp. 1210, 1219, 1228, 1237, 1244, 1251
	Spiral Review Book pp. SR116–SR121	Extension Book pp. E116–E121
	LAB Challenge LAB pp. 288, 290, 292, 294, 296, 298	LAB Challenge LAB pp. 288, 290, 292, 294, 296, 298
Lesson Notes Basic Level TG pp. 1209, 1224, 1232	Lesson Notes On Level TG pp. 1207, 1232	Lesson Notes Above Level TG p. 1207
Leveled Problem Solving Basic Level TG pp. 1210, 1219, 1228, 1237, 1244, 1251	Leveled Problem Solving On Level TG pp. 1210, 1219, 1228, 1237, 1244, 1251	Leveled Problem Solving Above Level TG pp. 1210, 1219, 1228, 1237, 1244, 1251

English Language Learners

Suggestions for addressing the needs of students learning English as a second language are included in the Developing Mathematical Language section at the beginning of most lessons.

ELL activities for this chapter can be found on TG pages 1205, 1213, 1221, 1231, 1239, and 1247.

The Multi-Age Classroom

Grade 4	• Students on this level should be able to complete the lessons in Chapter 15 but might need some additional practice with key concepts and skills. • Give students more practice with graphing on a coordinate grid.	See Grade 5, Intervention Activities, Lessons 15.1–15.6. See Grade 4, Lessons 12.3–12.7.
Grade 5	• Students on this level should be able to complete the lessons in Chapter 15 with minimal adjustments.	See Grade 5, Practice pages P116–P121.
Grade 6	• Students on this level should be able to complete the lessons in Chapter 15 and to extend concepts and skills related to graphing relationships on a coordinate grid. • Give students extended work with linear relationships.	See Grade 5, Extension pages E116–E121.

Cross Curricular Connections

Science Connection

Math Concept: proportional relationship between distance and time when speed is constant

Animal Speed

- Scientists calculate an animal's speed in miles per hour only to compare speeds. Animals do not run for a full hour. Most animals run in bursts to capture prey or to escape attack.

- Draw this table on the board. Tell students: Suppose a lion ran 220 feet in 3 seconds. 220 feet is $\frac{1}{24}$ mile.

Have students complete the table to find the lion's speed in miles per hour.

Distance (in miles)	$\frac{1}{24}$	$\frac{10}{24}$ or $\frac{5}{12}$	$\frac{10}{12}$ or $\frac{5}{6}$	50
Time	3 sec	30 sec ($\frac{1}{2}$ min)	60 sec (1 min)	60 min (1 hr)

Answer: 50 miles per hour

Lesson 15.4

Social Studies Connection

Math Concept: convert between Fahrenheit and Celsius temperatures

Temperature Extremes

- Tell students that temperatures are affected by a combination of airflow, conditions within the atmosphere, how close or far the land is from the equator or water, and the elevation of the land.

- Temperature also may determine the way people dress. If low temperatures are common, people may dress in heavy clothing. If high temperatures are common, people may dress in light clothing.

- Show students this table of some state temperature extremes and locate the states on a map.

Temperature Extreames (in °F)		
State	High	Low
Alaska	100	⁻80
Idaho	118	⁻60
Maine	105	⁻48

- Have students determine the range between high and low temperatures in °C for Alaska and Maine. Alaska: 100°C; Maine: 85°C

- Have students find the difference in high temperatures in °C between Alaska and Idaho. 10°C

Lesson 15.6

Literature Connection

Math Concept: converting distances

Natural Wonders of the World: Converting Distance Measurements to Metric Units
By Kerri O'Donnell

This book teaches students about converting between English standard and metric units. The use of natural wonders as the source for the measurements, provides an real life context for the math that is being taught.

Lesson 15.1

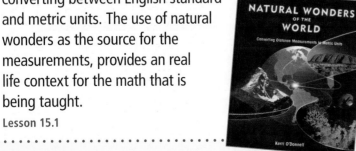

School-Home Connection

A reproducible copy of the School-Home Connection letter in English and in Spanish can be found in the Teacher Resource Book page SHC57–SHC60.

Encourage students to play *Travel Far,* found on the School-Home Connection page, with a family member. Students will work with graphs of distance over time in **Lessons 15.5** and **15.6**.

Assessment Options

There are many opportunities in *Think Math!* to assess students' understanding of concepts, skills, and problem solving. Learning Goals for Chapter 15 are provided below. The assessment options provide opportunities to evaluate whether or not students have retained learning from prior experiences. Choose the forms of assessment that best meet the needs of your students.

Chapter 15 Learning Goals

	Learning Goals	Lesson Number
15-A	Make and interpret tables and straight-line graphs of proportional measurement relationships, using both positive and negative coordinates	15.1–15.4, 15.6
15-B	Label the axes of a grid using a scale appropriate for the data to be graphed	15.3
15-C	Make and interpret graphs that show measurement units that change over time	15.1, 15.5
15-D	Apply problem solving strategies such as *make a table* to solve problems	15.7

✔ Informal Assessment

Ongoing Assessment
Provides insight into students' thinking to guide instruction (TG pp. 1209, 1214, 1225, 1236)

Reflect and Summarize the Lesson
Checks understanding of lesson concepts (TG pp. 1209, 1218, 1227, 1236, 1243, 1250, and 1254)

Snapshot Assessment
Mental Math and **Quick Write**
Offers a quick observation of students' progress on chapter concepts and skills (TG pp. 1258–1259)

Performance Assessment
Provides quarterly assessment of Chapters 12–15 concepts using real-life situations
Assessment Guide
pp. AG225–AG230

✔ Formal Assessment

Standardized Test Prep
Problem Solving Test Prep
Prepares students for standardized tests
Lesson Activity Book p. 300 (TG p. 1255)

Chapter 15 Review/Assessment
Reviews and assesses students' understanding of the chapter concepts and skills
Lesson Activity Book pp. 301–302 (TG p. 1260)

Chapter 15 Test
Assesses the chapter concepts and skills
Assessment Guide
Form A pp. AG121–AG122
Form B pp. AG123–AG124

Benchmark 4 Assessment
Provides quarterly assessment of Chapters 12–15 concepts and skills
Assessment Guide
Benchmark 4A pp. AG125–AG132
Benchmark 4B pp. AG133–AG140

World Almanac for Kids

Use the World Almanac for Kids feature, *Indy 500: Vroom!*, found on pp. 250–251 of the **Student Handbook,** to provide students with an opportunity to practice using their problem solving skills by solving real world problems.

FACT • ACTIVITY 1

❶ 200 miles

❷ 2 hours; $2\frac{1}{2}$ hours

❸ 100 miles; 300 miles

❹ Check student's graph.

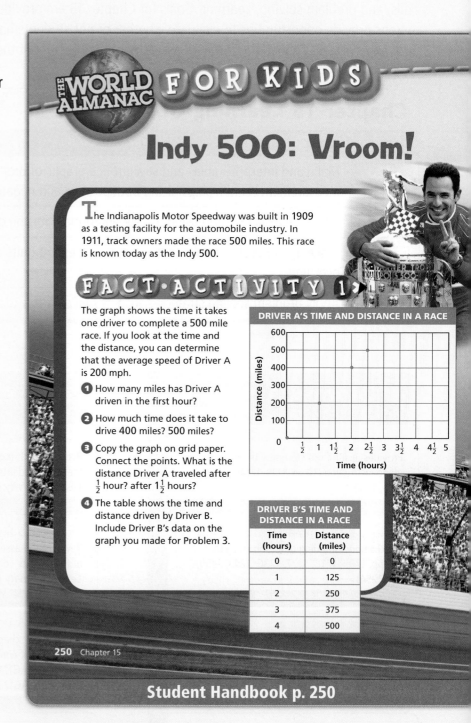

THE WORLD ALMANAC FOR KIDS

Indy 500: Vroom!

The Indianapolis Motor Speedway was built in 1909 as a testing facility for the automobile industry. In 1911, track owners made the race 500 miles. This race is known today as the Indy 500.

FACT • ACTIVITY 1

The graph shows the time it takes one driver to complete a 500 mile race. If you look at the time and the distance, you can determine that the average speed of Driver A is 200 mph.

❶ How many miles has Driver A driven in the first hour?

❷ How much time does it take to drive 400 miles? 500 miles?

❸ Copy the graph on grid paper. Connect the points. What is the distance Driver A traveled after $\frac{1}{2}$ hour? after $1\frac{1}{2}$ hours?

❹ The table shows the time and distance driven by Driver B. Include Driver B's data on the graph you made for Problem 3.

DRIVER A'S TIME AND DISTANCE IN A RACE

DRIVER B'S TIME AND DISTANCE IN A RACE	
Time (hours)	Distance (miles)
0	0
1	125
2	250
3	375
4	500

250 Chapter 15

Student Handbook p. 250

FACT·ACTIVITY 2

The drivers in a race do not drive at a constant speed. In a long race like the Indy 500, drivers usually stop for 1 to 3 "pit stops" for refueling, repairs, and tire changes.

Use the Race Story graph for 1–4.

❶ How long does it take the driver to finish the race?

❷ The driver went ■ miles in the first 60 minutes, so his speed was ■ miles per hour.

❸ When did the driver make pit stops? How can you tell from the graph?

❹ Between the first and second pit stops, the driver drove ■ miles in ■ minutes. Did he drive faster or slower than he did in the first part of the race? Explain.

RACE STORY

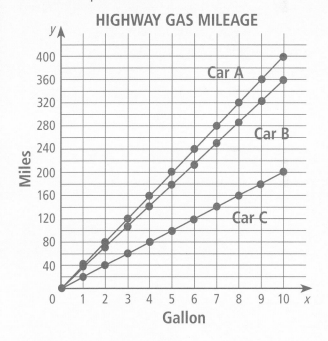

CHAPTER PROJECT

Research three different kinds of cars. Find each car's gas mileage for highway and city driving, and its fuel tank capacity. The gas mileage is the average number of miles the vehicle travels on a gallon of gas. The higher the gas mileage, the less you will spend on gas.

- Compare the gas mileage of the cars you chose. Draw a graph to display the results! Use 10 data points. You may put all three cars on the same graph.

ALMANAC Fact

The winner of the 2006 Indy 500 race reached a speed of 221 miles per hour. After crossing the finish line, the winner drove the car down Victory Lane and drank a glass of milk!

Student Handbook p. 251

FACT·ACTIVITY 2

❶ 200 minutes

❷ 170, 170

❸ Between 60 and 70 minutes and between 130 and 140 minutes; you can tell because the points indicating the distance traveled do not increase during these times.

❹ 150; 60; slower; the driver's speed in the first part of the race was 170 mph.

CHAPTER PROJECT

Possible Response:

HIGHWAY GAS MILEAGE

Vocabulary

To reinforce vocabulary concepts, invite students to complete the vocabulary activities on pp. 258–259 of the *Student Handbook.* Encourage students to record their answers in their math journals.

Many responses are possible.

12 Possible response: The points are on a line if the rates between pairs of points are the same, that is, if the y value changes the same way for the same change in x. For example, if the difference in the x values from point 1 to point 2 is 4, and the different in the x values from point 2 to point 3 is 8, then the difference in the y values from point 2 to point 3 needs be twice the difference in the y values from point 1 to point 2.

13 The conversion rate from Fahrenheit to Celsius is constant. For every 9 degrees of change in Fahrenheit temperature, the Celsius temperature changes by 5 degrees. For example, if the change in temperature is 36°F, $36 \div 9 = 4$ and $4 \times 5 = 20$, so the change is 20°C. The conversion rule for temperature changes, from °F to °C, is "Divide by 9, and multiply by 5."

Chapter 15 Vocabulary

Choose the best vocabulary term from Word List A for each sentence.

1 How one quantity changes in comparison to the change of another quantity is called ___?___. **rate**

2 The incline of a graphed line with respect to the axes is its ___?___. **steepness**

3 The difference between one number and the next on the scale of a graph is a(n) ___?___. **interval**

4 A common rate that compares distance over time is ___?___. **miles per hour**

5 The numbers placed at fixed distances on the axes of a graph form the ___?___. **scale**

6 The distance an object travels divided by the time it takes to travel the distance is the ___?___. **speed**

7 The operation or operations needed to convert one unit to another related unit is called a(n) ___?___. **conversion rule**

8 A diagram that shows the relationship between two measures is called a(n) ___?___. **conversion graph**

9 Changing kilograms to pounds is called ___?___. **converting measurements**

Word List A

conversion graph
conversion rule
converting measurements
coordinate grid
interval
miles per hour
rate
scale
slope
speed
steepness

Complete each analogy using the best term from Word List B.

10 Latitude and longitude are to a map as horizontal and vertical lines are to a ___?___. **coordinate grid**

11 Inches is to length as miles per hour is to ___?___. **speed**

Word List B

coordinate grid
interval
scale
slope
speed

💬 Talk Math

Discuss with a partner what you have learned about tables and graphs of measurement relationships. Use the vocabulary terms *conversion rule* and *rate*.

12 How can you tell whether the graph of three or more points will lie along a straight line?

13 Suppose you know how much the temperature has changed in degrees Fahrenheit. How can you find out how much it changed in degrees Celsius?

258 Chapter 15

Student Handbook p. 258

Word Definition Map

14 Create a word definition map for the term *coordinate grid.*

A What is it?

B What is it like?

C What are some examples?

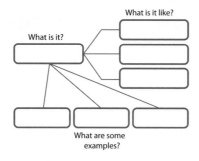

What is it?

What is it like?

What are some examples?

Degrees of Meaning Grid

15 Create a degrees of meaning grid using the terms *conversion rule* and *rate.* Use what you know and what you have learned about comparing units.

General	Less General	Specific	More Specific

What's in a Word?

SCALE In math, *scale* refers to the numbers set at fixed distances that label a graph. In music, a *scale* is a group of tones that go up or down in pitch with each tone relating to the others in a specific way. In daily life, a *scale* is a machine that measures the weight of something. A climber *scales* a cliff.

Scale has to do with intervals. A graph *scale* has intervals depending on what it measures. The tones in a musical *scale* are set at definite intervals. A weight *scale* has intervals in pounds or grams. A climber moves hands and feet at intervals in order to go forward.

Chapter 15   **259**

---

15 Many answers are possible. One example is provided.

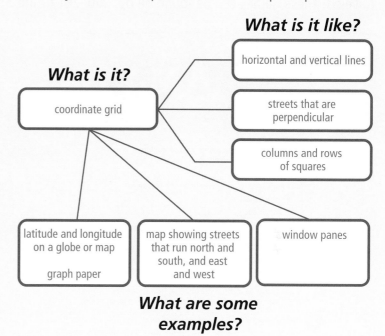

What is it like?

horizontal and vertical lines

streets that are perpendicular

columns and rows of squares

What is it?

coordinate grid

latitude and longitude on a globe or map

graph paper

map showing streets that run north and south, and east and west

window panes

What are some examples?

14 Many answers are possible. One example is provided.

General	Less General	Specific	More Specific
Conversion rule	Converting measurements	Quarts to gallons	8 quarts = 2 gallons
Rate	Speed	Miles per hour	8 miles per hour

Graphing Tic-Tac-Toe in **Lesson 15.1** provides an opportunity for students to recognize when points on a coordinate grid lie along a straight line. *The Great Race* in **Lesson 15.5** provides an opportunity for students to plot points to show time and the related distance traveled. These games can be found on pp. 260–261 of the ***Student Handbook.***

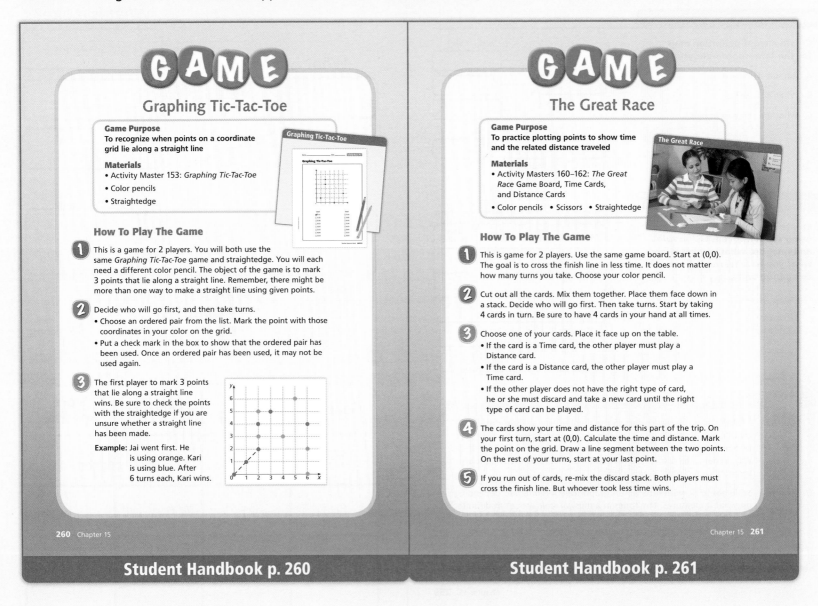

Challenge

The Challenge activity *Lots of Conversions* challenges students to complete measurement conversion tables, draw graphs to show the conversions, and then use the tables and graphs to answer questions. This activity can be found on p. 262 of the *Student Handbook.*

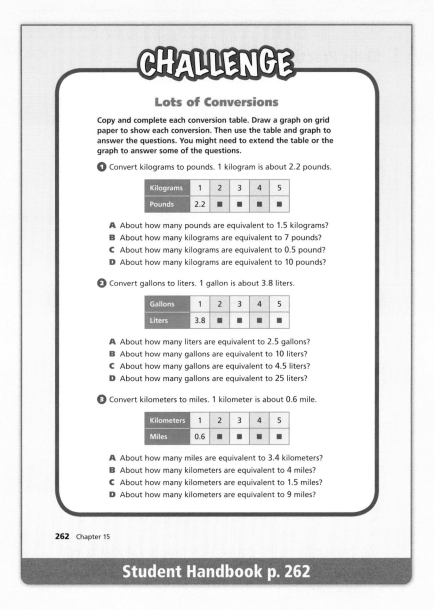

CHALLENGE

Lots of Conversions

Copy and complete each conversion table. Draw a graph on grid paper to show each conversion. Then use the table and graph to answer the questions. You might need to extend the table or the graph to answer some of the questions.

❶ Convert kilograms to pounds. 1 kilogram is about 2.2 pounds.

Kilograms	1	2	3	4	5
Pounds	2.2	■	■	■	■

  A About how many pounds are equivalent to 1.5 kilograms?
  B About how many kilograms are equivalent to 7 pounds?
  C About how many kilograms are equivalent to 0.5 pound?
  D About how many kilograms are equivalent to 10 pounds?

❷ Convert gallons to liters. 1 gallon is about 3.8 liters.

Gallons	1	2	3	4	5
Liters	3.8	■	■	■	■

  A About how many liters are equivalent to 2.5 gallons?
  B About how many gallons are equivalent to 10 liters?
  C About how many gallons are equivalent to 4.5 liters?
  D About how many gallons are equivalent to 25 liters?

❸ Convert kilometers to miles. 1 kilometer is about 0.6 mile.

Kilometers	1	2	3	4	5
Miles	0.6	■	■	■	■

  A About how many miles are equivalent to 3.4 kilometers?
  B About how many kilometers are equivalent to 4 miles?
  C About how many kilometers are equivalent to 1.5 miles?
  D About how many kilometers are equivalent to 9 miles?

262 Chapter 15

Student Handbook p. 262

❶ 4.4; 6.6; 8.8; 11; check students' graphs.

- about 3.3 lb
- about 3.2 kg
- about 0.2 kg
- about 4.5 kg

❷ 7.6; 11.4; 15.2; 19; check students' graphs.

- about 9.5 L
- about 2.6 gal
- about 1.2 gal
- about 6.6 gal

❸ 1.2; 1.8; 2.4; 3; check students' graphs.

- about 2 mi
- about 6.6 km
- about 2.5 km
- about 15 km

Lesson Planner

- To graph points on a coordinate grid
- To relate slope and rate of change

1 | Daily Activities (TG p. 1205)

Open-Ended Problem Solving/Headline Story	Skills Practice and Review— Converting Between Measurement Units

2 | Teach and Practice (TG pp. 1206–1209)

MATERIALS

Ⓐ **Reading the Student Letter** (TG p. 1206)

Ⓑ **Graphing Temperatures** (TG p. 1207)

Ⓒ **Playing a Game:** *Graphing Tic-Tac-Toe* (TG p. 1208)

Ⓓ **Graphing to Solve Problems** (TG p. 1209)

- TR: Activity Master, AM153
- transparency of AM152 (optional)
- straightedges
- color pencils
- 📖 LAB pp. 287–288
- 📖 SH pp. 249, 260

3 | Differentiated Instruction (TG p. 1210)

Leveled Problem Solving (TG p. 1210)	Practice Book P116
Intervention Activity (TG p. 1210)	Extension Book E116
Extension Activity (TG p. 1210)	Spiral Review Book SR116
Literature Connection (TG p. 1202)	

Lesson Notes

About the Lesson

Students study graphing in this chapter. They begin by plotting and finding points on coordinate grids in the context of temperature. They examine changes in temperature over time and note that when the temperature changes the same amount in the same amount of time, the points that indicate these temperatures lie along the same straight line. This idea will help students in upcoming lessons when they make conversion graphs, interpreting the straight line these graphs have as a constant relationship between the two units in the conversion graph. (Students will explore this idea further in later grades when they study functions.)

About the Mathematics

Students see that straight-line graphs mean constant rates of change. They also notice that the steeper the line, the faster the rate of change. In future lessons students will examine speed and will use this idea to determine when a person traveled the fastest.

Use with Lesson Activity Book pp. 287–288.

Developing Mathematical Language

Vocabulary: slope, rate

Students are likely familiar with these words from contexts outside of math class. Since the everyday meanings of these terms are very close to their mathematical meaning, use students' familiarity with these terms (e.g., the *slope* of a hill or the *rate* charged for mowing lawns) to help them understand the terms. The *slope* of a line is the line's incline with respect to the axes. A larger *slope* describes a steeper incline. *Rate* shows how a quantity changes in comparison to the change of another quantity. Speed is an example of a *rate* because it describes the change in distance over a certain change in time.

Familiarize students with the terms *slope* and *rate.*

Beginning Hold your forearm horizontally in front of you. Ask students to mirror you as you demonstrate changing the *slope* of your forearm from no *slope,* or completely flat, to a steep *slope.*

Intermediate Have students draw two hills on paper, one with a steep *slope* and one with a gentle *slope.*

Advanced Ask students what *rate* they would charge for any odd jobs they are capable of doing.

Open-Ended Problem Solving

You might use the Internet to look up average temperatures and extend this Headline Story. Students might consider the difference between the hottest and coldest temperatures on Mount Everest, for example.

 Headline Story

Susan claims that the average temperature decreases by 3°F for every 2,000 feet of elevation on Mount Everest. If she were correct, what would be the temperature at 29,000 feet if the temperature at the base camp at 17,000 feet is ____ °F.

Possible responses: If the base camp was 50°F, 29,000 feet would be 32°F. If the temperature at base camp was 0°F, the temperature at 29,000 feet would be ⁻18°F. There would be a difference of 18°F between base camp and 29,000 feet. The temperature at 21,000 feet would be 6°F less than at base camp.

Skills Practice and Review

Converting Between Measurement Units

Name a pair of related measurement units, such as feet and yards, cups and quarts, or ounces and pounds. Give an amount in one unit (such as 12 feet) and ask a student to tell you the equivalent amount in the other unit (in this case, 4 yards). Make sure to include some fractions (for example, $7\frac{1}{2}$ feet = $2\frac{1}{2}$ yards). If students are not sure about the conversion, ask someone to remind the class how many feet are in one yard. 3 Go through several examples, sometimes giving one unit and sometimes the other. You might make an input/output table and have students fill in either the output or the input.

whole class 5 MIN

NCTM Standards 3, 7, 8, 9

Ⓐ Reading the Student Letter

Purpose To introduce the content of the chapter

Introduce The Student Letter is designed to spur interest and curiosity. Have students read and discuss the letter. Ask students for the coordinates of Point C (5,3) to see how much they remember about finding and naming points on the coordinate grid. If necessary, remind them that the first coordinate refers to the horizontal distance from the vertical axis while the second coordinate refers to the vertical distance from the horizontal axis.

Share Have students share their thoughts about which point shows Sam's location after 1 second of walking 4 feet per second. (Point B because its coordinates indicate that 1 second of time has elapsed since Sam started moving and 4 feet of distance has been traveled.)

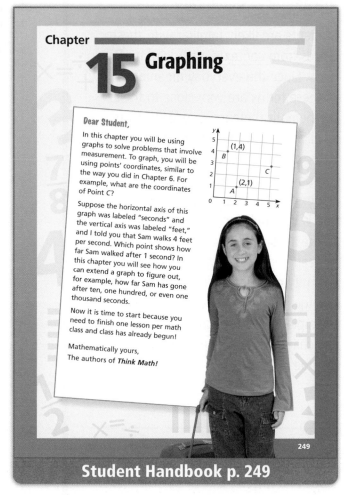

Student Handbook p. 249

Chapter

15 Graphing

Dear Student,

In this chapter you will be using graphs to solve problems that involve measurement. To graph, you will be using points' coordinates, similar to the way you did in Chapter 6. For example, what are the coordinates of Point C?

Suppose the horizontal axis of this graph was labeled "seconds" and the vertical axis was labeled "feet," and I told you that Sam walks 4 feet per second. Which point shows how far Sam walked after 1 second? In this chapter you will see how you can extend a graph to figure out, for example, how far Sam has gone after ten, one hundred, or even one thousand seconds.

Now it is time to start because you need to finish one lesson per math class and class has already begun!

Mathematically yours,
The authors of *Think Math!*

249

💬 Talk Math

❓ If Sam continues walking 4 feet per second, what would his coordinates be after 2 seconds? (2,8) because in 2 seconds he would have traveled 8 feet

❓ Suppose Sam only walked $\frac{1}{2}$ foot per second. What would be his coordinates after 1 second of walking? after 2 seconds of walking?
After 1 second of walking his coordinates would be $(1,\frac{1}{2})$ because he would have walked a half-foot in 1 second. After 2 seconds his coordinates would be (2,1).

B **Graphing Temperatures**

Purpose To practice graphing changes in temperature over time, and to recognize when change is constant by looking at a graph

Introduce Display AM152: Temperature Graph or sketch a similar grid on the board. Tell students that you will say the temperature on each day at 1 P.M. and that you want a volunteer to plot the corresponding point on the graph. Make sure to give temperatures so that once several points are on the graph you can connect the points with a straightedge. For example, you might say that on Day 1 the temperature is 0°C at 1 P.M., on Day 2 it's 2°C, on day 3 it's 4°C and that the temperature didn't change between Days 3 and 4. After recording temperatures for 8 days, you're graph might look like this:

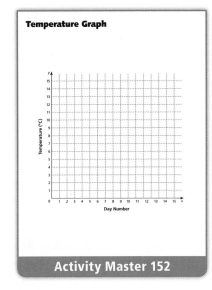

Temperature Graph

Activity Master 152

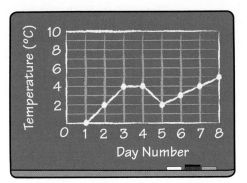

💬 **Talk Math**

❷ How did the temperature change between Days 1 and 2? between days 2 and 3? If you used the temperatures given above, the temperature increased 2°C between Days 1 and 2 and between Days 2 and 3.

Tell students that when the temperature changes by the same amount over the same period of time (as it did between Days 1 and 3), the change is constant. Point out that a straight line is formed by a constant change in one quantity (in this case temperature) over a constant change in another quantity (in this case time).

❷ Where else in the graph was there a constant change in temperature? If you used the temperatures given above, there was a constant increase in temperature from Day 1 to Day 3 and from Day 5 to Day 8 and a constant decrease between Day 4 and Day 5.

❷ What does the horizontal line between Days 3 and 4 indicate? A horizontal line indicates that there was no change in temperature over that time period.

❷ Did the temperature decrease between any of the days? Yes, the temperature decreased between Days 4 and 5.

❷ Did the temperature change faster between Days 1 and 3 or between Days 5 and 7? The temperature changed by 2°C each day between Days 1 and 3, but only by 1°C each day between Days 5 and 7, so the change was faster between Days 1 and 3.

Differentiated Instruction

On Level/Above Level Ask a volunteer to name a starting temperature for Day 1 and then have students name and plot points on the graph for

• possible temperatures between Days 1, 2, 3, and 4 that show a constant increase in temperature;

• a possible temperature for Day 5 that shows no change in temperature between Days 4 and 5, and

• possible temperatures between Days 5, 6, and 7 that show a constant decrease in temperature.

Practice Repeat this activity with new temperatures, this time using Fahrenheit instead of Celsius. You might sketch a new grid whose temperature scale begins around 60°F.

Materials

Concept Alert

Students may notice that straight lines are the results of moving a consistent number of spaces horizontally and a consistent number of spaces vertically between points on the line. Therefore, students can check that the points form a straight line even without a straightedge: by seeing if the number of horizontal spaces between the first and second points is the same as between the second and third points, and the number of vertical spaces between the first and second points is the same as between the second and third points.

C Playing a Game: *Graphing Tic-Tac-Toe*

Purpose To recognize when points on a coordinate grid lie along a straight line

Goal The object of the game, *Graphing Tic-Tac-Toe,* is to mark 3 points that lie along a straight line

Prepare the Materials Give each pair of students AM153: *Graphing Tic-Tac-Toe* and 2 color pencils. Explain that the goal of the game is to make a straight line using at least 3 points, and that there are many ways of making straight lines using the given points.

How to Play

❶ Students take turns choosing an ordered pair and marking a point on the grid with those coordinates. Each player marks their points with a different color. After an ordered pair has been selected, that player should put a check mark in the box beside it to indicate that it's no longer available.

❷ Play continues until one of the players has marked 3 points that lie along a straight line. If the players are unsure whether or not a straight line is formed, they can use a straightedge to check.

❸ The first player to mark three points that are on a straight line wins.

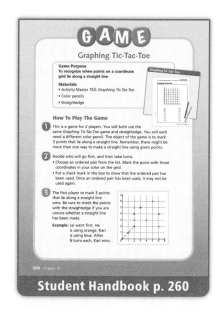

Student Handbook p. 260

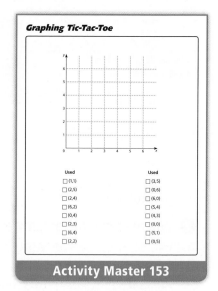

Activity Master 153

Purpose To practice making and interpreting graphs

NCTM Standards 1, 3, 6, 7, 8, 9, 10

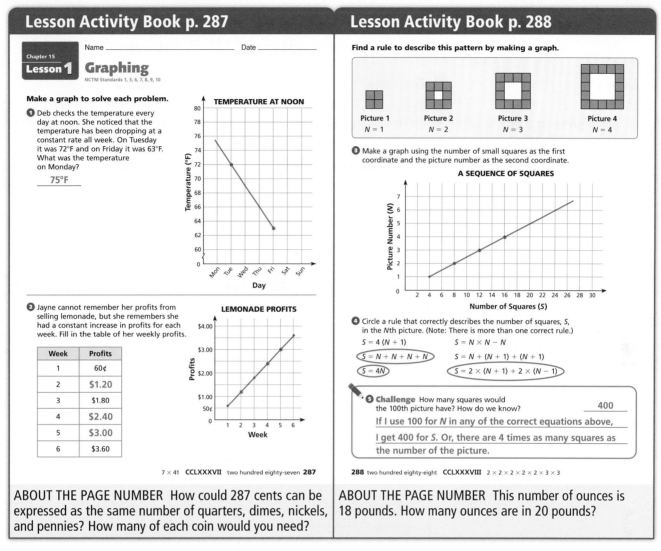

Teaching Notes for LAB page 287

Students graph temperature in one problem, and profit in the other. Each of these graphs show constant change, and students may decide to connect the points to show straight lines.

Differentiated Instruction Basic Level If students struggle with Problem 2, you might help by reminding them that a constant change results in a straight line on a graph. Then have them find the profit for Week 2 on the graph by connecting the points indicating the profits for Weeks 1 and 3 to form a straight line. Once they've found the profit for Week 2, it should be clear that the profits increase by 60¢ each week.

Teaching Notes for LAB page 288

Students use a graph to figure out a pattern. Graphing the number of squares for each successive picture helps students to see that there are 4 more squares in each successive unit in the pattern. Be sure students understand what the "Nth picture" means.

✓**Ongoing Assessment** The rules for the pattern are describing using equations with variables. This allows students to review some of the algebraic ideas they studied in **Chapter 13.**

Challenge Problem Students use a rule that describes the pattern to predict the number of squares in its 100th unit.

Reflect and Summarize the Lesson

Write Math **Taryn made a line graph to show the temperature at noon on Days 1–5. She labeled the horizontal axis with the days and the vertical axis with the temperatures. From Day 1 to Day 4 she drew a straight line sloping up and from Day 4 to Day 5 she drew a horizontal line. How would you describe the temperature change from Day 1 to Day 5?** Between Day 1 and Day 4 there was a constant increase in temperature; between Day 4 and Day 5 there was no change in temperature.

3 | Differentiated Instruction

Leveled Problem Solving

At noon, it was 7° on Sunday, 7° on Monday, 2° on Tuesday, 5° on Wednesday, 8° on Thursday, 11° on Friday, and 12° on Saturday.

❶ Basic Level

In a graph of these data, the horizontal axis represents days. Describe the graph of the line from Monday to Tuesday? Explain. Possible answer: It slopes down because the temperature drops from 7° to 2°.

❷ On Level

In a graph of these data, the horizontal axis represents days. Between which days is the graph a horizontal line? Explain. Sunday and Monday; the temperature has no change on those days.

❸ Above Level

In a graph of these data, the horizontal axis represents days. Which 3 days have the same constant increase in temperature? Explain. Wednesday through Friday; the temperature rises 3° each day.

Intervention	Practice	Extension

Activity Coordinate Relay

Ask students for ideas on how to remember that the first number of a coordinate pair is the horizontal distance and that the second number is the vertical distance. Suggest that they put *horizontal* and *vertical* in alphabetical order. Then have them practice plotting points on the board in a relay race between two teams.

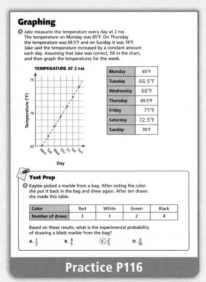

Practice P116

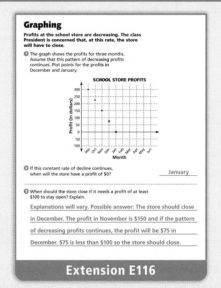

Extension E116

Spiral Review

Spiral Review Book page SR116 provides review of the following previously learned skills and concepts:

- dividing with large numbers using an area model
- applying the problem solving strategy *guess and check*

You may wish to have students work with partners to complete the page.

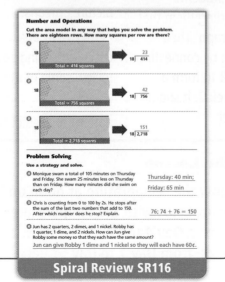

Spiral Review SR116

Extension Activity
The Plotting Game

Give each pair of students grid paper and have them draw a coordinate plane. Tell partners to take turns writing a coordinate pair, plotting it on the plane, and labeling it with a different letter. Then have students draw a line from the origin (0,0) to each point. The player with the steeper slope gets 1 point. Let students play several rounds. The winner is the player with the most points at the end of the game.

Teacher's Notes 🍎

Daily Notes . . .

Quick Notes

More Ideas

Lesson 2 Graphing Capacity Conversions

NCTM Standards 2, 3, 4, 5, 6, 7, 8, 9, 10

Lesson Planner

STUDENT OBJECTIVES
- To make straight-line graphs of proportional relationships
- To review the relationships among cups, pints, quarts, and gallons

1 Daily Activities (TG p. 1213)

Open-Ended Problem Solving/Headline Story	Skills Practice and Review— Converting Between Measurement Units

2 Teach and Practice (TG pp. 1214–1218)

	MATERIALS
(A) **Graphing Cups and Pints** (TG pp. 1214–1215)	• TR: Activity Masters, AM155–AM156
(B) **Making and Comparing Conversion Graphs** (TG p. 1216)	• transparencies of AM154–AM155 (optional) • straightedges
(C) **Making and Interpreting Conversion Graphs** (TG p. 1217)	• 📖 LAB pp. 289–290 • 📖 SH p. 252

3 Differentiated Instruction (TG p. 1219)

Leveled Problem Solving (TG p. 1219)	Practice Book P117
Intervention Activity (TG p. 1219)	Extension Book E117
Extension Activity (TG p. 1219)	Spiral Review Book SR117

Lesson Notes

About the Lesson

In this lesson, students continue making linear graphs by graphing proportional relationships between pairs of quantities. Throughout the rest of the chapter they will explore graphs of proportional relationships, such as the conversion between measurement units, or the distance covered in a certain amount of time when speed is constant. This lesson uses conversions among customary capacity units as the context for introducing linear graphs (graphs that consist of one unbroken straight line), giving students an opportunity to review what they know about these measurement units.

About the Mathematics

Graphs can be used to show, visually, the relationship between two variable quantities related by a mathematical rule. The conversion of pints to cups follows such a rule. Multiplying the number of pints by 2 tells how many cups that is. We can abbreviate all those words to *number of cups = 2 × number of pints.* We do not further abbreviate to $c = 2p$ to avoid confusing the units with variables. If we collect some pairs of values for the number of pints and the number of cups, we can use these pairs of numbers as coordinates of points on a graph. Because we know that this rule is true for *any* input, we can plot a few points, connect them with a straight line, and use the graph to get information about other input/output pairs.

Use with Lesson Activity Book pp. 289–290.

Developing Mathematical Language

Vocabulary: converting measurements, coordinate grid

When we need to convert many measurements from one unit to another, such as from quarts to gallons or from feet to inches, a table of conversions can eliminate repetitive computation. A graph can represent the same information visually: let each pair of values in the table be the horizontal and vertical coordinates of a point, and plot each point on a *coordinate grid.*

Familiarize students with the term *converting measurements.*

Beginning Tell students that the word *conversion* stems from the word *convert,* which means "to change." Show students a yardstick, and discuss converting inches into feet. Have students help you make a *conversion* table that converts feet to inches.

Intermediate Guide students to make a *conversion* table that converts pounds to ounces. Explain that they need to *convert,* or change, the amounts to be measured into ounces.

Advanced Have students choose two related units of measure and make a *conversion* table. Then have them switch tables with a partner and determine the two units.

Open-Ended Problem Solving

Read the Headline Story to your students. In responding to this story, you might tell students that they can pour measured amounts of water down the drain in order to reuse a container. However, if they use a container to measure out an exact amount, they can assume it's filled to the top without any spillage.

 Headline Story

Yoshi has a gallon jug, a quart jug, and a pint jug. The gallon jug is full of water; the other two jars are empty. He wants to measure out 5 pints of water. How can he do it?

Possible responses: He can fill up the quart jug and the pint jug from the gallon jug; that will leave 5 pints in the gallon jug. Or, he can use the pint jug to take a pint at a time out of the gallon jug until the gallon jug has 5 pints left. (He'd have to take out 3 pints, because there are 8 pints in a gallon.)

Skills Practice and Review

Converting Between Measurement Units

Name a pair of related measurement units, such as ounces and pounds, meters and centimeters, or milliliters and liters. Use different units than in the previous lesson. Give an amount in one unit (such as 32 ounces) and ask a student to tell you the equivalent amount in the other unit (in this case, 2 pounds). If students are not sure about the conversion, ask someone to remind the class how many ounces are in one pound (16). Go through several examples, sometimes giving one unit and sometimes the other. You might make an input/output table and have students fill in either the output or the input.

If you have time, introduce other related units and have students convert between them.

whole class 15 MIN

A Graphing Cups and Pints

Materials

- For the teacher: transparency of AM154 (optional), straightedge

NCTM Standards 2, 3, 4, 5, 6, 7, 8, 9, 10

Purpose To complete a table and make a graph for a linear relationship, and to interpret the graph

Introduce Tell students that a recipe calls for 6 cups of water, but that all you could find were pint containers. Show the class a transparency of Activity Master 154: Conversion Graph 1 or draw a similar grid on the board or on large chart paper. Also make an input/output table like the one below with rows (or columns) labeled *p* and *c* (or *pints* and *cups,* if you prefer.) Fill in one number in each pair, and invite a student to fill in the other. As you do this, suggest to students that they look for a pattern that can help them to figure out how many pints of water you need for your recipe. You might choose numbers deliberately out of order and include simple fractions.

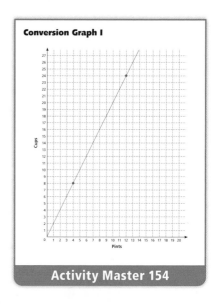

Activity Master 154

pints	4	1	$2\frac{1}{3}$	7	9	$3\frac{1}{2}$	12	$8\frac{1}{2}$
cups	8	2	$4\frac{2}{3}$	14	18	7	24	17

✔ **Ongoing Assessment**

- This lesson uses conversions between measurement units as a context for introducing graphs of linear relationships. Students are likely to remember the names of the U.S. customary capacity units (cups, pints, quarts, and gallons) but may have forgotten some of the relationships. You might use the Skills Practice and Review activity to share what students already know about conversions.

Task Once students have completed the table, plot the first pair of numbers as a point on the graph, and label that point with its coordinates.

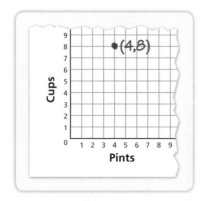

Invite students to plot the other points.

If you used the numbers suggested in the table, your graph should look like the one on the right.

💬 **Talk Math** Ask questions about the numbers in the table and the graph.

❓ **What patterns do you see in the table?** Possible answer: The number of cups is twice the number of pints; every time you add a pint, you add two more cups.

❓ **What patterns do you see in the graph?** Possible answers: The points all line up on the same straight line. The vertical coordinate of each point is twice the horizontal coordinate.

❓ **How do the patterns in the table relate to patterns on the graph?** Possible answer: The patterns are really the same because the graph is a pictorial version of the table.

Task Line a straightedge up carefully with (1,2) and (12,24), and draw the line between them and extending a bit beyond each "end." All points plotted so far should lie on the same straight line. If any points do not lie on this line, have students check the conversion and make sure they plotted the conversion correctly.

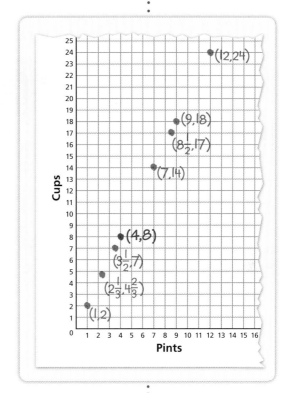

💬 **Talk Math** Then, ask questions about the line.

❓ **The line seems to go through the point (5,10). Explain what that tells us.** It tells us that 5 pints is equivalent to 10 cups.

❓ **What does the graph show about converting 12 cups into pints? Explain.** 12 cups converts into 6 pints. We look for the point on the line whose vertical coordinate is 12, and find its horizontal coordinate, 6.

❓ **Can you tell from the graph how many pints make 11 cups? Explain.** Yes; $5\frac{1}{2}$ pints contain 11 cups. Trace straight across from 11 on the "cups" axis to the line and then down to the "pints" axis. It's halfway between 5 and 6.

❓ **How can you use the graph to convert between cups and pints without using the rule? How can this help you figure out the number of pints in 6 cups for the recipe?** Whichever amount you know, trace from there up or across to the line, and then across or down to the other axis to find the corresponding amount. So, trace horizontally along the line corresponding to 6 cups until you hit the line, and then go down the vertical line to find out the number of pints, in this case, 3.

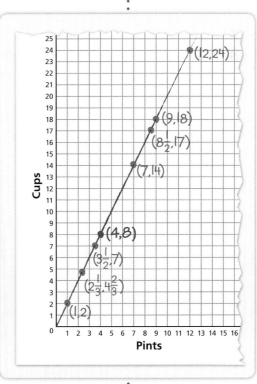

Materials
- For the teacher: transparencies of AM154–155 (optional), straightedge
- For each student: AM155, straightedge

NCTM Standards 2, 3, 4, 5, 6, 7, 8, 9, 10

B Making and Comparing Conversion Graphs

Purpose To make a table and a graph for a linear relationship, and to interpret the graph

Introduce Ask students what they remember about how quarts and gallons are related. When someone mentions that 1 gallon is equivalent to 4 quarts, write the relationship on the board.

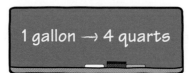

1 gallon → 4 quarts

Task Have students work in small groups first to make a table using AM156: Converting Quarts and Gallons and then to make a graph showing the conversion between quarts and gallons on Activity Master 155: Conversion Graph II. When they have made their graphs, ask the groups to share their graphs and any observations they have about them.

 Talk Math Ask questions such as these.

❓ How many gallons are equivalent to 8 quarts? Explain. 8 quarts are equivalent to 2 gallons. The coordinate pair for the point is (2,8); the vertical coordinate, 8, is four times the horizontal coordinate, 2.

❓ How can you tell from the graph how many gallons make 10 quarts? Trace straight across from 10 on the "quarts" axis to the line and down to the "gallons" axis. It's halfway between 2 and 3. So, 10 quarts contain $2\frac{1}{2}$ gallons.

❓ How is this graph (about quarts and gallons) similar to the cups/pints graph you made in the previous activity? Possible answer: In both graphs the points are on a straight line.

❓ How is this graph different from the cups/pints graph? Possible answers: The line that makes this graph is steeper because we multiply the first coordinate of each point by 4 to get the second coordinate, while we only multiplied by 2 in the cups/pints graph.

Extend You may want to graph a few points on a transparency of Activity Master 155: Conversion Graph II and lay it over the transparency of Activity Master 154: Conversion Graph I from Activity A to show how the quarts/gallon line and the cups/pints line compare.

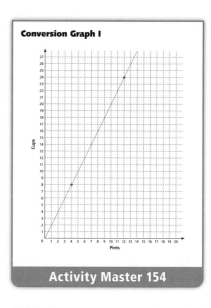

Conversion Graph I

Activity Master 154

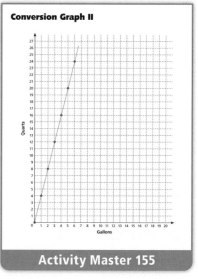

Conversion Graph II

Activity Master 155

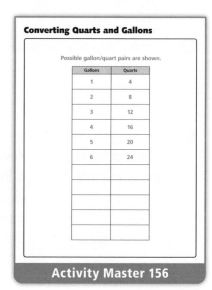

Converting Quarts and Gallons

Possible gallon/quart pairs are shown.

Gallons	Quarts
1	4
2	8
3	12
4	16
5	20
6	24

Activity Master 156

Use with Lesson Activity Book pp. 289–290.

Making and Interpreting
Conversion Graphs LAB pp. 289–290

Purpose To complete a table and make a graph for a linear relationship, and to interpret the graph

NCTM Standards 2, 3, 4, 5, 6, 7, 8, 9, 10

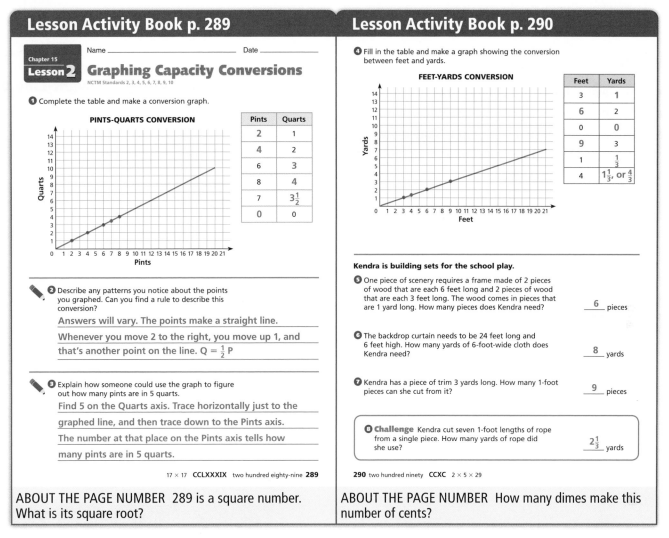

Lesson Activity Book p. 289

Name _____ Date _____

Chapter 15
Lesson 2 **Graphing Capacity Conversions**
NCTM Standards 2, 3, 4, 5, 6, 7, 8, 9, 10

❶ Complete the table and make a conversion graph.

PINTS-QUARTS CONVERSION

Pints	Quarts
2	1
4	2
6	3
8	4
7	$3\frac{1}{2}$
0	0

❷ Describe any patterns you notice about the points you graphed. Can you find a rule to describe this conversion?

Answers will vary. The points make a straight line.

Whenever you move 2 to the right, you move up 1, and that's another point on the line. $Q = \frac{1}{2} P$

❸ Explain how someone could use the graph to figure out how many pints are in 5 quarts.

Find 5 on the Quarts axis. Trace horizontally just to the graphed line, and then trace down to the Pints axis. The number at that place on the Pints axis tells how many pints are in 5 quarts.

17 × 17 CCLXXXIX two hundred eighty-nine **289**

ABOUT THE PAGE NUMBER 289 is a square number. What is its square root?

Lesson Activity Book p. 290

❹ Fill in the table and make a graph showing the conversion between feet and yards.

FEET-YARDS CONVERSION

Feet	Yards
3	1
6	2
0	0
9	3
1	$\frac{1}{3}$
4	$1\frac{1}{3}$, or $\frac{4}{3}$

Kendra is building sets for the school play.

❺ One piece of scenery requires a frame made of 2 pieces of wood that are each 6 feet long and 2 pieces of wood that are each 3 feet long. The wood comes in pieces that are 1 yard long. How many pieces does Kendra need?   __6__ pieces

❻ The backdrop curtain needs to be 24 feet long and 6 feet high. How many yards of 6-foot-wide cloth does Kendra need?   __8__ yards

❼ Kendra has a piece of trim 3 yards long. How many 1-foot pieces can she cut from it?   __9__ pieces

❽ **Challenge** Kendra cut seven 1-foot lengths of rope from a single piece. How many yards of rope did she use? $2\frac{1}{3}$ yards

290 two hundred ninety CCXC 2 × 5 × 29

ABOUT THE PAGE NUMBER How many dimes make this number of cents?

Teaching Notes for LAB page 289

Students complete a table and make a conversion graph relating pints and quarts.

They write about the patterns they find in the graph and explain how they can use the graph to determine the number of pints in 5 quarts.

Students will need a straightedge to draw the line connecting the points plotted on the grid.

Teaching Notes for LAB page 290

Students complete a table and make a conversion graph relating feet and yards, and then use the graph and table to solve word problems about converting between feet and yards.

Challenge Problem In the Challenge Problem the conversion of 7 feet gives a mixed number of yards.

Write Math

Keith made a graph to show how pints are related to quarts. He labeled the horizontal axis "Pints" and the vertical axis "Quarts." How can he use the graph to find the number of quarts in 9 pints? Possible answer: He can trace straight up from 9 on the "Pints" axis to the line and across to the "Quarts" axis. It will be halfway between 4 and 5. So, 9 pints contain $4\frac{1}{2}$ quarts.

Review Model

Refer students to Review Model: Making a Straight-Line Graph in the *Student Handbook* to see how to use pairs of numbers in an input-output table to make a line graph. Students will need copies of Activity Master 154: Conversion Graph I for the problems at the bottom of the page.

✔ **Check for Understanding**

❶ 16, 2, 20

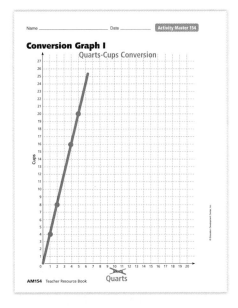

❷ 3, 18, 0, 12

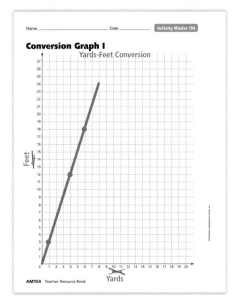

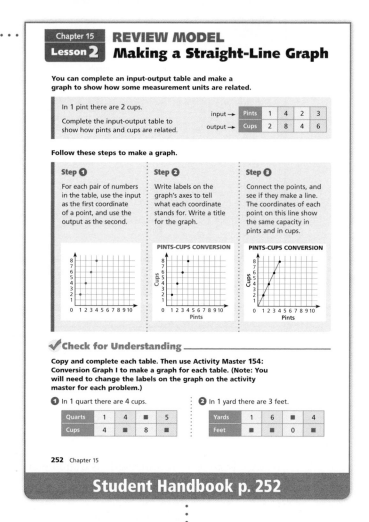

3 | Differentiated Instruction

**Randi makes a graph to show how feet are related to yards.
She labels the horizontal axis "Feet" and the vertical axis "Yards."**

❶ Basic Level

Which point will be on the graph, (9,3) or (3,9)? Explain. (9,3); Possible explanation: The number on the horizontal axis goes first and that's feet. 9 feet is as long as 3 yards, not the other way around.

❷ On Level

How many yards are in 12 feet? Explain how Randi can use the graph to answer the question. 4 yards; she can trace straight up from 12 on the "Feet" axis to the line and across to the "Yards" axis.

❸ Above Level

How many feet are in 9 yards? Explain how Randi can use the graph to answer the question. 27 feet; she can trace straight across from 9 on the "Yards" axis to the line and down to the "Feet" axis.

Intervention	Practice	Extension

Activity Weeks and Days

Have pairs or small groups of students make a conversion table that relates days and weeks. Tell them to assign weeks to the horizontal axis and days to the vertical axis. Have students write coordinates in the form (weeks,days) for each entry in the table and then plot the points. After students have completed this task, ask them to consider what it would mean if the coordinates were in the form (days,weeks).

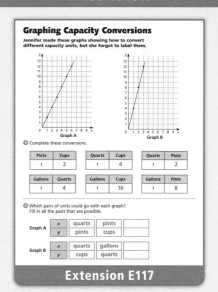

Practice P117

Extension E117

Extension Activity
Reverse Conversion

Have small groups of students make a conversion table using measures of their choice. Then have them make a conversion graph from the table.

Let groups switch graphs and make their own conversion table from the graph.

Spiral Review

Spiral Review Book page SR117 provides review of the following previously learned skills and concepts:

• writing a rule and naming the result of a number trick

• describing attributes of prisms and pyramids

You may wish to have students work with partners to complete the page.

Spiral Review SR117

Lesson **3** Changing the Scale of Graphs

NCTM Standards 2, 3, 4, 5, 6, 7, 8, 9, 10

Lesson Planner

STUDENT OBJECTIVES
- To vary the scale of graphs in order to better display data
- To further explore graphs of linear relationships
- To review and practice conversions between measurement units

1 | Daily Activities (TG p. 1221)

Open-Ended Problem Solving/Headline Story	Skills Practice and Review—Changing Temperatures

2 | Teach and Practice (TG pp. 1222–1227)

Ⓐ **Fitting a Graph into a Small Space** (TG pp. 1222–1223)

Ⓑ **Making and Comparing Conversion Graphs** (TG pp. 1224–1225)

Ⓒ **Determining an Appropriate Scale** (TG p. 1226)

MATERIALS
- transparency of AM157 (optional)
- TR: Activity Master, AM157
- straightedges
- 📖 LAB pp. 291–292
- 📖 SH pp. 253–254

3 | Differentiated Instruction (TG p. 1228)

Leveled Problem Solving (TG p. 1228)	Practice Book P118
Intervention Activity (TG p. 1228)	Extension Book E118
Extension Activity (TG p. 1228)	Spiral Review Book SR118

Lesson Notes

About the Lesson

Students continue to explore graphs of linear relationships in the context of conversions between measurement units. In this lesson, they learn that a graph can be scaled differently to better display data in a limited space.

About the Mathematics

This lesson continues to explore functions (rules) that make straight lines when you graph them. Students have already worked with functions in which some specified number is added to the input to produce the output. In this chapter, students work with functions in which the output is a multiple of the input.

Even if we combine these two types of rules—multiplying the input *(x)* by a fixed number (including 1 or 0), adding another fixed number (including negative numbers or 0), and outputting the result—the graph will be a straight line. This combination rule can be written as $y = mx + b$, where *x*, as always, can vary. The letters *m* and *b* stand for the fixed numbers, *m* being the multiplier of the input *x*, and *b* being the base to which this multiple of *x* is always added. As always, *y* is the output. For example, if *x* stands for a given number of pints and *y* stands for the corresponding number of cups, the multiplier would be 2 because there are twice as many cups for a given number of pints, and the base would be 0.

Use with Lesson Activity Book pp. 291–292.

Developing Mathematical Language

Vocabulary: interval, scale

An *interval* is the distance or space between two objects. On a coordinate graph, we generally number each axis in equal *intervals,* which may be 1, 2, 5, 100, or any other number that creates a graph at a convenient *scale* for the numbers that are involved.

Scale on a scale drawing or map, indicates how much "life-size" is represented within some particular space on the drawing or map, for example, how many miles are represented by a quarter inch on the map. *Scale,* on a graph, indicates how many units are represented by a move of one space along one axis. On a graph, *scale* is indicated in the way the axes are numbered.

Familiarize students with the term *interval.*

Beginning Have the class skip-count by threes, fours, and fives, starting with different numbers. Help students determine the *interval* of each counting exercise.

Intermediate Give each pair of students AM157: Conversion Graph III. Have each student choose an *interval.* One student fills in the boxes along the *x*-axis using the chosen *interval,* and the other student completes the *y*-axis.

Advanced Give each student AM157: Conversion Graph III. Guide them to use an *interval* of 2 on the *x*-axis and an *interval* of 1 on the *y*-axis.

Open-Ended Problem Solving

Read the Headline Story to the students and write the numbers so they can see them. See sample responses for ideas.

 Headline Story

The sum 10 + 10 + 10 can be rewritten as the sum of consecutive numbers: 9 + 10 + 11. How can you use this idea to find consecutive numbers that add up to 45?

Possible responses: We can make 45 as a sum of equal numbers. 45 = 5 × 9, or 9 + 9 + 9 + 9 + 9. Then, make the first ones smaller and the later ones larger so that the middle stays that same: 7 + 8 + 9 + 10 + 11. We can make 45 as 15 + 15 + 15, so also as 14 + 15 + 16.

Skills Practice and Review

Changing Temperatures

Have students practice using negative numbers in the context of changing temperatures. Draw a thermometer or number line on the board, marking multiples of 10 from ⁻20 to 40, and ask students questions about temperature changes.

- The temperature was 36°F and now is 8°F. By how many degrees did the temperature drop?
- The temperature was 12°C and dropped 30°C. What temperature, in degrees Celsius, is it now?
- The temperature was ⁻23°C and went up 7 degrees Celsius. What's the temperature now in degrees Celsius?
- At 4:00 in the afternoon, the temperature was only 6°C, but now it's ⁻12°C. How did the temperature change?

For a challenge, use numbers that aren't on your thermometer.

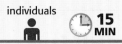 individuals **15 MIN**

Ⓐ Fitting a Graph into a Small Space

Materials
- For each student: AM157, straightedge

NCTM Standards 2, 3, 4, 5, 6, 7, 8, 9, 10

Purpose To choose an appropriate scale for a graph and then make the graph

Introduce Ask students what they know about how inches and feet are related. When someone mentions that 12 inches are equivalent to 1 foot, write the relationship on the board.

You may want to continue by having students help you begin to make an inches/ feet conversion table. Then, distribute Explore: Fitting the Graph on the Page and AM157: Conversion Graph III to students. Ask students to read the paragraphs at the top of the Explore page. Before they begin working on the activity independently, be sure students understand that they must first make a table of at least 6 data points. They use the blank table at the bottom of Activity Master 157 to record the data points.

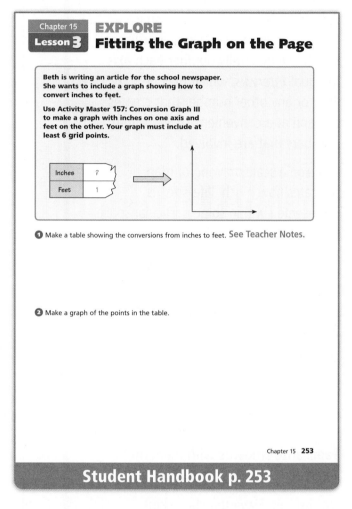

Student Handbook p. 253

Teacher Story

❝To simplify many activities on conversion between units and have students concentrate on the mathematical aspect of it, I am keeping the list of conversions on a chart on the wall, and my students can refer to it any time.❞

Task Have students work on Explore: Fitting the Graph on the Page independently. They make a graph relating inches to feet, using at least 6 data points, but must figure a way to scale the graph to show the relationship in limited space.

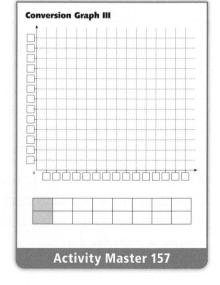

Activity Master 157

At first students are likely to fill in the blank vertical and horizontal axes with numbers in counting order (i.e., 1, 2, 3…), but Activity Master 157: Conversion Graph III does not have enough room to fit in 6 intervals of 12 along either axis. If students let each horizontal unit correspond to one inch, then after a foot or so they will run out of room on the graph. Even if they plot points at half-foot locations, they can't plot many points. If they let each space stand for two inches, more points fit on the graph. If each space stands for 3 or 4 or 6 or even 12 inches, students can plot yet more points. However, if they assign too many inches to a space, the graph again gets hard to read. The goal is to choose a scale that lets them see all of the data in a readable way. Students may need to be reminded to label their axes with the appropriate units.

Share When students have completed their graphs, have them share their graphs and explain how they fit 6 points on the graph.

Talk Math You may want to ask questions such as these to guide the discussion.

❷ What labels did you use for the axes? Possible answer: "Inches" for the horizontal axis and "Feet" for the vertical axis.

❷ Why is a scale with an interval of 1 difficult to use for this graph? Possible answer: If you use an interval of 1 for both the inches and the feet axes, you will run out of space before you can plot 6 data points.

❷ What scale did you use for the inches axis? for the feet axis? Answers will vary.

Encourage students to explain the scale they chose. Some students may have tried to pick points representing fractional numbers of feet so that they could have 6 points without any of them going above 15 inches. This strategy still requires thinking about scale: if each space on the feet axis stands for 1 foot, it's hard to subdivide them to show where $\frac{1}{3}$ foot or $\frac{1}{4}$ foot would be. Re-labeling the feet axis so that each space stands for $\frac{1}{4}$ or $\frac{1}{12}$ of a foot makes these points easier to plot.

Make sure students understand that they can label each axis with whatever size "jumps" are convenient, but that all intervals on one axis must be the same size so that it's easy to look at the points and see the same patterns you can see in the table of numbers. Also, help students see that their choice of the jump "size" determines which part of the graph they will see. For example, one could use the third graph to convert up to 72 inches into feet, while the first graph allows work with only up to 12 inches.

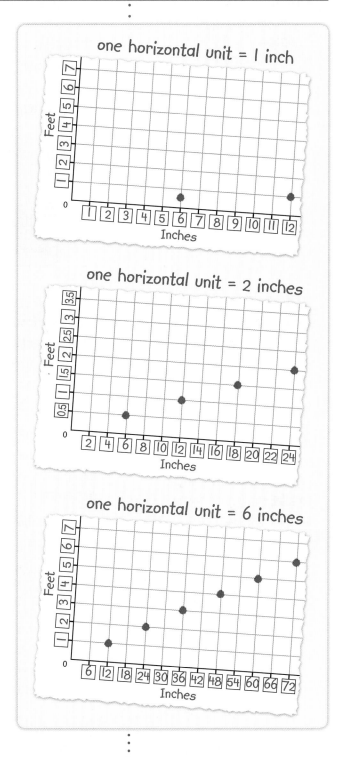

B Making and Comparing Conversion Graphs

Materials

- For the teacher: transparency of AM157 (optional)
- For each group of students: AM157, straightedge

NCTM Standards 2, 3, 4, 5, 6, 7, 8, 9, 10

Purpose To choose an appropriate scale for a conversion graph and then make the graph

Introduce Divide the class into small groups. Write these pairs of measurement units on the board and give each group a different pair of units to graph. Ask the students in each group to write a rule to show how the measurement units are related.

- Ounces and pounds
- Cups and quarts
- Quarts and gallons
- Cups and gallons
- Inches and feet
- Inches and yards
- Centimeters and meters
- Grams and kilograms
- Liters and milliliters

Differentiated Instruction

Basic Level You can vary the challenge level of Activity B by your choice of the unit conversions you assign to each group. You may want to assign familiar conversion rules, such as inches to feet, or conversions involving a smaller conversion factor, such as cups to quarts, to students who are less comfortable with conversions. Keep the conversion factor large enough, however, so that students need to think about the scale they choose for the graph.

Task Tell students to make a conversion table showing at least 6 pairs of numbers that go with their conversion rule. Using a new copy of Activity Master 157: Conversion Graph III, each group must find an appropriate scale to fit all their points onto the graph. They will need to label each axis with the name of the measurement unit it represents, and choose and show the scale.

Some students may choose points that cannot be nicely graphed together. For example, students could choose this set of points:

1 L = 1,000 mL;

2 L = 2,000 mL;

3 L = 3,000 mL; and

4,000 L = 4,000,000 mL.

In this case, you might encourage students to come up with the best scale they can or replace an inconvenient point with something that fits better.

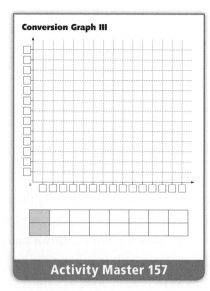

Activity Master 157

Share When students finish, have each group share its graph with the class. Students can explain the scale they used and why they chose it. Invite the class to compare the graphs of different units.

Talk Math You may want to ask questions such as these to guide the discussion.

❷ Do some graphs look the same? Answer will vary, but it is very possible that some graphs will look the same. Example: cups to quarts and quarts to gallons on the same scale

❷ If graphs do look the same, are the conversion rules for the two sets of units the same or different? Answers will vary. A graph of cups/quarts and a graph of cups/gallons could look the same, if the quarts axis is labeled in jumps of 2 for every 1 on the cups axis, while the gallons axis is labeled in jumps of 4 for every 1 on the cups axis.

❷ Do all the conversion rules that give the same pairs of numbers in the tables have graphs that look the same? No. The graphs of rules that give the same pairs of numbers in the tables can be the same or they can be different, depending on how the axes are labeled.

Practice Pick one graph as an example. Copy a few of its points onto a transparency of Activity Master 157: Conversion Graph III and draw the line, or plot the points and draw the line on the board or on chart-sized graph paper.

Ask students to suggest a different scale you could use for the same graph. Erase the original line and numbers along the axes, and graph the same points using a different scale. Repeat with another example. Sometimes, all the points may not fit on the graph; if so, show roughly where the point should be to emphasize that there isn't enough space to fit it when we use this scale.

Ongoing Assessment

You can assess your students' comfort and familiarity with measurement units (especially for capacity) that they may not have used in a while. If students have forgotten the conversions, you might briefly review them (either during the lesson or at some other time).

As students graph conversions between units, you can observe their facility with multiples and factors.

- Can they convert easily, or do they struggle with the arithmetic?

- Do they write each multiplication or division, or are they able to compute mentally?

Determining an Appropriate Scale LAB pp. 291–292

Purpose To determine appropriate scales for a graph

NCTM Standards 2, 3, 4, 5, 6, 7, 8, 9, 10

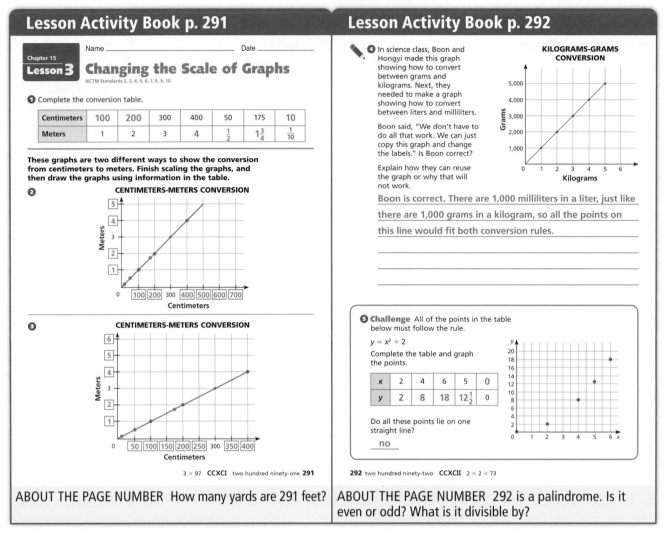

Lesson Activity Book p. 291

Name _____ Date _____

Chapter 15
Lesson 3 **Changing the Scale of Graphs**
NCTM Standards 2, 3, 4, 5, 6, 7, 8, 9, 10

1 Complete the conversion table.

Centimeters	100	200	300	400	50	175	10
Meters	1	2	3	4	$\frac{1}{2}$	$1\frac{3}{4}$	$\frac{1}{10}$

These graphs are two different ways to show the conversion from centimeters to meters. Finish scaling the graphs, and then draw the graphs using information in the table.

2 CENTIMETERS-METERS CONVERSION

3 CENTIMETERS-METERS CONVERSION

3 × 97 **CCXCI** two hundred ninety-one **291**

ABOUT THE PAGE NUMBER How many yards are 291 feet?

Lesson Activity Book p. 292

4 In science class, Boon and Hongyi made this graph showing how to convert between grams and kilograms. Next, they needed to make a graph showing how to convert between liters and milliliters.

Boon said, "We don't have to do all that work. We can just copy this graph and change the labels." Is Boon correct?

Explain how they can reuse the graph or why that will not work.

KILOGRAMS-GRAMS CONVERSION

Boon is correct. There are 1,000 milliliters in a liter, just like there are 1,000 grams in a kilogram, so all the points on this line would fit both conversion rules.

5 Challenge All of the points in the table below must follow the rule.

$y = x^2 \div 2$

Complete the table and graph the points.

x	2	4	6	5	0
y	2	8	18	$12\frac{1}{2}$	0

Do all these points lie on one straight line?

no

292 two hundred ninety-two **CCXCII** 2 × 2 × 73

ABOUT THE PAGE NUMBER 292 is a palindrome. Is it even or odd? What is it divisible by?

Teaching Notes for LAB page 291

Students complete a conversion table for meters and centimeters, finish scaling the graph, and then draw the graph from the information in the table.

Regardless of the scale used for the graph, not all of the points in the conversion table will be on intersections.

Other scales can be used for the graphs. For example, for the graph in Problem 2, the meters axis could be labeled in jumps of 2 and the centimeters axis in jumps of 200. Similarly, the graph in Problem 3 could be labeled in jumps of 2 and jumps of 100.

Teaching Notes for LAB page 292

Students explain why the kilograms/grams conversion graph can look like a liters/milliliters conversion graph. This problem emphasizes the fact that in the metric system, similar measurement units are related by powers of 10. There are 1,000 milliliters in a liter, 1,000 grams in a kilogram, and 1,000 milligrams in a gram. The prefix *milli-* means $\frac{1}{1000}$, and the prefix *kilo-* means 1,000.

Challenge Problem In the Challenge Problem, students graph points that fit the relationship $y = x^2 \div 2$ and notice that not all graphs form a straight line. Encourage students to use a straightedge to verify that the points are not on a line.

Reflect and Summarize the Lesson

Write Math

Explain how you would choose the scale for a graph. Give an example. Possible answer: Look at the numbers in the data. Choose a scale for each axis that allows you to graph several points and to show differences among the data points.

Review Model . . . .

Refer students to Review Model: Choosing an Appropriate Scale in the *Student Handbook* to see how to use the data being graphed to help you choose a reasonable scale for the axes. Students will need copies of Activity Master 157: Conversion Graph III for the problems at the bottom of the page.

✔ Check for Understanding

Scales and graphs may vary. See below for graphs.

❶ 3,000; 6,000; 2,000; 0

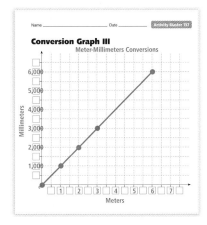

❷ 24; 60; 72, 0

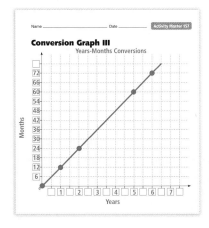

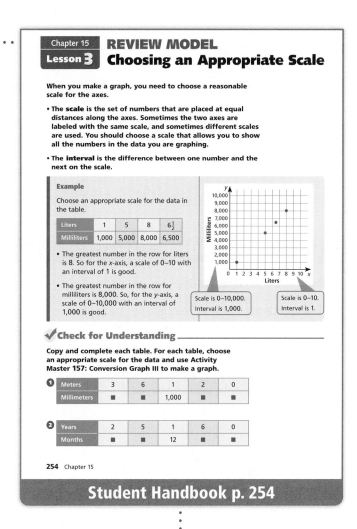

Student Handbook p. 254

3 | Differentiated Instruction

Abby knows a year has 12 months. Her graph has "Months" on the vertical axis and "Years" on the horizontal axis.

❶ Basic Level

She wants to graph the number of months in 6 years. Which interval scale seems the best for the vertical axis: 2, 12, or 36? Explain. 12; the vertical axis needs to go to 6 × 12, or 72 months.

❷ On Level

She numbered her horizontal axis from 0 to 6, and used an interval scale of 6 for the marks on her vertical axis. Which numbers will go along the vertical axis? Explain. The multiples of 6 from 0 to 72

❸ Above Level

The horizontal axis will be in intervals of $\frac{1}{4}$ year, and she wants to graph two years. What is an appropriate interval scale she might use for the vertical axis? Explain. 3; $\frac{1}{4}$ year is 3 months. Other answers are possible.

Intervention

Activity Scale Relay

Have students work in teams. Draw on the board a set of axes with 8 tick marks on the vertical axis. Tell students that you are going to name the greatest number on the vertical axis of this graph and they will complete the labeling. Give each team a multiple of 8 (such as 24, 32, or 56). Teams will decide on the interval and choose one member to go to the board to write the scale for the vertical axis.

Practice

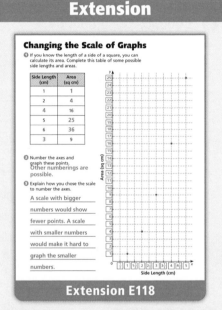

Practice P118

Extension

Extension E118

Extension Activity
Generalizing Scale

Have pairs of students write a paragraph describing how to determine the best scale for a graph. Ask them to address when an interval might need to be less than 1 and when an interval might need to be very large. Allow time for students to share their paragraphs in small groups.

Spiral Review

Spiral Review Book page SR118 provides review of the following previously learned skills and concepts:

• finding the area of the base and the volume of rectangular prisms

• listing possible outcomes of an experiment defining prisms and pyramids

You may wish to have students work with partners to complete the page.

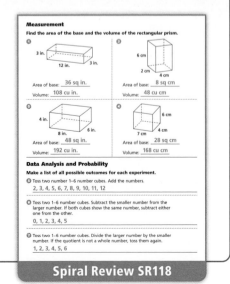

Spiral Review SR118

Teacher's Notes 🍎

Daily Notes . . .

Quick Notes

More Ideas

Lesson 4 Graphing Change Over Time

NCTM Standards 2, 3, 4, 5, 6, 7, 8, 9, 10

Lesson Planner

STUDENT OBJECTIVE ·
- To understand the proportional relationship between distance and time when the speed is constant

1 Daily Activities (TG p. 1231)

Open-Ended Problem Solving/Headline Story	Skills Practice and Review—Changing Temperature Chains

2 Teach and Practice (TG pp. 1232–1236)

	MATERIALS
Ⓐ **Distance and Time** (TG pp. 1232–1233) Ⓑ **Graphing Distance and Time** (TG pp. 1234–1235) Ⓒ **Solving Problems about Distance and Time** (TG p. 1236)	• transparency of AM34 (optional) • straightedges • 📖 LAB pp. 293–294 • 📖 SH p. 255

3 Differentiated Instruction (TG p. 1237)

Leveled Problem Solving (TG p. 1237)	Practice Book P119
Intervention Activity (TG p. 1237)	Extension Book E119
Extension Activity (TG p. 1237)	Spiral Review Book SR119
Science Connection (TG p. 1202)	

Lesson Notes

About the Lesson

Students continue to explore and graph linear rules, as they investigate how distance and time are related by the speed of travel. While virtually all students at this age will know "60 miles per hour" is a measure of speed, many do not quite realize what it means: if we drive at that speed for 1 hour, we would cover 60 miles or, if we drive at that speed and have 60 miles to go, it will take us an hour to get there. That last fact gives a great deal of power: If we have only *half* as far to go, it will take us *half* an hour; if we have $\frac{1}{60}$ as far to go (that is, one mile), it will take us $\frac{1}{60}$ of an hour (one minute).

About the Mathematics

If you travel at a constant speed, the relationship between the distance you travel and the time it takes

to do so is strictly proportional: graphing distance against time gives you a straight line.

The speedometer tells us the speed we're driving at any moment, but in real travel, speed often varies, and if we want to figure out "when are we going to get there," it is useful to estimate the average speed and pretend that, instead of going a bit faster for a few minutes and then slower for some other minutes, we're constantly going at that one intermediate speed. Speeds of 60 mph and 30 mph make calculations really easy, and are often close enough to the average speed we're going to be quite usable as estimates for highway or local travel.

(continued on page R6)

Use with Lesson Activity Book pp. 293–294.

Developing Mathematical Language

Vocabulary: miles per hour, speed

Computations involving *speed* can be simplified if we assume an average *speed* or a *speed* that does not change. We can then calculate the *speed* by dividing the distance the object travels by the time that it takes: for example, *miles per hour,* miles divided by hours.

The *speed* of a vehicle generally means its average, *speed,* "smoothing out" the effects of acceleration and deceleration to adjust for traffic, terrain, and so on.

The questions "What was the *speed?*" and "How fast was it going?" are identical; the answer requires units, such as *miles per hour,* or feet per second.

Familiarize students with the terms *miles per hour* and *speed.*

Beginning Write 55 *miles per hour* on the board. Ask students to suggest what might move at that *speed.* Repeat for other *miles per hour.*

Intermediate Ask students to suggest some fast *speeds* that cars might travel and then some slow *speeds.*

Advanced Have students suggest and then discuss reasonable *speeds* for activities that are familiar to them, such as: a car on a highway (60 mph), a car near a school (20 mph), a bicycle (8 to 16 mph), walking (2 to 4 mph).

Open-Ended Problem Solving

Read the Headline Story to the students. Encourage them to think of creative ways to answer the question.

 ### Headline Story

> Jessica takes the bus downtown to meet her mom. The bus stops at her apartment every 20 minutes, always on time. The bus trip takes between 15 and 20 minutes, and Jessica then walks 5 to 10 minutes from the bus to her mom's job. Today, when she arrived, it was exactly 4:00. What time could she have left her apartment today?

Possible responses: The longest this whole trip could take is 50 minutes. The shortest is 20 minutes. So, she could have left as early as 3:10, or as late as 3:40.

 ## Skills Practice and Review

Changing Temperature Chains

As in the previous lesson, draw a thermometer or number line on the board that includes negative numbers. Ask students to find the differences between various temperatures, asking questions like these.

- If the high temperature on Monday was 50 degrees Fahrenheit and it was 17 degrees Fahrenheit colder the next day, what was the high temperature on Tuesday?
- Today's high temperature is 12 degrees Celsius colder than yesterday's, which was 5 degrees Celsius. What is today's high temperature?

Let students make up their own questions, too.

individuals
or pairs

15 MIN

NCTM Standards 2, 3, 4, 5, 6, 7, 8, 9, 10

A Distance and Time

Purpose To investigate how distance and time are related by the speed of travel

Introduce Distribute Explore: Getting Home on Time to students and make sure they understand the setting given in the text at the top of the page. To ensure that students understand it, you might ask them to retell it in their own words.

Task **Have students work to answer the questions on the Explore page individually or with a partner.** After they have had some time to think about the questions, gather the class to discuss their answers. In order to answer the questions, students will have to have reasoned about Mrs. Singh's walking *speed*.

Chapter 15   **EXPLORE**
Lesson 4   **Getting Home on Time**

In nice weather, Mrs. Singh likes to walk home from work. She leaves work at 5:00. She needs to be home by 6:30. She works 6 miles from home.

Work

Home

❶ If it takes her 30 minutes to walk 1 mile, how long will it take her to get home? Will she be home in time?
It will take 3 hours. No; she will not be home until 8:00.

❷ If she can walk fast and jog a bit so that she covers 5 miles in 1 hour, how long will it take her to get home? Will she be home in time?
It will take $1\frac{1}{5}$ hours (1 hour, 12 minutes). Yes; she will be home at 6:12.

❸ What is the slowest speed at which she could walk and still make it home by 6:30?
She could walk 1 mile every quarter of an hour, or 4 miles per hour.

Chapter 15   **255**

Student Handbook p. 255

Talk Math Use questions such these to help students reason about Mrs. Singh's walking speed.

❓ What did you think about to help you answer Problem 1? Possible answer: It takes Mrs. Singh 30 minutes to walk 1 mile. She has 6 miles to go, so I must multiply the 30 minutes by 6. 30 minutes is half an hour. Six half-hours is 3 hours.

❓ If she walks a mile in 30 minutes, how many miles per hour is that? (How many miles in one hour?) 1 mile in 30 minutes is the same as 2 miles in an hour—2 miles per hour.

❓ If it takes her 3 hours to walk home, will Mrs. Singh be home in time? Explain. No. If she leaves work at 5:00 and needs to be home at 6:30 she has only 1 hour and 30 minutes, or $1\frac{1}{2}$ hours.

Differentiated Instruction

Basic Level/On Level Some students may find a drawing helpful in solving or understanding this problem.

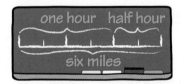

one hour   half hour

six miles

If the issue has not already come up during the course of the discussion, point out to the class that in thinking about these questions, you have been making the assumption that Mrs. Singh always walks at the same speed for the entire trip home, and never stops along the way.

Use with Lesson Activity Book pp. 293–294.

❷ What did you think about to help you answer Problem 3? Possible answer: If Mrs. Singh can walk 5 miles in an hour, then in the remaining half hour she could walk another 2.5 miles, and she doesn't need to walk even half that far to get home, so she'll certainly arrive in time.

❷ At what time will Mrs. Singh be home if she walks 5 miles in 1 hour? Explain. 6:12; if she walks 5 miles in 1 hour, it must take $\frac{1}{5}$ of an hour to walk 1 mile; so that's $1\frac{1}{5}$ hours (or 1 hour and 12 minutes) in all.

❷ What do the answers to Problems 1 and 2 tell you about the speed Mrs. Singh must walk to get home in time? Possible answer: Mrs. Singh needs to walk faster than she did in Problem 1 (because that was too slow to get home in time), but she can walk slower than described in Problem 2 (because she had time left over). The slowest speed she can go and still get home in time must be somewhere in between.

For Problem 3, students may not be sure what arithmetic to use to compute the speed exactly, or what language to use to describe that speed, but some will be able to figure out that if Mrs. Singh has an hour and a half in which to go 6 miles, she'll get home exactly on time if she takes a quarter-hour to go each mile.

When the class is ready, take a few minutes to talk about the idea of speed. Students are probably familiar with talking about driving at some number of miles per hour, for example, 60 miles per hour. What that means is that if you kept going at the same speed for an hour, you would go 60 miles. What if you were driving at 60 miles per hour, but you only drove for half an hour? You'd go half of 60 miles, or 30 miles. In Problem 3, if Mrs. Singh takes 15 minutes to walk each mile, she's going 1 mile per quarter-hour, or 4 miles per hour (a fast but possible walking speed).

Materials
- For the teacher: transparency of AM34 (optional), straightedge

NCTM Standards 2, 3, 4, 5, 6, 7, 8, 9, 10

B Graphing Distance and Time

Purpose To make a table and a graph for a time/distance linear relationship, and to explore how the steepness of the line on the graph changes when the speed changes

Introduce Draw an input-output table like the one below on the board and use a transparency of Activity Master 34: Quadrant 1 Grid or draw a blank coordinate grid.

Fill in 1 and 4 in the first row of the input/output table: let's say Mrs. Singh takes 1 hour to walk 4 miles. Have the class fill in some other time/distance pairs. (For example, she walks 8 miles in 2 hours; she walks 2 miles in $\frac{1}{2}$ hour.)

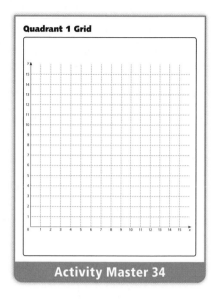

Activity Master 34

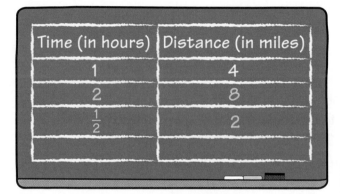

When you have at least four entries in the table, help students complete the task below.

Task **With students, graph the points on the blank grid.** You may want to mention that when we make graphs about time, we usually put time on the horizontal axis, and call it the time axis (or *t*-axis). (If you are using the grid on Activity Master 34, you may need to change the scale on at least one of the axes.)

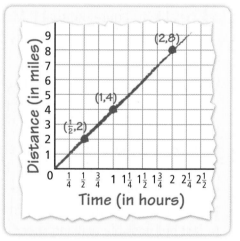

 Talk Math Then, ask questions such as these.

❓ How are the points plotted in this graph like the points we plotted in the measurement conversion graphs earlier in this chapter? Possible answer: The points all lie in a straight line.

❓ Does it make sense to connect the points as they did with those other graphs? Explain. Possible answer: Yes; because we can walk for *any* amount of time, not just whole numbers of hours—even fractions of seconds—and can plot a point for any of those amounts of time, there are no "gaps." This rule puts all of its points on the same line.

Use a straightedge to connect the points.

Practice Name a time that is not one of the points you graphed from the table and ask someone to find the point on the graph that corresponds to that time, and tell you how far Mrs. Singh walked in that amount of time. Have students use the 4-mile-per-hour rule to calculate the distance and verify that the answer is the same. Repeat this process with a few examples, including some that don't use whole numbers (for example, how far does Mrs. Singh walk in $3\frac{1}{4}$ hours?), and so the point on the graph does not fall on an intersection of the grid: have students estimate the distance by looking at the graph, and then calculate the exact answer. (Because she can go 4 miles in an hour, she can go 1 mile in a quarter of an hour. So, in the first three hours, she'll go 12 miles, and in the remaining quarter hour, another mile.)

Ask, "What if Mrs. Singh walked 3 miles per hour?" Have students help you generate some time/distance pairs and graph these new points.

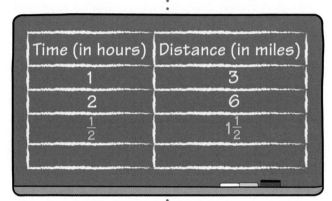

Time (in hours)	Distance (in miles)
1	3
2	6
$\frac{1}{2}$	$1\frac{1}{2}$

Talk Math Continue with questions such as these.

❷ How is this graph for walking 3 miles per hour similar to or different from the previous one we drew for walking 4 miles per hour? Possible answer: Both are straight lines slanting up to the right. The line in this graph is not as steep as the other one.

❷ How can you tell, just by looking at the lines, which one represents Mrs. Singh walking faster? Possible answer: The steeper line shows more miles covered in the same number of hours, so it represents the faster walk.

❷ How can you figure out, just by looking at the graph, how fast Mrs. Singh was walking? Possible answers: If you look at one hour's worth of walking on the time axis, and see how much the graph goes up in that interval, you'll know how many miles she walks in one hour, and that's her speed.

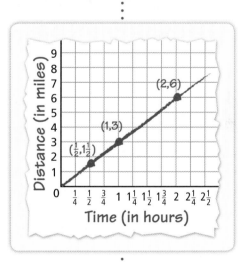

Extend Ask students what they think a graph of Mrs. Singh walking at 5 miles per hour will look like, compared to the lines you already have. If they don't suggest these two facts, you may want to mention them.

• Walking 5 miles per hour is faster than either 4 or 3 miles per hour, so the line should be even steeper than either of these two.

• At any given time, the point for the new line should be above the points on the other two lines.

Have students help you generate a few points, graph them, and see if their predictions were correct.

individuals
👤 ⏰ **20 MIN**

Purpose To solve problems about travel at a constant speed

NCTM Standards 2, 3, 4, 5, 6, 7, 8, 9, 10

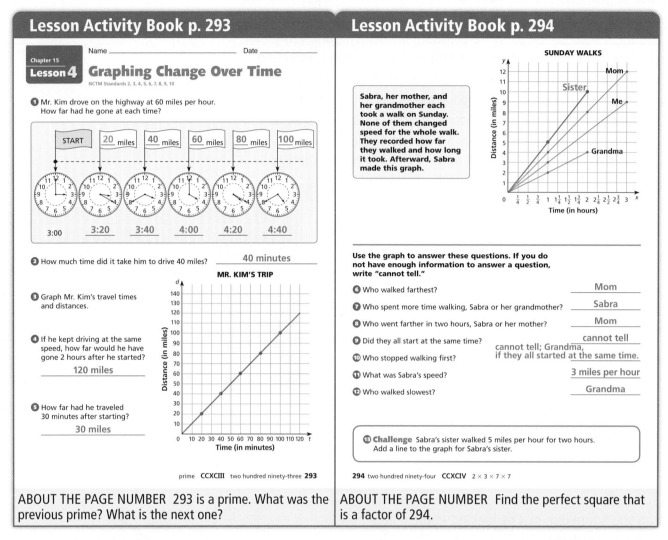

Teaching Notes for LAB page 293

Students make a distance/time graph. Because the problem involves a constant speed, they can connect the points with a straight line and, as for Problems 4 and 5, infer new times and distances from the ones they plotted.

✔**Ongoing Assessment** Working with proportional relationships and adjusting the scale of graphs both require students to multiply, divide, and use fractions. This lesson offers you an opportunity to notice how easily students handle these operations.

Teaching Notes for LAB page 294

Students compare three graphs of walking time, distance, and speed, and consider what kinds of questions can be answered by these graphs. Students distinguish among the total distance walked, the total time spent, and the speed of walking. The graph shows how many hours people walked, but not what times they started, so it doesn't give us enough information to answer Problems 9 and 10.

Challenge Problem The challenge asks students to add a line to the graph to show a new constant speed.

Reflect and Summarize the Lesson

Write Math

Suppose you use the same grid to graph two lines—one line to show how distance is related to time when someone walks 2 miles per hour and another line to show how distance is related to time when someone walks 4 miles per hour. How are the lines similar? How are they different? Possible answer: Both are straight lines slanting up to the right. The line for 2 miles per hour is not as steep as the one for 4 miles per hour.

Leveled Problem Solving

Richard is riding his bicycle across Pennsylvania at 18 miles per hour.

❶ Basic Level

How far will he travel in 5 hours? Explain. 90 miles; he travels 18 miles the first hour, 36 miles in 2 hours, 54 miles in 3 hours, 72 miles in 4 hours, and 90 miles in 5 hours.

❷ On Level

How far will he travel in 30 minutes? Explain. 9 miles; 30 minutes is $\frac{1}{2}$ hour, so he will travel half as far as he can travel in one hour.

❸ Above Level

How far will he travel in $4\frac{1}{2}$ hours? Explain. 81 miles; he travels 9 miles in $\frac{1}{2}$ hour and 18 miles each hour. $4 \times 18 = 72$, $72 + 9 = 81$

Intervention

Activity Distance and Time

Help students get a feel for the idea of "per hour." Have students suggest activities they can do in the classroom for 1 minute, such as snapping their fingers, jumping up and down, walking from the front to the back of the classroom. Time each activity for 1 minute and discuss how this translates into the number of snaps per hour, jumps per hour, and so on.

Practice

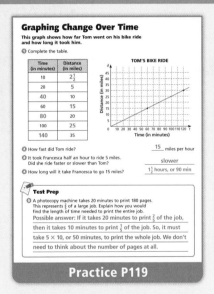

Practice P119

Extension

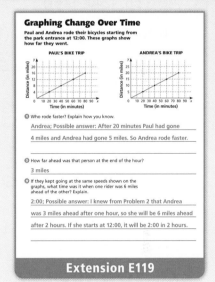

Extension E119

Spiral Review

Spiral Review Book page SR119 provides review of the following previously learned skills and concepts:

- finding the measurements of angles formed by two intersecting lines, given the measurement of one of the angles
- applying the problem solving strategy *make a table*

You may wish to have students work with partners to complete the page.

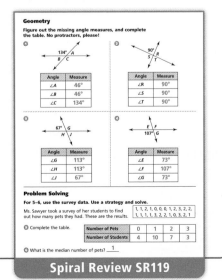

Spiral Review SR119

Extension Activity
Heart Rate

Have students place a finger on their necks to find a pulse and count the number of beats per minute. Then have students determine the number of beats per hour, per day, and per year. Challenge students to determine the number of beats their heart beats every 10 years.

Use with Lesson Activity Book pp. 293–294.

Lesson 5 Graphing the Story of a Trip

NCTM Standards 2, 3, 4, 5, 6, 7, 8, 9, 10

Lesson Planner

STUDENT OBJECTIVES
- To graph distance traveled over different time intervals
- To interpret story problems and graphs about speed, distance, and time

1 | Daily Activities (TG p. 1239)

| Open-Ended Problem Solving/Headline Story | Skills Practice and Review— Changing Temperatures Chains |

2 | Teach and Practice (TG pp. 1240–1243)

MATERIALS

- (A) **Graphing the Story of a Bike Race** (TG pp. 1240–1241)
- (B) **Interpreting Graphs** (TG p. 1242)
- (C) **Playing a Game: *The Great Race*** (TG p. 1243)

- transparency of AM159 (optional)
- TR: Activity Masters, AM158, AM160–AM162
- straightedges, color pencils, scissors
- 📖 LAB pp. 295–296
- 📖 SH p. 261

3 | Differentiated Instruction (TG p. 1244)

Leveled Problem Solving (TG p. 1244)	Practice Book P120
Intervention Activity (TG p. 1244)	Extension Book E120
Extension Activity (TG p. 1244)	Spiral Review Book SR120

Lesson Notes

About the Lesson

In the previous lesson students investigated situations when speed of traveling was constant. Now they consider stories about speed that changes over time. Students graph distance over time and interpret the graphs to answer questions about the situations in the stories.

About the Mathematics

When you graph a straight line on a coordinate plane, it has the same slope everywhere along the line. You can think of this as being related to its incline or angle relative to the axes. Because of this constant slope, a set of directions that moves you from one point to another on the line (such as left two spaces and up

one space) will *always* keep you on the line, regardless of where you apply those directions.

In the stories in this lesson, the speed is not constant: it changes at various points in time. However, the speed is still assumed to be constant *between* those points where we are told it changes. So, instead of one straight line, the graph is a series of line segments with different slopes. Looking at the graph of Meredith's bike race, we can tell when she was going more or less quickly by comparing the slopes of the line segments for different time intervals. The steeper the slope, the faster her speed is.

(continued on page R7)

Use with Lesson Activity Book pp. 295–296.

Developing Mathematical Language

Vocabulary: constant speed, steepness

In this lesson, we again use *constant speed*, but we notice when the speed changes abruptly. Though the speed varies from one time interval to another we assume that the speed is constant within each segment of the trip.

The *steepness* of the graph shows how quickly the *y*-values change (rise or fall) as the *x*-values increase. We choose the non-mathematical term *steepness* to take advantage of students' familiarity with the *steepness* of hills and to avoid technical detail in the related mathematical term, slope.

Review the term *steepness* with students, perhaps using a hill or drawing as a context.

Beginning Draw several pairs of slanted line segments on the board. Ask students to identify the steeper line segment in each pair.

Intermediate Have students draw two staircases on construction paper. One staircase should have 1-inch vertical risers and 2-inch horizontal steps. For the other staircase, reverse the dimensions of the riser and step. Ask students to identify the steeper staircase.

Advanced Have students work in small groups. Give students the dimensions of a staircase, such as 6 inches for the vertical riser and 10 inches for the horizontal step. Ask how they would make the staircase *steeper*.

1 | Daily Activities

Open-Ended Problem Solving

Read the Headline Story to the students. Encourage them to think of creative ways to answer the question.

 Headline Story

What could this graph represent? Suggest labels for the horizontal and vertical axes.

Possible responses: There are 3 of something on the vertical axis for every 1 on the horizontal axis; so you could put feet on the vertical axis and yards on the horizontal axis, because there are 3 feet in a yard. If the vertical axis was miles and the horizontal axis hours, it could be a graph of someone going 3 miles an hour.

Skills Practice and Review

Changing Temperature Chains

Repeat the skills practice from **Lesson 15.4**, giving a temperature question using small numbers so students can practice using negative numbers. Again, have students use temperatures from both scales, Celsius and Fahrenheit. Have students answer—and then ask—questions as before. You might challenge students by requiring they ask a different kind of question than the one they answered. For example, if they answer a question such as, "How did the temperature change when it went from ⁻15°C to 8°C?" they can't ask another question that directly asks for the change. (You might allow a question that is indirectly the same, such as, "How much warmer is 12°C than ⁻3°C?".)

whole class **10 MIN**

Ⓐ Graphing the Story of a Bike Race

Materials
- For the teacher:
  transparency of AM159
  (optional), straightedge
- For each student:
  AM158

NCTM Standards 2, 3, 4, 5, 6, 7, 8, 9, 10

Purpose To interpret the graph of distance over time when the speed is not constant

Introduce Give each student a copy of Activity Master 158: Training for a Bike Race to refer to. Ask a volunteer to read the paragraph at the top of the page aloud. Have a student explain what the data in the table shows.

Task **On a transparency of Activity Master 159: Graph of a Bike Race or a grid drawn on the board, help students to graph each data point.** (These points will *not* lie on a single straight line.)

💬 **Talk Math** When the points are plotted, ask these questions.

❓ Can you connect the points with one straight line, as in the past few lessons? (You may want to use a straightedge to check.) Explain. No. Although you can draw a line through some of the points, no single straight line will connect them all

❓ Why aren't these points in a straight line like the points were in previous lessons? Each of the points is 10 minutes apart in time, but they're not all the same amount apart in distance. Meredith wasn't always going the same speed.

We can get an *approximate* idea of how far Meredith had gone at any minute by connecting all the dots making a bent line—straight from "start" to the first "beep," and then straight from each dot to the next.

💬 **Talk Math** Continue with these questions.

❓ According to the graph, how far had Meredith traveled in the first 50 minutes? in the first 45 minutes? Possible answer: She traveled 20 miles in the first 50 minutes. After the first 45 minutes she was between her 40 minutes beep and 50 minutes beep, which is between 18 and 20 miles. The graph suggests she had traveled 19 miles.

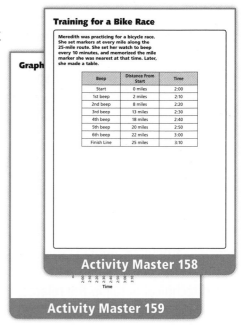

Training for a Bike Race

Meredith was practicing for a bicycle race. She set markers at every mile along the 25-mile route. She set her watch to beep every 10 minutes, and memorized the mile marker she was nearest at that time. Later, she made a table.

Beep	Distance From Start	Time
Start	0 miles	2:00
1st beep	2 miles	2:10
2nd beep	8 miles	2:20
3rd beep	13 miles	2:30
4th beep	18 miles	2:40
5th beep	20 miles	2:50
6th beep	22 miles	3:00
Finish Line	25 miles	3:10

Activity Master 158

Activity Master 159

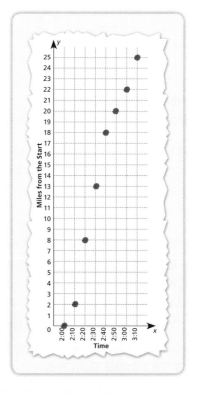

Use with Lesson Activity Book pp. 295–296.

❓ Why should we be less certain about how far Meredith traveled in 45 minutes than we are about how far she traveled in 50 minutes? Possible answer: We know she is changing speeds. We are told how far she went in 50 minutes, but we're only guessing about 45. Maybe she went the full 20 miles in 45 minutes and then had to stop to rest!

The problem doesn't actually tell us anything about what happened in between the beeps. That makes sense for real life: if Meredith just checked her mileage every time she heard a beep, the information in the table would be all she would know. If Meredith wanted to be able to say something about her speed, she would have to *assume* that she was going at a constant speed between each pair of beeps. Explain that the way you've connected the dots makes the assumption that between each pair of beeps, Meredith's speed was the same for the whole 10 minutes.

Talk Math Ask these questions about the graph.

❓ How much time passed between the 2nd beep and the 3rd beep? between the 3rd beep and the 6th beep? 10 minutes; 30 minutes

❓ How long did the whole race take? 1 hour 10 minutes

❓ When was Meredith going fastest? How can we figure that out? The faster the speed, the steeper the line on the graph. Meredith was going fastest between the 1st and 2nd beeps, 6 miles in 10 minutes.

❓ If there was a big uphill somewhere along the race course, where do you think it was? Explain. Meredith was probably going most slowly as she went up the hill, so wherever her speed was slowest, that was probably the hill. That would be between the Start and the 1st beep or between the 3rd and 5th beeps, where she went 2 miles for each 10 minutes. Perhaps she was going downhill between the 2nd and 4th beeps.

❓ How fast was Meredith going between the 1st and 2nd beeps? In 10 minutes, she traveled 6 miles. In 60 minutes at that speed, she would go 36 miles, so that's 36 miles per hour.

Possible Discussion

Another way to figure out when Meredith was going the fastest is to think about the distance she traveled between each beep. Since the time between each pair of beeps is 10 minutes, the time interval when she was going fastest is the one in which she covered the most distance. But the distances listed in the table are *total* distances. We need to know how much distance she covered between one beep and the next. We could figure that out from the table, by subtracting the total distance of the 2nd beep from the 3rd beep to find out what the distance between the 2nd and 3rd was. In effect, this is finding the change in the vertical coordinate for a 10 minute change in the horizontal coordinate. The greater the change in the vertical coordinate over the change in the horizontal coordinate, the greater the slope. So, usually it is where the slope of the line segment between 2 points is the greatest.

Concept Alert

When thinking about a story problem about a cyclist going up a hill, it is natural to confuse the steepness of the *hill* with the steepness of the *graph*. In fact, the steeper the hill, the more likely the cyclist will be going more slowly so the graph will be flatter.

Interpreting Graphs LAB pp. 295–296

Purpose To make graphs representing distance and time when speed is not constant, and to interpret the graphs to answer questions

NCTM Standards 2, 3, 4, 5, 6, 7, 8, 9, 10

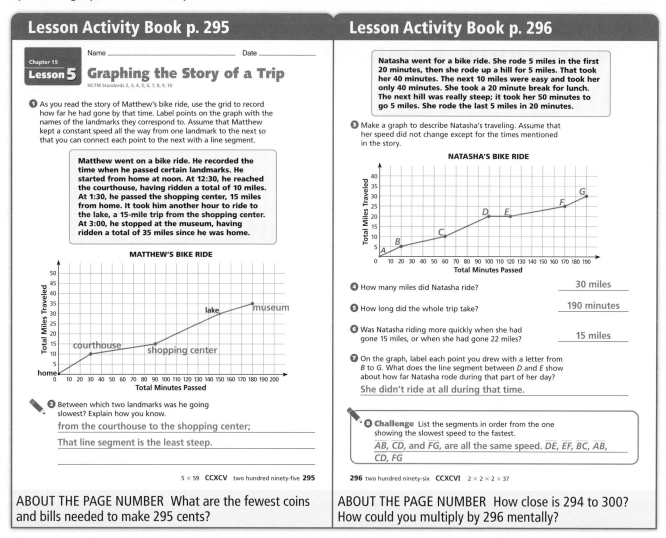

Lesson Activity Book p. 295

Name _____ Date _____

Chapter 15
Lesson 5 **Graphing the Story of a Trip**
NCTM Standards 2, 3, 4, 5, 6, 7, 8, 9, 10

❶ As you read the story of Matthew's bike ride, use the grid to record how far he had gone by that time. Label points on the graph with the names of the landmarks they correspond to. Assume that Matthew kept a constant speed all the way from one landmark to the next so that you can connect each point to the next with a line segment.

> Matthew went on a bike ride. He recorded the time when he passed certain landmarks. He started from home at noon. At 12:30, he reached the courthouse, having ridden a total of 10 miles. At 1:30, he passed the shopping center, 15 miles from home. It took him another hour to ride to the lake, a 15-mile trip from the shopping center. At 3:00, he stopped at the museum, having ridden a total of 35 miles since he was home.

MATTHEW'S BIKE RIDE

❷ Between which two landmarks was he going slowest? Explain how you know.

from the courthouse to the shopping center;

That line segment is the least steep.

5 × 59 **CCXCV** two hundred ninety-five **295**

Lesson Activity Book p. 296

> Natasha went for a bike ride. She rode 5 miles in the first 20 minutes, then she rode up a hill for 5 miles. That took her 40 minutes. The next 10 miles were easy and took her only 40 minutes. She took a 20 minute break for lunch. The next hill was really steep; it took her 50 minutes to go 5 miles. She rode the last 5 miles in 20 minutes.

❸ Make a graph to describe Natasha's traveling. Assume that her speed did not change except for the times mentioned in the story.

NATASHA'S BIKE RIDE

❹ How many miles did Natasha ride? _30 miles_

❺ How long did the whole trip take? _190 minutes_

❻ Was Natasha riding more quickly when she had gone 15 miles, or when she had gone 22 miles? _15 miles_

❼ On the graph, label each point you drew with a letter from B to G. What does the line segment between D and E show about how far Natasha rode during that part of her day?

She didn't ride at all during that time.

❽ **Challenge** List the segments in order from the one showing the slowest speed to the fastest.

$\overline{AB}$, $\overline{CD}$, and $\overline{FG}$ are all the same speed. $\overline{DE}$, $\overline{EF}$, $\overline{BC}$, $\overline{AB}$, $\overline{CD}$, $\overline{FG}$

296 two hundred ninety-six **CCXCVI** 2 × 2 × 2 × 37

ABOUT THE PAGE NUMBER What are the fewest coins and bills needed to make 295 cents?

ABOUT THE PAGE NUMBER How close is 294 to 300? How could you multiply by 296 mentally?

Teaching Notes for LAB page 295

Reading a complex mathematical problem requires a new kind of literacy skill—a systematic kind of reading—that your students might need your help with. You may want to begin this page with them, and then have them continue on their own.

Students must use the times given to figure out how much time has elapsed since the beginning of the ride to each landmark Matthew passes. Then they graph each time/distance pair. Because Matthew's speed is constant between each pair of landmarks, it is appropriate to connect the points with line segments.

Students can compare speeds by looking at the steepness of the line segments (the steeper the line, the more distance Matthew covers for each unit of time, so the faster he must be going). They can also compare how much distance was covered in equivalent amounts of time.

Teaching Notes for LAB page 296

Students need to be careful to remember that the times in the problem are the times between one point and the next, whereas the times marked on the horizontal axis on the graph are total times since the beginning of the trip.

Challenge Problem The Challenge Problem requires students to compare speeds at different times by comparing the steepness of the different line segments.

Playing a Game: *The Great Race*

Purpose To practice plotting points to show time and the related distance traveled

Goal The object of the game, *The Great Race*, is to cross the finish line (600 miles) in the least amount of time (measured on the horizontal axis). The number of *turns* to cross the finish line doesn't matter; all that matters is which car took the fewest *hours* to go the distance.

Prepare Materials Each pair of students will need 2 color pencils, a straightedge, scissors, and a game board and a set of cards from AM160–AM162.

How to Play

❶ Shuffle the Time and Distance Cards to make one draw deck. Deal each player 4 cards. One player chooses a card from his or her hand and plays it face up.

❷ The second player must play a card of the opposite type—Time if the first card was Distance, and *vice versa.* If the second player has no card of the appropriate type, he or she keeps discarding a card and drawing a new one, until it is possible to play.

❸ The two cards represent the first player's time and distance for this section of the trip. The first player starts at (0,0) on Activity Master 160: *The Great Race* Game Board and advances by the time and distance given on the cards. For example, if the cards were 2 hours and 50 miles, the player would advance to the point (2,50) on the game board. The player uses a color pencil to mark this stopping point and to draw a line segment connecting it to *that player's* previous stopping point. In later turns, the player calculates the new time and distance starting from their last turn's stopping point. For example, if this player's second set of cards were 1 hour and 50 miles, the player has now gone one hour more (now a total of 3 hours) and 50 miles more (a total of 100 miles) and so would move to the point (3,100), and connect it to (2,50).

❹ Each player draws a new card, bringing their hands back up to 4 cards.

❺ Players alternate turns, shuffling the discard piles to create new draw decks when necessary.

❻ The game continues until both players have crossed the Finish Line. The winner is the one whose total time (not the number of turns) at 600 miles is the least.

Materials

- For each pair of students: AM160–AM162, 2 color pencils, straightedge, scissors

NCTM Standards 2, 3, 4, 5, 6, 7, 8, 9, 10

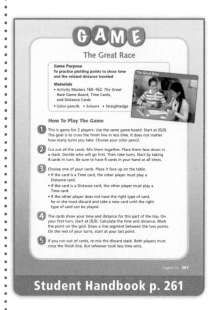

Student Handbook p. 261

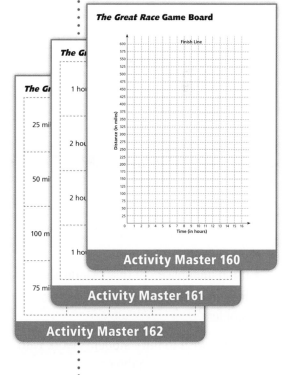

Activity Master 160
Activity Master 161
Activity Master 162

Reflect and Summarize the Lesson

Write Math **Marissa made a graph of her hiking trip. The graph is made up of line segments. By looking at the graph of her hike, how can you tell when she was hiking more or less quickly?** You can compare the steepness of the line segments that make up the graph. The steeper the line segment, the faster her speed is.

3 | Differentiated Instruction

Leveled Problem Solving

Gunther walked $3\frac{1}{2}$ miles in 1 hour, another 1 mile in 15 minutes, and another $\frac{3}{4}$ mile in the last 20 minutes. Suppose Gunther graphs his walk.

❶ Basic Level

Which part of the line will be steeper, the first part of his walk or the second part? Explain. second part; 1 mile in 15 min is the same as 4 miles in 1 hr.

❷ On Level

Which part of the line will be steeper, the first part of his walk or the last part? Explain. first part; $\frac{3}{4}$ mile in 20 min is the same as $\frac{3}{4}$ mile in $\frac{1}{3}$ hr, or $3 \times \frac{3}{4}$, or $2\frac{1}{4}$ miles in 1 hr.

❸ Above Level

Which part of the line will be the steepest? Explain. second part; 1 mile in 15 min = 4 miles in 1 hr. $\frac{3}{4}$ mile in 20 min = $2\frac{1}{4}$ miles in 1 hr; $4 > 3\frac{1}{2} > 2\frac{1}{4}$

Intervention

Activity Pencil Roll

Have small groups of students roll pencils down ramps made by a notebook. Tell each group to vary the steepness of the ramp with stacked books to vary the speed of the rolling pencil.

Help students make the connection between steepness and speed. Have them complete this sentence:

As the ramp gets _____ the pencil rolls faster. steeper

Practice

Graphing the Story of a Trip

The Callahan family went on a trip in their car. They changed speed at 4 points along the way, but kept a constant speed between one point and the next.

❶ Complete the table and graph of the Callahans' trip.

Point	Time on clock	Distance from Start
A	1:00	0
B	1:45	40
C	2:15	60
D	3:15	140
E	4:00	160

THE CALLAHANS' TRIP

❷ How long did it take them to drive from Point C to Point E?
1 hour and 45 minutes, or 105 minutes

❸ Were they driving faster between Point B and Point C, or between Point C and Point D? Explain how you know.
between C and D; The line segment from C to D is steeper.

Test Prep

❹ A restaurant has tables that seat 4 people. When the restaurant is full, it holds 152 people. How many people are in the restaurant if half of the tables are full and half have two people at them? Explain how you found your answer.
114 people; Possible explanation: There are 38 tables in the restaurant because 4 × 38 = 154. 19 tables have 4 people at them (which is 76 people) and 19 tables have 2 people at them (which is 38 people). 76 + 38 = 114

Practice P120

Extension

Graphing the Story of a Candle

Graph A   Graph B   Graph C   Graph D

A candle burned for a while and then was blown out. Which of the graphs above could show . . .

❶ How the height of the candle changed over time. C

❷ How the amount of light the candle gives off changed over time. A

❸ The amount of melted wax at the bottom of the candle. B

❹ Explain why you choose one of your answers.
Answers will vary.

Extension E120

Spiral Review

Spiral Review Book page SR120 provides review of the following previously learned skills and concepts:

• using multiplication to check division

• finding a rule for a situation in a story problem

You may wish to have students work with partners to complete the page.

Number and Operations

Each division was done on a calculator. Check the result by multiplying. If there is an error, please correct it.

❶ $56\overline{)1,568}$ 38

Check: 38 × 56 = 2,128
Is the quotient correct? no
If not, what is the correct quotient? 28

❷ $47\overline{)2,914}$ 62

Check: 62 × 47 = 2,914
Is the quotient correct? yes
If not, what is the correct quotient?

❸ $76\overline{)1,900}$ 25

Check: 25 × 76 = 1,900
Is the quotient correct? yes
If not, what is the correct quotient?

❹ $83\overline{)2,241}$ 31

Check: 31 × 83 = 2,573
Is the quotient correct? no
If not, what is the correct quotient? 27

Algebra

Write an equation to describe the situation.

❺ Admission to the amusement park is $8 for adults and $5 for children. Each ride costs $3. The Smiths are at the park. They go on 11 rides together. Use T to stand for the total cost, A for the number of adults, and C for the number of children. $T = 8A + 5C + 33$

❻ Alva's Bakery sells muffins for $2 each and cakes for $7 each. Find C, the total cost of buying M muffins and K cakes. $C = 2M + 7K$

❼ A football team gained an average of G yards on each of 4 plays. Then they lost 7 yards on the next play. Use T to stand for the total number of yards and G for the number of yards gained. $T = 4G - 7$

Spiral Review SR120

Extension Activity
How Far?

Have students write a word problem that involves walking at two different speeds for two different time intervals. Then have students share the problem with a partner who determines the total distance the person walked.

Teacher's Notes

Daily Notes . . .

Quick Notes

More Ideas

Lesson 6 — Graphing Temperature Conversions

NCTM Standards 1, 2, 3, 7, 8, 9, 10

Lesson Planner

STUDENT OBJECTIVES
- To further investigate linear graphs, using both positive and negative coordinates
- To review the Celsius and Fahrenheit systems for measuring temperature

1 Daily Activities (TG p. 1247)

Open-Ended Problem Solving/Headline Story	Skills Practice and Review— Elapsed Time Chain

2 Teach and Practice (TG pp. 1248–1250)

MATERIALS

Ⓐ **Creating a Temperature Conversion Table** (TG p. 1248)

Ⓑ **Graphing Temperature Conversions** (TG p. 1249)

Ⓒ **Using Graphs to Find Changes in Temperature** (TG p. 1250)

- transparency of AM163 (optional)
- 📖 LAB pp. 297–298

3 Differentiated Instruction (TG p. 1251)

Leveled Problem Solving (TG p. 1251)	Practice Book P121
Intervention Activity (TG p. 1251)	Extension Book E121
Extension Activity (TG p. 1251)	Spiral Review Book SR121
Social Studies Connection (TG p. 1202)	

Lesson Notes

About the Lesson

In this lesson, students continue making and using graphs of straight lines to show proportional relationships. Students use the conversion between Fahrenheit and Celsius as a context in which it makes sense to extend the line using negative numbers.

About the Mathematics

Like other conversions between measurement units, the relationship between Celsius and Fahrenheit is linear. However, the rule relating °F and °C is more complicated than the 12-to-1 rule relating inches to feet, or even the rule relating inches and centimeters. (See About the Mathematics in **Lesson 15.3**.)

A change of 5°C equals a change of 9°F. While this may sound similar to other conversions, there is also a shift in where the origin is for converting between °C and °F. 0 cm = 0 in., but 0°C ≠ 0°F. Therefore, to convert between Celsius and Fahrenheit, you make *two* changes—*multiplying* to account for the proportional relationship between the two units, and then *adding* an extra 32°F. Creating the Celsius and Fahrenheit systems involved choosing a temperature to call 0. Those zeros are arbitrary—they aren't anything like "an absence of temperature" in the way

(continued on page R8)

Developing Mathematical Language

Vocabulary: <u>conversion rule</u>, <u>conversion graph</u>

Some students might not recognize the word *conversion* as a form of the familiar verb *convert*. Remind students that they have converted between two measures, such as inches and feet, quarts and gallons, and days and weeks. Each conversion has a different *conversion rule*. The graph of the *conversion rule* is a *conversion graph* that relates one measure to the other. In this lesson, the *conversion graph* relates degrees Fahrenheit to degrees Celsius.

Familiarize students with the terms *conversion rule* and *conversion graph.*

Beginning Write the words *convert* and *conversion* on the board. Have students identify the parts of the words that are the same, *conver-*. Remind students that *convert* means "to change from one thing to another" and that a *conversion rule* is used for changing between units.

Intermediate Remind students that *convert* means, "to change from one thing to another" and that they have used *rule* with input-output tables. Have students write a *conversion rule* for two measures, such as months and years.

Advanced Have students discuss situations in which they would need to use a *conversion rule.*

Open-Ended Problem Solving

To extend this Headline Story, you might tell students how long it took to heat up the oven for different dishes Brett was making, and have them figure out the target temperatures.

 Headline Story

> Brett turned on the oven. He looked at the thermometer every 5 minutes and noticed the temperature had risen by the same amount each time. If the temperature in the oven was 75°F when he first turned it on, how long will it take to get to 450°F?

Possible responses: It depends how much the temperature goes up in 5 minutes. From 75° to 450° is a change of 375°. If it goes up 25° every 5 minutes, it will take 15 five-minute intervals, or 75 minutes. If it goes up 100° in 5 minutes, it will take $3\frac{3}{4}$ five-minute intervals, which is almost 20 minutes. I wouldn't wait over an hour for an oven to warm up. The temperature likely increases around 100° in each 5-minute interval.

Skills Practice and Review

Elapsed Time Chain

Give students a problem about elapsed time; for example, "I arrived at school today an hour before the first class started. When did I get here?" After a student answers, let them think of a time related question.

- Joanie arrived 20 minutes after Kate. Kate arrived at 7:42. When did Joanie arrive?

- Pearl dropped one of her pencils but didn't notice until 2:32. She remembered that she dropped it when Taisha presented her problem 25 minutes ago. When did Pearl drop it?

whole class 15 MIN

Materials
- For the teacher: transparency of AM163 (optional)

NCTM Standards 1, 2, 7, 8, 9

A Creating a Temperature Conversion Table

Purpose To review and relate the Fahrenheit and Celsius temperature scales

Introduce Ask students what they remember about the two systems for measuring temperature, Fahrenheit and Celsius. See if there are particular temperatures students remember in either system, such as the temperature at which water freezes 32°F or 0°C, the temperature at which water boils 212°F or 100°C, or normal body temperature. 98.6°F or 37°C Students may also have a general sense of what range of temperatures in each scale correspond to a warm or cold day outside.

Task Have students use a pattern to convert between Fahrenheit and Celsius.

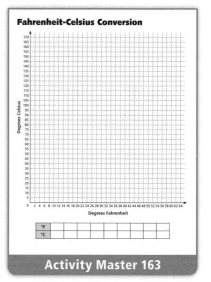

Display AM163: Fahrenheit-Celsius Conversion or sketch a similar table on the board. In the table, write the temperature at which water freezes: 32°F or 0°C. In the next column, write 41°F and 5°C. Without stating the rule that you are following, do another example, increasing °F by 9 and °C by 5. Then fill in another jump of 9 for °F, and ask a student to name the corresponding value for °C.

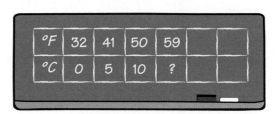

Do several more jumps like this, letting students follow the rule (without stating it) to fill in the missing numbers. Then try a skip of 18°F and see if students realize that the corresponding change in °C should be 10. When most of the class seems to have figured out the rule you're using, ask someone to explain it. Whenever °F goes up by 9°, °C goes up by 5.

💬 Talk Math

❓ The temperature was 0°C and then rose 10°. What is the temperature now in °C and °F? 10°C or 50°F

❓ It's 41°F and then drops to 0°C. How many degrees did the temperature change in Celsius degrees? in Fahrenheit degrees? 41°F is 5°C so the change in temperature in Celsius is ⁻5°. Since 0°C is 32°F, the change in temperature in Fahrenheit is ⁻9°.

Graphing Temperature Conversions

Purpose To review negative numbers and graph the relationship between the Fahrenheit and Celsius temperature scales

Materials
• For the teacher: transparency of AM163 (optional)

NCTM Standards 3, 7, 8, 9

Introduce Display AM163: Fahrenheit-Celsius Conversion or sketch the axes from the page on the board. Remind students of negative numbers by asking what numbers they would label on the axes if the axes were extended down or to the left.

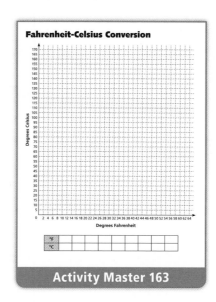

Fahrenheit-Celsius Conversion

Activity Master 163

Task **Using the table you just created with the class in Activity A, have students plot pairs of numbers from the table as points on the graph.** Ask them to name or write the coordinates of each point. You might ask them to predict what the graph will look like. Because the Fahrenheit axis is labeled in jumps of 2, not all points will fall on intersections of grid lines.

Talk Math

❓ Are all of the points on the same straight line? Is this what you expected? Yes. The points appear to lie on a straight line. We could expect this, because °F always changes by the same amount when °C changes by a certain amount.

❓ How is this graph different from the other linear graphs you have made in previous lessons of this chapter? The line doesn't pass through (0,0).

❓ Could you extend this graph into negative coordinates? Yes. If the temperature was 5° below 0° in Celsius, it would be 9° below 32°, or 23° in Fahrenheit, and so on.

Connect the points to form a straight line. Pick a Celsius temperature that is a multiple of 5 but that is not one of the points you graphed. Ask students to use the graph to figure out what the corresponding Fahrenheit reading should be. (Find that temperature on the Celsius axis, and then trace your finger horizontally along that grid line until you hit the line of the graph. Then trace your finger straight down to the Fahrenheit axis and read the value there.) Then choose one or two Celsius temperatures that are not multiples of 5. The corresponding Fahrenheit reading won't be a whole number and students will need to estimate. Also do the reverse, picking a Fahrenheit temperature and asking students to find the corresponding Celsius reading.

Concept Alert

Using a graph in this way to convert between Celsius and Fahrenheit temperatures that are not both whole numbers doesn't provide exact answers. Students will need to estimate.

Extend To challenge students you might ask them to convert between a negative temperature in Celsius and Fahrenheit. For example, ⁻10°C is 18° less than 32° in Fahrenheit.

Using Graphs to Find Changes in Temperature LAB pp. 297–298

Purpose To use a graph to solve problems involving changes in temperatures and converting between Celsius and Fahrenheit

NCTM Standards 1, 3, 7, 8, 9, 10

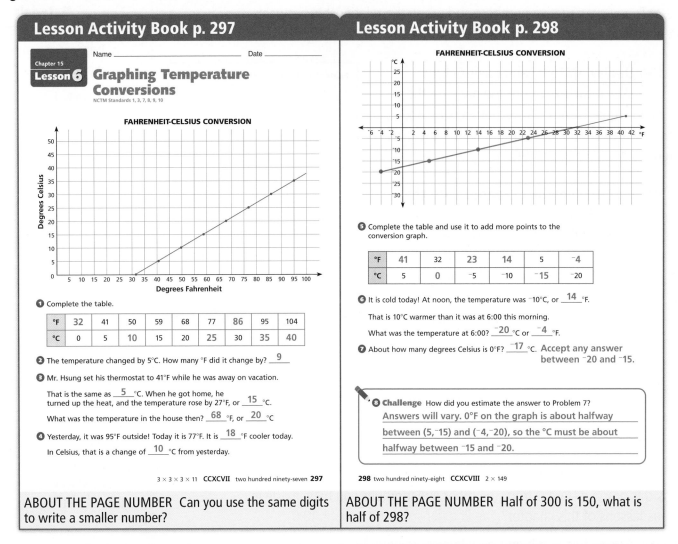

Teaching Notes for LAB page 297

Students use the conversion rule they discovered in class (a change of 9°F is the same as a change of 5°C) and the graph to complete a table of correspondences between Celsius and Fahrenheit temperatures. Students then use the graph, table, and/or the conversion rule to solve word problems involving changes in temperature.

Possible Discussion Discuss why the graphs on LAB pp. 297–298 look different. This lesson demonstrates some situations where different scales are useful. The Celsius graph on LAB p. 297 uses jumps of 5 to label both axes because the goal was to get more points onto the graph.

Teaching Notes for LAB page 298

On LAB p. 298, students need to estimate the Fahrenheit numbers, so the scale is in jumps of 2. Students extend the Fahrenheit-Celsius graph into negative temperatures and use the new data to solve problems. Problem 7 requires students to estimate the Celsius temperature corresponding to 0°F. They may use the graph to estimate visually (the point looks like it's about halfway between ⁻15° and ⁻20°).

Challenge Problem Students explain the strategy they used to estimate the answer in Problem 7.

Reflect and Summarize the Lesson

Write Math **If the temperature of water increases by 10 degrees Celsius by how much does it increase in Farhenheit degrees? Explain how you know.** The temperature increases by 18°F. A change of 5°C is the same as a change of 9°F, so a change of 10°C is the same as a change of 18°F.

3 | Differentiated Instruction

Today it is 25°C outside. Last night it was 15° cooler.

❶ Basic Level
What is the change in degrees Fahrenheit? Explain. 27°; for every 5° change in Celsius, there is a 9° change in Fahrenheit: $15 \div 5 = 3$, and $3 \times 9 = 27$.

❷ On Level
Last night's temperature was 50°F. What is today's temperature in degrees Fahrenheit? Explain. 77°F; $15 \div 5 = 3$, $3 \times 9 = 27$, $50 + 27 = 77$

❸ Above Level
Is 55°F closer to today's temperature or last night's temperature of 50°F? Explain. last night's temperature; $25°C = 77°F$, $77° - 55° = 22°F$ and $22°F > 5°F$

Intervention	Practice	Extension

Activity Celsius/Fahrenheit Thermometer

Have students draw a vertical thermometer using 14 lines of lined paper as tick marks. Have them label the left side *Celsius* and the right side *Fahrenheit.* At the ninth tick mark from the bottom, have students label the Celsius side 0° and the Fahrenheit side 32°. Tell students to label the entire thermometer by skip-counting by 5s for Celsius and 9s for Fahrenheit. Then have students convert various temperatures.

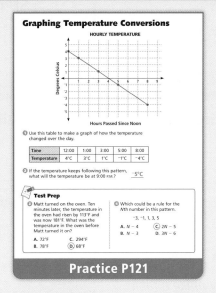

Practice P121

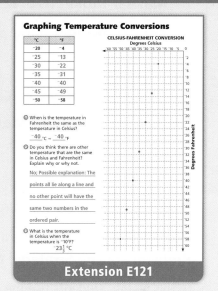

Extension E121

Spiral Review

Spiral Review Book page SR121 provides review of the following previously learned skills and concepts:

- estimating sums and differences of mixed numbers
- interpreting data in circle graphs

You may wish to have students work with partners to complete the page.

Spiral Review SR121

Extension Activity Conversion Graphs

Assign pairs of students different measurement conversions, such as feet and yards, weeks and days, pints and quarts. Use conversions having corresponding units of 12 or less. Have partners graph the conversions two different ways, once with the smaller unit on the horizontal axis and the larger unit on the vertical axis and *vice versa.* Tell students to use the same scale on each axis. Display pairs of graphs, and discuss patterns students notice.

Problem Solving Strategy and Test Prep

NCTM Standards 1, 2, 6, 7, 8, 10

Lesson Planner

- To practice the problem solving strategy *make a table*
- To articulate the steps and strategies used to solve problems
- To prepare for standardized tests

Problem Solving Strategy:
Make a Table (TG pp. 1253–1254, 1256–1257)

 **MATERIALS**

Ⓐ Discussing the Problem Solving Strategy: Make a Table (TG p. 1253)

Ⓑ Solving Problems by Applying the Strategy (TG p. 1254)

- 📖 LAB p. 299
- 📖 SH pp. 256–257

 Problem Solving Test Prep (TG pp. 1255)

Ⓒ Getting Ready for Standardized Tests (TG p. 1255)

- 📖 LAB p. 300

Lesson Notes

About Problem Solving

Problem Solving Strategy: Make a Table

In this lesson, students use the strategy *make a table* to solve problems involving patterns.

This lesson also gives you an opportunity to assess your students' ability to name and identify points on the coordinate plane, including points with negative coordinates; to graph data from tables and to interpret graphs; to recognize and graph linear relationships; and to choose an appropriate scale for a graph.

Skills Practice and Review

Elapsed Time Chain

Repeat this activity from **Lesson 15.6,** but now require students to ask a different type of question than the one they just answered. For example, if they answer a question with a time of day (like 11:34), they have to ask a question whose answer is a length of time, such as, "We started school at 8:00, and it's now 11:34. How long ago did we start school?"

(A) Discussing the Problem Solving Strategy: Make a Table

 whole class 15 MIN

NCTM Standards 1, 2, 6, 7, 8, 10

Purpose To share strategies for solving problems and focus on the problem solving strategy, *make a table*

Introduce Remind students that throughout this chapter they have been using the strategy *make a table* to help them look at patterns in sequences and in line graphs.

Record the following problem on the board or on a blank transparency. Ask a volunteer to read the problem. Then have the students begin working on the problem.

Problem Jake put 4 cubes together to make a train.

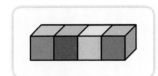

He counted the faces of the cube that were touching the table and those that were showing. There were 18 in all. How many faces would be on the table or showing if he made a train of 30 cubes?

Share Have students share their strategies for solving the problem. Students may suggest making a table to help them find the pattern.

 Talk Math

❓ How might making a table help you answer the question? A table helps you organize the data to make it easier to find a pattern in the relationship between the number of cubes and the number of faces on the table or showing.

❓ How would you make the table? One table is shown.

Number of Cubes	1	2	3	4	5	6	N	30
Number of Faces on the Table or Showing	6	10	14	18	22	26	$4N + 2$	$4 \times 30 + 2 = 122$

❓ How did you decide how many faces would be on the table or showing for *N* cubes? When I look at the 4-train cube I see that there are four sides of the train (top, bottom, and two sides) that each have 4 faces, so that's 4×4. There are also 2 faces on the ends. That's a total of $4 \times 4 + 2$ faces for a 4-cube train. For an *N*-cube train, there would be $4 \times N + 2$ faces.

Solving Problems by Applying the Strategy LAB p. 299

Purpose To practice the problem solving strategy, *make a table*

Teaching Notes for LAB page 299

Have students look at the first three problems that all go with the sequence of squares on LAB page 299 and, if available, put up a transparency of the page. Give students a few minutes to look at the five parts of the problem. Then have students share their strategies for solving the problem. Discuss how to use the problem solving strategy *make a table* to help find the pattern of the squares in the sequence. You may want to ask questions like these to guide the discussion.

Read to Understand

What do you know from reading the problem? the number of squares in the first three pictures of a sequence.

What do you need to find out? the rule for describing the number of squares in Picture *N* in this sequence.

Plan

How can you solve this problem? You can make a table and a graph to help you find a pattern in the number of squares in each picture in the sequence.

How could you make a table? Make two columns to list the number of squares for each successive picture in the sequence and once you notice a pattern, extend it in the table.

Solve

How might you use a table to solve the problem? You can use the number pairs in the table as coordinates of points on a graph and then look at the graph to find the way the number of squares increases in each successive picture in the sequence.

What pattern do you notice? The first picture has 1 square and each picture after that adds 4 more squares. The *N* th picture has 4 more squares then the picture before it. So, the *N* th picture will have $1 + 4 \times (N - 1)$ squares.

Check

Look back at the original problem. Do your answers make sense? How do you know?

Lesson Activity Book p. 299

Name _____ Date _____

Chapter 15
Lesson 7

Problem Solving Strategy
Make a Table
NCTM Standards 1, 2, 6, 7, 8, 10

Understand
Plan
Solve
Check

Find a rule to describe this pattern by making a graph.

❶ Draw the next picture in this sequence.

❷ Complete the table below.

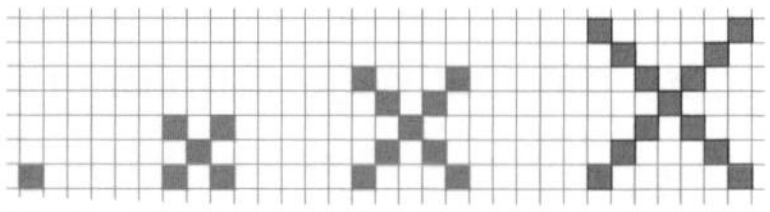

Picture 1   Picture 2   Picture 3   Picture 4

❸ Make a graph using the picture number as the first coordinate and the number of small squares as the second coordinate. Draw a line to connect the points.

Picture Number	Number of Squares
1	1
2	5
3	9
4	13
5	17
10	37
N	$4N - 3$, or $1 + 4 \times (N - 1)$

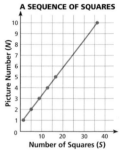

A SEQUENCE OF SQUARES

❹ Use the graph to find the number of squares in Picture 6 and in Picture 8.

Picture 6: __21__ squares   Picture 8: __29__ squares

❺ Describe in words how to predict the number of squares in Picture *N*.
Answer will vary. Possible answer: The first picture has only 1 square, and each picture after that adds 4 more squares. The *N*th picture has 4 more squares than the picture before it. So the *N*th picture will have $1 + 4 \times (N - 1)$ squares, which can be written $4N - 3$ squares.

13 × 23   **CCXCIX**   two hundred ninety-nine **299**

ABOUT THE PAGE NUMBER To add to this number, add to 300 and then take away 1.

Reflect and Summarize the Lesson

Write Math

How can using the strategy *make a table* help you solve a problem?
Possible answer: Making a table can help you find a pattern in the how numbers in a sequence are related.

Problem Solving Test Prep

(C) Getting Ready for Standardized Tests LAB p. 300

individuals

👤 🕐 **30 MIN**

Purpose To prepare students for standardized tests

NCTM Standards 2, 4, 5, 6, 7, 9, 10

Lesson Activity Book p. 300

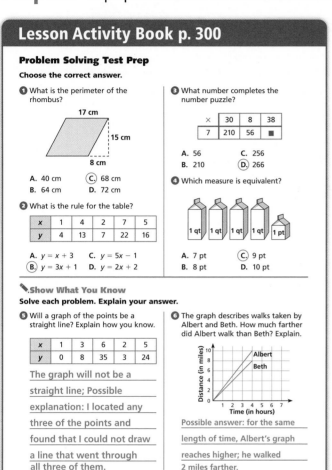

Problem Solving Test Prep

Choose the correct answer.

1 What is the perimeter of the rhombus?

17 cm / 15 cm / 8 cm

A. 40 cm   C. 68 cm
B. 64 cm   D. 72 cm

2 What is the rule for the table?

x	1	4	2	7	5
y	4	13	7	22	16

A. y = x + 3   C. y = 5x − 1
B. y = 3x + 1   D. y = 2x + 2

3 What number completes the number puzzle?

×	30	8	38
7	210	56	■

A. 56   C. 256
B. 210   D. 266

4 Which measure is equivalent?

1 qt 1 qt 1 qt 1 qt 1 pt

A. 7 pt   C. 9 pt
B. 8 pt   D. 10 pt

Show What You Know

Solve each problem. Explain your answer.

5 Will a graph of the points be a straight line? Explain how you know.

x	1	3	6	2	5
y	0	8	35	3	24

The graph will not be a straight line; Possible explanation: I located any three of the points and found that I could not draw a line that went through all three of them.

6 The graph describes walks taken by Albert and Beth. How much farther did Albert walk than Beth? Explain.

Albert / Beth — Distance (in miles) / Time (in hours)

Possible answer: for the same length of time, Albert's graph reaches higher; he walked 2 miles farther.

300 three hundred   CCC   2 × 2 × 3 × 5 × 5

ABOUT THE PAGE NUMBER 300 is a triangular number: 1 + 2 + . . . + 24. It has a horizontal line of symmetry.

Teaching Notes for LAB page 300

The test items on this page are written in the same style and arranged in the same format as those on many state assessments. The page is cumulative and is designed for students to apply a variety of problem solving strategies including *make a table, write an equation,* and *look for a pattern.* Have students share the strategies they use.

The Item Analysis Chart indicates one of the possible strategies that may be used for each test item.

Show What You Know

Short Response

Direct students' attention to Problems 5 and 6. Explain that they must decide how to solve the problems. Then have students write an explanation of how they know their answer is correct. To provide more space for students to communicate their thinking about these problems, you may wish to have them write their responses and explanations on a separate sheet of paper. Use the Scoring Rubric below to evaluate their understanding.

Item Analysis Chart

Item	Strategy
1	Write an equation
2	Look for a pattern
3	Write an equation
4	Look for a pattern, make a table or chart
5	Draw a picture or diagram
6	Use logical reasoning

Scoring Rubric

2	• Demonstrates complete understanding of the problem and chooses an appropriate strategy to determine the solution
1	• Demonstrates a partial understanding of the problem and chooses a strategy that does not lead to a complete and accurate solution
0	• Demonstrates little understanding of the problem and shows little evidence of using any strategy to determine a solution

Refer students to the Problem Solving Strategy Review Model: Make a Table in the *Student Handbook* pp. 256–257 to review a model of the four steps they can use with problem solving strategy, *make a table.*

Additional problem solving practice is also provided.

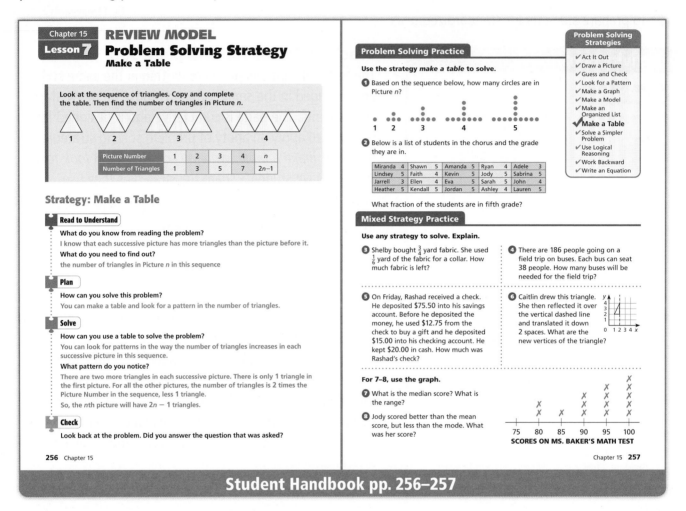

Student Handbook pp. 256–257

Task Have students read the problem at the top of the Review Model page. Then discuss.

💬 **Talk Math**

❓ Look at the pattern of triangles. What would Picture 5, the next picture in the sequence, look like? There would be one more triangle on each end of the figure. There would be 9 triangles in all.

❓ How does knowing the number of triangles in the *n*th picture, help you find the number of triangles in any picture in the sequence? Give an example. Once you know a rule for the *n*th picture, you can substitute the number for the picture you want for the *n* and find the number of triangles in that picture. For example, if you want to know the number of triangles in Picture 100, you would substitute 100 for *n*: $2 \times 100 - 1$ to find that the number of triangles in the 100th picture is 199.

successive picture in the sequence. Once you notice a pattern, extend it in the table.

❷ $\frac{3}{5}$; Possible explanation: You can use the strategy *make a table.* You can list the grades of the students in the chorus (3 through 5) and then make a tally mark for each student who is in each grade. Count the total number of tally marks and the number of tally marks next to fifth grade. There are 12 students out of 20 who are in the fifth grade. $\frac{12}{20}$ is equivalent to $\frac{3}{5}$.

subtract. $\frac{}{4}$ $\frac{}{6}$ $\frac{}{12}$ $\frac{}{12}$ $\frac{}{12}$

❹ 5 buses; Possible explanation: You can use the strategy *write an equation* to solve. To find the number of buses needed, divide 186, the number of people going on the field trip, by 38, the number of people who can ride each bus. The quotient is 4 with a remainder of 34. Since there is a remainder, another bus is needed for the field trip.

❺ $123.25; Possible explanation: You can *work backward* to solve. You can begin with $75.50, the amount Rashad deposited into the bank. Add $20.00, $15.00, and $12.75 to that amount to find the total amount of Rashad's check.

❻ (2,2), (2,0), (3,0); Possible explanation: You can use the strategy *act it out* or *draw a picture* to show where the figure will be after it has been transformed. After the triangle is reflected over the vertical dashed line, the vertices are at (2,4), (2,2), (3,2). After the figure is translated down 2 spaces, the vertices are at (2,2), (2,0), (3,0).

❼ median, 95; range, 20; Possible explanation: You can *act it out* to find the median and *write an equation* to find the range. To find the median, you need to find the middle value in the list of scores. To find the range, you find the difference between the minimum and maximum values. $100 - 80 = 20$.

❽ 95; Possible explanation: You can *write an equation* to solve. To find the mean, you add all the scores together and divide by the total number of scores. $1{,}395 \div 15 = 93$. Once you find the mean, determine the mode, or the most common value in the set of data. The number scored most often by the students was 100. Use the strategy *use logical reasoning* to find Jody's score. It is greater than the mean, 93, but less than the mode, 100.

Purpose To provide students with an opportunity to demonstrate understanding of Chapter 15 concepts and skills

MATERIALS
- LAB pp. 301–302
- Chapter 15 Test
  (Assessment Guide
  pp. AG121–AG122)

Chapter 15 Learning Goals and Assessment Options

These learning goals are assessed in many ways throughout the chapter. The chart below correlates each learning goal to specific formal and informal assessment options.

	Learning Goals	Lesson Number	Snapshot Assessment	Chapter Review Item Numbers	Chapter Test Item Numbers
			Item Number	LAB pp. 301–302	Assessment Guide pp. AG121–AG122
15-A	Make and interpret tables and straight-line graphs of proportional measurement relationships, using both positive and negative coordinates	15.1–15.4, 15.6	1, 5	1, 3, 7, 8	1-4, 8, 9
15-B	Label the axes of a grid using a scale appropriate for the data to be graphed	15.3	2, 6	2	2
15-C	Make and interpret graphs that show measurement units that change over time	15.1, 15.5	3, 4, 7	4, 5, 6	5-7
15-D	Apply problem solving strategies such as *make a table* to solve problems	15.7	8	9–11	10,11

📷 Snapshot Assessment

The following Mental Math and Quick Write questions and tasks provide a quick, informal assessment of students' understanding of Chapter 15 concepts, skills, and problem solving strategies.

whole class   10 MIN

Mental Math This oral assessment uses mental math strategies and can be used with the whole class.

❶ Which would result in a steeper line in a conversion graph in which both pairs of conversions are graphed with the same intervals? Explain.

- Pints to cups, or yards to feet? yards to feet: (multiply each yard by 3 to get feet, compared to multiplying each pint by 2 to get cups)
- Yards to feet, or feet to inches? feet to inches: (multiply each foot by 12 to get inches, compared to multiplying each yard by 3 to get feet)
- Minutes to seconds, or hours to minutes? the same: (both require multiplying by 60)
(Learning Goal 15-A)

❷ If setting up a graph to show a conversion of days to weeks.

- What labels would you likely use for the axes? Possible answer: days for the horizontal axis and weeks for the vertical axis.
- What scale would you likely use for the weeks axis? Answer will vary; possible answer: an interval of 1 would work.
- What scale would you use for the days axis? Answer will vary; possible answer: an interval of 7 would work since there are 7 days in every week.
(Learning Goal 15-B)

3 Joe starts riding his bike at noon. He bikes at the same speed throughout the entire trip. He travels 1 mile every $\frac{1}{2}$ hour. If he rides his bike for 2 hours, how far does he travel? Explain. He travels 4 miles, since he travels 1 mile each $\frac{1}{2}$ hour, or 2 miles each hour. He travels 2 hours at 2 miles each hour, which is 4 miles in all.
(Learning Goal 15-C)

4 Kyle runs cross country races and consistently runs a 4-minute mile. At that pace, how long will it take her to complete a 2.5-mile race? 10 minutes; possible explanation: each mile takes 4 minutes, therefore 2 whole miles would take 8 minutes. The other $\frac{1}{2}$ mile would take half as long, or 2 minutes. 8 minutes plus the 2 minutes equals 10 minutes in all.
(Learning Goal 15-C)

Quick Write This informal written assessment can be administered to small groups or the whole class. Read each question and have the students record responses on their write-on boards. Encourage students to listen and think about the questions before responding.

For 5–8 students will need graph paper and a red pencil or pen.
Draw the table on the board and fill in the answers together.

5

gallons	1	2	3	4
quarts	4	8	12	16

- What is the ordered pair of the first point you would plot on a graph? (1,4)
- Plot on your graph with the remaining ordered pairs
- Label the graph Check students' graphs for the ordered pairs on their graph and the labeled axis. The ordered pairs are (1,4), (2,8), (3,12), (4,16).
- Create a straight-line graph with these points. Students should connect the four points with a straightedge, resulting in a straight line.
(Learning Goal 15-A)

6

hours	1	2	3	4
minutes	60	120	180	240

- If you were setting up a conversion line graph with the above data, and the horizontal axis was labeled hours, how would you number the equal intervals? Start with 0 and use intervals of 1, since you only need to record up to 4 hours.
- Could a scale with an interval of 1 also be used for minutes on the vertical axis? Why or why not? No, if you used intervals of 1, you would run out of space before you could plot all 4 points.
- Plot the points on your graph; label the axes.
- What scale interval did you use on the vertical axis? Explain. Answers will vary; accept any reasonable intervals and explanations such as: 30, could cover all needed values from 0 to 240 in a reasonable space on the vertical axis.
(Learning Goal 15-B)

7 Complete the conversion table for a car trip:

time (hr.)	1	2	$2\frac{1}{2}$	3
distance (mi.)	50	100	125	150

- Graph a conversion table with the data given.
- What would happen to the distance if the time doubled? The distance would also double.
- On the same graph, add a red line to your graph to show a car traveling the same length of time but at 60 miles per hour. Which line would be steeper? red line since 60 mph is faster
(Learning Goal 15-C)

8 Make a table to solve the following problem:
If 4 cans of soup cost 82¢, how much will 22 cans of soup cost? Use pictures, numbers, or words to explain your answer. $4.51 Check students' tables. Possible explanation: 20 cans are 5 whole groups of cans, or 5 groups of 82¢, which equals $4.10. 2 more cans are needed to get to 22 cans. 2 cans, half of 4 cans, would cost half of 82¢, or 41¢. Add together $4.10 and 41¢ to get a total of $4.51 for 22 cans of soup.
(Learning Goal 15-D)

Formal Assessment

Chapter Review/Assessment The Chapter 15 Review/Assessment on *Lesson Activity Book* pages 301–302 assesses students' understanding of making and interpreting tables and graphs of both proportional measurement relationships and of measurement units that change over time. Students should be able to complete these pages independently.

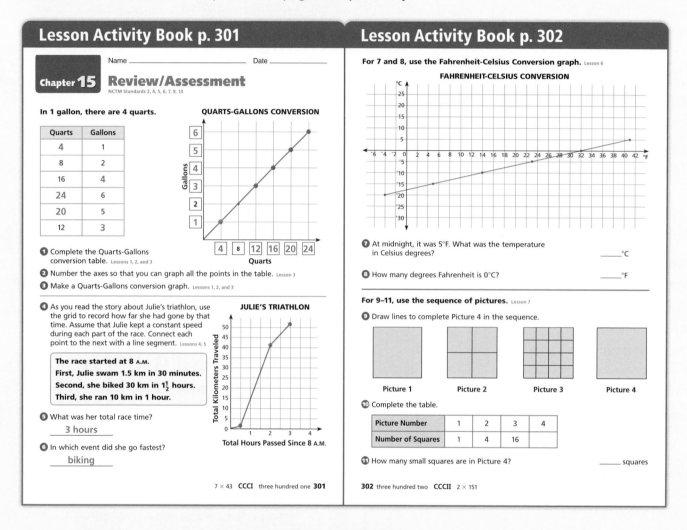

Extra Support Students who have difficulty with items on the Chapter 15 Review/Assessment may need review of the lesson where development of the concept was provided. You can use the Intervention Activity to increase students' understanding before the Chapter Test is given.

Chapter Test Use the Chapter 15 Test in the *Assessment Guide* to assess concepts, skills, and problem solving from the chapter and to prepare students for standardized tests. The Chapter Test and other test items are also available online.

Chapter Notes

Quick Notes

More Ideas

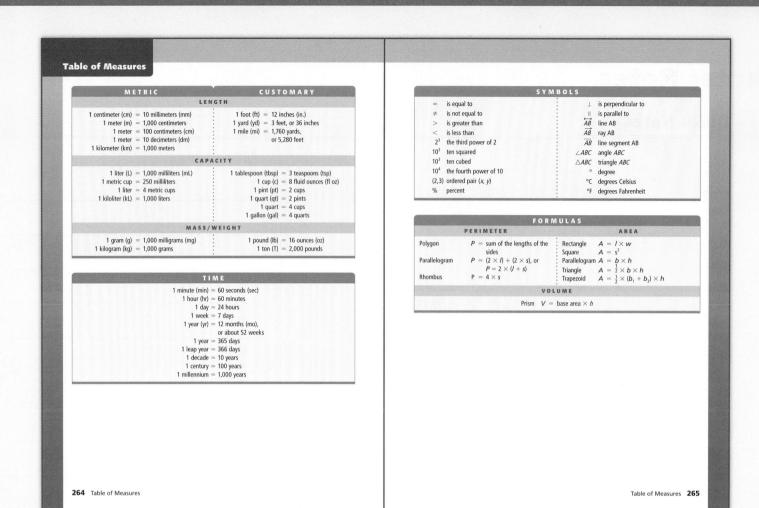

METRIC	CUSTOMARY
LENGTH	
1 centimeter (cm) = 10 millimeters (mm)	1 foot (ft) = 12 inches (in.)
1 meter (m) = 1,000 centimeters	1 yard (yd) = 3 feet, or 36 inches
1 meter = 100 centimeters (cm)	1 mile (mi) = 1,760 yards,
1 meter = 10 decimeters (dm)	or 5,280 feet
1 kilometer (km) = 1,000 meters	
CAPACITY	
1 liter (L) = 1,000 milliliters (mL)	1 tablespoon (tbsp) = 3 teaspoons (tsp)
1 metric cup = 250 milliliters	1 cup (c) = 8 fluid ounces (fl oz)
1 liter = 4 metric cups	1 pint (pt) = 2 cups
1 kiloliter (kL) = 1,000 liters	1 quart (qt) = 2 pints
	1 quart = 4 cups
	1 gallon (gal) = 4 quarts
MASS/WEIGHT	
1 gram (g) = 1,000 milligrams (mg)	1 pound (lb) = 16 ounces (oz)
1 kilogram (kg) = 1,000 grams	1 ton (T) = 2,000 pounds

TIME

1 minute (min) = 60 seconds (sec)
1 hour (hr) = 60 minutes
1 day = 24 hours
1 week = 7 days
1 year (yr) = 12 months (mo),
or about 52 weeks
1 year = 365 days
1 leap year = 366 days
1 decade = 10 years
1 century = 100 years
1 millennium = 1,000 years

SYMBOLS

=	is equal to	⊥	is perpendicular to
≠	is not equal to	∥	is parallel to
>	is greater than	$\overleftrightarrow{AB}$	line AB
<	is less than	$\overrightarrow{AB}$	ray AB
2^3	the third power of 2	$\overline{AB}$	line segment AB
10^2	ten squared	∠ABC	angle ABC
10^3	ten cubed	△ABC	triangle ABC
10^4	the fourth power of 10	°	degree
(2,3)	ordered pair (x, y)	°C	degrees Celsius
%	percent	°F	degrees Fahrenheit

FORMULAS

PERIMETER		AREA	
Polygon	P = sum of the lengths of the sides	Rectangle	$A = l \times w$
		Square	$A = s^2$
Parallelogram	$P = (2 \times l) + (2 \times s)$, or $P = 2 \times (l + s)$	Parallelogram	$A = b \times h$
		Triangle	$A = \frac{1}{2} \times b \times h$
Rhombus	$P = 4 \times s$	Trapezoid	$A = \frac{1}{2} \times (b_1 + b_2) \times h$

VOLUME

Prism $\quad V$ = base area × h

PRONUNCIATION KEY

a	add, map	f	fit, half	n	nice, tin	p	pit, stop	y◊ f	use, few
Σ	ace, rate	g	go, log	ng	ring, song	r	run, poor	v	vain, eve
â(r)	c are, air	h	hope, hate	o	odd, hot	s	see, pass	w	win, away
ä	palm, father	i	it, give	∫	open, so	sh	sure, rush	y	yet, yearn
b	bat, rub	π	ice, write	ô	order, jaw	t	talk, sit	z	zest, muse
ch	check, catch	j	joy, ledge	oi	oil, boy	th	thin, both	zh	vision, pleasure
d	dog, rod	k	cool, take	ou	pout, now	th	this, bathe		
e	end, pet	l	look, rule	‰	took, full	u	up, done		
∏	equal, tree	m	move, seem	◊ p	ool, food	û(r)	b urn, term		

∂ the schwa, an unstressed vowel representing the sound spelleda in above,e in sicken, i in possible,o in melon, u in circus

Other symbols:
- • separates words into syllables
- Δ indicates stress on a syllable

A

acute angle [∂-ky◊tΔ angΔg∂l] An angle that has a measure less than a right angle (less than 90°)

Example:

addends [adΔendz]Numbers that are added in an addition problem

adding products [Δad•ing präΔ•d∂kts]The process of adding partial products to find the total product

algebra [Δal•j∂-br∂] Mathematics that deals with the relationship between numbers

algebraic expression [Δal•j∂-brΣ•ik ik•Δspre•sh∂n]An incomplete number sentence where some of the variables are replaced with letters or symbols that represent numbers

Example: $x + 3$ $10 - x$ $x + 5$ are all algebraic expressions

algebraic notation [Δal•j∂-brΣ•ik n∫•ΔtΣ•sh∂n] Mathematical shorthand used to express numerical properties, patterns, and relationships

angle [angΔg∂l]A figure formed by two rays that meet at a common endpoint

Example:

approximation [∂prokΔs∂mΣΔsh∂n]An estimation

area [ârΔ∏•∂]The measurement of two-dimensional space inside a plane figure

area model [ârΔ∏•∂möΔd∂l]A rectangular diagram used to model multiplication and division of whole numbers and multiplication of fractions

Example: To find the product of 84 × 12, the area model becomes:

	80	4
10	800	40
2	160	8

area of a net [ârΔ∏•∂∂f ΔΣ net]The total area of all the faces of a net

array [∂-rΣΔ] An arrangement of objects in rows and columns

Example:

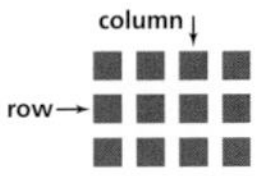

average [avΔrij] See *mean*

axis [akΔs∂s]The horizontal or vertical number line used in a graph or coordinate plane

B

balance [Δba•l∂n(t)s] verb To equalize in weight or number

balance scale [Δba•l∂n(t)s skΣl] An instrument used to weigh objects and to compare the weights of objects

base [bās] A two-dimensional figure's side or a three-dimensional figure's face by which the figure is measured or named

Example:

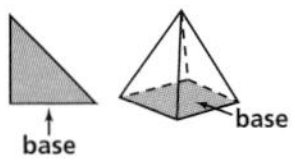

benchmark fraction [bench′märk frak′shən] A familiar fraction used as a point of reference

billion [bil′yən] One thousand million; written as 1,000,000,000

break [′brāk] To separate a number into smaller numbers that total the given number

C

certain [sur′tən] Sure to happen; will always happen

column [′kä•ləm] A vertical line in an array

Example:

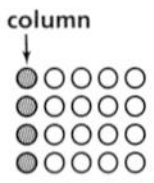

combination [kam•bə•nā′•shən]] A choice in which the order of items does not matter

combined partial products [′käm•bīnd ′pär•shûl prä•dəkts] A combination of any of the partial products (but not the final product) of a multiplication problem

common denominator [kä′mən di•nä′mə•nā•tòr] A number that may be evenly divided by each of the denominators of a given group of fractions

Example: 6, 12, and 18 are all common denominators of $\frac{1}{3}$ and $\frac{1}{2}$

common factor [kä′mən fak′tər] A number that is a factor of two or more numbers

common multiple [kä′mən mul′tə•pəl] A number that is a multiple of two or more numbers

common unit [kä′mən ′yü•nət] A unit that quantities have in common so that a calculation can be performed on them

comparing [kəm•′pār•ing] Describing whether two or more numbers are equal to, less than, or greater than each other

compatible numbers [kəm•pa′tə•bəl num′bərz] Numbers that are easy to compute mentally and are chosen to simplify the calculation of an estimate

composite [käm•pä′zət] A number having more than two factors

Example: 6 is a composite number, since its factors are 1, 2, 3, and 6.

concave [kän•′kāv] Used to describe a polygon with at least one angle measuring more than 180°; one or more line segments that are outside the polygon can always be drawn between two vertices

cone [kōn] A three-dimensional figure that has a flat, circular base and one apex

Example:

congruent [kən•grōō′ənt] Having the same size and shape

congruent figures [kən•grōō′ənt fi•′gûrz] Figures that have the same size and shape

Example:

The triangles are congruent

constant speed [′kän(t)•stənt ′spēd] The assumption that speed stays the same throughout each interval of distance or time

conversion graph [kən•′vər•zhən ′graf] A graph that shows how to convert between measurements

conversion rule [kən•′vər•zhən ′rül] A rule that describes how to convert between measurements

converting measurements [kən•′vərt•ing ′me•zhar•mənts] Changing measurements from one unit to another

convex [kän•′veks] Used to describe a polygon with all interior angles measuring less than 180°; all diagonals are inside the polygon

coordinate grid [k∫•ôrΔd∂-n∂t grid] A grid formed by two intersecting and perpendicular number lines called axes

Example:

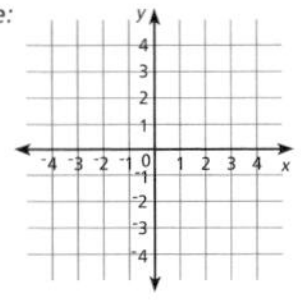

coordinates [k∫•ôrΔd∂-n∂ts] The numbers in an ordered pair

cubic unit [ky◊Δbik y◊Δn∂t] A unit of volume with dimensions 1 unit × 1 unit × 1 unit

cylinder [siΔl∂n•d∂r] A three-dimensional figure that has two parallel bases that are congruent circles

Example:

D

decimal [deΔs∂-m∂l] A number with one or more digits to the right of the decimal point

decimal part of a number [deΔs∂-m∂l pärt Δ∂f ΔΣ num•Δb∂r]The digit or digits to the right of a decimal point that represent a fraction whose denominator is either 10 or a power of 10 (10; 100; 1,000; and so on)

Example: 3.27 2 and 7 are the decimal parts

denominator [di•näΔm∂-nΣ•t∂r] The number below the bar in a fraction that tells how many equal parts are in the whole

Example: $\frac{3}{4}$ ← denominator

describing situations with diagrams [di•Δskrπb•ing Δsi•ch∂-ΔwΣ•sh∂ns Δwith Δdπ•∂-grams] Drawing pictures or diagrams to help describe and solve problems

describing situations with equations [di•Δskrπb•ing Δsi•ch∂-ΔwΣ•sh∂ns with i•ΔkwΣ•zh∂ns] Using equations to help describe and solve problems

difference [difΔ∂r•∂ns] The result of subtracting two numbers

digit [diΔjit] Any one of the ten symbols 0, 1, 2, 3, 4, 5, 6, 7, 8, 9 used to write numbers

digits in the same place-value position [diΔjits Δin the ΔsΣm plΣs val•Δy◊ p∂-Δzi•sh∂n]Digits with like place value in two numbers and are used to compare numbers

dividend [diΔv∂-dend]The number being divided in a division problem

Example: 36 ÷ 6; $6\overline{)36}$

The dividend is 36.

divisibility [d∂-Δvi•z∂-Δbi•l∂-t∏]The capacity of being divided, without a remainder

divisible [d∂-viΔzi•b∂l] A number is divisible by another number if the quotient is a whole number and the remainder is zero.

Example: 21 is *divisible* by 3.

divisible by [d∂-viΔz∂-b∂l Δbπ]Can be divided without a remainder

Example: Numbers divisible by 12 are 12, 24, 36. . .

division [d∂-viΔzh∂n] The process of sharing or grouping a number into equal parts; the operation that is the inverse of multiplication

divisor [d∂-vπΔz∂r]The number that divides the dividend

Example: 15÷ 3; $3\overline{)15}$

The divisor is 3.

dot sketch [Δdät Δskech]An array of small circles that is used to represent a fraction, to find equivalent fractions, to multiply fractions, and to show combinations

Example:

double [Δde•b∂l]When both addends are the same number

doubling products [′də•b(ə-)ling prä•dəkts] The process of finding the product of two numbers if one factor is even, by multiplying by half of the even number and then multiplying the result by 2.

Example: 6 × 15 = (3 × 15) × 2

E

edge [ej] The line segment where two or more faces of a three-dimensional figure meet

Example:

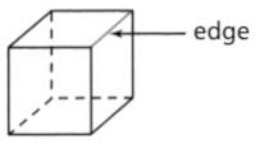

endpoint [end′•point′] The point marking the end of a line segment

equalize [′ē•kwə•′līz] Redistributing amounts so that everyone gets the same amount

equal to [′ē•kwəl tōō] Having the same value

equals [′ē•kwəlz] The statement when two variables are equivalent

equation [i•kwā′zhən] An algebraic or numerical sentence that shows that two quantities are equal

equilateral triangle [ē•kwə•la′tə•rəl trī′ang•gəl] A triangle with three congruent sides

Example:

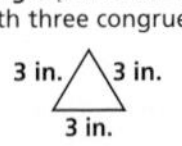

equivalent [ē-•kwiv′ə•lənt] Having the same value

equivalent decimals [ē•kwiv′ə•lənt de′sə•məlz] Decimals that name the same number or amount

Example: 0.4 = 0.40 = 0.400

equivalent fractions [ē•kwiv′ə•lənt frak′shən] Fractions that name the same number or amount

equivalent mixed number [ē•kwiv′ə•lənt mikst num′bər] Two or more mixed numbers that have the same value

Example: $2\frac{13}{8}$, $3\frac{5}{8}$, and $3\frac{10}{16}$ are all equivalent mixed numbers.

estimate [es′tə•mət] *noun* A number close to an exact amount

estimate [es′tə•māt] *verb* To find a number that is close to an exact amount

estimating [′es•ti•māt•ing] Finding a number that is close to an exact amount

estimation [′es•tə•′mā•shən] An educated guess at an answer

even [′ē•vən] A whole number that is divisible by 2

Examples: 2, 4, 6, 8, 10, 12, 14, 16, . . .

event [i•vent′] One outcome or a set of outcomes in an experiment

expanded notation [ik•′spand•id nō•′tā-shən] A way to write numbers by showing the value of each digit

Examples: 635 = 600 + 30 + 5
1,479 = 1,000 + 400 + 70 + 9

expanded form [ik•spand′id fôrm] A way to write numbers by showing the value of each digit

Example: 832 = 800 + 30 + 2

exponent [ek′spō•nənt] A number that shows how many times the base is used as a factor

Example: $10^3 = 10 \times 10 \times 10$; 3 is the exponent.

F

face [fās] A polygon that is a flat surface of a three-dimensional figure

Example:

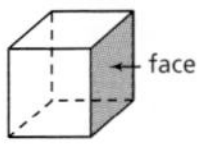

factor [fak′tər] A number multiplied by another number to find a product

factoring [fak′tər•ing] The process of finding factors of a number

flip [flip] A movement of a figure to a new position by flipping the figure over a line; a reflection

Example:

fraction of a fraction [frakΔshən ər ΔΣ frakΔshən] A smaller part of a fraction, where the larger fraction represents the whole

Example: One third of a *half* mile is one sixth of the *whole* mile.

fraction of a set [frakΔshən ər ΔΣ Δseə] A fraction of a group

fractions that add to 1 [frakΔshəns Δthat Δad Δtȯ Δwən] Two or more fractions that have a sum equal to 1

Example: $\frac{1}{8} + \frac{7}{8} = 1$

fractions that name tenths and hundredths [frakΔshəns Δthat ΔnΣm tenths Δand hunΔdrədths] Fractions that can be directly written in decimal form

Example: = $\frac{3}{10}$ can be written as 0.3 and $\frac{17}{100}$ can be written as 0.17

function [funkΔshən] A relationship between two quantities in which one quantity depends on the other

G

greater [grΣΔtər] Having a larger value

greater than (>) [grΣΔtər than] A symbol used to compare two numbers, with the greater number given first

Example: 6 > 4

H

height [hīt] The distance from the base to the farthest point of a two- or three-dimensional figure

Example:

height

horizontal axis [hȯr-ə-Δzän-tul] The horizontal number line on a coordinate plane

Example:

horizontal axis

horizontal coordinate [hȯr-ə-Δzän-tul kȯ-ȯrΔdə-nəts] In a coordinate pair, the value that is represented by x, which shows the horizontal location

Example: = In the coordinate pair (4,3) the horizontal coordinate is 4.

horizontal line [hȯr-ə-Δzän-tul līn] A line parallel to the horizon

hundredth [hunΔdrədth] One of one hundred equal parts

Examples: 0.56   fifty-six hundredths
$\frac{45}{100}$ forty-five hundredths

I

improbable [im-Δprä-bə-bəl] Not likely to happen

improper fraction [im-Δprä-pər frak Δshən] A fraction where the numerator is larger than the denominator

Example: = $\frac{4}{3}$ is an improper fraction.

input [inΔp%ot] The number that is the start of a process and then acted on

---

intersections [in-tər-Δsek-shən] The places where lines cross in dot sketches used to show combinations

Example:

interval [in-tər-vəl] The difference between one number and the next on the scale of a graph

inverse [in-Δvərs] Operations that undo each other, like addition and subtraction or multiplication and division

isosceles triangle [i-sä-sə-lēz tri-ang-gəl] A triangle with at least two congruent sides

Example: 10 in.   10 in.
7 in.

K

kite [kīt] A quadrilateral with no parallel sides, two pairs of congruent sides, two lines of symmetry, and all vertices are convex

Example:

L

largest product [lär-jest präΔdəkt] The product with the greatest value when multiple products are compared

least common denominator (LCD) [lēst kä-mən di-nä-mə-nā-tər] The least common multiple of two or more denominators

Example: The LCD for $\frac{1}{4}$ and $\frac{5}{6}$ is 12.

length [Δlenkth] The measure of a side of a figure

less [less] Having a smaller value

less than (<) [less than] A symbol used to compare two numbers, with the lesser number given first

Example: 4 < 6

like denominators [Δlīk di-nä-mə-tər] Two or more denominators that are the same number

like place values [Δlīk plās val'y%o] The same place-value position in two or more numbers

Example: 18.7
3.9
204.16

The digits that share a *like place value* with 8 are 3 and 4.

line [līn] A straight path in a plane, extending in both directions with no endpoints

Example:

line segment [līn segΔmənt] A part of a line between two endpoints

Example:

line of symmetry [līn of si-mə-trē] Line that separates a figure into two congruent parts

M

maximum [Δmak-sə-məm] The largest possible quantity or number

mean [mēn] The average of a set of numbers, found by dividing the sum of the set by the number of addends

measurements [Δme-zhər-mənts] The sizes, quantities, or amounts, found by measuring

measuring height of a parallelogram [Δme-zhə-ring Δhīt əf Δ pä-rə-lel'ə-gram] To measure the perpendicular difference from a base to the opposite side

Example: **Height of a parallelogram**

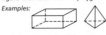

median [mē-dē-ən] The middle number in a set of data that are arranged in order

---

miles per hour [ΔmiΔ] A measurement of speed that shows the number of miles traveled for each hour (60 mins.)

million [milΔyən] One thousand thousands; written as 1,000,000

minimum [Δmi-nə-məm] The smallest possible quantity or number

mixed number [mikst numΔbər] A number that is made up of a whole number and a fraction

Example: $1\frac{5}{8}$

mobile [Δm%o-Δbīll] A structure that is balanced from a point; a representation of a balanced equation

Example:

mode [mōd] The number or item that occurs most often in a set of data

multiple [mulΔtə-pəl] The product of a given whole number and another whole number

Example: 3 × 9 = 27, so 27 is a multiple of 3 and 9.

N

negative [neΔgə-tiv] Any integer less than zero

Examples: ⁻4, ⁻5, and ⁻6 are negative integers.

neighbor numbers [Δnā-bər Δnem-bərz] Consecutive numbers one less and one greater than a certain number

Example: Neighbor numbers of 16 are 15 and 17

numerator [n%o-mə-rΣΔ-tər] The number above the bar in a fraction that tells how many equal parts of the whole are being considered

Example: $\frac{3}{4}$ = numerator

O

obtuse angle [äb-t%osΔ angΔgəl] An angle that has a measure is greater than 90° and less than 180°

Example:

odd [Δäd] A whole number that is not divisible by 2

Example: 27   95   3

operation [Δä-pə-Δrā-shən] The process of changing one number to another according to a rule

Example: operation signs: +, −, ÷, ×

opposite angles [Δä-pə-zət angΔgəl] Angles that touch only at their vertex and share the same lines as sides

Example:

These angles are *opposite angles.*

ordered pair [ȯrΔdərd pär] A pair of numbers used to locate a point on a grid. The first number tells the left-right position and the second number tells the up-down position.

ordering [ȯr-də-ring] Arranging according to size, amount, or value

organized list [ȯr-gə-nīzəd list] One way to organize data in order to solve a problem

origin [ȯr-ə-jən] The point where the two axes of a coordinate plane intersect, (0,0)

outcome [out-Δkum] A possible result of an experiment

outlier [out-Δlī-ər] A value separated from most of the rest in a set of data

output [out-p%ot] A number that is the result of some actions on an input

---

P

parallel [Δpar-ə-lel] Lines or figures in a plane that never intersect

Example:

parallel faces [Δpar-ə-lel Δfās-əs] Faces in a three-dimensional figure that are parallel to each other

parallelogram [Δpa-rə-lel'ə-gram] A quadrilateral with two pairs of parallel sides

Example:

part of a whole [Δpärt əf ä hōl] One or more equal sections of one unit

Example: A quarter hour is $\frac{1}{4}$ of an hour, and an hour has 4 such parts in it.

partial product [Δpär-shəl prä'dəkts] The product of parts (usually parts of different place values) of each factor

Example: 24
× 3
12 ← Multiply the ones: 3 × 4 = 12
+60 ← Multiply the tens: 3 × 20 = 60
72

partition [pär-Δti-shən] To break a number into smaller numbers that total the given number

percent [pər-Δsent] A fraction expressed in hundredths

Example: $\frac{1}{10} = \frac{10}{100} = 10\%$

perimeter [pə-rim'ə-tər] The distance around a closed two-dimensional figure

perpendicular lines [pər-pen-dik'yə-lər līns] Two lines that intersect to form right angles

Example:

perpendicular faces [pər-pen-dik'yə-lər fās-əs] Faces in a three-dimensional figure that are perpendicular to each other

place value [plās val'y%o] A system of writing numbers so that as you move to the left, the value of each place is 10 times greater than the value of the place at its right

place-value position [plās val'y%o pə-Δzi-shən] The place that a digit has in a number

polygon [pol'-i-gon] A closed two-dimensional figure formed by three or more line segments

Examples:

polyhedron [pol-i-hē'drən] A three-dimensional figure with faces that are polygons

Examples:

population [pä-pyə-lā'shən] The entire group of objects or individuals considered for a survey

positive [pä'zə-tiv] Any integer greater than zero

powers of 10 [pauΔərs 'əf tən] A number that results when 10 is used as a base with an exponent

Example: $10^1 = 10$; $10^2 = 10 \times 10 = 100$; $10^3 = 10 \times 10 \times 10 = 1{,}000$; and so on

prime [prīm] A number that has exactly two factors: 1 and itself

Examples: 5, 7, 11, 13, 17, and 19 are prime numbers.

prime factorization [prīm fak-tə-rə-Δzā-shən] A number written as the product of all its prime factors

Examples:

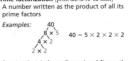
$40 = 5 \times 2 \times 2 \times 2$

prism [priz'əm] A three-dimensional figure that has two congruent, polygon-shaped bases, and other faces that are all rectangles

Examples:

rectangular   triangular
prism   prism

(continued from page 664)

About the Mathematics

On the left, students pull out whatever multiple of the divisor they recognize. On the right, students subtract the largest "simple" multiple of the divisor that they can. This lesson gives students an efficient approach that they can practice, but deliberately avoids giving them the most efficient approach. Delaying that until the next lesson gives students time to think about and make choices about how they will approach problems

like these, allowing them to clarify their ideas before mechanizing them.

The records are different from the one in the lesson, but use the same process. Here, partial quotients appear on the same line as the corresponding multiple of 19. The quotient is the sum of all the partial quotients.

(continued from page 752)

About the Mathematics

them to make a triangle. If you like, insert pipe cleaners to hold them together at the vertices. The triangle is *rigid*—it doesn't change shape as you push at the corners (as long as you don't bend the straws). If you perform the same type of experiment with a four-sided figure, you find that it is *not* rigid. It can squish and collapse in various ways and still have straight sides of the lengths you started with.

If you start with only two straws of some specified length, there are many triangles that you can describe

with them, each with a different-length third straw. But if you start with two straws of specified lengths and say exactly what angle must come between them, there is no further choice about the third side: exactly one triangle is possible. Two sides and the angle between them is enough information to specify exactly one triangle. Similarly, one side and an angle at each of its endpoints specify exactly one triangle.

(continued from page 774)

About the Mathematics

Start with a pair of intersecting lines, as shown below. Line *m* intersects line *l* at some angle we'll call $\angle F$.

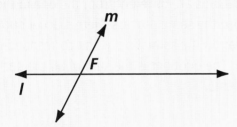

Draw a second line, *n,* parallel to line *m,* and intersecting at the $\angle S$.

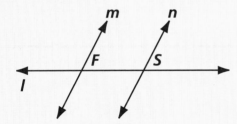

We want to show that if lines *m* and *n* are parallel, then $\angle F$ and $\angle S$ have equal measures.

Let's suppose, just for a moment, that the angles do not have equal measure. Then, $\angle S$ is either bigger or smaller than $\angle F$. If it is bigger, then the measure of $\angle F$ and the measure of $\angle R$ add up to less than 180° and lines *m* and *n* will meet somewhere above at an angle that makes 180° when added to the measure of $\angle F$ and $\angle R$.

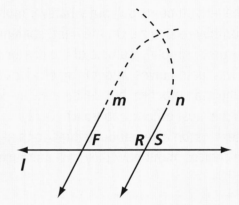

But this cannot happen, because parallel lines do not intersect! So, maybe $\angle S$ can be smaller than $\angle F$. Similar reasoning shows that in this case *m* and *n* have to cross below. So, $\angle S$ cannot be bigger than $\angle F$ and it cannot be smaller. Therefore, the measures of the two angles have to be equal!

How did we get into such a mess? Well, if lines *m* and *n* meet, then we get this impossible triangle. There can't be such a triangle, so lines *m* and *n* can't meet! This would be the case no matter what angle we chose initially. If $\angle F$ had been smaller, $\angle S$ would have been smaller too, so $\angle R$ would have been larger. The measures of $\angle R$ and $\angle S$ would still sum up to 180°.

(continued from page 1136)

About the Mathematics

the 6 equally likely possible outcomes. We expect, in the long run, that a tossed cube will turn up "even" half of the time. We can't assign a theoretical probability to flipping a bottle cap, because we don't know, without experimenting, whether the two outcomes (open-side up, open-side down) *are* equally likely. Scientific research often begins with a hypothesis—in this case, that the bottle cap *would* land open-side up half the time—and then accepts or rejects that hypothesis after testing it with an experiment.

In measuring probability with an experiment, we base the fraction on experimental results

$$\left(\frac{\text{number of occurrences of the event we are focusing on}}{\text{the number of trials}}\right)$$

instead of basing it on the theory

$$\left(\frac{\text{number of outcomes within the event we are focusing on}}{\text{the number of possible outcomes}}\right).$$

Experimental probabilities based on a small number of trials are likely to be poor estimates of the real probability. The larger the number of trials, the more precision and reliability you get. This is sometimes known as "The Law of Large Numbers."

(continued from page 1144)

About the Mathematics

That tells us that, on average, $\frac{1}{3}$ of all tosses will be a 2 or 5. (As always, the more tosses, the closer the experimental results are likely to be to the prediction based on the theoretical probability.)

If we are tossing two number cubes, not all sums are equally likely (e.g., 7 occurs more often than 2 or 12). It would be incorrect to reason that the probability of tossing a 7 is $\frac{1}{11}$ because there are 11 different sums

and 7 is one of them. Instead we must consider that there are 36 possible outcomes (because tossing a 3 with one cube and a 4 with the other is a different outcome than tossing a 4 with the first cube and a 3 with the other), and those whose sum is 7 comprise 6 out of the 36. Therefore, the probability of getting a sum of 7 is $\frac{6}{36}$, or $\frac{1}{6}$.

(continued from page 1230)

About the Mathematics

At 60 miles per hour, we travel 60 miles in 60 minutes—which is to say *one* mile each minute if we are going at a steady pace. From that, we conclude that 14 miles will take 14 minutes, and 90 miles will take an hour and a half.

If we travel slower, it will take us longer. How much longer? If we can go only 15 miles in the hour—that is, we are traveling at 15 mph—then 60 miles will take four hours, each of those miles taking four minutes. Another way of saying that is: if we go at $\frac{1}{4}$ the speed, it takes 4 times as long. If we were to go at 3 times the speed, it would take us $\frac{1}{3}$ the time!

Let's reason about how much longer a 15-mile trip takes if we travel at 45 mph instead of 60 mph. At 60 mph, a 15-mile trip takes 15 minutes. At $\frac{1}{4}$ that speed, 15 miles per hour, it takes an hour (60 minutes, 4 times as long). At 3 times *that* speed, 45 miles per hour, it takes a third of *that* time, $\frac{1}{3}$ hour, or 20 minutes.

Reviewing, we see a pattern. At 60 mph, the trip takes 15 minutes. At that $\frac{3}{4}$ speed, it takes $\frac{4}{3}$ the time! Over this short trip, that's only a 5-minute difference. For a longer trip, the difference might be significant.

When we make a graph, the horizontal axis typically represents the input and the vertical axis represents the consequence of that input—the output. By convention, most graphs involving time put time on the horizontal axis. If we were asking how much time it takes to travel a certain distance, or how the time would change for a particular trip if we varied the speed, then the amount of time would be the consequence of the thing we're varying, and it would be reasonable to put it on the vertical axis.

(continued from page 1238)

About the Mathematics

When students are working on LAB p. 295 you might want to have them read the story of Matthew's bike ride all the way through quickly, just to get a rough sense of what it is about, but there are too many tiny details in the story to make much sense out of it that way. To get those details, we must start over, and take notes from the beginning. Because the information that we want to collect is about distance and time traveled, our notes should ignore other details. One approach is to read a sentence, ask what we need to know, and put just that piece of information in a table or on a graph. Then move on to the next sentence, and so on, through the story. What information could we write down from "He started from home at noon"? We don't care about "home," but we do care to know that this is the start: no minutes have passed, and no miles have been traveled. We could enter that on a table, or plot the point (0,0) on the graph (or both). "At 12:30, he reached the court house, 10 miles from home." What do we write down or put on the graph? (30 minutes, 10 miles). After starting this with your students, let them see what they can do by themselves.

So that the changes in the steepness of the graph are clearly visible, students should use a straightedge to draw the line segments on the LAB pages.

The LAB pages present two story problems about bicycle trips, similar to the situation in Activity A. Students make graphs representing the distance and time each part of the trip took, and interpret the graphs. Problems 2, 6, and 8 ask students to compare the speed the cyclist was traveling during the different parts of the trip. Some ways students may do this include comparing the steepness of the line segments that represent different parts of the trip, or by figuring out how much distance was covered in equivalent amounts of time.

(continued from page 1246)

About the Mathematics

that zero units of length, weight, or volume are. This is why temperatures can be negative as well as positive: it's possible for things to get colder than the temperatures Celsius and Fahrenheit call 0.

These are equations that tell us how to convert between the two temperature systems: $F = (\frac{9}{5} C) + 32$ and $C = \frac{5}{9} (F - 32)$.

The $\frac{9}{5}$ or $\frac{5}{9}$ represents the relationship between a degree change in the two systems: a change of 5°C is equivalent to a change of 9°F. On a graph, when Fahrenheit is on the *x*-axis, you can count over 9° on the Fahrenheit axis and up 5° on the Celsius axis from one point on the line to find another. The 32° added or subtracted in the equation accounts for the fact that 0°C = 32°F.

Index

Correlations to NCTM Standards and Curriculum Focal Points

Standard	Grades 3–5 Expectations	Correlation to NCTM Standards
Instructional programs from prekindergarten through grade 12 should enable all students to—	*In grades 3–5 all students should—*	

1 NUMBER AND OPERATIONS

Content standards that develop focal points are in boldface type.

Standard	Grades 3–5 Expectations	Correlation to NCTM Standards
Understand numbers, ways of representing numbers, relationships among numbers, and number systems	• understand the place-value structure of the base-ten number system and be able to represent and compare whole numbers and decimals; • **recognize equivalent representations for the same number and generate them by decomposing and composing numbers;** • develop understanding of fractions as parts of unit wholes, as parts of a collection, as locations on number lines, and as divisions of whole numbers; • use models, benchmarks, and equivalent forms to judge the size of fractions; • **recognize and generate equivalent forms of commonly used fractions, decimals, and percents;** • **explore numbers less than 0 by extending the number line and through familiar applications;** • **describe classes of numbers according to characteristics such as the nature of their factors.**	**1.1, 1.5, 2.5, 3.1, 3.2, 3.3, 3.4, 3.5, 3.6, 3.7, 3.8, 4.3, 4.4, 4.5, 4.6, 4.7, 4.8, 4.9, 4.10, 7.4, 7.5, 7.6, 14.5, 14.6, 15.6,** 2.5, 4.1, 4.5, 4.6, 4.7, 4.8, 4.10, 7.1, 7.2, 7.3, 7.12, 14.1, 14.3, 14.7
Understand meanings of operations and how they relate to one another	• understand various meanings of multiplication and division; • **understand the effects of multiplying and dividing whole numbers;** • **identify and use relationships between operations, such as division as the inverse of multiplication, to solve problems;** • **understand and use properties of operations, such as the distributivity of multiplication over addition.**	**1.2, 1.4, 1.5, 1.7, 2.1, 2.2, 2.3, 2.4, 2.6, 2.8, 2.9, 2.10, 2.11, 2.12, 8.1, 8.2, 8.3, 8.4,** 2.4, 2.10, 3.6, 3.7, 3.8, 8.2
Compute fluently and make reasonable estimates	• **develop fluency with basic number combinations for multiplication and division and use these combinations to mentally compute related problems, such as 30 × 50;** • **develop fluency in adding, subtracting, multiplying, and dividing whole numbers;** • **develop and use strategies to estimate the results of whole-number computations and to judge the reasonableness of such results;** • develop and use strategies to estimate computations involving fractions and decimals in situations relevant to students' experience; • use visual models, benchmarks, and equivalent forms to add and subtract commonly used fractions and decimals; • select appropriate methods and tools for computing with whole numbers from among mental computation, estimation, calculators, and paper and pencil according to the context and nature of the computation and use the selected method or tools.	**1.1, 1.2, 1.3, 1.4, 1.5, 1.6, 1.7, 1.8, 2.1, 2.2, 2.3, 2.4, 2.6, 2.7, 2.8, 2.9, 2.10, 2.11, 2.12, 4.1, 4.2, 5.1, 5.2, 5.3, 5.4, 5.5, 5.6, 6.9, 6.10, 7.7, 7.8, 7.9, 7.10, 7.11, 7.12, 8.3, 8.4, 8.5, 8.6, 8.7, 8.8, 8.9, 8.10, 9.5, 9.6, 9.9, 10.1, 10.2, 10.3, 10.4, 10.5, 10.6, 10.7, 11.1, 11.2, 11.3, 11.4, 11.5, 11.6, 11.7, 11.8, 11.9, 11.10, 11.11, 12.4, 12.5, 12.6, 12.7, 12.8, 12.9, 13.1, 13.2, 13.3, 13.4, 13.5, 13.7, 13.8, 15.1, 15.6, 15.7**

Standard	Grades 3–5 Expectations	Correlation to NCTM Standards
Instructional programs from prekindergarten through grade 12 should enable all students to—	*In grades 3–5 all students should—*	

2 ALGEBRA

Content standards that develop focal points are in boldface type.

Standard	Grades 3–5 Expectations	Correlation to NCTM Standards
Understand patterns, relations, and functions	• **describe, extend, and make generalizations about geometric and numeric patterns;** • **represent and analyze patterns and functions, using words, tables, and graphs.**	**1.5, 1.6, 1.8,** 2.1, **2.3, 2.4, 2.5, 2.6, 2.8, 2.9, 2.10, 2.11,** 3.6, 3.7, 5.4, 5.6, 6.4, 7.1, 7.2, 7.3, 9.9, 11.8, 15.2, 15.3, 15.4, 15.5, 15.6, 15.7
Represent and analyze mathematical situations and structures using algebraic symbols	• **identify such properties as commutativity, associativity, and distributivity and use them to compute with whole numbers;** • represent the idea of a variable as an unknown quantity using a letter or a symbol; • **express mathematical relationships using equations.**	**1.2, 1.3, 1.4, 1.6, 1.7,** 4.2, 6.11, **8.1, 8.2, 8.6, 8.7, 8.8, 8.9, 10.2, 10.5, 11.3, 11.4, 11.5, 11.11, 12.2, 12.9, 13.3, 13.4, 13.7, 13.8,** 1.3, 1.5, 1.6, 6.1, 6.2, 6.10, 10.2, 10.5, 11.3, 12.2, 12.9, 13.2, 13.3, 13.4, 13.5, 13.6, 13.7
Use mathematical models to represent and understand quantitative relationships	• **model problem situations with objects and use representations such as graphs, tables, and equations to draw conclusions.**	**1.1,** 2.2, 2.7, **2.12,** 3.1, 3.2, 3.3, 3.4, 3.5, 3.8, 4.1, 4.3, 4.4, 4.5, 4.6, 4.7, 4.8, 4.9, 4.10, 5.1, 5.2, 5.3, 5.5, 7.1, 7.3, 7.4, 7.5, 7.6, 7.7, 7.8, 7.9, 7.10, 7.11, 7.12, 8.2, 8.3, 8.4, 8.5, 8.7, 8.10, 11.1, 11.2, 11.3, 13.1, 13.2, 13.3, 13.4, 15.2, 15.3, 15.4, 15.5, 15.6, 15.7
Analyze change in various contexts	• investigate how a change in one variable relates to a change in a second variable; • identify and describe situations with constant or varying rates of change and compare them.	6.1, 6.2, 15.2, 15.3, 15.4, 15.5, 15.6, 15.7

3 GEOMETRY

Content standards that develop focal points are in boldface type.

Standard	Grades 3–5 Expectations	Correlation to NCTM Standards
Analyze characteristics and properties of two- and three-dimensional geometric shapes and develop mathematical arguments about geometric relationships	• **identify, compare, and analyze attributes of two- and three-dimensional shapes and develop vocabulary to describe the attributes;** • **classify two- and three-dimensional shapes according to their properties and develop definitions of classes of shapes such as triangles and pyramids;** • **investigate, describe, and reason about the results of subdividing, combining, and transforming shapes;** • explore congruence and similarity; • **make and test conjectures about geometric properties and relationships and develop logical arguments to justify conclusions.**	**6.2, 6.3, 6.4, 6.5, 6.12, 9.1, 9.2, 9.3, 9.4, 9.5, 9.6, 9.7, 9.8, 9.9, 10.1, 10.2, 10.3, 10.4, 10.5, 10.6, 10.7, 12.1, 12.2, 12.3, 12.4, 12.5, 12.6, 12.7, 12.8, 12.9,** 6.1, 6.3, 6.5, 9.4
Specify locations and describe spatial relationships using coordinate geometry and other representational systems	• describe location and movement using common language and geometric vocabulary; • make and use coordinate systems to specify locations and to describe paths; • **find the distance between points along horizontal and vertical lines of a coordinate system.**	**6.2, 6.3, 6.7, 15.1,** 6.1, 6.2, 6.3, 6.4, 6.5, 6.6, 6.7, 6.12, 15.1
Apply transformations and use symmetry to analyze mathematical situations	• predict and describe the results of sliding, flipping, and turning two-dimensional shapes; • describe a motion or a series of motions that will show that two shapes are congruent; • **identify and describe line and rotational symmetry in two- and three-dimensional shapes and designs.**	**6.3, 6.4, 9.7,** 6.3, 6.4, 6.5, 6.12

Standard	Grades 3–5 Expectations	Correlation to NCTM Standards
Instructional programs from prekindergarten through grade 12 should enable all students to—	*In grades 3–5 all students should—*	
Use visualization, spatial reasoning, and geometric modeling to solve problems	• **build and draw geometric objects;** • **create and describe mental images of objects, patterns, and paths;** • **identify and build a three-dimensional object from two-dimensional representations of that object;** • **identify and draw a two-dimensional representation of a three-dimensional object;** • **use geometric models to solve problems in other areas of mathematics, such as number and measurement;** • recognize geometric ideas and relationships and apply them to other disciplines and to problems that arise in the classroom or in everyday life.	9.1, 9.8, 9.9, 10.1, 10.2, 10.3, 10.4, 10.5, 10.6, 10.7, 12.1, 12.4, 12.5, 12.6, 12.7, 12.8, 12.9, 15.1, 15.2, 15.3, 15.4, 15.5, 15.6

4 MEASUREMENT

*Content standards that develop focal points are in boldface type.

Standard	Grades 3–5 Expectations	Correlation to NCTM Standards
Understand measurable attributes of objects and the units, systems, and processes of measurement	• **understand such attributes as length, area, weight, volume, and size of angle and select the appropriate type of unit for measuring each attribute;** • **understand the need for measuring with standard units and become familiar with standard units in the customary and metric systems;** • **carry out simple unit conversions, such as from centimeters to meters, within a system of measurement;** • **understand that measurements are approximations and how differences in units affect precision;** • explore what happens to measurements of a two-dimensional shape such as its perimeter and area when the shape is changed in some way.	9.1, 9.2, 9.3, 9.4, 9.5, 9.6, 9.8, 9.9, 10.1, 10.2, 10.3, 10.4, 10.5, 10.6, 10.7, 11.4, 11.5, 11.6, 11.7, 12.4, 12.5, 12.6, 12.7, 12.8, 12.9, 15.2, 15.3, 15.4, 15.5, 10.6, 12.7
Apply appropriate techniques, tools, and formulas to determine measurements.	• **develop strategies for estimating the perimeters, areas, and volumes of irregular shapes;** • **select and apply appropriate standard units and tools to measure length, area, volume, weight, time, temperature, and the size of angles;** • **select and use benchmarks to estimate measurements;** • develop, understand, and use formulas to find the area of rectangles and related triangles and parallelograms; • **develop strategies to determine the surface areas and volumes of rectangular solids.**	2.6, 9.2, 9.3, 9.4, 9.5, 9.6, 9.8, 9.9, 10.1, 10.2, 10.3, 10.4, 10.5, 10.6, 10.7, 11.4, 11.5, 11.6, 11.7, 12.4, 12.5, 12.6, 12.7, 12.8, 12.9, 2.6, 10.3, 10.4, 10.5, 10.7

5 DATA ANALYSIS AND PROBABILITY

*Content standards that develop focal points are in boldface type.

Standard	Grades 3–5 Expectations	Correlation to NCTM Standards
Formulate questions that can be addressed with data and collect, organize, and display relevant data to answer them	• **design investigations to address a question and consider how data-collection methods affect the nature of the data set;** • **collect data using observations, surveys, and experiments;** • **represent data using tables and graphs such as line plots, bar graphs, and line graphs;** • **recognize the differences in representing categorical and numerical data.**	6.8, 6.9, 6.10, 6.11, 14.6, 14.7, 15.2, 15.3, 15.4, 15.5

Standard	Grades 3–5 Expectations	Correlation to NCTM Standards
Instructional programs from prekindergarten through grade 12 should enable all students to—0	In grades 3–5 all students should—	
Select and use appropriate statistical methods to analyze data	• describe the shape and important features of a set of data and compare related data sets, with an emphasis on how the data are distributed; • use measures of center, focusing on the median, and understand what each does and does not indicate about the data set; • compare different representations of the same data and evaluate how well each representation shows important aspects of the data.	**6.8, 6.9, 6.10, 6.11, 15.3**, 6.9, 6.10, 6.11, 13.8
Develop and evaluate inferences and predictions that are based on data	• propose and justify conclusions and predictions that are based on data and design studies to further investigate the conclusions or predictions.	**14.1, 14.2, 14.3, 14.4**
Understand and apply basic concepts of probability	• describe events as likely or unlikely and discuss the degree of likelihood using such words as certain, equally likely, and impossible; • predict the probability of outcomes of simple experiments and test the predictions; • understand that the measure of the likelihood of an event can be represented by a number from 0 to 1.	**14.1, 14.2, 14.3, 14.4**

6 PROBLEM SOLVING

Instructional programs from prekindergarten through grade 12 should enable all students to—	• Build new mathematical knowledge through problem solving • Solve problems that arise in mathematics and in other contexts • Apply and adapt a variety of appropriate strategies to solve problems • Monitor and reflect on the process of mathematical problem solving	1.1, 1.2, 1.3, 1.4, 1.5, 1.6, 1.7, 1.8, 2.1, 2.3, 2.6, 2.7, 2.12, 3.1, 3.2, 3.3, 3.4, 3.5, 3.8, 4.1, 4.2, 4.6, 4.8, 4.9, 4.10, 5.1, 5.3, 5.4, 5.5, 5.6, 6.1, 6.2, 6.4, 6.5, 6.6, 6.7, 6.8, 6.9, 6.10, 6.11, 6.12, 7.2, 7.3, 7.4, 7.5, 7.6, 7.7, 7.8, 7.9, 7.10, 7.11, 7.12, 8.1, 8.2, 8.3, 8.4, 8.5, 8.6, 8.7, 8.8, 8.9, 8.10, 9.2, 9.3, 9.4, 9.5, 9.6, 9.7, 9.8, 9.9, 10.1, 10.3, 10.4, 10.5, 10.6, 10.7, 11.1, 11.2, 11.3, 11.4, 11.5, 11.6, 11.8, 11.9, 11.10, 11.11, 12.1, 12.2, 12.4, 12.6, 12.8, 12.9, 13.5, 13.7, 13.8, 14.3, 14.6, 14.7, 15.1, 15.2, 15.3, 15.4, 15.5, 15.7

7 REASONING AND PROOF

Instructional programs from prekindergarten through grade 12 should enable all students to—	• Recognize reasoning and proof as fundamental aspects of mathematics • Make and investigate mathematical conjectures • Develop and evaluate mathematical arguments and proofs • Select and use various types of reasoning and methods of proof	1.1, 1.2, 1.3, 1.4, 1.5, 1.6, 1.7, 2.1, 2.2, 2.3, 2.4, 2.5, 2.6, 2.7, 2.8, 2.9, 2.10, 2.11, 2.12, 3.1, 3.3, 3.4, 3.6, 3.7, 3.8, 4.1, 4.2, 4.3, 4.4, 4.5, 4.6, 4.7, 4.8, 4.9, 4.10, 5.1, 5.3, 5.4, 5.5, 5.6, 6.1, 6.2, 6.3, 6.4, 6.5, 6.6, 6.7, 6.8, 6.9, 6.10, 7.1, 7.2, 7.3, 7.4, 7.5, 7.6, 7.7, 7.8, 7.9, 7.10, 7.11, 7.12, 8.1, 8.2, 8.3, 8.4, 8.5, 8.6, 8.7, 8.8, 8.9, 8.10, 9.1, 9.2, 9.5, 9.6, 9.7, 9.8, 9.9, 10.1, 10.2, 10.3, 10.4, 10.5, 10.6, 10.7, 11.1, 11.2, 11.3, 11.4, 11.5, 11.6, 11.7, 11.8, 11.9, 11.10, 11.11, 12.1, 12.2, 12.3, 12.4, 12.5, 12.6, 12.7, 12.8, 12.9, 13.1, 13.2, 13.3, 13.4, 13.5, 13.7, 13.8, 14.1, 14.2, 14.3, 14.4, 14.5, 14.6, 14.7, 15.1, 15.2, 15.3, 15.4, 15.5, 15.6, 15.7

Standards	Grades 3–5 Expectations	Correlation to NCTM Standards

8 COMMUNICATION

Standards	Grades 3–5 Expectations	Correlation to NCTM Standards
Instructional programs from prekindergarten through grade 12 should enable all students to—	• Organize and consolidate their mathematical thinking through communication • Communicate their mathematical thinking coherently and clearly to peers, teachers, and others • Analyze and evaluate the mathematical thinking and strategies of others; • Use the language of mathematics to express mathematical ideas precisely.	Opportunities to communicate mathematical thinking occur in every lesson. Some examples are: 1.1, 1.2, 1.3, 1.4, 1.5, 1.6, 1.7, 1.8, 2.1, 2.2, 2.3, 2.4, 2.5, 2.6, 2.7, 2.8, 2.9, 2.10, 2.11, 2.12, 3.1, 3.2, 3.3, 3.4, 3.5, 3.6, 3.7, 3.8, 4.1, 4.2, 4.3, 4.4, 4.5, 4.6, 4.7, 4.8, 4.9, 4.10, 5.1, 5.2, 5.3, 5.4, 5.5, 5.6, 6.1, 6.2, 6.3, 6.4, 6.5, 6.6, 6.7, 6.8, 6.9, 6.10, 6.11, 6.12, 7.1, 7.2, 7.3, 7.4, 7.5, 7.6, 7.7, 7.8, 7.9, 7.10, 7.11, 7.12, 8.1, 8.2, 8.3, 8.4, 8.5, 8.6, 8.7, 8.8, 8.9, 8.10, 9.1, 9.2, 9.3, 9.4, 9.5, 9.6, 9.7, 9.8, 9.9, 10.1, 10.2, 10.3, 10.4, 10.5, 10.6, 10.7, 11.1, 11.2, 11.3, 11.4, 11.5, 11.6, 11.7, 11.8, 11.9, 11.10, 11.11, 12.1, 12.2, 12.3, 12.4, 12.5, 12.6, 12.7, 12.8, 12.9, 13.1, 13.2, 13.3, 13.4, 13.5, 13.6, 13.7, 13.8, 14.1, 14.2, 14.3, 14.4, 14.5, 14.6, 14.7, 15.1, 15.2, 15.3, 15.4, 15.5, 15.6, 15.7

9 CONNECTIONS

Standards	Grades 3–5 Expectations	Correlation to NCTM Standards
Instructional programs from prekindergarten through grade 12 should enable all students to—	• Recognize and use connections among mathematical ideas • Understand how mathematical ideas interconnect and build on one another to produce a coherent whole • Recognize and apply mathematics in contexts outside of mathematics	1.1, 1.3, 1.4, 1.5, 1.6, 1.8, 2.1, 2.2, 2.3, 2.4, 2.5, 2.6, 2.7, 2.8, 2.9, 2.10, 2.11, 2.1, 2.2, 2.3, 2.4, 2.5, 2.6, 2.7, 2.8, 2.9, 2.10, 2.11, 2.12, 3.1, 3.3, 3.8, 4.1, 4.2, 4.3, 4.4, 4.5, 4.6, 4.7, 4.8, 4.9, 4.10, 5.1, 5.2, 5.3, 5.4, 5.5, 5.6, 6.1, 6.2, 6.3, 6.4, 6.5, 6.6, 6.7, 6.8, 6.9, 6.10, 6.11, 6.12, 7.1, 7.2, 7.3, 7.4, 7.5, 7.6, 7.7, 7.8, 7.9, 7.11, 7.12, 8.1, 8.2, 8.3, 8.4, 8.5, 8.6, 8.7, 8.8, 8.9, 8.10, 9.1, 9.5, 9.6, 9.7, 9.8, 10.1, 10.2, 10.3, 10.4, 10.5, 10.6, 10.7, 11.2, 11.3, 11.4, 11.5, 11.6, 11.7, 11.8, 11.9, 11.10, 11.11, 12.1, 12.2, 12.3, 12.4, 12.5, 12.6, 12.7, 12.8, 12.9, 13.1, 13.2, 13.3, 13.4, 13.5, 13.6, 13.7, 13.8, 14.1, 14.2, 14.3, 14.4, 14.5, 14.6, 14.7, 15.1, 15.2, 15.3, 15.4, 15.5, 15.6

10 REPRESENTATION

Standards	Grades 3–5 Expectations	Correlation to NCTM Standards
Instructional programs from prekindergarten through grade 12 should enable all students to—	• Create and use representations to organize, record, and communicate mathematical ideas • Select, apply, and translate among mathematical representations to solve problems • Use representations to model and interpret physical, social, and mathematical phenomena	1.1, 1.3, 1.5, 1.6, 1.7, 1.8, 2.1, 2.2, 2.3, 2.4, 2.5, 2.6, 2.8, 2.9, 2.10, 2.11, 2.12, 3.1, 3.2, 3.3, 3.4, 3.5, 3.8, 4.1, 4.2, 4.3, 4.4, 4.5, 4.6, 4.7, 4.8, 4.9, 4.10, 5.1, 5.2, 5.3, 5.4, 5.5, 5.6, 6.1, 6.2, 6.3, 6.4, 6.5, 6.6, 6.7, 6.8, 6.9, 6.10, 6.11, 6.12, 7.1, 7.3, 7.4, 7.5, 7.6, 7.7, 7.8, 7.10, 7.11, 7.12, 8.1, 8.2, 8.3, 8.4, 8.5, 8.6, 8.7, 8.8, 8.10, 9.3, 9.9, 10.4, 10.5, 11.1, 11.2, 11.3, 11.6, 11.7, 11.8, 11.10, 12.1, 12.2, 12.3, 12.4, 12.5, 12.6, 12.7, 12.8, 12.9, 13.1, 13.4, 13.5, 13.6, 13.8, 14.6, 14.7, 15.1, 15.2, 15.3, 15.4, 15.5, 15.6, 15.7